Front Plate 1 Three-Dimensional Sierpinski gasket computed with points.

(Courtesy of University of New Mexico.)

Front Plate 2 Three-Dimensional Sierpinski gasket computed by recursive subdivision of tetrahedra.

(Courtesy of University of New Mexico.)

Front Plate 3 Elevation data for Honolulu, Hawaii displayed using a quadmesh to define control points for a Bezier surface.

(Courtesy of Brian Wylie, University of New Mexico and Sandia National Laboratories.)

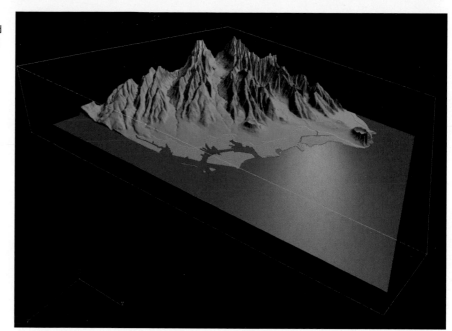

Front Plate 4 Wire frame of the quadmesh showing lower resolution in flat areas.

(Courtesy of Brian Wylie, University of New Mexico and Sandia National Laboratories.)

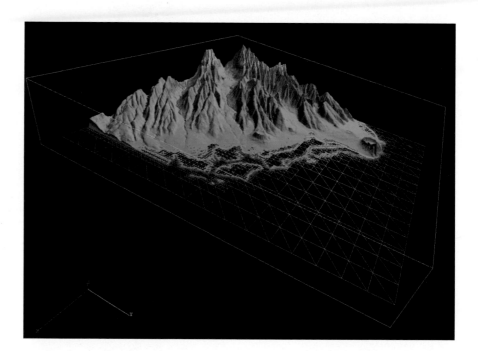

Fourth Edition

Interactive Computer Graphics

A
Top-Down
Approach
Using
OpenGL®

Fourth Edition

Interactive Computer Graphics

A
Top-Down
Approach
Using
OpenGL®

EDWARD ANGEL
University of New Mexico

PEARSON

Addison
Wesley

Boston San Francisco New York
London Toronto Sydney Tokyo Singapore Madrid
Mexico City Munich Paris Cape Town Hong Kong Montreal

Acquisitions Editor   *Matt Goldstein*
Project Editor   *Katherine Harutunian*
Production Supervisor   *Marilyn Lloyd*
Marketing Manager   *Michelle Brown*
Marketing Coordinator   *Jake Zavracky*
Project Management   *Windfall Software*
Composition   *Windfall Software, using ZzTEX*
Text Designer   *Sandra Rigney*
Copyeditor   *Yonie Overton*
Proofreader   *Jennifer McClain*
Technical Illustration   *LM Graphics*
Cover Design   *Joyce Cosentino Wells*
Cover Image   *© Hue Walker, Arts Technology Center, University of New Mexico*
Prepress and Manufacturing   *Caroline Fell*
Printer: *Courier Westford*

Access the latest information about Addison-Wesley titles from our World Wide Web site:
http://www.aw-bc.com/computing

ISBN 0-321-31252-X
2 3 4 5 6 7 8 9 10—CRW—08 07 06

To Rose Mary

CONTENTS

Preface   xxiii

CHAPTER **1** GRAPHICS SYSTEMS AND MODELS   1

1.1   Applications of Computer Graphics   2
1.1.1   Display of Information   2
1.1.2   Design   3
1.1.3   Simulation and Animation   3
1.1.4   User Interfaces   4
1.2   A Graphics System   5
1.2.1   Pixels and the Frame Buffer   6
1.2.2   Output Devices   7
1.2.3   Input Devices   10
1.3   Images: Physical and Synthetic   10
1.3.1   Objects and Viewers   11
1.3.2   Light and Images   12
1.3.3   Imaging Models   14
1.4   Imaging Systems   15
1.4.1   The Pinhole Camera   16
1.4.2   The Human Visual System   18
1.5   The Synthetic-Camera Model   19
1.6   The Programmer's Interface   21
1.6.1   The Pen-Plotter Model   22
1.6.2   Three-Dimensional APIs   24
1.6.3   A Sequence of Images   26
1.6.4   The Modeling–Rendering Paradigm   28
1.7   Graphics Architectures   29
1.7.1   Display Processors   29
1.7.2   Pipeline Architectures   30

1.7.3   The Graphics Pipeline   31
1.7.4   Vertex Processing   31
1.7.5   Clipping and Primitive Assembly   32
1.7.6   Rasterization   33
1.7.7   Fragment Processing   33
1.8   Programmable Pipelines   33
1.9   Performance Characteristics   34
         SUMMARY AND NOTES   35
         SUGGESTED READINGS   36
         EXERCISES   36

CHAPTER 2 GRAPHICS PROGRAMMING   39
2.1   The Sierpinski Gasket   39
2.2   Programming Two-Dimensional Applications   40
2.2.1   Coordinate Systems   45
2.3   The OpenGL API   46
2.3.1   Graphics Functions   47
2.3.2   The Graphics Pipeline and State Machines   48
2.3.3   The OpenGL Interface   49
2.4   Primitives and Attributes   50
2.4.1   Polygon Basics   52
2.4.2   Polygon Types in OpenGL   53
2.4.3   Approximating a Sphere   55
2.4.4   Text   56
2.4.5   Curved Objects   58
2.4.6   Attributes   58
2.5   Color   60
2.5.1   RGB Color   62
2.5.2   Indexed Color   64
2.5.3   Setting of Color Attributes   65
2.6   Viewing   66
2.6.1   The Orthographic View   67
2.6.2   Two-Dimensional Viewing   69
2.6.3   Matrix Modes   70
2.7   Control Functions   71
2.7.1   Interaction with the Window System   71
2.7.2   Aspect Ratio and Viewports   73
2.7.3   The main, display, and myinit Functions   74
2.7.4   Program Structure   76

2.8	The Gasket Program	76
2.9	Polygons and Recursion	77
2.10	The Three-Dimensional Gasket	80
2.10.1	Use of Three-Dimensional Points 80	
2.10.2	Use of Polygons in Three Dimensions 82	
2.10.3	Hidden-Surface Removal 84	
2.11	Plotting Implicit Functions	85
2.11.1	Marching Squares 86	
	SUMMARY AND NOTES	93
	SUGGESTED READINGS	94
	EXERCISES	95

CHAPTER 3	INPUT AND INTERACTION	**99**
3.1	Interaction	99
3.2	Input Devices	100
3.2.1	Physical Input Devices 101	
3.2.2	Logical Devices 104	
3.2.3	Input Modes 105	
3.3	Clients and Servers	107
3.4	Display Lists	108
3.4.1	Definition and Execution of Display Lists 110	
3.4.2	Text and Display Lists 112	
3.4.3	Fonts in GLUT 114	
3.5	Programming Event-Driven Input	115
3.5.1	Using the Pointing Device 116	
3.5.2	Window Events 119	
3.5.3	Keyboard Events 121	
3.5.4	The Display and Idle Callbacks 121	
3.5.5	Window Management 122	
3.6	Menus	122
3.7	Picking	124
3.7.1	Picking and Selection Mode 125	
3.8	A Simple Paint Program	131
3.9	Building Interactive Models	137
3.10	Animating Interactive Programs	140
3.10.1	The Rotating Square 140	
3.10.2	Double Buffering 142	
3.10.3	Using a Timer 144	

3.11   Design of Interactive Programs   145
3.11.1 Toolkits, Widgets, and the Frame Buffer   145
3.12   Logic Operations   146
3.12.1 Drawing Erasable Lines   147
3.12.2 XOR and Color   150
3.12.3 Cursors and Overlay Planes   151
        SUMMARY AND NOTES   151
        SUGGESTED READINGS   152
        EXERCISES   153

CHAPTER 4 GEOMETRIC OBJECTS AND
          TRANSFORMATIONS   157
4.1   Scalars, Points, and Vectors   158
4.1.1   Geometric Objects   158
4.1.2   Coordinate-Free Geometry   159
4.1.3   The Mathematical View: Vector and Affine Spaces   160
4.1.4   The Computer Science View   161
4.1.5   Geometric ADTs   162
4.1.6   Lines   162
4.1.7   Affine Sums   163
4.1.8   Convexity   164
4.1.9   Dot and Cross Products   164
4.1.10 Planes   165
4.2   Three-Dimensional Primitives   166
4.3   Coordinate Systems and Frames   168
4.3.1   Representations and N-Tuples   170
4.3.2   Change of Coordinate Systems   171
4.3.3   Example Change of Representation   173
4.3.4   Homogeneous Coordinates   174
4.3.5   Example Change in Frames   177
4.3.6   Working with Representations   179
4.4   Frames in OpenGL   180
4.5   Modeling a Colored Cube   185
4.5.1   Modeling the Faces   185
4.5.2   Inward- and Outward-Pointing Faces   186
4.5.3   Data Structures for Object Representation   187
4.5.4   The Color Cube   187
4.5.5   Bilinear Interpolation   189
4.5.6   Vertex Arrays   190

4.6   Affine Transformations   192
4.7   Translation, Rotation, and Scaling   194
4.7.1   Translation   195
4.7.2   Rotation   196
4.7.3   Scaling   197
4.8   Transformations in Homogeneous Coordinates   200
4.8.1   Translation   200
4.8.2   Scaling   201
4.8.3   Rotation   202
4.8.4   Shear   203
4.9   Concatenation of Transformations   204
4.9.1   Rotation About a Fixed Point   205
4.9.2   General Rotation   207
4.9.3   The Instance Transformation   208
4.9.4   Rotation About an Arbitrary Axis   209
4.10   OpenGL Transformation Matrices   212
4.10.1   The Current Transformation Matrix   213
4.10.2   Rotation, Translation, and Scaling   214
4.10.3   Rotation About a Fixed Point in OpenGl   214
4.10.4   Order of Transformations   215
4.10.5   Spinning of the Cube   216
4.10.6   Loading, Pushing, and Popping Matrices   217
4.11   Interfaces to Three-Dimensional Applications   218
4.11.1   Using Areas of the Screen   218
4.11.2   A Virtual Trackball   219
4.11.3   Smooth Rotations   222
4.11.4   Incremental Rotation   223
4.12   Quaternions   224
4.12.1   Complex Numbers and Quaternions   224
4.12.2   Quaternions and Rotation   225
         SUMMARY AND NOTES   227
         SUGGESTED READINGS   228
         EXERCISES   229

CHAPTER **5 VIEWING**   **233**
5.1   Classical and Computer Viewing   233
5.1.1   Classical Viewing   235
5.1.2   Orthographic Projections   236
5.1.3   Axonometric Projections   237

5.1.4   Oblique Projections   238
5.1.5   Perspective Viewing   239
5.2   Viewing with a Computer   240
5.3   Positioning of the Camera   242
5.3.1   Positioning of the Camera Frame   242
5.3.2   Two Viewing APIs   247
5.3.3   The Look-At Function   250
5.3.4   Other Viewing APIs   251
5.4   Simple Projections   252
5.4.1   Perspective Projections   252
5.4.2   Orthogonal Projections   255
5.5   Projections in OpenGL   256
5.5.1   Perspective in OpenGL   257
5.5.2   Parallel Viewing in OpenGL   258
5.6   Hidden-Surface Removal   260
5.6.1   Culling   262
5.7   Interactive Mesh Displays   262
5.7.1   Meshes   262
5.7.2   Walking Through a Scene   264
5.7.3   Polygon Offset   266
5.8   Parallel-Projection Matrices   267
5.8.1   Projection Normalization   268
5.8.2   Orthogonal-Projection Matrices   268
5.8.3   Oblique Projections   271
5.9   Perspective-Projection Matrices   274
5.9.1   Perspective Normalization   274
5.9.2   OpenGL Perspective Transformations   278
5.10   Projections and Shadows   279
         SUMMARY AND NOTES   282
         SUGGESTED READINGS   282
         EXERCISES   283

CHAPTER 6 SHADING   285
6.1   Light and Matter   286
6.2   Light Sources   289
6.2.1   Color Sources   290
6.2.2   Ambient Light   290
6.2.3   Point Sources   291

6.2.4   Spotlights   292

6.2.5   Distant Light Sources   292

6.3   The Phong Reflection Model   293

6.3.1   Ambient Reflection   295

6.3.2   Diffuse Reflection   295

6.3.3   Specular Reflection   297

6.3.4   The Modified Phong Model   298

6.4   Computation of Vectors   299

6.4.1   Normal Vectors   300

6.4.2   Angle of Reflection   302

6.5   Polygonal Shading   304

6.5.1   Flat Shading   304

6.5.2   Smooth and Gouraud Shading   306

6.5.3   Phong Shading   308

6.6   Approximation of a Sphere by Recursive Subdivision   309

6.7   Light Sources in OpenGL   312

6.8   Specification of Materials in OpenGL   314

6.9   Shading of the Sphere Model   316

6.10   Global Illumination   317

         SUMMARY AND NOTES   319

         SUGGESTED READINGS   320

         EXERCISES   320

CHAPTER **7** FROM VERTICES TO FRAGMENTS   **323**

7.1   Basic Implementation Strategies   324

7.2   Four Major Tasks   326

7.2.1   Modeling   326

7.2.2   Geometry Processing   327

7.2.3   Rasterization   328

7.2.4   Fragment Processing   329

7.3   Clipping   330

7.4   Line-Segment Clipping   330

7.4.1   Cohen-Sutherland Clipping   331

7.4.2   Liang-Barsky Clipping   333

7.5   Polygon Clipping   335

7.6   Clipping of Other Primitives   338

7.6.1   Bounding Boxes and Volumes   338

7.6.2   Curves, Surfaces, and Text   339
7.6.3   Clipping in the Frame Buffer   340
7.7   Clipping in Three Dimensions   **340**
7.8   Rasterization   **343**
7.9   Bresenham's Algorithm   **346**
7.10   Polygon Rasterization   **348**
7.10.1   Inside–Outside Testing   348
7.10.2   OpenGL and Concave Polygons   350
7.10.3   Fill and Sort   351
7.10.4   Flood Fill   351
7.10.5   Singularities   352
7.11   Hidden-Surface Removal   **352**
7.11.1   Object-Space and Image-Space Approaches   353
7.11.2   Sorting and Hidden-Surface Removal   354
7.11.3   Scanline Algorithms   355
7.11.4   Back-Face Removal   356
7.11.5   The z-Buffer Algorithm   357
7.11.6   Scan Conversion with the z-Buffer   359
7.11.7   Depth Sort and the Painter's Algorithm   361
7.12   Antialiasing   **363**
7.13   Display Considerations   **365**
7.13.1   Color Systems   366
7.13.2   The Color Matrix   369
7.13.3   Gamma Correction   370
7.13.4   Dithering and Halftoning   371
         SUMMARY AND NOTES   **372**
         SUGGESTED READINGS   **373**
         EXERCISES   **374**

CHAPTER **8 DISCRETE TECHNIQUES**   **379**
8.1   Buffers   **379**
8.2   Digital Images   **381**
8.3   Writing into Buffers   **384**
8.3.1   Writing Modes   385
8.3.2   Writing with XOR   387
8.4   Bit and Pixel Operations in OpenGL   **388**
8.4.1   OpenGL Buffers and the Pixel Pipeline   389
8.4.2   Bitmaps   390

8.4.3   Raster Fonts   391

8.4.4   Pixels and Images   393

8.4.5   Lookup Tables   394

8.5   Examples   395

8.5.1   The Mandelbrot Set   395

8.5.2   Testing Algorithms   398

8.5.3   Buffers for Picking   399

8.6   Mapping Methods   399

8.7   Texture Mapping   401

8.7.1   Two-Dimensional Texture Mapping   402

8.8   Texture Mapping in OpenGL   408

8.8.1   Two-Dimensional Texture Mapping   409

8.8.2   Texture Sampling   412

8.8.3   Working with Texture Coordinates   415

8.8.4   Texture Objects   417

8.8.5   Multitexturing   418

8.9   Texture Generation   418

8.10   Environment Maps   419

8.11   Compositing Techniques   425

8.11.1   Opacity and Blending   425

8.11.2   Image Compositing   426

8.11.3   Blending and Compositing in OpenGL   427

8.11.4   Antialiasing Revisited   428

8.11.5   Back-to-Front and Front-to-Back Rendering   430

8.11.6   Depth Cueing and Fog   431

8.12   Multirendering and the Accumulation Buffer   432

8.12.1   Scene Antialiasing   433

8.12.2   Bump Mapping and Embossing   433

8.12.3   Image Processing   434

8.12.4   Imaging Extensions   435

8.12.5   Other Multipass Methods   436

8.13   Sampling and Aliasing   437

8.13.1   Sampling Theory   437

8.13.2   Reconstruction   442

8.13.3   Quantization   444

         SUMMARY AND NOTES   444

         SUGGESTED READINGS   445

         EXERCISES   446

CHAPTER **9** PROGRAMMABLE SHADERS   **449**

9.1   Programmable Pipelines   449
9.2   Shading Languages   450
9.2.1   Shade Trees   451
9.3   Extending OpenGL   452
9.3.1   OpenGL Versions and Extensions   453
9.3.2   GLSL and Cg   454
9.4   The OpenGL Shading Language   454
9.4.1   Vertex Shaders   454
9.4.2   Fragment Shaders   457
9.5   The OpenGL Shading Language   458
9.5.1   GLSL Execution   458
9.5.2   Data Types and Qualifiers   459
9.5.3   Operators and Functions   462
9.6   Linking Shaders with OpenGL Programs   463
9.7   Moving Vertices   465
9.7.1   Scaling Vertex Positions   465
9.7.2   Morphing   467
9.7.3   Particle Systems   468
9.8   Lighting with Shaders   470
9.8.1   Phong Shading   470
9.8.2   Nonphotorealistic Shading   473
9.9   Fragment Shaders   474
9.10   Per-Vertex Versus Per-Fragment Phong Shading   474
9.11   Samplers   476
9.12   Cube Maps   480
9.12.1   Reflection Maps   480
9.12.2   Refraction   482
9.12.3   Normalization Maps   485
9.13   Bump Mapping   487
9.13.1   Finding Bump Maps   487
9.13.2   Bump Mapping with Height Fields   489
9.13.3   Bump Mapping with Fragment Shaders   490
9.13.4   Example   490
         SUMMARY AND NOTES   492
         SUGGESTED READINGS   493
         EXERCISES   493

CHAPTER **10** MODELING   **497**

10.1	Symbols and Instances	498
10.2	Hierarchical Models	499
10.3	A Robot Arm	501
10.4	Trees and Traversal	504
10.4.1	A Stack-Based Traversal 505	
10.5	Use of Tree Data Structures	508
10.6	Animation	512
10.7	Graphical Objects	513
10.7.1	Methods, Attributes, and Messages 514	
10.7.2	A Cube Object 516	
10.7.3	Implementing the Cube Object 518	
10.7.4	Objects and Hierarchy 519	
10.7.5	Geometric Objects 520	
10.8	Scene Graphs	521
10.9	A Simple Scene Graph API	523
10.9.1	The Node Class 523	
10.9.2	Geometry Nodes 525	
10.9.3	Camera Class 527	
10.9.4	Lights and Materials 528	
10.9.5	Transformations 529	
10.9.6	The Robot Figure 530	
10.9.7	Implementing the Viewer 532	
10.9.8	Implementing a Node 536	
10.10	Other Tree Structures	539
10.10.1	CSG Trees 539	
10.10.2	BSP Trees 541	
10.10.3	Quadtrees and Octrees 543	
10.11	Graphics and the Internet	545
10.11.1	Networks and Protocols 545	
10.11.2	Hypermedia and HTML 546	
10.11.3	Databases and VRML 547	
10.11.4	Java and Applets 548	
10.12	Procedural Methods	549
10.13	Physically Based Models and Particle Systems	551
10.14	Newtonian Particles	552
10.14.1	Independent Particles 554	

10.14.2   Spring Forces   554
10.14.3   Attractive and Repulsive Forces   556
10.15   Solving Particle Systems   557
10.16   Constraints   560
10.16.1   Collisions   560
10.16.2   Soft Constraints   563
          SUMMARY AND NOTES   564
          SUGGESTED READINGS   565
          EXERCISES   565

CHAPTER **11** CURVES AND SURFACES   **569**
11.1   Representation of Curves and Surfaces   569
11.1.1   Explicit Representation   569
11.1.2   Implicit Representations   571
11.1.3   Parametric Form   572
11.1.4   Parametric Polynomial Curves   573
11.1.5   Parametric Polynomial Surfaces   574
11.2   Design Criteria   575
11.3   Parametric Cubic Polynomial Curves   576
11.4   Interpolation   577
11.4.1   Blending Functions   579
11.4.2   The Cubic Interpolating Patch   581
11.5   Hermite Curves and Surfaces   583
11.5.1   The Hermite Form   583
11.5.2   Geometric and Parametric Continuity   585
11.6   Bézier Curves and Surfaces   586
11.6.1   Bézier Curves   586
11.6.2   Bézier Surface Patches   589
11.7   Cubic B-Splines   591
11.7.1   The Cubic B-Spline Curve   591
11.7.2   B-Splines and Basis   594
11.7.3   Spline Surfaces   595
11.8   General B-Splines   596
11.8.1   Recursively Defined B-Splines   597
11.8.2   Uniform Splines   598
11.8.3   Nonuniform B-Splines   599
11.8.4   NURBS   599

11.9	Rendering of Curves and Surfaces	600
11.9.1	Polynomial Evaluation Methods 601	
11.9.2	Recursive Subdivision of Bézier Polynomials 602	
11.9.3	Rendering of Other Polynomial Curves by Subdivision 605	
11.9.4	Subdivision of Bézier Surfaces 605	
11.10	The Utah Teapot	608
11.11	Algebraic Surfaces	610
11.11.1	Quadrics 610	
11.11.2	Rendering of Surfaces by Ray Casting 611	
11.11.3	Subdivision Curves and Surfaces 611	
11.11.4	Mesh Subdivision 612	
11.12	Curves and Surfaces in OpenGL	615
11.12.1	Bézier Curves 616	
11.12.2	Bézier Surfaces 617	
11.12.3	Displaying the Teapot 618	
11.12.4	NURBS Functions 620	
11.12.5	Quadrics 620	
	SUMMARY AND NOTES	621
	SUGGESTED READINGS	622
	EXERCISES	622

CHAPTER **12** **ADVANCED RENDERING**		**625**
12.1	Going Beyond Pipeline Rendering	625
12.2	Ray Tracing	626
12.3	Building a Simple Ray Tracer	630
12.3.1	Recursive Ray Tracing 630	
12.3.2	Calculating Intersections 632	
12.3.3	Ray-Tracing Variations 635	
12.4	The Rendering Equation	636
12.5	Radiosity	638
12.5.1	The Radiosity Equation 639	
12.5.2	Solving the Radiosity Equation 640	
12.5.3	Computing Form Factors 642	
12.5.4	Carrying Out Radiosity 644	
12.6	RenderMan	646
12.7	Large-Scale Rendering	647
12.7.1	Sort-Middle Rendering 648	
12.7.2	Sort-Last Rendering 650	

12.7.3 Sort-First Rendering 653

12.8 Image-Based Rendering 655

12.8.1 A Simple Example 655

SUMMARY AND NOTES 658

SUGGESTED READINGS 659

EXERCISES 659

APPENDIX A SAMPLE PROGRAMS 663

A.1 Sierpinski Gasket Program 664

A.2 Recursive Generation of Sierpinski Gasket 666

A.3 Recursive Three-Dimensional Sierpinski Gasket 667

A.4 Marching Squares 670

A.5 Square Drawing Program 674

A.6 Paint Program 677

A.7 Double-Buffering Example 684

A.8 Selection-Mode Picking Program 686

A.9 Rotating-Cube Program 689

A.10 Rotating Cube Using Vertex Arrays 691

A.11 Rotating Cube with a Virtual Trackball 693

A.12 Moving Viewer 697

A.13 Sphere Program 700

A.14 Mandelbrot Set Program 703

A.15 Bresenham's Algorithm 707

A.16 Rotating Cube with Texture 709

A.17 GLSL Example 712

A.18 Scene-Graph Example 716

A.19 Program for Drawing Bézier Curves 721

APPENDIX B SPACES 725

B.1 Scalars 725

B.2 Vector Spaces 726

B.3 Affine Spaces 728

B.4 Euclidean Spaces 729

B.5 Projections 730

B.6 Gram-Schmidt Orthogonalization 731

SUGGESTED READINGS 732

EXERCISES 732

APPENDIX **C** MATRICES   **735**

C.1   Definitions   735
C.2   Matrix Operations   736
C.3   Row and Column Matrices   737
C.4   Rank   738
C.5   Change of Representation   739
C.6   The Cross Product   741
C.7   Eigenvalues and Eigenvectors   742
      SUGGESTED READINGS   743
      EXERCISES   744

APPENDIX **D** SYNOPSIS OF OPENGL FUNCTIONS   **745**

D.1   Specifying Simple Geometry   745
D.2   Attributes   746
D.3   Working with the Window System   747
D.4   Interaction   748
D.5   Enabling Features   750
D.6   Transformations   750
D.7   Viewing   751
D.8   Defining Discrete Primitives   752
D.9   Display Lists   753
D.10 Picking   754
D.11 Lighting   755
D.12 Texture Mapping   755
D.13 State and Buffer Manipulation   757
D.14 Vertex Arrays   757
D.15 Blending Functions   758
D.16 Query Functions   758
D.17 Curve and Surface Functions   758
D.18 GLU Quadrics   759
D.19 GLSL Functions   760

References   763

Function Index   771

Subject Index   773

PREFACE

This book is an introduction to computer graphics, with an emphasis on applications programming. In the first edition, which was published in 1997, I noted that in the seven years since my previous graphics text, the field had experienced enormous growth—a rate of growth that exceeded most people's expectations, including my own. In the eight years (and three editions) since, we have seen even more changes. Feature-length computer-animated movies, have proved to be commercial and artistic successes. The use of computer effects in movies is standard and it is often almost impossible to distinguish live action from computer-generated effects. Recent hardware has blurred the distinction between computers and game boxes. Programmable graphics processors provide a level of flexibility in personal computers that was not available in the most expensive workstations just a few years ago.

Not only have graphics capabilities increased but costs have been reduced for both high- and low-end workstations. Within the last few years the cost of a graphics system that can generate over ten million three-dimensional polygons per second with lighting and texture mapping has gone from over $100,000 to less than $1000. The availability of special-purpose graphics boards for personal computers has been especially significant. These boards provide support for sophisticated three-dimensional applications, starting at about $100. On the software side, OpenGL remains the standard programmer's interface both for writing application programs and developing high-level products in the scientific community.

A Top-Down Approach

These recent advances and the success of the first three editions have reinforced my belief in a top-down, programming-oriented approach to introductory computer graphics. Although many computer science and engineering departments now support more than one course in the subject, most students will take only a single course. Such a course is placed in the curriculum after students have already studied programming, data structures, algorithms, software engineering, and basic mathematics. A class in computer graphics allows the instructor to build on these topics in a way that can be both informative and fun. I want these students to be programming three-dimensional applications as soon as possible. Low-level algorithms, such as those that draw lines or fill polygons, can be dealt with later, after students are creating graphics.

John Kemeny, a pioneer in computer education, used a familiar automobile analogy: You don't have to know what's under the hood to be literate, but unless you know how to program, you'll be sitting in the back seat instead of driving. That same analogy applies to the way we teach computer graphics. One approach—the algorithmic approach—is to teach everything about what makes a car function: the engine, the transmission, the combustion process. A second approach—the survey approach—is to hire a chauffeur, sit back, and see the world as a spectator. The third approach—the programming approach that I have adopted here—is to teach you how to drive and how to take yourself wherever you want to go. As the old auto-rental commercial used to say, "Let us put *you* in the driver's seat."

Programming with OpenGL and C

When I began teaching computer graphics 20 years ago, the greatest impediment to implementing a programming-oriented course, and to writing a textbook for that course, was the lack of a widely accepted graphics library or application programmer's interface (API). Difficulties included high cost, limited availability, lack of generality, and high complexity. The development of OpenGL resolved most of the difficulties many of us had experienced with other APIs (such as GKS and PHIGS) and with the alternative of using home-brewed software. OpenGL today is supported by most workstation suppliers and is available for most platforms through third-party vendors. It is bundled with all recent versions of Microsoft Windows and with the Apple Macintosh Operating System. There is also an OpenGL API called Mesa that is included with most Linux distributions.

A graphics class teaches far more than the use of a particular API, but a good API makes it easier to teach key graphics topics, such as three-dimensional graphics, shading, client–server graphics, modeling, and implementation algorithms. I believe that OpenGL's extensive capabilities and well-defined architecture lead to a stronger foundation for teaching both theoretical and practical aspects of the field and for teaching important new capabilities, such as texture mapping and compositing, that until recently were not supported in any API.

I switched my classes to OpenGL about 12 years ago, and the results astounded me. By the middle of the semester, *every* student was able to write a moderately complex three-dimensional program that required understanding of three-dimensional viewing and event-driven input. In 15 years of teaching computer graphics, I had never come even close to this result. That class led me to rewrite my previous book from scratch.

This book is a textbook on computer graphics; it is not an OpenGL manual. Consequently, I do not cover all aspects of the OpenGL API but rather explain only what is necessary for mastering this book's contents. I present OpenGL at a level that should permit users of other APIs to have little difficulty with the material. For students who want more detail on OpenGL, my recent book *OpenGL: A Primer,* Second Edition, (Addison-Wesley 2004) should be a valuable supplement.

In this edition, I use both C and C++, with C as the dominant language. There are two reasons for this decision. First, OpenGL is not object-oriented, so using C++ or Java would not add significantly to the basic presentation, unless I were to insert an object-oriented geometric library between OpenGL and the user. I have not taken this step, despite its appealing features, because it would detract from the graphics and would make the book less accessible to students who are good programmers but unfamiliar with object-oriented languages. Second, my experience has been that object-oriented approaches shield the user from what is going on inside (as they should), whereas in an introduction to computer graphics, I want readers to be aware of what is happening at the lowest levels. Although the use of computer graphics is a wonderful way to introduce students to object-oriented programming, in my view, an object-oriented approach is not the most effective way to teach graphics to computer science and engineering students. The exception to this view is when I introduce scene graphs which are object oriented and benefit from the use of C++. My undergraduate students use Java and C in their beginning courses but have no difficulty in using the code in this book with either C or C++.

Within the computer graphics community, there has been much discussion of the future of OpenGL and whether it will be replaced by DirectX. Among computer graphics educators, however, there is little doubt that OpenGL will continue to be the API of choice for their classes. Although DirectX is the standard for game development, in the opinion of many of us, it is not well suited for teaching computer graphics, nor for users who want to develop their own applications. In addition to being specific to Windows platforms, DirectX requires far more code for basic portable applications. At the higher levels, OpenGL and DirectX support similar functionality in similar ways. Hence, users of this book should be able to move to DirectX with little difficulty when required.

Intended Audience

This book is suitable for advanced undergraduates and first-year graduate students in computer science and engineering and for students in other disciplines who have good programming skills. The book also will be useful to many professionals. I have taught approximately 100 short courses for professionals; my experiences with those students have had a great influence on what I have chosen to include in the book.

Prerequisites for the book are good programming skills in C or C++, an understanding of basic data structures (linked lists, trees), and a rudimentary knowledge of linear algebra and trigonometry. I have found that the mathematical backgrounds of computer science students, whether of undergraduates or of graduates, vary considerably. Hence, I have chosen to integrate into the text much of the linear algebra and geometry that is required for fundamental computer graphics. I have also summarized this material in Appendices B and C.

Organization of the Book

The book is organized as follows. Chapter 1 overviews the field and introduces image formation by optical devices; thus, we start with three-dimensional concepts immediately. Chapter 2 introduces programming using OpenGL. Although the first example program that we develop—each chapter has one or more complete programming examples—is two-dimensional, it is embedded in a three-dimensional setting and leads to a three-dimensional extension. In Chapter 3, we discuss interactive graphics in a modern client–server setting and develop event-driven graphics programs. Chapters 4 and 5 concentrate on three-dimensional concepts; Chapter 4 is concerned with defining and manipulating three-dimensional objects, whereas Chapter 5 is concerned with viewing them. Chapter 6 introduces light–material interactions and shading. These chapters should be covered in order and can be done in about 10 weeks of a 15-week semester.

The next six chapters can be read in almost any order. All six are somewhat open ended and can be covered at a survey level, or individual topics can be pursued in depth. Chapter 7 surveys rasterization. It gives one or two major algorithms for each of the basic steps, including clipping, line generation, and polygon fill . Chapter 8 introduces many of the new discrete capabilities that are now supported in graphics hardware and by OpenGL. All these techniques involve working with various buffers. It concludes with a short discussion of aliasing problems in computer graphics. Chapter 9 is an introduction to programmable shaders using the OpenGL Shading Language (GLSL), which is now a standard part of OpenGL. We use programmable shaders to develop techniques, such as bump mapping, that can now be done in real time. Chapters 8 and 9 conclude the discussion of the standard viewing pipeline used by all interactive graphics systems.

Chapter 10 contains a number of topics that fit loosely under the heading of modeling. The topics range from building models that encapsulate the relationships between the parts of a model, to high-level approaches to graphics over the Internet, to procedural methods. It includes a simple scene graph API. Curves and surfaces, including subdivision surfaces, are discussed in Chapter 11. Chapter 12 surveys alternate approaches to rendering. It includes expanded discussions of ray tracing and radiosity and an introduction to image-based rendering and parallel rendering.

Programs, primarily from the first part of the book, are included in Appendix A. They are also available online (see Support Materials). Appendices B and C contain a review of the background mathematics. Appendix D is new and contains a synopsis of the OpenGL functions used in the book.

Changes from the Third Edition

The reaction of readers of the first three editions of this book was overwhelmingly positive, especially to the use of OpenGL and the top-down approach. But there are always improvements to be made and recent advances to be covered. The advent of programmable graphics processors has been a major advance, one that I believe should have a major impact on how we teach computer graphics. Besides forcing a rearrangement of material from earlier editions, techniques that were not possible to implement in most systems, and thus were covered only in a perfunctory manner, are now routine and can be taught in a first course in computer graphics. An additional benefit of the rearrangement of topics is that the chapters now follow the OpenGL pipeline more closely than in previous editions.

Programmable shaders are covered in the new Chapter 9 using the OpenGL Shading Language that is part of OpenGL 2.0. Using programmable shaders, many techniques now can be implemented in real time. Hence, some of the material has been moved around. Thus, bump mapping, which was covered with texture mapping in the third edition, is now covered with fragment shaders. Although some instructors may find this change to be a bit odd at first, I think that they will see the advantages when they start teaching about vertex and fragment shaders.

I have eliminated the separate chapters on scientific visualization and procedural methods from the third edition. Except for the most advanced sections, most of the material has been distributed through the other chapters in a way that should allow instructors to cover some advanced material at their option. For example, the marching squares method is now at the end of Chapter 2 to provide an example of a sophisticated two-dimensional application, but covering it is not necessary for proceeding to Chapter 3.

I believe that these changes should have minor effects on the teaching of a one-semester introductory course but should make it easier for instructors to use the book for a two-semester class.

Support Materials

The support for the book is on the Web, both through the author's Web site *www.cs.unm.edu/~angel* and Addison-Wesley's site *www.aw.com/cssupport*. Support material that is available to all readers of this book includes

- Sources of information on OpenGL.
- Instructions on how to get started with OpenGL on the most popular systems.
- Program code.
- Solutions to selected exercises.
- PowerPoint lectures.

Additional support materials, including solutions to all the nonprogramming exercises, are available only to instructors adopting this textbook for classroom use. Please contact your school's Addison-Wesley representative for information on obtaining access to this material.

Acknowledgments

I have been fortunate over the past few years to have worked with wonderful students at UNM. They were the first to get me interested in OpenGL, and I have learned much from them. They include Hue Bumgarner-Kirby (Walker), Ye Cong, Pat Crossno, Tommie Daniel, Chris Davis, Lisa Desjarlais, Kim Edlund, Lee Ann Fisk, Maria Gallegos, Brian Jones, Christopher Jordan, Max Hazelrigg, Sheryl Hurley, Thomas Keller, Ge Li, Pat McCormick, Al McPherson, Ken Moreland, Martin Muller, David Munich, Jim Pinkerton, Jim Prewett, Dave Rogers, Hal Smyer, Takeshi Hakamata, Dave Vick, Brian Wylie, and Jin Xiong. Many of the examples in the color plates were created by these students.

The first edition of this book was written during my sabbatical; various parts were written in five different countries. The experience speaks well for the versatility of portable computers and the universality of the Internet. Nevertheless, the task would not have been accomplished without the help of a number of people and institutions that made their facilities available to me. I am greatly indebted to Jonas Montilva and Chris Birkbeck of the Universidad de los Andes (Venezuela), to Rodrigo Gallegos and Aristides Novoa of the Universidad Tecnologica Equinoccial (Ecuador), to Long Wen Chang of the National Tsing Hua University (Taiwan), and to Kin Hong Wong and Pheng Ann Heng of the Chinese University of Hong Kong. Ramiro Jordan of ISTEC and the University of New Mexico made possible many of these visits. John Brayer and Jason Stewart at the University of New Mexico and Helen Goldstein at Addison-Wesley somehow managed to get a variety of items to me wherever I happened to be. My Web site contains a description of my adventures writing the first edition.

This edition was written in New Mexico and benefited greatly from the feedback of hundreds of instructors and students who used these editions and sent me their comments. Many of the changes from earlier editions are responses to their requests and comments.

David Kirk and Mark Kilgard at NVIDIA were kind enough to provide cards for testing many of the recent algorithms. A number of other people provided significant help. I thank Ben Bederson, Gonzalo Cartagenova, Tom Caudell, Kathi Collins, Kathleen Danielson, Roger Ehrich, Robert Geist, Chuck Hansen, Mark Henne, Bernard Moret, Dick Nordhaus, Helena Saona, Dave Shreiner, Vicki Shreiner, Gwen Sylvan, and Mason Woo. Mark Kilgard, Brian Paul, and Nate Robins are owed a great debt by the OpenGL community for creating software that enables OpenGL code to be developed over a variety of platforms.

At the University of New Mexico, the High Performance Computing Center and IBM provided support for many of my visualization projects. The Computer Science Department, the Arts Technology Center in the College of Fine

Arts, the National Science Foundation, Sandia National Laboratories, and Los Alamos National Laboratory have supported many of my students and research projects that led to parts of this book. David Beining and the Lodestar Planetarium have provided tremendous support for the Full Dome Project (Sheryl Hurley, Christopher Jordan, Laurel Ladwig, Hue (Bumgarner-Kirby) Walker) that provided some of the images in the color plates.

Reviewers of my manuscript drafts provided a variety of viewpoints on what I should include and what level of presentation I should use. These reviewers include Gur Saran Adhar (University of North Carolina at Wilmington), Mario Agrular (Jacksonville State University), Michael Anderson (University of Hartford), C. S. Bauer (University of Central Florida), Marty Barrett (East Tennessee State University), Robert P. Burton (Brigham Young University), Sam Buss (University of California, San Diego), Kai H. Chang (Auburn University), Ron DiNapoli (Cornell University), Eric Alan Durant (Milwaukee School of Engineering), David S. Ebert (Purdue University), Chenyi Hu (University of Central Arkansas), Mark Kilgard (NVIDIA Corporation), Lisa B. Lancor (Southern Connecticut State University), Chung Lee (CA Polytechnic University, Pomona), John L. Lowther (Michigan Technological University), R. Marshall (Boston University and Bridgewater State College), Bruce A. Maxwell (Swathmore College), James R. Miller (University of Kansas), Han-Wei Shen (The Ohio State University), Oliver Staadt (University of California, Davis), Stephen L. Stepoway (Southern Methodist University), Michael Wainer (Southern Illinois University, Carbondale), George Wolberg (City College of New York), Yang Wang (Southern Methodist State University), Steve Warren (Kansas State University), Mike Way (Florida Southern College), and Ying Zhu (Georgia State University). Although the final decisions may not reflect their views—which often differed considerably from one another—each reviewer forced me to reflect on every page of the manuscript.

I acknowledge the entire production team at Addison-Wesley. My editors, Peter Gordon, Maite Suarez-Rivas, and Matt Goldstein have been a pleasure to work with through four editions of this book and the OpenGL Primer. Katherine Harutunian has helped me through the production process on all my books with Addison-Wesley. Through four editions, Paul Anagnostopoulos at Windfall Software has always been more than helpful in assisting me with TEX problems. I am especially grateful to Lyn Dupré. I am not a natural writer. If the readers could see the original draft of the first edition, they would understand the wonders that Lyn does with a manuscript.

My wife, Rose Mary Molnar, did the figures for my first graphics book, many of which form the basis for the figures in this book. Probably only other authors can fully appreciate the effort that goes into the book production process and the many contributions and sacrifices our partners make to that effort. The dedication to the book is a sincere but inadequate recognition of all of Rose Mary's contributions to my work.

GRAPHICS SYSTEMS
AND MODELS

Over the past decade, computer and communication technologies have become dominant forces in our lives. Activities as wide-ranging as film making, publishing, banking, and education continue to undergo revolutionary changes as these technologies alter the ways in which we conduct our daily activities. The combination of computers, networks, and the complex human visual system, through computer graphics, has led to new ways of displaying information, seeing virtual worlds, and communicating with both other people and machines.

Computer graphics is concerned with all aspects of producing pictures or images using a computer. The field began humbly almost 50 years ago, with the display of a few lines on a **cathode-ray tube (CRT)**; now, we can generate images by computer that are nearly indistinguishable from photographs of real objects. We routinely train pilots with simulated airplanes, generating graphical displays of a virtual environment in real time. Feature-length movies made entirely by computer have been successful, both critically and financially.

In this chapter, we start our journey with a short discussion of applications of computer graphics. Then we overview graphics systems and imaging. Throughout this book, our approach stresses the relationships between computer graphics and image formation by familiar methods, such as drawing by hand and photography. We shall see that these relationships can help us to design application programs, graphics libraries, and architectures for graphics systems.

In this book, we introduce a particular graphics software system, **OpenGL**, which has become a widely accepted standard for developing graphics applications. Fortunately, OpenGL is easy to learn, and it possesses most of the characteristics of other popular graphics systems. Our approach is top-down. We want you to start writing, as quickly as possible, application programs that will generate graphical output. After you begin writing simple programs, we shall discuss how the underlying graphics library and the hardware are implemented. This chapter should give a sufficient overview for you to proceed to writing programs.

1.1 Applications of Computer Graphics

The development of computer graphics has been driven both by the needs of the user community and by advances in hardware and software. The applications of computer graphics are many and varied; we can, however, divide them into four major areas:

1. Display of information
2. Design
3. Simulation and animation
4. User interfaces

Although many applications span two or more of these areas, the development of the field was based on separate work in each.

1.1.1 Display of Information

Classical graphics techniques arose as a medium to convey information among people. Although spoken and written languages serve a similar purpose, the human visual system is unrivaled both as a processor of data and as a pattern recognizer. More than 4000 years ago, the Babylonians displayed floor plans of buildings on stones. More than 2000 years ago, the Greeks were able to convey their architectural ideas graphically, even though the related mathematics was not developed until the Renaissance. Today, the same type of information is generated by architects, mechanical designers, and draftspeople using computer-based drafting systems.

For centuries, cartographers have developed maps to display celestial and geographical information. Such maps were crucial to navigators as these people explored the ends of the earth; maps are no less important today in fields such as geographic information systems. Now, maps can be developed and manipulated in real time over the Internet.

Over the past 100 years, workers in the field of statistics have explored techniques for generating plots that aid the viewer in determining the information in a set of data. Now, we have computer plotting packages that provide a variety of plotting techniques and color tools and that can handle multiple large data sets. Nevertheless, it is still the human's ability to recognize visual patterns that ultimately allows us to interpret the information contained in the data. The field of information visualization is becoming increasingly more important as we have to deal with understanding complex phenomena from problems in bioinformatics to detecting security threats.

Medical imaging poses interesting and important data-analysis problems. Modern imaging technologies—such as computed tomography (CT), magnetic resonance imaging (MRI), ultrasound, and positron-emission tomography (PET)—generate three-dimensional data that must be subjected to algorithmic manipulation to provide useful information. Color Plate 20 shows an image of a person's head in which the skin is displayed as transparent and the internal structures are displayed as opaque. Although the data were collected by a medical imaging system, computer graphics produced the image that shows the structures.

Supercomputers now allow researchers in many areas to solve previously intractable problems. The field of scientific visualization provides graphical tools that help these researchers to interpret the vast quantity of data that they generate. In fields such as fluid flow, molecular biology, and mathematics, images generated by conversion of data to geometric entities that can be displayed have yielded new insights into complex processes. For example, Color Plate 19 shows fluid dynamics in the mantle of the earth. The system used a mathematical model to generate the data. We present various visualization techniques as examples throughout the rest of the text.

1.1.2 Design

Professions such as engineering and architecture are concerned with design. Starting with a set of specifications, engineers and architects seek a cost-effective and esthetic solution that satisfies the specifications. Design is an iterative process. Rarely in the real world is a problem specified such that there is a unique optimal solution. Design problems are either *overdetermined*, such that they possess no solution that satisfies all the criteria, much less an optimal solution, or *underdetermined*, such that they have multiple solutions that satisfy the design criteria. Thus, the designer works in an iterative manner. She generates a possible design, tests it, and then uses the results as the basis for exploring other solutions.

The power of the paradigm of humans interacting with images on the screen of a CRT was recognized by Ivan Sutherland over 40 years ago. Today, the use of interactive graphical tools in computer-aided design (CAD) pervades fields such as architecture and the design of mechanical parts and of very-large-scale integrated (VLSI) circuits. In many such applications, the graphics are used in a number of distinct ways. For example, in a VLSI design, the graphics provide an interactive interface between the user and the design package, usually by means of such tools as menus and icons. In addition, after the user produces a possible design, other tools analyze the design and display the analysis graphically. Color Plates 9 and 10 show two views of the same architectural design. Both images were generated with the same CAD system. They demonstrate the importance of having the tools available to generate different images of the same objects at different stages of the design process.

1.1.3 Simulation and Animation

Once graphics systems evolved to be capable of generating sophisticated images in real time, engineers and researchers began to use them as simulators. One of the most important uses has been in the training of pilots. Graphical flight simulators have proved both to increase safety and to reduce training expenses. The use of special VLSI chips has led to a generation of arcade games as sophisticated as flight simulators. Games and educational software for home computers are almost as impressive. Color Plate 16 shows a physical robot and the corresponding graphical simulation. The simulator can be used for designing the robot, for planning its path, and for simulating its behavior in complex environments.

The success of flight simulators led to the use of computer graphics for animation in the television, motion-picture, and advertising industries. Entire animated movies can now be made by computer at a cost less than that of movies made with traditional hand-animation techniques. The use of computer graphics with hand animation allows the creation of technical and artistic effects that are not possible with either alone. Whereas computer animations have a distinct look, we can also generate photorealistic images by computer. Often images that we see on television, in movies, and in magazines are so realistic that we cannot distinguish computer-generated or computer-altered images from photographs. In Chapters 6 and 9, we discuss many of the lighting effects used to produce computer animations. Color Plates 11 through 13 are three scenes from a computer-generated video. The artists and engineers who created these scenes used commercially available software. The plates demonstrate our ability to generate realistic environments, such as the factory in Plate 11; to simulate robots, as shown in Plate 12; and to create special effects, such as the sparks in Plate 13. The images in Color Plate 31 show another example of the use of computer graphics to generate an effect that, although it looks realistic, could not have been created otherwise. The images in Color Plates 23 and 24 also are realistic renderings.

The field of virtual reality (VR) has opened up many new horizons. A human viewer can be equipped with a display headset that allows her to see separate images with her right eye and her left eye so that she has the effect of stereoscopic vision. In addition, her body location and position, possibly including her head and finger positions, are tracked by the computer. She may have other interactive devices available, including force-sensing gloves and sound. She can then act as part of a computer-generated scene, limited only by the image-generation ability of the computer. For example, a surgical intern might be trained to do an operation in this way, or an astronaut might be trained to work in a weightless environment. Color Plate 22 shows one frame of a VR simulation of a simulated patient used for remote training of medical personnel.

1.1.4 User Interfaces

Our interaction with computers has become dominated by a visual paradigm that includes windows, icons, menus, and a pointing device, such as a mouse. From a user's perspective, windowing systems such as the X Window System, Microsoft Windows, and the Macintosh Operating System differ only in details. More recently, millions of people have become users of the Internet. Their access is through graphical network browsers, such as Netscape and Internet Explorer, that use these same interface tools. We have become so accustomed to this style of interface that we often forget that what we are doing is working with computer graphics.

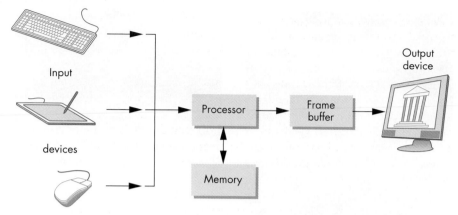

FIGURE 1.1 A graphics system.

Although we are familiar with the style of graphical user interface used on most workstations,[1] advances in computer graphics have made possible other forms of interfaces. Color Plate 14 shows the interface used with a high-level modeling package. It demonstrates the variety both of the tools available in such packages and of the interactive devices the user can employ in modeling geometric objects.

1.2 A Graphics System

A computer graphics system is a computer system; as such, it must have all the components of a general-purpose computer system. Let us start with the high-level view of a graphics system, as shown in the block diagram in Figure 1.1. There are five major elements in our system:

1. Input devices
2. Processor
3. Memory
4. Frame buffer
5. Output devices

This model is general enough to include workstations and personal computers, interactive game systems, and sophisticated image-generation systems. Although all the components, with the exception of the frame buffer, are present in a standard computer, it is the way each element is specialized for computer graphics that characterizes this diagram as a portrait of a graphics system.

---

1. Although personal computers and workstations evolved by somewhat different paths, at present, there is virtually no fundamental difference between them. Hence, we shall use the terms *personal computer* and *workstation* synonymously.

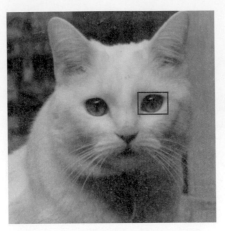
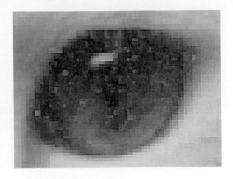

FIGURE 1.2   Pixels. (a) Image of Yeti the cat. (b) Detail of area around one eye showing individual pixels.

1.2.1   Pixels and the Frame Buffer

At present, almost all graphics systems are raster based. A picture is produced as an array—the **raster**—of picture elements, or **pixels**, within the graphics system. As we can see from Figure 1.2, each pixel corresponds to a location, or small area, in the image. Collectively, the pixels are stored in a part of memory called the **frame buffer**. The frame buffer can be viewed as the core element of a graphics system. Its **resolution**—the number of pixels in the frame buffer—determines the detail that you can see in the image. The **depth**, or **precision**, of the frame buffer, defined as the number of bits that are used for each pixel, determines properties such as how many colors can be represented on a given system. For example, a 1-bit-deep frame buffer allows only two colors, whereas an 8-bit-deep frame buffer allows 2^8 (256) colors. In **full-color** systems, there are 24 (or more) bits per pixel. Such systems can display sufficient colors to represent most images realistically. They are also called **true-color** systems, or **RGB-color** systems, because individual groups of bits in each pixel are assigned to each of the three primary colors—red, green, and blue—used in most displays.

The frame buffer usually is implemented with special types of memory chips that enable fast redisplay of the contents of the frame buffer. In software-based systems, such as those used for high-resolution rendering or to generate complex visual effects that cannot be produced in real time, the frame buffer is part of system memory.

In a very simple system, the frame buffer holds only the colored pixels that are displayed on the screen. In most systems, the frame buffer holds far more information, such as depth information needed for creating images from three-dimensional data. In these systems, the frame buffer comprises multiple buffers, one or more of which are **color buffers** that hold the colored pixels that are displayed. For now, we can use the terms *frame buffer* and *color buffer* synonymously without confusion.

In a simple system, there may be only one processor, the **central processing unit** (**CPU**) of the system, which must do both the normal processing and the graphical processing. The main graphical function of the processor is to take specifications of graphical primitives (such as lines, circles, and polygons) generated by application programs and to assign values to the pixels in the frame buffer that best represent these entities. For example, a triangle is specified by its three vertices, but to display its outline by the three line segments connecting the vertices, the graphics system must generate a set of pixels that appear as line segments to the viewer. The conversion of geometric entities to pixel colors and locations in the frame buffer is known as **rasterization**, or **scan conversion**. In early graphics systems, the frame buffer was part of the standard memory that could be directly addressed by the CPU. Today, virtually all graphics systems are characterized by special-purpose **graphics processing units** (**GPUs**), custom-tailored to carry out specific graphics functions. The GPU can be either on the mother board of the system or on a graphics card. The frame buffer is accessed through the graphics processing unit and may be included in the GPU.

1.2.2 Output Devices

The dominant type of display (or **monitor**), and the one that we assume is used on our system, is the **cathode-ray tube** (**CRT**). A simplified picture of a CRT is shown in Figure 1.3. When electrons strike the phosphor coating on the tube, light is emitted. The direction of the beam is controlled by two pairs of deflection plates. The output of the computer is converted, by digital-to-analog converters, to voltages across the x and y deflection plates. Light appears on the surface of the CRT when a sufficiently intense beam of electrons is directed at the phosphor.

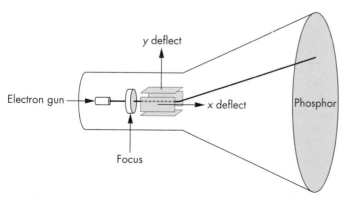

FIGURE 1.3   The cathode-ray tube (CRT).

If the voltages steering the beam change at a constant rate, the beam will trace a straight line, visible to a viewer. Such a device is known as the **random-scan**, **calligraphic**, or **vector** CRT, because the beam can be moved directly from any position to any other position. If intensity of the beam is turned off, the beam can be moved to a new position without changing any visible display. This configuration was the basis of early graphics systems that predated the present raster technology.

A typical CRT will emit light for only a short time—usually, a few milli-seconds—after the phosphor is excited by the electron beam. For a human to see a steady, flicker-free image on most CRT displays, the same path must be retraced, or **refreshed**, by the beam at a sufficiently high rate, the **refresh rate**. In older systems, the refresh rate is determined by the frequency of the power system, 60 cycles per second or 60 Hertz (Hz) in the United States and 50 Hz in much of the rest of the world. Modern displays are no longer coupled to these low frequencies and operate at rates up to about 85 Hz.

In a raster system, the graphics system takes pixels from the frame buffer and displays them as points on the surface of the display in one of two fundamental ways. In a **noninterlaced** system, the pixels are displayed row by row, or scan line by scan line, at the refresh rate. In an **interlaced** display, odd rows and even rows are refreshed alternately. Interlaced displays are used in commercial television. In an interlaced display operating at 60 Hz, the screen is redrawn in its entirety only 30 times per second, although the visual system is tricked into thinking the refresh rate is 60 Hz rather than 30 Hz. Viewers located near the screen, however, can tell the difference between the interlaced and noninterlaced displays. Noninterlaced displays are becoming more widespread, even though these displays process pixels at twice the rate of the interlaced display.

Color CRTs have three different colored phosphors (red, green, and blue), arranged in small groups. One common style arranges the phosphors in triangular groups called **triads**, each triad consisting of three phosphors, one of each primary. Most color CRTs have three electron beams, corresponding to the three types of phosphors. In the shadow-mask CRT (Figure 1.4), a metal screen with small holes—the **shadow mask**—ensures that an electron beam excites only phosphors of the proper color.

Although CRTs are still the most common display device, they are rapidly be-ing replaced by flat-screen technologies. Flat-panel monitors are inherently raster. Although there are multiple technologies available, including light-emitting diodes (LEDs), liquid-crystal displays (LCDs), and plasma panels, all use a two-dimensional grid to address individual light-emitting elements. Figure 1.5 shows a generic flat-panel monitor. The two outside plates each contain parallel grids of wires that are oriented perpendicular to each other. By sending electrical signals to the proper wire in each grid, the electrical field at a location, determined by the intersection of two wires, can be made strong enough to control the corre-sponding element in the middle plate. The middle plate in an LED panel contains light-emitting diodes that can be turned on and off by the electrical signals sent to the grid. In an LCD display, the electrical field controls the polarization of

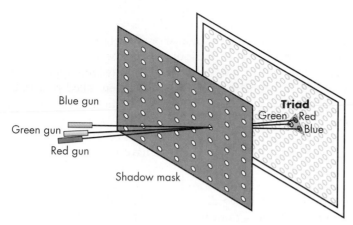

FIGURE 1.4 Shadow-mask CRT.

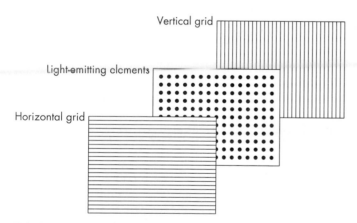

FIGURE 1.5 Generic flat-panel display.

the liquid crystals in the middle panel, thus turning on and off the light passing through the panel. A plasma panel uses the voltages on the grids to energize gases embedded between the glass panels holding the grids. The energized gas becomes a glowing plasma.

Most projection systems are also raster devices. These systems use a variety of technologies, including CRTs and digital light projection (DLP). From a user perspective, they act as standard monitors with similar resolutions and precisions. Hard-copy devices, such as printers and plotters, are also raster based but cannot be refreshed.

1.2.3   Input Devices

Most graphics systems provide a keyboard and at least one other input device. The most common input devices are the mouse, the joystick, and the data tablet. Each provides positional information to the system, and each usually is equipped with one or more buttons to provide signals to the processor. Often called **pointing devices**, these devices allow a user to indicate a particular location on the display. We study these devices in Chapter 3.

Game consoles lack keyboards but include a greater variety of input devices than a standard workstation. A typical console might have multiple buttons, a joy stick, and dials.

Games, CAD, and virtual reality applications have all generated the need for input devices that provide more than two-dimensional data. Three-dimensional locations on a real-world object can be obtained by a variety of devices, including laser range finders and acoustic sensors. Higher-dimensional data can be obtained by devices such as data gloves, which include many sensors, and computer vision systems.

1.3   Images: Physical and Synthetic

Until recently, the pedagogical approach to teaching computer graphics was focused on how to construct raster images of simple two-dimensional geometric entities (for example, points, line segments, and polygons) in the frame buffer. Next, most textbooks discussed how to define two- and three-dimensional mathematical objects in the computer and image them with the set of two-dimensional rasterized primitives.

This approach worked well for creating simple images of simple objects. In modern systems, however, we want to exploit the capabilities of the software and hardware to create realistic images of computer-generated three-dimensional objects—a task that involves many aspects of image formation, such as lighting, shading, and properties of materials. Because such functionality is supported directly by most present computer graphics systems, we prefer to set the stage for creating these images here, rather than to expand a limited model later.

Computer-generated images are synthetic or artificial, in the sense that the objects being imaged do not exist physically. In this chapter, we argue that the preferred method to form computer-generated images is similar to traditional imaging methods, such as cameras and the human visual system. Hence, before we discuss the mechanics of writing programs to generate images, we discuss the way images are formed by optical systems. We construct a model of the image-formation process that we can then use to understand and develop computer-generated imaging systems.

In this chapter, we make minimal use of mathematics. We want to establish a paradigm for creating images and to present a computer architecture for implementing that paradigm. Details are presented in subsequent chapters, where we shall derive the relevant equations.

1.3.1 Objects and Viewers

We live in a world of three-dimensional objects. The development of many branches of mathematics, including geometry and trigonometry, was in response to the desire to systematize conceptually simple ideas, such as the measurement of size of objects and distance between objects. Often, we seek to represent our understanding of such spatial relationships with pictures or images, such as maps, paintings, and photographs. Likewise, the development of many physical devices—including cameras, microscopes, and telescopes—was tied to the desire to visualize spatial relationships among objects. Hence, there always has been a fundamental link between the physics and the mathematics of image formation—one that we can exploit in our development of computer image formation.

Two basic entities must be part of any image-formation process, be it mathematical or physical: *object* and *viewer*. The object exists in space independent of any image-formation process and of any viewer. In computer graphics, where we deal with synthetic objects, we form objects by specifying the positions in space of various geometric primitives, such as points, lines, and polygons. In most graphics systems, a set of locations in space, or of **vertices**, is sufficient to define, or approximate, most objects. For example, a line can be defined by two vertices; a polygon can be defined by an ordered list of vertices; and a sphere can be specified by two vertices that specify its center and any point on its circumference. One of the main functions of a CAD system is to provide an interface that makes it easy for a user to build a synthetic model of the world. In Chapter 2, we show how OpenGL allows us to build simple objects; in Chapter 11, we learn to define objects in a manner that incorporates relationships among objects.

Every imaging system must provide a means of forming images from objects. To form an image, we must have someone or something that is viewing our objects, be it a human, a camera, or a digitizer. It is the **viewer** that forms the image of our objects. In the human visual system, the image is formed on the back of the eye. In a camera, the image is formed in the film plane. It is easy to confuse images and objects. We usually see an object from our single perspective and forget that other viewers, located in other places, will see the same object differently. Figure 1.6(a) shows two viewers observing the same

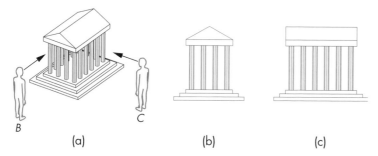

FIGURE 1.6   Image seen by three different viewers. (a) A's view. (b) B's view. (c) C's view.

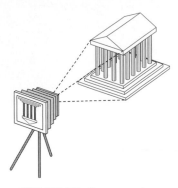

FIGURE 1.7   Camera system.

building. This image is what is seen by an observer A who is far enough away from the building to see both the building and the two other viewers, B and C. From A's perspective, B and C appear as objects, just as the building does. Figures 1.6(b) and (c) show the images seen by B and C, respectively. All three images contain the same building, but the image of the building is different in all three.

Figure 1.7 shows a camera system viewing a building. Here we can observe that both the object and the viewer exist in a three-dimensional world. However, the image that they define—what we find on the film plane—is two-dimensional. The process by which the specification of the object is combined with the specification of the viewer to produce a two-dimensional image is the essence of image formation, and we shall study it in detail.

1.3.2   Light and Images

The preceding description of image formation is far from complete. For example, we have yet to mention light. If there were no light sources, the objects would be dark, and there would be nothing visible in our image. Nor have we indicated how color enters the picture or what the effects of the surface properties of the objects are.

Taking a more physical approach, we can start with the arrangement in Figure 1.8, which shows a simple physical imaging system. Again, we see a physical object and a viewer (the camera); now, however, there is a light source in the scene. Light from the source strikes various surfaces of the object, and a portion of the reflected light enters the camera through the lens. The details of the interaction between light and the surfaces of the object determine how much light enters the camera.

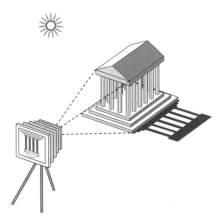

FIGURE 1.8   A camera system with an object and a light source.

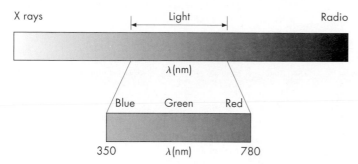

FIGURE 1.9   The electromagnetic spectrum.

Light is a form of electromagnetic radiation. Electromagnetic energy travels as waves that can be characterized by either their wavelengths or their frequencies.[2] The electromagnetic spectrum (Figure 1.9) includes radio waves, infrared (heat), and a portion that causes a response in our visual systems. This **visible spectrum**, which has wavelengths in the range of 350 to 780 nanometers (nm), is called (visible) **light**. A given light source has a color determined by the energy that it emits at various wavelengths. Wavelengths in the middle of the range, around 520 nm, are seen as green; those near 450 nm are seen as blue; and those near 650 nm are seen as red. Just as with a rainbow, light at wavelengths between red and green, we see as yellow, and wavelengths shorter than blue generate violet light.

Light sources can emit light either as a set of discrete frequencies or continuously. A laser, for example, emits light at a single frequency, whereas an incandescent lamp emits energy over a range of frequencies. Fortunately, in computer graphics, except for recognizing that distinct frequencies are visible as distinct colors, we rarely need to deal with the physical properties of light.

Instead, we can follow a more traditional path that is correct when we are operating with sufficiently high light levels and at a scale where the wave nature of light is not a significant factor. **Geometric optics** models light sources as emitters of light energy, each of which have a fixed intensity. Modeled geometrically, light travels in straight lines, from the sources to those objects with which it interacts. An ideal **point source** emits energy from a single location at one or more frequencies equally in all directions. More complex sources, such as a light bulb, can be characterized as emitting light over an area and by emitting more light in one direction than another. A particular source is characterized by the intensity of light that it emits at each frequency and by that light's directionality. We consider only point sources for now. More complex sources often can be

---

2. The relationship between frequency (f) and wavelength (λ) is $f\lambda = c$, where c is the speed of light.

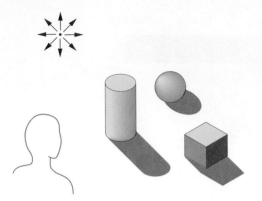

FIGURE 1.10   Scene with a single point light source.

approximated by a number of carefully placed point sources. Modeling of light sources is discussed in Chapter 6.

1.3.3   Imaging Models

There are multiple approaches to how we can form images from a set of objects, the light-reflecting properties of these objects, and the properties of the light sources in the scene. In this section, we introduce two physical approaches. Although these approaches are not suitable for the real-time graphics that we ultimately want, they will give us some insight into how we can build a useful imaging architecture. In fact, we return to these approaches in Chapter 12.

We can start building an imaging model by following light from a source. Consider the scene in Figure 1.10; it is illuminated by a single point source. We include the viewer in the figure because we are interested in the light that reaches her eye. The viewer can also be a camera, as shown in Figure 1.11. A **ray** is a semi-infinite line that emanates from a point and travels to infinity in a particular direction. Because light travels in straight lines, we can think in terms of rays of light emanating in all directions from our point source. A portion of these infinite rays contributes to the image on the film plane of our camera. For example, if the source is visible from the camera, some of the rays go directly from the source through the lens of the camera, and strike the film plane. Most rays, however, go off to infinity, neither entering the camera directly nor striking any of the objects. These rays contribute nothing to the image, although they may be seen by some other viewer. The remaining rays strike and illuminate objects. These rays can interact with the objects' surfaces in a variety of ways. For example, if the surface is a mirror, a reflected ray might—depending on the orientation of the surface—enter the lens of the camera and contribute to the image. Other surfaces scatter light in all directions. If the surface is transparent, the light ray from the source can pass through it and may interact with other objects, enter

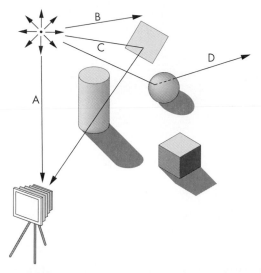

FIGURE 1.11 Ray interactions. Ray A enters camera directly. Ray B goes off to infinity. Ray C is reflected by a mirror. Ray D goes trough a transparent sphere.

the camera, or travel to infinity without striking another surface. Figure 1.11 shows some of the possibilities.

Ray tracing and **photon mapping** are image-formation techniques that are based on these ideas and that can form the basis for producing computer-generated images. We can use the ray-tracing idea to simulate physical effects as complex as we wish, as long as we are willing to carry out the requisite computing. Although tracing rays can provide a close approximation to the physical world, it is not well suited for real-time computation.

Other physical approaches to image formation are based on conservation of energy. The most important in computer graphics is **radiosity**. This method works best for surfaces that scatter the incoming light equally in all directions. Even in this case, radiosity requires more computation than can be done in real time. We defer discussion of these techniques until Chapter 12.

1.4 Imaging Systems

We now introduce two imaging systems: the pinhole camera and the human visual system. The pinhole camera is a simple example of an imaging system that will enable us to understand the functioning of cameras and of other optical imagers. We emulate it to build a model of image formation. The human visual system is extremely complex but still obeys the physical principles of other optical imaging systems. We introduce it not only as an example of an imaging system but also

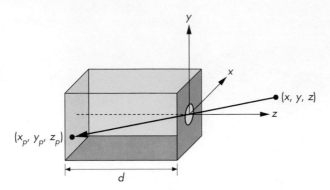

FIGURE 1.12   Pinhole camera.

because understanding its properties will help us to exploit the capabilities of computer-graphics systems.

1.4.1   The Pinhole Camera

The pinhole camera in Figure 1.12 provides an example of image formation that we can understand with a simple geometric model. A **pinhole camera** is a box with a small hole in the center of one side of the box; the film is placed inside the box on the side opposite the pinhole. Suppose that we orient our camera along the z-axis, with the pinhole at the origin of our coordinate system. We assume that the hole is so small that only a single ray of light, emanating from a point, can enter it. The film plane is located a distance d from the pinhole. A side view (Figure 1.13) allows us to calculate where the image of the point (x, y, z) is on the film plane $z = -d$. Using the fact that the two triangles in Figure 1.13 are similar, we find that the y coordinate of the image is at y_p, where

$$y_p = -\frac{y}{z/d}.$$

A similar calculation, using a top view, yields

$$x_p = -\frac{x}{z/d}.$$

The point $(x_p, y_p, -d)$ is called the **projection** of the point (x, y, z). In our idealized model, the color on the film plane at this point will be the color of the point (x, y, z). The **field**, or **angle, of view** of our camera is the angle made by the largest object that our camera can image on its film plane. We can calculate

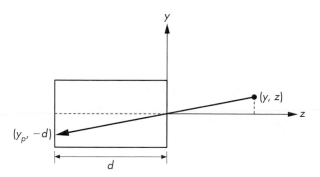

FIGURE 1.13   Side view of pinhole camera.

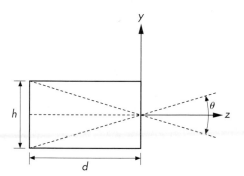

FIGURE 1.14   Angle of view.

the field of view with the aid of Figure 1.14.[3] If h is the height of the camera, the angle of view θ is

$$\theta = 2 \tan^{-1} \frac{h}{2d}.$$

The ideal pinhole camera has an infinite **depth of field**: Every point within its field of view is in focus. The image of a point is a point. The pinhole camera has two disadvantages. First, because the pinhole is so small—it admits only a single ray from a point source—almost no light enters the camera. Second, the camera cannot be adjusted to have a different angle of view.

The jump to more sophisticated cameras and to other imaging systems that have lenses is a small one. By replacing the pinhole with a lens, we solve the two

---

3. If we consider the problem in three, rather than two, dimensions, then the diagonal length of the film will substitute for h.

problems of the pinhole camera. First, the lens gathers more light than can pass through the pinhole. The larger the aperture of the lens, the more light the lens can collect. Second, by picking a lens with the proper focal length—a selection equivalent to choosing d for the pinhole camera—we can achieve any desired angle of view (up to 180 degrees). Lenses, however, do not have an infinite depth of field: Not all distances from the lens are in focus.

For our purposes, in this chapter, we can work with a pinhole camera whose focal length is the distance d from the front of the camera to the film plane. Like the pinhole camera, computer graphics produces images in which all objects are in focus.

1.4.2   The Human Visual System

Our extremely complex visual system has all the components of a physical imaging system, such as a camera or a microscope. The major components of the visual system are shown in Figure 1.15. Light enters the eye through the lens and cornea, a transparent structure that protects the eye. The iris opens and closes to adjust the amount of light entering the eye. The lens forms an image on a two-dimensional structure called the **retina** at the back of the eye. The rods and cones (so named because of their appearance when magnified) are light sensors and are located on the retina. They are excited by electromagnetic energy in the range of 350 to 780 nm.

The rods are low-level-light sensors that account for our night vision and are not color sensitive; the cones are responsible for our color vision. The sizes of the rods and cones, coupled with the optical properties of the lens and cornea, determine the **resolution** of our visual systems, or our **visual acuity**. Resolution is a measure of what size objects we can see. More technically, it is a measure of how close we can place two points and still recognize that there are two distinct points.

The sensors in the human eye do not react uniformly to light energy at different wavelengths. There are three types of cones and a single type of rod. Whereas intensity is a physical measure of light energy, **brightness** is a measure of how intense we perceive the light emitted from an object to be. The human visual system does not have the same response to a monochromatic (single-frequency) red light as to a monochromatic green light. If these two lights were to emit the same energy, they would appear to us to have different brightness, because of the unequal response of the cones to red and green light. We are most sensitive to green light, and least to red and blue.

Brightness is an overall measure of how we react to the intensity of light. Human color-vision capabilities are due to the different sensitivities of the three types of cones. The major consequence of having three types of cones is that instead of having to work with all visible wavelengths individually, we can use three standard primaries to approximate any color that we can perceive. Consequently, most image-production systems, including film and video, work with just three basic, or **primary**, colors. We discuss color in depth in Chapter 2.

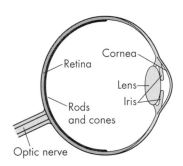

FIGURE 1.15 The human visual system.

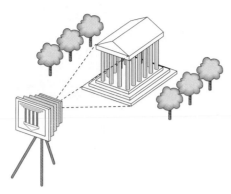

FIGURE 1.16   Imaging system.

The initial processing of light in the human visual system is based on the same principles used by most optical systems. However, the human visual system has a back end much more complex than that of a camera or telescope. The optic nerves are connected to the rods and cones in an extremely complex arrangement that has many of the characteristics of a sophisticated signal processor. The final processing is done in a part of the brain called the visual cortex, where high-level functions, such as object recognition, are carried out. We shall omit any discussion of high level processing; instead, we can think simply in terms of an image that is conveyed from the rods and cones to the brain.

1.5   The Synthetic-Camera Model

Our models of optical imaging systems lead directly to the conceptual foundation for modern three-dimensional computer graphics. We look at creating a computer-generated image as being similar to forming an image using an optical system. This paradigm has become known as the **synthetic-camera model**. Consider the imaging system shown in Figure 1.16. We again see objects and a viewer. In this case, the viewer is a bellows camera.[4] The image is formed on the film plane at the back of the camera. So that we can emulate this process to create artificial images, we need to identify a few basic principles.

First, the specification of the objects is independent of the specification of the viewer. Hence, we should expect that, within a graphics library, there will be separate functions for specifying the objects and the viewer.

---

4. In a bellows camera, the front plane of the camera, where the lens is located, and the back of the camera, the film plane, are connected by flexible sides. Thus, we can move the back of the camera independently of the front of the camera, introducing additional flexibility in the image-formation process. We use this flexibility in Chapter 5.

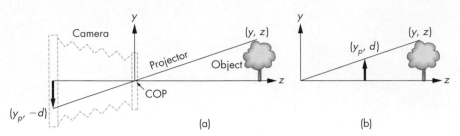

FIGURE 1.17 Equivalent views of image formation. (a) Image formed on the back of the camera. (b) Image plane moved in front of the camera.

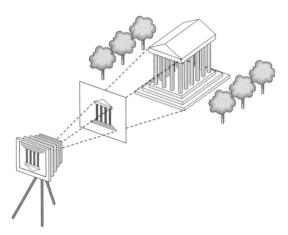

FIGURE 1.18 Imaging with the synthetic camera.

Second, we can compute the image using simple geometric calculations, just as we did with the pinhole camera. Consider the side view of the camera and a simple object in Figure 1.17. The view in part (a) of the figure is similar to that of the pinhole camera. Note that the image of the object is flipped relative to the object. Whereas with a real camera, we would simply flip the film to regain the original orientation of the object, with our synthetic camera we can avoid the flipping by a simple trick. We draw another plane in front of the lens (Figure 1.17(b)), and work in three dimensions, as shown in Figure 1.18. We find the image of a point on the object on the virtual image plane by drawing a line, called a **projector**, from the point to the center of the lens, or the **center of projection** (**COP**). Note that all projectors are rays emanating from the center of projection. In our synthetic camera, the virtual image plane that we have moved in front of the lens is called the **projection plane**. The image of the point is located where the projector passes through the projection plane. In Chapter 5, we discuss this process in detail and derive the relevant mathematical formulas.

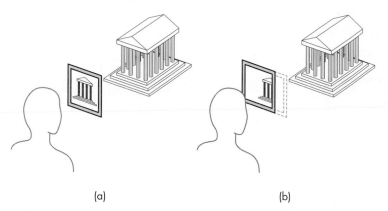

(a)   (b)

FIGURE 1.19   Clipping. (a) Window in initial position. (b) Window shifted.

We must also consider the limited size of the image. As we saw, not all objects can be imaged onto the pinhole camera's film plane. The angle of view expresses this limitation. In the synthetic camera, we can move this limitation to the front by placing a **clipping rectangle**, or **clipping window**, in the projection plane (Figure 1.19). This rectangle acts as a window, through which a viewer, located at the center of projection, sees the world. Given the location of the center of projection, the location and orientation of the projection plane, and the size of the clipping rectangle, we can determine which objects will appear in the image.

1.6 The Programmer's Interface

There are numerous ways that a user can interact with a graphics system. With completely self-contained packages, such as are used in the CAD community, a user develops images through interactions with the display using input devices, such as a mouse and a keyboard. In a typical application, such as the painting program in Figure 1.20, the user sees menus and icons that represent possible actions. By clicking on these items, the user guides the software and produces images without having to write programs.

Of course, someone has to develop the code for these applications, and many of us, despite the sophistication of commercial products, still have to write our own graphics application programs (and even enjoy doing so).

The interface between an application program and a graphics system can be specified through a set of functions that resides in a graphics library. These specifications are called the **application programmer's interface (API)**. The application programmer's model of the system is shown in Figure 1.21. The application programmer sees only the API and is thus shielded from the details of both the hardware and the software implementation of the graphics library. The software **drivers** are responsible for interpreting the output of the

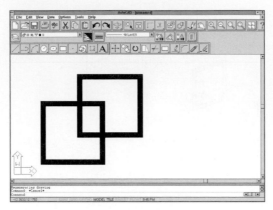

FIGURE 1.20   Interface for a painting program.

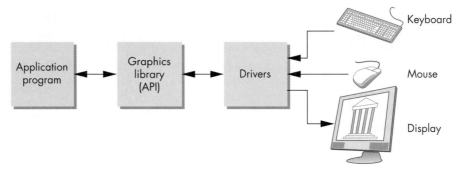

FIGURE 1.21   Application programmer's model of graphics system.

API and converting these data to a form that is understood by the particular hardware. From the perspective of the writer of an application program, the functions available through the API should match the conceptual model that the user wishes to employ to specify images.

1.6.1 The Pen-Plotter Model

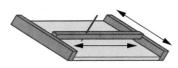

FIGURE 1.22   Pen plotter.

Historically, most early graphics systems were two-dimensional systems. The conceptual model that they used is now referred to as the *pen-plotter model*, referencing the output device that was available on these systems. A **pen plotter** (Figure 1.22) produces images by moving a pen held by a gantry, a structure that can move the pen in two orthogonal directions across the paper. The plotter can raise and lower the pen as required to create the desired image. Pen plotters are still in use; they are well suited for drawing large diagrams, such as blueprints. Various APIs—such as LOGO and PostScript—have their origins in this model. Although they differ from one another, they have a common view of the process of creating an image as being similar to the process of drawing on a pad of paper. The user works on a two-dimensional surface of some size. She moves a pen around on this surface, leaving an image on the paper.

We can describe such a graphics system with two drawing functions:

```
moveto(x,y)
lineto(x,y)
```

Execution of the moveto function moves the pen to the location (x, y) on the paper without leaving a mark. The lineto function moves the pen to (x, y) and draws a line from the old to the new location of the pen. Once we add a few initialization and termination procedures, as well as the ability to change pens to alter the drawing color or line thickness, we have a simple—but complete—graphics system. Here is a fragment of a simple program in such a system:

```
moveto(0, 0);
lineto(1, 0);
lineto(1, 1);
lineto(0, 1);
lineto(0,0);
```

This fragment would generate the output in Figure 1.23(a). If we added the code

```
moveto(0, 1);
lineto(0.5, 1.866);
lineto(1.5, 1.866);
lineto(1.5, 0.866);
lineto(1, 0);
moveto(1, 1);
lineto(1,5,1.866);
```

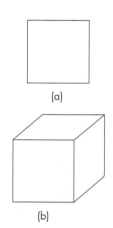

(a)

(b)

FIGURE 1.23 Output of pen-plotter program for (a) a square, and (b) a projection of a cube.

we would have the image of a cube formed by an oblique projection, as is shown in Figure 1.23(b).

For certain applications, such as page layout in the printing industry, systems built on this model work well. For example, the PostScript page-description language, a sophisticated extension of these ideas, is a standard for controlling typesetters and printers.

An alternate raster-based, but still limiting, two-dimensional model relies on writing pixels directly into a frame buffer. Such a system could be based on a single function of the form

```
write_pixel(x, y, color)
```

where x,y is the location of the pixel in the frame buffer and color gives the color to be written there. Such models are well suited to writing the algorithms for rasterization and processing of digital images.

We are much more interested, however, in the three-dimensional world. The pen-plotter model does not extend well to three-dimensional graphics systems. For example, if we wish to use the pen-plotter model to produce the image of a three-dimensional object on our two-dimensional pad, either by hand or by computer, then we have to figure out where on the page to place two-dimensional points corresponding to points on our three-dimensional object. These two-dimensional points are, as we saw in Section 1.5, the projections of points in three-dimensional space. The mathematical process of determining projections is an application of trigonometry. We develop the mathematics of projection in Chapter 5; understanding projection is crucial to understanding three-dimensional graphics. We prefer, however, to use an API that allows users to work directly in the domain of their problems and to use computers to carry out the details of the projection process automatically, without the users having to make any trigonometric calculations within the application program. That approach should be a boon to users who have difficulty learning to draw various projections on a drafting board or sketching objects in perspective. More important, users can rely on hardware and software implementations of projections within the implementation of the API that are far more efficient than any possible implementation of projections within their programs would be.

1.6.2 Three-Dimensional APIs

The synthetic-camera model is the basis for a number of popular APIs, including OpenGL, Direct3D, and Java3D. If we are to follow the synthetic-camera model, we need functions in the API to specify

- Objects
- A viewer
- Light sources
- Material properties

Objects are usually defined by sets of vertices. For simple geometric objects—such as line segments, rectangles, and polygons—there is a simple relationship between a list of **vertices**, or positions in space, and the object. For more complex objects, there may be multiple ways of defining the object from a set of vertices. A circle, for example, can be defined by three points on its circumference, or by its center and one point on the circumference.

Most APIs provide similar sets of primitive objects for the user. These primitives are usually those that can be displayed rapidly on the hardware. The usual sets include points, line segments, polygons, and sometimes text. OpenGL programs define primitives through lists of vertices. The following OpenGL code fragment specifies the triangular polygon in Figure 1.24 through five function calls:

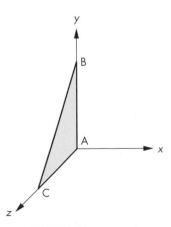

FIGURE 1.24   A triangle.

```
glBegin(GL_POLYGON);
    glVertex3f(0.0, 0.0, 0.0); /* vertex A */
    glVertex3f(0.0, 1.0, 0.0); /* vertex B */
    glVertex3f(0.0, 0.0, 1.0); /* vertex C */
glEnd( );
```

The function glBegin specifies the type of primitive that the vertices define. Each subsequent execution of glVertex defines the x, y, z coordinates of a location in space. The function glEnd ends the list of vertices. Note that by adding additional vertices, we can define an arbitrary polygon. If we change the type parameter, GL_POLYGON, we can use the same vertices to define a different geometric primitive. For example, the type GL_LINE_STRIP uses the vertices to define two connected line segments, whereas the type GL_POINTS uses the same vertices to define three points.

Some APIs let the user work directly in the frame buffer by providing functions that read and write pixels. Some APIs provide curves and surfaces as primitives; often, however, these types are approximated by a series of simpler primitives within the application program. OpenGL provides access to the frame buffer, curves, and surfaces.

We can define a viewer or camera in a variety of ways. Available APIs differ both in how much flexibility they provide in camera selection and in how many different methods they allow. If we look at the camera in Figure 1.25, we can identify four types of necessary specifications:

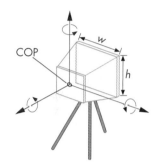

FIGURE 1.25 Camera specification.

1. **Position**   The camera location usually is given by the position of the center of the lens, which is the center of projection (COP).
2. **Orientation**   Once we have positioned the camera, we can place a camera coordinate system with its origin at the center of projection. We can then rotate the camera independently around the three axes of this system.
3. **Focal length**   The focal length of the lens determines the size of the image on the film plane or, equivalently, the portion of the world the camera sees.
4. **Film plane**   The back of the camera has a height and a width. On the bellows camera, and in some APIs, the orientation of the back of the camera can be adjusted independently of the orientation of the lens.

These specifications can be satisfied in various ways. One way to develop the specifications for the camera location and orientation uses a series of coordinate-system transformations. These transformations convert object positions represented in a coordinate system that specifies object vertices to object positions in a coordinate system centered at the COP. This approach is useful, both for doing implementation and for getting the full set of views that a flexible camera can provide. We use this approach extensively, starting in Chapter 5.

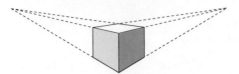

FIGURE 1.26   Two-point perspective of a cube.

Having many parameters to adjust, however, can also make it difficult to get a desired image. Part of the problem lies with the synthetic-camera model. Classical viewing techniques, such as are used in architecture, stress the *relationship* between the object and the viewer, rather than the *independence* that the synthetic-camera model emphasizes. Thus, the classical two-point perspective of a cube in Figure 1.26 is a *two-point* perspective because of a particular relationship between the viewer and the planes of the cube (see Exercise 1.7). Although the OpenGL API allows us to set transformations with complete freedom, it also provides helpful extra functions. For example, consider the two function calls

```
gluLookAt(cop_x, cop_y, cop_z, at_x, at_y, at_z, up_x, up_y, up_z);
glPerspective(field_of_view, aspect_ratio, near, far);
```

The first function call points the camera from a center of projection toward a desired point (the *at* point), with a specified *up* direction for the camera. The second selects a lens for a perspective view (the *field of view*) and how much of the world that the camera should image (the *aspect ratio* and the *near* and *far* distances). However, none of the APIs built on the synthetic-camera model provide functions for directly specifying a desired relationship between the camera and an object.

Light sources are defined by their location, strength, color, and directionality. APIs provide a set of functions to specify these parameters for each source. Material properties are characteristics, or attributes, of the objects, and such properties are specified through a series of function calls at the time that each object is defined. Both light sources and material properties depend on the models of light–material interactions supported by the API. We discuss such models in Chapter 6.

1.6.3   A Sequence of Images

In Chapter 2, we begin our detailed discussion of the OpenGL API that we will use throughout this book. The images defined by your OpenGL programs will be formed automatically by the hardware and software implementation of the image-formation process.

Here we look at a sequence of images that shows what we can create using the OpenGL API. We present these images as an increasingly more complex series of renderings of the same objects. The sequence not only loosely follows the order in which we present related topics but also reflects how graphics systems have developed over the past 30 years.

Color Plate 1 shows an image of an artist's creation of a sunlike object. Color Plate 2 shows the object rendered using only line segments. Although the object consists of many parts, and although the programmer may have used sophisticated data structures to model each part and the relationships among the parts, the rendered object shows only the outlines of the parts. This type of image is known as a **wireframe** image because we can see only the edges of surfaces: Such an image would be produced if the objects were constructed with stiff wires that formed a frame with no solid material between the edges. Before raster-graphics systems became available, wireframe images were the only type of computer-generated images that we could produce.

In Color Plate 3, the same object has been rendered with flat polygons. Certain surfaces are not visible because there is a solid surface between them and the viewer; these surfaces have been removed by a hidden-surface-removal (HSR) algorithm. Most raster systems can fill the interior of polygons with a solid color in approximately the same time that they can render a wireframe image. Although the objects are three-dimensional, each surface is displayed in a single color, and the image fails to show the three-dimensional shapes of the objects. Early raster systems could produce images of this form.

In Chapters 2 and 3, we show you how to generate images composed of simple geometric objects—points, line segments, and polygons. In Chapters 4 and 5, you will learn how to transform objects in three dimensions and how to obtain a desired three-dimensional view of a model, with hidden surfaces removed.

Color Plate 4 illustrates smooth shading of the polygons that approximate the object; it shows that the object is three-dimensional and gives the appearance of a smooth surface. We develop shading models that are supported by OpenGL in Chapter 6. These shading models are also supported in the hardware of most recent workstations; generating the shaded image on one of these systems takes approximately the same amount of time as does generating a wireframe image.

Color Plate 5 shows a more sophisticated wireframe model constructed using NURBS surfaces, which we introduce in Chapter 11. Such surfaces give the application programmer great flexibility in the design process but are ultimately rendered using line segments and polygons.

In Color Plates 6 and 7, we add surface texture to our object; texture is one of the effects that we discuss in Chapter 8. All recent graphics processors support texture mapping in hardware, so rendering of a texture-mapped image requires little additional time. In Color Plate 6, we use a technique called *bump mapping* that gives the appearance of a rough surface even though we render the same flat polygons as in the other examples. Color Plate 7 shows an *environment map* applied to the surface of the object, which gives the surface the appearance of a mirror. These techniques will be discussed in detail in Chapters 8 and 9.

Color Plate 8 shows a small area of the rendering of the object using an environment map. The image on the left shows the jagged artifacts known as aliasing errors that are due to the discrete nature of the frame buffer. The image

FIGURE 1.27 The modeling–rendering pipeline.

on the right has been rendered using a smoothing or antialiasing method that we shall study in Chapters 8 and 10.

Not only do these images show what is possible with available hardware and a good API, but they are also simple to generate, as we shall see in subsequent chapters. In addition, just as the images show incremental changes in the renderings, the programs are incrementally different from one another.

1.6.4 The Modeling–Rendering Paradigm

In many situations—especially in CAD applications and in the development of complex images, such as for movies—we can separate the modeling of the scene from the production of the image, or the **rendering** of the scene. Hence, we can look at image formation as the two-step process shown in Figure 1.27. Although the tasks are the same as those we have been discussing, this block diagram suggests that we might implement the modeler and the renderer with different software and hardware. For example, consider the production of a single frame in an animation. We first want to design and position our objects. This step is highly interactive, and we do not need to work with detailed images of the objects. Consequently, we prefer to carry out this step on an interactive workstation with good graphics hardware. Once we have designed the scene, we want to render it, adding light sources, material properties, and a variety of other detailed effects, to form a production-quality image. This step requires a tremendous amount of computation, so we prefer to use a number-cruncher machine. Not only is the optimal hardware different in the modeling and rendering steps, but the software that we use also may be different.

The interface between the modeler and renderer can be as simple as a file produced by the modeler that describes the objects and that contains additional information important only to the renderer, such as light sources, viewer location, and material properties. Pixar's RenderMan Interface follows this approach and uses a file format that allows modelers to pass models to the renderer in text format. One of the other advantages of this approach is that it allows us to develop modelers that, although they use the same renderer, are custom-tailored to particular applications. Likewise, different renderers can take as input the same interface file. It is even possible, at least in principle, to dispense with the modeler completely and to use a standard text editor to generate an interface file. For any but the simplest scenes, however, users cannot edit lists of information for a renderer. Rather, they use interactive modeling software. Because we must have at least a simple image of our objects to interact with a modeler, most modelers use the synthetic-camera model to produce these images in real time.

This paradigm has become popular as a method for generating computer games and images over the Internet. Models, including the geometric objects, lights, cameras, and material properties, are placed in a data structure called a **scene graph** that is passed to a renderer or game engine. We shall examine scene graphs in Chapter 10.

1.7 Graphics Architectures

On one side of the API is the application program. On the other is some combination of hardware and software that implements the functionality of the API. Researchers have taken various approaches to developing architectures to support graphics APIs.

Early graphics systems used general-purpose computers with the standard von Neumann architecture. Such computers are characterized by a single processing unit that processes a single instruction at a time. A simple model of these early graphics systems is shown in Figure 1.28. The display in these systems was based on a calligraphic CRT display that included the necessary circuitry to generate a line segment connecting two points. The job of the host computer was to run the application program and to compute the endpoints of the line segments in the image (in units of the display). This information had to be sent to the display at a rate high enough to avoid flicker on the display. In the early days of computer graphics, computers were so slow that refreshing even simple images, containing a few hundred line segments, would burden an expensive computer.

1.7.1 Display Processors

The earliest attempts to build special-purpose graphics systems were concerned primarily with relieving the general-purpose computer from the task of refreshing the display continuously. These **display processors** had conventional architectures (Figure 1.29) but included instructions to display primitives on the CRT. The main advantage of the display processor was that the instructions to generate the image could be assembled once in the host and sent to the display processor, where they were stored in the display processor's own memory as a **display list**,

FIGURE 1.28   Early graphics system.

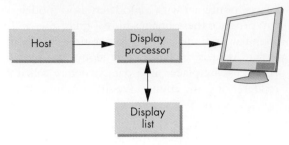

FIGURE 1.29   Display-processor architecture.

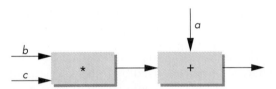

FIGURE 1.30   Arithmetic pipeline.

or **display file**. The display processor would then execute repetitively the program in the display list, at a rate sufficient to avoid flicker, independently of the host, thus freeing the host for other tasks. This architecture has become closely associated with the client–server architectures that we discuss in Chapter 3.

1.7.2   Pipeline Architectures

The major advances in graphics architectures parallel closely the advances in workstations. In both cases, the ability to create special-purpose VLSI chips was the key enabling technology development. In addition, the availability of inexpensive solid-state memory led to the universality of raster displays. For computer-graphics applications, the most important use of custom VLSI circuits has been in creating **pipeline** architectures.

The concept of pipelining is illustrated in Figure 1.30 for a simple arithmetic calculation. In our pipeline, there is an adder and a multiplier. If we use this configuration to compute $a + (b * c)$, the calculation takes one multiplication and one addition—the same amount of work required if we use a single processor to carry out both operations. However, suppose that we have to carry out the same computation with many values of a, b, and c. Now, the multiplier can pass on the results of its calculation to the adder and can start its next multiplication while the adder carries out the second step of the calculation on the first set of data. Hence, whereas it takes the same amount of time to calculate the results for any one set of data, when we are working on two sets of data at one time, our total time for calculation is shortened markedly. Here the rate at which data

FIGURE 1.31   Geometric pipeline.

flows through the system, the **throughput** of the system, has been doubled. Note that as we add more boxes to a pipeline, it takes more time for a single datum to pass through the system. This time is called the **latency** of the system; we must balance it against increased throughput in evaluating the performance of a pipeline.

We can construct pipelines for more complex arithmetic calculations that will afford even greater increases in throughput. Of course, there is no point in building a pipeline unless we will do the same operation on many data sets. But that is just what we do in computer graphics, where large sets of vertices must be processed in the same manner.

1.7.3   The Graphics Pipeline

We start with a set of objects. Each object comprises a set of graphical primitives. Each primitive comprises a set of vertices. We can think of the collection of primitive types and vertices as defining the **geometry** of the scene. In a complex scene, there may be thousands—even millions—of vertices that define the objects. We must process all these vertices in a similar manner to form an image in the frame buffer. If we think in terms of processing the geometry of our objects to obtain an image, we can employ the block diagram in Figure 1.31, which shows the four major steps in the imaging process:

1. Vertex processing
2. Clipping and primitive assembly
3. Rasterization
4. Fragment processing

In subsequent chapters, we discuss the details of these steps. Here we are content to overview these steps and show that they can be pipelined.

1.7.4   Vertex Processing

In the first block of our pipeline, each vertex is processed independently. The two major functions of this block are to carry out coordinate transformations and to compute a color for each vertex.

Many of the steps in the imaging process can be viewed as transformations between representations of objects in different coordinate systems. For example, in our discussion of the synthetic camera, we observed that a major part of viewing is to convert to a representation of objects from the system in which they were defined to a representation in terms of the coordinate system of the camera. A further example of a transformation arises when we finally put our images onto the output device. The internal representation of objects—whether in the camera coordinate system or perhaps in a system used by the graphics software—eventually must be represented in terms of the coordinate system of the display. We can represent each change of coordinate systems by a matrix. We can represent successive changes in coordinate systems by multiplying, or **concatenating**, the individual matrices into a single matrix. In Chapter 4, we examine these operations in detail. Because multiplying one matrix by another matrix yields a third matrix, a sequence of transformations is an obvious candidate for a pipeline architecture. In addition, because the matrices that we use in computer graphics will always be small (4×4), we have the opportunity to use parallelism within the transformation blocks in the pipeline.

Eventually, after multiple stages of transformation, the geometry is transformed by a projection transformation. We shall see in Chapter 5 that we can implement this step using 4×4 matrices, and thus projection fits in the pipeline. In general, we want to keep three-dimensional information as long as possible, as objects pass through the pipeline. Consequently, the projection transformation is somewhat more general than the projections in Section 1.5. In addition to retaining three-dimensional information, there is a variety of projections that we can implement. We shall see these projections in Chapter 5.

The assignment of vertex colors can be as simple as the program specifying a color or as complex as the computation of a color from a physically realistic shading model that incorporates the surface properties of the object and the characteristic light sources in the scene. We shall discuss shading models in Chapter 6.

1.7.5 Clipping and Primitive Assembly

The second fundamental block in the implementation of the standard graphics pipeline is for clipping and primitive assembly. We must do clipping because of the limitation that no imaging system can see the whole world at once. The human retina has a limited size corresponding to an approximately 90-degree field of view. Cameras have film of limited size, and we can adjust their fields of view by selecting different lenses.

We obtain the equivalent property in the synthetic camera by considering a **clipping volume**, such as the pyramid in front of the lens in Figure 1.18. The projections of objects in this volume appear in the image. Those that are outside do not and are said to be clipped out. Objects that straddle the edges of the clipping volume are partly visible in the image. Efficient clipping algorithms are developed in Chapter 7.

Clipping must be done on a primitive by primitive basis rather than on a vertex by vertex basis. Thus, within this stage of the pipeline, we must assemble sets of vertices into primitives, such as line segments and polygons, before clipping can take place. Consequently, the output of this stage is a set of primitives whose projections can appear in the image.

1.7.6 Rasterization

The primitives that emerge from the clipper are still represented in terms of their vertices and must be converted to pixels in the frame buffer. For example, if three vertices specify a triangle with a solid color, the rasterizer must determine which pixels in the frame buffer are inside the polygon. We discuss this rasterization (or scan-conversion) process in Chapter 8 for line segments and polygons. The output of the rasterizer is a set of **fragments** for each primitive. A fragment can be thought of as a potential pixel that carries with it information, including its color and location, that is used to update the corresponding pixel in the frame buffer. Fragments can also carry along depth information that allows later stages to determine if a particular fragment lies behind other previously rasterized fragments for a given pixel.

1.7.7 Fragment Processing

The final block in our pipeline takes in the fragments generated by the rasterizer and updates the pixels in the frame buffer. If the application generated three-dimensional data, some fragments may not be visible because the surfaces that they define are behind other surfaces. The color of a fragment may be altered by texture mapping or bump mapping as in Color Plates 6 and 7. The color of the pixel that corresponds to a fragment can also be read from the frame buffer and blended with the fragment's color to create translucent effects. These effects will be covered in Chapters 8 and 9.

1.8 Programmable Pipelines

Graphics architectures have gone through multiple cycles in which the importance of special-purpose hardware relative to standard CPUs has gone back and forth. However, the importance of the pipeline architecture has remained regardless of this cycle. None of the other approaches—ray tracing, radiosity, photon mapping—leads to real-time performance. Hence, the commodity graphics market is dominated by graphics cards that have pipelines built into the graphics processing unit. All of these commodity cards implement the pipeline that we have just described, albeit with more options, many of which we shall discuss in later chapters.

For many years, these pipeline architectures have had a fixed functionality. Although the application program could set many parameters, the basic operations available within the pipeline were fixed. Recently, there has been a major advance in pipeline architectures. Both the vertex processor and the fragment processor are now programable by the application program. One of the most exciting aspects of this advance is that many of the techniques that formerly could not be done in real time because they were not part of the fixed-function pipeline can now be done in real time. Bump mapping, which we illustrated in Color Plate 6, is but one example of an algorithm that is now programmable but formerly could only be done off-line.

Vertex programs can alter the location or color of each vertex as it flows through the pipeline . Thus, we can implement a variety light-material models or create new kinds of projections. Fragment programs allow us to use textures in new ways. Chapter 9 is devoted to these new methodologies.

1.9   Performance Characteristics

There are two fundamentally different types of processing in our architecture. At the front end, there is geometric processing, based on processing vertices through the various transformations, vertex shading, clipping, and primitive assembly. This processing is ideally suited for pipelining, and it usually involves floating-point calculations. The geometry engine developed by Silicon Graphics, Inc. (SGI) was a VLSI implementation for many of these operations in a special-purpose chip that became the basis for a series of fast graphics workstations. Later, floating-point accelerator chips put 4×4 matrix-transformation units on the chip, reducing a matrix multiplication to a single instruction. Nowadays, graphics workstations and commodity graphics cards use graphics processing units (GPUs) that perform most of the graphics operations at the chip level. Pipeline architectures are the dominant type of high-performance system.

Beginning with rasterization and including many features that we discuss later, processing involves a direct manipulation of bits in the frame buffer. This back-end processing is fundamentally different from front-end processing, and we implement it most effectively using architectures that have the ability to move blocks of bits quickly. The overall performance of a system is characterized by how fast we can move geometric entities through the pipeline and by how many pixels per second we can alter in the frame buffer. Consequently, the fastest graphics workstations are characterized by geometric pipelines at the front ends and parallel bit processors at the back ends. Until about 10 years ago, there was a clear distinction between front- and back-end processing and there were different components and boards dedicated to each. Now commodity graphics cards use GPUs that contain the entire pipeline within a single chip. The latest cards implement the entire pipeline using floating-point arithmetic and have floating-point frame buffers. These GPUs are so powerful that even the highest level systems, systems that incorporate multiple pipelines, use these processors.

Pipeline architectures dominate the graphics field, especially where real-time performance is of importance. Our presentation has made a case for using such an architecture to implement the hardware in a system. Commodity graphics cards incorporate the pipeline within their GPUs. Cards that cost less than $100 can render millions of shaded texture-mapped polygons per second. However, we can also make as strong a case for pipelining being the basis of a complete software implementation of an API. The power of the synthetic-camera paradigm is that the latter works well in both cases.

However, where realism is important, other types of renderers can perform better at the expense of requiring more computation time. Pixar's RenderMan interface was created to interface their off-line renderer. Physically based techniques, such as ray tracing and radiosity, can create photorealistic images with great fidelity, but not in real time.

Summary and Notes

In this chapter, we have set the stage for our top-down development of computer graphics. We presented the overall picture so that you can proceed to writing graphics applications programs in the next chapter without feeling that you are working in a vacuum.

We have stressed that computer graphics is a method of image formation that should be related to classical methods of image formation—in particular, to image formation in optical systems, such as in cameras. In addition to explaining the pinhole camera, we have introduced the human visual system; both are examples of imaging systems.

We described multiple image-formation paradigms, each of which has applicability in computer graphics. The synthetic-camera model has two important consequences for computer graphics. First, it stresses the independence of the objects and the viewer—a distinction that leads to a good way of organizing the functions that will be in a graphics library. Second, it leads to the notion of a pipeline architecture, in which each of the various stages in the pipeline performs distinct operations on geometric entities, then passes on the transformed objects to the next stage.

We also introduced the idea of tracing rays of light to obtain an image. This paradigm is especially useful in understanding the interaction between light and materials that is essential to physical image formation. Because ray tracing and other physically based strategies cannot render scenes in real time, we defer further discussion of them until Chapter 12.

The modeling–rendering paradigm is becoming increasingly important. A standard graphics workstation can generate millions of line segments or polygons per second at a resolution of up to 2048×1546 pixels. Such a workstation can shade the polygons using a simple shading model and can display only visible surfaces at this rate. However, realistic images may require a resolution of up to 4000×6000 pixels to match the resolution of film and may use light and material effects that cannot be implemented in real time. Even as the power of available hardware and software continues to grow, modeling and rendering have such different goals that we can expect the distinction between a modeling and a rendering to survive.

Our next step will be to explore the application side of graphics programming. We use the OpenGL API, which is powerful, is supported on most platforms, and has a distinct architecture that will allow us to use it to understand how computer graphics works, from an application program to a final image on a display.

Suggested Readings

There are many excellent graphics textbooks. The book by Newman and Sproull [New73] was the first to take the modern point of view of using the synthetic-camera model. The various versions of Foley et al. [Fol90, Fol94] have been the standard references for over a decade. Other good texts include Hearn and Baker [Hea04], Hill [Hil01], and Shirley [Shi02].

Good general references include *Computer Graphics*, the quarterly journal of SIGGRAPH (the Association for Computing Machinery's Special Interest Group on Graphics), *IEEE Computer Graphics and Applications*, and *Visual Computer*. The proceedings of the annual SIGGRAPH conference include the latest techiques. These proceedings formerly were published as the summer issue of *Computer Graphics*. Now, they are published as an issue of the *ACM Transactions on Graphics* and are available on DVD. Of particular interest to newcomers to the field are the state-of-the-art animations available from SIGGRAPH and the notes from tutorial courses taught at that conference, both of which are now available on DVD.

Sutherland's doctoral dissertation, published as *Sketchpad: A Man–Machine Graphical Communication System* [Sut63] was probably the seminal paper in the development of interactive computer graphics. Sutherland was the first person to realize the power of the new paradigm in which humans interacted with images on a CRT display. Videotape copies of film of his original work are still available.

Tufte's books [Tuf83, Tuf90, Tuf97] show the importance of good visual design and contain considerable historical information on the development of graphics. The article by Carlbom and Paciorek [Car78] gives a good discussion of some of the relationships between classical viewing, as used in fields such as architecture, and viewing by computer.

Many books describe the human visual system. Pratt [Pra78] gives a good short discussion for working with raster displays. Also see Glassner [Gla95], Wyszecki and Stiles [Wys82], and Hall [Hal89].

Exercises

1.1   The pipeline approach to image generation is nonphysical. What are the main advantages and disadvantages of such a nonphysical approach?

1.2   In computer graphics, objects such as spheres are usually approximated by simpler objects constructed from flat polygons (polyhedra). Using lines of longitude and latitude, define a set of simple polygons that approximate

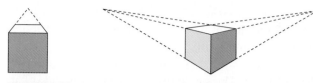

FIGURE 1.32   Perspectives of a cube.

a sphere centered at the origin. Can you use only quadrilaterals or only triangles?

1.3   A different method of approximating a sphere starts with a regular tetrahedron, which is constructed from four triangles. Find its vertices, assuming that it is centered at the origin and has one vertex on the y-axis. Derive an algorithm for obtaining increasingly closer approximations to a unit sphere, based on subdividing the faces of the tetrahedron.

1.4   Consider the clipping of a line segment in two dimensions against a rectangular clipping window. Show that you require only the endpoints of the line segment to determine whether the line segment is not clipped, is partially visible, or is clipped out completely.

1.5   For a line segment, show that clipping against the top of the clipping rectangle can be done independently of the clipping against the other sides. Use this result to show that a clipper can be implemented as a pipeline of four simpler clippers.

1.6   Extend Exercises 1.4 and 1.5 to clipping against a three-dimensional right parallelepiped.

1.7   Consider the perspective views of the cube shown in Figure 1.32. The one on the left is called a *one-point perspective* because parallel lines in one direction of the cube—along the sides of the top—converge to a *vanishing point* in the image. In contrast, the image on the right is a *two-point perspective*. Characterize the particular relationship between the viewer, or a simple camera, and the cube that determines why one is a two-point perspective and the other a one-point perspective.

1.8   The memory in a frame buffer must be fast enough to allow the display to be refreshed at a rate sufficiently high to avoid flicker. A typical workstation display can have a resolution of 1280×1024 pixels. If it is refreshed 72 times per second, how fast must the memory be? That is, how much time can we take to read one pixel from memory? What is this number for a 480×640 display that operates at 60 Hz but is interlaced?

1.9   Movies are generally produced on 35-mm film that has a resolution of approximately 2000×3000 pixels. What implication does this resolution have for producing animated images for television as compared with film?

1.10 Consider the design of a two-dimensional graphical API for a specific application, such as for VLSI design. List all the primitives and attributes that you would include in your system.

1.11 It is possible to design a color CRT that uses a single electron gun and does not have a shadow mask. The single beam is turned on and off at the appropriate times to excite the desired phosphors. Why might such a CRT be more difficult to design, as compared to the shadow-mask CRT?

1.12 In a typical shadow-mask CRT, if we want to have a smooth display, the width of a pixel must be about three times the width of a triad. Assume that a monitor displays 1280×1024 pixels, has a CRT diameter of 50 cm, and has a CRT depth of 25 cm. Estimate the spacing between holes in the shadow mask.

1.13 An interesting exercise that should help you understand how rapidly graphics performance has improved is to go to the Web sites of some of the GPU manufacturers, such as NVIDIA, ATI, and 3DLabs, and look at the specifications for their products. Often the specs for older cards and GPUs are still there. How rapidly has geometric performance improved? What about pixel processing? How has the cost per rendered triangle decreased?

GRAPHICS PROGRAMMING

Our approach to computer graphics is programming oriented. Consequently, we want you to get started programming graphics as soon as possible. To this end, we introduce a minimal application programmer's interface (API). This API is sufficient to allow you to program many interesting two- and three-dimensional problems and to familiarize you with the basic graphics concepts.

We regard two-dimensional graphics as a special case of three-dimensional graphics. This perspective allows us to get started, even though we touch on three-dimensional concepts lightly in this chapter. Our two-dimensional code will execute without modification on a three-dimensional system.

Our development uses a simple but informative problem: the Sierpinski gasket. It shows how we can generate an interesting and, to many people, unexpectedly sophisticated image using only a handful of graphics functions. We use OpenGL as our API, but our discussion of the underlying concepts is broad enough to encompass most modern systems. The functionality that we introduce in this chapter is sufficient to allow you to write basic two- and three-dimensional programs that do not require user interaction.

2.1 The Sierpinski Gasket

We use as a sample problem the drawing of the Sierpinski gasket—an interesting shape that has a long history and is of interest in areas such as fractal geometry. The Sierpinski gasket is an object that can be defined recursively and randomly; in the limit, however, it has properties that are not at all random. We start with a two-dimensional version, but as we shall see in Section 2.11, the three-dimensional version is almost identical.

Suppose that we start with three points in space. As long as the points are not collinear, they define a unique plane and define the vertices of a triangle. We assume that this plane is the plane $z = 0$ and that these points, as specified in some convenient coordinate system,[1] are $(x_1, y_1, 0)$, $(x_2, y_2, 0)$, and $(x_3, y_3, 0)$. The construction proceeds as follows:

1. Pick an initial point (x, y, z) at random inside the triangle.
2. Select one of the three vertices at random.
3. Find the location halfway between the initial point and the randomly selected vertex.
4. Display this new point by putting some sort of marker, such as a small circle, at the corresponding location on the display.
5. Replace the point at (x, y, z) with this new point.
6. Return to step 2.

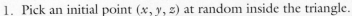

FIGURE 2.1 Generation of the Sierpinski gasket.

Thus, each time that we generate a new point, we display it on the output device. This process is illustrated in Figure 2.1, where $\mathbf{p}_0$ is the initial location, and $\mathbf{p}_1$ and $\mathbf{p}_2$ are the first two locations generated by our algorithm.

Before we develop the program, you might try to figure out what the resulting image will be. Try to construct it on paper; you might be surprised by your results.

A possible form for our graphics program might be this:

```
main( )
{
    initialize_the_system();

    for(some_number_of_points)
    {
        pt = generate_a_point();
        display_the_point(pt);
    }

    cleanup();
}
```

Although our final OpenGL program will have a slightly different organization, it will be almost that simple. We develop the program in stages. First, we concentrate on the core: generating and displaying points. There are two questions that we must answer: How do we represent points in space? and Should we use a two-dimensional, three-dimensional, or other representation?

2.2 Programming Two-Dimensional Applications

For two-dimensional applications, such as the Sierpinski gasket, although we could use a pen-plotter API, such an approach would limit us. Instead, we

---

1. In Chapter 4, we expand the concept of a coordinate system to the more general formulation of a *frame*.

choose to start with a three-dimensional world; we regard two-dimensional systems, such the one on which we will produce our image, as special cases. Mathematically, we view the two-dimensional plane, or a simple two-dimensional curved surface, as a subspace of a three-dimensional space. Hence, statements— both practical and abstract—about the bigger three-dimensional world will hold for the simpler two-dimensional one.

We can represent a point in the plane $z = 0$ as $\mathbf{p} = (x, y, 0)$ in the three-dimensional world, or as $\mathbf{p} = (x, y)$ in the two-dimensional plane. OpenGL, like most three-dimensional graphics systems, allows us to use either representation, with the underlying internal representation being the same, regardless of which form the user chooses. We can implement representations of points in a number of ways, but the simplest is to think of a three-dimensional point as being represented by a triplet $\mathbf{p} = (x, y, z)$ or a column matrix

$$\mathbf{p} = \begin{bmatrix} x \\ y \\ z \end{bmatrix}.$$

For now, we ignore the question of the coordinate system in which $\mathbf{p}$ is represented.

We use the terms *vertex* and *point* in a somewhat different manner in OpenGL. A **vertex** is a position in space; we use two-, three-, and four-dimensional spaces in computer graphics. We use vertices to define the atomic geometric primitives that are recognized by our graphics system. The simplest geometric primitive is a point in space, which is specified by a single vertex. Two vertices define a line segment, a second primitive object; three vertices can determine either a triangle or a circle; four determine a quadrilateral, and so on.

OpenGL has multiple forms for many functions. The variety of forms allows the user to select the one best suited for her problem. For the vertex function, we can write the general form

```
glVertex*()
```

where the * can be interpreted as either two or three characters of the form nt or ntv, where n signifies the number of dimensions (2, 3, or 4); t denotes the data type, such as integer (i), float (f), or double (d); and v, if present, indicates that the variables are specified through a pointer to an array, rather than through an argument list. We shall use whatever form is best suited for our discussion, leaving the details of the various other forms to the *OpenGL Reference Manual* [Ope04b]. Regardless of which form a user chooses, the underlying representation is the same, just as the plane on which we are constructing the gasket can be looked at as either a two-dimensional space or the subspace of three-dimensional space corresponding to the plane $z = 0$. In Chapter 4, we shall see that the underlying representation is four-dimensional; however, we do not need to worry about that fact yet.

In OpenGL, we often use basic OpenGL types, such as `GLfloat` and `GLint`, rather than the C types, such as `float` and `int`. These types are defined in the OpenGL header files and usually in the obvious way—for example,

```
#define GLfloat float
```

However, use of the OpenGL types allows additional flexibility for implementations where, for example, we might want to change floats to doubles without altering existing application programs.

Returning to the vertex function, if the user wants to work in two dimensions with integers, then the form

```
glVertex2i(GLint xi, GLint yi)
```

is appropriate, and

```
glVertex3f(GLfloat x, GLfloat y, GLfloat z)
```

specifies a position in three-dimensional space using floating-point numbers. Finally, if we use an array to store the information for a three-dimensional vertex,

```
GLfloat vertex[3]
```

then we can use

```
glVertex3fv(vertex)
```

Vertices can define a variety of geometric primitives; different numbers of vertices are required depending on the primitive. We can group as many vertices as we wish between the functions `glBegin` and `glEnd`. The argument of `glBegin` specifies the geometric type that we want our vertices to define. Hence, a line segment can be specified by

```
glBegin(GL_LINES);
  glVertex3f(x1,y1,z1);
  glVertex3f(x2,y2,z2);
glEnd();
```

We can use the same data to define a pair of points, by using the form

```
glBegin(GL_POINTS);
  glVertex3f(x1,y1,z1);
  glVertex3f(x2,y2,z2);
glEnd();
```

We can now look at the heart of our Sierpinski gasket program. Suppose that we choose to generate all our points within a 50×50 square whose lower-left-hand corner is at $(0, 0)$—a convenient, but easily altered, choice.

First, we must consider how we wish to represent geometric data in our program. We could employ the most basic representation of separate x, y, and z variables (in three dimensions). In this application, because we are working in the plane $z = 0$, we could use either the form

```
glVertex3f(x,y,0);
```

or the form

```
glVertex2f(x,y);
```

We could also define a new data type

```
typedef GLfloat point2[2];
```

and use something like[2]

```
point2 p;
glVertex2fv(p);
```

Generally, we shall find it easiest simply to define arrays to hold points using the glVertex3fv or glVertex2fv forms.

Returning to the Sierpinski gasket, we create a function, called display, that generates 5000 points each time it is called. We assume that an array of triangle vertices vertices[3] is defined in display:

```
void display()
{
   GLfloat vertices[3][3] = {{0.0, 0.0, 0.0}, {25.0, 50.0, 0.0}, {50.0,
   0.0, 0.0}};
           /* an arbitrary triangle in the plane z=0 */
   GLfloat p[3] = {7.5 ,5.0, 0.0};
           /* or set to any desired initial point inside the triangle */
   int j, k;
   int rand(); /* standard random-number generator */

   glBegin(GL_POINTS);
   for(k=0;k<5000;k++)
   {
     /* pick a random vertex from 0,1,2 */

     j=rand()%3;
```

---

2. Because OpenGL is not object oriented, we cannot do what we might really like, which is to define a point object with a corresponding set of overloaded operators (see Exercise 2.21).

```
/* compute new location */

p[0] = (p[0] + vertices[j][0])/2;
p[1] = (p[1] + vertices[j][1])/2;

/* display new point */


    glVertex3fv(p);
  }
  glEnd();
  glFlush();
}
```

Note that because all points are in the plane $z = 0$, we could have used two-dimensional points by changing only three lines of code in display to

```
GLfloat
vertices[3][2] = {{0.0, 0.0}, {25.0, 50.0}, {50.0, 0.0}};

GLfloat p[2] = {7.5 ,5.0};

glVertex2fv(p);
```

The function rand is a standard random-number generator that produces a new random integer each time it is called. We use the modulus operator to reduce these random integers to the three integers 0, 1, and 2. For a small number of iterations, the particular characteristics of the random-number generator are not crucial, and any other random-number generator should work at least as well as rand.

The call to glFlush ensures that points are rendered to the screen as soon as possible. If you leave it out, the program should work correctly, but you may notice a delay in a busy or networked environment. We still do not have a complete program; Figure 2.2 shows the output that we expect to see.

Note that because any three noncollinear points define a plane, had we started with three points (x_1, y_1, z_1), (x_2, y_2, z_2), and (x_3, y_3, z_3) along with an initial point in the same plane, then added the code

```
p[2]=(p[2]+vertices[j][2])/2.0;
```

to our code, the gasket would be generated in the plane defined by the original three vertices.

We have now written the core of the program. But we still have to worry about such issues as the following:

1. In what colors are we drawing?
2. Where on the screen does our image appear?

FIGURE 2.2   The Sierpinski gasket as generated with 5000 random points.

3. How large will the image be?
4. How do we create an area of the screen—a window—for our image?
5. How much of our infinite drawing surface will appear on the screen?
6. How long will the image remain on the screen?

The answers to all these questions are important, although initially they may appear to be peripheral to our major concerns. As we shall see, the basic code that we develop to answer these questions and to control the placement and appearance of our renderings will not change substantially across programs. Hence, the effort that we expend now will be repaid later.

2.2.1   Coordinate Systems

At this point, you may be puzzled about how to interpret the values of x, y, and z in our specification of vertices. In what units are they? Are they in feet, meters, microns? Where is the origin? In each case, the simple answer is that it is up to you.

Originally, graphics systems required the user to specify all information, such as vertex locations, directly in units of the display device. If that were true for high-level application programs, we would have to talk about points in terms of screen locations in pixels or centimeters from a corner of the display. There are obvious problems with this method, not the least of which is the absurdity of using distances on the computer screen to describe phenomena where the natural unit might be light years (such as in displaying astronomical data) or microns (for integrated-circuit design). One of the major advances in graphics software systems occurred when the graphics systems allowed users to work in any coordinate system that they desired. The advent of **device-independent graphics** freed application programmers from worrying about the details of input and output devices. The user's coordinate system became known as the **world coordinate system**, or the **application** or **problem coordinate system**. Within

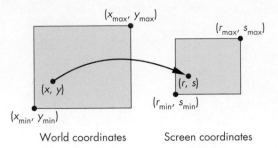

FIGURE 2.3   Mapping from world coordinates to screen coordinates.

the slight limitations of floating-point arithmetic on our computers, we can use any numbers that fit our application.

Units on the display were first called **physical-device coordinates** or just **device coordinates**. For raster devices, such as most CRT displays, we use the term **window coordinates** or **screen coordinates**.[3] Screen coordinates are always expressed in some integer type, because the center of any pixel in the frame buffer must be located on a fixed grid or, equivalently, because pixels are inherently discrete and we specify their locations using integers.

At some point, the values in world coordinates must be mapped to screen coordinates, as shown in Figure 2.3. The graphics system, rather than the user, is responsible for this task, and the mapping is performed automatically as part of the rendering process. As we shall see in the next few sections, the user needs to specify only a few parameters—such as the area of the world that she would like to see and the size of the display—to define this mapping.

2.3   The OpenGL API

We have the heart of a simple graphics program; now, we want to gain control over how our objects appear on the display. We also want to control the flow of the program, and we have to interact with the window system. Before completing our program, we describe the OpenGL API in more detail. Because vertices are represented in the same manner internally, whether they are specified as two- or three-dimensional entities, everything that we do here will be equally valid in three dimensions. Of course, we can do much more in three dimensions, but we are only getting started. In this chapter, we concentrate on how to specify primitives to be displayed; we leave interaction to Chapter 3.

OpenGL's structure is similar to that of most modern APIs, including Java3D and DirectX. Hence, any effort that you put into learning OpenGL will carry over

---

3. OpenGL makes a distinction between raster and screen coordinates, but this distinction will not be important until we work with how the OpenGL pipeline is implemented in Chapter 7.

to other software systems. Although OpenGL is easy to learn, compared with other APIs, it is nevertheless powerful. It supports the simple two- and three-dimensional programs that we develop in Chapters 2 through 6; it also supports the advanced rendering techniques that we study in Chapters 8 through 12.

Our prime goal is to study computer graphics; we are using an API to help us attain that goal. Consequently, we do not present all OpenGL functions, and we omit many details. However, our sample programs will be complete. More detailed information on OpenGL and on other APIs is given in the Suggested Readings section at the end of the chapter.

2.3.1 Graphics Functions

Our basic model of a graphics package is a **black box**, a term that engineers use to denote a system whose properties are described by only its inputs and outputs; we may know nothing about its internal workings. We can think of the graphics system as a box whose inputs are function calls from a user program; measurements from input devices, such as the mouse and keyboard; and possibly other input, such as messages from the operating system. The outputs are primarily the graphics sent to our output devices. For now, we can take the simplified view of inputs as function calls and outputs as primitives displayed on our monitor, as shown in Figure 2.4. Although OpenGL is the particular system that we use, all graphics APIs have a similar structure.

We describe an API through the functions in its library. A good API may contain hundreds of functions, so it is helpful to divide them into seven major groups:

1. Primitive functions
2. Attribute functions
3. Viewing functions
4. Transformation functions
5. Input functions
6. Control functions
7. Query functions

The **primitive functions** define the low-level objects or atomic entities that our system can display. Depending on the API, the primitives can include points, line segments, polygons, pixels, text, and various types of curves and surfaces.

If primitives are the *what* of an API—the primitive objects that can be displayed—then attributes are the *how*. That is, the attributes govern the way that a primitive appears on the display. **Attribute functions** allow us to perform

FIGURE 2.4 Graphics system as a black box.

operations ranging from choosing the color with which we display a line segment, to picking a pattern with which to fill the inside of a polygon, to selecting a typeface for the titles on a graph.

Our synthetic camera must be described if we are to create an image. As we saw in Chapter 1, we must describe the camera's position and orientation in our world and must select the equivalent of a lens. This process will not only fix the view but also allow us to clip out objects that are too close or too far away. The **viewing functions** allow us to specify various views, although APIs differ in the degree of flexibility they provide in choosing a view.

One of the characteristics of a good API is that it provides the user with a set of **transformation functions** that allows her to carry out transformations of objects, such as rotation, translation, and scaling. Our developments of viewing in Chapter 5 and of modeling in Chapter 10 will make heavy use of matrix transformations. In OpenGL, we obtain viewing functionality through transformations.

For interactive applications, an API must provide a set of **input functions** to allow us to deal with the diverse forms of input that characterize modern graphics systems. We need functions to deal with devices such as keyboards, mice, and data tablets. In Chapter 3, we introduce functions for working with different input modes and with a variety of input devices.

In any real application, we also have to worry about handling the complexities of working in a multiprocessing, multiwindow environment—usually an environment where we are connected to a network and there are other users. The **control functions** enable us to communicate with the window system, to initialize our programs, and to deal with any errors that take place during the execution of our programs.

If we are to write device-independent programs, we should expect the implementation of the API to take care of differences between devices, such as how many colors are supported or the size of the display. However, there are applications where we need to know some properties of the particular implementation. For example, we would probably chose to do things differently if we knew in advance that we were working with a display that could support only two colors rather than one with millions of colors. More generally, within our applications we can often use other information within the API, including camera parameters or values in the frame buffer. A good API will provide this information through a set of **query functions**.

2.3.2 The Graphics Pipeline and State Machines

If we put together some of these perspectives on graphics APIs, we can obtain another view, one closer to the way OpenGL, in particular, is actually organized and implemented. We can think of the entire graphics system as a **state machine**, a black box that contains a finite-state machine. This state machine has inputs that come from the application program and that may change the state of the machine or cause the machine to produce a visible output. From the perspective of the API, graphics functions are of two types: those that define primitives that flow through a pipeline inside the state machine and those that either change the state inside the machine or return state information. In OpenGL, functions such as glVertex are of the first type, whereas almost all other functions are of the second type.

One important consequence of this view is that in OpenGL most parameters are persistent; their values remain unchanged until we explicitly change them through functions that alter the state. For example, once we set a color, that color remains the *current color* until it is changed through a color-altering function. Another consequence of this view is that attributes that we may consider as bound to objects—a red line or a blue circle—are in fact part of the state, and a line will be drawn in red only if the current color state calls for drawing in red. Although within our applications it is usually harmless, and often preferable, to think of attributes as bound to primitives, there can be annoying consequences if we neglect to make state changes when needed or lose track of the current state.

2.3.3 The OpenGL Interface

OpenGL function names begin with the letters gl and are stored in a library usually referred to as GL (or OpenGL in Windows). There are a few related libraries that we also use. The first is the **OpenGL Utility Library (GLU)**. This library uses only GL functions but contains code for creating common objects, such as spheres, and other tasks that users prefer not to write repeatedly. The GLU library is available in all OpenGL implementations. The second library addresses the problems of interfacing with the window system. We use a readily available library called the **OpenGL Utility Toolkit (GLUT)** that provides the minimum functionality that should be expected in any modern windowing system. We introduce a few of its functions in this chapter and describe more of them in Chapter 3, where we consider input and interaction in detail. Figure 2.5 shows the organization of the libraries for an X Window System environment. The GLX library provides the minimum "glue" between OpenGL and the X Window System. GLX is used by GLUT, and thus this library and various others are called from the OpenGL libraries, but the application program does not need to refer to these libraries directly. A similar organization holds for other environments. For example, with Microsoft Windows a library called wgl replaces GLX; whereas for the Macintosh we use the library called agl.

OpenGL makes heavy use of macros to increase code readability and avoid the use of magic numbers. Thus, strings such as GL_FILL and GL_POINTS are defined in header (.h) files. In most implementations, one of the "include" lines

```
#include <GL/glut.h>
```

or

```
#include <glut.h>
```

is sufficient to read in glut.h, gl.h, and glu.h.

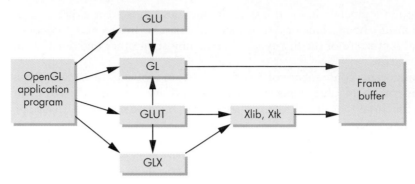

FIGURE 2.5   Library organization.

2.4   Primitives and Attributes

Within the graphics community, there has been an ongoing debate about which primitives should be supported in an API. The debate is an old one and has never been fully resolved. On the minimalist side, the contention is that an API should contain a small set of primitives that all hardware can be expected to support. In addition, the primitives should be orthogonal, each giving a capability unobtainable from the others. Minimal systems typically support lines, polygons, and some form of text (strings of characters), all of which can be generated efficiently in hardware. On the other end are systems that can also support a variety of primitives, such as circles, curves, surfaces, and solids. The argument here is that users need more complex primitives to build sophisticated applications easily. However, because few hardware systems can be expected to support the large set of primitives that is the union of all the desires of the user community, a program developed with such a system probably would not be portable, because few implementations could be expected to support the entire set of primitives.

OpenGL takes an intermediate position. The basic library has a small set of primitives. The GLU libary contains a richer set of objects derived from the basic library.

OpenGL supports two classes of primitives: **geometric primitives** and **image**, or **raster, primitives**. Geometric primitives are specified in the problem domain and include points, line segments, polygons, curves, and surfaces. These primitives pass through a geometric pipeline, as shown in Figure 2.6, where they are subject to series of geometric operations that determine whether a primitive is visible, where on the display it appears if it is visible, and the rasterization of the primitive into pixels in the frame buffer. Because geometric primitives exist in a two- or three-dimensional space, they can be manipulated by operations such as rotation and translation. In addition, they can be used as building blocks for other geometric objects using these same operations. Raster primitives, such as arrays of pixels, lack geometric properties and cannot be manipulated in space

Geometric Pipeline

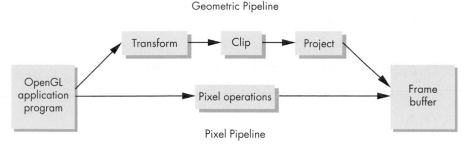

Pixel Pipeline

FIGURE 2.6   Simplified OpenGL pipeline.

in the same way as geometric primitives. They pass through a separate parallel pipeline on their way to the frame buffer. We shall defer our discussion of raster primitives until Chapter 8.

The basic OpenGL geometric primitives are specified by sets of vertices. Thus, the programmer defines her objects with sequences of the form

```
glBegin(type);
    glVertex*(...);
    .
    .
    .
    glVertex*(...);
glEnd();
```

The value of `type` specifies how OpenGL assembles the vertices to define geometric objects. Other code and OpenGL function calls can occur between `glBegin` and `glEnd`. For example, we can change attributes or perform calculations for the next vertex between `glBegin` and `glEnd`, or between two invocations of `glVertex`. A major conceptual difference between the basic geometric types is whether or not they have interiors. All the basic types are defined by sets of vertices.

Finite sections of lines between two vertices, called **line segments**—in contrast to lines that are infinite in extent—are of great importance in geometry and computer graphics. You can use line segments to define approximations to curves, or you can use a sequence of line segments to connect data values for a graph. You can also use line segments for the edges of closed objects, such as polygons, that have interiors. Consequently, it is often helpful to think in terms of both vertices and line segments.

If we wish to display points or line segments, we have a few choices in OpenGL (Figure 2.7). The primitives and their `type` specifications include the following:

Points (`GL_POINTS`) Each vertex is displayed at a size of at least one pixel.

Line segments (`GL_LINES`) The line-segment type causes successive pairs of vertices to be interpreted as the endpoints of individual segments. Note that

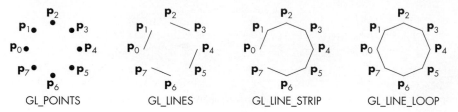

FIGURE 2.7   Point and line-segment types.

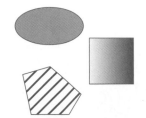

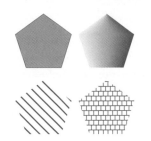

FIGURE 2.8   Filled objects.

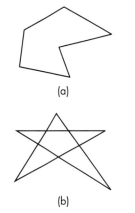

FIGURE 2.9   Methods of displaying a polygon.

FIGURE 2.10   Polygons. (a) Simple. (b) Nonsimple.

successive segments usually are disconnected because the interpretation is done on a pairwise basis.

Polylines (GL_LINE_STRIP, GL_LINE_LOOP) If successive vertices (and line segments) are to be connected, we can use the line strip, or **polyline** form. Many curves can be approximated via a suitable polyline. If we wish the polyline to be closed, we can locate the final vertex in the same place as the first, or we can use the GL_LINE_LOOP type, which will draw a line segment from the final vertex to the first, thus creating a closed path.

2.4.1 Polygon Basics

Line segments and polylines can model the edges of objects, but closed objects also may have interiors (Figure 2.8). We usually reserve the name **polygon** to refer to an object that has a border that can be described by a line loop but also has a well-defined interior.[4] Polygons play a special role in computer graphics because we can display them rapidly and use them to approximate arbitrary surfaces. The performance of graphics systems is measured by the number of polygons per second that can be rendered. We can render a polygon in a variety of ways. We can render only its edges. We can render its interior with a solid color or a pattern. And we can render or not render the edges, as shown in Figure 2.9. Although the outer edges of a polygon are defined easily by an ordered list of vertices, if the interior is not well defined, then the list of vertices may not be rendered at all or rendered in an undesirable manner. Three properties will ensure that a polygon will be displayed correctly: It must be simple, convex, and flat.

In two dimensions, as long as no two edges of a polygon cross each other, we have a **simple** polygon. As we can see from Figure 2.10, simple two-dimensional polygons have well-defined interiors. Although the locations of the vertices determine whether or not a polygon is simple, the cost of testing is sufficiently high (see Exercise 2.12) that most graphics systems require that the application program do any necessary testing. We can ask what a graphics system will do if it

_____

4. The term *fill area* is sometimes used instead of *polygon*.

is given a nonsimple polygon to display and whether there is a way to define an interior for a nonsimple polygon. We shall examine these questions in Chapter 8.

From the perspective of implementing a practical algorithm to fill the interior of a polygon, simplicity alone is often not enough. Some APIs guarantee a consistent fill from implementation to implementation only if the polygon is convex. An object is **convex** if all points on the line segment between any two points inside the object, or on its boundary, are inside the object (Figure 2.11). Although so far we have been dealing with only two-dimensional objects, this definition makes reference neither to the type of object nor to the number of dimensions. Convex objects include triangles, tetrahedra, rectangles, circles, spheres, and parallelepipeds (Figure 2.12). There are various tests for convexity (see Exercise 2.19). However, like simplicity testing, convexity testing is expensive and usually left to the application program.

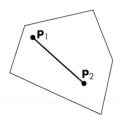

FIGURE 2.11   Convexity.

In three dimensions, polygons present a few more difficulties because, unlike all two-dimensional objects, all the vertices that define the polygon need not lie in the same plane. One property that most graphics systems exploit, and that we shall use, is that any three vertices that are not collinear determine both a triangle and the plane in which that triangle lies. Hence, if we always use triangles, we are safe—we can be sure that these objects will be rendered correctly. Often, we are almost forced to use triangles because typical rendering algorithms are guaranteed to be correct only if the vertices form a flat convex polygon. In addition, hardware and software often support a triangle type that is rendered much faster than is a polygon with three vertices.

2.4.2 Polygon Types in OpenGL

Let us return to the OpenGL types. For objects with interiors, we can specify the following types (Figure 2.13):

Polygons (`GL_POLYGON`) The edges are the same as they would be if we used line loops. Successive vertices define line segments, and a line segment connects the final vertex to the first. The interior is filled according to the state of the relevant attributes. Note that a mathematical polygon has an inside and an outside that

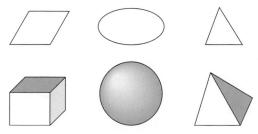

FIGURE 2.12   Convex objects.

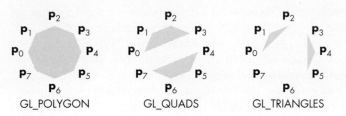

FIGURE 2.13   Polygon types.

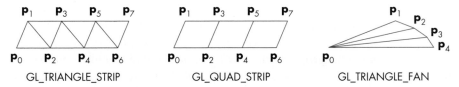

FIGURE 2.14   Triangle strip, quadrilateral strip, and triangle fan.

are separated by the edge. The edge itself has no width. Consequently, most graphics systems allow you to fill the polygon with a color or pattern or to draw lines around the edges, but not to do both. In OpenGL, we can use the function glPolygonMode to render the edges or just points for the vertices, instead of fill (the default). However, if we want to draw a polygon that is filled and to display its edges, then we have to render it twice, once in each mode, or to draw a polygon and a line loop with the same vertices.

Triangles and Quadrilaterals (GL_TRIANGLES, GL_QUADS)   These objects are special cases of polygons. Successive groups of three and four vertices are interpreted as triangles and quadrilaterals, respectively. Using these types may lead to a rendering more efficient than that obtained with polygons.

Strips and Fans (GL_TRIANGLE_STRIP, GL_QUAD_STRIP, GL_TRIANGLE_FAN)   These objects are based on groups of triangles or quadrilaterals that share vertices and edges. In the triangle strip, for example, each additional vertex is combined with the previous two vertices to define a new triangle (Figure 2.14). For the quadstrip, we combine two new vertices with the previous two vertices to define a new quadrilateral. A triangle fan is based on one fixed point. The next two points determine the first triangle, and subsequent triangles are formed from one new point, the previous point, and the first (fixed) point.

2.4.3 Approximating a Sphere

Fans and strips also allow us to approximate many curved surfaces simply. For example, one way to construct an approximation to a sphere is to use a set of polygons defined by lines of longitude and latitude as in Figure 2.15. We can do so very efficiently using either quad strips or triangle strips. Consider a unit sphere. We can describe it by the three equations

$$x(\theta, \phi) = \sin \theta \cos \phi,$$
$$y(\theta, \phi) = \cos \theta \cos \phi,$$
$$z(\theta, \phi) = \sin \phi.$$

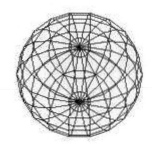

FIGURE 2.15 Sphere approximation with quadrilaterals.

If we fix θ and draw curves as we change ϕ, we get circles of constant longitude. Likewise, if we fix ϕ and vary θ, we obtain circles of constant latitude. By generating points at fixed increments of θ and ϕ, we can define quadrilaterals as in Figure 2.15. Remembering that we must convert degrees to radians for the standard trigonometric functions, the code for the quadrilaterals corresponding to increments of 20 degrees in θ and to 20 degrees in ϕ is

```
c=M_PI/180.0; //degrees to radians, M_PI = 3.14159...
for(phi=-80.0; phi<=80.0; phi+=20.0)
{
    phir=c*phi;
    phir20=c*(phi+20);
    glBegin(GL_QUAD_STRIP);
    for(theta=-180.0; theta<=180.0;theta+=20.0)
    {
        thetar=c*theta;
        x=sin(thetar)*cos(phir);
        y=cos(thetar)*cos(phir);
        z=sin(phir);
        glVertex3d(x,y,z);
        x=sin(thetar)*cos(phir20);
        y=cos(thetar)*cos(phir20);
        z=sin(phir20);
        glVertex3d(x,y,z);
    }
    glEnd();
}
```

However, we have a problem at the poles, where we can no longer use strips because all lines of longitude converge there. We can, however, use two triangle fans, one at each pole as follows:

```
glBegin(GL_TRIANGLE_FAN);
    glVertex3d(0.0, 0.0 , 1.0);
    c=M_PI/180.0;
```

```
    c80=c*80.0;
    z=sin(c80);
    for(thet=-180.0; theta<=180.0;theta+=20.0)
    {
        thetar=c*theta;
        x=sin(thetar)*cos(c80);
        y=cos(thetar)*cos(c80);
        glVertex3d(x,y,z);
    }
glEnd();

glBegin(GL_TRIANGLE_FAN);
    glVertex3d(0.0, 0.0, -1.0);
    z=-sin(c80);
    for(theta=-180.0;theta<=180.0;theta+=20.0)
    {
        thetar=c*theta;
        x=sin(thetar)*cos(c80);
        y=cos(thetar)*cos(c80);
        glVertex3d(x,y,z);
    }
glEnd();
```

2.4.4   Text

Graphical output in applications such as data analysis and display requires annotation, such as labels on graphs. Although, in nongraphical programs, textual output is the norm, text in computer graphics is problematic. In nongraphical applications, we are usually content with a simple set of characters, always displayed in the same manner. In computer graphics, however, we often wish to display text in a multitude of fashions by controlling type styles, sizes, colors, and other parameters. We also want to have available a choice of fonts. **Fonts** are families of type faces of a particular style, such as Times, Computer Modern, or Helvetica.

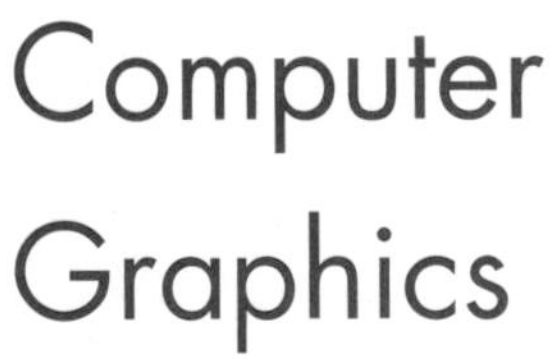

There are two forms of text: stroke and raster. **Stroke text** (Figure 2.16) is constructed as are other geometric objects. We use vertices to define line segments or curves that outline each character. If the characters are defined by closed boundaries, we can fill them. The advantage of stroke text is that it can be defined to have all the detail of any other object, and because it is defined in the same way as are other graphical objects, it can be manipulated by our standard transformations and viewed like any other graphical primitive. Using transformations, we can make a stroke character bigger or rotate it, retaining its detail and appearance. Consequently, we need to define a character only once and can use transformations to generate it at the desired size and orientation.

Computer

Graphics

FIGURE 2.16   Stroke text (Post-Script font).

Defining a full 128- or 256-character stroke font, however, can be complex, and the font can take up significant memory and processing time. The standard PostScript fonts are defined by polynomial curves, and they illustrate all the advantages and disadvantages of stroke text. The various PostScript fonts can be used for both high- and low-resolution applications. Often developers mitigate the problems of slow rendering of such stroke characters by putting considerable processing power in the printer. This strategy is related to the client–server concepts that we discuss in Chapter 3.

Raster text (Figure 2.17) is simple and fast. Characters are defined as rectangles of bits called **bit blocks**. Each block defines a single character by the pattern of 0 and 1 bits in the block. A raster character can be placed in the frame buffer rapidly by a **bit-block-transfer (bitblt)** operation, which moves the block of bits using a single command. We discuss bitblt in Chapter 8; OpenGL allows the application program to use functions that allow direct manipulation of the contents of the frame buffer.

You can increase the size of raster characters by **replicating** or duplicating pixels, a process that gives larger characters a blocky appearance (Figure 2.18). Other transformations of raster characters, such as rotation, may not make sense, because the transformation may move the bits defining the character to locations that do not correspond to the location of pixels in the frame buffer.

Because stroke and bitmap characters can be created from other primitives, OpenGL does not have a text primitive. However, the GLUT library provides

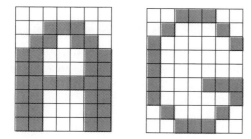

FIGURE 2.17   Raster text.

FIGURE 2.18   Raster-character replication.

a few predefined bitmap and stroke character sets that are defined in software and are portable. For example, we can put out a bitmap character that is 8×13 pixels by

```
glutBitmapCharacter(GLUT_BITMAP_8_BY_13, c)
```

where c is the number of the ASCII character that we wish to be placed on the display. The character is placed at the present **raster position** on the display (a location that is part of the graphics state), is measured in pixels, and can be altered by the various forms of the function `glRasterPos*`. We return to text in Chapter 3. There we shall see that both stroke and raster text can be implemented most efficiently through display lists.

2.4.5 Curved Objects

The primitives in our basic set have all been defined through vertices. With the exception of the point type, all either consist of line segments or use line segments to define the boundary of a region that can be filled with a solid color or a pattern. We can take two approaches to creating a richer set of objects.

First, we can use the primitives that we have to approximate curves and surfaces. For example, if we want a circle, we can use a regular polygon of n sides. Likewise, we have approximated a sphere with triangles and quadrilaterals. More generally, we approximate a curved surface by a mesh of convex polygons—a **tessellation**—which can occur either at the rendering stage or within the user program.

The other approach, which we explore in Chapter 11, is to start with the mathematical definitions of curved objects, then build graphics functions to implement those objects. Objects such as quadric surfaces and parametric polynomial curves and surfaces are well understood mathematically, and we can specify them through sets of vertices. For example, we can define a sphere by its center and a point on its surface, or we can define a cubic polynomial curve by four points.

Most graphics systems give us aspects of both approaches. In OpenGL, we can use the GLU or GLUT libraries for a collection of approximations to common curved surfaces, and we can write functions to define more of our own. We can also use the advanced features of OpenGL to work with parametric polynomial curves and surfaces.

2.4.6 Attributes

In a modern graphics system, there is a distinction between what the type of a primitive is and how that primitive is rendered. A red solid line and a green dashed line are the same geometric type, but each is rendered differently. An **attribute** is any property that determines how a geometric primitive is to be rendered. Color is an obvious attribute, as are the thickness of a line and the pattern used

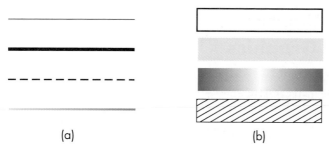

(a)   (b)

FIGURE 2.19   Attributes for (a) lines and (b) polygons.

to fill a polygon. Several of these attributes are shown in Figure 2.19 for lines and polygons.

Attributes may be associated with, or **bound** to, primitives at various points in the modeling and rendering pipeline. At this point, we are concerned with immediate-mode graphics. In **immediate mode**, primitives are not stored in the system but rather passed through the system for possible rendering as soon as they are defined. The current values of attributes are part of the state of the graphics system. When a primitive is rendered, the current attributes for that type are used, and it is displayed immediately. There is no memory of the primitive in the system. Only the primitive's effect on the frame buffer appears on the display; once erased from the display, it is lost. In Chapter 3, we introduce display lists, which will enable us to keep objects in memory so that these objects can be redisplayed.

OpenGL's emphasis on immediate-mode graphics and a pipeline architecture works well for interactive applications, but that emphasis is a fundamental difference between OpenGL and object-oriented systems in which objects can be created and recalled as desired. We shall discuss scene graphs, which are fundamental to systems such as Java3D, in Chapter 10 and there we shall see that they provide another higher-level approach to computer graphics.

Each geometric type has a set of attributes. For example, a point has a color attribute and a size attribute. Line segments can have color, thickness, and pattern (solid, dashed, or dotted). Filled primitives, such as polygons, have more attributes because we must use multiple parameters to specify how the fill should be done. We can fill with a solid color or a pattern. We can decide not to fill the polygon and to display only its edges. If we fill the polygon, we might also display the edges in a color different from that of the interior.

In systems that support stroke text as a primitive, there is a variety of attributes. Some of these attributes are demonstrated in Figure 2.20; they include the direction of the text string, the path followed by successive characters in the string, the height and width of the characters, the font, and the style (bold, italic, underlined).

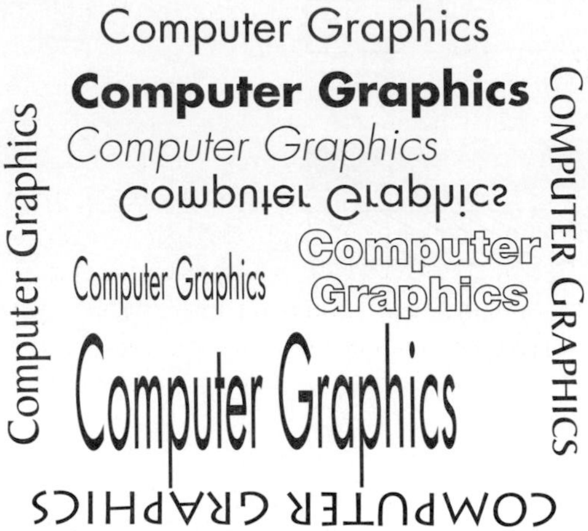

Computer Graphics

Computer Graphics

Computer Graphics

Computer Graphics (upside down)

Computer Graphics

Computer Graphics (outline)

Computer Graphics (vertical)

COMPUTER GRAPHICS (vertical)

Computer Graphics

COMPUTER GRAPHICS (upside down)

FIGURE 2.20   Stroke-text attributes.

2.5   Color

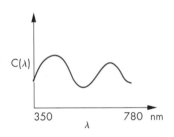

FIGURE 2.21   A color distribution.

Color is one of the most interesting aspects of both human perception and computer graphics. We can use the model of the human visual system from Chapter 1 to obtain a simple but useful color model. Full exploitation of the capabilities of the human visual system using computer graphics requires a far deeper understanding of the human anatomy, physiology, and psychophysics. We shall present a more sophisticated development in Chapter 7.

A visible color can be characterized by a function $C(\lambda)$ that occupies wavelengths from about 350 to 780 nm, as shown in Figure 2.21. The value for a given wavelength λ in the visible spectrum gives the intensity of that wavelength in the color.

Although this characterization is accurate in terms of a physical color whose properties we can measure, it does not take into account how we *perceive* color. As we noted in Chapter 1, the human visual system has three types of cones responsible for color vision. Hence, our brains do not receive the entire distribution $C(\lambda)$ for a given color but rather three values—the **tristimulus values**—that are the responses of the three types of cones to the color. This reduction of a color to three values leads to the **basic tenet of three-color theory**: *If two colors produce the same tristimulus values, then they are visually indistinguishable.*

A consequence of this tenet is that in principle, a display need have only three color, primaries to produce the three tristimulus values needed for a human observer. We vary the intensity of each primary to produce a color as we saw for the CRT in Chapter 1. The CRT is one example of **additive color** where the primary colors add together to give the perceived color. Other examples of additive color include projectors and slide (positive) film. In such systems, the primaries are usually red, green, and blue. With additive color, primaries add light to an initially black display, yielding the desired color.

For processes such as commercial printing and painting, a **subtractive color model** is more appropriate. Here we start with a white surface, such as a sheet of paper. Colored pigments remove color components from light that is striking the surface. If we assume that white light hits the surface, a particular point will be red if all components of the incoming light are absorbed by the surface except for wavelengths in the red part of the spectrum, which are reflected. In subtractive systems, the primaries are usually the **complementary colors**: cyan, magenta, and yellow (CMY; Figure 2.22). We shall not explore subtractive color here. You need to know only that an RGB additive system has a dual with a CMY subtractive system (see Exercise 2.8).

We can view a color as a point in a **color solid**, as shown in Figure 2.23 and in Color Plate 21. We draw the solid using a coordinate system corresponding to the three primaries. The distance along a coordinate axis represents the amount

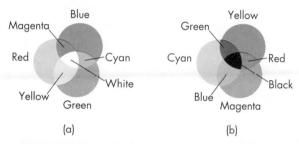

(a)   (b)

FIGURE 2.22   Color formation. (a) Additive color.
(b) Subtractive color.

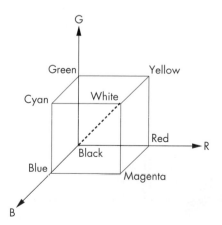

FIGURE 2.23   Color solid.

of the corresponding primary in the color. If we normalize the maximum value of each primary to be 1, then we can represent any color that we can produce with this set of primaries as a point in a unit cube. The vertices of the cube correspond to black (no primaries on); red, green, and blue (one primary fully on); the pairs of primaries, cyan (green and blue fully on), magenta (red and blue fully on), and yellow (red and green fully on); and white (all primaries fully on). The principal diagonal of the cube connects the origin (black) with white. All colors along this line have equal tristimulus values and appear as shades of gray.

There are many matters that we are not exploring fully here and will return to in Chapter 7. Most concern the differences among various sets of primaries or the limitations conferred by the physical constraints of real devices. In particular, the set of colors produced by one device—its **color gamut**—is not the same as for other devices, nor will match the human's color gamut. Nor will the tristimulus values used on one device produce the same visible color as the same tristimulus values on another device.

2.5.1   RGB Color

Now we can look at how color is handled in a graphics system from the programmer's perspective—that is, through the API. There are two different approaches. We shall stress the **RGB-color model** because an understanding of it will be crucial for our later discussion of shading. Historically, the **indexed color model** (Section 2.5.2) was easier to support in hardware because of its lower memory requirements and the limited colors available on displays, but in modern systems RGB color has become the norm.

In a three-primary-color, additive-color RGB system, there are conceptually separate buffers for red, green, and blue images. Each pixel has separate red, green, and blue components that correspond to locations in memory (Figure 2.24). In a typical system, there might be a 1280×1024 array of pixels, and each pixel might consist of 24 bits (3 bytes): 1 byte for each of red, green, and blue. With present commodity graphics cards having from 64MB to 256MB of

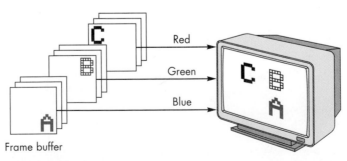

FIGURE 2.24   RGB color.

memory, there is no longer a problem of storing and displaying the contents of the frame buffer at video rates.

As programmers, we would like to be able to specify any color that can be stored in the frame buffer. For our 24-bit example, there are 2^{24} possible colors, sometimes referred to as 16 M colors. where M denotes 1024^2. Other systems may have as many as 12 (or more) bits per color or as few as 4 bits per color. Because our API should be independent of the particulars of the hardware, we would like to specify a color independently of the number of bits in the frame buffer and to let the drivers and hardware match our specification as closely as possible to the available display. A natural technique is to use the color cube and to specify color components as numbers between 0.0 and 1.0, where 1.0 denotes the maximum (or **saturated** value) of the corresponding primary, and 0.0 denotes a zero value of that primary. In OpenGL, we use the color cube as follows. To draw in red, we issue the function call

```
glColor3f(1.0, 0.0, 0.0);
```

The execution of this function will set the current drawing color to red. Because the color is part of the state, we continue to draw in red until the color is changed. The "3f" is used in a manner similar to the glVertex function: It conveys that we are using a three-color (RGB) model and that the values of the components are given as floats in C. If we use an integer or byte type to specify a color value, the maximum value of the chosen type corresponds to the primary fully on, and the minimum value corresponds to the primary fully off.

Later, we shall be interested in a four-color (RGBA) system. The fourth color (A, or **alpha**) also is stored in the frame buffer as are the RGB values; it can be set with four-dimensional versions of the color functions. In Chapter 7, we shall see various uses for alpha, such as for creating fog effects or for combining images. Here we need to specify the alpha value as part of the initialization of an OpenGL program. If blending is enabled (Chapter 8), then the alpha value will be treated by OpenGL as either an **opacity** or **transparency** value. Transparency and opacity are complements of each other. An opaque object passes no light through it; a transparent object passes all light. Opacity values can range from fully transparent (A=0.0) to fully opaque (A=1.0).

One of the first tasks that we must do in a program is to clear an area of the screen—a drawing window—in which to display our output. We also must clear this window whenever we want to draw a new frame. By using the four-dimensional (RGBA) color system, we can create effects where the drawing window interacts with other windows that may be beneath it by manipulating the opacity assigned to the window when it is cleared. The function call

```
glClearColor(1.0, 1.0, 1.0, 1.0);
```

defines a four-color clearing color that is white, because the first three components are set to 1.0, and is opaque, because the alpha component is 1.0. We can then use the function glClear to make the window on the screen solid and white. Note that by default blending is not enabled. Consequently, the alpha value can be set in glClearColor to a value other than 1.0 and the default window will still be opaque.

2.5.2 Indexed Color

Early graphics systems had frame buffers that were limited in depth. For example, we might have had a frame buffer with a spatial resolution of 1280×1024, but each pixel was only 8 bits deep. We could divide each pixel's 8 bits into smaller groups of bits to assign to each of red, green, and blue. Although this technique was adequate in a few applications, it usually did not give us enough flexibility in color assignment. Indexed color provided a solution that allowed applications to display a wide range of colors as long as the application did not need more colors than could be referenced by a pixel. This technique is still of use today.

We follow an analogy with an artist who paints in oils. The oil painter can produce an almost infinite number of colors by mixing together a limited number of pigments from tubes. We say that the painter has a potentially large color **palette**. At any one time, however, perhaps due to a limited number of brushes, the painter uses only a few colors. In this fashion, our painter can create an image that, although it contains a small number of colors, expresses the painter's desires because she can choose the few colors from a large palette.

Returning to the computer model, we can argue that if we can choose for each application a limited number of colors from a large selection (our palette), we should be able to create good-quality images most of the time.

We can select colors by interpreting our limited-depth pixels as indices into a table of colors rather than as color values. Suppose that our frame buffer has k bits per pixel. Each pixel value or index is an integer between 0 and $2^k - 1$. Suppose that we can display colors with a precision of m bits; that is, we can choose from 2^m reds, 2^m greens, and 2^m blues. Hence, we can produce any of 2^{3m} colors on the display, but the frame buffer can specify only 2^k of them. We handle the specification through a user-defined **color-lookup table** that is of size $2^k \times 3m$ (Figure 2.25). The user program fills the 2^k entries (rows) of the table with the desired colors, using m bits for each of red, green, and blue. Once the

Input		Red	Green	Blue
0		0	0	0
1		$2^m - 1$	0	0
·		0	$2^m - 1$	0
·		·	·	·
·		·	·	·
$2^k - 1$		·	·	·

$\longleftarrow$ *m* bits $\longrightarrow$ $\longleftarrow$ *m* bits $\longrightarrow$ $\longleftarrow$ *m* bits $\longrightarrow$

FIGURE 2.25   Color-lookup table.

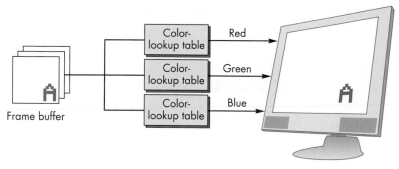

FIGURE 2.26 Indexed color.

user has constructed the table, she can specify a color by its index, which points to the appropriate entry in the color-lookup table (Figure 2.26). For $k = m = 8$, a common configuration, she can choose 256 out of 16 M colors. The 256 entries in the table constitute the user's color palette.

If we are in color-index mode, the present color is selected by a function such as

```
glIndexi(element);
```

that selects a particular color out of the table. Setting and changing the entries in the color-lookup table involves interacting with the window system, a topic discussed in Chapter 3. One difficulty arises if the window system and underlying hardware support only a limited number of colors because the window system may have only a single color table that must be used for all its windows, or it might have to juggle multiple tables, one for each window on the screen. GLUT allows us to set the entries in a color table for each window through the function

```
glutSetColor(int color, GLfloat red, GLfloat green, GLfloat blue)
```

Historically, color-index mode was important because it required less memory for the frame buffer and fewer other hardware components. However, cost is no longer an issue and color-index mode presents a few problems. When we work with dynamic images that must be shaded, we usually need more colors than are provided by color-index mode. In addition, the interaction with the window system is also more complex than with RGB color. Consequently, for the most part, we shall assume that we are using RGB color.

2.5.3 Setting of Color Attributes

For our simple example program, we use RGB color. We have three attributes to set. The first is the clear color, which is set to white by the function call

```
glClearColor(1.0, 1.0, 1.0, 1.0);
```

We can select the rendering color for our points by setting the color state variable to red through the function call

```
glColor3f(1.0, 0.0, 0.0);
```

We can set the size of our rendered points to be 2 pixels wide, by using

```
glPointSize(2.0);
```

Note that attributes, such as the point size and line width, are specified in terms of the pixel size. Hence, if two displays have different-sized pixels (due to their particular screen dimensions and resolutions), the rendered images may appear slightly different. Certain graphics APIs, in an attempt to ensure that identical displays will be produced on all systems with the same user program, specify all attributes in a device-independent manner. Unfortunately, ensuring that two systems produce the same display has proved to be a difficult implementation problem. OpenGL has chosen a more practical balance between desired behavior and realistic constraints.

2.6   Viewing

We can now put a variety of graphical information into our world, and we can describe how we would like these objects to appear, but we do not yet have a method for specifying exactly which of these objects should appear on the screen. Just as what we record in a photograph depends on where we point the camera and what lens we use, we have to make similar viewing decisions in our program.

A fundamental concept that emerges from the synthetic-camera model that we introduced in Chapter 1 is that the specification of the objects in our scene is completely independent of our specification of the camera. Once we have specified both the scene and the camera, we can compose an image. The camera forms an image by exposing the film, whereas the computer system forms an image by carrying out a sequence of operations in its pipeline. The application program needs to worry only about specification of the parameters for the objects and the camera, just as the casual photographer does not have to worry about how the shutter works or the details of the photochemical interaction of film with light.

There are default viewing conditions in computer image formation that are similar to the settings on a basic camera with a fixed lens. However, a camera that has a fixed lens and sits in a fixed location forces us to distort our world to take a picture. We can create pictures of elephants only if we place the animals sufficiently far from the camera, or of ants if we put the insects relatively close to the lens. We prefer to have the flexibility to change the lens to make it easier to form an image of a collection of objects. The same is true when we use our graphics system.

2.6.1 The Orthographic View

The simplest and OpenGL's default view is the orthographic projection. We discuss this projection and others in detail in Chapter 5, but we want to introduce the orthographic projection here so that you can get started writing three-dimensional programs. Mathematically, the orthographic projection is what we would get if the camera in our synthetic-camera model had an infinitely long telephoto lens and we could then place the camera infinitely far from our objects. We can approximate this effect as in Figure 2.27 by leaving the image plane fixed and moving the camera far from this plane. In the limit, all the projectors become parallel and the center of projection is replaced by a **direction of projection**.

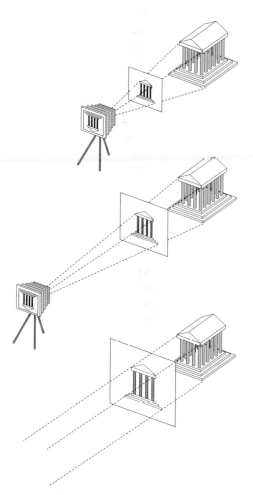

FIGURE 2.27 Creating an orthographic view by moving the camera away from the projection plane.

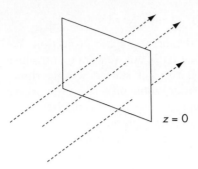

FIGURE 2.28   Orthographic projectors with projection plane $z = 0$.

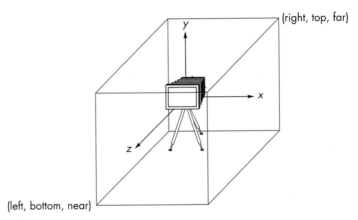

(right, top, far)

(left, bottom, near)

FIGURE 2.29   The default camera and an orthographic view volume.

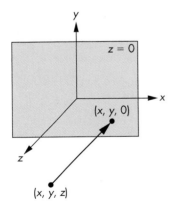

FIGURE 2.30   Orthographic projection.

Rather than worrying about cameras an infinite distance away, suppose that we start with projectors that are parallel to the positive z-axis and the projection plane at $z = 0$, as in Figure 2.28. Note that not only are the projectors perpendicular or orthogonal to the projection plane, but we can slide the projection plane along the z-axis without changing where the projectors intersect this plane.

For orthographic viewing, we can think of there being a special orthographic camera that resides in the projection plane, something that is not possible for other views. Perhaps more accurately stated, there is a reference point in the projection plane from which we can make measurements of a view volume and a direction of projection. In OpenGL, the reference point starts off at the origin and the camera points in the negative z direction, as in Figure 2.29. The orthographic projection takes a point (x, y, z) and projects it into the point $(x, y, 0)$ as shown in Figure 2.30. Note that if we are working in two dimensions with all vertices in the plane $z = 0$, a point and its projection are the same; however, we can employ the machinery of a three-dimensional graphics system to produce our image. In OpenGL, an orthographic projection with a right-parallelepiped viewing volume is specified via

```
void glOrtho(GLdouble left, GLdouble right, GLdouble bottom,
    GLdouble top, GLdouble near, GLdouble far)
```

Note that all the parameters are distances measured *from* the camera. The orthographic projection "sees" only those objects in the volume specified by viewing volume. Unlike a real camera, the orthographic projection can include objects behind the camera. Thus, as long as the plane $z = 0$ is located between near and far, the two-dimensional plane will intersect the viewing volume.

If we do not specify a viewing volume, OpenGL uses its default, a $2 \times 2 \times 2$ cube, with the origin in the center. In terms of our two-dimensional plane, the bottom-left corner is at $(-1.0, -1.0)$, and the upper-right corner is at $(1.0, 1.0)$.

2.6.2 Two-Dimensional Viewing

Remember that, in our view, two-dimensional graphics is a special case of three-dimensional graphics. Our viewing rectangle is in the plane $z = 0$ within a three-dimensional **viewing volume**, as shown in Figure 2.31. If using a three-dimensional volume seems strange in a two-dimensional application, the function

```
void gluOrtho2D(GLdouble left, GLdouble right,
    GLdouble bottom, GLdouble top)
```

in the utility library may make your program more consistent with its two-dimensional structure. This function is equivalent to glOrtho, with near and far set to -1.0 and 1.0, respectively. In Chapters 4 and 5, we discuss moving the camera and creating more complex views.

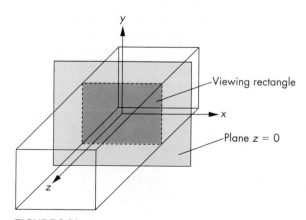

FIGURE 2.31   Viewing volume.

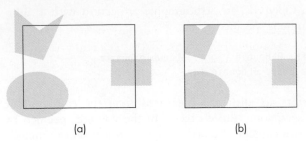

(a)   (b)

FIGURE 2.32   Two-dimensional viewing. (a) Objects before clipping. (b) Image after clipping.

We could also consider two-dimensional viewing directly by taking a rectangular area of our two-dimensional world and transferring its contents to the display, as shown in Figure 2.32. The area of the world that we image is known as the **viewing rectangle**, or **clipping rectangle**. Objects inside the rectangle are in the image; objects outside are **clipped out** and are not displayed. Objects that straddle the edges of the rectangle are partially visible in the image. The size of the window on the display and where this window is placed on the display are independent decisions that we examine in Section 2.7.

2.6.3   Matrix Modes

Pipeline graphics systems have an architecture that depends on multiplying together, or **concatenating**, a number of transformation matrices to achieve the desired image of a primitive. Like most other OpenGL variables, the values of these matrices are part of the state of the system and remain in effect until changed. The two most important matrices are the **model-view** and **projection** matrices. At any time, the state includes values for both of these matrices, which are initially set to identity matrices. In Chapter 4, we study a set of OpenGL functions to manipulate these matrices. The usual sequence is to modify the initial identity matrix by applying a sequence of transformations. There is only a single set of functions that can be applied to any type of matrix. We select the matrix to which the operations apply by first setting the **matrix mode**, a variable that is set to one type of matrix and is also part of the state. The default matrix mode is to have operations apply to the model-view matrix, so to alter the projection matrix, we must first switch modes. The following sequence is common for setting a two-dimensional viewing rectangle:

```
glMatrixMode(GL_PROJECTION);
glLoadIdentity();
gluOrtho2D(0.0, 50.0, 0.0, 50.0);
glMatrixMode(GL_MODELVIEW);
```

This sequence defines a 50.0×50.0 viewing rectangle with the lower-left corner of the rectangle at the origin of the two-dimensional system. It then switches the matrix mode back to model-view mode. In complex programs, it is always a good idea to return to a given matrix mode, in this case model-view mode, to avoid problems caused by losing track of which matrix mode the program is in at a given time.

2.7 Control Functions

We are almost done with our first program, but we still must discuss the minimal interactions with the window and operating systems. If we look at the details for a specific environment, such as the X Window System on a linux platform or Windows on a PC, we see that the programmer's interface between the graphics system and the operating and window systems can be complex. Exploitation of the possibilities open to the application programmer requires knowledge specific to these systems. In addition, the details can be different for two different environments, and discussing these differences will do little to enhance our understanding of computer graphics.

Rather than deal with these issues in detail, we look at a minimal set of operations that must take place from the perspective of the graphics application program. Earlier we discussed the OpenGL Utility Toolkit (GLUT); it is a library of functions that provides a simple interface between the systems. Details specific to the underlying windowing or operating system are inside the implementation, rather than being part of its API. Operationally, we add another library to our standard library search path. Both here and in Chapter 3, GLUT will help us to understand the interactions that characterize modern interactive graphics systems, including a wide range of APIs, operating systems, and window systems. The application programs that we produce using GLUT should run under multiple window systems.

2.7.1 Interaction with the Window System

The term *window* is used in a number of different ways in the graphics and work-station literature. We use **window**, or **screen window**, to denote a rectangular area of our display. We are concerned only with raster displays. A window has a height and width, and because the window displays the contents of the frame buffer, positions in the window are measured in **window** or **screen coordinates**,[5] where the units are pixels.

---

5. In OpenGL, window coordinates are three-dimensional, whereas screen coordinates are two-dimensional. Both systems use units measured in pixels, but window coordinates retain depth information.

In a modern environment, we can display many windows on the monitor. Each can have a different purpose, ranging from editing a file to monitoring our system. We use the term *window system* to refer to the multiwindow environment provided by systems such as the X Window System and Microsoft Windows. The window in which the graphics output appears is one of the windows managed by the window system. Hence, to the window system, the graphics window is a particular type of window—one in which graphics can be displayed or rendered. References to positions in this window are relative to one corner of the window. We have to be careful about which corner is the origin. In science and engineering, the lower-left corner is the origin and has window coordinates (0,0). However, virtually all raster systems display their screens in the same way as commercial television systems do—from top to bottom, left to right. From this perspective, the top-left corner should be the origin. Our OpenGL commands assume that the origin is bottom left, whereas information returned from the windowing system, such as the mouse position, often has the origin at the top left and thus requires us to convert the position from one coordinate system to the other.

Although our screen may have a resolution of, say, 1280×1024 pixels, the window that we use can have any size. Thus, the frame buffer must have a resolution equal to the screen size. Conceptually, if we use a window of 300×400 pixels, we can think of it as corresponding to a 300×400 frame buffer, even though it uses only a part of the real frame buffer.

Before we can open a window, there must be interaction between the windowing system and OpenGL. In GLUT, this interaction is initiated by the function call

```
glutInit(int *argcv, char **argv)
```

The two arguments allow the user to pass command-line arguments, as in the standard C main function, and are usually the same as in main. We can now open an OpenGL window using the GLUT function

```
glutCreateWindow(char *title)
```

where the title at the top of the window is given by the string title.

The window that we create has a default size, a position on the screen, and characteristics such as use of RGB color. We can also use GLUT functions before window creation to specify these parameters. For example, the code

```
glutInitDisplayMode(GLUT_RGB | GLUT_DEPTH | GLUT_DOUBLE);
glutInitWindowSize(640, 480);
glutInitWindowPosition(0,0);
```

specifies a 480×640 window in the top-left corner of the display. We specify RGB rather than indexed (GLUT_INDEX) color, a depth buffer for hidden-surface removal, and double rather than single (GLUT_SINGLE) buffering. The defaults, which are all we need for now, are RGB color, no hidden-surface removal, and single buffering. Thus, we do not need to request these options explicitly, but specifying them makes the code clearer. Note that parameters are logically OR'ed together in the argument to glutInitDisplayMode.

2.7.2 Aspect Ratio and Viewports

The **aspect ratio** of a rectangle is the ratio of the rectangle's width to its height. The independence of the object, viewing, and workstation window specifications can cause undesirable side effects if the aspect ratio of the viewing rectangle, specified by glOrtho, is not the same as the aspect ratio of the window specified by glutInitWindowSize. If they differ, as depicted in Figure 2.33, objects are distorted on the screen. This distortion is a consequence of our default mode of operation, in which the entire clipping rectangle is mapped to the display window. The only way that we can map the entire contents of the clipping rectangle to the entire display window is to distort the contents of the former to fit inside the latter. We can avoid this distortion if we ensure that the clipping rectangle and display window have the same aspect ratio.

Another, more flexible method is to use the concept of a viewport. A **viewport** is a rectangular area of the display window. By default, it is the entire window, but it can be set to any smaller size in pixels via the function

```
void glViewport(GLint x, GLint y, GLsizei w, GLsizei h)
```

where (x,y) is the lower-left corner of the viewport (measured relative to the lower-left corner of the window), and w and h give the height and width, respectively. The types are all integers that allow us to specify positions and distances in pixels. Primitives are displayed in the viewport, as shown in Figure 2.34. For a given window, we can adjust the height and width of the viewport to match the aspect ratio of the clipping rectangle, thus preventing any object distortion in the image.

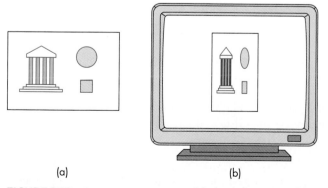

(a)   (b)

FIGURE 2.33 Aspect-ratio mismatch. (a) Viewing rectangle. (b) Display window.

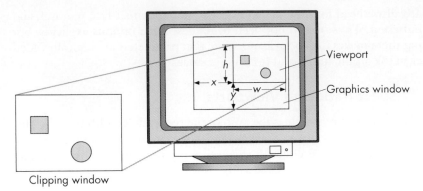

Clipping window

FIGURE 2.34   A mapping to the viewport.

The viewport is part of the state. If we change the viewport between rendering objects or rerendering the same objects with the viewport changed, we achieve the effect of multiple viewports with different images in different parts of the window. We see further uses of the viewport in Chapter 3, where we consider interactive changes in the size and shape of the window.

2.7.3   The main, display, and myinit Functions

In principle, we should be able to combine the simple initialization code with our code from Section 2.1 to form a complete OpenGL program that generates the Sierpinski gasket. Unfortunately, life in a modern system is not that simple. There are two problems: One is generic to all graphics systems; the second has more to do with problems of interacting with the underlying windowing system.

In immediate-mode graphics, a primitive is rendered into the frame buffer as soon as it is specified; the system uses the present state to determine the primitive's appearance. Subsequently, the program goes on to the next statement. In an interactive program, we would continue to generate more primitives. However, for an application such as our sample program, we draw a few primitives and are finished. As the application ends, the application window may disappear from the display before we have even had a chance to see our output. A simple solution for our simple program might be to insert a delay, for example, via a standard function such as sleep(enough_time). For any but the most trivial applications, however, we need a more sophisticated mechanism. In Chapter 3, we discuss event processing, which will give us greater interactive control in our programs. For now, we can use the GLUT function

```
void glutMainLoop();
```

whose execution will cause the program to begin an event-processing loop. If there are no events to process, the program will sit in a wait state, with our graphics on the screen, until we terminate the program through some external means—say, by hitting a special key or a combination of keys, such as control-c—that terminates the execution of the program.

Graphics are sent to the screen through a function called the **display callback**. This function is named through the GLUT function

```
void glutDisplayFunc(void (*func)(void))
```

and **registered** with the window system. Here the function named func will be called whenever the windowing system determines that the OpenGL window needs to be redisplayed. One of these times is when the window is first opened; thus, if we put all our graphics into this function (for our noninteractive example), func will be executed once and our gasket will be drawn. Although it may appear that our use of the display function is merely a convenience for organizing our program, the display function is required by GLUT. A display callback also occurs, for example, when the window is moved from one location on the screen to another and when a window in front of the OpenGL window is destroyed, making visible the whole OpenGL window.

Following is a main program that works for most noninteractive applications:

```
#include <GL/glut.h>

void main(int argc, char **argv)
{

    glutInit(&argc,argv);
    glutInitDisplayMode (GLUT_SINGLE | GLUT_RGB);
    glutInitWindowSize(500,500);
    glutInitWindowPosition(0,0);
    glutCreateWindow("simple  OpenGL example");
    glutDisplayFunc(display);
    myinit();
    glutMainLoop();
}
```

We use an initialization function myinit()[6] to set the OpenGL state variables dealing with viewing and attributes—parameters that we prefer to set once, independently of the display function. The standard "include" (.h) file for GLUT is loaded before the beginning of the function definitions. In most implementations, the compiler directive

```
#include <GL/glut.h>
```

---

6. We hope to avoid confusion by using the same function names as those in the *OpenGL Programming Guide* [Ope04a] and in the GLUT documentation [Kil94a].

will add in the header files for the GLUT library, the OpenGL library (gl.h), and the OpenGL utility library (glu.h). The macro definitions for our standard values, such as GL_LINES and GL_RGB, are in these files.

2.7.4 Program Structure

Every program we write will have the same structure as our gasket program. We shall always use the GLUT toolkit. The main function will then consist of calls to GLUT functions to set up our window(s) and to make sure that the local environment supports the required display properties. The main will also name the required callbacks and callback functions. Every program must have a display callback, and most will have other callbacks to set up interaction. The myinit function will set up user options, usually through OpenGL functions on the GL and GLU libraries. Although these options could be set in main, it is clearer to keep GLUT functions separate from OpenGL functions. In the majority of programs, the graphics output will be generated in the display callback.

2.8 The Gasket Program

Using our main function, we can now write the myinit and display functions and thus complete the program that will generate the Sierpinski gasket. We draw red points on a white background. We also set up a two-dimensional coordinate system so that our points are defined within a 50.0×50.0 square with the origin in the lower-left corner. In this version, we use two-dimensional representations of points.

Here are the two functions:

```
void myinit()
{
/* attributes */

    glClearColor(1.0, 1.0, 1.0, 1.0); /* white background */
    glColor3f(1.0, 0.0, 0.0); /* draw in red */

/* set up viewing */

    glMatrixMode(GL_PROJECTION);
    glLoadIdentity();
    gluOrtho2D(0.0, 50.0, 0.0, 50.0);
    glMatrixMode(GL_MODELVIEW);
}
```

```
void display()
{
   GLfloat vertices[3][2]={{0.0,0.0},{25.0,50.0},{50.0,0.0}};
      /* triangle */
   int i, j, k;
   int rand(); /* standard random-number generator */
   GLfloat p[2] ={7.5 , 5.0}; /* arbitrary point
                                  inside triangle */

   glClear(GL_COLOR_BUFFER_BIT);  /* clear the window */

 /* compute and output 5000 new points */

   glBegin(GL_POINTS);

   for( k=0; k<5000; k++)
   {
       j=rand()%3; /* pick a vertex at random */

 /* compute point halfway between vertex and old point */

       p[0] = (p[0]+vertices[j][0])/2.0;
       p[1] = (p[1]+vertices[j][1])/2.0;

 /* plot point */

       glVertex2fv(p);
   }
   glEnd();
   glFlush();
}
```

Our display function has an arbitrary three vertices defined in it, and an arbitrary initial point is defined within the triangle that they define. Note that we picked the values in glOrtho so that the clipping window barely contains the triangle and there is no relationship between the size of the window on the display and the size of the clipping window; although by making both these windows square, there is no shape distortion of the gasket. A call to the OpenGL function glFlush has been included; it forces the system to plot the points on the display as soon as possible. A complete listing of this program, and of the other example programs that we generate in subsequent chapters, is given in Appendix A.

2.9 Polygons and Recursion

The output from our gasket program (Figure 2.2) shows considerable structure. If we were to run the program with more iterations, then much of the

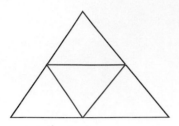

FIGURE 2.35   Bisecting the sides of a triangle.

randomness in the image would disappear. Examining this structure, we see that regardless of how many points we generate, there are no points in the middle. If we draw line segments connecting the midpoints of the sides of the original triangle, then we divide the original triangle into four triangles, the middle one containing no points (Figure 2.35).

Looking at the other three triangles, we see that we can apply the same observation to each of them; that is, we can subdivide each of these triangles into four triangles by connecting the midpoints of the sides, and each middle triangle will contain no points.

This structure suggests a second method for generating the Sierpinski gasket— one that uses polygons instead of points and does not require the use of a random-number generator. One advantage of using polygons is that we can fill solid areas on our display. Our strategy is to start with a single triangle, to subdivide it into four smaller triangles by bisecting the sides, and then to remove the middle triangle from further consideration. We repeat this procedure on the remaining triangles until the size of the triangles that we are removing is small enough—about the size of one pixel—that we can draw the remaining triangles.

We can implement the process that we just described through a recursive program. We start its development with a simple function that draws a single triangular polygon given three arbitrary vertices:

```
void triangle(GLfloat *a, GLfloat *b, GLfloat *c)


{
     glVertex2fv(a);
     glVertex2fv(b);
     glVertex2fv(c);
}
```

Suppose that the vertices of our original triangle are given by the array

```
GLfloat v[3][2];
```

Then the midpoints of the sides are given by the array m[3][3], which can be computed using the code

```
for(j=0; j<2; j++) m[0][j]=(v[0][j]+v[1][j])/2.0;
for(j=0; j<2; j++) m[1][j]=(v[0][j]+v[2][j])/2.0;
for(j=0; j<2; j++) m[2][j]=(v[1][j]+v[2][j])/2.0;
```

With these six locations, we can use triangle to draw the three triangles formed by (v[0], m[0], m[1]); (v[2], m[1], m[2]); and (v[1], m[2], m[0]). We do not simply want to draw these triangles; we want to subdivide them. Hence, we make the process recursive. We define a recursive function

```
divide_triangle(float *a, float *b, float *c, int k)
```

that will draw the triangles only if k is zero. Otherwise, it will subdivide the triangle specified by a, b, and c and decrease k. Here is the code:

```
void divide_triangle(GLfloat *a, GLfloat *b, GLfloat *c, int k)
{
    GLfloat ab[2], ac[2], bc[2];
    int j;
    if(k>0)
    {
 /* compute midpoints of sides */

        for(j=0; j<2; j++) ab[j]=(a[j]+b[j])/2;
        for(j=0; j<2; j++) ac[j]=(a[j]+c[j])/2;
        for(j=0; j<2; j++) bc[j]=(b[j]+c[j])/2;

 /* subdivide all but inner triangle */

        divide_triangle(a, ab, ac, k-1);
        divide_triangle(c, ac, bc, k-1);
        divide_triangle(b, bc, ab, k-1);
    }
    else triangle(a,b,c); /* draw triangle at
                          end of recursion */
}
```

The display function is now almost trivial. It uses a global[7] value of n determined by the main program to fix the number of subdivision steps we would like, and it calls divide_triangle once.

```
void display()
{
    glClear(GL_COLOR_BUFFER_BIT);
    glBegin(GL_TRIANGLES);
        divide_triangle(v[0], v[1], v[2], n);
    glEnd();
    glFlush();
}
```

Note that we have put a single glBegin() and glEnd() in the display callback rather that the perhaps more intuitive placement of glBegin() and glEnd() in the triangle function. We can do this only because we are using the GL_TRIANGLES

---

7. Note that often we have no convenient way to pass variables to GLUT callbacks other than through global parameters. Although we prefer not to pass values in such a manner, because the form of these functions is fixed, we have no good alternative.

FIGURE 2.36   Triangles after five subdivisions.

type, which generates a new triangle primitive after each three vertices, rather than the GL_POLYGON type. This placement makes the program far more efficient.

The rest of the program is the same as our previous gasket program except that we read in the value of n. Output for five subdivision steps is shown in Figure 2.36. The complete program is given in Appendix A.

2.10   The Three-Dimensional Gasket

We have argued that two-dimensional graphics is a special case of three-dimensional graphics, but we have not yet seen a complete three-dimensional program. Next, we convert our two-dimensional Sierpinski gasket program to a program that will generate a three-dimensional gasket, that is, one that is not restricted to a plane. We can follow either of the two approaches that we used for the two-dimensional gasket. Both extensions start in a similar manner, replacing the initial triangle with a tetrahedron (Figure 2.37).

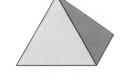

FIGURE 2.37   Tetrahedron.

2.10.1   Use of Three-Dimensional Points

Because every tetrahedron is convex, the midpoint of a line segment between a vertex and any point inside a tetrahedron is also inside the tetrahedron. Hence, we can follow the same procedure as before, but this time, instead of the three vertices required to define a triangle, we need four initial vertices to define the tetrahedron. Note that as long as no three vertices are collinear, we can choose the four vertices of the tetrahedron at random without affecting the character of the result.

The required changes are primarily in the function display. We define and initialize an array to hold the vertices

```
                    /* vertices of an arbitrary tetrahedron */
GLfloat vertices[4][3]={{0.0,0.0,0.0},{25.0,50.0,10.0},
                    {50.0,25.0,25.0},{25.0,10.0,25.0}};

                /* arbitrary initial location inside triangle */
GLfloat p[3] ={25.0,10.0,25.0};
```

We now use the function glVertex3fv to define points. One problem with the three-dimensional gasket that we did not have with the two-dimensional gasket occurs because points are not restricted to a single plane; thus, it may be difficult to envision the three-dimensional structure from the two-dimensional image displayed. To get around this problem, we have added a color function that makes the color of each point depend on that point's location, so we can understand the resulting image more easily. Here is the display function:

```
void display()
{
/* computes and plots a single new location */

  int rand();
  int i;
  j=rand()%4; /* pick a vertex at random */

/* compute point halfway between vertex and old location */

  p[0] = (p[0]+vertices[j][0])/2.0;
  p[1] = (p[1]+vertices[j][1])/2.0;
  p[2] = (p[2]+vertices[j][2])/2.0;

/* plot point */

  glBegin(GL_POINTS);
   glColor3f(p[0]/250.0,p[1]/250.0,p[2]/250.0);
   glVertex3fv( p );
  glEnd();

  glFlush();

}
```

We are now working in three dimensions, so we define a three-dimensional clipping volume (in main.c) by

```
glOrtho(-50.0 , 50.0, -50.0, 50.0 ,-50.0, 50.0);
```

Figure 2.38 and Front Plate 1 show that if we generate enough points, the resulting figure will look like the initial tetrahedron with increasingly smaller tetrahedrons removed.

FIGURE 2.38   Three-dimensional Sierpinski gasket.

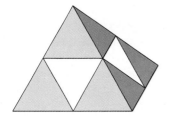

FIGURE 2.39   Subdivided tetrahedron.

2.10.2   Use of Polygons in Three Dimensions

There is a more interesting approach that uses both polygons and subdivision of a tetrahedron into smaller tetrahedrons. Suppose that we start with a tetrahedron and find the midpoints of its six edges and connect these midpoints as in Figure 2.39. There are now four smaller tetrahedrons, one for each of the original vertices, and another area in the middle that we will discard.

Following our second approach to a single triangle, we will use recursive subdivision to subdivide the four tetrahedrons that we keep. Because the faces of a tetrahedron are the four triangles determined by its four vertices, at the end of the subdivisions, we can render each of the final tetrahedrons by drawing four triangles.

Most of our code is almost the same as in two dimensions. Our triangle routine now uses points in three dimensions rather than in two dimensions:

```
void triangle(GLfloat *a, GLfloat *b, GLfloat *c)
{
      glVertex3fv(a);
      glVertex3fv(b);
      glVertex3fv(c);
}
```

We draw each tetrahedron, coloring each face with a different color by using the following function:

```
void tetra(GLfloat *a, GLfloat *b, GLfloat *c, GLfloat *d)
{
        glColor3fv(colors[0]);
        triangle(a, b, c);
        glColor3fv(colors[1]);
        triangle(a, c, d);
        glColor3fv(colors[2]);
        triangle(a, d, b);
        glColor3fv(colors[3]);
        triangle(b, d, c);
}
```

We subdivide a tetrahedron in a manner similar to subdividing a triangle.
Our code for divide_triangle does the same:

```
void divide_tetra(GLfloat *a, GLfloat *b, GLfloat *c, GLfloat *d, int m)
{

    GLfloat mid[6][3];
    int j;
    if(m>0)
    {
        /* compute six midpoints */

        for(j=0; j<3; j++) mid[0][j]=(a[j]+b[j])/2;
        for(j=0; j<3; j++) mid[1][j]=(a[j]+c[j])/2;
        for(j=0; j<3; j++) mid[2][j]=(a[j]+d[j])/2;
        for(j=0; j<3; j++) mid[3][j]=(b[j]+c[j])/2;
        for(j=0; j<3; j++) mid[4][j]=(c[j]+d[j])/2;
        for(j=0; j<3; j++) mid[5][j]=(b[j]+d[j])/2;

        /* create 4 tetrahedrons by subdivision */

        divide_tetra(a, mid[0], mid[1], mid[2], m-1);
        divide_tetra(mid[0], b, mid[3], mid[5], m-1);
        divide_tetra(mid[1], mid[3], c, mid[4], m-1);
        divide_tetra(mid[2], mid[4], d, mid[5], m-1);

    }
    else(tetra(a,b,c,d)); /* draw tetrahedron at end of recursion */
}
```

We can now start with four vertices and do n subdivisions with the display callback

```
{
    glClear(GL_COLOR_BUFFER_BIT);
    glBegin(GL_TRIANGLES);
```

```
            divide_tetra(v[0], v[1], v[2], v[3], n);
        glEnd();
        glFlush();
    }
```

There is just one more problem that we must address before we have a useful three-dimensional program.

2.10.3 Hidden-Surface Removal

If you execute the code in the previous section, you might be confused by the results. The program draws triangles in the order that they are specified in the program. This order is determined by the recursion in our program and not by the geometric relationships among the triangles. Each triangle is drawn (filled) in a solid color and is drawn over those triangles that have already been rendered to the display.

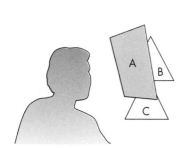

FIGURE 2.40 The hidden-surface problem.

Contrast this order to the way that we would see the triangles if we were to construct the three-dimensional Sierpinski gasket out of small solid tetrahedra. We would see only those faces of tetrahedra that were in front of all other faces as seen by a viewer. Figure 2.40 shows a simplified version of this **hidden-surface** problem. From the viewer's position, she sees quadrilateral A clearly, but triangle B is blocked from her view, and triangle C is only partially visible. Without going into the details of any specific algorithm, you should be able to convince yourself that given the position of the viewer and the triangles, we should be able to draw the triangles such that the correct image is obtained. Algorithms for ordering objects so that they are drawn correctly are called **visible-surface algorithms** or **hidden-surface–removal algorithms**, depending on how we look at the problem. We discuss such algorithms in detail in Chapters 4 and 7.

For now, we can simply use a particular hidden-surface–removal algorithm, called the **z-buffer** algorithm, that is supported by OpenGL. This algorithm can be turned on (enabled) and off (disabled) easily. In our main program, we must request the auxiliary storage, a z (or depth) buffer, by modifying the initialization of the display mode to the following:

```
glutInitDisplayMode(GLUT_SINGLE | GLUT_RGB | GLUT_DEPTH);
```

Note that the z buffer is one of the buffers that make up the frame buffer. We enable the algorithm by the function call

```
glEnable(GL_DEPTH_TEST)
```

either in main.c or in an initialization function such as myinit.c. Because the algorithm stores information in the depth buffer, we must clear this buffer whenever we wish to redraw the display; thus, we modify the clear procedure in the display function:

```
glClear(GL_COLOR_BUFFER_BIT | GL_DEPTH_BUFFER_BIT);
```

FIGURE 2.41   Three-dimensional gasket after five recursion steps.

The display callback is

```
void display()
{
  glClear(GL_COLOR_BUFFER_BIT | GL_DEPTH_BUFFER_BIT);
  glBeginGL_TRIANGLES;
      divide_tetra(v[0], v[1], v[2], v[3], n);
  glEnd();
  glFlush();
}
```

The results are shown in Figure 2.41 and Front Plate 2 for a recursion of four steps. The complete program is given in Appendix A.

2.11 Plotting Implicit Functions[8]

Before we move on to interactive graphics, let's consider a nontrivial example that illustrates both data visualization and that two-dimensional graphics applications can be far from trivial. The problem with which we are concerned here is how to display data defined by an **implicit function** of the form

$$g(x, y) = 0,$$

8. This section may be skipped on a first reading.

where the function g is known analytically, such as the equation for a unit circle centered at the origin:

$$g(x, y) = x^2 + y^2 - 1 = 0.$$

Display of **explicit functions** of the form

$$y = h(x)$$

is fairly straightforward because we can evaluate y for a set of values of x and then write a simple program to display these (x, y) pairs connected by line segments. However, for implicit functions, we can neither solve for a value of y corresponding to a given x, nor can we say in general whether such a value exists. For example, depending on the values of a and b, the implicit equation

$$g(x, y) = (x^2 + y^2 + a^2)^2 - 4a^2x^2 - b^4$$

may generate no, one, or two closed curves, known as the Ovals of Cassini.

A more general version of the problem is the display of the function

$$z = f(x, y),$$

where f is the height of a surface for a given position on, say, the surface of the earth. Often we want **contour curves** that correspond to a set of fixed values of z. Thus, for a value z equal to c, we have to solve the implicit equation

$$g(x, y) = f(x, y) - c = 0.$$

Such curves should be familiar as the topographic maps used by hikers and geologists.

Returning to the original problem, rather than trying to solve an implicit equation, we start by computing values (samples) of g. Some of the samples will be greater than zero, while others will be less than zero. Our problem will be to find an approximation of the desired function from this set of samples. We solve the problem for sampled data by a technique called **marching squares**. We shall develop the method for the slightly more general contour mapping problem.

2.11.1 Marching Squares

Suppose that we sample the function $f(x, y)$ at evenly spaced points on a rectangular array (or lattice or grid) in x and y, thus creating a set of samples $\{f_{ij} = f(x_i, y_j)\}$ for

$$x_i = x_0 + i\Delta x, \quad i = 0, 1, \ldots, N - 1,$$
$$y_j = y_0 + j\Delta y, \quad j = 0, 1, \ldots, M - 1,$$

where Δx and Δy are the spacing between samples in the x and y directions, respectively. Other than for simplifying the development, the equal spacing is not necessary. Equivalently, we might have obtained a set of $N \times M$ samples by making measurements of some physical quantity on a regular grid, or the samples might have come directly from a device such as a laser range finder or a satellite.

Suppose that we would like to find an approximation to the implicit curve

$$z = f(x, y)$$

for a particular value of z that we denote by c, our contour value. For a given value of c, there may be no contour curve, a single contour curve, or multiple contour curves. If we are working with sampled data, then we can only approximate a contour curve. Our strategy for constructing an approximate contour curve is to construct a curve of connected line segments—a **piecewise linear curve**. We start with the rectangular **cell** determined by the four grid points (x_i, y_j), (x_{i+1}, y_j), (x_{i+1}, y_{j+1}), (x_i, y_{j+1}), as shown in Figure 2.42. Our algorithm finds the line segments on a cell-by-cell basis, using only the values of z at the corners of a cell to determine whether the desired contour passes through the cell.

In general, the sampled values that we have at the corners of the cell are not equal to the contour value. However, the contour curve might still pass through the cell. Consider the simple case where only one of the values at the corners— say, f_{ij}—is greater than c, and the values at the other vertices of the cell are less than c:

$$f_{ij} > c,$$
$$f_{i+1,j} < c,$$
$$f_{i+1,j+1} < c,$$
$$f_{i,j+1} < c.$$

We can show this situation either as in Figure 2.43(a), where we have indicated the values relative to c, or as in Figure 2.43(b), where we have colored black the vertices for which the value is less than c and have colored white the vertex whose value is greater than c. By looking at this situation, we can see that if the function f that generated the data is reasonably well behaved, then the contour curve must cross the two edges that have one white vertex and one black vertex. Equivalently, if the function $f(x, y) - c$ is greater than 0 at one vertex and less than 0 at an adjacent vertex, it must be equal to 0 somewhere in between. This situation is shown in Figure 2.44(a).

Figure 2.44(a) shows only one way that the contour might cross the edge. The contour also might cross three times, as shown in Figure 2.44(b), or any odd number of times. Each of these interpretations is consistent with the sampled data. We shall always use the interpretation that a single crossing of an edge by a contour is more likely for smooth functions than are multiple crossings. This choice is an example of the **principle of Occam's razor**, which states that *if there are multiple possible explanations of a phenomenon that are consistent with the data, choose the simplest one*.

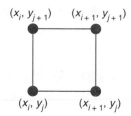

FIGURE 2.42   Rectangular cell.

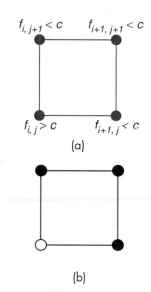

FIGURE 2.43   Labeling the vertices of a cube. (a) Thresholding of the vertices. (b) Coloring of the vertices.

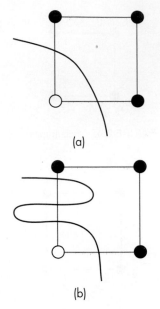

(a)

(b)

FIGURE 2.44 Contour crossing a cell edge. (a) Once. (b) Multiple times.

Returning to our example cell, if we can estimate where the contour intersects the two edges, then we can join the points of intersection with a line segment. We can even draw this line segment immediately because the computation for other cells is independent of what we do with this cell. But where do we place the intersections? There are two simple strategies. We could simply place the intersection halfway between the black and the white vertices. However, if a is only slightly greater than c and b is much less than c, then we expect the intersection of the contour with the edge of a cell to be closer to (x_i, y_j) than to (x_{i+1}, y_j). A more sophisticated strategy uses interpolation. Consider two vertices that share an edge of a cell and have values on opposite sides of c—for example,

$$f(x_i, y_i) = a, \quad a > c,$$
$$f(x_{i+1}, y_j) = b, \quad b < c.$$

If the two vertices are separated by an x spacing Δx, then we can interpolate the point of intersection using a line segment, as shown in Figure 2.45.

This line segment intersects the x-axis at

$$x = x_i + \frac{(a - c)\Delta x}{a - b}.$$

We use this point for one endpoint of our line segment approximation to the contour in this cell, and we do a similar calculation for the intersection on the other edge with a black and a white vertex.

Our discussion thus far has been in terms of a particular cell for which one vertex is colored white and the others are colored black. There are 16 ($= 2^4$) ways that we can color the vertices of a cell using only black and white. All could arise in our contour problem. These cases are shown in Figure 2.46, as is a simple way of drawing line segments consistent with the data. If we study these cases, numbered 0–15 from left to right, we see that there are two types of symmetry. One is rotational. All cases that can be converted to the same cube by rotation, such as cases 1 and 2, have a single line segment cutting off one of the vertices. There is also symmetry between cases that we can convert to each other by switching all black vertices to white vertices and vice versa, such as cases

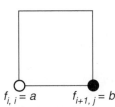

$f_{i,i} = a$ $f_{i+1,j} = b$

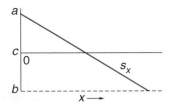

FIGURE 2.45 Interpolation of the intersection of a cell edge.

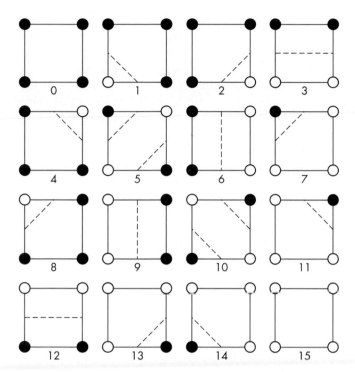

FIGURE 2.46 Sixteen cases of vertex labelings with contours.

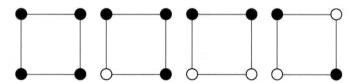

FIGURE 2.47 Four unique cases of vertex labelings.

0 and 15. Once we take symmetry into account, only four cases are truly unique. These cases are shown in Figure 2.47. Hence, we need code that can draw line segments for only four cases, and we can map all other cases into these four.

The first case is trivial because the simplest interpretation is that the contour does not pass through the cell, and we draw no line segments. The second case is the one that we just discussed; it generates one line segment. The third case is also simple: We can draw a single line segment that goes from one edge to the opposite edge.

The final case is more difficult and more interesting because it contains an ambiguity. We have the two equally simple interpretations shown in Figure 2.48;

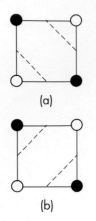

(a)

(b)

FIGURE 2.48 Ambiguous interpretation.

we must decide which one to use. If we have no other information, we have no reason to prefer one over the other, and we can pick one at random. Alternatively, we could always use only one of the possibilities. But as Figure 2.49 shows, we get different results depending on which interpretation we choose. Another possibility is to subdivide the cell into four smaller cells, as shown in Figure 2.50, generating a new data point in the center. We can obtain the value at this point either from the function, if we know it analytically, or by averaging the values at the corners of the original cell. Hopefully, none of these smaller cells is an ambiguous case. If any is ambiguous, we can further subdivide it.

The code for creating a contour plotter is fairly simple. Suppose that the values at the four vertices are a, b, c, and d. We loop over all cells. If a, b, c, and d are the values at the corners of a cell, then the code to compute which cell type we have is

```
int cell(double a, double b, double c , double d)
{
/* THRESHOLD = contour value */
    int n=0;
    if(a>THRESHOLD) n+=1;
    if(b>THRESHOLD) n+=8;
    if(c>THRESHOLD) n+=4;
    if(d>THRESHOLD) n+=2;
    return n;
}
```

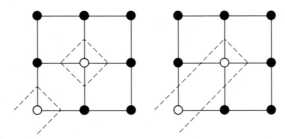

FIGURE 2.49   Example of different contours with the same labeling.

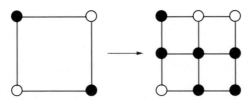

FIGURE 2.50   Subdivision of a cube.

We then can assign the cell to one of the four canonical cases by

```
switch(n)
{
  case 1: case 2: case 4: case 7: case 8:
              case 11: case 13: case 14:
   /* contour cuts off one corner */
   draw_one(num, i,j,a,b,c,d);
   break;
  case 3: case 6: case 9: case 12: /* contour crosses cell */
   draw_adjacent(num,i,j,a,b,c,d);
   break;
  case 5: case 10: /* ambiguous cases */
    draw_opposite(num, i,j,a,b,c,d);
    break;
  case 0: case 15: break; /* no contour in cell */
}
```

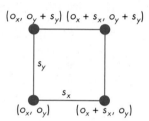

FIGURE 2.51 Drawing the line segment for the adjacent case.

Finally, we write the functions that draw the three cases that have line segments in them. For example, the function draw_one deals with the eight cases that draw a line segment from one edge to an adjacent edge of the cell. If the cell has side lengths of s_x and s_y in the x and y directions, respectively, and the lower-left corner of the cell is at (ox,oy) as shown in Figure 2.51, then the code is in part

```
void draw_one(int num, int i, int j, double a, double b,
                     double c, double d)
{

/* num = cell type */
/* i, j = coordinates of cell in array */
/* a, b, c, d values at four corners of cell */

/* s_x, s_y = side length of cell */
/* compute the lower left-corner of cell here */

  switch(num) /* case type */
  {
   case 1: case 14:
       x1=ox;
       y1=oy+s_y;
       x2=ox+s_x;
       y2=oy;
       break;

/* the other cases go here */

  }
```

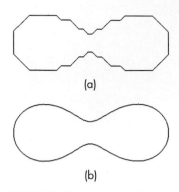

(a)

(b)

FIGURE 2.52 An Oval of Cassini. (a) Using the midpoint. (b) Using interpolation.

```
/* draw the line segment */

    glVertex2d(x1, y1);
    glVertex2d(x2, y2);
}
```

The full code is given in `contour.c`. Figure 2.52 shows two curves corresponding to a single contour value for the Ovals of Cassini function

$$f(x, y) = (x^2 + y^2 + a^2)^2 - 4a^2x^2 - b^4,$$

with $a = 0.49$ and $b = 0.5$. We constructed the curve in part (a) always using the midpoint for the point of intersection of the curve with an edge of a cell. We constructed the curve in part (b) using interpolation to obtain the point of intersection. The function was sampled on a 50×50 grid. Figure 2.53 shows the Hononolu data-set display with multiple contours at equally spaced contour values.

There are other ways to construct contour curves. One is to start with a cell that is known to have a piece of the contour and then follow this contour to adjacent cells as necessary to complete the contour. However, the marching-squares method has the advantage that all cells can be dealt with independently—we march through the data—and the extension to three dimensions for volumetric data is straightforward.

FIGURE 2.53 Contour plot of Honolulu data.

Summary and Notes

In this chapter, we introduced the OpenGL API and applied the basic concepts that we learned in Chapter 1. Although the first application we used to develop our first program was two-dimensional, we took the path of looking at two-dimensional graphics as a special case of three-dimensional graphics. We then were able to extend the example to three dimensions with minimal work.

The Sierpinski gasket provides a nontrivial beginning application. A few extensions and mathematical issues are presented in the exercises at the end of this chapter. The texts in the Suggested Readings section provide many other examples of interesting curves and surfaces that can be generated with simple programs.

The historical development of graphics APIs and graphical models illustrates the importance of starting in three dimensions. The pen-plotter model from Chapter 1 was used for many years and is the basis of many important APIs, such as PostScript. Work to define an international standard for graphics APIs began in the 1970s and culminated with the adoption of GKS by the International Standards Organization (ISO) in 1984. However, GKS had its basis in the pen-plotter model and as a two-dimensional API was of limited utility in the CAD community. Although the standard was extended to three dimensions with GKS-3D, the limitations imposed by the original underlying model led to a standard that was lacking in many aspects. The PHIGS and PHIGS+ APIs, started in the CAD community, are inherently three-dimensional and are based on the synthetic-camera model.

OpenGL is derived from the GL API, which is based on implementing the synthetic-camera model with a pipeline architecture. GL was developed for Silicon Graphics, Inc. (SGI) workstations, which incorporated a pipeline architecture originally implemented with special-purpose VLSI chips. Hence, although PHIGS and GL have much in common, GL was designed specifically for high-speed real-time rendering. OpenGL was a result of application users realizing the advantages of GL programming and wanting to carry these advantages to other platforms. Because it removed input and windowing functions from GL and concentrated on rendering, OpenGL emerged as a new API that was portable while retaining the features that make GL such a powerful API.

Although most application programmers who use OpenGL prefer to program in C, there is a fair amount of interest in higher-level interfaces. Using C++ rather than C requires minimal code changes but does not provide a true object-oriented interface to OpenGL. Among object-oriented programmers, there has been much interest in both OpenGL and higher-level APIs. Although there is no official Java binding to OpenGL, there have been multiple efforts to come up with one. The problem is not simple because application users want to make use of the object orientation of Java and various Java toolkits, together with a non–object-oriented OpenGL specification. There are a few bindings available on the Internet, and Sun Microsystems recently released their Java bindings.

In Chapter 10, we shall introduce scene graphs, which provide a much higher-level, object-oriented interface to graphics hardware. Most scene graph APIs are built on top of OpenGL.

Within the game community, the dominance of Windows makes it possible for game developers to write code for a single platform. DirectX runs only on Windows platforms and is optimized for speed on these systems. Although much DirectX code looks like OpenGL code, the coder can make use of device-dependent features that are available in commodity graphics cards. Consequently, applications written in DirectX do not have the portability and stability of OpenGL applications. Thus, we see DirectX dominating the game world, whereas scientific and engineering applications generally are written in OpenGL. For OpenGL programmers who want to use features specific to certain hardware, OpenGL has an extension mechanism for accessing these features but at the cost of portability. Programming pipelines that are accessible through the OpenGL Shading Language and Cg (Chapter 9) are leading to small performance differences between OpenGL and DirectX for high-end applications.

Our examples and programs have shown how we describe and display geometric objects in a simple manner. In terms of the modeling–rendering paradigm that we presented in Chapter 1, we have focused on the modeling. However, our models are completely unstructured. Representations of objects are lists of vertices and attributes. In Chapter 10, we shall learn to construct hierarchical models that can represent relationships among objects. Nevertheless, at this point, you should be able to write interesting programs. Complete the exercises at the end of the chapter and extend a few of the two-dimensional problems to three dimensions.

The marching-squares method is a special case of the marching-cubes method [Lor87] that was developed for the visualization of volumetric data.

Suggested Readings

The Sierpinski gasket provides a good introduction to the mysteries of fractal geometry; there are good discussions in several texts [Bar93, Hil01, Man82, Pru90].

The pen-plotter API is used by PostScript [Ado85] and LOGO [Pap81]. LOGO provides turtle graphics, an API that is both simple to learn and capable of describing several of the two-dimensional mathematical curves that we use in Chapter 10 (see Exercise 2.4).

GKS [ANSI85], GKS-3D [ISO88], PHIGS [ANSI88], and PHIGS+ [PHI89] are both U.S. and international standards. Their formal descriptions can be obtained from the American National Standards Institute (ANSI) and from ISO. Numerous textbooks use these APIs [Ang90, End84, Fol94, Hea04, Hop83, Hop91].

The X Window System [Sch88] has become the standard on UNIX workstations and has influenced the development of window systems on other platforms. The RenderMan interface is described in [Ups89].

The two standard references for OpenGL are the *OpenGL Programming Guide* [Ope04a] and the *OpenGL Reference Manual* [Ope04b]. There is also a formal specification of OpenGL [Seg92]. Starting with the second edition and continuing through the present fourth edition, the *Programming Guide* uses the GLUT library that was developed by Mark Kilgard [Kil94b]. The *Programming Guide* provides many more code examples using OpenGL. GLUT was developed for use with the X Window System [Kil96], but there are also versions for Windows and the Macintosh. Much of this information and many of the example programs are available over the Internet. Representative sites are listed at the beginning of Appendix A.

OpenGL: A Primer [Ang04], the companion book to this text, contains details of the OpenGL functions used here and more example programs.

The graphics part of the DirectX API was originally known as Direct3D. The present version is Version 9.0 [Gra03].

Exercises

2.1 A slight variation on generating the Sierpinski gasket with triangular polygons yields the *fractal mountains* used in computer-generated animations. After you find the midpoint of each side of the triangle, perturb this location before subdivision. Generate these triangles without fill. Later, you can do this exercise in three dimensions and add shading. After a few subdivisions, you should have generated sufficient detail that your triangles look like a mountain.

2.2 The Sierpinski gasket, as generated in Exercise 2.1, demonstrates many of the geometric complexities that are studied in fractal geometry [Man82]. Suppose that you construct the gasket with mathematical lines that have length but no width. In the limit, what percentage of the area of the original triangle remains after the central triangle has been removed after each subdivision? Consider the perimeters of the triangles remaining after each central triangle is removed. In the limit, what happens to the total perimeter length of all remaining triangles?

2.3 At the lowest level of processing, we manipulate bits in the frame buffer. OpenGL has pixel-oriented commands that allow users to access the frame buffer directly. You can experiment with simple raster algorithms, such as drawing lines or circles, by using the OpenGL function glPoint as the basis of a simple virtual-frame-buffer library. Write a library that will allow you to work in a frame buffer that you create in memory. The core functions should be WritePixel and ReadPixel. Your library should allow

FIGURE 2.54   Generation of the Koch snowflake.

you to set up and display your frame buffer and to run a user program that reads and writes pixels.

2.4   *Turtle graphics* is an alternative positioning system that is based on the concept of a turtle moving around the screen with a pen attached to the bottom of his shell. The turtle's position can be described by a triplet (x, y, θ), giving the location of the center and the orientation of the turtle. A typical API for such a system includes functions such as

```
init(x,y,theta); /* initialize position and orientation
                          of turtle */
forward(distance);
right(angle);
left(angle);
pen(up_down);
```

Implement a turtle-graphics library using OpenGL.

2.5   Use your turtle-graphics library from Exercise 2.4 to generate the Sierpinski gasket and fractal mountains of Exercises 2.1 and 2.2.

2.6   Space-filling curves have interested mathematicians for centuries. In the limit, these curves have infinite length, but they are confined to a finite rectangle and never cross themselves. Many of these curves can be generated iteratively. Consider the "rule" pictured in Figure 2.54 that replaces a single line segment with four shorter segments. Write a program that starts with a triangle and iteratively applies the replacement rule to all the line segments. The object that you generate is called the Koch snowflake. For other examples of space-filling curves, see [Hil01] and [Bar93].

2.7   You can generate a simple maze starting with a rectangular array of cells. Each cell has four sides. You remove sides (except from the perimeter of all the cells) until all the cells are connected. Then you create an entrance and an exit by removing two sides from the perimeter. A simple example is shown in Figure 2.55. Write a program using OpenGL that takes as input the two integers N and M and then draws an $N \times M$ maze.

2.8   Describe how you would adapt the RGB color model in OpenGL to allow you to work with a subtractive color model.

2.9   We saw that a fundamental operation in graphics systems is to map a point (x, y) that lies within a clipping rectangle to a point (x_s, y_s) that

FIGURE 2.55   Maze.

lies in the viewport of a window on the screen. Assume that the two rectangles are defined by OpenGL function calls

```
glViewport(u, v, w, h);
gluOrtho2D(x_min, x_max, y_min, y_max);
```

Find the mathematical equations that map (x, y) into (x_s, y_s).

2.10 Many graphics APIs use relative positioning. In such a system, the API contains functions such as

```
move_rel(x,y);
line_rel(x,y);
```

for drawing lines and polygons. The move_rel function moves an internal position, or cursor, to a new position; the line_rel function moves the cursor and defines a line segment between the old cursor position and the new position. What are the advantages and disadvantages of relative positioning as compared to the absolute positioning used in OpenGL? Describe how you would add relative positioning to OpenGL.

2.11 In practice, testing each point in a polygon to determine whether it is inside or outside the polygon is extremely inefficient. Describe the general strategies that you might pursue to avoid point-by-point testing.

2.12 Devise a test to determine whether a two-dimensional polygon is simple.

2.13 Figure 2.56 shows a set of polygons called a *mesh*; these polygons share some edges and vertices. Find one or more simple data structures that represent the mesh. A good data structure should include information on shared vertices and edges. Using OpenGL, find an efficient method for displaying a mesh represented by your data structure.

2.14 In Section 2.4, we saw that OpenGL defines polygons using lists of vertices. Why might it be better to define polygons by their edges? *Hint:* Consider how you might represent a mesh efficiently.

2.15 In OpenGL, we can associate a color with each vertex. If the endpoints of a line segment have different colors assigned to them, OpenGL will

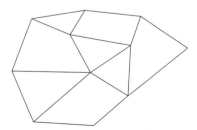

FIGURE 2.56 Polygonal mesh.

interpolate between the colors as it renders the line segment. It will do the same for polygons. Use this property to display the *Maxwell triangle*: an equilateral triangle whose vertices are red, green, and blue. What is the relationship between the Maxwell triangle and the color cube?

2.16 We can simulate many realistic effects using computer graphics by incorporating simple physics in the model. Simulate a bouncing ball in two dimensions incorporating both gravity and elastic collisions with a surface. You can model the ball with a closed polygon that has a sufficient number of sides to look smooth.

2.17 An interesting but difficult extension of Exercise 2.16 is to simulate a game of pool or billiards. You will need to have multiple balls that can interact with the sides of the table and with one another. *Hint:* Start with two balls and consider how to detect possible collisions.

2.18 A certain graphics system with a CRT display is advertised to display any four out of 64 colors. What does this statement tell you about the frame buffer and about the quality of the monitor?

2.19 Devise a test for the convexity of a two-dimensional polygon.

2.20 One problem for beginning users of OpenGL is the number of forms of the basic functions such as glVertex. In a language such as C++, we can use a single name and let the compiler pick the correct version by the type of the arguments. In C++, write a library to sit between OpenGL and a user program that minimizes the number of functions that the application programmer needs.

2.21 Another approach to the three-dimensional gasket is based on subdividing only the faces of an initial tetrahedron. Write a program that takes this approach. How do the results differ from the program that we developed in Section 2.10?

2.22 Each time that we subdivide the tetrahedron and keep only the four smaller tetrahedrons corresponding to the original vertices, we decrease the volume by a factor f. Find f. What is the ratio of the new surface area of the four tetrahedrons to the surface area of the original tetrahedron?

2.23 If we extend the marching-squares argument to surfaces in three dimensions, we get a method called *marching cubes*. We look at the possible ways that a surface can intersect a cube and color the cube's vertices accordingly. How many black and white colorings of the cube are there? How many unique colorings remain when we remove symmetries?

INPUT AND INTERACTION

We now turn to the development of interactive graphics programs. Interactive computer graphics opens up a myriad of applications, ranging from interactive design of buildings, to control of large systems through graphical interfaces, to virtual reality systems, to computer games.

Our discussion has three main parts. First, we introduce the variety of devices available for interaction. We consider input devices from two different perspectives: (1) the way that the physical devices can be described by their real-world properties, and (2) the way that these devices appear to the application program. We then consider client–server networks and client–server graphics. We use these ideas to develop event-driven input for our graphics programs. Finally, we develop a paint program that demonstrates the important features of interactive graphics programming.

3.1 Interaction

One of the most important advances in computer technology was enabling users to interact with computer displays. More than any other event, Ivan Sutherland's Sketchpad project launched the present era of *interactive* computer graphics. The basic paradigm that he introduced is deceptively simple. The user sees an image on the display. She reacts to this image by means of an interactive device, such as a mouse. The image changes in response to her input. She reacts to this change, and so on. Whether we are writing programs using the tools available in a modern window system or using the human–computer interface in an interactive museum exhibit, we are making use of this paradigm.

In the 40 years since Sutherland's work, there have been many advances in both hardware and software, but the viewpoint and ideas that he introduced still dominate interactive computer graphics. These influences range from how we conceptualize the human–computer interface to how we can employ graphical data structures that allow for efficient implementations.

In this chapter, we take an approach slightly different from that in the rest of the book. Although rendering is the prime concern of most modern APIs, including OpenGL, interactivity is an important component of many applications.

OpenGL, however, does not support interaction directly. The major reason for this omission is that the system architects who designed OpenGL wanted to increase its portability by allowing the system to work in a variety of environments. Consequently, window and input functions were left out of the API. Although this decision makes renderers portable, it makes more difficult discussions of interaction that do not include specifics of the window system. In addition, because any application program must have at least a minimal interface to the window environment, we cannot avoid such issues completely if we want to write complete, nontrivial programs. If interaction is omitted from the API, the application programmer is forced to worry about the often arcane details of her particular environment.

We can avoid such potential difficulties by using a simple library, or toolkit, as we did in Chapter 2. The toolkit can provide the minimal functionality that is expected on virtually all systems, such as opening of windows, use of the keyboard and mouse, and creation of pop-up menus through the toolkit's API. We adopt this approach, even though it may not provide all the features of any particular windowing system and may produce code that neither makes use of the full capabilities of the window system nor proves as efficient as code written for a particular environment.

We use the term *window system*, as we did in Chapter 2, to include the total environment provided by systems such as the X Window System, Microsoft Windows, and the Macintosh Operating System. Graphics programs that we develop will render into a window within one of these environments. The terminology used in the window system literature may obscure the distinction between, for example, an X window and the OpenGL window into which our graphics are rendered. However, you will usually be safe if you regard the OpenGL window as a particular type of window on your system that can display output from OpenGL programs. Our use of the GLUT toolkit will enable us to avoid the complexities inherent in the interactions among the window system, the window manager, and the graphics system. Just as it did in Chapter 2, GLUT will allow our sample programs to be independent of any particular window system.

We start by describing several interactive devices and the variety of ways that we can interact with them. We then put these devices in the setting of a client–server network and introduce an API for minimal interaction. Finally, we shall generate sample programs.

3.2   Input Devices

We can think about input devices in two distinct ways. The obvious one is to look at them as physical devices, such as a keyboard or a mouse, and to discuss how they work. Certainly, we need to know something about the physical properties of our input devices, so such a discussion is necessary if we are to obtain a full understanding of input. However, from the perspective of an application programmer, we should not need to know the details of a particular physical device to write an application program. Rather, we prefer to treat input devices as *logical* devices whose properties are specified in terms of what they do from the perspective of the application program. A **logical device** is characterized by its high-level interface with the user program rather than by its physical characteristics. Logical devices are familiar to all writers of high-level programs. For example, data input and output in C are done through functions such as `printf`, `scanf`, `getchar`, and `putchar`, whose arguments use the standard C data types, and through input (`cin`) and output (`cout`) streams in C++. When we output a string using `printf`, the physical device on which the output appears could be a printer, a terminal, or a disk file. This output could even be the input to another program. The details of the format required by the destination device are of minor concern to the writer of the application program.

In computer graphics, the use of logical devices is slightly more complex because the forms that input can take are more varied than the strings of bits or characters to which we are usually restricted in nongraphical applications. For example, we can use the mouse—a physical device—either to select a location on the screen of our CRT or to indicate which item in a menu we wish to select. In the first case, an x, y pair (in some coordinate system) is returned to the user program; in the second, the application program may receive an integer as the identifier of an entry in the menu. The separation of physical from logical devices allows us to use the same physical devices in multiple markedly different logical ways. It also allows the same program to work, without modification, if the mouse is replaced by another physical device, such as a data tablet or trackball.

3.2.1 Physical Input Devices

From the physical perspective, each input device has properties that make it more suitable for certain tasks than for others. We take the view used in most of the workstation literature that there are two primary types of physical devices: pointing devices and keyboard devices. The **pointing device** allows the user to indicate a position on the screen and almost always incorporates one or more buttons to allow the user to send signals or interrupts to the computer. The **keyboard device** is almost always a physical keyboard but can be generalized to include any device that returns character codes. We use the American Standard Code for Information Interchange (ASCII) in our examples. ASCII assigns a single unsigned byte to each character. Nothing we do restricts us to this particular choice, other than that ASCII is the prevailing code used. Note, however, that other codes, especially those used for Internet applications, use multiple bytes for each character, thus allowing for a much richer set of supported characters.

The mouse (Figure 3.1) and trackball (Figure 3.2) are similar in use and often in construction as well. A typical mechanical mouse when turned over looks like a trackball. In both devices, the motion of the ball is converted to signals sent

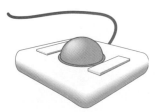

FIGURE 3.1   Mouse.

FIGURE 3.2   Trackball.

back to the computer by pairs of encoders inside the device that are turned by the motion of the ball. The encoders measure motion in two orthogonal directions.

There are many variants of these devices. Some use optical detectors rather than mechanical detectors to measure motion. Small trackballs are popular with portable computers because they can be incorporated directly into the keyboard. There are also various pressure-sensitive devices used in keyboards that perform similar functions to the mouse and trackball but that do not move; their encoders measure the pressure exerted on a small knob that often is located between two keys in the middle of the keyboard.

We can view the output of the mouse or trackball as two independent values provided by the device. These values can be considered as positions and converted—either within the graphics system or by the user program—to a two-dimensional location in either screen or world coordinates. If it is configured in this manner, we can use the device to position a marker (cursor) automatically on the display; however, we rarely use these devices in this direct manner.

It is not necessary that the output of the mouse or trackball encoders be interpreted as a position. Instead, either the device driver or a user program can interpret the information from the encoder as two independent velocities (see Exercise 3.4). The computer can then integrate these values to obtain a two-dimensional position. Thus, as a mouse moves across a surface, the integrals of the velocities yield x, y values that can be converted to indicate the position for a cursor on the screen, as shown in Figure 3.3. By interpreting the distance traveled by the ball as a velocity, we can use the device as a variable-sensitivity input device. Small deviations from rest cause slow or small changes; large deviations cause rapid large changes. With either device, if the ball does not rotate, then there is no change in the integrals and a cursor tracking the position of the mouse will not move. In this mode, these devices are **relative-positioning** devices because changes in the position of the ball yield a position in the user program; the absolute location of the ball (or the mouse) is not used by the application program.

Relative positioning, as provided by a mouse or trackball, is not always desirable. In particular, these devices are not suitable for an operation such as tracing a diagram. If, while the user is attempting to follow a curve on the screen with a mouse, she lifts and moves the mouse, the absolute position on the curve

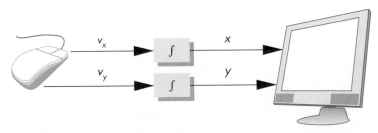

FIGURE 3.3   Cursor positioning.

being traced is lost. **Data tablets** provide absolute positioning. A typical data tablet (Figure 3.4) has rows and columns of wires embedded under its surface. The position of the stylus is determined through electromagnetic interactions between signals traveling through the wires and sensors in the stylus. Touch-sensitive transparent screens that can be placed over the face of a CRT have many of the same properties as the data tablet. Small, rectangular, pressure-sensitive touchpads are embedded in the keyboards of many portable computers. These touchpads can be configured as either relative- or absolute-positioning devices.

FIGURE 3.4   Data tablet.

The **lightpen** has a long history in computer graphics. It was the device used in Sutherland's original Sketchpad. The lightpen contains a light-sensing device, such as a photocell (Figure 3.5). If the lightpen is positioned on the face of the CRT at a location opposite where the electron beam strikes the phosphor, the light emitted exceeds a threshold in the photodetector and a signal is sent to the computer. Because each redisplay of the frame buffer starts at a precise time, we can use the time at which this signal occurs to determine a position on the CRT screen (see Exercise 3.19). Hence, we have a direct-positioning device. The lightpen is not as popular as the mouse, data tablet, and trackball. One of its major deficiencies is that it has difficulty obtaining a position that corresponds to a dark area of the screen.

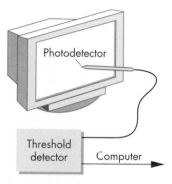

FIGURE 3.5   Lightpen.

One other device, the **joystick** (Figure 3.6), is particularly worthy of mention. The motion of the stick in two orthogonal directions is encoded, interpreted as two velocities, and integrated to identify a screen location. The integration implies that if the stick is left in its resting position, there is no change in the cursor position and that the farther the stick is moved from its resting position, the faster the screen location changes. Thus, the joystick is a variable-sensitivity device. The other advantage of the joystick is that the device can be constructed with mechanical elements, such as springs and dampers, that give resistance to a user who is pushing the stick. Such a mechanical feel, which is not possible with the other devices, makes the joystick well suited for applications such as flight simulators and games.

FIGURE 3.6   Joystick.

For three-dimensional graphics, we might prefer to use three-dimensional input devices. Although various such devices are available, none have yet won the widespread acceptance of the popular two-dimensional input devices. A **space-ball** looks like a joystick with a ball on the end of the stick (Figure 3.7); however, the stick does not move. Rather, pressure sensors in the ball measure the forces applied by the user. The spaceball can measure not only the three direct forces (up–down, front–back, left–right) but also three independent twists. The device measures six independent values and thus has six **degrees of freedom**. Such an input device could be used, for example, both to position and to orient a camera.

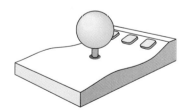

FIGURE 3.7   Spaceball.

Other three-dimensional devices, such as laser-based structured-lighting systems and laser-ranging systems, measure three-dimensional positions. Numerous tracking systems used in virtual reality applications sense the position of the user. Virtual reality and robotics applications often need more degrees of freedom than the two to six provided by the devices that we have described. Devices such as data gloves can sense motion of various parts of the human body, thus providing many additional input signals.

3.2.2 Logical Devices

We can now return to looking at input from inside the application program—that is, from the logical point of view. Two major characteristics describe the logical behavior of an input device: (1) the measurements that the device returns to the user program, and (2) the time when the device returns those measurements.

Some earlier APIs defined six classes of logical input devices. Because input in a modern window system cannot always be disassociated completely from the properties of the physical devices, OpenGL does not take this approach. Nevertheless, we describe the six classes briefly because they illustrate the variety of input forms available to a developer of graphical applications. We shall see how OpenGL can provide the functionality of each of these classes.

1. **String**   A string device is a logical device that provides ASCII strings to the user program. Usually, this logical device is implemented by means of a physical keyboard. In this case, the terminology is consistent with that used in most window systems and OpenGL, which do not distinguish between the logical string device and the keyboard.

2. **Locator**   A locator device provides a position in world coordinates to the user program. It is usually implemented by means of a pointing device, such as a mouse or a trackball. In OpenGL, we usually use the pointing device in this manner, although we have to do the conversion from screen coordinates to world coordinates within our own programs.

3. **Pick**   A pick device returns the identifier of an object on the display to the user program. It is usually implemented with the same physical device as a locator but has a separate software interface to the user program. In OpenGL, we can use a process called *selection* to accomplish picking.

4. **Choice**   Choice devices allow the user to select one of a discrete number of options. In OpenGL, we can use various widgets provided by the window system. A **widget** is a graphical interactive device, provided by either the window system or a toolkit. Typical widgets include menus, scrollbars, and graphical buttons. Most widgets are implemented as special types of windows. For example, a menu with n selections acts as a choice device, allowing us to select one of n alternatives.

5. **Valuators**   Valuators provide analog input to the user program. On some graphics systems, there are boxes or dials to provide valuator input. Here again, widgets within various toolkits usually provide this facility through graphical devices, such as slidebars.

6. **Stroke**   A stroke device returns an array of locations. Although we can think of a stroke device as similar to multiple uses of a locator, it is often implemented such that an action, say, pushing down a mouse button, starts the transfer of data into the specified array, and a second action, such as releasing the button, ends this transfer.

3.2.3 Input Modes

The manner by which physical and logical input devices provide input to an application program can be described in terms of two entities: a measure process and a device trigger. The **measure** of a device is what the device returns to the user program. The **trigger** of a device is a physical input on the device with which the user can signal the computer. For example, the measure of a keyboard contains a string, and the trigger can be the Return or Enter key. For a locator, the measure includes the position, and the associated trigger can be a button on the pointing device.

We can obtain the measure of a device in three distinct modes. Each mode is defined by the relationship between the measure process and the trigger. Once the measure process is started, the measure is taken and placed in a buffer, even though the contents of the buffer may not yet be available to the program. For example, the position of a mouse is tracked continuously by the underlying window system, regardless of whether the application program needs mouse input.

In **request mode**, the measure of the device is not returned to the program until the device is triggered. This input mode is standard in nongraphical applications. For example, if a typical C program requires character input, we use a function such as scanf. When the program needs the input, it halts when it encounters the scanf statement and waits while we type characters at our terminal. We can backspace to correct our typing, and we can take as long as we like. The data are placed in a keyboard buffer whose contents are returned to our program only after a particular key, such as the Enter key (the trigger), is depressed. For a logical device, such as a locator, we can move our pointing device to the desired location and then trigger the device with its button; the trigger will cause the location to be returned to the application program. The relationship between measure and trigger for request mode is shown in Figure 3.8.

Sample-mode input is immediate. As soon as the function call in the user program is encountered, the measure is returned. Hence, no trigger is needed (Figure 3.9). In sample mode, the user must have positioned the pointing device

FIGURE 3.8   Request mode.

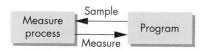

FIGURE 3.9   Sample mode.

or entered data using the keyboard before the function call, because the measure is extracted immediately from the buffer.

One characteristic of both request- and sample-mode input in APIs that support them is that the user must identify which device is to provide the input. Consequently, we ignore any other information that becomes available from any input device other than the one specified. Both request and sample modes are useful for situations where the program guides the user but are not useful in applications where the user controls the flow of the program. For example, a flight simulator or computer game might have multiple input devices—such as a joystick, dials, buttons, and switches—most of which can be used at any time. Writing programs to control the simulator with only sample- and request-mode input is nearly impossible, because we do not know what devices the pilot will use at any point in the simulation. More generally, sample- and request-mode input are not sufficient for handling the variety of possible human–computer interactions that arise in a modern computing environment.

Our third mode, **event mode**, can handle these other interactions. We introduce it in three steps. First, we show how event mode can be described as another mode within our measure–trigger paradigm. Second, we discuss the basics of client and servers where event mode is the preferred interaction mode. Third, we show an event-mode interface to OpenGL using GLUT, and we write demonstration programs using this interface.

Suppose that we are in an environment with multiple input devices, each with its own trigger and each running a measure process. Each time that a device is triggered, an **event** is generated. The device measure, including the identifier for the device, is placed in an **event queue**. This process of placing events in the event queue is completely independent of what the application program does with these events. One way that the application program can work with events is shown in Figure 3.10. The user program can examine the front event in the queue or, if the queue is empty, can wait for an event to occur. If there is an event in the queue, the program can look at the event's type and then decide what to do.

Another approach is to associate a function called a **callback** with a specific type of event. From the perspective of the window system, the operating system queries or polls the event queue regularly and executes the callbacks corresponding to events in the queue. We take this approach because it is the one currently used with the major window systems and has proved effective in client–server environments.

FIGURE 3.10   Event–mode model.

3.3 Clients and Servers

So far, our approach to input has been isolated from all other activities that might be happening in our computing environment. We have looked at our graphics system as a monolithic box with limited connections to the outside world, other than through our carefully controlled input devices and a display. Networks and multiuser computing have changed this picture dramatically, and to such an extent that, even if we had a single-user isolated system, its software probably would be configured as a simple client–server network.

If computer graphics is to be useful for a variety of real applications, it must function well in a world of distributed computing and networks. In this world, our building blocks are entities called **servers** that can perform tasks for **clients**. Clients and servers can be distributed over a network (Figure 3.11) or contained entirely within a single computational unit. Familiar examples of servers include print servers, which can allow sharing of a high-speed printer among users; compute servers, such as remotely located supercomputers, accessible from user programs; file servers that allow users to share files and programs, regardless of the machine they are logged into; and terminal servers that handle dial-in access. Users and user programs that make use of these services are clients or client programs.

It is less obvious what we should call a workstation connected to the network: It can be both a client and a server, or perhaps more to the point, a workstation may run client programs and server programs concurrently.

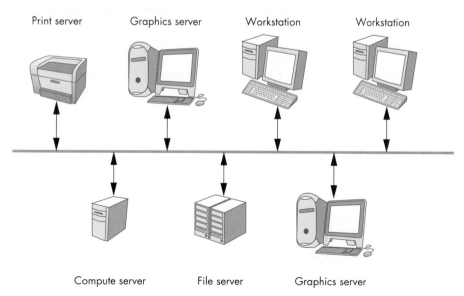

FIGURE 3.11 Network.

The model that we use here was popularized by the X Window System. We use much of that system's terminology, which is now common to most window systems and fits well with graphical applications.

A workstation with a raster display, a keyboard, and a pointing device, such as a mouse, is a **graphics server**. The server can provide output services on its display and input services through the keyboard and pointing device. These services are potentially available to clients anywhere on the network.

Our OpenGL application programs are clients that use the graphics server. Within an isolated system, this distinction may not be apparent as we write, compile, and run the software on a single machine. However, we also can run the same application program using other graphics servers on the network.

3.4   Display Lists

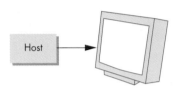

FIGURE 3.12   Simple graphics architecture.

Display lists illustrate how we can use clients and servers on a network to improve interactive graphics performance. Display lists have their origins in the early days of computer graphics. As we saw in Chapter 1, the original architecture of a graphics system was based on a general-purpose computer (or host) connected to a display (Figure 3.12). The computer would send out the necessary information to redraw the display at a rate sufficient to avoid noticeable flicker.[1] At that time (circa 1960), computers were slow and expensive, so the cost of keeping even a simple display refreshed was prohibitive for all but a few applications.

The solution to this problem was to build a special-purpose computer, called a **display processor**, with an organization like that illustrated in Figure 3.13. The display processor had a limited instruction set, most of which was oriented toward drawing primitives on the display. The user program was processed in the host computer, resulting in a compiled list of instructions that was then sent to the display processor, where the instructions were stored in a **display memory** as a **display file**, or **display list**. For a simple noninteractive application, once the display list was sent to the display processor, the host was free for other tasks, and the display processor would execute its display list repeatedly at a rate sufficient to avoid flicker. In addition to resolving the bottleneck due to burdening the host, the display processor introduced the advantages of special-purpose rendering hardware.

Today, the display processor of old has become a graphics server, and the user program on the host computer has become a client. The major bottleneck is no longer the rate at which we have to refresh the display (although that is still a significant problem), but rather the amount of traffic that passes between

---

1. This rate depends on the phosphors in the CRT, but usually is in the range of 60 to 85 Hz or one-half that rate if the display is interlaced.

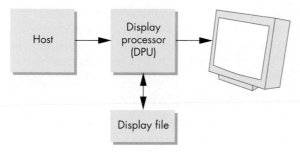

FIGURE 3.13   Display-processor architecture.

the client and server. In addition, the use of special-purpose hardware now characterizes high-end systems.

We can send graphical entities to a display in one of two ways. We can send the complete description of our objects to the graphics server. For our typical geometric primitives, this transfer entails sending vertices, attributes, and primitive types, in addition to viewing information. In our fundamental mode of operation, **immediate mode**, as soon as the program executes a statement that defines a primitive, that primitive is sent to the server for possible display and no memory of it is retained in the system.[2] To redisplay the primitive after a clearing of the screen, or in a new position after an interaction, the program must redefine the primitive and then must resend the primitive to the display. For complex objects in highly interactive applications, this process can cause a considerable quantity of data to pass from the client to the server.

Display lists offer an alternative to this method of operation. This second method is called **retained-mode** graphics. We define the object once, then put its description in a display list. The display list is stored in the server and redisplayed by a simple function call issued from the client to the server. In addition to conferring the obvious advantage of reduced network traffic, this model also allows much of the overhead in executing commands to be done once and have the results stored in the display list on the graphics server. Thus, in many situations, the optimum configuration consists of a good numerical-processing computer that executes the client program and a special-purpose graphics computer for the server—an old idea used with great efficiency in modern systems.

There are, of course, a few disadvantages to the use of display lists. Display lists require memory on the server, and there is the overhead of creating a display list. Although this overhead is often offset by the efficiency of the execution of the display list, it might not be if the data are changing.

---

2. The *image* of a displayed primitive is retained in the frame buffer, but objects and images are not the same.

In modern workstations that use commodity graphics cards in which the GPU carries out most rendering commands, there may not be a performance advantage in using display lists. However, display lists provide an elegant method for building models out of components that are each defined by a display list.

3.4.1   Definition and Execution of Display Lists

Display lists have much in common with ordinary files. There must be a mechanism to define (create) and manipulate (place information in) them. The definition of which contents of a display list are permissible should be flexible enough to allow considerable freedom to the user. OpenGL has a small set of functions to manipulate display lists and places only a few restrictions on display-list contents. We develop several simple examples to show the functions' uses.

Display lists are defined similarly to geometric primitives. There is a glNewList at the beginning and a glEndList at the end, with the contents in between. Each display list must have a unique identifier—an integer that is usually macro-defined in the C program by means of a #define directive to an appropriate name for the object in the list. For example, the following code defines a red box. The code is similar to code from Chapter 2, but this time it places the information in a display list:

```
#define BOX 1 /* or some other unused integer */

glNewList(BOX,  GL_COMPILE);
    glBegin(GL_POLYGON);
        glColor3f(1.0, 0.0, 0.0);
        glVertex2f(-1.0, -1.0);
        glVertex2f( 1.0, -1.0);
        glVertex2f( 1.0,  1.0);
        glVertex2f(-1.0,  1.0);
    glEnd();
glEndList();
```

The flag GL_COMPILE tells the system to send the list to the server but not to display its contents. If we want an immediate display of the contents while the list is being constructed, we can use the GL_COMPILE_AND_EXECUTE flag instead.

Each time that we wish to draw the box on the server, we execute the function

```
glCallList(BOX);
```

Just as it does with other OpenGL functions, the present state determines which transformations are applied to the primitives in the display list. Thus, if we change the model-view or projection matrices between executions of the display list, the box will appear in different places or will no longer even appear, as the following code fragment demonstrates:

```
glMatrixMode(GL_PROJECTION);
for(i= 1 ; i<5; i++)
{
    glLoadIdentity();
    gluOrtho2D(-2.0*i  , 2.0*i , -2.0*i , 2.0*i );
    glCallList(BOX);
}
```

Each time that glCallList is executed, the box is redrawn, albeit with a different clipping rectangle.

In succeeding chapters, we introduce various transformation matrices that will enable us to use display lists for modeling. Because we can change state from within a display list, we have to be careful to avoid allowing these changes to have undesirable—and often unexpected—effects later. For example, our box display list changes the drawing color. Each time that the display list is executed, the drawing color is set to red; unless the color is set to some other value, primitives defined subsequently in the program also will be colored red.

The easiest safeguard is to use the matrix and attribute stacks provided by OpenGL. A **stack** is a data structure in which the item placed most recently in the structure is the first removed. We can save the present values of attributes and matrices by placing, or **pushing**, them on the top of the appropriate stack; we can recover them later by removing, or **popping**, them from the stack. A standard—and safe—procedure is always to push both the attributes and matrices on their own stacks when we enter a display list, and to pop them when we exit. Thus, we usually see the function calls

```
glPushAttrib(GL_ALL_ATTRIB_BITS);
glPushMatrix();
```

at the beginning of a display list and

```
glPopAttrib();
glPopMatrix();
```

at the end. We use matrix and attributes stacks extensively in Chapter 10 to build and display hierarchical models. Note that although stacks provide a convenient programming aid for modeling, there is a performance cost every time that we push or pop matrices and attributes.

A few additional functions are available that make it easier to work with display lists. Often, we want to work with multiple display lists, as we demonstrate with the next example. We can create multiple lists with consecutive identifiers more easily if we use the function glGenLists(number), which returns the first integer (or base) of number consecutive integers that are unused labels. The function glCallLists allows us to execute multiple display lists with a single function call. Text generation is a good example of how we can make excellent use of the options available through display lists. Section 3.4.2 contains many OpenGL details; you may want to skip it the first time that you read this chapter. It illustrates the flexibility that the API provides to the application programmer for dealing with troublesome problems that arise in working with text. We encounter many of these issues again in Chapter 10 when we discuss graphics and the Internet.

3.4.2 Text and Display Lists

In Chapter 2, we introduced both stroke and raster text. Regardless of which type we choose to use, we need a reasonable amount of code to describe a set of characters. For example, suppose that we use a raster font in which each character is stored as a 8×13 pattern of bits. It takes 13 bytes to store each character. If we want to display a string by the most straightforward method, we can send each character to the server each time that we want it displayed. This transfer requires the movement of at least 13 bytes per character. If we define a stroke font using only line segments, each character can require a different number of lines. If we use filled polygons for characters, as in Figure 3.14, we see that an "I" is fairly simple to define, but we may need many line segments to get a sufficiently smooth "O." On the average, we need many more than 13 bytes per character to represent a stroke font. For applications that display large quantities of text, sending each character to the display every time that it is needed can place a significant burden on our graphics systems.

A more efficient strategy is to define the font once, using a display list for each character, and then to store the font on the server using these display lists. This solution is similar to what is done for bitmap fonts on standard alphanumeric display terminals. The patterns are stored in read-only memory (ROM) in the terminal, and each character is selected and displayed based on a single byte: its ASCII code. The difference here is one of both quantity and quality. We can define as many fonts as our display memory can hold, and we can treat stroke fonts like other graphical objects, allowing us to translate, scale, and rotate them as desired.

The basics of defining and displaying a character string (1 byte per character) using a stroke font and display lists provide a simple but important example of the use of display lists in OpenGL. The procedure is essentially the same for a raster font. We can define either the standard 96 printable ASCII characters or we can define patterns for a 256-character extended ASCII character set.

First, we define a function OurFont(char c), which will draw any ASCII character c that can appear in our string. The function might have a form like

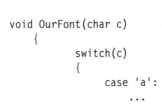

FIGURE 3.14 Stroke characters. (a) Filled strings. (b) Magnified outlines.

```
void OurFont(char c)
   {
       switch(c)
       {
          case 'a':
             ...
```

```
                break;
                case 'A':
                    ...
                break;
                    ...
            }
        }
```

Within each case, we have to be careful about the spacing; each character in the string must be displayed to the right of the previous character. We can use the translate function that we introduce in Chapter 4 to get the desired spacing or shift the vertex positions. Suppose that we are defining the letter "O," and we wish it to fit in a unit square. The corresponding part of OurFont might be

```
case 'O':
    glTranslatef(0.5, 0.5, 0.0); /* move to center */
    glBegin{GL_QUAD_STRIP);
    for (i=0; i<=12; i++)  /* 12 vertices */
    {
            angle = 3.14159 /6.0 * i; /* 30 degrees in radians */
            glVertex2f(0.4*cos(angle)+0.5; 0.4*sin(angle)+0.5);
            glVertex2f(0.5*cos(angle)+0.5, 0.5*sin(angle)+0.5);
    }
    glEnd();
    break;
```

This code approximates the circle with 12 quadrilaterals. Each will be filled according to the present state. Although we do not discuss the full power of transformations until Chapter 4, here we explain the use of the translation function in this code. We are working with two-dimensional characters. Hence, each character is defined in the plane $z = 0$, and we can use whatever coordinate system we wish to define our characters. We assume that each character fits inside a box.[3] The usual strategy is to start at the lower-left corner of the first character in the string and to draw one character at a time, drawing each character such that we end at the lower-right corner of that character's box, which is the lower-left corner of the successor's box.

The first translation moves us to the center of the "O" character's box, which we set to be a unit square. We then define our vertices using two concentric circles centered at this point (Figure 3.15). One way to envision the translation function is to say that it shifts the origin for all the drawing commands that follow. After the 12 quadrilaterals in the strip are defined, we move to the lower-right corner of the box. The two translations accumulate; as a result of these translations, we

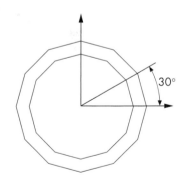

FIGURE 3.15 Drawing of the letter "O."

---

3. Each character may have a different size and thus be in a box of unique dimensions, or if we are defining a fixed-width monotype font (such as the one used to set code in this book), all characters will have boxes of the same size.

are in the proper position to start the next character. Note that, in this example, we do not want to push and pop the matrices. Other characters can be defined in a similar manner.

Although our code is inelegant, its efficiency is of little consequence because the characters are generated only once and then are sent to the graphics server as a compiled display list.

Suppose that we want to generate a 256-character set. The required code, using the OurFont function, is as follows:

```
base = glGenLists(256); /* return index of first of 256
                         consecutive available ids */
for(i=0; i<256; i++)
{
      glNewList(base + i, GL_COMPILE);
      OurFont(i);
      glEndList();
}
```

When we wish to use these display lists to draw individual characters, rather than offsetting the identifier of the display lists by base each time, we can set an offset with

```
glListBase(base);
```

Finally, our drawing of a string is accomplished in the server by the function call

```
char *text_string;

glCallLists( (GLint) strlen(text_string), GL_BYTE, text_string);
```

which makes use of the standard C library function strlen to find the length of input string text_string. The first argument in the function glCallLists is the number of lists to be executed. The third is a pointer to an array of a type given by the second argument. The identifier of the kth display list executed is the sum of the list base (established by glListBase) and the value of the kth character in the array of characters.

3.4.3 Fonts in GLUT

In general, we prefer to use an existing font rather than to define our own. GLUT provides a few raster and stroke fonts.[4] They do not make use of display lists; in the final example in this chapter, however, we create display lists to contain

---

4. We can also access fonts that are provided by the window system but at the expense of code portability.

one of these GLUT fonts. We can access a single character from a **monotype**, or evenly spaced, font by the function call

```
glutStrokeCharacter(GLUT_STROKE_MONO_ROMAN, int character)
```

GLUT_STROKE_ROMAN provides proportionally spaced characters. You should use these fonts with caution. Their size (approximately 120 units maximum) may have little to do with the units of the rest of your program; thus, they may have to be scaled. We usually control the position of a character by using a translation before the character function is called. In addition, each invocation of glutStrokeCharacter includes a translation to the bottom right of the character's box, to prepare for the next character. Scaling and translation affect the OpenGL state, so here we should be careful to use glPushMatrix and glPopMatrix as necessary to prevent undesirable positioning of objects defined later in the program. Our discussion of transformations in Chapter 4 should enable you to use stroke fonts effectively.

Raster and bitmap characters are produced in a similar manner. For example, a single 8×13 character is obtained using

```
glutBitmapCharacter(GLUT_BITMAP_8_BY_13, int character)
```

Positioning of bitmap characters is considerably simpler than is that of stroke characters because bitmap characters are drawn directly in the frame buffer and are not subject to geometric transformations, whereas stroke characters are. OpenGL keeps, within its state, a **raster position**. This position identifies where the next raster primitive will be placed; it can be set using the function glRasterPos*(). The user program typically moves the raster position to the desired location before the first character in a string defined by glutBitmapCharacter is invoked. This change does not affect subsequent rendering of geometric primitives. If characters have different widths, we can use the function glutBitmapWidth(font, char) to return the width of a particular character. However, the function glutBitmapCharacter automatically advances the raster position, so typically we need not manipulate the raster position until we want to define a string of characters elsewhere on the display. We use bitmap characters in our example of a painting program later in this chapter, using display lists.

We shall return to display lists when we discuss hierarchical modeling in Chapter 10. Because most OpenGL code can be encapsulated between a glNewList and glEndList, you should be able to convert most code to use display lists with little effort.

3.5 Programming Event-Driven Input

In this section, we develop event-driven input through a number of simple examples that use the callback mechanism that we introduced in Section 3.2. We examine various events that are recognized by the window system and, for those of interest to our application, we write callback functions that govern how the application program responds to these events.

3.5.1 Using the Pointing Device

We start by altering the `main` function in the gasket program from Chapter 2. In the original version, we used functions in the GLUT library to put a window on the screen and then entered the event loop by executing the function `glutMainLoop`. In that chapter, we entered the loop but did nothing. We could not even terminate the program, except through an external mechanism. Our first example will remedy this omission by using the pointing device to terminate a program. We accomplish this task by having the program execute a standard termination function called `exit` when a particular mouse button is depressed.

We discuss only those events recognized by GLUT. A window system such as the X Window System recognizes many more events. However, the GLUT library will recognize a set of events that is common to most window systems and is sufficient for developing basic interactive graphics programs that can be used with multiple window systems. Two types of events are associated with the pointing device, which is conventionally assumed to be a mouse. A **move event** is generated when the mouse is moved with one of the buttons depressed. If the mouse is moved without a button being held down, this event is classified as a **passive move event**. After a move event, the position of the mouse—its measure—is made available to the application program. A **mouse event** occurs when one of the mouse buttons is either depressed or released. A button being held down does not generate a mouse event until the button is released. The information returned includes the button that generated the event, the state of the button after the event (up or down), and the position of the cursor tracking the mouse in window coordinates (with the origin in the upper-left corner of the window). We register the mouse callback function, usually in the `main` function, by means of the GLUT function

```
glutMouseFunc(mouse);
```

The mouse callback must have the form

```
void mouse(int button, int state, int x, int y)
```

Within the callback function, we define the actions that we want to take place if the specified event occurs. There may be multiple actions defined in the mouse callback function corresponding to the many possible button and state combinations. For our simple example, we want the depression of the left mouse button to terminate the program. The required callback is the single-line function

```
void mouse(int button, int state, int x, int y)
{
    if(button == GLUT_LEFT_BUTTON && state == GLUT_DOWN)
            exit(0);
}
```

If any other mouse event—such as a depression of one of the other buttons—occurs, no response action will occur, because no action corresponding to these events has been defined in the callback function.

Our next example illustrates the benefits of the program structure that we introduced in the previous chapter. We write a program to draw a small box at each location on the screen where the mouse cursor is located at the time that the left button is pushed. A push of the middle button terminates the program.

First, we look at the main program, which is much the same as our previous examples.[5]

```
int main(int argc, char **argv)
{

    glutInit(&argc,argv);
    glutInitWindowSize(ww, wh); /*globally defined initial window size */
    glutInitDisplayMode(GLUT_SINGLE | GLUT_RGB);
    glutCreateWindow("square");
    myinit();
    glutReshapeFunc(myReshape);
    glutMouseFunc(mouse);
    glutDisplayFunc(display);
    glutMainLoop();
}
```

The **reshape event** is generated whenever the window is resized, such as by a user interaction; we discuss it next. We do not need the required display callback for drawing in this example because the only time that primitives will be generated is when a mouse event occurs. Because GLUT requires that every program have a display callback, we must include this callback, although it can have a simple body:

```
void display()
{
    glClear(GL_COLOR_BUFFER_BIT);
}
```

---

5. We use naming conventions for callbacks similar to those in the *OpenGL Programming Guide* [Ope04a].

The mouse callbacks are again in the function mouse.

```
void mouse(int btn, int state, int x, int y)
{
  if(btn==GLUT_LEFT_BUTTON && state==GLUT_DOWN) drawSquare(x,y);
  if(btn==GLUT_RIGHT_BUTTON && state==GLUT_DOWN) exit();
}
```

Because only the primitives are generated in drawSquare, the desired attributes must have been set elsewhere, such as in our initialization function myinit.

We need three global variables. The size of the window may change dynamically, and its present size should be available, both to the reshape callback and to the drawing function drawSquare. If we want to change the size of the squares we draw, we may find it beneficial to make the square-size parameter global as well. Our initialization routine selects a clipping window that is the same size as the window created in main and selects the viewport to correspond to the entire window. This window is cleared to black. Note that we could omit the setting of the window and viewport here because we are merely setting them to the default values. However, it is illustrative to compare this code with what we do in the reshape callback in Section 3.5.2.

```
/* globals */

GLsizei wh = 500, ww = 500; /* initial window size */
GLfloat size = 3.0;   /*one-half of side length of square */

void myinit()
{
   /* set initial viewing conditions */

      glViewport(0,0,ww,wh);
      glMatrixMode(GL_PROJECTION);
      glLoadIdentity();
      gluOrtho2D(0.0, (GLdouble) ww , 0.0, (GLdouble) wh);
      glMatrixMode(GL_MODELVIEW);
      glClearColor (0.0, 0.0, 0.0, 1.0);
}
```

Our square-drawing routine has to take into account that the position returned from the mouse event is in the window system's coordinate system, which has its origin at the top left of the window. Hence, we have to flip the y value returned, using the present height of the window (the global wh). We pick a random color using the standard random-number generator rand().

```
void drawSquare(int x, int y)
{

      y=wh-y;
```

```
glColor3ub( (char) rand()%256, (char) rand()%256,
                 (char) rand()%256);
glBegin(GL_POLYGON);
    glVertex2f(x+size, y+size);
    glVertex2f(x-size, y+size);
    glVertex2f(x-size, y-size);
    glVertex2f(x+size, y-size);
glEnd();
glFlush();
}
```

After we insert the necessary include statements, we have a program that works, as long as the window size remains unchanged.

3.5.2 Window Events

Most window systems allow a user to resize the window, usually by using the mouse to drag a corner of the window to a new location. This event is an example of a **window event**. If such an event occurs, the user program can decide what to do.[6] If the window size changes, we have to consider three questions:

1. Do we redraw all the objects that were in the window before it was resized?
2. What do we do if the aspect ratio of the new window is different from that of the old window?
3. Do we change the sizes or attributes of new primitives if the size of the new window is different from that of the old?

There is no single answer to any of these questions. If we are displaying the image of a real-world scene, our reshape function probably should make sure that no shape distortions occur. But this choice may mean that part of the resized window is unused or that part of the scene cannot be displayed in the window. If we want to redraw the objects that were in the window before it was resized, we need a mechanism for storing and recalling them. Often we do this recall by encapsulating all drawing in a single function, such as the display function used in Chapter 2, which was registered as the display callback function. In the present example, however, that is probably not the best choice, because we decide what we draw interactively.

In our square-drawing example, we ensure that squares of the same size are drawn, regardless of the size or shape of the window. We clear the screen each time it is resized, and we use the entire new window as our drawing area. The reshape event returns in its measure the height and width of the new window.

---

6. Unlike most other callbacks, there is a default reshape callback that simply changes the viewport to the new window size, an action that might not be what the user desires.

We use these values to create a new OpenGL clipping window using `gluOrtho2D`, as well as a new viewport with the same aspect ratio. We then clear the window to black. Thus, we have the callback

```
void myReshape(GLsizei w, GLsizei h)
{

    /* adjust clipping box */

    glMatrixMode(GL_PROJECTION);
    glLoadIdentity();
    gluOrtho2D(0.0, (GLdouble)w, 0.0, (GLdouble)h);
    glMatrixMode(GL_MODELVIEW);
    glLoadIdentity();

    /* adjust viewport and clear */

    glViewport(0,0,w,h);

    /* save new window size in global variables */

    ww=w;
    wh=h;
}
```

The complete square-drawing program is given in Appendix A.

There are other possibilities here. We could change the size of the squares to match the increase or decrease of the window size. We have not considered other events, such as a window movement without resizing, an event that can be generated by a user who drags the window to a new location. And we have not specified what to do if the window is hidden behind another window and then is exposed (brought to the front). There are callbacks for these events, and we can write simple functions similar to `myReshape` for them or we can rely on the default behavior of GLUT. Another simple change that we can make to our program is to have new squares generated as long as one of the mouse buttons is held down. The relevant callback is the motion callback, which we set through the function

```
glutMotionFunc(drawSquare);
```

Each time the system senses the motion, a new square is drawn—an action that allows us to draw pictures using a brush with a square tip.

Note that the reshape callback generates a display call back. Our simple display callback clears the window so that any squares that are on the display are lost. If we want to retain the squares and redraw them on the resized window, we must create a mechanism to store their descriptions so they can be redrawn on the resized window. We return to this issue in Section 3.9.

3.5.3 Keyboard Events

We can also use the keyboard as an input device. Keyboard events are generated when the mouse is in the window and one of the keys is depressed. The pressing and releasing of keys are two distinct events. The GLUT function `glutKeyboardFunc` is the callback for events generated by depressing a key, whereas `glutKeyboardUpFunc` is the callback for events generated by release of a key.

When a keyboard event occurs, the ASCII code for the key that generated the event and the location of the mouse are returned. All the key press callbacks are registered in a single callback function, such as

```
glutKeyboardFunc(myKey);
```

For example, if we wish to use the keyboard only to exit the program, we can use the callback function

```
void myKey(unsigned char key, int x, int y)
{
    if(key=='q' || key == 'Q') exit( );
}
```

GLUT includes a function `glutGetModifiers` that allows the user to define actions using the meta keys, such as the Control and Alt keys. These special keys can be important when we are using one- or two-button mice because we can then define the same functionality as having left, right, and middle buttons as we have assumed in this chapter. More information about these functions is in the Suggested Readings section at the end of the chapter.

3.5.4 The Display and Idle Callbacks

Of the remaining callbacks, two merit special attention. We have already seen the display callback, which we used in Chapter 2. This callback is specified in GLUT by the function call

```
glutDisplayFunc(display);
```

It is invoked when GLUT determines that the window should be redisplayed. One such situation occurs when the window is opened initially, another is after a resize event. Because we know that a display event will be generated when the window is first opened, the display callback is a good place to put the code that generates most noninteractive output.

The display callback can be used in other contexts, such as in animations, where various values defined in the program may change. We can also use GLUT to open multiple windows. The state includes the present window, and we can render different objects into different windows by changing the present window.

We can also **iconify** a window by replacing it with a small symbol or picture. Consequently, interactive and animation programs will contain many calls for the reexecution of the display function. Rather than call it directly, we use the GLUT function

```
glutPostRedisplay();
```

Using this function, rather than invoking the display callback directly, avoids extra or unnecessary drawings of the screen by setting a flag inside GLUT's main loop indicating that the display needs to be redrawn. At the end of each execution of the main loop, GLUT uses this flag to determine whether the display function will be executed. Thus, using `glutPostRedisplay` ensures that the display will be drawn once each time the program goes through the event loop.

The **idle callback** is invoked when there are no other events. Its default is the null function pointer. A typical use of the idle callback is to continue to generate graphical primitives through a display function while nothing else is happening (see Exercise 3.2). We illustrate both the display and the idle callbacks in the paint programs that we develop in Sections 3.8 and 3.9.

We can change most callback functions during program execution by specifying a new callback function. We can also disable a callback by setting its callback function to NULL.

3.5.5 Window Management

GLUT also supports both multiple windows and subwindows of a given window. We can open a second top-level window (with the label "second window") by

```
id=glutCreateWindow("second window");
```

The returned integer value allows us to select this window as the current window into which objects will be rendered by

```
glutSetWindow(id);
```

We can make this window have properties different from those of other windows by invoking the `glutInitDisplayMode` before `glutCreateWindow`. Furthermore, each window can have its own set of callback functions because callback specifications refer to the present window.

3.6 Menus

We could use our graphics primitives and our mouse callbacks to construct various graphical input devices. For example, we could construct a slidebar as shown in Figure 3.16, using filled rectangles for the device, text for any labels, and

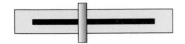

FIGURE 3.16   Slidebar.

the mouse to get the position. However, much of the code would be tedious to develop, especially if we tried to create visually appealing and effective graphical devices (widgets). Most window systems provide a toolkit that contains a set of widgets, but because our philosophy is not to restrict our discussion to any particular window system, we shall not discuss the specifics of such widget sets. Fortunately, GLUT provides one additional feature, **pop-up menus**, that we can use with the mouse to create sophisticated interactive applications.

Using menus involves taking a few simple steps. We must define the actions corresponding to each entry in the menu. We must link the menu to a particular mouse button. Finally, we must register a callback function for each menu. We can demonstrate simple menus with the example of a pop-up menu that has three entries. The first selection allows us to exit our program. The second and third change the size of the squares in our drawSquare function. We name the menu callback demo_menu. The function calls to set up the menu and to link it to the right mouse button should be placed in our main function. They are

```
glutCreateMenu(demo_menu);
glutAddMenuEntry("quit",1);
glutAddMenuEntry("increase square size", 2);
glutAddMenuEntry("decrease square size", 3);
glutAttachMenu(GLUT_RIGHT_BUTTON);
```

The function glutCreateMenu registers the callback function demo_menu.

The second argument in each entry's definition is the identifier passed to the callback when the entry is selected. Hence, our callback function is

```
void demo_menu(int id)
{
    switch(id)
    {
        case 1: exit(0);
        break;
        case 2: size = 2 * size;
        break;
        case 3: (size > 1) size = size/2;
        break;
    }
    glutPostRedisplay( );
}
```

The call to glutPostRedisplay requests a redraw through the glutDisplayFunc callback, so that the screen is drawn again without the menu.

GLUT also supports hierarchical menus, as shown in Figure 3.17. For example, suppose that we want the main menu that we create to have only two entries. The first entry still causes the program to terminate, but now the second causes a submenu to pop up. The submenu contains the two entries for changing the

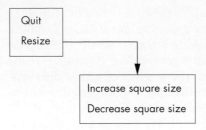

FIGURE 3.17   Structure of hierarchical menus.

size of the square in our square-drawing program. The following code for the menu (which is in main) should be clear:

```
sub_menu = glutCreateMenu(size_menu);
glutAddMenuEntry("Increase square size", 2);
glutAddMenuEntry("Decrease square size", 3);
glutCreateMenu(top_menu);
glutAddMenuEntry("Quit",1);
glutAddSubMenu("Resize", sub_menu);
glutAttachMenu(GLUT_RIGHT_BUTTON);
```

Writing the callback functions, size_menu and top_menu, should be a simple exercise for you (Exercise 3.5).

3.7 Picking

Picking is the logical input operation that allows the user to identify an object on the display. Although the action of picking uses the pointing device, the information that the user wants returned to the application program is not a position. A pick device is considerably more difficult to implement on a modern system than is a locator.

Such was not always the case. Old display processors could accomplish picking easily by means of a lightpen. Each redisplay of the screen would start at a precise time. The lightpen would generate an interrupt when the redisplay passed its sensor. By comparing the time of the interrupt with the time that the redisplay began, the processor could identify an exact place in the display list and subsequently could determine which object was being displayed.

One reason for the difficulty of picking in modern systems is the forward nature of the systems' rendering pipelines. Primitives are defined in an application program and move forward through a sequence of geometric operations, rasterization, and fragment operations on their way to the frame buffer. Although much of this process is reversible in a mathematical sense, the hardware is not reversible. Hence, converting from a location on the display to the corresponding primitive is not a direct calculation. There are also potential uniqueness problems (see Exercises 3.11 and 3.12).

There are at least three ways to deal with this difficulty. One process, known as **selection**, involves adjusting the clipping region and viewport such that we can keep track of which primitives in a small clipping region are rendered into a region near the cursor. These primitives go into a **hit list** that can be examined later by the user program. OpenGL supports this approach, and we shall discuss it after we examine two simpler, but less general strategies.

A simple approach is to use (**axis-aligned**) **bounding boxes**, or **extents**, for objects of interest. The extent of an object is the smallest rectangle, aligned with the coordinates axes, that contains the object. It is relatively easy to determine which rectangles in world coordinates correspond to a particular point in screen coordinates. If the application program maintains a simple data structure to relate objects and bounding boxes, approximate picking can be done within the application program. We demonstrate a simple example of this approach in Section 3.8.

Another simple approach involves using the back buffer and an extra rendering. When we use double buffering (Section 3.10.2), we use two color buffers: a front buffer and a back buffer. Because the back buffer is not displayed, we can use it for purposes other than for rendering the scene that we wish to display. Suppose that we render our objects into the back buffer, each in a distinct color. The application programmer is free to determine an object's contents by simply changing colors wherever a new object definition appears in the program.

We can perform picking in four steps that are initiated by a user-defined pick function in the application. First, we draw the objects into the back buffer with the pick colors. Second, we get the position of the mouse using the mouse callback. Third, we use the function `glReadPixels()` to find the color at the position in the frame buffer corresponding to the mouse position. Finally, we search a table of colors to find which object corresponds to the color read. We must follow this process by a normal rendering into the back buffer. There are some subtleties to the use of `glReadPixels()`, which we shall consider in Chapter 8.

3.7.1 Picking and Selection Mode

The difficult problem in implementing picking within the OpenGL pipeline is that we cannot go backward directly from the position of the mouse to primitives that were rendered close to that point on the screen. OpenGL provides a somewhat complex process using a rendering mode called **selection mode** to do picking at the cost of an extra rendering each time that we do a pick. The basic idea of selection mode is that the objects in a scene can be rendered but not necessarily to a color buffer. As we render objects, OpenGL can keep track of which objects render to any chosen area by determining whether they are in a specified clipping volume, which does not have to be the same as the clipping volume that we use to display our scene. There are a number of steps and functions that are required to do picking using selection mode. We shall examine each step and then put them together in a simple program. The function glRenderMode lets us select one of three modes: normal rendering to the color buffer (GL_RENDER), selection mode (GL_SELECT), or feedback mode (GL_FEEDBACK). Feedback mode can be used to obtain a list of the primitives that were rendered. We will not discuss this mode. The return value from glRenderMode can be used to determine the number of primitives that were in the clipping volume.

When we enter selection mode and render a scene, each primitive within the clipping volume generates a message called a **hit** that is stored in a buffer called the **name stack**. We use the function glSelectBuffer to identify an array for the selection data. There are four functions for initializing the name stack, for pushing and popping information on it, and for manipulating the top entry on the stack. The information that we produce is called the **hit list** and can be examined after the rendering to obtain the information needed for picking. The function

```
void glSelectBuffer(GLsizei n, GLuint *buff)
```

specifies the array buff of size n in which to place selection data. The function

```
void glInitNames( )
```

initializes the name stack. The function

```
void glPushName(GLuint name)
```

pushes name on the name stack. The function

```
void glPopName( )
```

pops the top name from the name stack. Finally, the function

```
void glLoadName(GLuint name)
```

replaces the top of the name stack with name. In general, each object that we wish to identify is a set of primitives to which we assign the same integer name. Before we render the object, we load its name on the name stack. We cannot load a name onto an empty stack, so we usually enter an unused name onto the stack when we initialize it, for example, by

```
glInitNames();
glPushName(0);
```

We typically use the mouse callback to enter selection mode and leave selection mode before the end of the mouse callback. When we return to render mode, glRenderMode returns the number of hits that have been processed. We then examine the hit list. We also change the clipping volume within the mouse callback so that we obtain hits in the desired region, usually an area that is close to the location of the mouse. We can set the clipping volume in two ways. We can simply define a view volume through gluOrtho2D (or use other viewing functions). We would probably first want to save the present clipping volume with a glPushMatrix. Then any primitive that fell within this new clipping volume would generate a hit regardless of where the mouse is located. This option works for selection, but when we pick we want only those objects that render near the cursor.

Suppose that we want all the objects that render into a small user-defined rectangle centered at the cursor. The size of the rectangle is a measure of how sensitive we want our picking to be. This rectangle is a small part of the viewport. Given the viewport, the location of the cursor, the size of the rectangle, and the clipping window, we can find a new clipping window such that all the objects in the new clipping window render into the full viewport. Mathematically, this is an exercise in proportions and involves the inverse of the projection matrix. We can let OpenGL do this calculation for us through the GLU function gluPickMatrix, which is applied before glOrtho2D when we are in selection mode. The function call has the form

```
gluPickMatrix( x,y,w,h,*vp);
```

and it creates a projection matrix for picking that restricts drawing to a w × h area centered at (x,y) in window coordinates within the viewport vp. Figure 3.18 illustrates the process for a two-dimensional application. In part (a) we see the normal window and the image on the display. We also see the cursor with a small box around it indicating the area in which, if a primitive is rendered, we will count it as a hit. Part (b) of the figure shows the window and display after the window has been changed by gluPickMatrix. Note that the world window has been changed so that only those objects that were in the pick rectangle are in the new window and these objects now occupy the whole viewport. It is for this reason that we do not want this image to appear on the screen.

Assuming that we have set up the viewing conditions for normal rendering during initialization or in the reshape callback, the mouse and display callbacks are of the form

```
#define N 2 /* N x N pixels around cursor for pick area */

 void mouse(int button, int state, int x, int y )
{
    GLuint nameBuffer[SIZE]; /* define SIZE elsewhere */
    GLint hits;
    GLint viewport[4];
    If( button == GLUT_LEFT_BUTTON && state == GLUT_DOWN)
    {
```

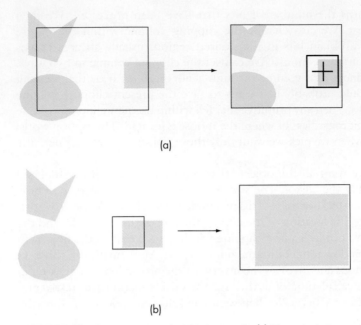

FIGURE 3.18 Two-dimensional picking example. (a) Normal window and display. (b) Window and display after applying pick matrix.

```
/* initialize the name stack */

glInitNames( );
glPushName( 0 );
glSelectBuffer( SIZE, nameBuffer);

/* set up viewing for selection mode */

glGetIntegerv(GL_VIEWPORT, viewport);
glMatrixMode(GL_PROJECTION);

/* save original viewing matrix */

glPushMatrix();
glLoadIdentity( );

/* N x N pick area around cursor */
/* must invert mouse y to get in world coords */
gluPickMatrix( (GLdouble) x, (GLdouble)
    ( viewport[3] - y), N, N, viewport);

/* same clipping window as in reshape callback */
```

```
            gluOrtho2D (xmin, xmax, ymin, ymax);

            draw_objects(GL_SELECT);
            glMatrixMode(GL_PROJECTION);

            /* restore viewing matrix */

            glPopMatrix();
            glFlush();

            /* return to normal render mode */

            hits = glRenderMode(GL_RENDER);

            /* process hits from selection mode rendering */

            processHits(hits, nameBuff);

            /* normal render */

            glutPostRedisplay();
        }
}

void display( )
{
    glClear( GL_COLOR_BUFFER_BIT);
    draw_objects(GL_RENDER);
    glFlush();
}
```

Note that we have to call the function that draws the objects directly rather than use glutPostRedisplay twice in the mouse callback because GLUT will do only one execution of the display callback each time through the event loop. Here is a simple function that draws two partially overlapping rectangles:

```
void drawObjects(GLenum mode)
{
    if(mode == GL_SELECT) glLoadName(1);
    glColor3f(1.0, 0.0, 0.0);
    glRectf(-0.5, -0.5, 1.0, 1.0);

    if(mode == GL_SELECT) glLoadName(2);
    glColor3f(0.0, 0.0, 1.0);
    glRectf(-1.0, -1.0, 0.5, 0.5);
}
```

Here we have introduced the glRectf(xmin, ymin, xmax, ymax), which specifies an axis-aligned rectangle in a single function.

Note that we need to change only the top element on the name stack. If we had a hierarchical object, as we shall discuss in Chapter 10, we could use glPushName to allow multiple names on the stack for a given hit. For an object with multiple parts, all the parts that were close to the cursor would have their names placed in the same stack. The final piece we need to write is the function that examines the name stack. We will have it print out how many primitives were placed in the stack for each left mouse click and the names of any objects that were picked. The hit buffer contains one record for each hit. Thus, every object that is rendered near the mouse cursor will generate a record. If there are no names on the hit list because no primitives were rendered near the mouse cursor, then there is a zero for the hit record. Otherwise, we find three types of information, all stored as integers. First, there is the number of names on the name stack when there was a hit. For our example, this number can only be 1. It is followed by two integers which give scaled minimum and maximum depths for the hit primitive. Because we are working in two dimensions, these values will not provide useful information. For three-dimensional applications, we can use these values to determine the front object that was picked. These three integers are followed by entries in the name stack. For our example, we will find the identifier of either the red or the blue rectangle here (a 1 or a 2). The following function will print out this information.

```
void processHits (GLint hits, GLuint buffer[])
{
    unsigned int i, j;
    GLuint names, *ptr;

    printf ("hits = %d\n", hits);
    ptr = (GLuint *) buffer;

     /* loop over number of hits */

    for (i = 0; i < hits; i++)
     {
        names = *ptr;

        /* skip over number of names and depths */

        ptr += 3;

        /* check each name in record */

      for (j = 0; j < names; j++)
        {
         if(*ptr==1) printf ("red rectangle\n");
         else printf ("blue rectangle\n");
```

```
        /* go to next hit record */

        ptr++;
    }
  }
}
```

Picking presents a number of other difficulties for the implementor. For example, if an object is defined hierarchically (like those we discuss in Chapter 10), then it is a member of a set of objects. When the object is indicated by the pointing device, a list of all objects in the set of which it is a member should be returned to the user program.

Graphics APIs usually do not specify how close to an object we must point for the object to be identified. One reason for this omission is to allow multiple ways of picking. For example, if we use the bounding-box strategy, we might not point to any point contained in the object. Another reason for this lack of precision is that humans are not accurate with positioning devices. Although the display at which we point might have a high resolution, we may find it difficult to indicate reliably with our pointing device the location on the screen corresponding to a given pixel.

3.8 A Simple Paint Program

We illustrate the use of callbacks, display lists, and interactive program design by developing a simple paint program. Paint programs have most of the features of sophisticated CAD programs. Any paint program should demonstrate most of the following features:

- It should have the ability to work with geometric objects, such as line segments and polygons. Given that geometric objects are defined through vertices, the paint program should allow us to enter vertices interactively.
- It should have the ability to manipulate pixels, and thus to draw directly into the frame buffer.
- It should provide control of attributes such as color, line type, and fill patterns.
- It should include menus for controlling the application.
- It should behave correctly when the window is moved or resized.

Our sample program demonstrates these principles and incorporates many of the features that we introduced in the small examples that we have developed.

Figure 3.19 shows the initial display that a user sees. The five boxes are buttons that select from the five drawing modes: line segment, rectangle, triangle, pixel, and text. The left mouse button selects the mode. If line-segment mode is selected, the next two clicks of the left mouse button while the cursor is outside the menu area give the locations of the endpoints. After the second

FIGURE 3.19   Initial display of paint program.

endpoint is located, the line segment is drawn in the present color. Rectangle and triangle modes are similar: In rectangle mode, we select the diagonal corners; in triangle mode, we locate the three vertices. A new mode can be selected at any time. In pixel mode, successive mouse clicks give positions for randomly colored rectangles that can have a side length of two or more pixels. In text mode, the user types in a string of characters that appear on the display, starting where the mouse was clicked most recently.

The menus (Figure 3.20) are controlled by the middle and right mouse buttons. The right button allows us to either clear the screen or terminate the program. The middle button allows us to change the drawing color, select between fill and no fill for the triangles and rectangles, and change the size of the pixel rectangles.

The most difficult part of the design process is deciding what functionality to place in each of the functions. The decisions reflected in our code are consistent with our previous examples. Many of the functions in our program are the same as those in our previous examples. We employ the following functions:

```
void mouse(int btn, int state , int x, int y); /* mouse callback */
void key( unsigned char c, int x, int y);      /* keyboard callback */
void display();                                 /* display callback */
void drawSquare(int x, int y);                  /* random-color square
                                                   function*/

void myReshape(GLsizei, GLsizei);               /* reshape callback */
void myinit();                                 /* initialization function */
void screen_box(int x, int y, int s);          /* box-drawing
                                                   function */
```

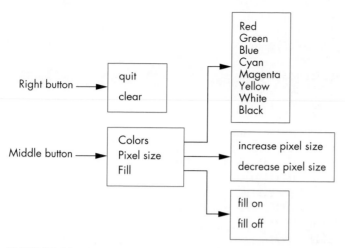

FIGURE 3.20   Menu structure of paint program.

```
void right_menu(int id);                    /* menu callbacks */
void middle_menu(int id);
void color_menu(int id);
void pixel_menu(int id);
void fill_menu(int id);
int pick(int x, int y);                     /* mode-selection
                                               function */
```

We have used most of these functions in our previous examples; thus, the main function is similar to the main function in our other examples:

```
/* object types */

#define NULL 0
#define LINE 1
#define RECTANGLE 2
#define TRIANGLE  3
#define POINTS 4
#define TEXT 5

int main(int argc, char **argv)
{
    int c_menu, p_menu, f_menu;

    glutInit(&argc,argv);
    glutInitDisplayMode (GLUT_SINGLE | GLUT_RGB);
    glutCreateWindow("Paint");
    glutDisplayFunc(display);
    c_menu = glutCreateMenu(color_menu);
```

```
        glutAddMenuEntry("Red",1);
        glutAddMenuEntry("Green",2);
        glutAddMenuEntry("Blue",3);
        glutAddMenuEntry("Cyan",4);
        glutAddMenuEntry("Magenta",5);
        glutAddMenuEntry("Yellow",6);
        glutAddMenuEntry("White",7);
        glutAddMenuEntry("Black",8);
        p_menu = glutCreateMenu(pixel_menu);
        glutAddMenuEntry("increase pixel size", 1);
        glutAddMenuEntry("decrease pixel size", 2);
        f_menu = glutCreateMenu(fill_menu);
        glutAddMenuEntry("fill on", 1);
        glutAddMenuEntry("fill off", 2);
        glutCreateMenu(right_menu);
        glutAddMenuEntry("quit",1);
        glutAddMenuEntry("clear",2);
        glutAttachMenu(GLUT_RIGHT_BUTTON);
        glutCreateMenu(middle_menu);
        glutAddSubMenu("Colors", c_menu);
        glutAddSubMenu("Pixel size", p_menu);
        glutAddSubMenu("Fill", f_menu);
        glutAttachMenu(GLUT_MIDDLE_BUTTON);
        myinit ();
        glutReshapeFunc (myReshape);
        glutMouseFunc (mouse);
        glutKeyboardFunc(key);
        glutMainLoop();
}

void display()
{
   glClear(GL_COLOR_BUFFER_BIT);
}
```

The function myinit clears the window, sets up global variables, and defines and compiles display lists for 128 characters.

```
void myinit()
{
/* set up a font in display list */
        int i;
        base = glGenLists(128);
        for(i=0;i<128;i++)
        {
                glNewList(base+i, GL_COMPILE);
                glutBitmapCharacter(GLUT_BITMAP_9_BY_15, i);
                glEndList();
        }
```

```
        glListBase(base);

        glViewport(0,0,ww,wh);

/* set clear color to white */

        glClearColor (1.0, 1.0, 1.0, 1.0);
}
```

The function display clears the window, sets the background to white, and then draws the buttons. The buttons are drawn as rectangles with sides that are 10 percent of the window height and width; they thus change size when the window is resized. Otherwise, the code here draws only simple primitives. The function myReshape is similar to the reshape callback that we introduced in Section 3.5.

```
void myReshape(GLsizei w, GLsizei h)
{

    /* pick 2D clipping window to match size of display window. */

    glMatrixMode(GL_PROJECTION);
    glLoadIdentity();
    gluOrtho2D(0.0, (GLdouble)w, 0.0, (GLdouble)h);
    glMatrixMode(GL_MODELVIEW);

    /* adjust viewport and clear */

    glViewport(0,0,w,h);

    /* save new window size in global variables */

    ww=w;
    wh=h;
}
```

The function pick detects which object on the screen has been selected by the mouse and thus works in conjunction with the mouse callback function mouse. When we are interested in only rectangular areas of the screen, such as the drawing area and the buttons, it is simpler to implement our own pick method within the application program rather than use selection mode picking.

Our procedure works as follows. Once a mouse event is detected, mouse uses pick to identify on which part of the screen the mouse is located. Because the buttons are rectangular boxes, we can detect directly whether the mouse is inside a button or in the drawing area; we return this information to mouse, which then does most of the work of drawing. Once an area has been identified by means of pick, the code chooses a proper mode, and determines whether it needs to output a primitive or to store the mouse location. For example, if the user indicated a triangle by first clicking on the appropriate button, the program must store two positions; then, when it receives the third position, it can draw the triangle. The appropriate code in mouse is

```
case (TRIANGLE):        /* pick detected click in triangle box */
    switch(count)       /* switch on number of vertices */
    {
      case(0):          /* store first vertex */
        count++;
        xp[0] = x;
        yp[0] = y;
        break;
      case(1):          /* store second vertex */
        count++;
        xp[1] = x;
        yp[1] = y;
        break;
      case(2):          /* third vertex: draw triangle */
        if(fill) glBegin(GL_POLYGON);
        else
        {
           glBegin(GL_LINE_LOOP);
           glVertex2i(xp[0],wh-yp[0]);
           glVertex2i(xp[1],wh-yp[1]);
           glVertex2i(x,wh-y);
           glEnd();
        }
        draw_mode=0;  /* reset mode */
        count=0;
        break;
    }
```

Note that the first mouse click selects triangle mode; subsequent clicks count and store vertices. However, if another mouse button is clicked on before the third vertex is selected, a new object is selected and drawn.

The function key renders characters entered from the keyboard to characters on the display:

```
void key(unsigned char k, int xx, int yy)
{
   if(draw_mode!=TEXT) return; /* draw characters until
                                      mode changes */
   glRasterPos2i(rx,ry);
   glCallList(k);  /* display list for character k */
}
```

A typical display from the middle of a drawing is shown in Figure 3.21. Although our paint program is simple and limited in the facilities that it provides

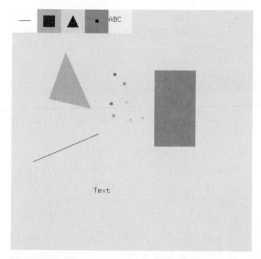

FIGURE 3.21 Output from painting program.

the user, we should be able to add more functionality easily. Straightforward exercises include adding the ability to switch from raster to stroke text, allowing multiple fonts, adding line attributes (width and type), allowing selection of fill methods (solid or patterns), and adding more objects (arbitrary polygons, circle approximations, and curves). However, making the paint program function as smoothly as commercial products do is much more difficult (although possible) for reasons that we discuss in Section 3.9.

The complete program is given in Appendix A.

3.9 Building Interactive Models

One of the many things missing from our paint program is the ability to save, manipulate, and even destroy the objects that we create interactively. Let's examine an approach that can be combined with the paint program but adds display lists and the idea of instancing.

Suppose that we want to build a complex image using a set of predefined building blocks. For the paint program, these can be simple geometric shapes. For an application such as interior design, the building blocks might consist of chairs, tables, and other household items. For circuit design, the objects might include resistors, capacitors, and voltage sources. Each occurrence of one of the basic items is known as an **instance**. In Chapter 4, we shall combine instancing with transformations, but here it will suffice to place objects directly into our scene.

Let's start with a few simple building blocks similar to the ones that we used in the paint program: an equilateral triangle, a square, a horizontal line segment, and a vertical line segment. For now, we can assume that each is defined with a simple size and centered at the origin. We can also assume that each is specified through some OpenGL code, such as

```
void square(float x0, float y0))
{
  glBegin(GL_QUAD);
    glVertex2f(x0-1.0, y0-1.0);
    glVertex2f(x0+1.0, y0-1.0);
    glVertex2f(x0+1.0, y0+1.0);
    glVertex2f(x0-1.0, y0+1.0);
  glEnd();
}
```

which draws a square centered at $(x0, y0)$. We can get the interactivity through the menus and picking as with the paint program; the user selects the desired item and then clicks the mouse where she would like it placed, which gives us the required $(x0, y0)$. The difference now is that we want to store the objects for later manipulation or even save the scene in a file.

First, we create a structure to hold the information needed to draw a single simple object

```
typedef struct object
{
    int type;
    float x, y;
    float color[3];
} object;
```

Here the structure contains room for an object type, the location of the center of the object, and its color. We reserve the type 0 to mean that an object no longer exists or alternately exists but should not be rendered. We can then store a set of 100 objects through an array called an **instance table**,

```
object table[100];
```

and an index to the last object in the list,

```
int last_object;
```

Adding objects to the table is simple. Suppose that the user indicates a square, to which we can assign type SQUARE:

```
#define SQUARE 1;
```

Once the user uses the menus to indicate the object type and its color and then uses the mouse to indicate where to place the object, the code to enter this information in the table looks something like

```
table[last_object].type = SQUARE;
table[last_object].x = x0;
table[last_object].y = y0;
table[last_object].color[0] = red;
table[last_object].color[1] = green;
table[last_object].color[2] = blue;
last_object++;
```

Now, whenever we want to display all the objects, we execute code such as

```
for(i=0; i<last_object; i++)
{
  switch(table[i].type)
  {
    case 0: break;
    case 1:
      {
      glColor3fv(table[i].color);
      triangle(table[i].x, table[i].y);
      break;
      }
      /* other types */
  }
}
```

So far, all is simple, but now let's consider how we might edit the table interactively to eliminate objects. We can use one of the picking methods discussed in this chapter to allow the user to identify an object that she wants to eliminate. Perhaps the simplest method to implement uses bounding boxes as in the paint program. We can start the implementation by adding two locations to the object structure that define the lower-left and upper-right corners of the bounding box:

```
/* in struct defintion */
float bb[2][2];
```

Thus when the user specifies a square, we add the code

```
bb[0][0] = x0-1,0;
bb[0][1] = y0-1,0;
bb[1][1] = x0+1,0;
bb[1][1] = y0+1,0;
```

Now suppose that the user has indicated through a menu that she wishes to eliminate an object and uses the mouse to locate the object. The program can now search the table for the first object whose bounding box contains the object and set the type of this object to zero. Hence, the next time that the display process goes through the instance table, that object will not be displayed.

Although this strategy will work if there are never more objects defined than can be contained in an array of a predetermined size, such might not always be the case. A better data structure will help. A simple exercise (see Exercise 3.26) is to implement the instance table with a linked list of objects. Each new object would add an element to the list, whereas deleting an object would require searching the list and then deleting the corresponding element from the list.

Our structure for storing each object can be expanded to allow for many other options. For example, we can add a size parameter that allows the user to expand or contract each object. We can add other structure members for other attributes besides color.

Another option (Exercise 3.27) would be to use display lists to store multiple objects and to increase the efficiency of the rendering. For example, we could add a menu to initiate and end a display list. As objects are created on the screen, pointers to them are placed in the display list. However, because OpenGL display lists can only be deleted and not edited, if we create a display list with multiple objects, the only available deletion operation is to delete the entire display list.

3.10 Animating Interactive Programs

So far, our programs have been static; once a primitive was placed on the display, its image did not change until the screen was cleared. Suppose that we want to create a picture in which one or more objects are changing or moving and thus their images must change. For example, we might want to have an animated character walk across the display, or we might want to move the viewer over time. We can gain insight into how we can handle these cases through a simple example in which we have a single rotating object.

3.10.1 The Rotating Square

Consider a two-dimensional point where

$$x = \cos \theta,$$

$$y = \sin \theta.$$

This point lies on a unit circle regardless of the value of θ. The three points $(-\sin \theta, \cos \theta)$, $(-\cos \theta, -\sin \theta)$, and $(\sin \theta, -\cos \theta)$ also lie on the unit circle. These four points are equidistant along the circumference of the circle, as shown in Figure 3.22. Thus, if we connect the points to form a polygon, we will have a square centered at the origin whose sides are of length $\sqrt{2}$.

Assuming that the value of θ is a global variable, we can display this cube with the display function

```
void display()
{
  glClear(GL_COLOR_BUFFER_BIT);
```

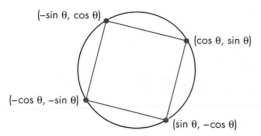

FIGURE 3.22   Square constructed from four points on a circle.

```
glBegin(GL_POLYGON);
  thetar = theta/(3.14159/180.0); /* convert degrees to radians */
  glVertex2f(cos(thetar), sin(thetar));
  glVertex2f(-sin(thetar), cos(thetar));
  glVertex2f(-cos(thetar), -sin(thetar));
  glVertex2f(sin(thetar), -cos(thetar));
glFnd();
}
```

Our display function will work for any value of θ, but suppose that we change θ as the program is running, thus rotating the square about the origin. We can display the rotated cube by simply reexecuting the display function through a call to `glutPostRedisplay`.

Now suppose that we want to increase θ by a fixed amount whenever nothing else is happening. We can use the idle callback for this operation. Thus, in our main program, we register the idle callback

```
glutIdleFunc(idle);
```

and define the function as

```
void idle()
{
  theta+=2; /* or some other amount */
  if(theta >= 360.0 theta-=360.0;
  glutPostRedisplay();
}
```

This program will work, but we want to make one further change: We would like to be able to turn on and turn off the rotation feature. We can accomplish this change by using the mouse function to change the idle function. We identify the mouse callback as

```
glutMouseFunc(mouse);
```

Then this function can be written as

```
void mouse(int button, int state, int x, int y)
{
  if(button==GLUT_LEFT_BUTTON&&state==GLUT_DOWN)
      glutIdleFunc(idle);
  if(button==GLUT_MIDDLE_BUTTON&&state=GLUT_DOWN)
      glutIdleFunc(NULL);
}
```

Thus, the left mouse button starts the cube rotating, and the middle mouse button stops the rotation. We call the full program single_double.c; it is given in Appendix A. If you run the program, the display probably will not look like a rotating square. Rather, you will see parts of squares changing over time. What went wrong? We consider this question next.

3.10.2 Double Buffering

When we redisplay the contents of our frame buffer, we want to do so at a rate sufficiently high that we cannot notice the clearing and redrawing of the screen. Most monitors must be refreshed at a rate between 60 and 85 times per second or we will notice the display flickering. As long as the contents of the frame buffer are unchanged and we refresh at the 60- to 85-Hz rate, we should not notice the refresh taking place.[7] However, if we change the contents of the frame buffer during a refresh, we may see undesirable artifacts of how we generate the display.

One manifestation of this problem occurs if the display being drawn is complex and cannot be drawn in a single refresh cycle. In this case, we see different parts of objects on successive refreshes. If an object is moving, its image may be distorted on the display. Another example occurs with the repetitive clearing and redrawing of an area of the screen, as occurs in our rotating-square program. Even though the square is a simple object and is rendered in a refresh cycle, in our program there is no coupling between when new squares are drawn into the frame buffer and when the frame buffer is redisplayed by the hardware. Thus, depending on exactly when the frame buffer is displayed, only part of the square may be in this buffer.

Double buffering provides a solution to these problems. Suppose that we have two color buffers at our disposal, conventionally called the front and back buffers. The **front buffer** is always the one displayed, whereas the **back buffer** is the one into which we draw. We can swap the front and back buffers at will from the application program. Only when the program issues an explicit function call are the buffers swapped. The buffer-swap function using GLUT is

```
glutSwapBuffers();
```

---

7. If the display is interlaced, the odd and even lines in the frame buffer are displayed alternately, giving a true refresh rate of one-half of the specified rate. On such displays, you probably will notice the slight shifts of objects up and down on alternate refresh cycles.

We set up double buffering by using the option GLUT_DOUBLE, instead of GLUT_SINGLE in glutInitDisplayMode. Hence, if we put our rendering into the display callback, the effect will be to update the back buffer. When the rendering is done, we execute glutSwapBuffers and the results will be displayed, thus guaranteeing a smooth display, even if it takes multiple refresh cycles to render the image into the frame buffer. Within the display callback, the first step is to clear the back buffer through glClear, and the final step is to invoke glutSwapBuffers.

Double buffering is standard in animation, where the primitives, attributes, and viewing conditions may change continuously. For our rotating square, we have to make two small changes to go from single to double buffering. First, we request a double buffered display in our main function by

```
glutInitDisplayMode(GLUT_RGB | GLUT_DOUBLE);
```

In our display function, we add the line

```
glutSwapBuffers();
```

after we have finished drawing our cube.

Double buffering does not solve all problems that we encounter with animated displays. If the display is complex, we still may need multiple frames to draw the image into the frame buffer. Double buffering does not speed up this process; it only ensures that we never see a partial display. However, we are often able to have visibly acceptable displays at rates as low as 10 to 20 frames per second if we use double buffering.

With fast GPUs that can display tens of millions of polygons per second, unless we have a very large number of primitives, the graphics system can render the full data set multiple times in a single refresh cycle. Visually, such displays are too fast for many applications. Most graphics processors now allow the user to synchronize the swapping of the buffers with the video frame rate.

There are other problems that arise in interactive programming that cannot be solved with double buffering alone. With interactive programs, such as the paint program, in which primitives can be defined outside of the display callback, we may want to render objects into more than one buffer.

The front and back buffers are color buffers that hold information that can be displayed on the screen. Normally, when we use double buffering, we would like OpenGL to draw into the back buffer, but we can control which color buffer is used for drawing through the function glDrawBuffer(). The default, when double buffering has been enabled, is equivalent to

```
glDrawBuffer(GL_BACK);
```

If we use

```
glDrawBuffer(GL_FRONT_AND_BACK);
```

primitives will be rendered into both the front and back buffers. In Chapter 8, we shall introduce other buffers that can be used to create new effects by writing into them instead of the back buffer.

3.10.3   Using a Timer

Before leaving the topic of rendering a smooth display, we want to consider the converse problem to having more primitives than can be rendered in one refresh cycle. Modern GPUs can render tens of millions of primitives per second, a number that is far higher than is needed in many applications. Consider what happens if we take a simple program such as the rotating cube and execute on a fast GPU. Whether or not we use double buffering, the cube will be rendered thousands of times per second and we will see a blur on the display. Not only is such a display fairly useless, we would like to control the speed of the rotation.

There are at least three approaches to the problem. We could use various timing mechanisms provided by libraries or the operating system to put delays into the application program. Another approach is provided by many commodity cards that allow the user to set an option under which swapping of buffers is locked to the refresh rate.

GLUT provides a third option through the timer function

```
glutTimerFunc(int delay, void (*timer_func)(int), int value)
```

Execution of this function starts a timer in the event loop that delays the event loop for delay milliseconds. When the timer has counted down the callback, the function time_func is executed. The value parameter allows us to pass a variable into the timer callback. A standard way to use the timer callback is to initiate a new timer by calling glutTimer. Because GLUT allows only a single timer, using this recursive mechanism allows the program to execute the display callback at a fixed rate. Thus, suppose that we have a simple program such as the rotating cube and can neglect the time it takes to render the primitives. If we want it to execute at n frames per second, we can set the timer by registering the callback

```
int n = 60; /* desired frame rate */
glutTimerFunc(100, myTimer, n);
```

in main and then define the callback by

```
void myTimer(int v)
{
  glutPostRedisplay);
  glutTimerFunc(1000/n, myTimer, v);
}
```

3.11 Design of Interactive Programs

Defining what characterizes a good interactive program is difficult, but recognizing and appreciating a good interactive program is easy. Such programs include features such as these:

1. A smooth display, showing neither flicker nor any artifacts of the refresh process
2. A variety of interactive devices on the display
3. A variety of methods for entering and displaying information
4. An easy-to-use interface that does not require substantial effort to learn
5. Feedback to the user
6. Tolerance for user errors
7. A design that incorporates consideration of both the visual and motor properties of the human

The importance of these features and the difficulty of designing a good interactive program should never be underestimated. The field of human–computer interaction (HCI) is an active one, and we shall not shortchange you by condensing it into a few pages. Our concern in this book is computer graphics; within this topic, our primary interest is rendering. However, there are a few topics common to computer graphics and HCI that we can pursue to improve our interactive programs.

3.11.1 Toolkits, Widgets, and the Frame Buffer

In our paint program, we have used interactive tools, such as pop-up menus, that were provided by GLUT, and graphical buttons that we constructed in our programs. There are many more possibilities, such as slidebars, dials, hot areas of the screen, sound, and icons. Usually, these tools are supplied with various toolkits, although there is nothing to prevent us from writing our own. In general, these toolkits use callbacks to interface with application programs and should be a simple extension of our development.

However, the simple model of rendering geometric objects into a color buffer is not sufficient to support many of these operations. Two examples illustrate the limitations of geometric rendering and show why, at times, we need to work directly in the frame buffer. First, consider our pop-up menus. When a menu callback is invoked, the menu appears over whatever was on the display. After we make our selection, the menu disappears and the screen is restored to the state in which it was before the menu was displayed.

Our second example is **rubberbanding**, a technique used for displaying line segments (and other primitives) that change as they are manipulated interactively. In our painting program, we indicated the endpoints of our desired line segment by two successive mouse locations. We did not have a mechanism for ensuring that any particular relationship would hold between these two locations, and we were not able to interact with the display to help us place the points. Suppose

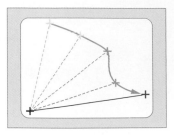

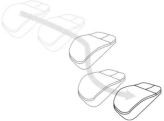

FIGURE 3.23 Rubberband line.

that after we locate the first point, as we move the mouse, a line segment is drawn automatically (and is updated on each refresh) from the first location to the present position of the mouse, as shown in Figure 3.23. This proccss is called **rubberbanding** because the line segment that we see on the display appears to be an elastic band, with one end fixed to the first location and the second end stretched to wherever the cursor moves. Note that before each new line segment appears, the previous line segment must be erased. Usually, the rubberbanding begins when a mouse button is depressed and continues until the button is released, at which time a final line segment is drawn.

We cannot implement this sequence of operations using only what we have presented so far. One way to implement these operations is to store the part of the display under the menu (or line) and to copy it back when the menu (or line) is no longer needed. Unfortunately, this description of what we want to do is in terms of what bits are on the display or, equivalently, of what is contained in the frame buffer. One potential solution does not involve primitives in the application program; it involves only their scan-converted images. Consequently, a set of operations for implementing such operations should be described in terms of the contents of the frame buffer—that is, in terms of blocks of bits with what are called bit-block-transfer (bitblt) operations. We can take this approach once we have discussed bits and pixels in Chapter 8. There is another approach, supported by most OpenGL implementations that can provide many of these capabilities in a simple manner that we shall explore next.

3.12 Logic Operations

When a program specifies a primitive that is visible, OpenGL renders it into a set of colored pixels that are written into the present drawing buffer. In the default mode of operation, these pixels simply replace the corresponding pixels that are already in the frame buffer. Thus, if we start with a color buffer that has been cleared to black and draw a blue rectangle that is 10×10 pixels, then 100 blue pixels are copied into the color buffer, replacing 100 black pixels. In this mode, called **copy, or replacement, mode**, it does not matter what color the original pixels under the rectangle were before they were colored blue, because the blue pixels replace pixels of any color that were there. Although this mode of writing into a buffer may seem obvious, it is not the only way to do the write operation.

Consider the model in Figure 3.24, where we consider the writing of a single pixel into a color buffer. The pixel that we want to write is called the **source pixel**. The pixel in the drawing buffer that the source pixel will affect is called the **destination pixel**. In copy mode, the source pixel replaces the destination pixel. But suppose that the implementation can first look at the destination pixel and use its value in combination with the source pixel to determine the value to place in the color buffer.

Although we could pick the function that combines the source and destination pixels in an infinite number of ways, most hardware supports only limited ways

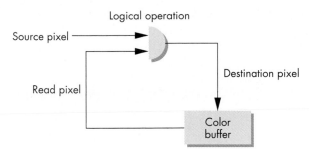

FIGURE 3.24 Pixel-writing model.

to combine source and destination pixels. In this chapter, we consider bitwise operations between the pixels. When we consider blending in Chapter 8, we shall introduce other options. There are 16 possible functions between two bits. Each defines a **writing mode**. We shall discuss these modes in more detail in Chapter 7. At this point, we are interested in two of these functions. The first is replacement mode, in which each bit in the source pixel replaces the corresponding bit in the destination pixel.

The other mode is the **exclusive OR** or **XOR mode** in which corresponding bits in each pixel are combined using the exclusive or logical operation. If s and d are corresponding bits in the source and destination pixels, we can denote the new destination bit as d', and it is given by

$$d' = d \oplus s,$$

where $\oplus$ denotes the XOR operation. The most interesting property of the XOR operation is that if we apply it twice, we return to the original state. That is,

$$d = (d \oplus s) \oplus s.$$

Thus, if we draw something in XOR mode, we can erase it by simply drawing it a second time.

OpenGL supports all 16 logic modes. Copy mode (GL_COPY) is the default. If we wish to change modes, we must enable logic operations:

    glEnable(GL_COLOR_LOGIC_OP);

and change to XOR mode when desired by

    glLogicOp(GL_XOR);

3.12.1 Drawing Erasable Lines

Using the XOR drawing mode, we can draw erasable lines in a variety of ways. Here is one simple method. Suppose that the OpenGL window is 500×500 pixels and the clipping window is a unit square with the origin at the lower-left corner. We use the mouse to get the first endpoint and store this point in world coordinates

```
xm = x/500.;
ym = (500-y)/500.;
```

We then can get the second point and draw a line segment in XOR mode:

```
xmm = x/500.;
ymm = (500-y)/500.;
glLogicOp(GL_XOR);
glBegin(GL_LINES);
    glVertex2f(xm, ym);
    glVertex2f(xmm, ymm);
glLogicOp(GL_COPY);
glEnd();
glFlush();
```

We switch back to copy mode in case we want to draw other objects in the normal mode. If we enter another point with the mouse, we first draw the same line in XOR mode and then a second line using the first endpoint and the mouse input

```
glLogicOp(GL_XOR);
glBegin(GL_LINES);
    glVertex2f(xm, ym);
    glVertex2f(xmm, ymm);
glEnd();
glFlush();
xmm = x/500.0;
ymm = (500-y)/500.0;
glBegin(GL_LINES);
    glVertex2f(xm, ym);
    glVertex2f(xmm, ymm);
glEnd();
glLogicOp(GL_COPY);
glFlush();
```

We can sequence these operations by using the right mouse button to enter these data and the left mouse button to indicate that we accept the line segment and wish to draw it in its final form

```
glLogicOp(GL_COPY);
glBegin(GL_LINES);
    glVertex2f(xm, ym);
    glVertex2f(xmm, ymm);
glEnd();
glFlush();
glLogicOp(GL_XOR);
```

We can keep track of vertices by adding a counter, as in the paint program, to store which endpoint is expected next.

This example is not quite a rubberband line, which is drawn continuously as the user moves the mouse. We can get a rubberband line by using the same operations in conjunction with a motion callback. Thus, when the user first depresses a designated mouse button, the first location is saved through the mouse callback. As the mouse moves with the key depressed, line segments are drawn from the first point to a second point determined through the motion callback, first redrawing the previous line segment each time to erase it. When the mouse button is released, a final line segment is drawn in copy mode from the mouse callback. We use the mouse callback to get the first corner when the left mouse button is first depressed. Then as long as the mouse button is held down and the mouse is moved, we use the motion callback to get successive values for the second corner. The first time we draw a single rectangle in XOR mode. After that, each time that we get a vertex, we first erase the existing rectangle by redrawing, then draw a new rectangle using the new vertex. Finally, when the mouse button is released, the mouse callback is executed once again. We then do a final erase and draw, and go back to replacement mode.

Note that we must define the counter and the corners of the rectangle as globals:

```
float xm, ym, xmm, ymm; /* the corners of the rectangle */
int first = 0; /* vertex the counter */
```

The callbacks are registered as

```
glutMouseFunc(mouse);
glutMotionFunc(move);
```

Here is the code for the callbacks:

```
void mouse(int btn, int state, int x, int y)
{

    if(btn==GLUT_LEFT_BUTTON && state == GLUT_DOWN)
    {
        xm = x/500.;
        ym = (500-y)/500.;
        glColor3f(0.0, 0.0, 1.0);
        glLogicOp(GL_XOR);
        first = 0;
    }
    if(btn==GLUT_LEFT_BUTTON && state == GLUT_UP)
    {
        glRectf(xm, ym, xmm, ymm);
        glFlush();
        glColor3f(0.0, 1.0, 0.0);
```

```
            glLogicOp(GL_COPY);
            xmm = x/500.0;
            ymm = (500-y)/500.0;
            glLogicOp(GL_COPY);
            glRectf(xm, ym, xmm, ymm);
            glFlush();
        }
}

void move(int x, int y)
{
    if( first == 1)
    {
        glRectf(xm, ym, xmm, ymm);
        glFlush();
    }
    xmm = x/500.0;
    ymm = (500-y)/500.0;
    glRectf(xm, ym, xmm, ymm);
    glFlush();
    first = 1;
}
```

3.12.2   XOR and Color

If you run our previous example, you should notice some odd color combinations where the temporary lines are drawn over pixels that have already been colored. In the example, we used blue for the temporary color as we did the rubberbanding and green for the final color. Suppose that we are using a system that stores color components to eight bits so that blue is stored as the 24-bit RGB values (00000000, 00000000, 11111111). Suppose that the screen is cleared to white or (11111111, 11111111, 11111111). Then when we draw the blue line using XOR mode, we will see a line in the RGB color (11111111, 11111111, 00000000) or yellow, rather than blue, because the XOR operation is applied bitwise. If the line crosses a red object, it will be colored magenta inside the object. These possibly annoying visual effects are a consequence of our use of the XOR write mode and should make it clear why a final drawing using copy mode is required.

Another common use of the XOR mode is for drawing a cursor on the display. Cursors can be small rectangles, small crosses, or other shapes. Often in CAD programs, we use crosshairs, two perpendicular lines that can extend to rulers on the edge of the display. If these objects are drawn in XOR mode, then we can move them around the screen without distorting anything else on the display. However, if there are objects on the display, the color of the objects under the cursor will be altered as the cursor moves across them.

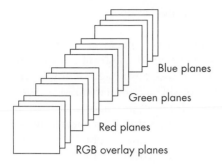

FIGURE 3.25   Color buffer with overlay planes.

3.12.3   Cursors and Overlay Planes

Rubberbanding and cursors can place a significant burden on graphics systems as they require the display to be updated constantly. Although the use of XOR mode appears to simplify the process, XOR requires the system to read the present destination pixels before computing the new destination pixels. These operations are slower than simply copying source pixels to the frame buffer.

An alternative is to provide hardware support for these types of interaction by providing extra bits in the color buffers by adding what are called **overlay planes**. Thus, a typical color buffer, as depicted in Figure 3.25, may have 8 bits for each of red, green, and blue and one red, one green, and one blue overlay plane.

The contents of the overlay planes are independent of what is in the color buffer. In addition, when the color buffer and overlay planes are displayed, the contents of the overlay planes act as if their values were copied into the color buffer. In other words, if there is a bit set in the red overlay plane and the corresponding bits in the blue and green overlay planes are not set, the corresponding point in the window will be red, regardless of what is in the matching 24 bits of the RGB-color buffer.

Overlay planes are a hardware feature and are not present in all systems. GLUT provides support for overlay planes if they are supported by the hardware.

Summary and Notes

In this chapter, we have touched on a number of topics related to interactive computer graphics. These interactive aspects make the field of computer graphics exciting and fun. Although our API, OpenGL, is independent of any operating or window system, we recognize that any program must have at least minimal interaction with the rest of the computer system. We handled simple interactions by using a simple toolkit, GLUT, whose API provides the necessary additional functionality, without being dependent on a particular operating or window system.

We have been heavily influenced by the client–server perspective. Not only does it allow us to develop programs within a networked environment but also to design programs that are portable yet can still take advantage of any special features available in the hardware. These concepts will be crucial in our discussion of object-oriented graphics and graphics for the Internet in Chapter 10.

From the application programmer's perspective, various characteristics of interactive graphics are shared by most systems. We see the graphics part of the system as a server, consisting of a raster display, a keyboard, and a pointing device. In almost all workstations, we have to work within a multiprocessing, windowed environment. Most likely, many processes are executing concurrently with the execution of your graphics program. However, the window system allows us to write programs for a specific window that act as though that window were the display device of a single-user system.

The overhead of setting up a program to run in this environment is small. Each application program contains a set of function calls that is virtually the same in every program. The use of logical devices within the application program frees the programmer from worrying about the details of particular hardware.

Within the environment that we have described, event-mode input is the norm. Although the other forms are available—request mode is the normal method used for keyboard input—event-mode input gives us far more flexibility in the design of interactive programs.

The speed of the latest generation of graphics processors not only allows us to carry out interactive applications that were not possible even a few years ago but also makes us rethink (as we should periodically) whether the techniques we have been using are still the best ones. For example, while hardware features such as logical operations and overlay planes made possible many interactive techniques, now with a fast GPU we can often simply draw the entire display fast enough that these features are no longer necessary.

Interactive computer graphics is a powerful tool with unlimited applications. At this point, you should be able to write fairly sophisticated interactive programs. Probably the most helpful exercise that you can do now is to write one. The exercises at the end of the chapter provide suggestions.

Suggested Readings

Many of the conceptual foundations for the windows-icons-menus-pointing interfaces that we now consider routine were developed at the Xerox Palo Alto Research Center (PARC) during the 1970s (see [Sch97]). The mouse also was developed there [Eng68]. The familiar interfaces of today—such as the Macintosh Operating System, the X Window System, and Microsoft Windows—all have their basis in this work.

The volume by Foley and associates [Fol94] contains a thorough description of the development of user interfaces with an emphasis on the graphical aspects. The books by Schneiderman [Sch97] and Nielson [Nie94] provide an introduction to HCI.

The X Window System [Sch88] was developed at the Massachusetts Institute of Technology and is the de facto standard in the UNIX workstation community. Recently, the development of the LINUX version for PCs has allowed the X Window System to run on these platforms too.

The input and interaction modes that we discussed in this chapter grew out of the standards that led to GKS [ANSI85] and PHIGS [ANSI88]. These standards were developed for both calligraphic and raster displays; thus, they do not take advantage of the possibilities available on raster-only systems (see [Pik84] and [Gol83]).

Although we have used the GLUT toolkit [Kil94b] exclusively, we can also interface directly with the X Window System with various X Window toolkits [Kil94a, OSF89] and with Microsoft Windows. Also of interest is the use of scripting languages, such as tcl/tk [Ost94], to develop user interfaces that work with OpenGL. Additional details on GLUT are in the OpenGL Primer [Ang04]. Other interface toolkits are also available for OpenGL; see the OpenGL Web site, *www.opengl.org*. To end where we began, Sutherland's Sketchpad is described in [Sut63].

Exercises

3.1   Explain problems that you face in defining a stroke font. Create a simple data structure that will allow you to define a set of stroke characters using only line segments.

3.2   Rewrite the Sierpinski gasket program from Chapter 2 such that the left mouse button will start the generation of points on the screen, the right mouse button will halt the generation of new points, and the middle mouse button will terminate the program. Include a reshape callback.

3.3   Construct slidebars to allow users to define colors in the paint program. Your interface should let the user see a color before that color is used.

3.4   We can construct a virtual trackball from a mouse by mapping the mouse pad onto a ball. A major use of such a device is to allow the user to obtain velocities by using the mouse to "spin" the ball. Construct such a virtual device and write a graphical application to demonstrate its use.

3.5   Alter the square-drawing program (Section 3.5) to incorporate menus like those described in Section 3.6.

3.6   Add an elapsed-time indicator in the paint program (Section 3.8) using a clock of your own design.

3.7   Creating simple games is a good way to become familiar with interactive graphics programming. Program the game of checkers. You can look at each square as an object that can be picked by the user. You can start with a program in which the user plays both sides.

3.8   Write a program that allows a user to play a simple version of solitaire. First, design a simple set of cards using only our basic primitives. Your program can be written in terms of picking rectangular objects.

3.9   Simulating a pool or billiards game presents interesting problems. As in Exercise 2.18, you must compute trajectories and detect collisions. The interactive aspects include initiating movement of the balls via a graphical cue stick, ensuring that the display is smooth and creating a two-person game.

3.10   Rather than using buttons or menus to select options in an interactive program, we can make selections based on where in the window the mouse is located. Use this mechanism in the paint program (Section 3.8).

3.11   The mapping from a point in object or world coordinates to one in screen coordinates is well defined. It is not invertible because we go from three dimensions to two dimensions. Suppose, however, that we are working with a two-dimensional application. Is the mapping invertible? What problem can arise if you use a two-dimensional mapping to return to a position in object or world coordinates by a locator device?

3.12   How do the results of Exercise 3.11 apply to picking?

3.13   In a typical application program, the programmer must decide whether or not to use display lists. Consider at least two applications. For each, list at least two factors in favor and two against the use of display lists. Using the fonts provided by GLUT, test whether what you wrote down is correct in practice.

3.14   Write an interactive program that will allow you to guide a graphical rat through the maze you generated in Exercise 2.7. You can use the left and right buttons to turn the rat and the middle button to move him forward.

3.15   Add rubberband lines and rectangles to the paint program.

3.16   Inexpensive joysticks, such as those used in toys and games, often lack encoders and contain only a pair of three-position switches. How might such devices function?

3.17   The orientation of an airplane is described by a coordinate system oriented as shown in Figure 3.26. The forward–backward motion of the joystick controls the up–down rotation with respect to the axis running along the length of the airplane, called the **pitch**. The right–left motion of the joystick controls the rotation about this axis, called the **roll**. Write a program that uses the mouse to control pitch and roll for the view seen by a pilot. You can do this exercise in two dimensions by considering a

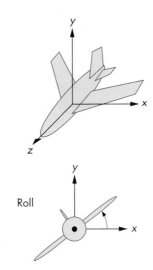

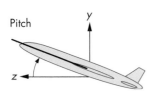

FIGURE 3.26   Airplane coordinate system.

set of objects to be located far from the airplane, then having the mouse control the two-dimensional viewing of these objects.

3.18 Consider a table with a two-dimensional sensing device located at the end of two linked arms, as shown in Figure 3.27. Suppose that the lengths of the two arms are fixed and the arms are connected by simple (1-degree-of-freedom) pivot joints. Determine the relationship between the joint angles θ and ϕ and the position of the sensor.

3.19 Suppose that a CRT has a square face of 40×40 centimeters and is refreshed in a noninterlaced manner at a rate of 60 Hz. Ten percent of the time that the system takes to draw each scan line is used to return the CRT beam from the right edge to the left edge of the screen (the horizontal-retrace time), and 10 percent of the total drawing time is allocated for the beam to return from the lower-right corner of the screen to the upper-left corner after each refresh is complete (the vertical-retrace time). Assume that the resolution of the display is 1024×1024 pixels. Find a relationship between the time at which a lightpen detects the beam and the lightpen's position. Give the result using both centimeters and screen coordinates for the location on the screen.

3.20 Circuit-layout programs are variants of paint programs. Consider the design of logical circuits using the Boolean AND, OR, and NOT functions. Each of these functions is provided by one of the three types of integrated circuits (gates), the symbols for which are shown in Figure 3.28. Write a program that allows the user to design a logical circuit by selecting gates from a menu and positioning them on the screen. Consider methods for connecting the outputs of one gate to the inputs of others.

3.21 Extend Exercise 3.20 to allow the user to specify a sequence of input signals. Have the program display the resulting values at selected points in the circuit.

3.22 Extend Exercise 3.20 to have the user enter a logical expression. Have the program generate a logical diagram from that expression.

3.23 Use the methods of Exercise 3.20 to form flowcharts for programs or images of graphs that you have studied in a data-structures class.

3.24 Plotting packages offer a variety of methods for displaying data. Write an interactive plotting application for two-dimensional curves. Your application should allow the user to choose the mode (polyline display of the data, bar chart, or pie chart), colors, and line styles.

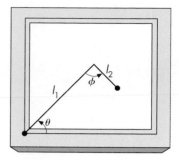

FIGURE 3.27 Two-dimensional sensing arm.

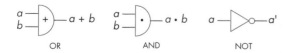

FIGURE 3.28 Symbols for logical circuits.

3.25 The required refresh rate for CRT displays of 50 to 85 Hz is based on the use of short-persistence phosphors that emit light for extremely short intervals when excited. Long-persistence phosphors are available. Why are long-persistence phosphors not used in most workstation displays? In what types of applications might such phosphors be useful?

3.26 Write a paint program such as that described in Section 3.9 using a linked list rather than an array to store the objects. Your program should allow the user to both add and delete objects interactively.

3.27 Redo the paint program using display lists to store objects.

GEOMETRIC OBJECTS AND TRANSFORMATIONS

We are now ready to concentrate on three-dimensional graphics. Much of this chapter is concerned with such matters as how to represent basic geometric types, how to convert between various representations, and what statements we can make about geometric objects independent of a particular representation.

We begin with an examination of the mathematical underpinnings of computer graphics. This approach should avoid much of the confusion that arises from a lack of care in distinguishing among a geometric entity, its representation in a particular reference system, and a mathematical abstraction of it.

We use the notions of affine and Euclidean vector spaces to create the necessary mathematical foundation for later work. One of our goals is to establish a method for dealing with geometric problems that is independent of coordinate systems. The advantages of such an approach will be clear when we worry about how to represent the geometric objects with which we would like to work. The coordinate-free approach will prove to be far more robust than one based on representing the objects in a particular coordinate system or frame. This coordinate-free approach also leads to the use of homogeneous coordinates, a system that not only enables us to explain this approach, but also leads to efficient implementation techniques.

We use the terminology of abstract data types to reinforce the distinction between an object and its representation. Our development will show that the mathematics arise naturally from our desire to manipulate a few basic geometric data types. Much of what we present here is an application of vector spaces, geometry, and linear algebra. Appendices B and C cover the formalities of vector spaces and matrix algebra, respectively.

In a vein similar to the approach we took in Chapters 2 and 3, we develop a simple application program to illustrate the basic principles and to see how the concepts are realized within an API. In this chapter, our example is focused on the representation and transformations of a cube. We also consider how to specify transformations interactively and apply them smoothly.

4.1   Scalars, Points, and Vectors

In computer graphics, we work with sets of geometric objects, such as lines, polygons, and polyhedra. Such objects exist in a three-dimensional world and have properties that can be described by concepts such as length and angles. As we discovered working in two dimensions, we can define most geometric objects using a limited set of simple entities. These basic geometric objects and the relationships among them can be described using three fundamental types: scalars, points, and vectors.

Although we shall consider each type from a geometric perspective, each of these types also can be defined formally, as in Appendix B, as obeying a set of axioms. Although ultimately we will use the geometric instantiation of each type, we want to take great care in distinguishing between the abstract definition of each entity and any particular example, or implementation, of it. By taking care here, we can avoid many subtle pitfalls later. Although we shall work in three-dimensional spaces, virtually all our results will hold in n-dimensional spaces.

4.1.1   Geometric Objects

Our fundamental geometric object is a point. In a three-dimensional geometric system, a **point** is a position in space. The only property that a point possesses is that point's position; a mathematical point has neither a size nor a shape.

Points are useful in specifying geometric objects but are not sufficient by themselves. We need real numbers to specify quantities such as the distance between two points. Real numbers—and complex numbers which we shall use occasionally—are examples of **scalars**. Scalars are objects that obey a set of rules that are abstractions of the operations of ordinary arithmetic. Thus, addition and multiplication are defined and obey the usual rules such as commutivity and associativity. Every scalar has multiplicative and additive inverses, which implicitly define subtraction and division.

We need one additional type—the **vector**—to allow us to work with directions. Physicists and mathematicians use the term *vector* for any quantity with direction and magnitude. Physical quantities, such as velocity and force, are vectors. A vector does not, however, have a fixed position in space.

In computer graphics, we often connect points with directed line segments, as shown in Figure 4.1. A line segment has both magnitude—its length—and direction—its orientation—and thus is a vector. Because vectors have no fixed position, the directed line segments shown in Figure 4.2 are identical because they have the same direction and magnitude. We shall often use the terms *vector* and *directed line segment* synonymously.

Vectors can have their lengths changed by real numbers. Thus, in Figure 4.3(a), line segment A has the same direction as line segment B, but B has twice the length that A has, so we can write $B = 2A$. We can also combine directed line segments by the **head-to-tail rule**, as in Figure 4.3(b). Here, we connect the head of vector A to the tail of vector C to form a new vector D,

FIGURE 4.1   Directed line segment that connects points.

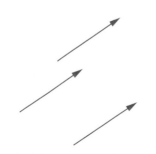

FIGURE 4.2   Identical vectors.

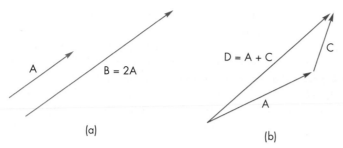

(a)

(b)

FIGURE 4.3   (a) Parallel line segments. (b) Addition of line segments.

whose magnitude and direction are determined by the line segment from the tail of A to the head of C. We can call this new vector, D, the **sum** of A and C and write $D = A + C$. Because vectors have no fixed positions, we can move any two vectors as necessary to form their sum graphically. Note that we have described two fundamental operations: the addition of two vectors and the multiplication of a vector by a scalar.

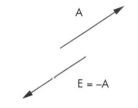

FIGURE 4.4   Inverse vectors.

If we consider two directed line segments, A and E in Figure 4.4, with the same length but opposite directions, their sum as defined by the head-to-tail addition has no length. This sum forms a special vector called the **zero vector**, which we denote **0**, that has a magnitude of zero. Because it has no length, the orientation of this vector is undefined. We say that E is the **inverse** of A and we can write $E = -A$. By similar reasoning, scalar-vector expressions such as $A + 2B - 3C$ make sense.

Although we can multiply a vector by a scalar to change its length, there are no obvious sensible operations between two points that produce another point. Nor are there operations between a point and a scalar that produce a point. There is, however, an operation between points and directed line segments (vectors), as is illustrated in Figure 4.5. We can use a directed line segment to move from one point to another. We call this operation **point-vector addition**, and it produces a new point. We can write this operation as $P = Q + v$. We see that the vector v displaces the point Q to the new location P.

FIGURE 4.5   Point-vector addition.

Looking at things slightly differently, any two points define a line segment or vector between them. We call this operation **point-point subtraction**, and we can write it as $v = P - Q$. Because vectors can be multiplied by scalars, some expressions involving scalars, vectors, and points make sense, such as $P + 3v$, or $2P - Q + 3v$, whereas others, such as $P + 3Q - v$, do not.

4.1.2   Coordinate-Free Geometry

Points exist in space regardless of any reference or coordinate system. Thus, we do not need a reference or coordinate system to define a point. This fact may seem counter to your experiences, but it is crucial to understanding geometry and how to build graphics systems. Consider the two-dimensional example in

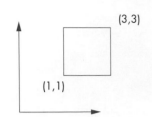

FIGURE 4.6 Object and coordinate system.

FIGURE 4.7 Object without coordinate system.

Figure 4.6. Here we see a coordinate system defined by two axes and a simple geometric object, a square. We can refer to the point at the lower-left corner of the square as having coordinates $(1,1)$ and note that the sides of the square are orthogonal to each other and that the point at $(3,1)$ is two units from the point at $(1,1)$. Now suppose that we remove the axes as in Figure 4.7. We can no longer specify where the points are. But those locations were relative to an arbitrary location and orientation of the original axes. What is more important is that the fundamental geometric relationships are preserved. The square is still a square; orthogonal lines are still orthogonal; distances between points remain the same.

Of course, we may find it inconvenient, at best, to refer to a specific point as "that point over there" or "the blue point to the right of the red one." Coordinate systems and frames (see Section 4.3) solve this reference problem, but for now we want to see just how far we can get following a coordinate-free approach that does not require an arbitrary reference system.

4.1.3 The Mathematical View: Vector and Affine Spaces

We can regard scalars, points, and vectors as members of mathematical sets; then we look at a variety of abstract spaces for representing and manipulating these sets of objects. Mathematicians have explored a variety of such spaces for applied problems, ranging from the solution of differential equations to the approximation of mathematical functions. The formal definitions of the spaces of interest to us—vector spaces, affine spaces, and Euclidean spaces—are given in Appendix B. We are concerned with only those examples in which the elements are geometric types.

We start with a set of scalars, any pair of which can be combined to form another scalar through two operations, called *addition* and *multiplication*. If these operations obey the closure, associativity, commutivity, and inverse properties described in Appendix B, the elements form a **scalar field**. Familiar examples of scalars include the real numbers, complex numbers, and rational functions.

Perhaps the most important mathematical space is the **(linear) vector space**. A vector space contains two distinct types of entities: vectors and scalars. In addition to the rules for combining scalars, within a vector space, we can combine scalars and vectors to form new vectors through **scalar–vector multiplication** and vectors with vectors through **vector–vector addition**. Examples of mathematical vector spaces include n-tuples of real numbers and the geometric operations on our directed line segments.

In a linear vector space, we do not necessarily have a way of measuring a scalar quantity. A **Euclidean space** is an extension of a vector space that adds a measure of size or distance and allows us to define such things as the length of a line segment.

An **affine space** is an extension of the vector space that includes an additional type of object: the point. Although there are no operations between two points or between a point and a scalar that yield points, there is an operation of *vector–*

point addition that produces a new point. Alternately, we can say there is an operation called *point–point subtraction* that produces a vector from two points. Examples of affine spaces include the geometric operations on points and directed line segments that we introduced in Section 4.1.1.

In these abstract spaces, objects can be defined independently of any particular representation; they are simply members of various sets. One of the major vector-space concepts is that of representing a vector in terms of one or more sets of basis vectors. Representation provides the tie between abstract objects and their implementation. Conversion between representations leads us to geometric transformations.

4.1.4 The Computer Science View

Although the mathematician may prefer to think of scalars, points, and vectors as members of sets that can be combined according to certain axioms, the computer scientist prefers to see them as **abstract data types** (**ADTs**). An ADT is a set of operations on data; the operations are defined independently of how the data are represented internally or of how the operations are implemented. The notion of *data abstraction* is fundamental to modern computer science. For example, the operation of adding an element to a list or of multiplying two polynomials can be defined independently of how the list is stored or of how real numbers are represented on a particular computer. People familiar with this concept should have no trouble distinguishing between objects (and operations on objects) and objects' representations (or implementations) in a particular system. From a computational point of view, we should be able to declare geometric objects through code such as

```
vector u,v;
point p,q;
scalar a,b;
```

regardless of the internal representation or implementation of the objects on a particular system. In object-oriented languages, such as C++, we can use language features, such as classes and overloading of operators, so we can write lines of code, such as

```
q = p+a*v;
```

using our geometric data types. Of course, first we must define functions that perform the necessary operations; so that we can write them, we must look at the mathematical functions that we wish to implement. First, we shall define our objects. Then we shall look to certain abstract mathematical spaces to help us with the operations among them.

4.1.5 Geometric ADTs

The three views of scalars, points, and vectors leave us with a mathematical and computational framework for working with our geometric entities. In summary, for computer graphics our scalars are the real numbers using ordinary addition and multiplication. Our geometric points are locations in space, and our vectors are directed line segments. These objects obey the rules of an affine space. We can also create the corresponding ADTs in a program.

Our next step is to show how we can use our types to perform geometrical operations and to form geometric objects. We shall use the following notation: Greek letters $\alpha, \beta, \gamma, \ldots$ denote scalars; upper-case letters $P, Q, R, \ldots$ define points; and lower-case letters $u, v, w, \ldots$ denote vectors. We have not as yet introduced any reference system, such as a coordinate system; thus, for vectors and points, this notation refers to the abstract objects, rather than to these objects' representations in a particular reference system. We use boldface letters for the latter in Section 4.3. The **magnitude** of a vector v is a real number denoted by $|v|$. The operation of vector–scalar multiplication (see Appendix B) has the property that

$$|\alpha v| = |\alpha||v|,$$

and the direction of αv is the same as the direction of v if α is positive and the opposite direction if α is negative.

We have two equivalent operations that relate points and vectors. First, there is the subtraction of two points, P and Q—an operation that yields a vector v denoted by

$$v = P - Q.$$

As a consequence of this operation, given any point Q and vector v, there is a unique point, P, that satisfies the preceding relationship. We can express this statement as follows: Given a point Q and a vector v, there is a point P such that

$$P = Q + v.$$

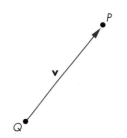

FIGURE 4.8 Point–point subtraction.

Thus, P is formed by a point–vector addition operation. Figure 4.8 shows a visual interpretation of this operation. The head-to-tail rule gives us a convenient way of visualizing vector–vector addition. We obtain the sum $u + v$ as shown in Figure 4.9(a) by drawing the sum vector as connecting the tail of u to the head of v. However, we can also use this visualization, as demonstrated in Figure 4.9(b), to show that for any three points P, Q, and R,

$$(P - Q) + (Q - R) = P - R.$$

4.1.6 Lines

The sum of a point and a vector (or the subtraction of two points) leads to the notion of a line in an affine space. Consider all points of the form

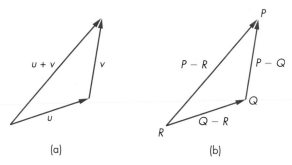

FIGURE 4.9   Use of the head-to-tail rule. (a) For vectors. (b) For points.

$$P(\alpha) = P_0 + \alpha d,$$

where P_0 is an arbitrary point, d is an arbitrary vector, and α is a scalar that can vary over some range of values. Given the rules for combining points, vectors, and scalars in an affine space, for any value of α, the function $P(\alpha)$ yields a point. For geometric vectors (directed line segments), these points lie on a line, as shown in Figure 4.10. This form is known as the **parametric form** of the line because we generate points on the line by varying the parameter α. For $\alpha = 0$, the line passes through the point P_0, and as α is increased, all the points generated lie in the direction of the vector d. If we restrict α to nonnegative values, we get the **ray** emanating from P_0 and going in the direction of d. Thus, a line is infinitely long in both directions, a line segment is a finite piece of a line between two points, and a ray is infinitely long in one direction.

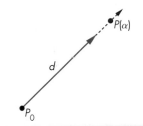

FIGURE 4.10   Line in an affine space.

4.1.7   Affine Sums

Whereas in an affine space the addition of two vectors, the multiplication of a vector by a scalar, and the addition of a vector and a point are defined, the addition of two arbitrary points and the multiplication of a point by a scalar are not. However, there is an operation called **affine addition** that has certain elements of these latter two operations. For any point Q, vector v, and positive scalar α,

$$P = Q + \alpha v$$

describes all points on the line from Q in the direction of v, as shown in Figure 4.11. However, we can always find a point R such that

$$v = R - Q;$$

thus

$$P = Q + \alpha(R - Q) = \alpha R + (1 - \alpha)Q.$$

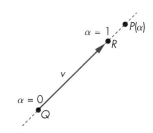

FIGURE 4.11   Affine addition.

This operation looks like the addition of two points and leads to the equivalent form

$$P = \alpha_1 R + \alpha_2 Q,$$

where

$$\alpha_1 + \alpha_2 = 1.$$

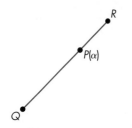

FIGURE 4.12   Line segment that connects two points.

4.1.8   Convexity

A **convex** object is one for which any point lying on the line segment connecting any two points in the object is also in the object. We saw the importance of convexity for polygons in Chapter 2. We can use affine sums to help us gain a deeper understanding of convexity. For $0 \leq \alpha \leq 1$, the affine sum defines the line segment connecting R and Q, as shown in Figure 4.12; thus, this line segment is a convex object. We can extend the affine sum to include objects defined by n points $P_1, P_2, \ldots, P_n$. Consider the form

$$P = \alpha_1 P_1 + \alpha_2 P_2 + \ldots + \alpha_n P_n.$$

We can show, by induction, that this sum is defined if and only if

$$\alpha_1 + \alpha_2 + \ldots + \alpha_n = 1.$$

The set of points formed by the affine sum of n points, under the additional restriction

$$\alpha_i \geq 0, \quad i = 1, 2, \ldots, n,$$

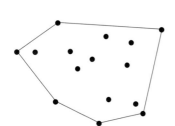

FIGURE 4.13   Convex hull.

is called the **convex hull** of the set of points (Figure 4.13). It is easy to verify that the convex hull includes all line segments connecting pairs of points in $\{P_1, P_2, \ldots, P_n\}$. Geometrically, the convex hull is the set of points that we form by stretching a tight-fitting surface over the given set of points—**shrink-wrapping** the points. It is the smallest convex object that includes the set of points. The notion of convexity is extremely important in the design of curves and surfaces; we return to it later in Chapter 11.

4.1.9   Dot and Cross Products

Many of the geometric concepts relating the orientation between two vectors are in terms of the **dot** (**inner**) and **cross** (**outer**) **products** of two vectors. The dot product of u and v is written $u \cdot v$ (see Appendix B). If $u \cdot v = 0$, u and v are said to be **orthogonal**. In a Euclidean space, the magnitude of a vector is defined. The square of the magnitude of a vector is given by the dot product

$$|u|^2 = u \cdot u.$$

The angle between two vectors is given by

$$\cos\theta = \frac{u \cdot v}{|u||v|}.$$

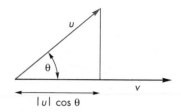

In addition, $|u|\cos\theta = u \cdot v/|v|$ is the length of the orthogonal projection of u onto v, as shown in Figure 4.14. Thus, the dot product expresses the geometric result that the shortest distance from a point (the end of the vector u) to the line segment v is obtained by drawing the vector orthogonal to v from the end of u. We can also see that the vector u is composed of the sum of the orthogonal projection on v and a vector orthogonal to v.

FIGURE 4.14 Dot product and projection.

In vector space, vectors are **linearly independent** if we cannot write one in terms of the others using scalar-vector addition. A vector space has a **dimension**, which is the maximum number of linearly independent vectors that we can find. Given any three linearly independent vectors in a three-dimensional space, we can use the dot product to construct three vectors, each of which is orthogonal to the other two. This process is outlined in Appendix B. We can also use two nonparallel vectors, u and v, to determine a third vector n that is orthogonal to them (Figure 4.15). This vector is determined by the **cross product**

$$n = u \times v.$$

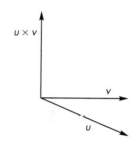

FIGURE 4.15 Cross product.

Note that we can use the cross product to derive three mutually orthogonal vectors in a three-dimensional space from any two nonparallel vectors. Starting again with u and v, we first compute n as before. Then, we can compute w by

$$w = u \times n,$$

and u, n, and w are mutually orthogonal.

The cross product is derived in Appendix C, using the representation of the vectors that gives a direct method for computing it. The magnitude of the cross product gives the sine of the angle θ between u and v,

$$|\sin\theta| = \frac{|u \times v|}{|u||v|}.$$

Note that the vectors u, v, and n form a **right-handed coordinate system**; that is, if u points in the direction of the thumb of the right hand and v points in the direction of the index finger, then n points in the direction of the middle finger.

4.1.10 Planes

A **plane** in an affine space can be defined as a direct extension of the parametric line. From simple geometry, we know that three points not on the same line determine a unique plane. Suppose that P, Q, and R are three such points in an affine space. The line segment that joins P and Q is the set of points of the form

$$S(\alpha) = \alpha P + (1 - \alpha)Q, \qquad 0 \le \alpha \le 1.$$

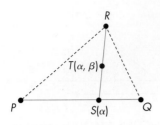

FIGURE 4.16 Formation of a plane.

Suppose that we take an arbitrary point on this line segment and form the line segment from this point to R, as shown in Figure 4.16. Using a second parameter β, we can describe points along this line segment as

$$T(\beta) = \beta S + (1 - \beta)R, \qquad 0 \le \beta \le 1.$$

Such points are determined by both α and β and form the plane determined by P, Q, and R. Combining the preceding two equations, we obtain one form of the equation of a plane:

$$T(\alpha, \beta) = \beta[\alpha P + (1 - \alpha)Q] + (1 - \beta)R.$$

We can rearrange this equation in the form

$$T(\alpha, \beta) = P + \beta(1 - \alpha)(Q - P) + (1 - \beta)(R - P).$$

Noting that $Q - P$ and $R - P$ are arbitrary vectors, we have shown that a plane can also be expressed in terms of a point, P_0, and two nonparallel vectors, u and v, as

$$T(\alpha, \beta) = P_0 + \alpha u + \beta v.$$

We can also observe that for $0 \le \alpha, \beta \le 1$, all the points $T(\alpha, \beta)$ lie in the triangle formed by P, Q, and R. If a point P lies in the plane, then

$$P - P_0 = \alpha u + \beta v.$$

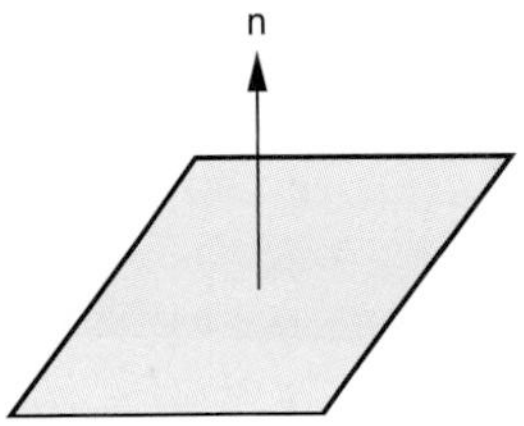

We can find a vector w that is orthogonal to both u and v, as shown in Figure 4.17. If we use the cross product

$$n = u \times v,$$

then the equation of the plane becomes

$$n \cdot (P - P_0) = 0.$$

FIGURE 4.17 Normal to a plane.

The vector n is perpendicular, or orthogonal, to the plane; it is called the **normal** to the plane. The forms $P(\alpha)$, for the line, and $T(\alpha, \beta)$, for the plane, are known as **parametric forms** because they give the value of a point in space for each value of the parameters α and β.

4.2 Three-Dimensional Primitives

In a three-dimensional world, we can have a far greater variety of geometric objects than we could in two dimensions. When we worked in a two-dimensional plane in Chapter 2, we considered objects that were simple curves, such as line segments, and objects that had interiors, such as polygons. In three dimensions, we retain these objects, but they are no longer restricted to lie in the same plane. Hence, curves become curves in space (Figure 4.18), and objects with interiors

FIGURE 4.18 Curves in three dimensions.

can become surfaces in space (Figure 4.19). In addition, we can have objects with volumes, such as parallelepipeds and ellipsoids (Figure 4.20).

We face two problems when we expand our graphics system to incorporate all these possibilities. First, the mathematical definitions of these objects can become complex. Second, we are interested in only those objects that lead to efficient implementations in graphics systems. The full range of three-dimensional objects cannot be supported on existing graphics systems, except by approximate methods.

Three features characterize three-dimensional objects that fit well with existing graphics hardware and software:

1. The objects are described by their surfaces and can be thought of as being hollow.
2. The objects can be specified through a set of vertices in three dimensions.
3. The objects either are composed of or can be approximated by flat, convex polygons.

FIGURE 4.19 Surfaces in three dimensions.

We can understand why we set these conditions if we consider what most modern graphics systems do best: They render triangular, or other flat, polygons. Commodity graphics cards can render 100 million small, flat polygons per second.[1]

The first condition implies that we need only two-dimensional primitives to model three-dimensional objects because a surface is a two- rather than a three-dimensional entity. The second condition is an extension of our observations in Chapters 1 and 2. If an object is defined by vertices, we can use a pipeline architecture to process these vertices at high rates, and we can use the hardware to generate the images of the objects only during rasterization. The final condition is an extension from our discussion of two-dimensional polygons. Most graphics systems are optimized for the processing of points and polygons. In three dimensions, a polygon can be defined by an ordered list of vertices. However, if there are more than three vertices, they do not have to lie in the same plane; if they do not, there is no simple way to define the interior of the object. Consequently, most graphics systems require that the user specify simple planar polygons, or the results of rasterizing the polygon are not guaranteed to be what the programmer might desire. Because triangular polygons are always flat, either the modeling system is designed to always produce triangles, or the graphics system provides a method to divide, or **tessellate**, an arbitrary polygon into triangular polygons. If we apply this same argument to a curved object, such as a sphere, we realize that we should use an approximation to the sphere composed of small, flat polygons.

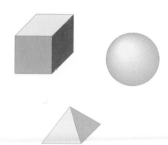

FIGURE 4.20 Volumetric objects.

---

1. Performance claims for graphics systems usually are quoted for three-dimensional triangles that can be generated by triangle strips. In addition, these triangles are shaded, lit, and texture mapped, because these functions can be implemented in hardware.

Hence, even if our modeling system provides curved objects, we assume that a polygonal approximation is used for implementation.

The major exception to this approach is **constructive solid geometry** (**CSG**). In such systems, we build objects from a small set of volumetric objects through set operations such as union and intersection. We consider CSG models in Chapter 10. Although this approach is an excellent one for modeling, rendering CSG models is more difficult than is rendering surface-based polygonal models. Although this situation may not hold in the future, we discuss in detail only surface rendering.

All the primitives with which we work can be specified through a set of vertices. As we move away from abstract objects to real objects, we must consider how we represent points in space in a manner that can be used within our graphics systems.

4.3   Coordinate Systems and Frames

So far, we have considered vectors and points as abstract objects, without representing them in an underlying reference system. In a three-dimensional vector space, we can represent any vector w uniquely in terms of any three linearly independent vectors, v_1, v_2, and v_3 (see Appendix B), as

$$w = \alpha_1 v_1 + \alpha_2 v_2 + \alpha_3 v_3.$$

The scalars $\alpha_1, \alpha_2,$ and α_3 are the **components** of w with respect to the **basis** v_1, v_2, and v_3. These relationships are shown in Figure 4.21. We can write the **representation** of w with respect to this basis as the column matrix

$$\mathbf{a} = \begin{bmatrix} \alpha_1 \\ \alpha_2 \\ \alpha_3 \end{bmatrix},$$

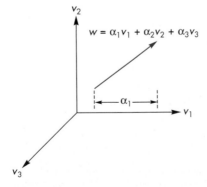

FIGURE 4.21   Vector derived from three basis vectors.

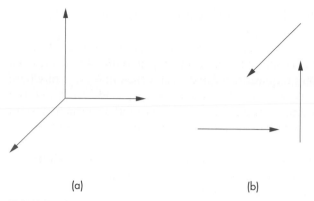

(a)   (b)

FIGURE 4.22 Coordinate systems. (a) Vectors emerging from a common point. (b) Vectors moved.

where boldface letters denote a representation in a particular basis, as opposed to the original abstract vector w. We can also write this relationship as

$$w = \mathbf{a}^T \begin{bmatrix} v_1 \\ v_2 \\ v_3 \end{bmatrix}.$$

We usually think of the basis vectors, v_1, v_2, v_3, as defining a **coordinate system**. However, for dealing with problems using points, vectors, and scalars, we need a more general method. Figure 4.22 shows one aspect of the problem. The three vectors form a coordinate system that is shown in Figure 4.22(a) as we would usually draw it, with the three vectors emerging from a single point. We could use these three basis vectors as a basis to represent any vector in three dimensions. Vectors, however, have direction and magnitude, but lack a position attribute. Hence, Figure 4.22(b) is equivalent, because we have moved the basis vectors, leaving their magnitudes and directions unchanged. Most people find this second figure confusing, even though mathematically it expresses the same information as the first figure. We are still left with the problem of how to represent points— entities that have fixed positions.

Because an affine space contains points, once we fix a particular reference point—the origin—in such a space, we can represent all points unambiguously. The usual convention for drawing coordinate axes as emerging from the origin, as shown in Figure 4.22(a), makes sense in the affine space where both points and vectors have representations. However, this representation requires us to know *both* the reference point and the basis vectors. The origin and the basis vectors determine a **frame**. Loosely, this extension fixes the origin of the vector coordinate system at some point P_0. Within a given frame, every vector can be written uniquely as

$$w = \alpha_1 v_1 + \alpha_2 v_2 + \alpha_3 v_3,$$

just as in a vector space; in addition, every point can be written uniquely as

$$P = P_0 + \beta_1 v_1 + \beta_2 v_2 + \beta_3 v_3.$$

Thus, the representation of a particular vector in a frame requires three scalars; the representation of a point requires three scalars and the knowledge of where the origin is located. As we shall see in Section 4.3.4, by abandoning the more familiar notion of a coordinate system and a basis in that coordinate system in favor of the less familiar notion of a frame, we avoid the difficulties caused by vectors having magnitude and direction but no fixed position. In addition, we shall be able to represent points and vectors in a manner that will allow us to use matrix representations but that maintains a distinction between the two geometric types.

Because points and vectors are two distinct geometric types, graphical representations that equate a point with a directed line segment drawn from the origin to that point (Figure 4.23) should be regarded with suspicion. Thus, a correct interpretation of Figure 4.23 is that a given vector can be defined as going from a fixed reference point (the origin) to a particular point in space. Note that a vector, like a point, exists regardless of the reference system, but as we shall see with both points and vectors, we eventually have to work with their representation in a particular reference system.

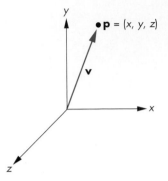

FIGURE 4.23 A dangerous representation of a vector.

4.3.1 Representations and N-Tuples

Suppose that vectors e_1, e_2, and e_3 form a basis. The representation of any vector, v, is given by the components $(\alpha_1, \alpha_2, \alpha_3)$, where

$$v = \alpha_1 e_1 + \alpha_2 e_2 + \alpha_3 e_3.$$

The basis vectors[2] must themselves have representations that we can denote $\mathbf{e}_1$, $\mathbf{e}_2$, and $\mathbf{e}_3$, given by

$$\mathbf{e_1} = (1, 0, 0)^T,$$
$$\mathbf{e_2} = (0, 1, 0)^T,$$
$$\mathbf{e_3} = (0, 0, 1)^T.$$

Consequently, in terms of representations, we can write the representation of any vector v as a column matrix $\mathbf{a}$ or as the 3-tuple $(\alpha_1, \alpha_2, \alpha_3)$ where

$$\mathbf{a} = \alpha_1 \mathbf{e}_1 + \alpha_2 \mathbf{e}_2 + \alpha_3 \mathbf{e}_3.$$

From this perspective, working with representations is equivalent to working with 3-tuples of scalars. These 3-tuples form a vector space known as the Eu-

---

2. Many textbooks on vectors refer to these vectors as the unit basis $\mathbf{i}, \mathbf{j}, \mathbf{k}$ and write other vectors in the form $v = \alpha_1 \mathbf{i} + \alpha_2 \mathbf{j} + \alpha_2 \mathbf{k}$.

clidean space $\mathbf{R}^3$ that is equivalent (or **homomorphic**) to the vector space of our original geometric vectors. From a practical perspective, it is almost always easier to work with 3-tuples than with other representations.

4.3.2 Change of Coordinate Systems

Frequently, we are required to find how the representation of a vector changes when we change the basis vectors. For example, in OpenGL, we define our geometry using the coordinate system or frame that is natural for the model, which is known as the **object** or **model frame**. Models are then brought into the **world frame**. At some point, we want to know how these objects appear to the camera. It is natural at that point to convert from the world frame to the **camera** or **eye frame**. The conversion from the object frame to the eye frame is done by the model-view matrix.

Let us consider changing representations for vectors first. Suppose that $\{v_1, v_2, v_3\}$ and $\{u_1, u_2, u_3\}$ are two bases. Each basis vector in the second set can be represented in terms of the first basis (and vice versa). Hence, there exist nine scalar components, $\{\gamma_{ij}\}$, such that

$$u_1 = \gamma_{11}v_1 + \gamma_{12}v_2 + \gamma_{13}v_3,$$
$$u_2 = \gamma_{21}v_1 + \gamma_{22}v_2 + \gamma_{23}v_3,$$
$$u_3 = \gamma_{31}v_1 + \gamma_{32}v_2 + \gamma_{33}v_3.$$

The 3×3 matrix

$$\mathbf{M} = \begin{bmatrix} \gamma_{11} & \gamma_{12} & \gamma_{13} \\ \gamma_{21} & \gamma_{22} & \gamma_{23} \\ \gamma_{31} & \gamma_{32} & \gamma_{33} \end{bmatrix}$$

is defined by these scalars, and

$$\begin{bmatrix} u_1 \\ u_2 \\ u_3 \end{bmatrix} = \mathbf{M} \begin{bmatrix} v_1 \\ v_2 \\ v_3 \end{bmatrix}.$$

The matrix $\mathbf{M}$ contains the information to go from a representation of a vector in one basis to its representation in the second basis. The inverse of $\mathbf{M}$ gives the matrix representation of the change from $\{u_1, u_2, u_3\}$ to $\{v_1, v_2, v_3\}$. Consider a vector w that has the representation $\{\alpha_1, \alpha_2, \alpha_3\}$ with respect to $\{v_1, v_2, v_3\}$; that is,

$$w = \alpha_1 v_1 + \alpha_2 v_2 + \alpha_3 v_3.$$

Equivalently,

$$w = \mathbf{a}^T \begin{bmatrix} v_1 \\ v_2 \\ v_3 \end{bmatrix},$$

where

$$\mathbf{a} = \begin{bmatrix} \alpha_1 \\ \alpha_2 \\ \alpha_3 \end{bmatrix}.$$

Assume that $\mathbf{b}$ is the representation of w with respect to $\{u_1, u_2, u_3\}$; that is,

$$w = \beta_1 u_1 + \beta_2 u_2 + \beta_3 u_3,$$

or

$$w = \mathbf{b}^T \begin{bmatrix} u_1 \\ u_2 \\ u_3 \end{bmatrix},$$

where

$$\mathbf{b} = \begin{bmatrix} \beta_1 \\ \beta_2 \\ \beta_3 \end{bmatrix}.$$

Then, using our representation of the second basis in terms of the first, we find that

$$w = \mathbf{b}^T \begin{bmatrix} u_1 \\ u_2 \\ u_3 \end{bmatrix} = \mathbf{b}^T \mathbf{M} \begin{bmatrix} v_1 \\ v_2 \\ v_3 \end{bmatrix} = \mathbf{a}^T \begin{bmatrix} v_1 \\ v_2 \\ v_3 \end{bmatrix}.$$

Thus,

$$\mathbf{a} = \mathbf{M}^T \mathbf{b}.$$

The matrix $(\mathbf{M}^T)^{-1}$ takes us from $\mathbf{a}$ to $\mathbf{b}$:

$$\mathbf{b} = (\mathbf{M}^T)^{-1} \mathbf{a}.$$

Thus, rather than working with our original vectors, typically directed line segments, we can work instead with their representations, which are 3-tuples or elements of $\mathbf{R}^3$. This result is important because it moves us from considering abstract vectors to working with column matrices of scalars—the vectors' representations. The important point to remember is that whenever we work with columns of real numbers as "vectors," there is an underlying basis of which we must not lose track, lest we end up working in the wrong coordinate system.

These changes in basis leave the origin unchanged. We can use them to represent rotation and scaling of a set of basis vectors to derive another basis set, as shown in Figure 4.24. However, a simple translation of the origin, or change of frame as shown in Figure 4.25, cannot be represented in this way. After we complete a simple example, we introduce homogeneous coordinates, which allow us to change frames yet still use matrices to represent the change.

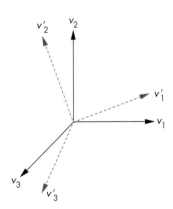

FIGURE 4.24 Rotation and scaling of a basis.

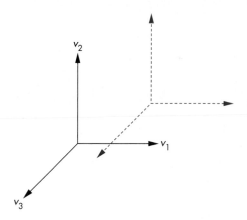

FIGURE 4.25 Translation of a basis.

4.3.3 Example Change of Representation

Suppose that we have a vector w whose representation in some basis is

$$\mathbf{a} = \begin{bmatrix} 1 \\ 2 \\ 3 \end{bmatrix}.$$

We can denote the three basis vectors as v_1, v_2, and v_3. Hence,

$$w = v_1 + 2v_2 + 3v_3.$$

Now suppose that we want to make a new basis from the three vectors v_1, v_2, and v_3:

$$u_1 = v_1,$$
$$u_2 = v_1 + v_2,$$
$$u_3 = v_1 + v_2 + v_3.$$

The matrix $\mathbf{M}$ is

$$\mathbf{M} = \begin{bmatrix} 1 & 0 & 0 \\ 1 & 1 & 0 \\ 1 & 1 & 1 \end{bmatrix}.$$

The matrix that converts a representation in v_1, v_2, and v_3 to one in which the basis vectors are u_1, u_2, and u_3 is

$$A = (M^T)^{-1}$$

$$= \begin{bmatrix} 1 & 1 & 1 \\ 0 & 1 & 1 \\ 0 & 0 & 1 \end{bmatrix}^{-1}$$

$$= \begin{bmatrix} 1 & -1 & 0 \\ 0 & 1 & -1 \\ 0 & 0 & 1 \end{bmatrix}.$$

In the new system, the representation of w is

$$b = Aa = \begin{bmatrix} -1 \\ -1 \\ 3 \end{bmatrix}.$$

That is,

$$w = -u_1 - u_2 + 3u_3.$$

If we are working in the space of 3-tuples ($\mathbf{R}^3$), rather than in an abstract setting, then we can associate v_1, v_2, and v_3 with the unit basis in $\mathbf{R}^3$:

$$e_1 = \begin{bmatrix} 1 \\ 0 \\ 0 \end{bmatrix}, \qquad e_2 = \begin{bmatrix} 0 \\ 1 \\ 0 \end{bmatrix}, \qquad e_3 = \begin{bmatrix} 0 \\ 0 \\ 1 \end{bmatrix}.$$

We can make this example a little more concrete by considering the following variant. Suppose that we are working with the default (x, y, z) coordinate system, which happens to be orthogonal. We are given the three direction vectors whose representations are $(1, 0, 0)$, $(1, 1, 0)$, and $(1, 1, 1)$. Thus, the first vector points along the x-axis, the second points in a direction parallel to the plane $z = 0$, and the third points in a direction symmetric to the three basis directions. These three new vectors, although they are not mutually orthogonal, are linearly independent and thus define a new coordinate system that we can call the x', y', z' system. The original directions have representations in the x', y', z' given by the rows of the matrix A.

4.3.4 Homogeneous Coordinates

Suppose that we start with the frame defined by the point P_0 and the vectors v_1, v_2, and v_3. Usually, our first inclination is to represent a point P located at (x, y, z) with the column matrix

$$p = \begin{bmatrix} x \\ y \\ z \end{bmatrix},$$

where x, y, and z are the components of the basis vectors for this point, so that

$$P = P_0 + xv_1 + yv_2 + zv_3.$$

If we represent the point this way, then its representation is of the same form as the *vector*

$$w = xv_1 + yv_2 + zv_3;$$

Many references associate the point (x, y, z) with the vector defined by a directed line segment from the origin to this point. This association can cause confusion. For example, the vector from the point $(1, 1, 1)$ to $(2, 3, 4)$ is the same as the vector from $(0, 0, 0)$ to $(1, 2, 3)$ because they have the same magnitude and direction, but we would not associate the first vector with point $(1, 2, 3)$ unless we fixed one end of it to $(0, 0, 0)$. We prefer to maintain points and vectors as distinct geometric types.

In addition, failure to distinguish between points and vectors can make implementation more difficult because a matrix multiplication in three dimensions cannot represent a change in frames. We take a different approach.

We use homogeneous coordinates to avoid these difficulties by using four-dimensional column matrices to represent both points and vectors in three dimensions. In the frame specified by (v_1, v_2, v_3, P_0), any point P can be written uniquely as

$$P = \alpha_1 v_1 + \alpha_2 v_2 + \alpha_3 v_3 + P_0.$$

If we agree to define the "multiplication" of a point by the scalars 0 and 1 as

$$0 \cdot P = \mathbf{0},$$
$$1 \cdot P = P,$$

then we can express this relation formally, using a matrix product, as

$$P = \begin{bmatrix} \alpha_1 & \alpha_2 & \alpha_3 & 1 \end{bmatrix} \begin{bmatrix} v_1 \\ v_2 \\ v_3 \\ P_0 \end{bmatrix}.$$

Strictly speaking, this expression is not a dot or inner product, because the elements of the matrices are dissimilar; nonetheless, the expression is computed as though it were an inner product by multiplying corresponding elements and summing the results. The four-dimensional row matrix on the right side of the equation is the **homogeneous-coordinate representation** of the point P in the frame determined by $v_1, v_2, v_3,$ and P_0. Equivalently, we can say that P is represented by the column matrix

$$\mathbf{p} = \begin{bmatrix} \alpha_1 \\ \alpha_2 \\ \alpha_3 \\ 1 \end{bmatrix}.$$

In the same frame, any vector w can be written

$$w = \delta_1 v_1 + \delta_2 v_2 + \delta_3 v_3$$

$$= [\, \delta_1 \quad \delta_2 \quad \delta_3 \quad 0 \,]^T \begin{bmatrix} v_1 \\ v_2 \\ v_3 \\ P_0 \end{bmatrix}.$$

Thus, w can be is represented by the column matrix

$$\mathbf{w} = \begin{bmatrix} \delta_1 \\ \delta_2 \\ \delta_3 \\ 0 \end{bmatrix}.$$

There are numerous ways to interpret this formulation geometrically. We simply note that we can carry out operations on points and vectors using their homogeneous-coordinate representations and ordinary matrix algebra. Consider, for example, a change of frames—a problem that caused difficulties when we used three-dimensional representations. If (v_1, v_2, v_3, P_0) and (u_1, u_2, u_3, Q_0) are two frames, then we can express the basis vectors and reference point of the second frame in terms of the first as

$$u_1 = \gamma_{11} v_1 + \gamma_{12} v_2 + \gamma_{13} v_3,$$
$$u_2 = \gamma_{21} v_1 + \gamma_{22} v_2 + \gamma_{23} v_3,$$
$$u_3 = \gamma_{31} v_1 + \gamma_{32} v_2 + \gamma_{33} v_3,$$
$$Q_0 = \gamma_{41} v_1 + \gamma_{42} v_2 + \gamma_{43} v_3 + P_0.$$

These equations can be written in the form

$$\begin{bmatrix} u_1 \\ u_2 \\ u_3 \\ Q_0 \end{bmatrix} = \mathbf{M} \begin{bmatrix} v_1 \\ v_2 \\ v_3 \\ P_0 \end{bmatrix},$$

where now $\mathbf{M}$ is the 4×4 matrix

$$\mathbf{M} = \begin{bmatrix} \gamma_{11} & \gamma_{12} & \gamma_{13} & 0 \\ \gamma_{21} & \gamma_{22} & \gamma_{23} & 0 \\ \gamma_{31} & \gamma_{32} & \gamma_{33} & 0 \\ \gamma_{41} & \gamma_{42} & \gamma_{43} & 1 \end{bmatrix}.$$

$\mathbf{M}$ is called the **matrix representation** of the change of frames.

We can also use $\mathbf{M}$ to compute the changes in the representations directly. Suppose that $\mathbf{a}$ and $\mathbf{b}$ are the homogeneous-coordinate representations either of two points or of two vectors in the two frames. Then

$$\mathbf{b}^T \begin{bmatrix} u_1 \\ u_2 \\ u_3 \\ Q_0 \end{bmatrix} = \mathbf{b}^T \mathbf{M} \begin{bmatrix} v_1 \\ v_2 \\ v_3 \\ P_0 \end{bmatrix} = \mathbf{a}^T \begin{bmatrix} v_1 \\ v_2 \\ v_3 \\ P_0 \end{bmatrix}.$$

Hence,

$$\mathbf{a} = \mathbf{M}^T \mathbf{b}.$$

When we work with representations, as is usually the case, we are interested in $\mathbf{M}^T$, which is of the form

$$\mathbf{M}^T = \begin{bmatrix} \alpha_{11} & \alpha_{12} & \alpha_{13} & \alpha_{14} \\ \alpha_{21} & \alpha_{22} & \alpha_{23} & \alpha_{24} \\ \alpha_{31} & \alpha_{32} & \alpha_{33} & \alpha_{34} \\ 0 & 0 & 0 & 1 \end{bmatrix},$$

and is determined by 12 coefficients.

There are other advantages to using homogeneous coordinates that we explore extensively in later chapters. Perhaps the most important is that all affine (line-preserving) transformations can be represented as matrix multiplications in homogeneous coordinates. Although we have to work in four dimensions to solve three-dimensional problems when we use homogeneous-coordinate representations, less arithmetic work is involved. The uniform representation of all affine transformations makes carrying out successive transformations (concatenation) far easier than in three-dimensional space. In addition, modern hardware implements homogeneous-coordinate operations directly, using parallelism to achieve high-speed calculations.

4.3.5 Example Change in Frames

Consider again the example of Section 4.3.3. If we again start with the basis vectors v_1, v_2, and v_3 and convert to a basis determined by the same u_1, u_2, and u_3, then the three equations are the same:

$$u_1 = v_1,$$
$$u_2 = v_1 + v_2,$$
$$u_3 = v_1 + v_2 + v_3.$$

The reference point does not change, so we add the equation

$$Q_0 = P_0.$$

Thus, the matrices in which we are interested are the matrix

$$\mathbf{M} = \begin{bmatrix} 1 & 0 & 0 & 0 \\ 1 & 1 & 0 & 0 \\ 1 & 1 & 1 & 0 \\ 0 & 0 & 0 & 1 \end{bmatrix},$$

its transpose, and their inverses.

Suppose that in addition to changing the basis vectors, we also want to move the reference point to the point that has the representation $(1, 2, 3, 1)$ in the original system. The displacement vector $v = v_1 + 2v_2 + 3v_3$ moves P_0 to Q_0. The fourth component identifies this entity as a point. Thus, we add to the three equations from the previous example the equation

$$Q_0 = P_0 + v_1 + 2v_2 + 3v_3,$$

and the matrix $\mathbf{M}^T$ becomes

$$\mathbf{M}^T = \begin{bmatrix} 1 & 1 & 1 & 1 \\ 0 & 1 & 1 & 2 \\ 0 & 0 & 1 & 3 \\ 0 & 0 & 0 & 1 \end{bmatrix}.$$

Its inverse is

$$\mathbf{A} = (\mathbf{M}^T)^{-1} = \begin{bmatrix} 1 & -1 & 0 & 1 \\ 0 & 1 & -1 & 1 \\ 0 & 0 & 1 & -3 \\ 0 & 0 & 0 & 1 \end{bmatrix}.$$

This pair of matrices allows us to move back and forth between representations in the two frames. Note that $\mathbf{A}$ takes the *point* $(1,2,3)$ in the original frame, whose representation is

$$\mathbf{p} = \begin{bmatrix} 1 \\ 2 \\ 3 \\ 1 \end{bmatrix},$$

to

$$\mathbf{p}' = \begin{bmatrix} 0 \\ 0 \\ 0 \\ 1 \end{bmatrix},$$

the origin in the new system. However, the *vector* $(1, 2, 3)$, which is represented as

$$\mathbf{a} = \begin{bmatrix} 1 \\ 2 \\ 3 \\ 0 \end{bmatrix}$$

in the original system, is transformed to

$$\mathbf{b} = \begin{bmatrix} -1 \\ -1 \\ 3 \\ 0 \end{bmatrix},$$

a transformation that is consistent with the results from our example of change in coordinate systems and that also demonstrates the importance of distinguishing between points and vectors.

4.3.6 Working with Representations

We usually work with representations rather than abstract points. Thus, when we specify a point, for example by `glVertex3f(x,y,z)`, we are actually giving the representation of the point in some frame, usually the object frame used by the application. Changes of representation are thus given as in Section 4.3.2 by a relationship of the form

$$\mathbf{a} = \mathbf{C}\mathbf{b},$$

where $\mathbf{a}$ and $\mathbf{b}$ are the two representations of a point or vector in homogeneous coordinates. The problem is how to find $\mathbf{C}$ when we are working with representations. It turns out to be quite easy. Suppose that we are working in some frame and we specify another frame by its representation in this frame. Thus, if in the original system we specify a frame by the representations of three vectors, u, v, and n, and give the origin of the new frame as the point p, in homogeneous coordinates all four of these entities are 4-tuples or elements of $\mathbf{R}^4$.

Let's consider the inverse problem. The matrix

$$\mathbf{D} = \mathbf{C}^{-1}$$

converts from representations in the (u, v, n, p) frame to representations in the original frame. Thus, we must have

$$\mathbf{D}\begin{bmatrix} 1 \\ 0 \\ 0 \\ 0 \end{bmatrix} = \mathbf{u} = \begin{bmatrix} u_1 \\ u_2 \\ u_3 \\ 0 \end{bmatrix}.$$

Likewise,

$$\mathbf{D}\begin{bmatrix} 0 \\ 1 \\ 0 \\ 0 \end{bmatrix} = \mathbf{v} = \begin{bmatrix} v_1 \\ v_2 \\ v_3 \\ 0 \end{bmatrix},$$

$$\mathbf{D}\begin{bmatrix} 0 \\ 0 \\ 1 \\ 0 \end{bmatrix} = \mathbf{n} = \begin{bmatrix} n_1 \\ n_2 \\ n_3 \\ 0 \end{bmatrix},$$

$$\mathbf{D}\begin{bmatrix} 0 \\ 0 \\ 0 \\ 1 \end{bmatrix} = \mathbf{p} = \begin{bmatrix} p_1 \\ p_2 \\ p_3 \\ 1 \end{bmatrix}.$$

Putting these results together, we find

$$\mathbf{DI} = \mathbf{D} = [\; u \quad v \quad n \quad p \;] = \begin{bmatrix} u_1 & v_1 & n_1 & p_1 \\ u_2 & v_2 & n_2 & p_2 \\ u_3 & v_3 & n_3 & p_3 \\ 0 & 0 & 0 & 1 \end{bmatrix},$$

or

$$\mathbf{C} = [\; u \quad v \quad n \quad p \;]^{-1} = \begin{bmatrix} u_1 & v_1 & n_1 & p_1 \\ u_2 & v_2 & n_2 & p_2 \\ u_3 & v_3 & n_3 & p_3 \\ 0 & 0 & 0 & 1 \end{bmatrix}^{-1}.$$

Thus, the representation of a frame in terms of another frame gives us the inverse of the matrix we need to convert from representations in the first frame to representations in the second. Of course, we must compute this inverse, but computing the inverse of a 4×4 matrix of this form should not present a problem.

4.4 Frames in OpenGL

As we have seen, OpenGL is based on a pipeline model, the first part of which is sequence of operations on vertices. We can characterize these geometric operations by a sequence of transformations or, equivalently, as a sequence of changes of representations of the objects defined by a user program. In a typical application, there are six representations embedded in the pipeline, although normally the programmer will not see more than a few of them directly. In each of these representations, a vertex has different coordinates. In the order they occur in the pipeline, the systems are

1. Object or model coordinates
2. World coordinates
3. Eye (or camera) coordinates
4. Clip coordinates
5. Normalized device coordinates
6. Window (or screen) coordinates

Let's consider what happens when a user specifies a vertex in a program through the function glVertex3f(x, y, z). This vertex may be defined directly in the application program or indirectly through an instantiation of some basic object, as we discussed in Chapter 3. In most applications, we tend to define or use objects with a convenient size and orientation and centered in their own frames. The coordinates in the corresponding function calls are in **object** or **model coordinates**.

Each object must be brought into an application that might contain hundreds or thousands of individual objects. The application program generally applies a sequence of transformations to each object to size, orient, and position it within a frame that is appropriate for the particular application. For example, if we were using an instance of a square for a window in an architectural application, we would scale it to have the correct proportions and units, which would probably be in feet or meters. The origin of application coordinates might be a location in the center of the bottom floor of the building. This application frame is called the **world frame** and the values are in **world coordinates**. Note that if we do not model with predefined objects or apply any transformations before we execute the glVertex function, object and world coordinates are the same.

Although object and world coordinates make sense to the application, the image that is produced depends on what the camera or viewer sees. Virtually all graphics systems use a frame whose origin is the center camera's lens[3] and whose axes are aligned with the sides of the camera. This frame is called the **camera frame** or **eye frame**. Because there is an affine transformation that corresponds to each change of frame, there are 4×4 matrices that represent the transformation from model coordinates to world coordinates and from world coordinates to eye coordinates. In OpenGL, these transformations are concatenated together into the model-view transformation, which is defined by the model-view matrix. Usually, the use of the model-view matrix instead of the individual matrices does not pose any problems for the application programmer. In Chapter 9, where we discuss programmable pipelines, we shall see situations where we must separate the two transformations.

OpenGL uses three other representations that we shall need later but, for completeness, we introduce them here. Once objects are in eye coordinates, OpenGL must check whether they lie with the viewing or clipping volumes. If they do not, they are clipped from the scene prior to rasterization. OpenGL can carry out this process most efficiently if it first carries out a projection transformation that brings all potentially visible objects into a cube centered at the origin in **clip coordinates**. We shall study this transformation in Chapter 5. After this transformation, vertices are still represented in homogeneous coordinates. The division by the w component, called **perspective division**, yields three-dimensional representations in **normalized device coordinates**. The final transformation takes a position in normalized device coordinates and, taking into account the viewport, creates a three-dimensional representation in **window coordinates**. Window coordinates are measured in units of pixels on the display but retain depth information.

From the application programmer's perspective, OpenGL starts with two frames: the eye frame and the object frame. The model-view matrix positions the object frame relative to the eye frame. Thus, the model-view matrix converts the homogeneous-coordinate representations of points and vectors to their

---

3. For a perspective view, the center of the lens is the center of projection (COP) whereas for an orthogonal view (the default), the direction of projection is aligned with the sides of the camera.

representations in the eye frame. Because the model-view matrix is part of the state of the system, there is always a present camera frame and a present object frame. OpenGL provides matrix stacks, so we can store model-view matrices or, equivalently, frames.

Initially, the model-view matrix is an identity matrix, so the object frame and eye frame are identical. Thus, if we do not change the model-view matrix, we are working in eye coordinates. As we saw in Chapter 2, the camera is at the origin of its frame, as in Figure 4.26(a). The three basis vectors in eye space correspond to (1) the up direction of the camera, the y direction; (2) the direction the camera is pointing, the negative z direction; and (3) a third orthogonal direction, x, placed so that the x, y, z directions form a right-handed coordinate system. We obtain other frames in which to place objects by performing homogeneous coordinate transformations that define new frames relative to the camera frame. We learn in Section 4.5 how to define these transformations; in Section 5.3 we use them to position the camera relative to our objects. Because changes of frame are represented by model-view matrices that can be stored, we can save frames and move between frames by changing the present model-view matrix.

When first working with multiple frames, there can be some confusion about which frames are fixed and which are varying. Because the model-view matrix positions the camera *relative* to the objects, it is usually a matter of convenience as to which frame we regard as fixed. Most of the time, we shall regard the camera as fixed and the other frames as moving relative to the camera, but you may prefer to adopt a different view.

Before beginning a detailed discussion of what transformations are and how we use them in OpenGL, we present two simple examples. In the default settings shown in Figure 4.26(a), the camera and object frames coincide with the camera pointing in the negative z direction. In many applications, it is natural to define objects as near the origin, such as a square centered at the origin or perhaps a group of objects whose center of mass is at the origin. It is also natural to set up our viewing conditions so that the camera sees only those objects that are in front of it. Consequently, to form images that contain all these objects, we must either move the camera away from the objects or move the objects away from the camera. Equivalently, we move the camera frame relative to the object frame. If we regard the camera frame as fixed and the model-view matrix as positioning the object frame relative to the camera frame, then the model-view matrix,

$$\mathbf{A} = \begin{bmatrix} 1 & 0 & 0 & 0 \\ 0 & 1 & 0 & 0 \\ 0 & 0 & 1 & -d \\ 0 & 0 & 0 & 1 \end{bmatrix},$$

moves a point (x, y, z) in the object frame to the point $(x, y, z - d)$ in the camera frame. Thus, by making d a suitably large positive number, we "move" the objects in front of the camera by moving the world frame relative to the camera frame,

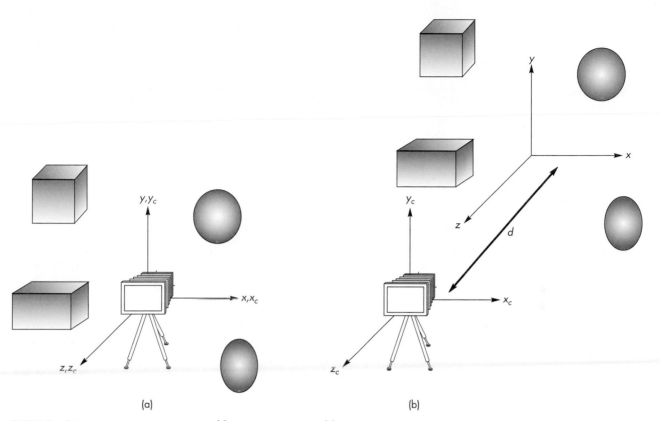

FIGURE 4.26 Camera and object frames. (a) In default positions. (b) After applying model-view matrix.

as in Figure 4.26(b). Note that, as far as the user—who is working in world coordinates—is concerned, she is positioning objects as before. The model-view matrix takes care of the relative positioning of the frames. Using this strategy is almost always better than attempting to alter the positions of the object by changing their vertices to place them in front of the camera.

Let's look at another example working directly with representations. When we define our objects through vertices, we are working in the application frame (or world frame). The vertices specified by glVertex3f(x,y,z) are the representation of a point in that frame. Thus, we do not use the world frame directly but rather implicitly by representing points (and vectors) in it. Consider the situation in Figure 4.27.

Here we see the camera as positioned in the object frame. Using homogeneous coordinates, it is centered at a point $p = (1, 0, 1, 1)^T$ in world coordinates and points at the origin in the world frame. Thus the vector whose representation in the world frame is $\mathbf{n} = (-1, 0, -1, 0)^T$ is orthogonal to the back of the camera

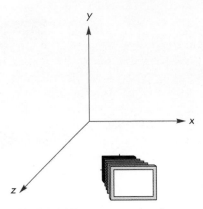

FIGURE 4.27   Camera at (1,0,1) pointing toward the origin.

and points toward the origin. The camera is oriented so that its up direction is the same as the up direction in world coordinates and has the representation $\mathbf{v} = (0, 1, 0, 0)^T$. We can form an orthogonal coordinate system for the camera by using the cross product to determine a third orthogonal direction for the camera, which is $\mathbf{u} = (1, 0, -1, 0)^T$. We can now proceed as in Section 4.3.4 and derive the matrix $\mathbf{M}$ that converts the representation of points and vectors in the world frame to their representations in the camera frame. This matrix in homogenous coordinates is given by

$$
(\mathbf{M}^T)^{-1} =
\begin{bmatrix}
1 & 0 & -1 & 1 \\
0 & 1 & 0 & 0 \\
-1 & 0 & -1 & 1 \\
0 & 0 & 0 & 1
\end{bmatrix}^{-1}
=
\begin{bmatrix}
\frac{1}{2} & 0 & -\frac{1}{2} & 0 \\
0 & 1 & 0 & 0 \\
-\frac{1}{2} & 0 & -\frac{1}{2} & 1 \\
0 & 0 & 0 & 1
\end{bmatrix}.
$$

Note that the origin in the original frame is now one unit in the n direction from the origin in the camera frame or, equivalently, at the point whose representation is $(0,0,1,1)$ in the camera frame.

In OpenGL, we can set a model-view matrix by sending an array of 16 elements to glLoadMatrix. For situations like the preceding, where we have the representation of one frame in terms of another through the specification of the basis vectors and the origin, it is a direct exercise to find the required coefficients. However, such is not usually the case. For most geometric problems, we usually go from one frame to another by a sequence of geometric transformations such as rotations, translations, and scales. We shall follow this approach in subsequent sections. But first, we shall look at a few simple approaches to building geometric objects.

4.5   Modeling a Colored Cube

We now have the tools we need to build three-dimensional graphical applications. Our tools are both conceptual and practical. We once again follow the pipeline approach that we pursued in our two-dimensional examples. Objects will again be defined in terms of sets of vertices. These vertices will pass through a number of transformations before the primitives that they define are rasterized in the frame buffer. The use of homogeneous coordinates not only will enable us to explain this process but will also lead to efficient implementation techniques.

FIGURE 4.28   One frame of cube animation.

We are going to produce a program to draw a rotating cube. One frame of an animation is shown in Figure 4.28. However, before we can rotate the cube, we shall consider how we can model it efficiently. First, we shall see that three-dimensional objects can be represented, like two-dimensional objects, through a set of vertices. We shall also see that data structures will help us to incorporate the relationships among the vertices, edges, and faces of geometric objects. Such data structures are supported in OpenGL through a facility called *vertex arrays* that we introduce at the end of this section.

After we have modeled the cube, we can animate it using affine transformations. We introduce these transformations in Section 4.6. We use these transformations to alter OpenGL's model-view matrix. In Chapter 5, we use these transformations again as part of the viewing process. Our pipeline model will serve us well. Vertices will flow through a number of transformations in the pipeline, all of which will use our homogeneous-coordinate representation. At the end of the pipeline awaits the rasterizer. At this point, we can assume it will do its job automatically, provided we perform the preliminary steps correctly.

4.5.1   Modeling the Faces

The cube is as simple a three-dimensional object as we might expect to model and display. There are a number of ways, however, to model it. A CSG system would regard it as a single primitive. At the other extreme, the hardware processes the cube as an object consisting of eight vertices. Our decision to use surface-based models implies that we regard a cube either as the intersection of six planes or as the six polygons, called **facets**, that define its faces. We start by assuming that the vertices of the cube are available through an array of vertices; for example, we could use

```
GLfloat vertices[8][3] = {{-1.0,-1.0,-1.0},{1.0,-1.0,-1.0},
   {1.0,1.0,-1.0}, {-1.0,1.0,-1.0}, {-1.0,-1.0,1.0},
   {1.0,-1.0,1.0}, {1.0,1.0,1.0}, {-1.0,1.0,1.0}};
```

We can adopt a more object-oriented form if we first define a three-dimensional point type

```
typedef GLfloat point3[3];
```

The vertices of the cube can be defined as

```
point3 vertices[8] ={{-1.0,-1.0,-1.0},{1.0,-1.0,-1.0},
    {1.0,1.0,-1.0}, {-1.0,1.0,-1.0}, {-1.0,-1.0,1.0},
    {1.0,-1.0,1.0}, {1.0,1.0,1.0}, {-1.0,1.0,1.0}};
```

OpenGL represents all vertices internally in four-dimensional homogeneous coordinates. Function calls using a three-dimensional type, such as glVertex3fv, have the values placed into four-dimensional form within the graphics system.

We can then use the list of points to define the faces of the cube. For example, one face is

```
glBegin(GL_POLYGON);
   glVertex3fv(vertices[0]);
   glVertex3fv(vertices[3]);
   glVertex3fv(vertices[2]);
   glVertex3fv(vertices[1]);
glEnd();
```

and we can define the other five faces in a similar manner. Note that we have defined three-dimensional polygons with exactly the same mechanism that we used to define two-dimensional polygons.

4.5.2 Inward- and Outward-Pointing Faces

We have to be careful about the order in which we specify our vertices when we are defining a three-dimensional polygon. We used the order 0, 3, 2, 1 for the first face. The order 1, 0, 3, 2 would be the same, because the final vertex in a polygon definition is always linked back to the first. However, the order 0, 1, 2, 3 is different. Although it describes the same boundary, the edges of the polygon are traversed in the reverse order—0, 3, 2, 1—as shown in Figure 4.29. In addition, each polygon has two sides. We can display either or both of them. First, however, we need a consistent way of identifying the faces.

We call a face **outward facing** if the vertices are traversed in a counterclockwise order when the face is viewed from the outside. This method is also known as the **right-hand rule** because if you orient the fingers of your right hand in the direction the vertices are traversed, the thumb points outward.

In our example it was important to have defined the order as 0, 3, 2, 1, rather than as 0, 1, 2, 3, so that we could define the outer side of the back of the cube correctly.[4] By defining front and back correctly, we shall be able to eliminate (or **cull**) faces that are not visible or to use different attributes to display front and back faces.

FIGURE 4.29 Traversal of the edges of a polygon.

---

4. Here *back* means as seen from the positive *z* direction. However, each face of an enclosed object, such as our cube, is an inside or outside face, regardless of from where we view it, as long as we view the face from outside the object.

4.5.3   Data Structures for Object Representation

We could now describe our cube through a set of vertex specifications. For example, we could use

```
glBegin(GL_POLYGON)
```

six times, each time followed by four vertices (via `glVertex`) and a `glEnd`, or we could use

```
glBegin(GL_QUADS)
```

followed by 24 vertices and a `glEnd`. Both of these methods work, but both fail to capture the essence of the cube's **topology**, as opposed to the cube's **geometry**. If we think of the cube as a polyhedron, we have an object—the cube—that is composed of six faces. The faces are each quadrilaterals that meet at vertices; each vertex is shared by three faces. In addition, pairs of vertices define edges of the quadrilaterals; each edge is shared by two faces. These statements describe the topology of a six-sided polyhedron. All are true, regardless of the location of the vertices—that is, regardless of the geometry of the object.[5]

Throughout the rest of this book, we shall see that there are numerous advantages to building for our objects data structures that separate the topology from the geometry. In this example we use a structure, the vertex list, that is both simple and useful and can be expanded later.

The data specifying the location of the vertices specify the geometry and can be stored as a simple list or array, such as in `vertices[8]`—the **vertex list**. The top-level entity is a cube; we regard it as being composed of six faces. Each face consists of four ordered vertices. Each vertex can be specified indirectly through its index. This data structure is shown in Figure 4.30. One of the advantages of this structure is that each geometric location appears only once, instead of being repeated each time it is used for a facet. If, in an interactive application, the location of a vertex is changed, the application needs to change that location only once, rather than searching for multiple occurrences of the vertex.

4.5.4   The Color Cube

We can use the vertex list to define a color cube. We assign the colors of the vertices of the color solid of Chapter 2 (black, white, red, green, blue, cyan, magenta, yellow) to the vertices. We define a function `quad` to draw quadrilateral polygons specified by pointers into the vertex list. We assign a color for the face using the index of the first vertex. Finally, the `colorcube` specifies the six faces, taking care to make them all outward-facing.

---

5. We are ignoring special cases (singularities) that arise, for example, when three or more vertices lie along the same line or when the vertices are moved so that we no longer have nonintersecting faces.

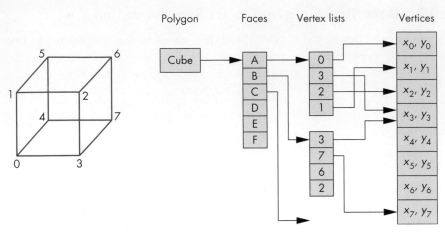

FIGURE 4.30 Vertex-list representation of a cube.

```
GLfoat vertices[8][3] ={{-1.0,-1.0,1.0},{-1.0,1.0,1.0},
   {1.0,1.0,1.0}, {1.0,-1.0,1.0}, {-1.0,-1.0,-1.0},
   {-1.0,1.0,-1.0}, {1.0,1.0,-1.0}, {1.0,-1.0,-1.0}};

GLfloat colors[8][3] = {{0.0,0.0,0.0},{1.0,0.0,0.0},
   {1.0,1.0,0.0}, {0.0,1.0,0.0}, {0.0,0.0,1.0},
   {1.0,0.0,1.0}, {1.0,1.0,1.0}, {0.0,1.0,1.0}};

void quad(int a, int b, int c, int d)
{
  glBegin(GL_QUADS);
    glColor3fv(colors[a]);
    glVertex3fv(vertices[a]);
    glColor3fv(colors[b]);
    glVertex3fv(vertices[b]);
    glColor3fv(colors[c]);
    glVertex3fv(vertices[c]);
    glColor3fv(colors[d]);
    glVertex3fv(vertices[d]);
  glEnd();
}

void colorcube()
{
   quad(0,3,2,1);
   quad(2,3,7,6);
   quad(0,4,7,3);
   quad(1,2,6,5);
   quad(4,5,6,7);
   quad(0,1,5,4);
}
```

4.5.5 Bilinear Interpolation

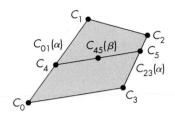

FIGURE 4.31 Bilinear interpolation.

Although we have specified colors for the vertices of the cube, the graphics system must decide how to use this information to assign colors to points inside the polygon. There are many ways to use the colors of the vertices to fill in, or **interpolate**, colors across a polygon. Probably the most common methods—ones that we use in other contexts—are based on **bilinear interpolation**.

Consider the polygon in Figure 4.31. The colors C_0, C_1, C_2, and C_3 are the ones assigned to the vertices in the application program. We can use linear interpolation to interpolate colors[6] along the edges between vertices 0 and 1, and between 2 and 3, by using

$$C_{01}(\alpha) = (1 - \alpha)C_0 + \alpha C_1,$$

$$C_{23}(\alpha) = (1 - \alpha)C_2 + \alpha C_3.$$

As α goes from 0 to 1, we generate colors, $C_{01}(\alpha)$ and $C_{23}(\alpha)$, along these two edges. For a given value of α, we obtain two colors, C_4 and C_5, on these edges. We can now interpolate colors along the line connecting the two points on the edges corresponding to C_4 and C_5:

$$C_{45}(\beta) = (1 - \beta)C_4 + \beta C_5.$$

For a flat quadrilateral, each color generated by this method corresponds to a point on the polygon. If the four vertices are not all in the same plane, then although a color is generated, its location on a surface is not clearly defined. We can avoid this problem by breaking up the quadrilateral into two triangles, as in Figure 4.32, and interpolating colors across each triangle. Thus, for the the triangle with vertex colors C_0, C_1, and C_2, we can interpolate between C_0 and C_1 as before and between C_0 and C_2, generating colors

$$C_{01}(\alpha) = (1 - \alpha)C_0 + \alpha C_1,$$

$$C_{02}(\alpha) = (1 - \alpha)C_0 + \alpha C_2.$$

Now we can proceed computing C_4 and C_5 along the edges and interpolating between them for interior colors along the line between them. We repeat the process for the second triangle using C_0, C_2, and C_3.

OpenGL uses variants of bilinear interpolation, not only for colors but, as we shall see in Chapters 6 and 8, for other values that can be assigned on a vertex-by-vertex basis as well.

We now have an object that we can display much as we did the three-dimensional Sierpinski gasket in Section 2.9, using glOrtho to provide a basic orthographic projection. In Section 4.5, we introduce transformations, enabling

---

6. Assume we are using RGB color and that the interpolation is applied individually to each primary color.

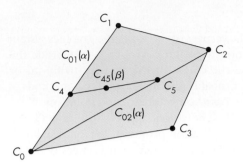

FIGURE 4.32   Bilinear interpolation of a triangle.

us to animate the cube and also to construct more complex objects. First, however, we introduce an OpenGL 1.1 feature that not only reduces the overhead of generating our cube but also gives us a higher-level method of working with the cube and with other polyhedral objects.

4.5.6 Vertex Arrays

Although we used vertex lists to model our cube, when we draw the cube we are making many calls to OpenGL functions. If we assign a color to each vertex, we make 60 OpenGL calls: six faces, each of which needs a `glBegin`, a `glEnd`, four calls to `glColor`, and four calls to `glVertex`. Each call involves overhead and data transfer. If, as we shall do in Chapter 6, we also specify a different normal vector at each vertex, we make even more function calls to draw our cube. Hence, although we have used a data structure that helps us to conceptualize the cube as a three-dimensional geometric object, the code to draw it may not execute quickly.

Vertex arrays provide a method for encapsulating the information in our data structure such that we can draw polyhedral objects with only a few function calls. They allow us to define a data structure using vertices and pass this structure to the implementation. When the objects defined by these arrays need to be drawn, we can ask OpenGL to traverse the structure with just a few function calls.

There are three steps in using vertex arrays. First, we enable the functionality of vertex arrays. Second, we tell OpenGL where and in what format the arrays are. Third, we render the object. The first two steps can be part of the initialization; the third is typically part of the display callback. We illustrate for the cube.

OpenGL allows many different types of arrays, including vertex, color, color index, normal, and texture coordinate, corresponding to items that can be set between a `glBegin` and a `glEnd`. Any given application usually requires only a subset of these types. For our rotating cube, we need only colors and vertices. We enable the corresponding arrays by

```
glEnableClientState(GL_COLOR_ARRAY);
glEnableClientState(GL_VERTEX_ARRAY);
```

Note that, unlike most OpenGL state information, the information for vertex arrays resides on the client side, not the server side—hence the function name `glEnableClientState`. The arrays are the same as before and can be set up as globals:

```
GLfloat vertices[8][3] = {{-1.0,-1.0,-1.0},{1.0,-1.0,-1.0},
{1.0,1.0,-1.0}, {-1.0,1.0,-1.0}, {-1.0,-1.0,1.0},
{1.0,-1.0,1.0}, {1.0,1.0,1.0}, {-1.0,1.0,1.0}};

GLfloat colors[8][3] = {{0.0,0.0,0.0},{1.0,0.0,0.0},
{1.0,1.0,0.0}, {0.0,1.0,0.0}, {0.0,0.0,1.0},
{1.0,0.0,1.0}, {1.0,1.0,1.0}, {0.0,1.0,1.0}};
```

We next identify where the arrays are by

```
glVertexPointer(3, GL_FLOAT, 0, vertices);
glColorPointer(3, GL_FLOAT, 0, colors);
```

The first three arguments state that the elements are three-dimensional colors and vertices stored as floats and that the elements are contiguous in the arrays. The fourth argument is a pointer to the actual array.

Now we have to provide the information in our data structure about the relationship between the vertices and the faces of the cube. We do so by specifying an array that holds the 24 ordered vertex indices for the six faces:

```
GLubyte cubeIndices[24]={0,3,2,1,      /* Face 0 */
                         2,3,7,6,      /* Face 1 */
                         0,4,7,3,      /* Face 2 */
                         1,2,6,5,      /* Face 3 */
                         4,5,6,7,      /* Face 4 */
                         0,1,5,4};     /* Face 5 */
```

Thus, the first face is determined by the indices (0, 3, 2, 1), the second by (2, 3, 7, 6), and so on. Note that we have put the indices in an order that preserves outside-facing polygons. The index array can also be specified as a global.

Now we can render the cube through use of the arrays. When we draw elements of the arrays, all the enabled arrays (in this example, colors and vertices) are rendered. We have a few options regarding how to draw the arrays. We can use the function

```
glDrawElements(GLenum type, GLsizei n, GLenum format, void *pointer)
```

Here type is the type of element, such as a line or polygon, that the arrays define; n is the number of elements that we wish to draw; format specifies the form of the data in the index array; and pointer points to the first index to use.

For our cube, within the display callback we could make six calls to `glDrawElements`, one for each face:

```
for(i=0;i<6;i++)
    glDrawElements(GL_POLYGON, 4, GL_UNSIGNED_BYTE, &cubeIndex[4*i]);
```

Thus, once we have set up and initialized the arrays, each time that we draw the cube, we have only six function calls. We can rotate the cube as before; glDrawElements uses the present state when it draws the cube.

We can do even better though. Each face of the cube is a quadrilateral. Thus, if we use GL_QUADS, rather than GL_POLYGON, we can draw the cube with the single function call

```
glDrawElements(GL_QUADS, 24, GL_UNSIGNED_BYTE, cubeIndices);
```

because GL_QUADS starts a new quadrilateral after each four vertices.

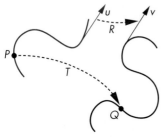

FIGURE 4.33 Transformation.

4.6 Affine Transformations

A **transformation** is a function that takes a point (or vector) and maps that point (or vector) into another point (or vector). We can picture such a function by looking at Figure 4.33 or by writing down the functional form

$$Q = T(P)$$

for points, or

$$v = R(u)$$

for vectors. If we can use homogeneous coordinates, then we can represent both vectors and points as four-dimensional column matrices and can define the transformation with a single function,

$$\mathbf{q} = f(\mathbf{p}),$$
$$\mathbf{v} = f(\mathbf{u}),$$

that transforms the representations of both points and vectors in a given frame.

This formulation is too general to be useful, as it encompasses all single-valued mappings of points and vectors. In practice, even if we were to have a convenient description of the function f, we would have to carry out the transformation on every point on a curve. For example, if we transform a line segment, a general transformation might require us to carry out the transformation for every point between the two endpoints.

Consider instead a restricted class of transformations. Let us assume that we are working in four-dimensional, homogeneous coordinates. In this space, both points and vectors are represented as 4-tuples.[7] We can obtain a useful class of transformations if we place restrictions on f. The most important restriction is

---

7. We consider only those functions that map vertices to other vertices and that obey the rules for manipulating points and vectors that we have developed in this chapter and in Appendix B.

linearity. A function f is a **linear function** if and only if, for any scalars α and β and any vertices p and q,

$$f(\alpha p + \beta q) = \alpha f(p) + \beta f(q).$$

The importance of such functions is that if we know the transformations of p and q, we can obtain the transformations of linear combinations of p and q by taking linear combinations of their transformations. Hence, we avoid having to calculate transformations for every linear combination.

Using homogeneous coordinates, we work with the representations of points and vectors. A linear transformation then transforms the representation of a given point (or vector) into another representation of that point (or vector) and can always be written in terms of the two representations, $\mathbf{u}$ and $\mathbf{v}$, as a matrix multiplication:

$$\mathbf{v} = \mathbf{A}\mathbf{u},$$

where $\mathbf{A}$ is a square matrix. Comparing this expression with what we obtained in Section 4.3 for changes in frame, we can observe that as long as $\mathbf{A}$ is nonsingular, each linear transformation corresponds to a change in frame. Hence, we can view a linear transformation in two equivalent ways: (1) as a change in the underlying representation, or frame, that yields a new representation of our vertices, or (2) as a transformation of the vertices within the same frame.

When we work with homogeneous coordinates, $\mathbf{A}$ is a 4×4 matrix that leaves unchanged the fourth (w) component of a representation. The matrix $\mathbf{A}$ is of the form

$$\mathbf{A} = \begin{bmatrix} \alpha_{11} & \alpha_{12} & \alpha_{13} & \alpha_{14} \\ \alpha_{21} & \alpha_{22} & \alpha_{23} & \alpha_{24} \\ \alpha_{31} & \alpha_{32} & \alpha_{33} & \alpha_{34} \\ 0 & 0 & 0 & 1 \end{bmatrix}.$$

The 12 values can be set arbitrarily, and we say this transformation has 12 **degrees of freedom**. However, points and vectors have slightly different representations in our affine space. Any vector is represented as

$$\mathbf{u} = \begin{bmatrix} \alpha_1 \\ \alpha_2 \\ \alpha_3 \\ 0 \end{bmatrix}.$$

Any point can be written as

$$\mathbf{p} = \begin{bmatrix} \beta_1 \\ \beta_2 \\ \beta_3 \\ 1 \end{bmatrix}.$$

If we apply an arbitrary $\mathbf{A}$ to a vector,

$$\mathbf{v} = \mathbf{Au},$$

we see that only nine of the elements of $\mathbf{A}$ affect $\mathbf{u}$, and thus there are only nine degrees of freedom in the transformation of vectors. Affine transformations of points have the full 12 degrees of freedom.

We can also show that affine transformations preserve lines. Suppose that we write a line in the form

$$P(\alpha) = P_0 + \alpha d,$$

where P_0 is a point and d is a vector. In any frame, the line can be expressed as

$$\mathbf{p}(\alpha) = \mathbf{p}_0 + \alpha \mathbf{d},$$

where $\mathbf{p}_0$ and $\mathbf{d}$ are the representations of P_0 and d in that frame. For any affine transformation matrix $\mathbf{A}$,

$$\mathbf{Ap}(\alpha) = \mathbf{Ap}_0 + \alpha \mathbf{Ad}.$$

Thus, we can construct the transformed line by first transforming $\mathbf{p}_0$ and $\mathbf{d}$ and using whatever line-generation algorithm we choose when the line segment must be displayed. If we use the two-point form of the line,

$$\mathbf{p}(\alpha) = \alpha \mathbf{p}_0 + (1 - \alpha)\mathbf{p}_1,$$

a similar result holds. We transform the representations of $\mathbf{p}_0$ and $\mathbf{p}_1$ and then construct the transformed line. Because there are only 12 elements in $\mathbf{M}$ that we can select arbitrarily, there are 12 degrees of freedom in the affine transformation of a line or line segment.

We have expressed these results in terms of abstract mathematical spaces. However, their importance in computer graphics is practical. We need only to transform the homogeneous-coordinate representation of the endpoints of a line segment to determine completely a transformed line. Thus, we can implement our graphics systems as a pipeline that passes endpoints through affine-transformation units, and we can finally generate the line at the rasterization stage.

Fortunately, most of the transformations that we need in computer graphics are affine. These transformations include rotation, translation, and scaling. With slight modifications, we can also use these results to describe the standard parallel and perspective projections in Chapter 5.

4.7   Translation, Rotation, and Scaling

We have been going back and forth between looking at geometric objects as abstract entities and working with their representation in a given frame. When we work with application programs, we have to work with representations.

In this section, first we show how we can describe the most important affine transformations independently of any representation. Then, we find matrices that describe these transformations by acting on the representations of our points and vectors. In Section 4.8, we shall see how these transformations are implemented in OpenGL.

We look at transformations as ways of moving the points that describe one or more geometric objects to new locations. Although there are many transformations that will move a particular point to a new location, there will almost always be only a single way to transform a collection of points to new locations while preserving the spatial relationships among them. Hence, although we can find many matrices that will move one corner of our color cube from P_0 to Q_0, only one of them, when applied to all the vertices of the cube, will result in a cube of the same size.

4.7.1 Translation

Translation is an operation that displaces points by a fixed distance in a given direction, as shown in Figure 4.34. To specify a translation, we need only to specify a displacement vector d, because the transformed points are given by

$$P' = P + d$$

for all points P on the object. Note that this definition of translation makes no reference to a frame or representation. Translation has three degrees of freedom because we can specify the three components of the displacement vector arbitrarily.

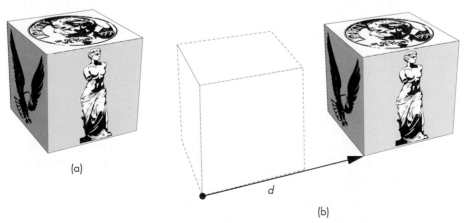

(a)

(b)

FIGURE 4.34 Translation. (a) Object in original position. (b) Object translated.

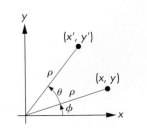

FIGURE 4.35 Two-dimensional rotation.

4.7.2 Rotation

Rotation is more difficult to specify than translation because more parameters are involved. We start with the simple example of rotating a point about the origin in a two-dimensional plane, as shown in Figure 4.35. Having specified a particular point—the origin—we are in a particular frame. A two-dimensional point at (x, y) in this frame is rotated about the origin by an angle θ to the position (x', y'). We can obtain the standard equations describing this rotation by representing (x, y) and (x', y') in polar form:

$$x = \rho \cos \phi,$$

$$y = \rho \sin \phi,$$

$$x' = \rho \cos(\theta + \phi),$$

$$y' = \rho \sin(\theta + \phi).$$

Expanding these terms using the trigonometric identities for the sine and cosine of the sum of two angles, we find

$$x' = \rho \cos \phi \cos \theta - \rho \sin \phi \sin \theta = x \cos \theta - y \sin \theta,$$

$$y' = \rho \cos \phi \sin \theta + \rho \sin \phi \cos \theta = x \sin \theta + y \cos \theta.$$

These equations can be written in matrix form as

$$\begin{bmatrix} x' \\ y' \end{bmatrix} = \begin{bmatrix} \cos \theta & -\sin \theta \\ \sin \theta & \cos \theta \end{bmatrix} \begin{bmatrix} x \\ y \end{bmatrix}.$$

We expand this form to three dimensions in Section 4.7.

Note three features of this transformation that extend to other rotations:

1. There is one point—the origin, in this case—that is unchanged by the rotation. We call this point the **fixed point** of the transformation. Figure 4.36 shows a two-dimensional rotation about a different fixed point.
2. Knowing that the two-dimensional plane is part of three-dimensional space, we can reinterpret this rotation in three dimensions. In a right-handed system, when we draw the x- and y-axes in the standard way, the positive z-axis comes out of the page. Our definition of a positive direction of rotation is counterclockwise when we look down the positive z-axis toward the origin. We use this definition to define positive rotations about other axes.
3. Two-dimensional rotation in the plane is equivalent to three-dimensional rotation about the z-axis. Points in planes of constant z all rotate in a similar manner, leaving their z values unchanged.

We can use these observations to define a general three-dimensional rotation that is independent of the frame. We must specify the three entities shown in Figure 4.37: a fixed point (P_f), a rotation angle (θ), and a line or vector about

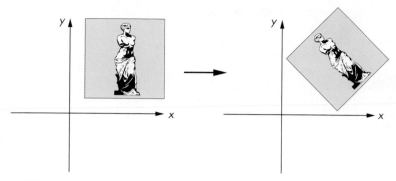

FIGURE 4.36 Rotation about a fixed point.

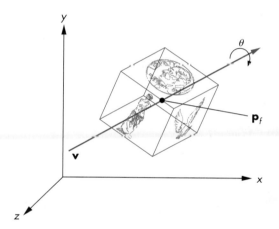

FIGURE 4.37 Three-dimensional rotation.

which to rotate. For a given fixed point, there are three degrees of freedom: the two angles necessary to specify the orientation of the vector and the angle that specifies the amount of rotation about the vector.

Rotation and translation are known as **rigid-body transformations**. No combination of rotations and translations can alter the shape or volume of an object; they can alter only the object's location and orientation. Consequently, rotation and translation alone cannot give us all possible affine transformations. The transformations in Figure 4.38 are affine, but they are not rigid-body transformations.

4.7.3 Scaling

Scaling is an affine non–rigid-body transformation. We can combine a properly chosen sequence of scalings, translations, and rotations to form any affine

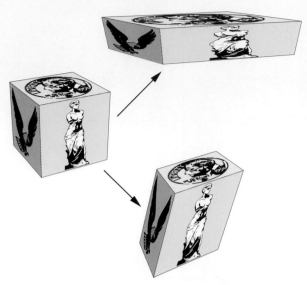

FIGURE 4.38   Non–rigid-body transformations.

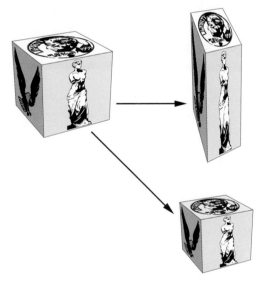

FIGURE 4.39   Uniform and nonuniform scaling.

transformation. Scaling can make an object bigger or smaller, as shown in Figure 4.39, which illustrates both uniform scaling in all directions and scaling in a single direction. We need nonuniform scaling to build up the full set of affine transformations that we use in modeling and viewing.

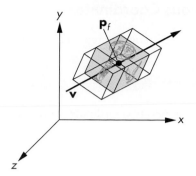

FIGURE 4.40 Effect of scale factor.

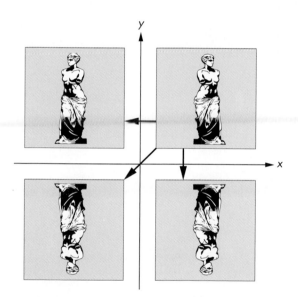

FIGURE 4.41 Reflection.

Scaling transformations have a fixed point, as we can see from Figure 4.40. Hence, to specify a scaling, we can specify the fixed point, a direction in which we wish to scale, and a scale factor (α). For $\alpha > 1$, the object gets longer in the specified direction; for $0 \leq \alpha < 1$, the object gets smaller in that direction. Negative values of α give us **reflection** (Figure 4.41) about the fixed point, in the scaling direction. Scaling has six degrees of freedom because we can specify an arbitrary fixed point and three independent scaling factors.

4.8   Transformations in Homogeneous Coordinates

All graphics APIs force us to work within some reference system. Hence, we cannot work with high-level expressions such as

$$Q = P + \alpha v.$$

Instead, we work with representations in homogeneous coordinates and with expressions such as

$$\mathbf{q} = \mathbf{p} + \alpha \mathbf{v}.$$

Within a frame, each affine transformation is represented by a 4×4 matrix of the form

$$\mathbf{A} = \begin{bmatrix} \alpha_{11} & \alpha_{12} & \alpha_{13} & \alpha_{14} \\ \alpha_{21} & \alpha_{22} & \alpha_{23} & \alpha_{24} \\ \alpha_{31} & \alpha_{32} & \alpha_{33} & \alpha_{34} \\ 0 & 0 & 0 & 1 \end{bmatrix}.$$

4.8.1   Translation

Translation displaces points to new positions defined by a displacement vector. If we move the point $\mathbf{p}$ to $\mathbf{p}'$ by displacing by a distance $\mathbf{d}$, then

$$\mathbf{p}' = \mathbf{p} + \mathbf{d}.$$

Looking at their homogeneous-coordinate forms

$$\mathbf{p} = \begin{bmatrix} x \\ y \\ z \\ 1 \end{bmatrix}, \qquad \mathbf{p}' = \begin{bmatrix} x' \\ y' \\ z' \\ 1 \end{bmatrix}, \qquad \mathbf{d} = \begin{bmatrix} \alpha_x \\ \alpha_y \\ \alpha_z \\ 0 \end{bmatrix},$$

we see that these equations can be written component by component as

$$x' = x + \alpha_x,$$
$$y' = y + \alpha_y,$$
$$z' = z + \alpha_z.$$

This method of representing translation using the addition of column matrices does not combine well with our representations of other affine transformations. However, we can also get this result using the matrix multiplication:

$$\mathbf{p}' = \mathbf{T}\mathbf{p},$$

where

$$\mathbf{T} = \begin{bmatrix} 1 & 0 & 0 & \alpha_x \\ 0 & 1 & 0 & \alpha_y \\ 0 & 0 & 1 & \alpha_z \\ 0 & 0 & 0 & 1 \end{bmatrix}.$$

$\mathbf{T}$ is called the **translation matrix**. We sometimes write it as $\mathbf{T}(\alpha_x, \alpha_y, \alpha_z)$ to emphasize the three independent parameters.

It might appear that using a fourth fixed element in the homogeneous representation of a point is not necessary. However, if we use the three-dimensional forms

$$\mathbf{q} = \begin{bmatrix} x \\ y \\ z \end{bmatrix}, \qquad \mathbf{q}' = \begin{bmatrix} x' \\ y' \\ z' \end{bmatrix},$$

it is not possible to find a 3×3 matrix $\mathbf{D}$ such that $\mathbf{q}' = \mathbf{D}\mathbf{q}$ for the given displacement vector $\mathbf{d}$. For this reason, the use of homogeneous coordinates is often seen as a clever trick that allows us to convert the addition of column matrices in three dimensions to matrix–matrix multiplication in four dimensions.

We can obtain the inverse of a translation matrix either by applying an inversion algorithm or by noting that if we displace a point by the vector d, we can return to the original position by a displacement of $-d$. By either method, we find that

$$\mathbf{T}^{-1}(\alpha_x, \alpha_y, \alpha_z) = \mathbf{T}(-\alpha_x, -\alpha_y, -\alpha_z) = \begin{bmatrix} 1 & 0 & 0 & -\alpha_x \\ 0 & 1 & 0 & -\alpha_y \\ 0 & 0 & 1 & -\alpha_z \\ 0 & 0 & 0 & 1 \end{bmatrix}.$$

4.8.2 Scaling

For both scaling and rotation, there is a fixed point that is unchanged by the transformation. We let the fixed point be the origin, and we show how we can concatenate transformations to obtain the transformation for an arbitrary fixed point.

A scaling matrix with a fixed point of the origin allows for independent scaling along the coordinate axes. The three equations are

$$x' = \beta_x x,$$
$$y' = \beta_y y,$$
$$z' = \beta_z z.$$

These three equations can be combined in homogeneous form as

$$\mathbf{p}' = \mathbf{S}\mathbf{p},$$

where

$$\mathbf{S} = \mathbf{S}(\beta_x, \beta_y, \beta_z) = \begin{bmatrix} \beta_x & 0 & 0 & 0 \\ 0 & \beta_y & 0 & 0 \\ 0 & 0 & \beta_z & 0 \\ 0 & 0 & 0 & 1 \end{bmatrix}.$$

As is true of the translation matrix and, indeed, of all homogeneous coordinate transformations, the final row of the matrix does not depend on the particular transformation, but rather forces the fourth component of the transformed point to retain the value 1.

We obtain the inverse of a scaling matrix by applying the reciprocals of the scale factors:

$$\mathbf{S}^{-1}(\beta_x, \beta_y, \beta_z) = \mathbf{S}\left(\frac{1}{\beta_x}, \frac{1}{\beta_y}, \frac{1}{\beta_z}\right).$$

4.8.3 Rotation

We first look at rotation with a fixed point at the origin. There are three degrees of freedom corresponding to our ability to rotate independently about the three coordinate axes. We have to be careful, however, because matrix multiplication is not a commutative operation (Appendix C). Rotation about the x-axis by an angle θ followed by rotation about the y-axis by an angle ϕ does not give us the same result as the one that we obtain if we reverse the order of the rotations.

We can find the matrices for rotation about the individual axes directly from the results of the two-dimensional rotation that we developed in Section 4.7.2. We saw that the two-dimensional rotation was actually a rotation in three dimensions about the z-axis and that the points remained in planes of constant z. Thus, in three dimensions, the equations for rotation about the z-axis by an angle θ are

$$x' = x \cos \theta - y \sin \theta,$$

$$y' = x \sin \theta + y \cos \theta,$$

$$z' = z;$$

or, in matrix form,

$$\mathbf{p}' = \mathbf{R}_z \mathbf{p},$$

where

$$\mathbf{R}_z = \mathbf{R}_z(\theta) = \begin{bmatrix} \cos \theta & -\sin \theta & 0 & 0 \\ \sin \theta & \cos \theta & 0 & 0 \\ 0 & 0 & 1 & 0 \\ 0 & 0 & 0 & 1 \end{bmatrix}.$$

We can derive the matrices for rotation about the x- and y-axes through an identical argument. If we rotate about the x-axis, the x values are unchanged, and we have a two-dimensional rotation in which points rotate in planes of constant x; for rotation about the y-axis, the y values are unchanged. The matrices are

$$\mathbf{R}_x = \mathbf{R}_x(\theta) = \begin{bmatrix} 1 & 0 & 0 & 0 \\ 0 & \cos\theta & -\sin\theta & 0 \\ 0 & \sin\theta & \cos\theta & 0 \\ 0 & 0 & 0 & 1 \end{bmatrix},$$

$$\mathbf{R}_y = \mathbf{R}_y(\theta) = \begin{bmatrix} \cos\theta & 0 & \sin\theta & 0 \\ 0 & 1 & 0 & 0 \\ -\sin\theta & 0 & \cos\theta & 0 \\ 0 & 0 & 0 & 1 \end{bmatrix}.$$

The signs of the sine terms are consistent with our definition of a positive rotation in a right-handed system.

Suppose that we let $\mathbf{R}$ denote any of our three rotation matrices. A rotation by θ can always be undone by a subsequent rotation by $-\theta$; hence,

$$\mathbf{R}^{-1}(\theta) = \mathbf{R}(-\theta).$$

In addition, noting that all the cosine terms are on the diagonal and the sine terms are off-diagonal, we can use the trigonometric identities $\cos(-\theta) = \cos\theta$ and $\sin(-\theta) = -\sin\theta$ to find

$$\mathbf{R}^{-1}(\theta) = \mathbf{R}^T(\theta).$$

In Section 4.8, we show how to construct any desired rotation matrix, with a fixed point at the origin, as a product of individual rotations about the three axes

$$\mathbf{R} = \mathbf{R}_z\mathbf{R}_y\mathbf{R}_x.$$

Using the fact that the transpose of a product is the product of the transposes in the reverse order, we see that for any rotation matrix,

$$\mathbf{R}^{-1} = \mathbf{R}^T.$$

A matrix whose inverse is equal to its transpose is called an **orthogonal matrix**. Normalized orthogonal matrices correspond to rotations about the origin.

4.8.4 Shear

Although we can construct any affine transformation from a sequence of rotations, translations, and scalings, there is one more affine transformation—the **shear** transformation—that is of such importance that we regard it as a basic type, rather than deriving it from the others. Consider a cube centered at the

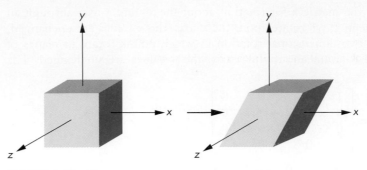

FIGURE 4.42   Shear.

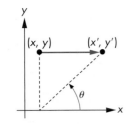

FIGURE 4.43   Computation of the shear matrix.

origin, aligned with the axes and viewed from the positive z-axis, as shown in Figure 4.42. If we pull the top to the right and the bottom to the left, we shear the object in the x direction. Note that neither the y nor the z values are changed by the shear, so we can call this operation x shear to distinguish it from shears of the cube in other possible directions. Using simple trigonometry on Figure 4.43, we see that each shear is characterized by a single angle θ; the equations for this shear are

$$x' = x + y \cot \theta,$$

$$y' = y,$$

$$z' = z,$$

leading to the shearing matrix

$$\mathbf{H}_x(\theta) = \begin{bmatrix} 1 & \cot \theta & 0 & 0 \\ 0 & 1 & 0 & 0 \\ 0 & 0 & 1 & 0 \\ 0 & 0 & 0 & 1 \end{bmatrix}.$$

We can obtain the inverse by noting that we need to shear in only the opposite direction; hence,

$$\mathbf{H}_x^{-1}(\theta) = \mathbf{H}_x(-\theta).$$

4.9   Concatenation of Transformations

In this section, we create examples of affine transformations by multiplying together, or **concatenating**, sequences of the basic transformations that we just introduced. Using this strategy is preferable to attempting to define an arbitrary transformation directly. The approach fits well with our pipeline architectures for implementing graphics systems.

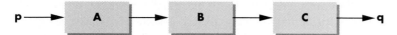

FIGURE 4.44   Application of transformations one at a time.

Suppose that we carry out three successive transformations on a point **p**, creating a new point **q**. Because the matrix product is associative, we can write the sequence as

$$\mathbf{q} = \mathbf{CBAp},$$

without parentheses. However, the order in which we carry out the transformations does affect the efficiency of the calculation. In one view, shown in Figure 4.44, we can carry out **A**, followed by **B**, followed by **C**—an order that corresponds to the grouping

$$\mathbf{q} = (\mathbf{C}(\mathbf{B}(\mathbf{Ap}))).$$

If we are to transform a single point, this order is the most efficient because each matrix multiplication involves multiplying a column matrix by a square matrix. If we have many points to transform, then we can proceed in two steps. First, we calculate

$$\mathbf{M} = \mathbf{CBA}.$$

Then, we use this matrix on each point

$$\mathbf{q} = \mathbf{Mp}.$$

This order corresponds to the pipeline in Figure 4.45, where we compute **M** first, then load it into a pipeline transformation unit. If we simply count operations, we see that although we do a little more work in computing **M** initially, because **M** may be applied to tens of thousands of points, this extra work is insignificant compared with the savings we obtain by using a single matrix multiplication for each point. We now derive examples of computing **M**.

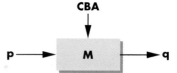

FIGURE 4.45   Pipeline transformation.

4.9.1   Rotation About a Fixed Point

Our first example shows how we can alter the transformations that we defined with a fixed point at the origin (rotation, scaling, shear) to have an arbitrary fixed point. We demonstrate for rotation about the z-axis; the technique is the same for the other cases.

Consider a cube with its center at $\mathbf{p}_f$ and its sides aligned with the axes. We want to rotate the cube about the z-axis, but this time about its center $\mathbf{p}_f$, which becomes the fixed point of the transformation, as shown in Figure 4.46. If $\mathbf{p}_f$ were the origin, we would know how to solve the problem: We would simply use $\mathbf{R}_z(\theta)$. This observation suggests the strategy of first moving the cube to the origin. We can then apply $\mathbf{R}_z(\theta)$ and finally move the object back such that its center is again at $\mathbf{p}_f$. This sequence is shown in Figure 4.47. In terms of our basic affine transformations, the first is $\mathbf{T}(-\mathbf{p}_f)$, the second is $\mathbf{R}_z(\theta)$, and the final is $\mathbf{T}(\mathbf{p}_f)$. Concatenating them together, we obtain the single matrix

$$\mathbf{M} = \mathbf{T}(\mathbf{p}_f)\mathbf{R}_z(\theta)\mathbf{T}(-\mathbf{p}_f).$$

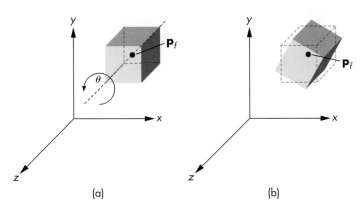

(a)   (b)

FIGURE 4.46   Rotation of a cube about its center.

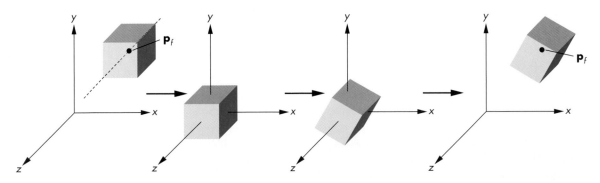

FIGURE 4.47   Sequence of transformations.

If we multiply out the matrices, we find that

$$
\mathbf{M} = \begin{bmatrix}
\cos\theta & -\sin\theta & 0 & x_f - x_f\cos\theta + y_f\sin\theta \\
\sin\theta & \cos\theta & 0 & y_f - x_f\sin\theta - y_f\cos\theta \\
0 & 0 & 1 & 0 \\
0 & 0 & 0 & 1
\end{bmatrix}.
$$

4.9.2 General Rotation

We now show that an arbitrary rotation about the origin can be composed of three successive rotations about the three axes. The order is not unique (see Exercise 4.10), although the resulting rotation matrix is. We form the desired matrix by first doing a rotation about the z-axis, then doing a rotation about the y-axis, and concluding with a rotation about the x-axis.

Consider the cube, again centered at the origin with its sides aligned with the axes, as shown in Figure 4.48(a). We can rotate it about the z-axis by an angle α to orient it as shown in Figure 4.48(b). We then rotate the cube by an angle β about the y-axis, as shown in a top view in Figure 4.49. Finally, we rotate the cube by an angle γ about the x-axis, as shown in a side view in Figure 4.50. Our final rotation matrix is

$$
\mathbf{R} = \mathbf{R}_x \mathbf{R}_y \mathbf{R}_z.
$$

A little experimentation should convince you that we can achieve any desired orientation by proper choice of α, β, and γ, although as we shall see in the example of Section 4.9.4, finding these angles can be tricky.

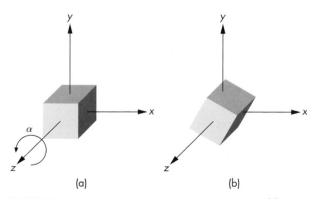

(a)   (b)

FIGURE 4.48   Rotation of a cube about the z-axis. (a) Cube before rotation. (b) Cube after rotation.

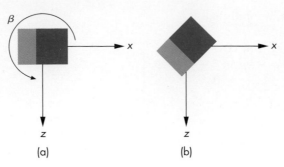

FIGURE 4.49   Rotation of a cube about the *y*-axis.

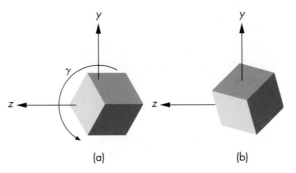

FIGURE 4.50   Rotation of a cube about the *x*-axis.

4.9.3 The Instance Transformation

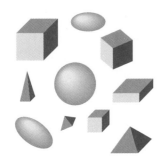

FIGURE 4.51   Scene of simple objects.

Our example of a cube that can be rotated to any desired orientation suggests a generalization appropriate for modeling. Consider a scene composed of many simple objects, such as that shown in Figure 4.51. One option is to define each of these objects, through its vertices, in the desired location with the desired orientation and size. An alternative is to define each of the object types once at a convenient size, in a convenient place, and with a convenient orientation. Each occurrence of an object in the scene is an **instance** of that object's prototype, and we can obtain the desired size, orientation, and location by applying an affine transformation—the **instance transformation**—to the prototype. We can build a simple database to describe a scene from a list of object identifiers (such as 1 for a cube and 2 for a sphere) and of the instance transformation to be applied to each object.

The instance transformation is applied in the order shown in Figure 4.52. Objects are usually defined in their own frames, with the origin at the center of mass and the sides aligned with the axes. First, we scale the object to

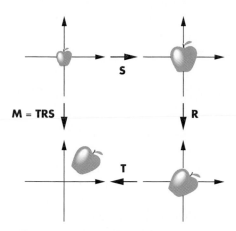

FIGURE 4.52 Instance transformation.

the desired size. Then we orient it with a rotation matrix. Finally, we translate it to the desired orientation. Hence, the instance transformation is of the form

$$\mathbf{M} = \mathbf{TRS}.$$

Modeling with the instance transformation works well not only with our pipeline architectures but also with the display lists that we introduced in Chapter 3. A complex object that is used many times can be loaded into the server once as a display list. Displaying each instance of it requires only sending the appropriate instance transformation to the server.

4.9.4 Rotation About an Arbitrary Axis

Our final rotation example illustrates not only how we can achieve a rotation about an arbitrary point and line in space but also how we can use direction angles to specify orientations. Consider rotating a cube, as shown in Figure 4.53. We need three entities to specify this rotation. There is a fixed point $\mathbf{p}_0$ that we assume is the center of the cube, a vector about which we rotate, and an angle of rotation. Note that none of these entities relies on a frame and that we have just specified a rotation in a coordinate-free manner. Nonetheless, to find an affine matrix to represent this transformation, we have to assume that we are in some frame.

The vector about which we wish to rotate the cube can be specified in various ways. One way is to use two points, $\mathbf{p}_1$ and $\mathbf{p}_2$, defining the vector

$$\mathbf{u} = \mathbf{p}_2 - \mathbf{p}_1.$$

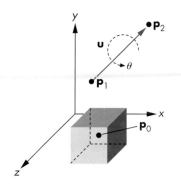

FIGURE 4.53 Rotation of a cube about an arbitrary axis.

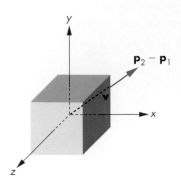

FIGURE 4.54 Movement of the fixed point to the origin.

Note that the order of the points determines the positive direction of rotation for θ and that even though we draw **u** as passing through $\mathbf{p}_0$, only the orientation of **u** matters. Replacing **u** with a unit-length vector

$$\mathbf{v} = \frac{\mathbf{u}}{|\mathbf{u}|} = \begin{bmatrix} \alpha_x \\ \alpha_y \\ \alpha_z \end{bmatrix}$$

in the same direction simplifies the subsequent steps. We have already seen that moving the fixed point to the origin is a helpful technique. Thus, our first transformation is the translation $\mathbf{T}(-\mathbf{p}_0)$, and the final one is $\mathbf{T}(\mathbf{p}_0)$. After the initial translation, the required rotation problem is as shown in Figure 4.54. Our previous example (see Section 4.8.2) showed that we could get an arbitrary rotation from three rotations about the individual axes. This problem is more difficult because we do not know what angles to use for the individual rotations. Our strategy is to carry out two rotations to align the axis of rotation, **v**, with the z-axis. Then we can rotate by θ about the z-axis, after which we can undo the two rotations that did the aligning. Our final rotation matrix will be of the form

$$\mathbf{R} = \mathbf{R}_x(-\theta_x)\mathbf{R}_y(-\theta_y)\mathbf{R}_z(\theta)\mathbf{R}_y(\theta_y)\mathbf{R}_x(\theta_x).$$

This sequence of rotations is shown in Figure 4.55. The difficult part of the process is determining θ_x and θ_y.

We proceed by looking at the components of **v**. Because **v** is a unit-length vector,

$$\alpha_x^2 + \alpha_y^2 + \alpha_z^2 = 1.$$

We draw a line segment from the origin to the point $(\alpha_x, \alpha_y, \alpha_z)$. This line segment has unit length and the orientation of **v**. Next, we draw the perpendiculars

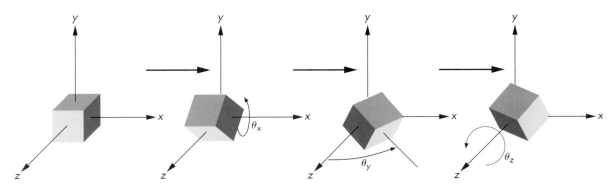

FIGURE 4.55 Sequence of rotations.

from the point $(\alpha_x, \alpha_y, \alpha_z)$ to the coordinate axes, as shown in Figure 4.56. The three **direction angles**—ϕ_x, ϕ_y, ϕ_z—are the angles between the line segment (or **v**) and the axes. The **direction cosines** are given by

$$\cos \phi_x = \alpha_x,$$
$$\cos \phi_y = \alpha_y,$$
$$\cos \phi_z = \alpha_z.$$

Only two of the direction angles are independent because

$$\cos^2 \phi_x + \cos^2 \phi_y + \cos^2 \phi_z = 1.$$

We can now compute θ_x and θ_y using these angles. Consider Figure 4.57. It shows that the effect of the desired rotation on the point $(\alpha_x, \alpha_y, \alpha_z)$ is to rotate the line segment into the plane $y = 0$. If we look at the projection of the line segment (before the rotation) on the plane $x = 0$, we see a line segment of length d on this plane. Another way to envision this figure is to think of the plane $x = 0$ as a wall and consider a distant light source located far down the positive x-axis. The line that we see on the wall is the shadow of the line segment from the origin to $(\alpha_x, \alpha_y, \alpha_z)$. Note that the length of the shadow is less than the length of the line segment. We can say the line segment has been **foreshortened** to $d = \sqrt{\alpha_y^2 + \alpha_z^2}$. The desired angle of rotation is determined by the angle that this shadow makes with the z-axis. However, the rotation matrix is determined by the sine and cosine of θ_x; thus, we never need to compute θ_x; rather, we need to compute only

$$\mathbf{R}_x(\theta_x) = \begin{bmatrix} 1 & 0 & 0 & 0 \\ 0 & \alpha_z/d & -\alpha_y/d & 0 \\ 0 & \alpha_y/d & \alpha_z/d & 0 \\ 0 & 0 & 0 & 1 \end{bmatrix}.$$

We compute $\mathbf{R}_y$ in a similar manner. Figure 4.58 shows the rotation. This angle is clockwise about the y-axis, therefore we have to be careful of the sign of the sine terms in the matrix, which is

$$\mathbf{R}_y(\theta_y) = \begin{bmatrix} d & 0 & -\alpha_x & 0 \\ 0 & 1 & 0 & 0 \\ \alpha_x & 0 & d & 0 \\ 0 & 0 & 0 & 1 \end{bmatrix}.$$

Finally, we concatenate all the matrices to find

$$\mathbf{M} = \mathbf{T}(\mathbf{p}_0)\mathbf{R}_x(-\theta_x)\mathbf{R}_y(-\theta_y)\mathbf{R}_z(\theta)\mathbf{R}_y(\theta_y)\mathbf{R}_x(\theta_x)\mathbf{T}(-\mathbf{p}_0).$$

Let us look at a specific example. Suppose that we wish to rotate an object by 45 degrees about the line passing through the origin and the point

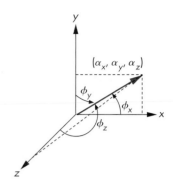

FIGURE 4.56   Direction angles.

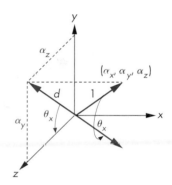

FIGURE 4.57   Computation of the x rotation.

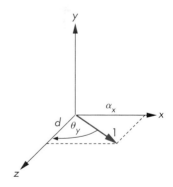

FIGURE 4.58   Computation of the y rotation.

$(1, 2, 3)$. We leave the fixed point at the origin. The first step is to find the point along the line that is a unit distance from the origin. We obtain it by normalizing $(1, 2, 3)$ to $(1/\sqrt{14}, 2/\sqrt{14}, 3/\sqrt{14})$, or $(1/\sqrt{14}, 2/\sqrt{14}, 3/\sqrt{14}, 1)$ in homogeneous coordinates. The first part of the rotation takes this point to $(0, 0, 1, 1)$. We first rotate about the x-axis by the angle $\cos^{-1} \frac{3}{\sqrt{13}}$. This matrix carries $(1/\sqrt{14}, 2/\sqrt{14}, 3/\sqrt{14}, 1)$ to $(1/\sqrt{14}, 0, \sqrt{13/14}, 1)$, which is in the plane $y = 0$. The y rotation must be by the angle $\cos^{-1}(\sqrt{13/14})$. This rotation aligns the object with the z-axis, and now we can rotate about the z-axis by the desired 45 degrees. Finally, we undo the first two rotations. If we concatenate these five transformations into a single rotation matrix $\mathbf{R}$, we find that

$$\mathbf{R} = \mathbf{R}_x\left(-\cos^{-1}\frac{3}{\sqrt{13}}\right)\mathbf{R}_y\left(-\cos^{-1}\sqrt{\frac{13}{14}}\right)\mathbf{R}_z(45)\mathbf{R}_y\left(\cos^{-1}\sqrt{\frac{13}{14}}\right)$$

$$\mathbf{R}_x\left(\cos^{-1}\frac{3}{\sqrt{13}}\right)$$

$$= \begin{bmatrix} \frac{2+13\sqrt{2}}{28} & \frac{2-\sqrt{2}-3\sqrt{7}}{14} & \frac{6-3\sqrt{2}+4\sqrt{7}}{28} & 0 \\ \frac{2-\sqrt{2}+3\sqrt{7}}{14} & \frac{4+5\sqrt{2}}{14} & \frac{6-3\sqrt{2}-\sqrt{7}}{14} & 0 \\ \frac{6-3\sqrt{2}-4\sqrt{7}}{28} & \frac{6-3\sqrt{2}+\sqrt{7}}{14} & \frac{18+5\sqrt{2}}{28} & 0 \\ 0 & 0 & 0 & 1 \end{bmatrix}.$$

This matrix does not change any point on the line passing through the origin and the point $(1, 2, 3)$. If we want a fixed point other than the origin, we form the matrix

$$\mathbf{M} = \mathbf{T}(\mathbf{p}_f)\mathbf{R}\mathbf{T}(-\mathbf{p}_f).$$

This example is not simple. It illustrates the powerful technique of applying many simple transformations to get a complex one. The problem of rotation about an arbitrary point or axis arises in many applications. The major variants lie in the manner in which the axis of rotation is specified. However, we can usually employ techniques similar to the ones that we have used here to determine direction angles or direction cosines.

4.10   OpenGL Transformation Matrices

We can now focus on the implementation of a homogeneous-coordinate transformation package and of that package's interface to the user. In OpenGL, there are several matrices that are part of the state. We shall use only the model-view matrix in this chapter. The matrix state is manipulated by a common set of functions, and we use the `glMatrixMode` function to select the matrix to which the operations apply. In OpenGL, the model-view matrix normally is an affine-transformation matrix and has only 12 degrees of freedom, as discussed in Section 4.5. The projection matrix, as we shall see in Chapter 5, is also a 4×4 matrix, but it is

FIGURE 4.59   Current transformation matrix (CTM).

not affine. OpenGL allows you to work with arbitrary 4×4 matrices and make use of all 16 degrees of freedom.

4.10.1   The Current Transformation Matrix

The generalization common to most graphics systems is the **current transformation matrix** (**CTM**). It is the matrix that is applied to any vertex that is defined subsequent to its setting. If we change the CTM, we change the state of the system. The CTM is part of the pipeline (Figure 4.59); thus, if **p** is a vertex, the pipeline produces **Cp**. The CTM is a 4×4 matrix; it can be altered by a set of functions provided by the graphics package.

Let **C** denote the CTM. Initially, it is set to the 4×4 identity matrix; it can be reinitialized as needed. If we use the symbol $\leftarrow$ to denote replacement, we can write this initialization operation as

$$\mathbf{C} \leftarrow \mathbf{I}.$$

The functions that alter **C** are of two forms: those that load it with some matrix and those that modify it by premultiplication or postmultiplication by a matrix. OpenGL uses only postmultiplication. The three transformations supported in most systems are translation, scaling with a fixed point of the origin, and rotation with a fixed point of the origin. Symbolically, we can write these operations in postmultiplication form as

$$\mathbf{C} \leftarrow \mathbf{CT},$$
$$\mathbf{C} \leftarrow \mathbf{CS},$$
$$\mathbf{C} \leftarrow \mathbf{CR},$$

and in load form as

$$\mathbf{C} \leftarrow \mathbf{T},$$
$$\mathbf{C} \leftarrow \mathbf{S},$$
$$\mathbf{C} \leftarrow \mathbf{R}.$$

Most systems allow us to load the CTM with an arbitrary matrix **M**,

$$\mathbf{C} \leftarrow \mathbf{M},$$

or to postmultiply by an arbitrary matrix **M**,

$$\mathbf{C} \leftarrow \mathbf{CM}.$$

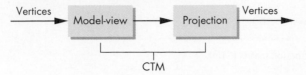

FIGURE 4.60   Model-view and projection matrices.

4.10.2   Rotation, Translation, and Scaling

In OpenGL, the matrix that is applied to all primitives is the product of the model-view matrix (`GL_MODELVIEW`) and the projection matrix (`GL_PROJECTION`). We can think of the CTM as the product of these matrices (Figure 4.60), and we can manipulate each individually by selecting the desired matrix by `glMatrixMode`. We can load a matrix with the function

```
glLoadMatrixf(pointer_to_matrix);
```

or a set a matrix to the identity matrix with the function

```
glLoadIdentity();
```

Arbitrary 4×4 matrices can be specified by a pointer to a one-dimensional array of 16 entries organized by the *columns* of the desired matrix.[8] We can alter the selected matrix with `glMultMatrixf(pointer_to_matrix)`. Rotation, translation, and scaling are provided through the three functions

```
glRotatef(angle, vx, vy, vz);
glTranslatef(dx, dy, dz);
glScalef(sx ,sy, sz);
```

All three alter the selected matrix by postmultiplication. For rotation, the angle is specified in degrees, and the variables vx, vy, and vz are the components of a vector about which we wish to rotate. In the translation function, the variables are the components of the displacement vector; for scaling, the variables determine the scale factors along the coordinate axes.

4.10.3   Rotation About a Fixed Point in OpenGL

In Section 4.8, we showed that we can perform a rotation about a fixed point, other than the origin, by first moving the fixed point to the origin, then rotating about the origin, and finally moving the fixed point back to its original location. The following sequence sets the matrix mode, then forms the required matrix

---

8. Note that this organization differs from C, which organizes two-dimensional arrays by rows.

for a 45-degree rotation about the line through the origin and the point $(1, 2, 3)$ with a fixed point of $(4, 5, 6)$:

```
glMatrixMode(GL_MODELVIEW);
glLoadIdentity();
glTranslatef(4.0, 5.0, 6.0);
glRotatef(45.0, 1.0, 2.0, 3.0);
glTranslatef(-4.0, -5.0, -6.0);
```

Note that we do not have to form the rotation matrix about an arbitrary axis, as we did in Section 4.8, although you might test your skill with transformations by doing so, forming the same matrix by concatenation of rotations about the three axes.

4.10.4 Order of Transformations

You might be bothered by what appears to be a reversal of the required function calls. The rule in OpenGL is this: *The transformation specified last is the one applied first.* A little examination shows that this order is a consequence of multiplying the CTM on the right by the specified affine transformation and thus is both correct and reasonable. The sequence of operations that we specified was

$$\mathbf{C} \leftarrow \mathbf{I},$$

$$\mathbf{C} \leftarrow \mathbf{CT}(4.0, 5.0, 6.0),$$

$$\mathbf{C} \leftarrow \mathbf{CR}(45.0, 1.0, 2.0, 3.0),$$

$$\mathbf{C} \leftarrow \mathbf{CT}(-4.0, -5.0, -6.0).$$

In each step, we postmultiply at the end of the existing CTM, forming the matrix

$$\mathbf{C} = \mathbf{T}(4.0, 5.0, 6.0)\mathbf{R}(45.0, 1.0, 2.0, 3.0)\mathbf{T}(-4.0, -5.0, -6.0),$$

which is the matrix that we expect from Section 4.8. Each vertex $\mathbf{p}$ that is specified *after* the model-view matrix has been set will be multiplied by $\mathbf{C}$, thus forming the new vertex

$$\mathbf{q} = \mathbf{Cp}.$$

There are other ways to think about the order of operations. One way is in terms of a stack. Altering the CTM is similar to pushing matrices onto a stack; when we apply the final transformation, the matrices are popped off the stack in the reverse order in which they were placed there. The analogy is conceptual rather than exact because when we call a transformation function in OpenGL, the matrix is altered immediately. However, OpenGL provides stacks to store matrices. When we discuss hierarchical modeling in Chapter 10, we shall need the operations

```
glPushMatrix();
glPopMatrix();
```

to traverse our data structures. In addition, as we did when we used the pushing and popping attributes in Chapter 3, we shall often find it helpful to bracket changes in state with a push and a pop of the matrix.

4.10.5 Spinning of the Cube

In this program, we take the cube that we defined in Section 4.5 and we rotate it using the three buttons of the mouse. We shall define three callback functions:

```
glutDisplayFunc(display);
glutIdleFunc(spincube);
glutMouseFunc(mouse);
```

The function display first sets a model-view matrix using the values of three angles determined by the mouse callback. It then draws a cube, using the colorcube function from Section 4.5.4. This example uses double buffering. Each time that the display callback is executed, it starts by clearing the frame buffer and the depth buffer—for hidden-surface removal; it finishes with a buffer swap.

```
void display()
{
   glClear(GL_COLOR_BUFFER_BIT | GL_DEPTH_BUFFER_BIT);
   glLoadIdentity();
   glRotatef(theta[0], 1.0, 0.0, 0.0);
   glRotatef(theta[1], 0.0, 1.0, 0.0);
   glRotatef(theta[2], 0.0, 0.0, 1.0);
   colorcube();
   glutSwapBuffers();
}
```

The mouse callback selects the axis for rotation:

```
void mouse(int btn, int state, int x, int y)
{
    if(btn==GLUT_LEFT_BUTTON && state == GLUT_DOWN) axis = 0;
    if(btn==GLUT_MIDDLE_BUTTON && state == GLUT_DOWN) axis = 1;
    if(btn==GLUT_RIGHT_BUTTON && state == GLUT_DOWN) axis = 2;
}
```

The idle callback increments the angle associated with the chosen axis by 2 degrees each time:

```
void spinCube()
{
   theta[axis] += 2.0;
   if( theta[axis] > 360.0 ) theta[axis] -= 360.0;
   glutPostRedisplay();
}
```

We can terminate the program using the keyboard with the simple keyboard callback

```
void mykey(char key, int mousex, int mousey)
{
    if(key=='q'||key=='Q') exit();
}
```

We shall not discuss hidden-surface removal until Chapter 5, but we note here that using it in OpenGL is almost trivial. We need only to clear the depth buffer and to enable the function by glEnable(GL_DEPTH_TEST). For the complete program, see Appendix A.

4.10.6 Loading, Pushing, and Popping Matrices

For most purposes, we can use rotation, translation, and scaling to form a desired transformation matrix. In some circumstances, however, such as with forming a shear matrix, it is easier to set up the matrix directly. Just as we load an identity matrix, we can load a 4×4 homogeneous-coordinate matrix as the current matrix by

```
glLoadMatrixf(myarray)
```

We can also multiply on the right of the current matrix by a user-defined matrix using the function

```
glMultMatrixf(myarray)
```

The array myarray is a one-dimensional array of 16 elements arranged by *columns*. Thus, if we want to multiply by the 4×4 matrix m, we can form myarray by

```
GLfloat m[4][4];
GLfloat myarray[16];

for(i=0;i<3;i++) for(j=0;j<3;j++)
   myarray[4*j+i]= m[i][j];
```

Sometimes we want to perform a transformation and then return to the same state as before its execution. This situation occurs when we execute an instance transformation that applies to a particular object and does not apply to the following objects in the code. Rather than recompute the transformation that existed before the instance transformation, we can push the transformation matrix on a stack with glPushMatrix before we multiply by the instance transformation and recover it later with glPopMatrix. Thus, we often see the sequence

```
glPushMatrix();
glTranslatef(....);
glRotatef(.....);
glScalef(.....);

/* draw object here */

glPopMatrix();
```

One place where pushing and popping of matrices and of attributes is extremely important is encountered when we use display lists. By pushing state variables on their stacks when we begin a display list and popping them at the end of the display list, we avoid any subsequent side affects due to state changes in the display list.

4.11   Interfaces to Three-Dimensional Applications

In Section 4.10.5, we used a three-button mouse to control the direction of rotation of our cube. This interface is limited. Rather than use all three mouse buttons to control rotation, we might want to use the mouse to control functions, such as exiting the program, that we would have had to assign to keys in our previous example.

We noted in Section 4.8 that there were many ways to obtain a given orientation. Rather than do rotations about the x-, y-, and z-axes in that order, we could do a rotation about the x-axis, followed by a rotation about the y-axis, and finish with another rotation about the x-axis. If we do our orientation this way, we can obtain our desired orientation using only two mouse buttons. However, there is still a problem: Our rotations are in a single direction. It would be easier to orient an object if we could rotate either forward or backward about an axis and could stop the rotation once we reached a desired orientation.

GLUT allows us to use the keyboard in combination with the mouse. We could, for example, use the left mouse button for a forward rotation about the x-axis and the control key in combination with the left mouse button for a backward rotation about the x-axis.

However, neither of these options provides a good user interface, which should be more intuitive and less awkward. Let's consider a few options that provide a more interesting and smoother interaction.

4.11.1   Using Areas of the Screen

Suppose that we want to use one mouse button for orienting an object, one for getting closer to or farther from the object, and one for translating the object to the left or right. We can use the motion callback to achieve all these functions. The callback returns which button has been activated and where the mouse is located. We can use the location of the mouse to control how fast and in which direction we rotate or translate and to move in or out.

As we just noted, we need the ability to rotate about only two axes to achieve any orientation. We could then use the left mouse button and the mouse position to control orientation. We can use the distance from the center of the screen to control the x and y rotations. Thus, if the left mouse button is held down but the mouse is located in the center of the screen, there will be no rotation; if the mouse is moved up, the object will be rotated about the y-axis in a clockwise manner; if the mouse is moved down, the object will be rotated about the y-axis in a counterclockwise manner. Likewise, motion to the right or left will cause rotation about the x-axis. The distance from the center can control the speed of rotation. Motion toward the corners can cause simultaneous rotations about the x- and y-axes.

Using the right mouse button in a similar manner, we can translate the object right to left and up to down. We might use the middle mouse button to move the object toward or away from the viewer by having the mouse position control a translation in the z direction. The code for such an interface is straightforward in GLUT; we leave it as an exercise (Exercise 4.19).

4.11.2 A Virtual Trackball

The use of the mouse position to control rotation about two axes provides us with most of the functionality of a trackball (Section 3.2). We can go one step further and create a graphical or virtual trackball using our mouse and the screen. One of the benefits of such a device is that we can create a frictionless trackball that, once we start it rotating, will continue to rotate until stopped by the user. Thus, the device will support continuous rotations of objects but will still allow changes in the speed and orientation of the rotation. We could also do the same for translation and other parameters that we can control from the mouse.

We start by mapping the position of a trackball to that of a mouse. Consider the trackball in Figure 4.61. We assume that the ball has a radius of 1 unit. We can map a position on its surface to the plane $y = 0$ by doing an orthogonal projection to the plane, as shown in Figure 4.62. The position (x, y, z) on the

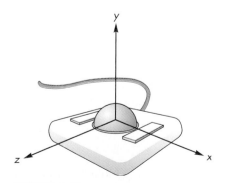

FIGURE 4.61   Trackball frame.

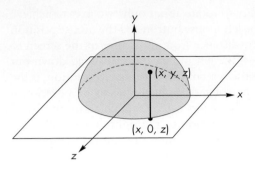

FIGURE 4.62   Projection of the trackball position to the plane.

surface of the ball is mapped to $(x, 0, z)$ on the plane. This projection is reversible because we know that the three-dimensional point that is projected to the point on the plane must satisfy the equation of the sphere

$$x^2 + y^2 + z^2 = 1.$$

Thus, given the point on the plane $(x, 0, z)$, the corresponding point on the hemisphere must be (x, y, z), where

$$y = \sqrt{1 - x^2 - z^2}.$$

We can compute the three-dimensional information and track it as the mouse moves. Suppose we have two positions on the hemisphere $\mathbf{p}_1$ and $\mathbf{p}_2$; then, the vectors from the origin to these points determine the orientation of a plane, as in Figure 4.63, whose normal is defined by their cross product

$$\mathbf{n} = \mathbf{p}_1 \times \mathbf{p}_2.$$

The motion of the trackball that moves from $\mathbf{p}_1$ to $\mathbf{p}_2$ can be achieved by a rotation about $\mathbf{n}$. The angle of rotation is the angle between the vectors $\mathbf{p}_1$ and $\mathbf{p}_2$, which we can compute using the magnitude of the cross product. Because both $\mathbf{p}_1$ and $\mathbf{p}_2$ have unit length,

$$|\sin \theta| = |\mathbf{n}|.$$

If we are tracking the mouse at a high rate, then the changes in position that we detect will be small; rather than use an inverse trigonometric function to find θ, we can use an approximation, such as

$$\sin \theta \approx \theta.$$

We can implement the virtual trackball through use of the idle, motion, and mouse callbacks in GLUT. We can think of the process in terms of three logical

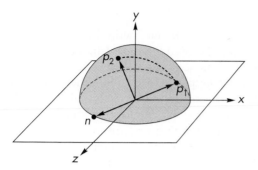

FIGURE 4.63 Computation of the plane of rotation.

variables, or flags, that control the tracking of the mouse and of the display redrawing. These are set initially as[9]

```
bool trackingMouse = false;
bool trackballMove = false;
bool redrawContinue = false;
```

If redrawContinue is true, the idle function posts a redisplay. If trackingMouse is true, we update the trackball position as part of the motion callback. If trackballMove is true, we update the rotation matrix that we use in our display routine.

The changes in these variables are controlled through the mouse callback. When we push a mouse button—either a particular button or any button depending on exactly what we want—then we start updating the trackball position by initializing it, then letting the motion callback update it and post redisplays in response to changes in the position of the mouse. When the mouse button is released, we stop tracking the mouse. We can use the two most recent mouse positions to define a velocity vector so that we can continually update the rotation matrix. Thus, once the mouse button is released, the object will continue to rotate at a constant velocity—an effect that we could achieve with an ideal frictionless trackball, but not directly with either a real mouse or a real trackball.

The code for the rotating cube with a virtual trackball is in trackball.c. This code has a few simple approximations to speed it up; it also takes care of a few problems, such as what happens if the mouse position is not directly below the hemisphere of the trackball—for example, when it is located in the corner of the window.

---

9. If the compiler does not support the Boolean type, we can use #define bool int and then define true and false as 1 and 0, respectively.

4.11.3 Smooth Rotations

The trackball example illustrates a problem with our method of computing rotations. Our approach to orienting objects is based on angles (the Euler angles) measured with respect to the three coordinate axes. This perspective led to our forming rotation matrices by concatenating simple rotations about the x-, y-, and z-axes to obtain a desired rotation about an arbitrary axis. Although OpenGL allows us to rotate about an arbitrary axis, we usually employ our concatenation strategy to determine this axis and the corresponding angle of rotation.

Consider what happens if we wish to move between two orientations as part of an animation. In principle, we can determine an appropriate rotation matrix as the product of rotations about the three axes,

$$\mathbf{R}(\theta) = \mathbf{R}_x(\theta_x)\mathbf{R}_y(\theta_y)\mathbf{R}_z(\theta_z).$$

If we want to create a sequence of images that move between the two orientations, we can change the individual angles in small increments, either individually or simultaneously. Such a sequence would not appear smooth to a viewer; she would detect the individual rotations about each of the three axes.

With the trackball, we saw that we could rotate the cube directly from one orientation to another in a smooth manner. We did so by exploiting the equivalence between the two orientations of the cube and two points on a unit circle. A smooth rotation between the two orientations corresponds to a great circle on the surface of a sphere. This circle corresponds to a single rotation about a suitable axis that is the normal to the plane determined by the two points on the sphere and that sphere's center. If we increase this angle smoothly, our viewer will see a smooth rotation.

In one sense, what has failed us is our mathematical formulation, which relies on the use of coordinate axes. However, a deeper and less axis-dependent method is embedded within the matrix formulation. Suppose that we start with an arbitrary rotation matrix $\mathbf{R}$. All points on a line in the direction $\mathbf{d}$ are unaffected by the rotation. Thus, for any such point $\mathbf{p}$,

$$\mathbf{Rp} = \mathbf{p}.$$

In terms of the matrix $\mathbf{R}$, the column matrix $\mathbf{p}$ is an **eigenvector** of the matrix corresponding to the **eigenvalue** 1 (see Appendix C). In addition, for the direction $\mathbf{d}$

$$\mathbf{Rd} = \mathbf{d}$$

so that its direction is unaffected by the rotation. Consequently, $\mathbf{d}$ is also an eigenvector of $\mathbf{R}$ corresponding to another eigenvalue of 1. The point $\mathbf{p}$ must be the fixed point of the rotation, and the vector $\mathbf{d}$ must be the normal to a plane perpendicular to the direction of rotation. In terms of the trackball, computing the axis of rotation was equivalent to finding a particular eigenvector of the desired rotation matrix. We could also go the other way. Given an arbitrary rotation matrix, by finding its eigenvalues and eigenvectors, we also determine the axis of rotation and the fixed point.

4.11.4 Incremental Rotation

Suppose that we are given two orientations of an object such as a camera and we want to go smoothly from one to the other. One approach is to find the great circle path as we did with the virtual trackball and make incremental changes in the angle that rotates us along this path. Thus, we start with the axis of rotation, a start angle, a final angle, and a desired increment in the angle determined by the number of steps we wish to take. The main loop in the code will be of the form

```
for(i=0, i<imax; i++)
{
    glRotatef(delta_theta, dx, dy, dz);
    draw object()
}
```

One problem with this approach is that the calculation of the rotation matrix requires the evaluation of the sines and cosines of three angles. We would do better if we compute the rotation matrix once and reuse it through code such as

```
GLfloat m[16];
glRotatef(dx, dy, dz, delta_theta);
glGetFloatv(GL_MODELVIEW, m);

for(i=0, i<imax; i++)
{
    glMultMatrixf(m);
    draw_object()
}
```

We could also use the small angle approximations

$$\sin \theta \approx \theta,$$

$$\cos \theta \approx 1.$$

If we form an arbitrary rotation matrix through the Euler angles

$$\mathbf{R} = \mathbf{R}_z(\psi)\mathbf{R}_y(\phi)\mathbf{R}_x(\theta),$$

then we can use the approximations to write $\mathbf{R}$ as

$$\mathbf{R} = \begin{bmatrix} \cos\psi & -\sin\psi & 0 & 0 \\ \sin\psi & \cos\psi & 0 & 0 \\ 0 & 0 & 1 & 0 \\ 0 & 0 & 0 & 1 \end{bmatrix} \begin{bmatrix} \cos\phi & 0 & \sin\phi & 0 \\ 0 & 1 & 0 & 0 \\ -\sin\phi & 0 & \cos\phi & 0 \\ 0 & 0 & 0 & 1 \end{bmatrix}$$

$$\begin{bmatrix} 1 & 0 & 0 & 0 \\ 0 & \cos\theta & -\sin\theta & 0 \\ 0 & \sin\theta & \cos\theta & 0 \\ 0 & 0 & 0 & 1 \end{bmatrix}$$

$$\approx \begin{bmatrix} 1 & -\psi & \phi & 0 \\ \psi & 1 & -\theta & 0 \\ -\phi & \theta & 1 & 0 \\ 0 & 0 & 0 & 1 \end{bmatrix}.$$

4.12   Quaternions

Quaternions are an extension of complex numbers that provide an alternative method for describing and manipulating rotations. Although less intuitive than our original approach, quaternions provide advantages for animation and hardware implementation of rotation.

4.12.1   Complex Numbers and Quaternions

In two dimensions, the use of complex numbers to represent operations such as rotation is well known to most students of engineering and science. For example, suppose that we let $\mathbf{i}$ denote the pure imaginary number such that $\mathbf{i}^2 = -1$. Recalling Euler's identity,

$$e^{i\theta} = \cos\theta + \mathbf{i}\sin\theta,$$

we can write the polar representation of a complex number $\mathbf{c}$ as

$$\mathbf{c} = a + \mathbf{i}b = re^{i\theta},$$

where $r = \sqrt{a^2 + b^2}$ and $\theta = \tan^{-1} b/a$.

If we rotate $\mathbf{c}$ about the origin by ϕ to $\mathbf{c}'$, we can find $\mathbf{c}'$ using a rotation matrix, or we can use the polar representation to write

$$\mathbf{c}' = re^{i(\theta+\phi)} = re^{i\theta}e^{i\phi}.$$

Thus $e^{i\phi}$ is a rotation operator in the complex plane and provides an alternative to using transformations that may prove more efficient in practice.

However, we are really interested in rotations in a three-dimensional space. In three dimensions, the problem is more difficult because to specify a rotation about the origin we need to specify both a direction (a vector) and the amount of rotation about it (a scalar). One solution is to use a representation that consists of both a vector and a scalar. Usually, this representation is written as the **quaternion**

$$a = (q_0, q_1, q_2, q_3) = (q_0, \mathbf{q}),$$

where $\mathbf{q} = (q_1, q_2, q_3)$. The operations among quaternions are based on the use of three "complex" numbers $\mathbf{i}, \mathbf{j},$ and $\mathbf{k}$ with the properties

$$\mathbf{i}^2 = \mathbf{j}^2 = \mathbf{k}^2 = \mathbf{ijk} = -1.$$

These numbers are analogous to the unit vectors in three dimensions, and we can write $\mathbf{q}$ as

$$\mathbf{q} = q_1 \mathbf{i} + q_2 \mathbf{j} + q_3 \mathbf{k}.$$

Now we can use the relationships among $\mathbf{i}, \mathbf{j},$ and $\mathbf{k}$ to derive quaternion addition and multiplication. If the quaternion b is given by

$$b = (p_0, \mathbf{p}),$$

then using the dot and cross products for vectors:

$$a + b = (p_0 + q_0, \mathbf{p} + \mathbf{q}),$$
$$ab = (p_0 q_0 - \mathbf{q} \cdot \mathbf{p}, q_0 \mathbf{p} + p_0 \mathbf{q} + \mathbf{q} \times \mathbf{p}).$$

We can also define a magnitude for quaternions in the normal manner as

$$|a|^2 = q_0^2 + q_1^2 + q_2^2 + q_3^2 = q_0^2 + \mathbf{q} \cdot \mathbf{q}.$$

Quaternions have a multiplicative identity, the quaternion $(1, \mathbf{0})$, and it is easy to verify that the inverse of a quaternion is given by

$$a^{-1} = \frac{1}{|a|^2} (q_0, -\mathbf{q}).$$

4.12.2 Quaternions and Rotation

So far we have only defined a new mathematical object. For it to be of use to us, we must relate it to our geometric entities and show how it can be used to carry out operations such as rotation. Suppose that we use the vector part of a quaternion to represent a point in space

$$p = (0, \mathbf{p}).$$

Thus, the components of $\mathbf{p} = (x, y, z)$ give the location of the point. Consider the quaternion

$$r = \left(\cos \frac{\theta}{2}, \sin \frac{\theta}{2} \mathbf{v} \right),$$

where $\mathbf{v}$ has unit length. We can then show that the quaternion r is a unit quaternion ($|r| = 1$), and therefore

$$r^{-1} = \left(\cos \frac{\theta}{2}, - \sin \frac{\theta}{2} \mathbf{v} \right).$$

If we consider the quaternion product of the quaternion p that represents a point with r, we obtain the quaternion

$$p' = rpr^{-1}.$$

This quaternion has the form $(0, \mathbf{p}')$, where

$$\mathbf{p}' = \cos^2 \frac{\theta}{2} \mathbf{p} + \sin^2 \frac{\theta}{2} (\mathbf{p} \cdot \mathbf{v}) \mathbf{v} + 2 \sin \frac{\theta}{2} \cos \frac{\theta}{2} (\mathbf{v} \times \mathbf{p}) - \sin \frac{\theta}{2} (\mathbf{v} \times \mathbf{p}) \times \mathbf{v}$$

and thus p' is the representation of a point. What is less obvious is that p' is the result of rotating the point $\mathbf{p}$ by θ degrees about the vector $\mathbf{v}$. However, we can verify that this indeed is the case by comparing terms in p' with those of the general rotation. Before doing so, consider the implication of this result. Because we get the same result, the quaternion product formed from r and p is an alternate to transformation matrices as a representation of rotation with a fixed point of the origin about an arbitrary axis. If we count operations, quaternions are faster and have been built into both hardware and software implementations.

Let us consider a few examples. Suppose that we consider the rotation about the z axis by θ with a fixed point at the origin. The desired unit vector v is $(0,0,1)$ yielding the quaternion

$$r = \cos \frac{\theta}{2} + \sin \frac{\theta}{2}(0, 0, 1).$$

The rotation of an arbitrary point $\mathbf{p} = (x, y, z)$ yields the quaternion

$$p' = rpr^{-1} = r(0, \mathbf{p})r^{-1} = (0, \mathbf{p}'),$$

where

$$\mathbf{p}' = (x \cos \theta - y \sin \theta, x \sin \theta + y \cos \theta, z).$$

Thus, we get the expected result but with fewer operations. If we consider a sequence of rotations about the coordinate axes that in matrix form yields the matrix $\mathbf{R} = \mathbf{R}_x(\theta_x)\mathbf{R}_y(\theta_y)\mathbf{R}_z(\theta_z)$, we instead can use the product of the corresponding quaternions to form $r_x r_y r_z$.

Returning to the rotation about an arbitrary axis, in Section 4.8.4, we derived a matrix of the form

$$\mathbf{M} = \mathbf{T}(\mathbf{p}_0)\mathbf{R}_x(-\theta_x)\mathbf{R}_y(-\theta_y)\mathbf{R}_z(\theta_z)\mathbf{R}_y(\theta_y)\mathbf{R}_x(\theta_x)\mathbf{T}(-\mathbf{p}_0).$$

Because of the translations at the beginning and end, we cannot use quaternions for the entire operation. We can, however, recognize that the elements of $p' = rpr^{-1}$ can be used to find the elements of the homogeneous coordinate rotation matrix embedded in $\mathbf{M}$. Thus, if again $r = (\cos\frac{\theta}{2}, \sin\frac{\theta}{2}\mathbf{v})$, then

$$
\mathbf{R} = \begin{bmatrix}
1 - 2\sin^2\frac{\theta}{2}(v_y^2 + v_z^2) & 2\sin^2\frac{\theta}{2}v_xv_y - 2\cos\frac{\theta}{2}\sin\frac{\theta}{2}v_z \\
2\sin^2\frac{\theta}{2}v_xv_y + 2\cos\frac{\theta}{2}\sin\frac{\theta}{2}v_z & 1 - 2\sin^2\frac{\theta}{2}(v_x^2 + v_z^2) \\
2\sin^2\frac{\theta}{2}v_xv_z - 2\cos\frac{\theta}{2}\sin\frac{\theta}{2}v_y & 2\sin^2\frac{\theta}{2}v_yv_z + 2\cos\frac{\theta}{2}\sin\frac{\theta}{2}v_x \\
0 & 0
\end{bmatrix}
$$

$$
\begin{bmatrix}
2\sin^2\frac{\theta}{2}v_xv_z + 2\cos\frac{\theta}{2}\sin\frac{\theta}{2}v_y & 0 \\
2\sin^2\frac{\theta}{2}v_yv_z - 2\cos\frac{\theta}{2}\sin\frac{\theta}{2}v_a & 0 \\
1 - 2\sin^2\frac{\theta}{2}(v_x^2 + v_y^2) & 0 \\
0 & 1
\end{bmatrix}.
$$

This matrix can be made to look more familiar if we use the trigonometric identities

$$\cos\theta = \cos^2\frac{\theta}{2} - \sin^2\frac{\theta}{2} = 1 - 2\sin^2\frac{\theta}{2},$$

$$\sin\theta = 2\cos\frac{\theta}{2}\sin\frac{\theta}{2},$$

and recall that $\mathbf{v}$ is a unit vector so that

$$v_x^2 + v_y^2 + v_z^2 = 1.$$

Thus, we can use quaternion products to form r and then form the rotation part of $\mathbf{M}$ by matching terms between $\mathbf{R}$ and r. We then use our normal transformation operations to add in the effect of the two translations.

In addition to the efficiency of using quaternions instead of rotation matrices, quaternions can be interpolated to obtain smooth sequences of rotations for animation. We shall see additional examples that require smooth rotation in Chapter 10.

Summary and Notes

In this chapter, we have presented two different—but ultimately complementary—points of view regarding the mathematics of computer graphics. One is that mathematical abstraction of the objects with which we work in computer graphics is necessary if we are to understand the operations that we carry out in our programs. The other is that transformations—and the techniques for carrying them out, such as the use of homogeneous coordinates—are the basis for implementations of graphics systems.

Our mathematical tools come from the study of vector analysis and linear algebra. For computer-graphics purposes, however, the order in which we have chosen to present these tools is the reverse of the order that most students learn. In particular, linear algebra is studied first, then vector-space concepts are linked to the study of n-tuples in $\mathbf{R}^n$. In contrast, our study of representation in mathematical spaces led to our use of linear algebra as a tool for implementing abstract types.

We pursued a coordinate-free approach for two reasons. First, we wanted to show that all the basic concepts of geometric objects and of transformations are independent of the ways the latter are represented. Second, as object-oriented languages become more prevalent, application programmers will work directly with the objects, instead of with those objects' representations. The references in Suggested Readings contain examples of geometric programming systems that illustrate the potential of this approach.

Homogeneous coordinates provided a wonderful example of the power of mathematical abstraction. By going to an abstract mathematical space—the affine space—we were able to find a tool that led directly to efficient software and hardware methods.

Finally, we provided the set of affine transformations supported in OpenGL and discussed ways that we could concatenate them to provide all affine transformations. The strategy of combining a few simple types of matrices to build a desired transformation is a powerful one; you should use it for a few of the exercises at the end of this chapter. In Chapter 5, we build on these techniques to develop viewing for three-dimensional graphics; in Chapter 10 we use our transformations to build hierarchical models.

Suggested Readings

There are many texts on vector analysis and linear algebra, although most treat the two topics separately. Within the geometric-design community the vector-space approach of coordinate-free descriptions of curves and surfaces has been popular; see the book by Faux and Pratt [Fau80]. See DeRose [DeR88, DeR89] for an introduction to geometric programming. Homogeneous coordinates arose in geometry [Max51] and were later discovered by the graphics community [Rie81]. Their use in hardware started with Silicon Graphics' Geometry Engine [Cla82]. Modern hardware architectures use application-specific integrated circuits (ASICs) that include homogeneous coordinate transformations.

Quaternions were introduced to computer graphics by Shoemaker [Sho85] for use in animation. See the book by Kuipers [Kui99] for many examples of the use of rotation matrices and quaternions.

Software tools such as Mathematica [Wol91] and MATLAB [Mat95] are excellent aids for learning to manipulate transformation matrices.

Exercises

4.1   Show that the following sequences commute:
   a. A rotation and a uniform scaling
   b. Two rotations about the same axis
   c. Two translations

4.2   *Twist* is similar to rotation about the origin except that the amount of rotation increases by a factor f the farther a point is from the origin. Write a program to twist the triangle-based Sierpinski gasket by a user-supplied value of f. Observe how the shape of the gasket changes with the number of subdivisions.

4.3   Write a library of functions that will allow you to do geometric programming. Your library should contain functions for manipulating the basic geometric types (points, lines, vectors) and operations on those types, including dot and cross products. It should allow you to change frames. You can also create functions to interface with OpenGL so that you can display the results of geometric calculations.

4.4   If we are interested in only two-dimensional graphics, we can use three-dimensional homogeneous coordinates by representing a point as $\mathbf{p} = [x \, y \, 1]^T$ and a vector as $\mathbf{v} = [a \, b \, 0]^T$. Find the 3×3 rotation, translation, scaling, and shear matrices. How many degrees of freedom are there in an affine transformation for transforming two-dimensional points?

4.5   We can specify an affine transformation by considering the location of a small number of points both before and after these points have been transformed. In three dimensions, how many points must we consider to specify the transformation uniquely? How does the required number of points change when we work in two dimensions?

4.6   How must we change the rotation matrices if we are working in a left-handed system and we retain our definition of a positive rotation?

4.7   Show that any sequence of rotations and translations can be replaced by a single rotation about the origin followed by a translation.

4.8   Derive the shear transformation from the rotation, translation, and scaling transformations.

4.9   In two dimensions, we can specify a line by the equation $y = mx + h$. Find an affine transformation to reflect two-dimensional points about this line. Extend your result to reflection about a plane in three dimensions.

4.10 In Section 4.8, we showed that an arbitrary rotation matrix could be composed from successive rotations about the three axes. How many ways can we compose a given rotation if we can do only three simple rotations? Are all three of the simple rotation matrices necessary?

4.11 Add shear to the instance transformation. Show how to use this expanded instance transformation to generate parallelepipeds from a unit cube.

4.12 Find a homogeneous-coordinate representation of a plane.

4.13 Determine the rotation matrix formed by glRotate. That is, assume that the fixed point is the origin and that the parameters are those of the function.

4.14 Consider the solution of either constant-coefficient linear differential or difference equations (recurrences). Show that the solutions of the homogeneous equations form a vector space. Relate the solution for a particular inhomogeneous equation to an affine space.

4.15 Write a program to generate a Sierpinski gasket as follows. Start with a white triangle. At each step, use transformations to generate three similar triangles that are drawn over the original triangle, leaving the center of the triangle white and the three corners black.

4.16 Start with a cube centered at the origin and aligned with the coordinate axes. Find a rotation matrix that will orient the cube symmetrically, as shown in Figure 4.64.

4.17 We have used vertices in three dimensions to define objects such as three-dimensional polygons. Given a set of vertices, find a test to determine whether the polygon that they determine is planar.

4.18 Three vertices determine a triangle if they do not lie in the same line. Devise a test for collinearity of three vertices.

4.19 We defined an instance transformation as the product of a translation, a rotation, and a scaling. Can we accomplish the same effect by applying these three types of transformations in a different order?

4.20 Write a program that allows you to orient the cube with one mouse button, to translate it with a second, and to zoom in and out with a third.

4.21 Given two nonparallel, three-dimensional vectors u and v, how can we form an orthogonal coordinate system in which u is one of the basis vectors?

4.22 An incremental rotation about the z-axis is determined by the matrix

$$\begin{bmatrix} 1 & -\theta & 0 & 0 \\ \theta & 1 & 0 & 0 \\ 0 & 0 & 1 & 0 \\ 0 & 0 & 0 & 1 \end{bmatrix}.$$

What negative aspects are there if we use this matrix for a large number of steps? Can you suggest a remedy? *Hint:* Consider points a distance of 1 from the origin.

4.23 Find the quaternions for 90-degree rotations about the x- and y-axes. Determine their product.

FIGURE 4.64 Symmetric orientation of cube.

4.24 Determine the rotation matrix $\mathbf{R} = \mathbf{R}(\theta_x)\mathbf{R}(\theta_y)\mathbf{R}(\theta_z)$. Find the corresponding quaternion.

4.25 Redo the trackball program using quaternions instead of rotation matrices.

4.26 Implement a simple package in C++ that can do the required mathematical operations for transformations. Such a package might include matrices, vectors, and frames.

4.27 In principle, an object-oriented system could provide scalars, vectors, and points as basic types, none of the popular APIs does so. Why do you think this is the case?

VIEWING

We have completed our discussion of the first half of the synthetic camera model—specifying objects in three dimensions. We now investigate the multitude of ways in which we can describe our virtual camera. Along the way, we examine related topics, such as the relationship between classical viewing techniques and computer viewing and how projection is implemented using projective transformations.

There are three parts to our approach. First, we look at the types of views that we can create and why we need more than one type of view. Then we examine how an application program can specify a particular view within OpenGL. We shall see that the viewing process has two parts. In the first, we use the model-view matrix to switch vertex representations from the object frame in which we defined our objects to their representation in the eye frame, in which the camera is at the origin. This representation of the geometry will allow us to use canonical viewing procedures. The second part of the process deals with the type of projection we prefer (parallel or perspective) and the part of the world we wish to image (the clipping or view volume). These specifications will allow us to form a projection matrix that is concatenated with the model-view matrix. Once more, we use a simple example program to demonstrate how the OpenGL API handles viewing. Finally, we derive the projection matrices that describe the most important parallel and perspective views.

5.1 Classical and Computer Viewing

Before looking at the interface between computer-graphics systems and application programs for three-dimensional viewing, we take a slight diversion to consider classical viewing. There are two reasons for examining classical viewing. First, many of the jobs that were formerly done by hand drawing—such as animation in movies, architectural rendering, drafting, and mechanical-parts design—are now routinely done with the aid of computer graphics. Practitioners of these fields need to be able to produce classical views—such as isometrics, elevations, and various perspectives—and thus must be able to use the computer

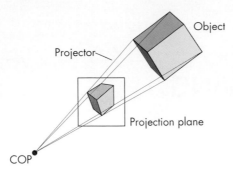

FIGURE 5.1   Viewing.

system to produce such renderings. Second, the relationships between classical and computer viewing show many advantages of, and a few difficulties with, the approach used by most APIs.

When we introduced the synthetic-camera model in Chapter 1, we pointed out the similarities between classical and computer viewing. The basic elements in both cases are the same. We have objects, a viewer, projectors, and a projection plane (Figure 5.1). The projectors meet at the **center of projection** (**COP**). The COP corresponds to the center of the lens in the camera or in the eye, and in a computer-graphics system, it is the origin of the **camera frame** for perspective views. All standard graphics systems follow the model that we described in Chapter 1, which is based on geometric optics. The projection surface is a plane, and the projectors are straight lines. This situation is the one we usually encounter and is easiest to implement, especially with our pipeline model.

Both classical and computer graphics allow the viewer to be an infinite distance from the objects. Note that as we move the COP to infinity, the projectors become parallel, and the COP can be replaced by a **direction of projection** (**DOP**), as shown in Figure 5.2. Note also that as the COP moves to infinity, we can leave the projection plane fixed and the size of the image remains about the same, even though the COP is infinitely far from the objects. Views with a finite COP are called **perspective views**; views with a COP at infinity are called **parallel views**. For parallel views, the origin of the camera frame usually lies in the projection plane.

Color Plates 9 and 10 show a parallel and a perspective rendering, respectively. These plates illustrate the importance of having both types of view available in applications such as architecture; in an API that supports both types of viewing, the user can switch easily between various viewing modes. Most modern APIs support both parallel and perspective viewing. The class of projections produced by these systems is known as **planar geometric projections** because the projection surface is a plane and the projectors are lines. Both perspective and parallel projections preserve lines; they do not, in general, preserve angles. Although the parallel views are the limiting case of perspective viewing, both

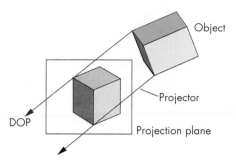

Object

Projector

DOP

Projection plane

FIGURE 5.2   Movement of the center of projection (COP) to infinity.

classical and computer viewing usually treat them as separate cases. For classical views, the techniques that people use to construct the two types by hand are different, as anyone who has taken a drafting class surely knows. From the computer perspective, there are differences in how we specify the two types of views. Rather than looking at a parallel view as the limit of the perspective view, we derive the limiting equations and use those equations directly to form the corresponding projection matrix. In modern pipeline architectures, the projection matrix corresponding to either type of view can be loaded into the pipeline.

Although computer graphics systems have two fundamental types of viewing (parallel and perspective), classical graphics appears to permit a host of different views, ranging from multiview orthographic projections to one-, two-, and three-point perspectives. This seeming discrepancy arises in classical graphics as a result of the desire to show a specific relationship among an object, the viewer, and the projection plane, as opposed to the computer graphics approach of complete independence of all specifications.

5.1.1 Classical Viewing

When an architect draws an image of a building, she knows which side she wishes to display and thus where she should place the viewer in relationship to the building. Each classical view is determined by a specific relationship between the objects and the viewer.

In classical viewing, there is the underlying notion of a **principal face**. The types of objects viewed in real-world applications, such as architecture, tend to be composed of a number of planar faces, each of which can be thought of as a principal face. For a rectangular object, such as a building, there are natural notions of the front, back, top, bottom, right, and left faces. In addition, many real-world objects have faces that meet at right angles; thus, such objects often have three orthogonal directions associated with them.

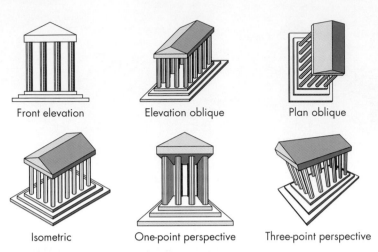

FIGURE 5.3   Classical views.

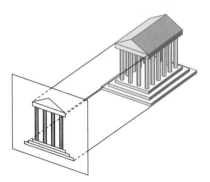

FIGURE 5.4   Orthographic projections.

Figure 5.3 shows some of the main types of views. We start with the most restrictive view for each of the parallel and perspective types, then move to the less restrictive conditions.

5.1.2 Orthographic Projections

Our first classical view is the **orthographic projection** shown in Figure 5.4. In all orthographic (or orthogonal) views, the projectors are perpendicular to the projection plane. In a **multiview orthographic projection**, we make multiple projections, in each case with the projection plane parallel to one of the principal faces of the object. Usually, we use three views—such as the front, top, and right—to display the object. The reason that we produce multiple views should be clear from Figure 5.5. For a boxlike object, only the faces parallel to the

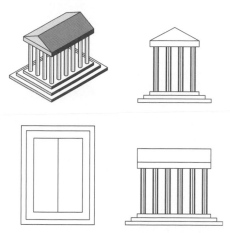

FIGURE 5.5   Temple and three multiview orthographic projections.

projection plane appear in the image. A viewer usually needs more than two views to visualize what an object looks like from its multiview orthographic projections. Visualization from these images can take skill on the part of the viewer. The importance of this type of view is that it preserves both distances and angles, and because there is no distortion of either distance or shape, multiview orthographic projections are well suited for working drawings.

5.1.3 Axonometric Projections

If we want to see more principal faces of our boxlike object in a single view, we must remove one of our restrictions. In **axonometric** views, the projectors are still orthogonal to the projection plane, as they are in Figure 5.6, but the projection plane can have any orientation with respect to the object. If the projection plane is placed symmetrically with respect to the three principal faces that meet at a corner of our rectangular object, we have an **isometric** view. If the projection plane is placed symmetrically with respect to two of the principal faces, the view is **dimetric**. The general case is a **trimetric** view. These views are shown in Figure 5.7. Note that in an isometric view, a line segment's length in the image space is shorter than its length measured in the object space. This **foreshortening** of distances is the same in the three principal directions, so we can still make distance measurements. In the dimetric view, however, there are two different foreshortening ratios; in the trimetric view, there are three. Also, although parallel lines are preserved in the image, angles are not. A circle is projected into an ellipse. This distortion is the price we pay for the ability to see more than one principal face in a view that can be produced easily either by hand or by computer. Axonometric views are used extensively in architectural and mechanical design.

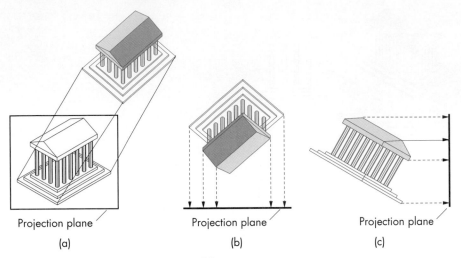

Projection plane   Projection plane   Projection plane

(a)   (b)   (c)

FIGURE 5.6   Axonometric projections. (a) Construction of trimetric-view projections. (b) Top view. (c) Side view.

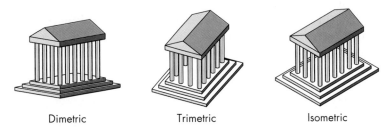

Dimetric   Trimetric   Isometric

FIGURE 5.7   Axonometric views.

5.1.4   Oblique Projections

The **oblique** views are the most general parallel views. We allow the projectors to make an arbitrary angle with the projection plane, as shown in Figure 5.8. In an oblique projection, angles in planes parallel to the projection plane are preserved. A circle in a plane parallel to the projection plane is projected into a circle, yet we can see more than one principal face of the object. Oblique views are the most difficult to construct by hand. They are also somewhat unnatural. Most physical viewing devices, including the human visual system, have a lens that is in a fixed relationship with the image plane—usually, the lens is parallel to the plane. Although these devices produce perspective views, if the viewer is far from the object, the views are approximately parallel, but orthogonal, because the projection plane is parallel to the lens. The bellows camera that we used to develop the synthetic-camera model in Section 1.6 has the flexibility to produce approximations to parallel oblique views.

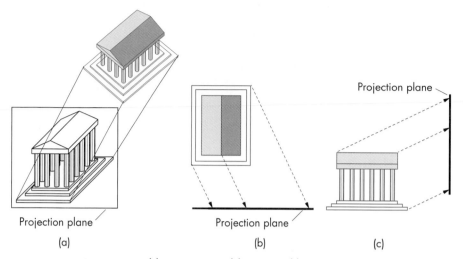

FIGURE 5.8 Oblique view. (a) Construction. (b) Top view. (c) Side view.

From the application programmer's point of view, there is no significant difference among the different parallel views. The application programmer specifies a type of view—parallel or perspective—and a set of parameters that describe the camera. The problem for the application programmer is how to specify these parameters in the viewing procedures so as best to view an object or to produce a specific classical view.

5.1.5 Perspective Viewing

All perspective views are characterized by **diminution** of size. When objects are moved farther from the viewer, their images become smaller. This size change gives perspective views their natural appearance; however, because the amount by which a line is foreshortened depends on how far the line is from the viewer, we cannot make measurements from a perspective view. Hence, the major use of perspective views is in applications such as architecture and animation, where it is important to achieve real-looking images.

In the classical perspective views, the viewer is located symmetrically with respect to the projection plane, as shown in Figure 5.9. Thus, the pyramid determined by the window in the projection plane and the center of projection is a symmetric or right pyramid. This symmetry is caused by the fixed relationship between the back (retina) and lens of the eye for human viewing, or between the back and lens of a camera for standard cameras, and by similar fixed relationships in most physical situations. Some cameras, such as the bellows camera, have movable film backs and can produce general perspective views. The model used in computer graphics includes this general case.

The classical perspective views are usually known as **one-**, **two-**, and **three-point perspectives**. The differences among the three cases are based on how

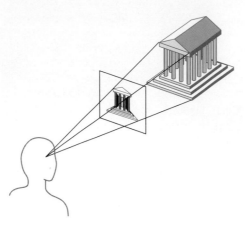

FIGURE 5.9   Perspective viewing.

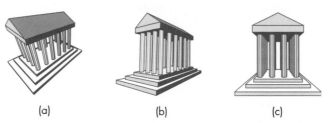

(a)   (b)   (c)

FIGURE 5.10   Classical perspective views. (a) Three-point. (b) Two-point. (c) One-point.

many of the three principal directions in the object are parallel to the projection plane. Consider the three perspective projections of the building in Figure 5.10. Any corner of the building includes the three principal directions. In the most general case—the three-point perspective—parallel lines in all three principal directions converge at three **vanishing points** (Figure 5.10(a)). If we allow one of the principal directions to become parallel to the projection plane, we have a two-point projection (Figure 5.10(b)), in which lines in only two of the principal directions converge. Finally, in the one-point perspective (Figure 5.10(c)), two of the principal directions are parallel to the projection plane, and we have only a single vanishing point. As with parallel viewing, it should be apparent from the programmer's point of view that the three situations are merely special cases of general perspective viewing, which we implement in Section 5.4.

5.2   Viewing with a Computer

We can now return to three-dimensional graphics from a computer perspective. Because viewing in computer graphics is based on the synthetic-camera model, we should be able to construct any of the classical views. However, there is a fundamental difference. All the classical views were based on a particular relationship among the objects, the viewer, and the projectors. In computer graphics, we stress the independence of the object specifications and camera parameters. In OpenGL, we shall have the choice of a perspective camera or an orthogonal camera. Whether a perspective view is a one-, two-, or three-point perspective is not something that is understood by OpenGL, as it would require knowing the relationships between objects and the camera. On balance, we prefer this independence, but if an application needs a particular type of view, the application programmer may well have to determine where to place the camera.

In terms of the pipeline architecture, viewing consists of two fundamental operations. First, we must position and orient the camera. This operation is the job of the model-view transformation. After vertices pass through this transformation, they are represented in eye or camera coordinates. The second step is the application of the projection transformation. This step applies the specified projection—orthographic or perspective—to the vertices and puts objects within the specified clipping volume in a normalized clipping volume. We shall examine these steps in detail in the next few sections, but at this point it would help to review the default camera, that is, the camera that OpenGL uses if we do not specify any viewing functions.

OpenGL starts with the camera at the origin of the object frame, pointing in the negative z direction. This camera is set up for orthogonal views and has a viewing volume that is a cube, centered at the origin and with sides of length 2. The default projection plane is the plane $z = 0$ and the direction of the projection is along the z-axis. Thus, objects within this box are visible and projected as in Figure 5.11. Until now, we were able to ignore any complex viewing procedures by exploiting our knowledge of this camera. Thus, we were able to define objects in the application programs that fit inside this cube and knew that they would

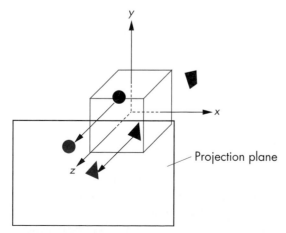

FIGURE 5.11   Imaging using the default camera.

be visible. In this approach, both the model-view and projection matrices were left as the default identity matrices.

Subsequently, we altered the model-view matrix, initially an identity matrix, by rotations and translations, so as to place the camera where we desired. The parameters that we set in glOrtho alter the projection matrix, also initially an identity matrix, so as to allow us to see objects inside an arbitrary right parallelepiped. In this chapter, we shall generate a wider variety of views by using the model-view matrix to position the camera and the projection matrix to produce both orthographic and perspective views.

5.3   Positioning of the Camera

We shall focus on the API that OpenGL provides for three-dimensional graphics. In this section, we deal with positioning the camera; in Section 5.4, we discuss how we specify the desired projection. We also see how other APIs specify a camera.

In OpenGL, the model-view and projection matrices are concatenated together to form the matrix that applies to geometric entities such as vertices. We have seen one use of the model-view matrix—to position objects in space. The other is to convert from the object frame to the frame of the camera.

5.3.1   Positioning of the Camera Frame

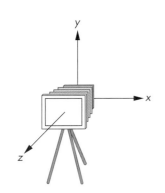

y

x

z

FIGURE 5.12   Initial camera position.

As we saw in Chapter 4, we can specify vertices in any units we choose, and we can define a model-view matrix by a sequence of affine transformations that reposition these vertices. The model-view transformation is the concatenation of a modeling transformation that takes instances of objects in object coordinates and brings them into the world frame. The second part transforms world coordinates to eye coordinates. Because we usually do not need to access world coordinates, we can use the model-view matrix rather than separate modeling and viewing matrices.

Initially, the model-view matrix is an identity matrix, so the camera frame and the object frame are identical. In OpenGL, the camera is initially pointing in the negative z direction (Figure 5.12).

In most applications, we model our objects as being located around the origin, so a camera located at the default position with the default orientation does not see all the objects in the scene. Thus, either we must move the camera away from the objects that we wish to have in our image, or the objects must be moved in front of the camera. These are equivalent operations, as either can be looked at as positioning the frame of the camera with respect to the frame of the objects.

It might help to think of a scene in which we have initially defined several objects, with the model-view matrix as the identity, by specifying all vertices through glVertex. Subsequent changes to the model view move the object frame relative to the camera and affect the camera's view of all objects defined *afterward*, as their vertices are specified relative to the repositioned object frame.

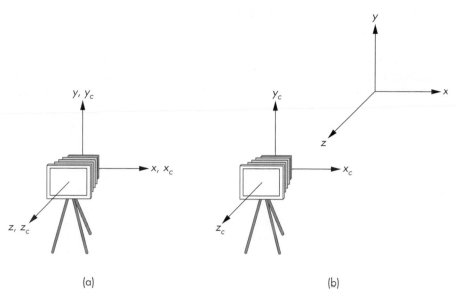

FIGURE 5.13   Movement of the camera and object frames. (a) Initial configuration. (b) Configuration after change in the model-view matrix.

Equivalently, in terms of the flow of an application program, the projection and model-view matrices are part of the state; when a primitive is defined, the system uses the present state to obtain the matrices that apply to it.

Consider the sequence in Figure 5.13. In part (a), we have the initial configuration. A vertex specified at $\mathbf{p}$ has the same representation in both frames. In part (b), we have changed the model-view matrix to $\mathbf{C}$ by a sequence of transformations. The two frames are no longer the same, although $\mathbf{C}$ contains the information to move from the camera frame to the object frame or, equivalently, contains the information that moves the camera away from its initial position at the origin of the object frame. A vertex specified at $\mathbf{q}$ through glVertex, *after* the change to the model-view matrix, is at $\mathbf{q}$ in the object frame. However, its position in the camera frame is $\mathbf{Cq}$ and is known internally to OpenGL; OpenGL converts positions to the camera frame through the viewing pipeline. The equivalent view is that the camera is still at the origin of its own frame, and the model-view matrix is applied to primitives specified in this system. In practice, you can use either view. But be sure to take great care regarding where in the program the primitives are specified relative to changes in the model-view matrix.

At any given time, the state of the model-view matrix encapsulates the relationship between the camera frame and the object frame. Although combining the modeling and viewing transformations into a single matrix may initially cause confusion, on closer examination this approach is a good one. If we regard the camera as an object with geometric properties, then transformations that alter the position and orientation of objects should also affect the position and orientation of the camera relative to these objects.

The obvious next problems are how we specify the desired position of the camera and how we implement camera positioning in OpenGL. Here we find it convenient to think in terms of moving the default camera relative to the object frame. We outline three approaches, one in this section and two in Section 5.3.2. Two others are given as exercises (Exercises 5.2 and 5.3).

Our first approach is to specify the position indirectly by applying a sequence of rotations and translations to the model-view matrix. This approach is a direct application of the instance transformation that we presented in Chapter 4, but we must be careful for two reasons. First, we usually want to define the camera *before* we position any objects in the scene.[1] Second, transformations on the camera may appear to be backward from what you might expect.

Consider an object centered at the origin. The camera is in its initial position, also at the origin, pointing down the negative z-axis. Suppose that we want an image of the faces of the object that point in the positive x direction. We must move the camera *away* from the origin. If we allow the camera to remain pointing in the negative z direction, then we want to move the camera backward along the positive z-axis, and the proper transformation is

```
glTranslatef(0.0, 0.0, -d);
```

where d is a positive number.

Many people find it helpful to interpret this operation as moving the camera frame relative to the object frame. This point of view has a basis in classical viewing. In computer graphics, we usually think of objects as being positioned in a fixed frame, and it is the viewer who must move to the right position to achieve the desired view. In classical viewing, the viewer dominates. Conceptually, we do viewing by picking up the object, orienting it as desired, and bringing it to the desired location. One consequence of the classical approach is that distances are measured from the viewer to the object, rather than—as in most physically based systems—from the object to the viewer. Classical viewing often resulted in a left-handed camera frame. Early graphics systems followed the classical approach by having modeling in right-handed coordinates and viewing in left-handed coordinates—a decision that, although technically correct, caused confusion among users. Although in OpenGL, distances from the camera, such as in glOrtho, are measured *from* the camera, which is consistent with classical viewing, OpenGL maintains a right-handed camera frame.

Suppose that we want to look at the same object from the positive x-axis. Now we not only have to move away from the object but also have to rotate the

---

1. In an animation, where in the program we define the position of the camera depends on whether we wish to attach the camera to a particular object or to place the camera in a fixed position in the scene (see Exercise 5.3).

camera about the y-axis, as shown in Figure 5.14. We must do the translation after we rotate the camera by 90 degrees about the y-axis. In the program, the calls must be in the reverse order, as we discussed in Section 4.8, so we expect to see code like the following:

```
glMatrixMode(GL_MODELVIEW);
glLoadIdentity();
glTranslatef(0.0, 0.0, -d);
glRotatef(-90.0, 0.0, 1.0, 0.0);
```

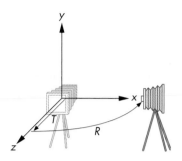

FIGURE 5.14 Positioning of the camera.

In terms of the two frames, we first rotate the object frame relative to the camera frame; then we move the two frames apart.

In Chapters 2 and 4, we were able to show simple three-dimensional examples by using the default projection matrix. The projection matrix, which we study in detail in Section 5.4, is set initially to an identity matrix. The default setting has the effect of creating an orthographic projection with the camera at the origin, pointed in the negative z direction. In our cube example in Chapter 4, we rotated the cube to see the desired faces. As we just discussed, rotating the cube is equivalent to rotating the frame of the cube with respect to the frame of the camera; we could have achieved the same view by rotating the camera relative to the cube. We can extend this strategy of translating and rotating the camera to create other orthographic views. Perspective views require changes to the projection matrix.

Consider creating an isometric view of the cube. Suppose that we again start with a cube centered at the origin and aligned with the axes. As the default camera is in the middle of the cube, we eventually want to move the camera away from the cube by a translation. We have an isometric view when the camera is located symmetrically with respect to three adjacent faces of the cube. We can rotate the cube to achieve this orientation and then move the camera away.

Even though we have yet to move the default camera, suppose that we are now looking at the cube from somewhere on the positive z-axis. We can obtain one of the eight isometric views—there is one for each vertex—by first rotating the cube about the x-axis until we see the two faces symmetrically, as in Figure 5.15(a). Clearly, we obtain this view by rotating the cube by 45 degrees. The second rotation is about the y-axis. We rotate the cube until we get the desired isometric. The required angle of rotation is -35.26 degrees about the y-axis. This second angle of rotation may not seem obvious. Consider what happens to the cube after the first rotation. From our position on the positive z-axis, the cube appears as in Figure 5.15(a). The original corner vertex at $(-1, 1, 1)$ has been transformed to $(-1, 0, \sqrt{2})$. If we look at the cube from the x-axis as in Figure 5.15(b), we see that we want to rotate the right vertex to the y-axis. The right triangle that determines this angle has sides of 1 and $\sqrt{2}$, which correspond to an angle of 35.26 degrees. However, we need a clockwise rotation, so the angle must be negative. Finally, we move the camera away from the origin. Thus, our strategy is to first rotate the frame of the camera relative to the frame of the object and

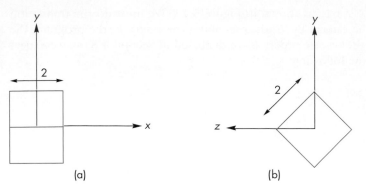

FIGURE 5.15 Cube after rotation about x-axis. (a) View from positive z-axis.
(b) View from positive y-axis.

then to separate the two frames; the model-view matrix is of the form

$$\mathbf{M} = \mathbf{TR}_x\mathbf{R}_y.$$

We obtain this model-view matrix for an isometric by multiplying the matrices
in homogeneous coordinates. The concatenation of the rotation matrices yields

$$\mathbf{R} = \mathbf{R}_x\mathbf{R}_y = \begin{bmatrix} 1 & 0 & 0 & 0 \\ 0 & \sqrt{6}/3 & -\sqrt{3}/3 & 0 \\ 0 & \sqrt{3}/3 & \sqrt{6}/3 & 0 \\ 0 & 0 & 0 & 1 \end{bmatrix} \begin{bmatrix} \sqrt{2}/2 & 0 & \sqrt{2}/2 & 0 \\ 0 & 1 & 0 & 0 \\ -\sqrt{2}/2 & 0 & \sqrt{2}/2 & 0 \\ 0 & 0 & 0 & 1 \end{bmatrix}$$

$$= \begin{bmatrix} \sqrt{2}/2 & 0 & \sqrt{2}/2 & 0 \\ \sqrt{6}/6 & \sqrt{6}/3 & -\sqrt{6}/6 & 0 \\ -\sqrt{3}/3 & \sqrt{3}/3 & \sqrt{3}/3 & 0 \\ 0 & 0 & 0 & 1 \end{bmatrix}.$$

It is simple to verify that the original vertex $(-1, 1, 1)$ is correctly transformed
to $(0, 0, \sqrt{3})$ by this matrix. If we concatenate in the translation by $(0, 0, -d)$,
the matrix becomes

$$\mathbf{TR} = \begin{bmatrix} \sqrt{2}/2 & 0 & \sqrt{2}/2 & 0 \\ \sqrt{6}/6 & \sqrt{6}/3 & -\sqrt{6}/6 & 0 \\ -\sqrt{3}/3 & \sqrt{3}/3 & \sqrt{3}/3 & -d \\ 0 & 0 & 0 & 1 \end{bmatrix}.$$

In OpenGL, the code for setting the model-view matrix is thus

```
glMatrixMode(GL_MODELVIEW);
glLoadIdentity();
glTranslatef(0.0, 0.0, -d);
glRotatef(35.26, 1.0, 0.0, 0.0);
glRotatef(45.0, 0.0, 1.0, 0.0);
```

Note that the clipping volume as set by glOrtho is relative to the camera frame. Thus, for an orthographic view, the translation of the camera does not affect the size of the image, but it can affect whether or not objects are clipped because the clipping volume is measured relative to the camera.

5.3.2 Two Viewing APIs

The construction of the model-view matrix for an isometric view is a little unsatisfying. Although the approach was intuitive, an interface that requires us to compute the individual angles before specifying the transformations is a poor one for an application program. We can take a different approach to positioning the camera—an approach that is similar to that used by PHIGS and GKS-3D, two of the original standard APIs for three-dimensional graphics. Our starting point is again the object frame. We describe the camera's position and orientation in this frame. The precise type of image that we wish to obtain—perspective or parallel—is determined separately by the specification of the equivalent of the projection matrix in OpenGL. This second part of the viewing process is often called the **normalization transformation**. We approach this problem as one of a change in frames. We again think of the camera as positioned initially at the origin, pointed in the negative *z* direction. Its desired location is centered at a point called the **view-reference point** (**VRP**; Figure 5.16), whose position is given in the object frame. The user executes a function such as

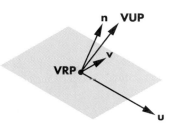

FIGURE 5.16   Camera frame.

```
set_view_reference_point(x, y, z);
```

to specify this position. Next, we want to specify the orientation of the camera. We can divide this specification into two parts: specification of the **view-plane normal** (**VPN**) and specification of the **view-up vector** (**VUP**). The VPN (**n** in Figure 5.16) gives the orientation of the projection plane or back of the camera. The orientation of a plane is determined by that plane's normal, and thus part of the API is a function

```
set_view_plane_normal(nx, ny, nz);
```

The orientation of the plane does not specify what direction is up from the camera's perspective. Given only the VPN, we can rotate the camera with its back in this plane. The specification of the VUP fixes the camera and is performed by

```
set_view_up(vup_x, vup_y, vup_z);
```

We project the VUP vector on the view plane to obtain the up-direction vector **v** (Figure 5.17). Use of the projection allows the user to specify any vector not parallel to **v**, rather than being forced to compute a vector lying in the projection plane. The vector **v** is orthogonal to **n**. We can use the cross product to obtain a third orthogonal direction **u**. This new orthogonal coordinate system usually is

FIGURE 5.17   Determination of the view-up vector.

referred to as either the **viewing-coordinate system** or the **u-v-n system**. With the addition of the VRP, we have the desired camera frame. The matrix that does the change of frames is the **view-orientation matrix**.

We can derive this matrix using rotations and translations in homogeneous coordinates. We start with the specifications of the view-reference point,

$$\mathbf{p} = \begin{bmatrix} x \\ y \\ z \\ 1 \end{bmatrix},$$

the view-plane normal,

$$\mathbf{n} = \begin{bmatrix} n_x \\ n_y \\ n_z \\ 0 \end{bmatrix},$$

and the view-up vector,

$$\mathbf{v_{up}} = \begin{bmatrix} v_{up_x} \\ v_{up_y} \\ v_{up_z} \\ 0 \end{bmatrix}.$$

We construct a new frame with the view-reference point as its origin, the view-plane normal as one coordinate direction, and two other orthogonal directions that we call **u** and **v**. Our default is that the original x, y, z axes become u, v, n, respectively. This choice corresponds to the default model-view matrix in OpenGL. The view-reference point can be handled through a simple translation $\mathbf{T}(-x, -y, -z)$ from the viewing frame to the original origin. The rest of the model-view matrix is determined by a rotation so that the model-view matrix $\mathbf{V}$ is of the form

$$\mathbf{V} = \mathbf{TR}.$$

The direction **v** must be orthogonal to **n**; hence,

$$\mathbf{n} \cdot \mathbf{v} = 0.$$

Figure 5.17 shows that **v** is the projection of $\mathbf{v_{up}}$ into the plane formed by **n** and $\mathbf{v_{up}}$ and thus must be a linear combination of these two vectors,

$$\mathbf{v} = \alpha \mathbf{n} + \beta \mathbf{v_{up}}.$$

If we temporarily ignore the length of the vectors, we can set $\beta = 1$ and solve for

$$\alpha = -\frac{\mathbf{v_{up}} \cdot \mathbf{n}}{\mathbf{n} \cdot \mathbf{n}}$$

and

$$\mathbf{v} = \mathbf{v}_{up} - \frac{\mathbf{v}_{up} \cdot \mathbf{n}}{\mathbf{n} \cdot \mathbf{n}} \mathbf{n}.$$

We can find the third orthogonal direction by taking the cross product

$$\mathbf{u} = \mathbf{v} \times \mathbf{n}.$$

These vectors do not generally have unit length. We can normalize each independently, obtaining three unit-length vectors $\mathbf{u}'$, $\mathbf{v}'$, and $\mathbf{n}'$. The matrix

$$\mathbf{A} = \begin{bmatrix} u'_x & v'_x & n'_x & 0 \\ u'_y & v'_y & n'_y & 0 \\ u'_z & v'_z & n'_z & 0 \\ 0 & 0 & 0 & 1 \end{bmatrix}$$

is a rotation matrix that orients a vector in the $\mathbf{u}'\mathbf{v}'\mathbf{n}'$ system with respect to the original system. However, we really want to go in the other direction to get the representation of vectors in the original system in the $\mathbf{u}'\mathbf{v}'\mathbf{n}'$ system. We want $\mathbf{A}^{-1}$, but because $\mathbf{A}$ is a rotation matrix, the desired matrix $\mathbf{R}$ is

$$\mathbf{R} = \mathbf{A}^{-1} = \mathbf{A}^T.$$

Finally, multiplying by the translation matrix $\mathbf{T}$, we have

$$\mathbf{V} = \mathbf{RT} = \begin{bmatrix} u'_x & u'_y & u'_z & -xu'_x - yu'_y - zu'_z \\ v'_x & v'_y & v'_z & -xv'_x - yv'_y - zv'_z \\ n'_x & n'_y & n'_z & -xn'_x - yn'_y - zn'_z \\ 0 & 0 & 0 & 1 \end{bmatrix}.$$

Note that, in this case, the translation matrix is on the right, whereas in our first derivation it was on the left. One way to interpret this difference is that in our first derivation, we rotated the frames and then pushed them apart in a direction represented in the camera frame. In the second derivation, the camera position was specified in the object frame. Another way to understand this difference is to note that the matrices $\mathbf{RT}$ and $\mathbf{TR}$ have similar forms. The rotation parts of the product—the upper-left 3×3 submatrices—are identical, as are the bottom rows. The top three elements in the right column differ because the frame of the rotation affects the translation coefficients in $\mathbf{RT}$ and does not affect them in $\mathbf{TR}$. For our isometric example,

$$\mathbf{n} = \begin{bmatrix} -1 \\ 1 \\ 1 \\ 0 \end{bmatrix},$$

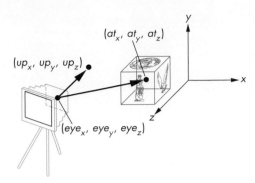

FIGURE 5.18   Look-at positioning.

$$\mathbf{v_{up}} = \begin{bmatrix} 0 \\ 1 \\ 0 \\ 0 \end{bmatrix}.$$

The camera position must be along a diagonal in the original frame. If we use

$$\mathbf{p} = \frac{\sqrt{3}}{3} \begin{bmatrix} -d \\ d \\ d \\ 1 \end{bmatrix},$$

we obtain the same model-view matrix that we derived in Section 5.3.1.

5.3.3   The Look-At Function

The use of the VRP, VPN, and VUP is but one way to provide an API for specifying the position of a camera. In many situations, a more direct method is appropriate. Consider the situation in Figure 5.18. Here a camera is located at a point **e** called the **eye point**, specified in the object frame, and it is pointed at a second point **a**, called the **at point**. These points determine a VPN and a VRP. The VPN is given by the vector formed by point subtraction between the eyepoint and the at point[2]

$$\mathbf{vpn} = \mathbf{e} - \mathbf{a}.$$

The view-reference point is the eye point. Hence, we need only to add the desired up direction for the camera. The OpenGL utility function

---

2. Note that subtracting the points in this order creates a left-handed camera frame as in Figure 5.18. OpenGL uses a right-handed camera frame that we obtain by simply reversing the direction of the normal vector.

```
void gluLookAt(GLdouble eyex, GLdouble eyey, GLdouble eyez, /* eye point */
        GLdouble atx, GLdouble aty, GLdouble atx, /* at point */
        GLdouble upx, GLdouble upy, GLdouble upz) /* up direction */
```

alters the model-view matrix for a camera pointed along this line. Thus, we usually use the sequence

```
glMatrixMode(GL_MODELVIEW);
glLoadIdentity();
gluLookAt(eyex,eyey,eyez,
        atx, aty, atx,
        upx, upy, upz);

/* define objects here */
```

Note that we can use the standard rotations, translations, and scalings as part of defining our objects. Although these transformations will also alter the model view matrix, it is often helpful conceptually to consider the use of gluLookAt as positioning the objects and subsequent operations that affect the model-view matrix as positioning the camera.

5.3.4   Other Viewing APIs

In many applications, neither of the viewing interfaces that we have presented is appropriate. Consider a flight-simulation application. The pilot using the simulator usually uses three angles—**roll**, **pitch**, and **yaw**—to specify her orientation. These angles are specified relative to the center of mass of the vehicle and to a coordinate system aligned along the axes of the vehicle, as shown in Figure 5.19. Hence, the pilot sees an object in terms of the three angles and of the distance from the object to the center of mass of her vehicle. A viewing transformation can be constructed (Exercise 5.2) from these specifications from a translation and three simple rotations.

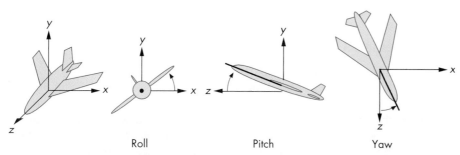

Roll   Pitch   Yaw

FIGURE 5.19   Roll, pitch, and yaw.

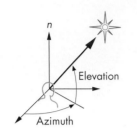

FIGURE 5.20 Elevation and azimuth.

Viewing in many applications is most naturally specified in polar— rather than rectilinear—coordinates. Applications involving objects that rotate about other objects fit this category. For example, consider the specification of a star in the sky. Its direction from a viewer is given by its elevation and azimuth (Figure 5.20). The **elevation** is the angle above the plane of the viewer at which the star appears. By defining a normal at the point that the viewer is located and using this normal to define a plane, we define the elevation, regardless of whether or not the viewer is actually standing on a plane. We can form two other axes in this plane, creating a viewing-coordinate system. The **azimuth** is the angle measured from an axis in this plane to the projection onto the plane of the line between the viewer and the star. The camera can still be rotated about the direction it is pointed by a **twist angle**.

5.4   Simple Projections

With a real camera, once we position it, we still must select a lens. As we saw in Chapter 1, it is the combination of the lens and the size of the film (or of the back of the camera) that determines how much of the world in front of a camera appears in the image. In computer graphics, we make an equivalent choice when we select the type of projection and the viewing parameters.

With a physical camera, a wide-angle lens gives the most dramatic perspectives, with objects near the camera appearing large compared to objects far from the lens. A telephoto lens gives an image that appears flat and is close to a parallel view. Most APIs distinguish between parallel and perspective views by providing different functions for the two cases. OpenGL does the same, even though the implementation of the two can use the same pipeline, as we shall see in Sections 5.9 and 5.10.

Just as we did with the model-view matrix, we can set the projection matrix with the glLoadMatrix function. Alternatively, we can use OpenGL functions for the most common viewing conditions. First, we consider the mathematics of projection. We can extend our use of homogeneous coordinates to the projection process, which allows us to characterize a particular projection with a 4×4 matrix.

5.4.1   Perspective Projections

Suppose that we are in the camera frame with the camera located at the origin, pointed in the negative z direction. Figure 5.21 shows two possibilities. In Figure 5.21(a), the back of the camera is orthogonal to the z direction and is parallel to the lens. This configuration corresponds to most physical situations, including those of the human visual system and of simple cameras. The situation in Figure 5.21(b) is more general; the back of the camera can have any orientation with respect to the front. We consider the first case in detail because it is simpler.

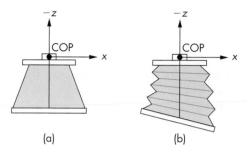

(a)   (b)

FIGURE 5.21 Two cameras. (a) Back parallel to front. (b) Back not parallel to front.

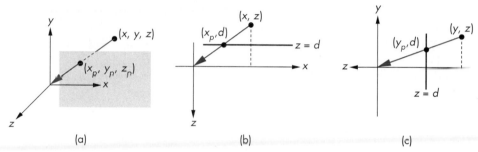

(a)   (b)   (c)

FIGURE 5.22 Three views of perspective projection. (a) Three-dimensional view. (b) Top view. (c) Side view.

However, the derivation of the general result follows the same steps and should be a direct exercise (Exercise 5.6).

As we saw in Chapter 1, we can place the projection plane in front of the center of projection. If we do so for the configuration of Figure 5.21(a), we get the views shown in Figure 5.22. A point in space (x, y, z) is projected along a projector into the point (x_p, y_p, z_p). All projectors pass through the origin and, because the projection plane is perpendicular to the z-axis,

$$z_p = d.$$

Because the camera is pointing in the negative z direction, the projection plane is in the negative half-space $z < 0$, and the value of d is negative.

From the top view shown in Figure 5.22(b), we see two similar triangles whose tangents must be the same. Hence,

$$\frac{x}{z} = \frac{x_p}{d},$$

and

$$x_p = \frac{x}{z/d}.$$

Using the side view shown in Figure 5.22(c), we obtain a similar result for y_p,

$$y_p = \frac{y}{z/d}.$$

These equations are nonlinear. The division by z describes **nonuniform fore-shortening**: The images of objects farther from the center of projection are reduced in size (diminution) compared to the images of objects closer to the COP.

We can look at the projection process as a transformation that takes points (x, y, z) to other points (x_p, y_p, z_p). Although this **perspective transformation** preserves lines, it is not affine. It is also irreversible: Because all points along a projector project into the same point, we cannot recover a point from its projection. In Sections 5.8 and 5.9, we shall develop OpenGL's use of an invertible variant of the projection transformation that preserves distances that are needed for hidden-surface removal.

We can extend our use of homogeneous coordinates to handle projections. When we introduced homogeneous coordinates, we represented a point in three dimensions (x, y, z) by the point $(x, y, z, 1)$ in four dimensions. Suppose that, instead, we replace (x, y, z) by the four-dimensional point

$$\mathbf{p} = \begin{bmatrix} wx \\ wy \\ wz \\ w \end{bmatrix}.$$

As long as $w \neq 0$, we can recover the three-dimensional point from its four-dimensional representation by dividing the first three components by w. In this new homogeneous-coordinate form, points in three dimensions become lines through the origin in four dimensions. Transformations are again represented by 4×4 matrices, but now the final row of the matrix can be altered—and thus w can be changed by such a transformation.

Obviously, we would prefer to keep $w = 1$ to avoid the divisions otherwise necessary to recover the three-dimensional point. However, by allowing w to change, we can represent a broader class of transformations, including perspective projections. Consider the matrix

$$\mathbf{M} = \begin{bmatrix} 1 & 0 & 0 & 0 \\ 0 & 1 & 0 & 0 \\ 0 & 0 & 1 & 0 \\ 0 & 0 & 1/d & 0 \end{bmatrix}.$$

The matrix $\mathbf{M}$ transforms the point

$$\mathbf{p} = \begin{bmatrix} x \\ y \\ z \\ 1 \end{bmatrix}$$

FIGURE 5.23   Projection pipeline.

to the point

$$\mathbf{q} = \begin{bmatrix} x \\ y \\ z \\ z/d \end{bmatrix}.$$

At first glance, $\mathbf{q}$ may not seem sensible; however, when we remember that we have to divide the first three components by the fourth to return to our original three-dimensional space, we obtain the results

$$x_p = \frac{x}{z/d},$$

$$y_p = \frac{y}{z/d},$$

$$z_p = \frac{z}{z/d} = d,$$

which are the equations for a simple perspective projection. In homogeneous coordinates, dividing $\mathbf{q}$ by its w component replaces $\mathbf{q}$ by the equivalent point

$$\mathbf{q}' = \begin{bmatrix} \frac{x}{z/d} \\ \frac{y}{z/d} \\ d \\ 1 \end{bmatrix} = \begin{bmatrix} x_p \\ y_p \\ z_p \\ 1 \end{bmatrix}.$$

We have shown that we can do at least a simple perspective projection, by defining a 4×4 projection matrix that we apply after the model-view matrix. However, we must perform a **perspective division** at the end. This division can be made a part of the pipeline, as shown in Figure 5.23.

5.4.2 Orthogonal Projections

Orthogonal or **orthographic** projections are a special case of parallel projections, in which the projectors are perpendicular to the view plane. In terms of a camera, orthogonal projections correspond to a camera with a back plane parallel to the lens, which has an infinite focal length. However, rather than using limiting relations as the COP moves to infinity, we can derive the projection equations directly. Figure 5.24 shows an orthogonal projection with the projection plane $z = 0$. As points are projected into this plane, they retain their x and y values, and the equations of projection are

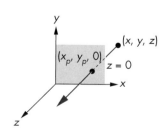

FIGURE 5.24   Orthogonal projection.

$$x_p = x,$$
$$y_p = y,$$
$$z_p = 0.$$

We can write this result using our original homogeneous coordinates:

$$
\begin{bmatrix} x_p \\ y_p \\ z_p \\ 1 \end{bmatrix} =
\begin{bmatrix} 1 & 0 & 0 & 0 \\ 0 & 1 & 0 & 0 \\ 0 & 0 & 0 & 0 \\ 0 & 0 & 0 & 1 \end{bmatrix}
\begin{bmatrix} x \\ y \\ z \\ 1 \end{bmatrix}.
$$

In this case, a division is unnecessary, although in hardware implementations, we can use the same pipeline for both perspective and orthogonal transformations.

We can expand both our simple projections to general perspective and parallel projections by preceding the projection by a sequence of transformations that converts the general case to one of the two cases that we know how to apply. First, we examine the API that the application programmer uses in OpenGL to specify a projection.

5.5 Projections in OpenGL

The projections that we developed in Section 5.4 did not take into account the properties of the camera—the focal length of its lens or the size of the film plane. Figure 5.25 shows the **angle of view** for a simple pinhole camera, like the one that we discussed in Chapter 1. Only those objects that fit within the angle of view of the camera appear in the image. If the back of the camera is rectangular, only objects within a semi-infinite pyramid—the **view volume**— whose apex is at the COP can appear in the image. Objects not within the view volume are said to be **clipped** out of the scene. Hence, our description of simple projections has been incomplete; we did not include the effects of clipping.

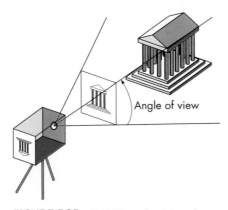

FIGURE 5.25   Definition of a view volume.

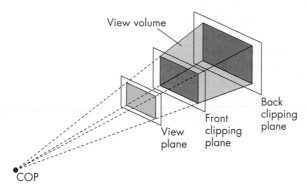

View volume

Back
clipping
plane

Front
clipping
plane

View
plane

View
plane

COP

FIGURE 5.26 Front and back clipping planes.

Most graphics APIs define clipping parameters through the specification of a projection. In a computer-graphics system, we allow a finite clipping volume by specifying front and back clipping planes, in addition to the angle of view, as shown in Figure 5.26. The resulting view volume is a **frustum**—a truncated pyramid. We have fixed only one parameter: We have specified that the COP is at the origin in the camera frame. We should be able to define each of the six sides of the frustum to have almost any orientation and position. If we did so, however, we would make it difficult to specify a view and rarely do we need this flexibility. We examine the OpenGL API. Other APIs differ in their function calls but incorporate similar restrictions.

Note that whereas the OpenGL functions, such as `gluLookAt`, that position the camera alter the model-view matrix and are specified in object coordinates, the functions that we introduce now will alter the projection matrix. The parameters for these functions will be specified in eye coordinates.

5.5.1 Perspective in OpenGL

In OpenGL, we have two functions for specifying perspective views and one for specifying parallel views. Alternatively, we can form the projection matrix directly, either by loading it, or by applying rotations, translations, and scalings to an initial identity matrix. We can specify our camera view by the function

```
glFrustum(GLdouble left, GLdouble right, GLdouble bottom, GLdouble top,
        GLdouble near, GLdouble far)
```

These parameters are shown in Figure 5.27 in the camera frame. The near and far distances must be positive and are measured from the COP (the origin in eye coordinates) to these planes, both of which are parallel to the plane $z = 0$. Because the camera is pointing in the negative z direction, the front (near) clipping plane is the plane $z = -near$, and the back (far) clipping plane is the plane $z = -far$. The plane $x = left$ is to the left of the camera as viewed from the COP in the

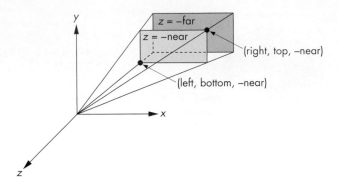

FIGURE 5.27 Specification of a frustum.

direction the camera is pointing. Similar statements hold for `right`, `bottom`, and `top`.

The projection matrix determined by these specifications multiplies the present matrix, thus we must first select the matrix mode. A typical sequence is

```
glMatrixMode(GL_PROJECTION);
glLoadIdentity();
glFrustum(left, right, bottom, top, near, far);
```

Note that these specifications do not have to be symmetric with respect to the z-axis and that the resulting frustum also does not have to be symmetric (a right frustum). In Section 5.9, we show how the projection matrix for this projection can be derived from the simple perspective-projection matrix of Section 5.4.

In many applications, it is natural to specify the angle of view, or field of view. However, if the projection plane is rectangular, rather than square, then we see a different angle of view in the top and side views (Figure 5.28). The angle *fov* is the angle between the top and bottom planes of the clipping volume. The OpenGL utility function

```
gluPerspective(GLdouble fovy, GLdouble aspect, GLdouble near, GLdouble far)
```

allows us to specify the angle of view in the up (y) direction, as well as the aspect ratio—width divided by height—of the projection plane. The near and far planes are specified as in `glFrustum`. This matrix also alters the present matrix, so we must again select the matrix mode, and usually must load an identity matrix, before invoking this function.

5.5.2 Parallel Viewing in OpenGL

The only parallel-viewing function provided by OpenGL is the orthogonal (orthographic) viewing function

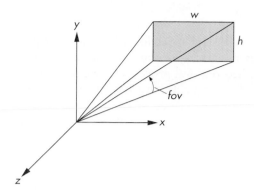

FIGURE 5.28   Specification using the field of view.

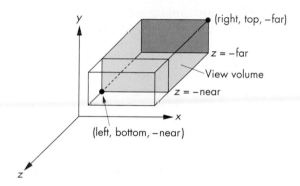

FIGURE 5.29   Orthographic viewing.

```
glOrtho(GLdouble left, GLdouble right, GLdouble bottom, GLdouble top,
        GLdouble near, GLdouble far)
```

Its parameters are identical to those of glFrustum. The view volume is a right parallelepiped, as shown in Figure 5.29. The near and far clipping planes are again at $z = -near$ and $z = -far$, respectively.

In perspective viewing, we require the distances to both the near and far planes to be positive because all projectors pass through the COP at the origin, and objects behind the COP are projected upside down, as compared with objects in front of the COP. Points in the camera frame plane $z = 0$ cannot be projected at all and lead to division by zero. This problem does not exist in parallel viewing, and there are thus no restrictions on the sign of the near and far distances in glOrtho.

5.6 Hidden-Surface Removal

We can now return to our rotating-cube program of Section 4.9 and add perspective viewing and movement of the camera. First, we can use our development of viewing to understand the hidden-surface–removal process that we used in our first version of the program. When we look at a cube that has opaque sides, we see only its three front-facing sides. From the perspective of our basic viewing model, we can say that we see only these faces because they block the projectors from reaching any other surfaces.

From the perspective of computer graphics, however, all the faces of the cube have been specified and travel down the graphics pipeline; thus, the graphics system must be careful about which surfaces it displays. Conceptually, we seek algorithms that either remove those surfaces that should not be visible to the viewer, called **hidden-surface–removal algorithms**, or find which surfaces are visible, called **visible-surface algorithms**. There are many approaches to the problem, several of which we investigate in Chapter 7. OpenGL has a particular algorithm associated with it, the z-**buffer algorithm**, to which we can interface through three function calls. Hence, we introduce that algorithm here, and we return to the topic in Chapter 8.

Hidden-surface–removal algorithms can be divided into two broad classes. **Object-space algorithms** attempt to order the surfaces of the objects in the scene such that drawing surfaces in a particular order provides the correct image. For example, for our cube, if we were to draw the back-facing surfaces first, we could "paint" over them with the front surfaces and would produce the correct image. This class of algorithms does not work well with pipeline architectures in which objects are passed down the pipeline in an arbitrary order. In order to decide on a proper order in which to render the objects, the graphics system must have all the objects available so it can sort them into the desired order.

Image-space algorithms work as part of the projection process and seek to determine the relationship among object points on each projector. The z-buffer algorithm is of the latter type and fits in well with the rendering pipeline in most graphics systems because we can save partial information as each object is rendered.

The basic idea of the z-buffer algorithm is shown in Figure 5.30. A projector from the COP passes through two surfaces. Because the circle is closer to the viewer than the triangle, it is the circle's color that determines the color placed in the color buffer at the location corresponding to where the projector pierces the projection plane. The difficulty is determining how we can make this idea work regardless of the order in which the triangle and the circle pass through the pipeline.

Let's assume that all the objects are polygons. If, as the polygons are rasterized, we can keep track of the distance from the COP or the projection plane to the closest point on each projector, then we can update this information as successive polygons are projected and filled. Ultimately, we display only the closest point on each projector. The algorithm requires a **depth** or z **buffer** to store the necessary depth information as polygons are rasterized. Because we must keep depth information for each pixel in the color buffer, the z buffer has the same spatial resolution as the color buffers. Its depth corresponds to the amount of depth resolution that is supported, usually 16, 24, or 32 bits. This buffer can come from the standard memory in the system, or special memory can be added at the end of a hardware pipeline. In OpenGL, the z buffer is one of the buffers that constitute the frame buffer.

The depth buffer is initialized to a value that corresponds to the farthest distance from the viewer. When each polygon inside the clipping volume is rasterized, the depth of each fragment—how far the corresponding point on the polygon is from the viewer—is calculated. If this depth is greater than the value at that fragment's location in the depth buffer, then a polygon that has already been rasterized is closer to the viewer along the projector corresponding to the fragment. Hence, for this fragment we ignore the color of the polygon and go on to the next fragment for this polygon, where we make the same test. If, however, the depth is less than what is already in the z buffer, then along this projector the polygon being rendered is closer than any one we have seen so far. Thus, we use the color of the polygon to replace the color of the pixel in the color buffer and update the depth in the z buffer.

For the example in Figure 5.30, we see that if the triangle passes through the pipeline first, its colors and depths will be placed in the color and z buffers. When the circle passes through the pipeline, its colors and depths will replace the colors and depths of the triangle where they overlap. If the circle is rendered first, its colors and depths will be placed in the buffers. When the triangle is rendered, in the areas where there is overlap, the depths of the triangle are greater than the depth of the circle, and at the corresponding pixels no changes will be made to the color or depth buffers.

Major advantages of this algorithm are that its complexity is proportional to the number of fragments generated by the rasterizer and that it can be

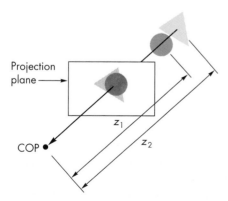

FIGURE 5.30 The z-buffer algorithm.

implemented with a small number of additional calculations over what we have to do to project and display polygons without hidden-surface removal. We shall return to this issue in Chapter 7.

From the application programmer's perspective, she must initialize the depth buffer and enable hidden-surface removal by using

```
glutInitDisplayMode(GLUT_DOUBLE | GLUT_RGB | GLUT_DEPTH);
glEnable(GL_DEPTH_TEST);
```

Here we use the GLUT library for the initialization and specify a depth buffer in addition to our usual RGB color and double buffering. The programmer can clear the color and depth buffers as necessary for a new rendering by using

```
glClear(GL_COLOR_BUFFER_BIT | GL_DEPTH_BUFFER_BIT);
```

5.6.1 Culling

For a convex object, such as the cube, we could simply remove all the faces pointing away from the viewer, and we could render only the ones facing the viewer. We consider this special case further in Chapter 7. We can turn on culling in OpenGL by enabling it:

```
glEnable(GL_CULL);
```

However, culling produces a correct image only if we have a convex object. Often we can use culling in addition to the z-buffer algorithm (which works with any collection of polygons). For example, suppose that we have a scene composed of a collection of n cubes. If we use only the z-buffer algorithm, we pass $6n$ polygons through the pipeline. If we enable culling, half the polygons can be eliminated early in the pipeline, and thus only $3n$ polygons pass through all stages of the pipeline.

5.7 Interactive Mesh Displays

We can now combine our understanding of projections and modeling three-dimensional concepts to build an interactive application. We will use a simple mesh model that has many of the features of complex CAD models.

5.7.1 Meshes

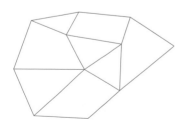

FIGURE 5.31 Mesh.

We now have the tools to walk through a scene interactively by having the camera parameters change in response to user input. Before introducing the interface, let's consider another example of data display: mesh plots. A **mesh** is a set of polygons that share vertices and edges. A general mesh, as shown in Figure 5.31, may contain polygons with any number of vertices and require a moderately

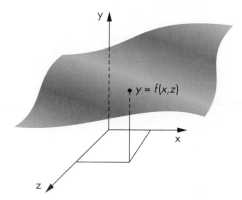

FIGURE 5.32 Height field.

sophisticated data structure to store and display efficiently. Rectangular and triangular meshes, such as we introduced in Chapter 2 for modeling a sphere, are much simpler to work with and are useful for a wide variety of applications. Here, we introduce rectangular meshes for the display of height data.

One way to represent surfaces is through a function of the form

$$y = f(x, z).$$

Thus, for each x, z we get exactly one y as in Figure 5.32. Such surfaces are sometimes called **2-1/2–dimensional surfacess** or **height fields**. Although not all surfaces can be represented this way, these surfaces have many applications. For example, if we use an x, y coordinate system to give positions on the surface of the earth, then we can use a function to represent the height or altitude at each location. In many situations, such as when we discussed contour maps in Chapter 2, the function f is known only discretely, and we have a set of samples or measurements of experimental data of the form

$$y_{ij} = f(x_i, z_j).$$

We assume that these data points are equally spaced such that

$$x_i = x_0 + i\Delta x, \quad i = 0, \ldots, N,$$
$$z_j = z_0 + j\Delta z, \quad j = 0, \ldots, M,$$

where Δx and Δz are the spacing between the samples in the x and z directions, respectively. If f is known analytically, then we can sample it to obtain a set of discrete data with which to work.

One simple way to generate a surface is through either a triangular or a quadrilateral mesh. We can use the four points $y_{ij}, y_{i+1, j}, y_{i+1, j+1}$, and $y_{i, j+1}$ to generate either a quadrilateral or two triangles. Thus, the data define a mesh of either NM quadrilaterals or $2NM$ triangles. The corresponding OpenGL

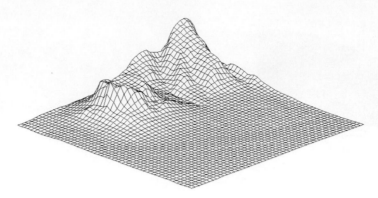

FIGURE 5.33   Mesh plot of Honolulu data.

programs are simple. The display callback need only go through the array forming alternately quads, triangles, quads, or quad strips from adjacent rows. For quads, the heart of the display callback is simply

```
for(i=0;i<N-1;i++) for(j=1;j<M-1;j++)

    glBegin(GL_QUADS)
      glVertex3i(i,y[i][j],j);
      glVertex3i(i+1,y[i+1][j],j);
      glVertex3i(i+1,y[i+1][j+1],j+1);
      glVertex3i(i,y[i][j+1],j+1);
    glEnd();
```

Figure 5.33 shows a rectangular mesh from height data for a part of Honolulu, Hawaii. These data are available on the Web site for the book.

5.7.2 Walking Through a Scene

The next step is to specify the camera and add interactivity. In this version, we use perspective viewing, and we allow the viewer to move the camera by depressing the x, X, y, Y, z, and Z keys on the keyboard, but we have the camera always pointing at the center of the cube. The gluLookAt function provides a simple way to reposition and reorient the camera.

The changes that we have to make to our previous program (Section 4.9) are minor. We define an array viewer[3] to hold the camera position. Its contents are altered by the simple keyboard callback function keys

```
void keys(unsigned char key, int x, int y)
{
    if(key == 'x') viewer[0]-= 1.0;
```

```
   if(key == 'X') viewer[0]+= 1.0;
   if(key == 'y') viewer[1]-= 1.0;
   if(key == 'Y') viewer[1]+= 1.0;
   if(key == 'z') viewer[2]-= 1.0;
   if(key == 'Z') viewer[2]+= 1.0;
   glutPostRedisplay();
}
```

The display function calls LookAt using viewer for the camera position and uses the origin for the "at" position. The cube is rotated, as before, based on the mouse input. Note the order of the function calls in display that alter the model-view matrix:

```
void display()
{
   glClear(GL_COLOR_BUFFER_BIT | GL_DEPTH_BUFFER_BIT);
   glLoadIdentity();
   gluLookAt(viewer[0],viewer[1],viewer[2],
             0.0, 0.0, 0.0,
             0.0, 1.0, 0.0);
   glRotatef(theta[0], 1.0, 0.0, 0.0);
   glRotatef(theta[1], 0.0, 1.0, 0.0);
   glRotatef(theta[2], 0.0, 0.0, 1.0);

/* draw mesh or other objects here */
   mesh();

   glutSwapBuffers();
}
```

We can invoke glFrustum from the reshape callback to specify the camera lens through the following code:

```
void myReshape(int w, int h)
{
   glViewport(0, 0, w, h);
   glMatrixMode(GL_PROJECTION);
   glLoadIdentity();
   if(w<=h) glFrustum(-2.0, 2.0, -2.0 * (GLfloat) h/ (GLfloat)
       w,2.0* (GLfloat) h / (GLfloat) w, 2.0, 20.0);
   else glFrustum(-2.0, 2.0, -2.0 * (GLfloat) w/ (GLfloat) h,
       2.0* (GLfloat) w / (GLfloat) h, 2.0, 20.0);
   glMatrixMode(GL_MODELVIEW);
}
```

Note that we chose the values of the parameters in glFrustum based on the aspect ratio of the window. Other than the added specification of a keyboard callback function in main, the rest of the program is the same as the program in Section 4.10. The complete program is given in Appendix A. If you run this program, you should note the effects of moving the camera, the lens, and the sides of the viewing frustum. Note what happens as you move toward the mesh. You should also consider the effect of always having the viewer look at the center of the mesh as she is moving.

Note that we could have used the mouse buttons to move the viewer. We could use the mouse buttons to move the user forward or to turn her right or left (see Exercise 5.14). However, by using the keyboard for moving the viewer, we can use the mouse to move the object as with the rotating cube in Chapter 4.

In this example, we are using direct positioning of the camera through gluLookAt. There are other possibilities. One is to use rotation and translation matrices to alter the model-view matrix incrementally. If we want to move the viewer through the scene without having her looking at a fixed point, this option may be more appealing. We could also keep a position variable in the program and change it as the viewer moves. In this case, the model-view matrix would be computed from scratch rather than changed incrementally. Which option we choose depends on the particular application, and often on other factors, such as the possibility that numerical errors might accumulate if we were to change the model-view matrix incrementally many times.

5.7.3 Polygon Offset

There are interesting aspects to and modifications we can make to the OpenGL program. First, if we use all the data, the resulting plot may contain many small polygons. The resulting density of lines in the display may be annoying and can contain moiré patterns. Hence, we might prefer to subsample the data either by using every kth point for some k or by averaging groups of data points to obtain a new set of samples with smaller N and M.

Second, the data in Figure 5.33 were drawn both as black lines and as white filled polygons. The lines are necessary to display the mesh. The polygons are necessary so that data in the front hide the data in the back. Although we can use OpenGL's hidden-surface–removal algorithm to display the polygons correctly, because these data are given in a structured order, we do not need to carry out a standard hidden-surface–removal process. If we display the data by first drawing those in back and then proceeding toward the front, the front polygons automatically hide the polygons farther back. In a system in which hidden-surface removal is done in software, not using a software z buffer and displaying the data in this manner may be faster. Data that are structured in such a manner are 2-1/2–dimensional as in Section 5.7.1. This special organization leads to efficient rendering algorithms. This structure is not sufficient to represent all three-dimensional surfaces.

There is one additional trick that we used in the display of Figure 5.33. If we draw both a polygon and a line loop with the same data, such as in the code

```
glColor3f(1.0, 1.0, 1.0);
glBegin(GL_QUADS)
  glVertex3i(i,z[i][j],j);
  glVertex3i(i+1,z[i+1][j],j);
  glVertex3i(i+1,z[i+1][j+1],j+1);
  glVertex3i(i,z[i][j+1],j+1);
glEnd();
glColor3f(0.0, 0.0, 0.0);
glBegin(GL_LINE_LOOP)
  glVertex3i(i,z[i][j],j);
  glVertex3i(i+1,z[i+1][j],j);
  glVertex3i(i+1,z[i+1][j+1],j+1);
  glVertex3i(i,z[i][j+1],j+1);
glEnd();
```

then the polygon and line loop are in the same plane. Even though the line loop is rendered after the polygon, numerical inaccuracies in the renderer often cause parts of a line loop to be blocked by the polygon with the same vertices. Although OpenGL lacks a mode to draw a filled polygon with its edges displayed in a different color, we can enable the **polygon offset mode** and set the offset parameters as in

```
glEnable(GL_POLYGON_OFFSET_FILL);
glPolygonOffset(1.0, 0.5);
```

The first parameter determines the offset; the second is an implementation-dependent scale factor. These functions move the polygons slightly away from the viewer, so all the desired lines should be visible.

The basic mesh rendering can be extended in many ways. In Chapter 6, we shall learn to add lights and surface properties to create a more realistic image; in Chapter 8, we shall learn to add a texture to the surface. The texture map might be an image of the terrain from a photograph or other data that might be obtained by digitization of a map. If we combine these techniques, we can generate a display in which we can make the image depend on the time of day by changing the position of the light source. It is also possible to obtain smoother surfaces by using the data to define a smoother surface with the aid of one of the surface types that we shall introduce in Chapter 11.

5.8 Parallel-Projection Matrices

The OpenGL projection matrices are not quite as simple as the projection matrices that we derived in Section 5.4. In this section and the next, we derive the OpenGL projection matrices. Because projections are such a key part of three-dimensional computer graphics, understanding projections is crucial for both writing user applications and implementing a graphics system. Furthermore, although the OpenGL projection functions that we introduced are sufficient for

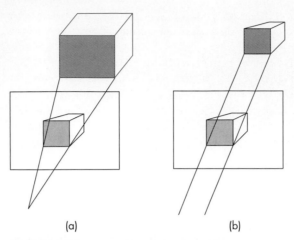

(a)   (b)

FIGURE 5.34   Predistortion of objects. (a) Perspective view. (b) Orthographic projection of distorted object.

FIGURE 5.35   Normalization transformation.

most viewing situations, views such as parallel oblique are not provided directly by the OpenGL API. We can obtain such views by setting up a projection matrix from scratch or by modifying one of the standard views. We can apply either of these approaches using the matrices that we derive.

5.8.1   Projection Normalization

Our approach is based on a technique called **projection normalization**, which converts all projections into orthogonal projections by first distorting the objects such that the orthogonal projection of the distorted objects is the same as the desired projection of the original objects. This technique is shown in Figure 5.34. However, because the distortion of the objects is described by a homogeneous-coordinate matrix, rather than distorting the objects, we can concatenate this matrix with a simple orthogonal-projection matrix to form the desired projection matrix, as shown in Figure 5.35.

5.8.2   Orthogonal-Projection Matrices

Although parallel viewing is a special case of perspective viewing, we start with orthogonal parallel viewing and extend the normalization technique to perspective viewing. We have shown that projection converts points in three-dimensional space to points on the projection plane and, further, that the transformation that does this operation is not reversible because all points along a projector project into the same point on the projection plane.

Our development breaks projection into two parts. The first converts the specified viewing volume to standard volume by a nonsingular homogeneous-coordinate transformation. We apply the transformation that does this conversion to all our objects by concatenating the transformation matrix with the model-view matrix. Objects are distorted in a manner that yields the desired projection through the second step, which is an orthogonal projection on the transformed objects and volume:

$$x_p = x,$$
$$y_p = y,$$
$$z_p = 0.$$

Note that carrying out this orthographic projection only requires setting the z value to zero or, equivalently, just neglecting it because it is not needed. The real work in the projection process is in the first transformation. The reasons for separating the projection process into two parts have to do with many of the other tasks that we do as part of the viewing pipeline. In particular, we shall see in Chapter 7 that clipping must be done in three dimensions and that the use of the nonsingular transformation matrix allows us to retain depth information along projectors that is necessary for hidden-surface removal and shading (Chapter 6). The first part of the process defines what most systems, including OpenGL, call the **projection matrix**. OpenGL also distinguishes between *screen coordinates*, which are two-dimensional and lack depth information, and *window coordinates*, which are three-dimensional and retain the depth information. In OpenGL, the projection matrix and the subsequent perspective division convert vertices to window coordinates.

For orthographic projections, the simplest clipping volume to deal with is a cube whose center is at the origin and whose sides are given by the six planes

$$x = \pm 1,$$
$$y = \pm 1,$$
$$z = \pm 1.$$

This cube is the default OpenGL view volume; equivalently, we can use the function calls

```
glMatrixMode(GL_PROJECTION);
glLoadIdentity();
glOrtho(-1.0, 1.0, -1.0, 1.0, -1.0, 1.0);
```

We call this volume the **canonical view volume**. The final two parameters in glOrtho are distances to the near and far planes measured from a camera at the origin pointed in the negative z direction. The near plane is at $z = 1.0$, which is behind the camera; the far plane is at $z = -1.0$, which is in front of

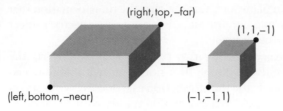

FIGURE 5.36   Mapping a view volume to the canonical view volume.

the camera. Although the projectors are parallel and an orthographic projection is conceptually akin to having a camera with a long telephoto lens located far from the objects, the importance of the near and far distances in glOrtho is that they determine which objects are clipped out.

Now suppose that, instead, we set the glOrtho parameters by the function call

```
glOrtho(left, right, bottom, top, near, far);
```

We now have specified a right parallelepiped view volume whose right side (relative to the camera) is the plane $x = left$, whose left side is the plane $x = right$, whose top is the plane $y = top$, and whose bottom is the plane $y = bottom$. The front is the near clipping plane $z = -near$, and the back is the far clipping plane $z = -far$. The projection matrix that OpenGL sets up is the matrix that transforms this volume to the cube centered at the origin with sides of length 2, which is shown in Figure 5.36. This matrix converts the vertices that specify our objects, such as through calls to glVertex, to vertices within this canonical view volume, by scaling and translating them. Consequently, vertices are transformed such that vertices within the specified view volume are transformed to vertices within the canonical view volume, and vertices outside the specified view volume are transformed to vertices outside the canonical view volume. Putting everything together, we see that the projection matrix is determined by the type of view and the view volume specified in glOrtho and that these specifications are relative to the camera. The positioning and orientation of the camera are determined by the model-view matrix. These two matrices are concatenated together, and objects have their vertices transformed by this matrix product.

We can use our knowledge of affine transformations to find this projection matrix. There are two tasks that we need to do. First, we must move the center of the specified view volume to the center of the canonical view volume (the origin) by doing a translation. Second, we must scale the sides of the specified view volume to each have a length of 2 (see Figure 5.36). Hence, the two transformations are $\mathbf{T}(-(right + left)/2, -(top + bottom)/2, +(far + near)/2)$ and $\mathbf{S}(2/(right - left), 2/(top - bottom), 2/(near - far))$, and they can be concatenated together (Figure 5.37) to form the projection matrix

FIGURE 5.37 Affine transformations for normalization.

$$
\mathbf{P} = \begin{bmatrix}
\dfrac{2}{left-right} & 0 & 0 & -\dfrac{left+right}{left-right} \\[2ex]
0 & \dfrac{2}{top-bottom} & 0 & -\dfrac{top+bottom}{top-bottom} \\[2ex]
0 & 0 & -\dfrac{2}{far-near} & \dfrac{far+near}{far-near} \\[2ex]
0 & 0 & 0 & 1
\end{bmatrix}.
$$

Because the camera is pointing in the negative z direction, the projectors are directed from infinity on the negative z-axis toward the origin.

5.8.3 Oblique Projections

Through glOrtho OpenGL provides a limited class of parallel projections—namely, only those for which the projectors are orthogonal to the projection plane. As we saw earlier in this chapter, oblique parallel projections are useful in many fields.[3] We could develop an oblique projection matrix directly; instead, however, we follow the process that we used for the general orthogonal projection. We convert the desired projection to a canonical orthogonal projection of distorted objects.

An oblique projection can be characterized by the angle that the projectors make with the projection plane, as shown in Figure 5.38. In APIs that support general parallel viewing, the view volume for an oblique projection has the near and far clipping planes parallel to the view plane, and the right, left, top, and bottom planes parallel to the direction of projection, as shown in Figure 5.39. We can derive the equations for oblique projections by considering the top and side views in Figure 5.40, which shows a projector and the projection plane $z = 0$. The angles θ and ϕ characterize the degree of obliqueness. In drafting, projections such as the cavalier and cabinet projections are determined by specific values of these angles. However, these angles are not the only possible interface (see Exercises 5.9 and 5.10).

If we consider the top view, we can find x_p by noting that

$$
\tan \theta = \frac{z}{x - x_p},
$$

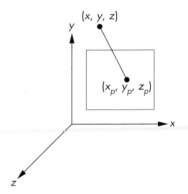

FIGURE 5.38 Oblique projection.

---

3. Note that without oblique projections we cannot draw coordinate axes in the way that we have been doing in this book (see Exercise 5.15).

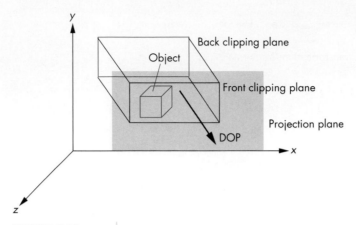

FIGURE 5.39   Oblique clipping volume.

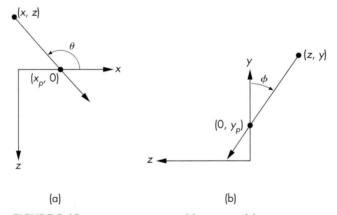

(a)   (b)

FIGURE 5.40   Oblique projection. (a) Top view. (b) Side view.

and thus

$$x_p = x - z \cot \theta .$$

Likewise,

$$y_p = y - z \cot \phi .$$

Using the equation for the projection plane

$$z_p = 0 ,$$

we can write these results in terms of a homogeneous-coordinate matrix

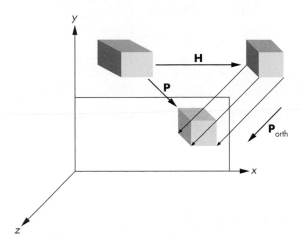

FIGURE 5.41   Effect of shear transformation.

$$\mathbf{P} = \begin{bmatrix} 1 & 0 & -\cot\theta & 0 \\ 0 & 1 & -\cot\phi & 0 \\ 0 & 0 & 0 & 0 \\ 0 & 0 & 0 & 1 \end{bmatrix}.$$

Following our strategy of the previous example, we can break $\mathbf{P}$ into the product

$$\mathbf{P} = \mathbf{M}_{\text{orth}}\mathbf{H}(\theta, \phi) = \begin{bmatrix} 1 & 0 & 0 & 0 \\ 0 & 1 & 0 & 0 \\ 0 & 0 & 0 & 0 \\ 0 & 0 & 0 & 1 \end{bmatrix} \begin{bmatrix} 1 & 0 & -\cot\theta & 0 \\ 0 & 1 & -\cot\phi & 0 \\ 0 & 0 & 1 & 0 \\ 0 & 0 & 0 & 1 \end{bmatrix},$$

where $\mathbf{H}(\theta, \phi)$ is a shearing matrix. Thus, we can implement an oblique projection by first doing a shear of the objects by $\mathbf{H}(\theta, \phi)$ and then doing an orthographic projection. Figure 5.41 shows the effect of $\mathbf{H}(\theta, \phi)$ on an object—a cube—inside an oblique view volume. The sides of the clipping volume become orthogonal to the view plane, but the sides of the cube become oblique as they are affected by the same shear transformation. However, the orthographic projection of the distorted cube is identical to the oblique projection of the undistorted cube.

We are not finished, because the view volume created by the shear is not our canonical view volume. We have to apply the same scaling and translation matrices that we used in Section 5.8.1. Hence, the transformation

$$\mathbf{ST} = \begin{bmatrix} \frac{2}{right-left} & 0 & 0 & -\frac{right+left}{right-left} \\ 0 & \frac{2}{top-bottom} & 0 & -\frac{top+bottom}{top-bottom} \\ 0 & 0 & -\frac{2}{far-near} & +\frac{far+near}{near-far} \\ 0 & 0 & 0 & 1 \end{bmatrix}$$

must be inserted after the shear and before the final orthographic projection, so the final matrix is

$$\mathbf{P} = \mathbf{M}_{\text{orth}}\mathbf{STH}.$$

The values of *left*, *right*, *bottom*, and *top* are the vertices of the right parallelepiped view volume created by the shear. These values depend on how the sides of the original view volume are communicated through the application program; they may have to be determined from the results of the shear to the corners of the original view volume.

5.9   Perspective-Projection Matrices

For perspective projections, we follow a path similar to the one that we used for parallel projections: We find a transformation that allows us, by distorting the vertices of our objects, to do a simple canonical projection to obtain the desired image. Our first step is to decide what this canonical viewing volume should be. We then introduce a new transformation, the **perspective-normalization transformation**, that converts a perspective projection to an orthogonal projection. Finally, we derive the perspective-projection matrix used in OpenGL.

5.9.1   Perspective Normalization

In Section 5.4, we introduced a simple perspective-projection matrix that, for the projection plane at $z = -1$ and the center of projection at the origin, is

$$\mathbf{M} = \begin{bmatrix} 1 & 0 & 0 & 0 \\ 0 & 1 & 0 & 0 \\ 0 & 0 & 1 & 0 \\ 0 & 0 & -1 & 0 \end{bmatrix}.$$

Suppose that to form an image, we also need to specify a clipping volume. Suppose that we fix the angle of view at 90 degrees by making the sides of the viewing volume intersect the projection plane at a 45-degree angle. Equivalently, the view volume is the semi-infinite view pyramid formed by the planes

$$x = \pm z,$$

$$y = \pm z,$$

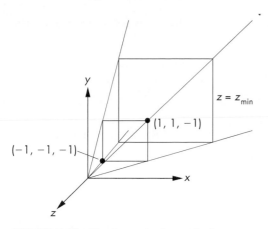

FIGURE 5.42 Simple perspective projection.

shown in Figure 5.42. We can make the volume finite by specifying the near plane to be $z = max$ and the far plane to be $z = z_{min}$, where both these values are negative (the near and far distances) and

$$z_{max} < z_{min}.$$

Consider the matrix

$$\mathbf{N} = \begin{bmatrix} 1 & 0 & 0 & 0 \\ 0 & 1 & 0 & 0 \\ 0 & 0 & \alpha & \beta \\ 0 & 0 & -1 & 0 \end{bmatrix},$$

which is similar to $\mathbf{M}$ but is nonsingular. For now, we leave α and β unspecified (but nonzero). If we apply $\mathbf{N}$ to the homogeneous-coordinate point $\mathbf{p} = [\, x \quad y \quad z \quad 1 \,]^{T}$, we obtain the new point $\mathbf{q} = [\, x' \quad y' \quad z' \quad w' \,]^{T}$, where

$$x' = x,$$
$$y' = y,$$
$$z' = \alpha z + \beta,$$
$$w' = -z.$$

After dividing by w', we have the three-dimensional point

$$x'' = -\frac{x}{z},$$
$$y'' = -\frac{y}{z},$$
$$z'' = -\left(\alpha + \frac{\beta}{z} \right).$$

If we apply an orthographic projection along the z-axis to $\mathbf{N}$, we obtain the matrix

$$\mathbf{M}_{\text{orth}}\mathbf{N} = \begin{bmatrix} 1 & 0 & 0 & 0 \\ 0 & 1 & 0 & 0 \\ 0 & 0 & 0 & 0 \\ 0 & 0 & -1 & 0 \end{bmatrix},$$

which is a simple perspective-projection matrix, and the projection of the arbitrary point $\mathbf{p}$ is

$$\mathbf{p}' = \mathbf{M}_{\text{orth}}\mathbf{N}\mathbf{p} = \begin{bmatrix} x \\ y \\ 0 \\ -z \end{bmatrix}.$$

After we do the perspective division, we obtain the desired values for x_p and y_p:

$$x_p = -\frac{x}{z},$$

$$y_p = -\frac{y}{z}.$$

We have shown that we can apply a transformation $\mathbf{N}$ to points, and after an orthogonal projection, we obtain the same result as we would have for a perspective projection. This process is similar to how we converted oblique projections to orthogonal projections by first shearing the objects.

The matrix $\mathbf{N}$ is nonsingular and transforms the original viewing volume into a new volume. We choose α and β such that the new volume is the canonical clipping volume. Consider the sides

$$x = \pm z.$$

They are transformed by $x'' = -x/z$ to the planes

$$x'' = \pm 1.$$

Likewise, the sides $y = \pm z$ are transformed to

$$y'' = \pm 1.$$

The front of the view volume $z = z_{\text{max}}$ is transformed to the plane

$$z'' = -\left(\alpha + \frac{\beta}{z_{\text{max}}}\right).$$

Finally, the far plane $z = z_{\text{min}}$ is transformed to the plane

$$z'' = -\left(\alpha + \frac{\beta}{z_{\text{min}}}\right).$$

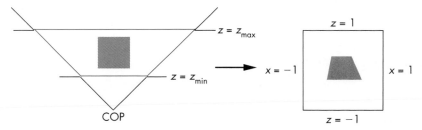

FIGURE 5.43   Perspective normalization of view volume.

If we select

$$\alpha = -\frac{z_{max} + z_{min}}{z_{max} - z_{min}},$$

$$\beta = -\frac{2z_{max}z_{min}}{z_{max} - z_{min}},$$

then the plane $z = z_{min}$ is mapped to the plane $z'' = -1$; the plane $z = z_{max}$ is mapped to the plane $z'' = 1$; and we have our canonical clipping volume. Figure 5.43 shows this transformation and the distortion to a cube within the volume. Thus, **N** has transformed the viewing frustum to a right parallelepiped, and an orthographic projection in the transformed volume yields the same image as does the perspective projection. The matrix **N** is called the **perspective-normalization matrix**. The mapping

$$z'' = -\left(\alpha + \frac{\beta}{z}\right)$$

is nonlinear but preserves the ordering of depths. Thus, if z_1 and z_2 are the depths of two points within the original viewing volume and

$$z_1 > z_2,$$

then their transformations satisfy

$$z_1'' > z_2''.$$

Consequently, hidden-surface removal works in the normalized volume, although the nonlinearity of the transformation can cause numerical problems because the depth buffer has a limited resolution, usually 24 or 32 bits. Note that, although the original projection plane we placed at $z = -1$ has been transformed by **N** to the plane $z'' = \beta - \alpha$, there is little consequence to this result because we follow **N** by an orthographic projection.

Although we have shown that both perspective and parallel transformations can be converted to orthographic transformations, the effects of this conversion are greatest in implementation. As long as we can put a carefully chosen

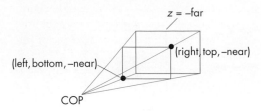

FIGURE 5.44   OpenGL perspective.

projection matrix in the pipeline before the vertices are defined, we need only one viewing pipeline for all possible views. In Chapter 7, where we discuss implementation in detail, we shall see how converting all view volumes to right parallelepipeds by our normalization process simplifies both clipping and hidden-surface removal.

5.9.2   OpenGL Perspective Transformations

The OpenGL function glFrustum does not restrict the view volume to a symmetric (or right) frustum. The parameters are as shown in Figure 5.44. We can form the OpenGL perspective matrix by first converting this frustum to the symmetric frustum with 45-degree sides (see Figure 5.42). The process is similar to the conversion of an oblique parallel view to an orthogonal view. First, we do a shear to convert the asymmetric frustum to a symmetric one. Figure 5.44 shows the desired transformation. The shear angle is determined by our desire to skew (shear) the point $((left + right)/2, (top + bottom)/2, -far)$ to $(0, 0, -near)$. The required shear matrix is

$$\mathbf{H}(\theta, \phi) = \mathbf{H}\left(\cot^{-1}\left(\frac{left + right}{-2far}\right), \cot^{-1}\left(\frac{top + bottom}{-2far}\right)\right).$$

The resulting frustum is described by the planes

$$x = \pm\frac{right - left}{-2far},$$

$$y = \pm\frac{top - bottom}{-2far},$$

$$z = -near,$$

$$z = -far.$$

The next step is to scale the sides of this frustum to

$$x = \pm z,$$

$$y = \pm z,$$

without changing either the near plane or the far plane. The required scaling matrix is $\mathbf{S}(-2near/(right - left), -2near/(top - bottom), 1)$. Note that this transformation is determined uniquely without reference to the location of the far plane $z = -far$ because in three dimensions, an affine transformation is determined by the results of the transformation on four points. In this case, these points are the four vertices where the sides of the frustum intersect the near plane.

To get the far plane to the plane $z = -1$ and the near plane to $z = 1$ after applying a projection normalization, we use the projection-normalization matrix $\mathbf{N}$:

$$\mathbf{N} = \begin{bmatrix} 1 & 0 & 0 & 0 \\ 0 & 1 & 0 & 0 \\ 0 & 0 & \alpha & \beta \\ 0 & 0 & -1 & 0 \end{bmatrix},$$

with α and β as in Section 5.9.1. The resulting projection matrix is in terms of the near and far distances,

$$\mathbf{P} = \mathbf{NSH} = \begin{bmatrix} \dfrac{-2far}{right-left} & 0 & \dfrac{right+left}{right-left} & 0 \\ 0 & \dfrac{-2far}{top-bottom} & \dfrac{top+bottom}{top-bottom} & 0 \\ 0 & 0 & -\dfrac{far+near}{far-near} & \dfrac{2far*near}{far-near} \\ 0 & 0 & -1 & 0 \end{bmatrix}.$$

5.10 Projections and Shadows

The creation of simple shadows is an interesting application of projection matrices. Although shadows are not geometric objects, they are important components of realistic images and give many visual clues to the spatial relationships among the objects in a scene. Starting from a physical point of view, shadows require a light source to be present. A point is in shadow if it is not illuminated by any light source, or equivalently if a viewer at that point cannot see any light sources. However, if the only light source is at the center of projection, there are no visible shadows, because any shadows are behind visible objects. This lighting strategy has been called the "flashlight in the eye" model and corresponds to the simple lighting we have used thus far.

To add physically correct shadows, we must understand the interaction between light and materials, a topic that we investigate in Chapter 6. There we show that global calculations are difficult; normally, they cannot be done in real time.

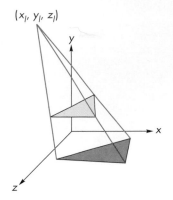

(x_l, y_l, z_l)

FIGURE 5.45 Shadow from a single polygon.

Nevertheless, the importance of shadows in applications such as flight simulators led to a number of special approaches that can be used in many circumstances. Consider the shadow generated by the point source in Figure 5.45. We assume for simplicity that the shadow falls on the ground or the surface,

$$y = 0.$$

Not only is the shadow a flat polygon, called a **shadow polygon**, but it is also the projection of the original polygon onto the surface. Specifically, the shadow polygon is the projection of the polygon onto the surface with the center of projection at the light source. Thus, if we do a projection onto the plane of a surface in a frame in which the light source is at the origin, we obtain the vertices of the shadow polygon. These vertices must then be converted back to a representation in the object frame. Rather than do the work as part of an application program, we can find a suitable projection matrix and use OpenGL to compute the vertices of the shadow polygon.

Suppose that we start with a light source at (x_l, y_l, z_l), as in Figure 5.46(a). If we reorient the figure such that the light source is at the origin, as in Figure 5.46(b), by a translation matrix $\mathbf{T}(-x_l, -y_l, -z_l)$, then we have a simple perspective projection through the origin. The projection matrix is

$$\mathbf{M} = \begin{bmatrix} 1 & 0 & 0 & 0 \\ 0 & 1 & 0 & 0 \\ 0 & 0 & 1 & 0 \\ 0 & \frac{1}{-y_l} & 0 & 0 \end{bmatrix}.$$

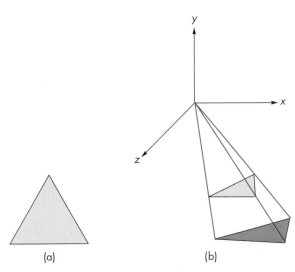

(a) (b)

FIGURE 5.46 Shadow polygon projection. (a) From a light source. (b) With source moved to the origin.

Finally, we translate everything back with $\mathbf{T}(x_l, y_l, z_l)$. The concatenation of this matrix and the two translation matrices projects the vertex (x, y, z) to

$$x_p = x_l - \frac{x - x_l}{(y - y_l)/y_l},$$

$$y_p = 0,$$

$$z_p = z_l - \frac{z - z_l}{(y - y_l)/y_l}.$$

However, with an OpenGL program, we can alter the model-view matrix to form the desired polygon:

```
GLfloat m[16];              /* shadow projection matrix */
for(i=0;i<15;i++) m[i]=0.0;
m[0]=m[5]=m[10]=1.0;
m[7]= -1.0/yl;

glColor3fv(polygon_color)
glBegin(GL_POLYGON)
  .
  .                         /* draw the polygon normally */
  .
glEnd();
glMatrixMode(GL_MODELVIEW);
glPushMatrix();             /* save state */
glTranslatef(xl,yl,zl);     /* translate back */
glMultMatrixf(m);           /* project */
glTranslate(-xl,-yl,-zl);   /* move light to origin */
glColor3fv(shadow_color);
glBegin(GL_POLYGON);
  .
  .                         /* draw the polygon again */
  .
glEnd();
glPopMatrix();              /* restore state */
```

Note that although we are performing a projection with respect to the light source, the matrix that we use is the model-view matrix. We render the same polygon twice: the first time as usual and the second time with an altered model-view matrix that transforms the vertices. The same viewing conditions are applied to both the polygon and its shadow polygon. The results of computing shadows for the cube are shown in Back Plate 3. The code is in the program cubes.c on the companion Web site.

For a simple environment, such as an airplane flying over flat terrain casting a single shadow, this technique works well. It is also easy to convert from point sources to distant (parallel) light sources (see Exercise 5.17). However, when objects can cast shadows on other objects, this method becomes impractical. In

Chapter 12, we address more general, but slower, rendering methods that will create shadows automatically as part of the rendering process.

Summary and Notes

We have come a long way. We can now write complete, nontrivial, three-dimensional applications. Probably the most instructive activity that you can do now is to write such an application. Developing skill with manipulating the model-view and projection functions takes practice.

We have presented the mathematics of the standard projections. Although most APIs obviate the user from writing projection functions, understanding the mathematics leads to understanding a pipeline implementation based on concatenation of 4×4 matrices. Until recently, user programs had to do the projections within the applications, and most hardware systems did not support perspective projections.

There are three major themes in the remainder of this book. First, we explore modeling further by expanding our basic set of primitives. In Chapter 10, we incorporate more complex relationships between simple objects through hierarchical models. We also explore approaches to modeling that do not force us to describe objects through procedures rather than as geometric objects. This approach allows us to model objects with only as much detail as is needed, to incorporate physical laws into our models, and to model natural phenomena that cannot be described by polygons. In Chapter 11, we leave the world of flat objects, adding curves and curved surfaces. These objects are defined by vertices, and we can implement them by breaking them into small flat primitives, so we can use the same viewing pipeline.

The second major theme is realism. Although more complex objects allow us to build more realistic models, we also explore more complex rendering options. In Chapter 6, we consider the interaction of light with the materials that characterize our objects. We look more deeply at hidden-surface–removal methods, at shading models, and in Chapters 8 and 9 at techniques such as texture mapping that allow us to create complex images from simple objects using advanced rendering techniques.

Third, we look more deeply at implementation in Chapter 7. At this point, we have introduced the major functional units of the graphics pipeline. We discuss the details of the algorithms used in each unit. We shall also see additional possibilities for creating images by working directly in the frame buffer.

Suggested Readings

Carlbom and Paciorek [Car78] discuss the relationships between classical and computer viewing. Rogers and Adams [Rog90] give many examples of the projection matrices corresponding to the standard views used in drafting. Foley et al. [Fol90], Watt [Wat00], and Hearn and Baker [Hea04] derive canonical projection transformations. All follow a PHIGS orientation, so the API is slightly different from the one used here, although Foley derives the most general case. The references differ in whether they use column or row matrices, in where the COP is located, and in whether the projection is in the positive or negative z direction. See the *OpenGL Programming Guide* [Ope04a] for a further discussion of the use of the model-view and projection matrices in OpenGL.

Exercises

5.1   Not all projections are planar geometric projections. Give an example of a projection in which the projection surface is not a plane and another in which the projectors are not lines.

5.2   Consider an airplane whose position is specified by the roll, pitch, and yaw and by the distance from an object. Find a model-view matrix in terms of these parameters.

5.3   Consider a satellite orbiting around the earth. Its position above the earth is specified in polar coordinates. Find a model-view matrix that keeps the viewer looking at the earth. Such a matrix could be used to show the earth as it rotates.

5.4   Show how to compute u and v directions from the VPN, VRP, and VUP using only cross products.

5.5   Can we obtain an isometric of the cube by a single rotation about a suitably chosen axis? Explain your answer.

5.6   Derive the perspective-projection matrix when the COP can be at any point and the projection plane can be at any orientation.

5.7   Show that perspective projection preserves lines.

5.8   Any attempt to take the projection of a point in the same plane as the COP will lead to a division by zero. What is the projection of a line segment that has endpoints on either side of the projection plane?

5.9   Define one or more APIs to specify oblique projections. You do not need to write the functions; just decide which parameters the user must specify.

5.10 Derive an oblique-projection matrix from specification of front and back clipping planes and top-right and bottom-left intersections of the sides of the clipping volume with the front clipping plane.

5.11 Our approach of normalizing all projections seems to imply that we could predistort all objects and support only orthographic projections. Explain any problems we would face if we took this approach to building a graphics system.

5.12   How do the OpenGL projection matrices change if the COP is not at the origin? Assume that the COP is at $(0, 0, d)$ and the projection plane is $z = 0$.

5.13   We can create an interesting class of three-dimensional objects by extending two-dimensional objects into the third dimension by extrusion. For example, a circle becomes a cylinder, a line becomes a quadrilateral, and a quadrilateral in the plane becomes a parallelepiped. Use this technique to convert the two-dimensional maze from Exercise 2.8 to a three-dimensional maze.

5.14   Extend the maze program of Exercise 5.13 to allow the user to walk through the maze. A click on the middle mouse button should move the user forward; a click on the right or left button should turn the user 90 degrees to the right or left, respectively.

5.15   If we were to use orthogonal projections to draw the coordinate axes, the x- and y-axes would lie in the plane of the paper, but the z-axis would point out of the page. Instead, we can draw the x- and y-axes meeting at a 90-degree angle, with the z-axis going off at -135 degrees from the x-axis. Find the matrix that projects the original orthogonal-coordinate axes to this view.

5.16   Write a program to display a rotating cube in a box with three light sources. Each light source should project the cube onto one of the three visible sides of the box.

5.17   Find the projection of a point onto the plane $ax + by + cz + d = 0$ from a light source located at infinity in the direction (d_x, d_y, d_z).

5.18   Using one of the three-dimensional interfaces discussed in Chapter 4, write a program to move the camera through a scene composed of simple objects.

5.19   Write a program to fly through the three-dimensional Sierpinski gasket formed by subdividing tetrahedra. Can you prevent the user from flying through walls?

5.20   In animation, often we can save effort by working with two-dimensional patterns that are mapped onto flat polygons that are always parallel to the camera. Write a program that will keep a simple polygon facing the camera as the camera moves.

5.21   Stereo images are produced by creating two images with the viewer in two slightly different positions. Consider a viewer who is at the origin but whose eyes are separated by Δx units. What are the appropriate viewing specifications to create the two images?

SHADING

We have learned to build three-dimensional graphical models and to display them. However, if you render one of our models, you might be disappointed to see images that look flat and thus fail to show the three-dimensional nature of the model. This appearance is a consequence of our unnatural assumption that each surface is lit such that it appears to a viewer in a single color. Under this assumption, the orthographic projection of a sphere is a uniformly colored circle, and a cube appears as a flat hexagon. If we look at a photograph of a lit sphere, we see not a uniformly colored circle but rather a circular shape with many gradations or **shades** of color. It is these gradations that give two-dimensional images the appearance of being three-dimensional.

What we have left out is the interaction between light and the surfaces in our models. This chapter begins to fill that gap. We develop separate models of light sources and of the most common light–material interactions. Our aim is to add shading to a fast pipeline graphics architecture, so we develop only a local lighting model. Such models, as opposed to global lighting models, allow us to compute the shade to assign to a point on a surface, independent of any other surfaces in the scene. The calculations depend only on the material properties assigned to the surface, the local geometry of the surface, and the locations and properties of the light sources. In this chapter, we introduce the lighting model used by OpenGL in its fixed-function pipeline and applied to each vertex. In Chapter 9, we consider how we can use other models if we can apply programs to each vertex and how we can apply lighting to each fragment, rather than each vertex.

Following our previous development, we investigate how we can apply shading to polygonal models. We develop a recursive approximation to a sphere that will allow us to test our shading algorithms. We then discuss how light and material properties are specified in OpenGL and can be added to our sphere-approximating program.

We conclude the chapter with a short discussion of the two most important methods for handling global lighting effects: ray tracing and radiosity.

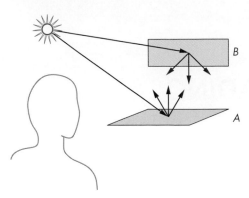

FIGURE 6.1 Reflecting surfaces.

6.1 Light and Matter

In Chapters 1 and 2, we presented the rudiments of human color vision, delaying until now any discussion of the interaction between light and surfaces. Perhaps the most general approach to rendering is based on physics, where we use principles such as conservation of energy to derive equations that describe how light is reflected from surfaces.

From a physical perspective, a surface can either emit light by self-emission, as a light bulb does, or reflect light from other surfaces that illuminate it. Some surfaces may both reflect light and emit light from internal physical processes. When we look at a point on an object, the color that we see is determined by multiple interactions among light sources and reflective surfaces. These interactions can be viewed as a recursive process. Consider the simple scene in Figure 6.1. Some light from the source that reaches surface A is scattered. Some of this reflected light reaches surface B, and some of it is then scattered back to A, where some of it is again reflected back to B, and so on. This recursive scattering of light between surfaces accounts for subtle shading effects, such as the bleeding of colors between adjacent surfaces. Mathematically, this recursive process results in an integral equation, the **rendering equation**, which in principle we could use to find the shading of all surfaces in a scene. Unfortunately, this equation generally cannot be solved analytically. Numerical methods are not fast enough for real-time rendering. There are various approximate approaches, such as radiosity and ray tracing, each of which is an excellent approximation to the rendering equation for particular types of surfaces. Unfortunately, neither ray tracing nor radiosity can yet be used to render scenes at the rate at which we can pass polygons through the modeling-projection pipeline. Consequently, we focus on a simpler rendering model, based on the Phong reflection model, that provides a compromise between physical correctness and efficient calculation. We shall consider the rendering equation, radiosity, and ray tracing in greater detail in Chapter 12.

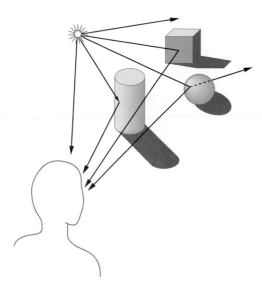

FIGURE 6.2   Light and surfaces.

Rather than looking at a global energy balance, we follow rays of light from light-emitting (or self-luminous) surfaces that we call **light sources**. We then model what happens to these rays as they interact with reflecting surfaces in the scene. This approach is similar to ray tracing, but we consider only single interactions between light sources and surfaces. There are two independent parts of the problem. First, we must model the light sources in the scene. Then we must build a reflection model that deals with the interactions between materials and light.

To get an overview of the process, we can start following rays of light from a point source, as shown in Figure 6.2. As we noted in Chapter 1, our viewer sees only the light that leaves the source and reaches her eyes—perhaps through a complex path and multiple interactions with objects in the scene. If a ray of light enters her eye directly from the source, she sees the color of the source. If the ray of light hits a surface visible to our viewer, the color she sees is based on the interaction between the source and the surface material: She sees the color of the light reflected from the surface toward her eyes.

In terms of computer graphics, we replace the viewer by the projection plane, as shown in Figure 6.3. Conceptually, the clipping window in this plane is mapped to the screen; thus, we can think of the projection plane as ruled into rectangles, each corresponding to a pixel. The color of the light source and of the surfaces determines the color of one or more pixels in the frame buffer.

We need to consider only those rays that leave the source and reach the viewer's eye, either directly or through interactions with objects. In the case of computer viewing, these are the rays that reach the center of projection (COP) after passing through the clipping rectangle. Note that most rays leaving a source do not

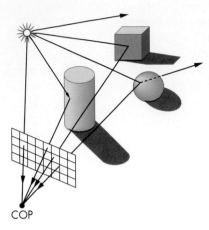

FIGURE 6.3   Light, surfaces, and computer imaging.

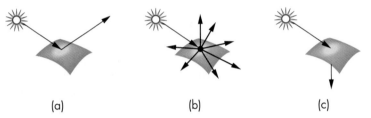

(a)   (b)   (c)

FIGURE 6.4   Light–material interactions. (a) Specular surface. (b) Diffuse surface. (c) Translucent surface.

contribute to the image and are thus of no interest to us. We make use of this observation in Section 6.10.

Figure 6.2 shows both single and multiple interactions between rays and objects. It is the nature of these interactions that determines whether an object appears red or brown, light or dark, dull or shiny. When light strikes a surface, some of it is absorbed and some of it is reflected. If the surface is opaque, reflection and absorption account for all the light striking the surface. If the surface is translucent, some of the light is transmitted through the material and emerges to interact with other objects. These interactions depend on wavelength. An object illuminated by white light appears red because it absorbs most of the incident light but reflects light in the red range of frequencies. A shiny object appears so because its surface is smooth. Conversely, a dull object has a rough surface. The shading of objects also depends on the orientation of their surfaces, a factor that we shall see is characterized by the normal vector at each point. These interactions between light and materials can be classified into the three groups depicted in Figure 6.4.

1. **Specular surfaces** appear shiny because most of the light that is reflected or **scattered** is in a narrow range of angles close to the angle of reflection. Mirrors are **perfectly specular surfaces**; the light from an incoming light ray may be partially absorbed, but all reflected light emerges at a single angle, obeying the rule that the angle of incidence is equal to the angle of reflection.

2. **Diffuse surfaces** are characterized by reflected light being scattered in all directions. Walls painted with matte or flat paint are diffuse reflectors, as are many natural materials, such as terrain viewed from an airplane or a satellite. **Perfectly diffuse surfaces** scatter light equally in all directions and thus appear the same to all viewers.

3. **Translucent surfaces** allow some light to penetrate the surface and to emerge from another location on the object. This process of **refraction** characterizes glass and water. Some incident light may also be reflected at the surface.

We shall model all these surfaces in Section 6.3 and Chapter 9. First, we consider light sources.

6.2 Light Sources

Light can leave a surface through two fundamental processes: self-emission and reflection. We usually think of a light source as an object that emits light only through internal energy sources. However, a light source, such as a light bulb, can also reflect some light that is incident on it from the surrounding environment. We neglect the emissive term in our simple models. When we discuss OpenGL lighting in Section 6.7, we shall see that we can easily simulate a self-emission term.

If we consider a source such as the one in Figure 6.5, we can look at it as an object with a surface. Each point (x, y, z) on the surface can emit light that is characterized by the direction of emission (θ, ϕ) and the intensity of energy emitted at each wavelength λ. Thus, a general light source can be characterized by a six-variable **illumination function** $I(x, y, z, \theta, \phi, \lambda)$. Note that we need two angles to specify a direction, and we are assuming that each frequency can be considered independently. From the perspective of a surface illuminated by this source, we can obtain the total contribution of the source (Figure 6.6) by integrating over its surface, a process that accounts for the emission angles that reach this surface and must also account for the distance between the source and the surface. For a distributed light source, such as a light bulb, the evaluation of this integral is difficult, whether we use analytic or numerical methods. Often, it is easier to model the distributed source with polygons, each of which is a simple source, or with an approximating set of point sources.

We consider four basic types of sources: ambient lighting, point sources, spotlights, and distant light. These four lighting types are sufficient for rendering most simple scenes.

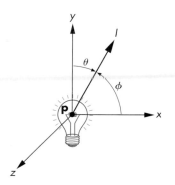

FIGURE 6.5 Light source.

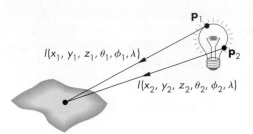

FIGURE 6.6 Adding the contribution from a source.

6.2.1 Color Sources

Not only do light sources emit different amounts of light at different frequencies, but their directional properties can vary with frequency as well. Consequently, a physically correct model can be complex. However, our model of the human visual system is based on three-color theory that tells us we perceive three tristimulus values, rather than a full color distribution. For most applications, we can thus model light sources as having three components—red, green, and blue—and can use each of the three color sources to obtain the corresponding color component that a human observer sees.

We describe a source through a three-component intensity or **luminance** function

$$\mathbf{I} = \begin{bmatrix} I_r \\ I_g \\ I_b \end{bmatrix},$$

each of whose components is the intensity of the independent red, green, and blue components. Thus, we use the red component of a light source for the calculation of the red component of the image. Because light–material computations involve three similar but independent calculations, we tend to present a single scalar equation, with the understanding that it can represent any of the three color components.

6.2.2 Ambient Light

In some rooms, such as in certain classrooms or kitchens, the lights have been designed and positioned to provide uniform illumination throughout the room. Often such illumination is achieved through large sources that have diffusers whose purpose is to scatter light in all directions. We could create an accurate simulation of such illumination, at least in principle, by modeling all the distributed sources and then integrating the illumination from these sources at each point on a reflecting surface. Making such a model and rendering a scene with it would be a daunting task for a graphics system, especially one for which real-time performance is desirable. Alternatively, we can look at the desired effect of the sources: to achieve a uniform light level in the room. This uniform lighting is called **ambient light**. If we follow this second approach, we can postulate an ambient intensity at each point in the environment. Thus, ambient illumination is characterized by an intensity, I_a, that is identical at every point in the scene.

Our ambient source has three color components:

$$\mathbf{I}_a = \begin{bmatrix} I_{ar} \\ I_{ag} \\ I_{ab} \end{bmatrix}.$$

We use the *scalar* I_a to denote any one of the red, green, or blue components of $\mathbf{I}_a$. Although every point in our scene receives the same illumination from $\mathbf{I}_a$, each surface can reflect this light differently.

6.2.3 Point Sources

An ideal **point source** emits light equally in all directions. We can characterize a point source located at a point $\mathbf{p}_0$ by a three-component color matrix:

$$\mathbf{I}(\mathbf{p}_0) = \begin{bmatrix} I_r(\mathbf{p}_0) \\ I_g(\mathbf{p}_0) \\ I_b(\mathbf{p}_0) \end{bmatrix}.$$

The intensity of illumination received from a point source is proportional to the inverse square of the distance between the source and surface. Hence, at a point $\mathbf{p}$ (Figure 6.7), the intensity of light received from the point source is given by the matrix

$$\mathbf{i}(\mathbf{p}, \mathbf{p}_0) = \frac{1}{|\mathbf{p} - \mathbf{p}_0|^2} \mathbf{I}(\mathbf{p}_0).$$

As we did with ambient light, we use $I(\mathbf{p}_0)$ to denote any of the components of $\mathbf{I}(\mathbf{p}_0)$.

The use of point sources in most applications is determined more by their ease of use than by their resemblance to physical reality. Scenes rendered with only

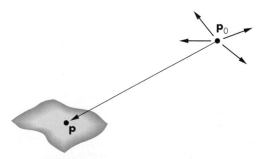

FIGURE 6.7 Point source illuminating a surface.

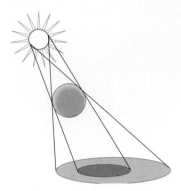

FIGURE 6.8 Shadows created by finite-size light source.

point sources tend to have high contrast; objects appear either bright or dark. In the real world, it is the large size of most light sources that contributes to softer scenes, as we can see from Figure 6.8, which shows the shadows created by a source of finite size. Some areas are fully in shadow, or in the **umbra**, whereas others are in partial shadow, or in the **penumbra**. We can mitigate the high-contrast effect from point-source illumination by adding ambient light to a scene.

The distance term also contributes to the harsh renderings with point sources. Although the inverse-square distance term is correct for point sources, in practice it is usually replaced by a term of the form $(a + bd + cd^2)^{-1}$, where d is the distance between $\mathbf{p}$ and $\mathbf{p}_0$. The constants a, b, and c can be chosen to soften the lighting. Note that if the light source is far from the surfaces in the scene, the intensity of the light from the source is sufficiently uniform that the distance term is constant over the surfaces.

6.2.4 Spotlights

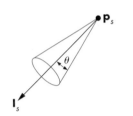

FIGURE 6.9 Spotlight.

Spotlights are characterized by a narrow range of angles through which light is emitted. We can construct a simple spotlight from a point source by limiting the angles at which light from the source can be seen. We can use a cone whose apex is at $\mathbf{p}_s$, which points in the direction $\mathbf{l}_s$, and whose width is determined by an angle θ, as shown in Figure 6.9. If $\theta = 180$, the spotlight becomes a point source.

More realistic spotlights are characterized by the distribution of light within the cone—usually with most of the light concentrated in the center of the cone. Thus, the intensity is a function of the angle ϕ between the direction of the source and a vector $\mathbf{s}$ to a point on the surface (as long as this angle is less than θ; Figure 6.10). Although this function could be defined in many ways, it is usually defined by $\cos^e \phi$, where the exponent e (Figure 6.11) determines how rapidly the light intensity drops off.

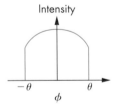

FIGURE 6.10 Attenuation of a spotlight.

As we shall see throughout this chapter, cosines are convenient functions for lighting calculations. If $\mathbf{u}$ and $\mathbf{v}$ are any unit-length vectors, we can compute the cosine of the angle θ between them with the dot product

$$\cos \theta = \mathbf{u} \cdot \mathbf{v},$$

a calculation that requires only three multiplications and two additions.

6.2.5 Distant Light Sources

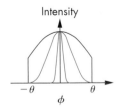

FIGURE 6.11 Spotlight exponent.

Most shading calculations require the direction from the point on the surface to the light source position. As we move across a surface, calculating the intensity at each point, we should recompute this vector repeatedly—a computation that is a significant part of the shading calculation. However, if the light source is far from the surface, the vector does not change much as we move from point to point, just as the light from the sun strikes all objects that are in close proximity to one another at the same angle. Figure 6.12 illustrates that we are effectively replacing a point source of light with a source that illuminates objects with parallel rays of light—a parallel source. In practice, the calculations for distant light sources are similar to the calculations for parallel projections; they replace the *location* of the light source with the *direction* of the light source. Hence, in homogeneous coordinates, a point light source at $\mathbf{p}_0$ is represented internally as a four-dimensional column matrix:

$$\mathbf{p}_0 = \begin{bmatrix} x \\ y \\ z \\ 1 \end{bmatrix},$$

FIGURE 6.12 Parallel light source.

In contrast, the distant light source is described by a direction vector whose representation in homogeneous coordinates is the matrix

$$\mathbf{p}_0 = \begin{bmatrix} x \\ y \\ z \\ 0 \end{bmatrix}.$$

The graphics system can carry out rendering calculations more efficiently for distant light sources than for near ones. Of course, a scene rendered with distant light sources looks different from a scene rendered with near sources. Fortunately, OpenGL allows both types of sources.

6.3   The Phong Reflection Model

Although we could approach light–material interactions through physical models, we have chosen to use a model that leads to efficient computations, especially when we use it with our pipeline-rendering model. The reflection model that we present was introduced by Phong and later modified by Blinn. It has proved to be efficient and to be a close enough approximation to physical reality to produce good renderings under a variety of lighting conditions and material properties.

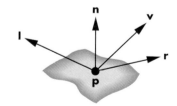

FIGURE 6.13 Vectors used by the Phong model.

The Phong model uses the four vectors shown in Figure 6.13 to calculate a color for an arbitrary point $\mathbf{p}$ on a surface. If the surface is curved, all four vectors can change as we move from point to point. The vector $\mathbf{n}$ is the normal at $\mathbf{p}$; we discuss its calculation in Section 6.4. The vector $\mathbf{v}$ is in the direction from $\mathbf{p}$ to the viewer or COP. The vector $\mathbf{l}$ is in the direction of a line from $\mathbf{p}$ to an arbitrary point on the source for a distributed light source or, as we are assuming for now, to the point-light source. Finally, the vector $\mathbf{r}$ is in the direction that a perfectly reflected ray from $\mathbf{l}$ would take. Note that $\mathbf{r}$ is determined by $\mathbf{n}$ and $\mathbf{l}$. We calculate it in Section 6.4.

The Phong model supports the three types of material–light interactions—ambient, diffuse, and specular—that we introduced in Section 6.1. Suppose that we have a set of point sources. We assume that each source can have separate ambient, diffuse, and specular components for each of the three primary colors. Although this assumption may appear unnatural, remember that our goal is to create realistic shading effects in as close to real time as possible. We use a local model to simulate effects that can be global in nature. Thus, our light-source model has ambient, diffuse, and specular terms. We need nine coefficients to characterize these terms at any point $\mathbf{p}$ on the surface. We can place these nine coefficients in a 3×3 illumination matrix for the ith light source:

$$\mathbf{L}_i = \begin{bmatrix} L_{ira} & L_{iga} & L_{iba} \\ L_{ird} & L_{igd} & L_{ibd} \\ L_{irs} & L_{igs} & L_{ibs} \end{bmatrix}.$$

The first row of the matrix contains the ambient intensities for the red, green, and blue terms from source i. The second row contains the diffuse terms; the third contains the specular terms. We assume that any distance-attenuation terms have not yet been applied.

We construct the model by assuming that we can compute how much of each of the incident lights is reflected at the point of interest. For example, for the red diffuse term from source i, L_{ird}, we can compute a reflection term R_{ird}, and the latter's contribution to the intensity at $\mathbf{p}$ is $R_{ird}L_{ird}$. The value of R_{ird} depends on the material properties, the orientation of the surface, the direction of the light source, and the distance between the light source and the viewer. Thus, for each point, we have nine coefficients that we can place in a matrix of reflection terms of the form

$$\mathbf{R}_i = \begin{bmatrix} R_{ira} & R_{iga} & R_{iba} \\ R_{ird} & R_{igd} & R_{ibd} \\ R_{irs} & R_{igs} & R_{ibs} \end{bmatrix}.$$

We can then compute the contribution for each color source by adding the ambient, diffuse, and specular components. For example, the red intensity that we see at $\mathbf{p}$ from source i is

$$I_{ir} = R_{ira}L_{ira} + R_{ird}L_{ird} + R_{irs}L_{irs}$$
$$= I_{ira} + I_{ird} + I_{irs}.$$

We obtain the total intensity by adding the contributions of all sources and, possibly, a global ambient term. Thus, the red term is

$$I_r = \sum_i (I_{ira} + I_{ird} + I_{irs}) + I_{ar},$$

where I_{ar} is the red component of the global ambient light.

We can simplify our notation by noting that the necessary computations are the same for each source and for each primary color. They differ depending on whether we are considering the ambient, diffuse, or specular terms. Hence, we can omit the subscripts i, r, g, and b. We write

$$I = I_a + I_d + I_s = L_a R_a + L_d R_d + L_s R_s,$$

with the understanding that the computation will be done for each of the primaries and each source; the global ambient term can be added at the end.

6.3.1 Ambient Reflection

The intensity of ambient light L_a is the same at every point on the surface. Some of this light is absorbed and some is reflected. The amount reflected is given by the ambient reflection coefficient, $R_a = k_a$. Because only a positive fraction of the light is reflected, we must have

$$0 \le k_a \le 1,$$

and thus

$$I_a = k_a L_a.$$

Here L_a can be any of the individual light sources, or it can be a global ambient term.

A surface has, of course, three ambient coefficients—k_{ar}, k_{ag}, and k_{ab}—and they can differ. Hence, for example, a sphere appears yellow under white ambient light if its blue ambient coefficient is small and its red and green coefficients are large.

6.3.2 Diffuse Reflection

A perfectly diffuse reflector scatters the light that it reflects equally in all directions. Hence, such a surface appears the same to all viewers. However, the amount of light reflected depends both on the material—because some of the incoming light is absorbed—and on the position of the light source relative to the surface. Diffuse reflections are characterized by rough surfaces. If we were to magnify a cross section of a diffuse surface, we might see an image like that shown in Figure 6.14. Rays of light that hit the surface at only slightly different angles are reflected back at markedly different angles. Perfectly diffuse surfaces are so rough that there is no preferred angle of reflection. Such surfaces, sometimes called **Lambertian surfaces**, can be modeled mathematically with Lambert's law.

Consider a diffuse planar surface, as shown in Figure 6.15, illuminated by the sun. The surface is brightest at noon and dimmest at dawn and dusk because, according to Lambert's law, we see only the vertical component of the incoming light. One way to understand this law is to consider a small parallel light source striking a plane, as shown in Figure 6.16. As the source is lowered in the (artificial) sky, the same amount of light is spread over a larger area, and the surface appears

FIGURE 6.14   Rough surface.

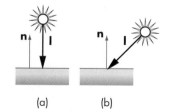

(a)   (b)

FIGURE 6.15   Illumination of a diffuse surface. (a) At noon. (b) In the afternoon.

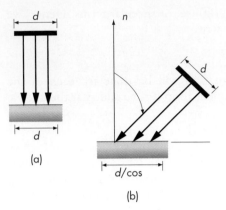

FIGURE 6.16 Vertical contributions by Lambert's law. (a) At noon. (b) In the afternoon.

dimmer. Returning to the point source of Figure 6.15, we can characterize diffuse reflections mathematically. Lambert's law states that

$$R_d \propto \cos \theta,$$

where θ is the angle between the normal at the point of interest $\mathbf{n}$ and the direction of the light source $\mathbf{l}$. If both $\mathbf{l}$ and $\mathbf{n}$ are unit-length vectors,[1] then

$$\cos \theta = \mathbf{l} \cdot \mathbf{n}.$$

If we add in a reflection coefficient k_d representing the fraction of incoming diffuse light that is reflected, we have the diffuse reflection term:

$$I_d = k_d (\mathbf{l} \cdot \mathbf{n}) L_d.$$

If we wish to incorporate a distance term, to account for attenuation as the light travels a distance d from the source to the surface, we can again use the quadratic attenuation term:

$$I_d = \frac{k_d}{a + bd + cd^2} (\mathbf{l} \cdot \mathbf{n}) L_d.$$

There is a potential problem with this expression because $(\mathbf{l} \cdot \mathbf{n}) L_d$ will be negative if the light source is below the horizon. In this case, we want to use zero rather than a negative value. Hence, in practice we use $\max((\mathbf{l} \cdot \mathbf{n}) L_d, 0)$.

---

1. Direction vectors, such as $\mathbf{l}$ and $\mathbf{n}$, are used repeatedly in shading calculations through the dot product. In practice, both the programmer and the graphics software should seek to normalize all such vectors as soon as possible.

6.3.3 Specular Reflection

If we employ only ambient and diffuse reflections, our images will be shaded and will appear three-dimensional, but all the surfaces will look dull, somewhat like chalk. What we are missing are the highlights that we see reflected from shiny objects. These highlights usually show a color different from the color of the reflected ambient and diffuse light. For example, a red plastic ball viewed under white light has a white highlight that is the reflection of some of the light from the source in the direction of the viewer (Figure 6.17).

FIGURE 6.17 Specular highlights.

Whereas a diffuse surface is rough, a specular surface is smooth. The smoother the surface is, the more it resembles a mirror. Figure 6.18 shows that as the surface gets smoother, the reflected light is concentrated in a smaller range of angles centered about the angle of a perfect reflector—a mirror or a perfectly specular surface. Modeling specular surfaces realistically can be complex because the pattern by which the light is scattered is not symmetric. It depends on the wavelength of the incident light, and it changes with the reflection angle.

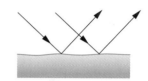

FIGURE 6.18 Specular surface.

Phong proposed an approximate model that can be computed with only a slight increase over the work done for diffuse surfaces. The model adds a term for specular reflection. Hence, we consider the surface as being rough for the diffuse term and smooth for the specular term. The amount of light that the viewer sees depends on the angle ϕ between **r**, the direction of a perfect reflector, and **v**, the direction of the viewer. The Phong model uses the equation

$$I_s = k_s L_s \cos^\alpha \phi.$$

The coefficient k_s ($0 \leq k_s \leq 1$) is the fraction of the incoming specular light that is reflected. The exponent α is a **shininess** coefficient. Figure 6.19 shows how, as α is increased, the reflected light is concentrated in a narrower region centered on the angle of a perfect reflector. In the limit, as α goes to infinity, we get a mirror; values in the range 100 to 500 correspond to most metallic surfaces, and smaller values (< 100) correspond to materials that show broad highlights.

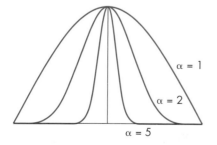

FIGURE 6.19 Effect of shininess coefficient.

The computational advantage of the Phong model is that if we have normalized $\mathbf{r}$ and $\mathbf{n}$ to unit length, we can again use the dot product, and the specular term becomes

$$I_s = k_s L_s \max((\mathbf{r} \cdot \mathbf{v})^\alpha, 0).$$

We can add a distance term, as we did with diffuse reflections. What is referred to as the **Phong model**, including the distance term, is written

$$I = \frac{1}{a + bd + cd^2}(k_d L_d \max(\mathbf{l} \cdot \mathbf{n}, 0) + k_s L_s \max((\mathbf{r} \cdot \mathbf{v})^\alpha, 0)) + k_a L_a.$$

This formula is computed for each light source and for each primary.

It might seem to make little sense either to associate a different amount of ambient light with each source or to allow the components for specular and diffuse lighting to be different. Because we cannot solve the full rendering equation, we must use various tricks in an attempt to obtain realistic renderings.

Consider, for example, an environment with many objects. When we turn on a light, some of that light hits a surface directly. These contributions to the image can be modeled with specular and diffuse components of the source. However, much of the rest of the light from the source is scattered from multiple reflections from other objects and makes a contribution to the light received at the surface under consideration. We can approximate this term by having an ambient component associated with the source. The shade that we should assign to this term depends on *both* the color of the source and the color of the objects in the room—an unfortunate consequence of our use of approximate models. To some extent, the same analysis holds for diffuse light. Diffuse light reflects among the surfaces, and the color that we see on a particular surface depends on other surfaces in the environment. Again, by using carefully chosen diffuse and specular components with our light sources, we can approximate a global effect with local calculations.

We have developed the Phong model in object space. The actual shading, however, is not done until the objects have passed through the model-view and projection transformations. These transformations can affect the cosine terms in the model (see Exercise 6.20). Consequently, to make a correct shading calculation, we must either preserve spatial relationships as vertices and vectors pass through the pipeline, perhaps by sending additional information through the pipeline from object space, or go backward through the pipeline to obtain the required shading information.

6.3.4 The Modified Phong Model

If we use the Phong model with specular reflections in our rendering, the dot product $\mathbf{r} \cdot \mathbf{v}$ should be recalculated at every point on the surface. We can obtain an interesting approximation by using the unit vector halfway between the viewer vector and the light-source vector:

$$\mathbf{h} = \frac{\mathbf{l} + \mathbf{v}}{|\mathbf{l} + \mathbf{v}|}.$$

Figure 6.20 shows all five vectors. Here we have defined ψ as the angle between $\mathbf{n}$ and $\mathbf{h}$, the **halfway angle**. When $\mathbf{v}$ lies in the same plane as do $\mathbf{l}$, $\mathbf{n}$, and $\mathbf{r}$, we can show (see Exercise 6.7) that

$$2\psi = \phi.$$

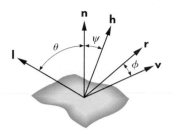

FIGURE 6.20 Determination of the halfway vector.

If we replace $\mathbf{r} \cdot \mathbf{v}$ with $\mathbf{n} \cdot \mathbf{h}$, we avoid calculation of $\mathbf{r}$. However, the halfway angle ψ is smaller than ϕ, and if we use the same exponent e in $(\mathbf{n} \cdot \mathbf{h})^e$ that we used in $(\mathbf{r} \cdot \mathbf{v})^e$, then the size of the specular highlights will be smaller. We can mitigate this problem by replacing the value of the exponent e with a value e' so that $(\mathbf{n} \cdot \mathbf{h})^{e'}$ is closer to $(\mathbf{r} \cdot \mathbf{v})^e$. It is clear that avoiding recalculation of $\mathbf{r}$ is desirable. However, to appreciate fully where savings can be made, you should consider all the cases of flat and curved surfaces, near and far light sources, and near and far viewers (see Exercise 6.8).

When we use the halfway vector in the calculation of the specular term, we are using the **Blinn-Phong**, or **modified Phong, shading model**. This model is the default in OpenGL and is the one carried out on each vertex as it passes down the pipeline.

Color Plate 25 shows a group of Utah teapots (Section 12.10) that have been rendered in OpenGL using the modified Phong model. Note that it is only our ability to control material properties that makes the teapots appear different from one another. The various teapots demonstrate how the modified Phong model can create a variety of surface effects, ranging from dull surfaces to highly reflective surfaces that look like metal.

6.4   Computation of Vectors

The illumination and reflection models that we have derived are sufficiently general that they can be applied to either curved or flat surfaces, to parallel or perspective views, and to distant or near surfaces. Most of the calculations for rendering a scene involve the determination of the required vectors and dot products. For each special case, simplifications are possible. For example, if the surface is a flat polygon, the normal is the same at all points on the surface. If the light source is far from the surface, the light direction is the same at all points.

In this section, we examine how the vectors are computed for the general case. In Section 6.5, we see what additional techniques can be applied when our objects are composed of flat polygons. This case is especially important because most renderers, including OpenGL, render curved surfaces by approximating those surfaces with many small, flat polygons.

6.4.1 Normal Vectors

For smooth surfaces, the vector normal to the surface exists at every point and gives the local orientation of the surface. Its calculation depends on how the surface is represented mathematically. Two simple cases—the plane and the sphere—illustrate both how we compute normals and where the difficulties lie.

A plane can be described by the equation

$$ax + by + cz + d = 0.$$

As we saw in Chapter 4, this equation could also be written in terms of the normal to the plane, $\mathbf{n}$, and a point, $\mathbf{p}_0$, known to be on the plane as

$$\mathbf{n} \cdot (\mathbf{p} - \mathbf{p}_0) = 0,$$

where $\mathbf{p}$ is any point (x, y, z) on the plane. Comparing the two forms, we see that the vector $\mathbf{n}$ is given by

$$\mathbf{n} = \begin{bmatrix} a \\ b \\ c \end{bmatrix},$$

or, in homogeneous coordinates,

$$\mathbf{n} = \begin{bmatrix} a \\ b \\ c \\ 0 \end{bmatrix}.$$

However, suppose that instead we are given three noncollinear points—$\mathbf{p}_0$, $\mathbf{p}_1$, $\mathbf{p}_2$—that are in this plane and thus are sufficient to determine it uniquely. The vectors $\mathbf{p}_2 - \mathbf{p}_0$ and $\mathbf{p}_1 - \mathbf{p}_0$ are parallel to the plane, and we can use their cross product to find the normal

$$\mathbf{n} = (\mathbf{p}_2 - \mathbf{p}_0) \times (\mathbf{p}_1 - \mathbf{p}_0).$$

We must be careful about the order of the vectors in the cross product: Reversing the order changes the surface from outward pointing to inward pointing, and that reversal can affect the lighting calculations. Some graphics systems use the first three vertices in the specification of a polygon to determine the normal automatically. OpenGL does not do so, but as we shall see in Section 6.5, forcing users to compute normals creates more flexibility in how we apply our lighting model.

For curved surfaces, how we compute normals depends on how we represent the surface. In Chapter 11, we discuss three different methods for representing curves and surfaces. We can see a few of the possibilities by considering how we represent a unit sphere centered at the origin. The usual equation for this sphere is the **implicit equation**

$$f(x, y, z) = x^2 + y^2 + z^2 - 1 = 0,$$

or in vector form,

$$f(\mathbf{p}) = \mathbf{p} \cdot \mathbf{p} - 1 = 0.$$

The normal is given by the **gradient vector**, which is defined by the column matrix

$$\mathbf{n} = \begin{bmatrix} \frac{\partial f}{\partial x} \\ \frac{\partial f}{\partial y} \\ \frac{\partial f}{\partial z} \end{bmatrix} = \begin{bmatrix} 2x \\ 2y \\ 2z \end{bmatrix} = 2\mathbf{p}.$$

The sphere could also be represented in **parametric form**. In this form, the x, y, and z values of a point on the sphere are represented independently in terms of two parameters u and v:

$$x = x(u, v),$$
$$y = y(u, v),$$
$$z = z(u, v).$$

As we shall see in Chapter 11, this form is preferable in computer graphics, especially for representing curves and surfaces; although, for a particular surface, there may be multiple parametric representations. One parametric representation for the sphere is

$$x(u, v) = \cos u \sin v,$$
$$y(u, v) = \cos u \cos v,$$
$$z(u, v) = \sin u.$$

As u and v vary in the range $-\pi/2 < u < \pi/2$, $-\pi < v < \pi$, we get all the points on the sphere. When we are using the parametric form, we can obtain the normal from the **tangent plane**, shown in Figure 6.21, at a point $\mathbf{p}(u, v) = [\, x(u, v) \quad y(u, v) \quad z(u, v)\,]^T$ on the surface. The tangent plane gives the local orientation of the surface at a point; we can derive it by taking the linear terms of the Taylor series expansion of the surface at $\mathbf{p}$. The result is that at $\mathbf{p}$, lines in the directions of the vectors represented by

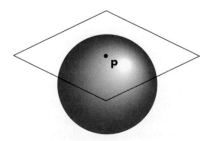

FIGURE 6.21 Tangent plane to sphere.

$$\frac{\partial \mathbf{p}}{\partial u} = \begin{bmatrix} \frac{\partial x}{\partial u} \\ \frac{\partial y}{\partial u} \\ \frac{\partial z}{\partial u} \end{bmatrix}, \qquad \frac{\partial \mathbf{p}}{\partial v} = \begin{bmatrix} \frac{\partial x}{\partial v} \\ \frac{\partial y}{\partial v} \\ \frac{\partial z}{\partial v} \end{bmatrix}$$

lie in the tangent plane. We can use their cross product to obtain the normal

$$\mathbf{n} = \frac{\partial \mathbf{p}}{\partial u} \times \frac{\partial \mathbf{p}}{\partial v}.$$

For our sphere, we find that

$$\mathbf{n} = \cos u \begin{bmatrix} \cos u \sin v \\ \cos u \cos v \\ \sin u \end{bmatrix} = (\cos u)\mathbf{p}.$$

We are interested in only the direction of $\mathbf{n}$; thus, we can divide by $\cos u$ to obtain the unit normal to the sphere

$$\mathbf{n} = \mathbf{p}.$$

In Section 6.9, we use this result to shade a polygonal approximation to a sphere.

Within a graphics system, we usually work with a collection of vertices, and the normal vector must be approximated from some set of points close to the point where the normal is needed. The pipeline architecture of real-time graphics systems makes this calculation difficult because we process one vertex at a time, and thus the graphics system may not have the information available to compute the approximate normal at a given point. Consequently, graphics systems often leave the computation of normals to the user program.

In OpenGL, we can associate a normal with a vertex through functions such as

```
glNormal3f(nx, ny, nz);
glNormal3fv(pointer_to_normal);
```

Normals are state variables. If we define a normal before a sequence of vertices through glVertex calls, this normal is associated with all the vertices and is used for the lighting calculations at all the vertices. The problem remains, however, that we have to determine these normals ourselves.

6.4.2 Angle of Reflection

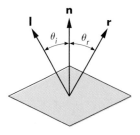

FIGURE 6.22   A mirror.

Once we have calculated the normal at a point, we can use this normal and the direction of the light source to compute the direction of a perfect reflection. An ideal mirror is characterized by the following statement: *The angle of incidence is equal to the angle of reflection.* These angles are as pictured in Figure 6.22. The **angle of incidence** is the angle between the normal and the light source (assumed to be a point source); the **angle of reflection** is the angle between the normal and the direction in which the light is reflected. In two dimensions, there is but a single angle satisfying the angle condition. In three dimensions, however, our statement is insufficient to compute the required angle: There is an infinite number of angles satisfying our condition. We must add the following statement: *At a point* **p** *on the surface, the incoming light ray, the reflected light ray, and the normal at the point must all lie in the same plane.* These two conditions are sufficient for us to determine **r** from **n** and **l**. Our primary interest is the direction, rather than the magnitude, of **r**. However, many of our rendering calculations will be easier if we deal with unit-length vectors. Hence, we assume that both **l** and **n** have been normalized such that

$$|\mathbf{l}| = |\mathbf{n}| = 1.$$

We also want

$$|\mathbf{r}| = 1.$$

If $\theta_i = \theta_r$, then

$$\cos \theta_i = \cos \theta_r.$$

Using the dot product, the angle condition is

$$\cos \theta_i = \mathbf{l} \cdot \mathbf{n} = \cos \theta_r = \mathbf{n} \cdot \mathbf{r}.$$

The coplanar condition implies that we can write **r** as a linear combination of **l** and **n**:

$$\mathbf{r} = \alpha \mathbf{l} + \beta \mathbf{n}.$$

Taking the dot product with **n**, we find that

$$\mathbf{n} \cdot \mathbf{r} = \alpha \mathbf{l} \cdot \mathbf{n} + \beta = \mathbf{l} \cdot \mathbf{n}.$$

We can get a second condition between α and β from our requirement that **r** also be of unit length; thus,

$$1 = \mathbf{r} \cdot \mathbf{r} = \alpha^2 + 2\alpha\beta \mathbf{l} \cdot \mathbf{n} + \beta^2.$$

Solving these two equations, we find that

$$\mathbf{r} = 2(\mathbf{l} \cdot \mathbf{n})\mathbf{n} - \mathbf{l}.$$

Although, the fixed-function OpenGL pipeline uses the modified Phong model and thus avoids having to calculate the reflection vector, in Chapter 9, we introduce programmable shaders that can use the reflection vector. Methods such as environment maps will use the reflected-view vector (see Exercise 6.24) that is used to determine what a viewer would see if she looked at a reflecting surface such as a highly polished sphere.

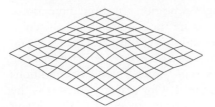

FIGURE 6.23   Polygonal mesh.

6.5   Polygonal Shading

Assuming that we can compute normal vectors, given a set of light sources and a viewer, the lighting models that we have developed can be applied at every point on a surface. Unfortunately, even if we have simple equations to determine normal vectors, as we did in our example of a sphere (Section 6.4), the amount of computation required can be large. We have already seen many of the advantages of using polygonal models for our objects. A further advantage is that for flat polygons, we can significantly reduce the work required for shading. Most graphics systems, including OpenGL, exploit the efficiencies possible for rendering flat polygons by decomposing curved surfaces into many small, flat polygons.

Consider a polygonal mesh, such as that shown in Figure 6.23, where each polygon is flat and thus has a well-defined normal vector. We consider three ways to shade the polygons: flat shading, smooth or Gouraud shading, and Phong shading.

6.5.1   Flat Shading

The three vectors—$\mathbf{l}$, $\mathbf{n}$, and $\mathbf{v}$—can vary as we move from point to point on a surface. For a flat polygon, however, $\mathbf{n}$ is constant. If we assume a distant viewer,[2] $\mathbf{v}$ is constant over the polygon. Finally, if the light source is distant, $\mathbf{l}$ is constant. Here *distant* could be interpreted in the strict sense of meaning that the source is at infinity. The necessary adjustments, such as changing the *location* of the source to the *direction* of the source, could then be made to the shading equations and to their implementation. *Distant* could also be interpreted in terms of the size of the polygon relative to how far the polygon is from the source or viewer, as shown in Figure 6.24. Graphics systems or user programs often exploit this definition.

If the three vectors are constant, then the shading calculation needs to be carried out only once for each polygon, and each point on the polygon is assigned

---

2. We can make this assumption in OpenGL by setting the local-viewer flag to false.

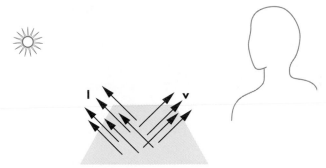

FIGURE 6.24   Distant source and viewer.

FIGURE 6.25   Flat shading of polygonal mesh.

the same shade. This technique is known as **flat,** or **constant, shading**. In OpenGL, we specify flat shading through

```
glShadeModel(GL_FLAT);
```

If flat shading is in effect, OpenGL uses the normal associated with the first vertex of a single polygon for the shading calculation. For primitives such as a triangle strip, OpenGL uses the normal of the third vertex for the first triangle, the normal of the fourth for the second, and so on. Similar rules hold for other primitives, such as quadrilateral strips.

Flat shading will show differences in shading for the polygons in our mesh. If the light sources and viewer are near the polygon, the vectors **l** and **v** will be different for each polygon. However, if our polygonal mesh has been designed to model a smooth surface, flat shading will almost always be disappointing because we can see even small differences in shading between adjacent polygons, as shown in Figure 6.25. The human visual system has a remarkable sensitivity to small differences in light intensity, due to a property known as **lateral inhibition**. If we see an increasing sequence of intensities, as is shown in Figure 6.26, we

FIGURE 6.26   Step chart.

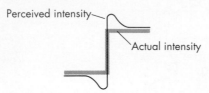

FIGURE 6.27   Perceived and actual intensities at an edge.

perceive the increases in brightness as overshooting on one side of an intensity step and undershooting on the other, as shown in Figure 6.27. We see stripes, known as **Mach bands**, along the edges. This phenomenon is a consequence of how the cones in the eye are connected to the optic nerve, and there is little that we can do to avoid it, other than to look for smoother shading techniques that do not produce large differences in shades at the edges of polygons.

6.5.2 Smooth and Gouraud Shading

In our rotating-cube example of Section 4.9, we saw that OpenGL interpolates colors assigned to vertices across a polygon. If we set the shading model to be smooth via

```
glShadeModel(GL_SMOOTH);
```

then OpenGL interpolates colors for other primitives such as lines. Suppose that we have enabled both smooth shading and lighting and that we assign to each vertex the normal of the polygon being shaded. The lighting calculation is made at each vertex using the material properties and the vectors $\mathbf{v}$ and $\mathbf{l}$ computed for each vertex. Note that if the light source is distant, and either the viewer is distant or there are no specular reflections, then smooth (or interpolative) shading shades a polygon in a constant color.

If we consider our mesh, the idea of a normal existing at a vertex should cause concern to anyone worried about mathematical correctness. Because multiple polygons meet at interior vertices of the mesh, each of which has its own normal, the normal at the vertex is discontinuous. Although this situation might complicate the mathematics, Gouraud realized that the normal at the vertex could be *defined* in such a way as to achieve smoother shading through interpolation. Consider an interior vertex, as shown in Figure 6.28, where four polygons meet. Each has its own normal. In **Gouraud shading**, we define the normal at a vertex to be the normalized average of the normals of the polygons that share the vertex. For our example, the **vertex normal** is given by

$$\mathbf{n} = \frac{\mathbf{n}_1 + \mathbf{n}_2 + \mathbf{n}_3 + \mathbf{n}_4}{|\mathbf{n}_1 + \mathbf{n}_2 + \mathbf{n}_3 + \mathbf{n}_4|}.$$

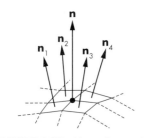

FIGURE 6.28   Normals near interior vertex.

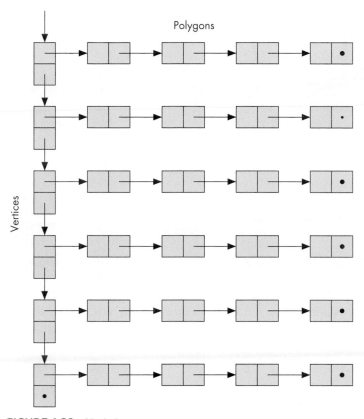

FIGURE 6.29 Mesh data structure.

From an OpenGL perspective, Gouraud shading is deceptively simple. We need only to set the vertex normals correctly. Often, the literature makes no distinction between smooth and Gouraud shading. However, the lack of a distinction causes a problem: How do we find the normals that we should average together? If our program is linear, specifying a list of vertices (and other properties), we do not have the necessary information about which polygons share a vertex. What we need, of course, is a data structure for representing the mesh. Traversing this data structure can generate the vertices with the averaged normals. Such a data structure should contain, at a minimum, polygons, vertices, normals, and material properties. One possible structure is the one shown in Figure 6.29. The key information that must be represented in the data structure is which polygons meet at each vertex.

Color Plates 4 and 5 show the shading effects available in OpenGL. In Color Plate 4, there is a single light source, but each polygon has been rendered with a single shade (constant shading), computed using the Phong model. In Color Plate 5, normals have been assigned to all the vertices. OpenGL has then

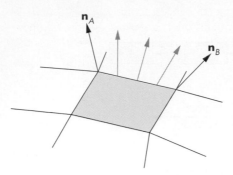

FIGURE 6.30   Edge normals.

computed shades for the vertices and has interpolated these shades over the faces of the polygons.

Color Plate 21 contains another illustration of the smooth shading provided by OpenGL. We used this color cube as an example in both Chapters 2 and 3, and the programs are in Appendix A. The eight vertices are colored black, white, red, green, blue, cyan, magenta, and yellow. Once smooth shading is enabled, OpenGL interpolates the colors across the faces of the polygons automatically.

6.5.3   Phong Shading

Even the smoothness introduced by Gouraud shading may not prevent the appearance of Mach bands. Phong proposed that instead of interpolating vertex intensities, as we do in Gouraud shading, we interpolate normals across each polygon. Consider a polygon that shares edges and vertices with other polygons in the mesh, as shown in Figure 6.30. We can compute vertex normals by interpolating over the normals of the polygons that share the vertex. Next, we can use bilinear interpolation, as we did in Chapter 4, to interpolate the normals over the polygon. Consider Figure 6.31. We can use the interpolated normals at vertices A and B to interpolate normals along the edge between them:

$$\mathbf{n}(\alpha) = (1 - \alpha)\mathbf{n}_A + \alpha\mathbf{n}_B.$$

We can do a similar interpolation on all the edges. The normal at any interior point can be obtained from points on the edges by

$$\mathbf{n}(\alpha, \beta) = (1 - \beta)\mathbf{n}_C + \beta\mathbf{n}_D.$$

Once we have the normal at each point, we can make an independent shading calculation. Usually, this process can be combined with rasterization of the polygon. Until recently, Phong shading could only be carried out off-line because it requires the interpolation of normals across each polygon. In terms of the pipeline, Phong shading requires that the lighting model be applied to each fragment, hence, the name **per fragment shading**. The latest graphics cards

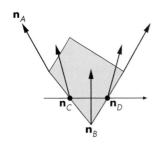

FIGURE 6.31   Interpolation of normals in Phong shading.

allow the programmer to write programs that operate on each fragment as it is generated by the rasterizer. Consequently, we can now do per fragment operations and thus implement Phong shading in real time. We shall discuss this topic in detail in Chapter 9.

6.6 Approximation of a Sphere by Recursive Subdivision

We have used the sphere as an example curved surface to illustrate shading calculations. However, the sphere is not an object supported within OpenGL. Both the GL utility library (GLU) and the GL Utility Toolkit (GLUT) contain spheres, the former by supporting quadric surfaces, a topic we discuss in Chapter 11, and the latter through a polygonal approximation.

Here we develop our own polygonal approximation to a sphere. It provides a basis for us to write simple programs that illustrate the interactions between shading parameters and polygonal approximations to curved surfaces. We introduce **recursive subdivision**, a powerful technique for generating approximations to curves and surfaces to any desired level of accuracy.

Our starting point is a tetrahedron, although we could start with any regular polyhedron whose facets could be divided initially into triangles.[3] The regular tetrahedron is composed of four equilateral triangles, determined by four vertices. We start with the four vertices $(0, 0, 1)$, $(0, 2\sqrt{2}/3, -1/3)$, $(-\sqrt{6}/3, -\sqrt{2}/3, -1/3)$, and $(\sqrt{6}/3, -\sqrt{2}/3, -1/3)$. All four lie on the unit sphere, centered at the origin. (Exercise 6.6 suggests one method for finding these points.)

We get a first approximation by drawing a wireframe for the tetrahedron. We define the four vertices by

```
GLfloat v[4][3]={{0.0, 0.0, 1.0}, {0.0, 0.942809, -0.333333},
                 {-0.816497, -0.471405, -0.333333},
                 {0.816497, -0.471405, -0.333333}};
```

We can draw triangles using the function

```
void triangle( GLfloat *a, GLfloat *b, GLfloat *c)
{
  glBegin(GL_LINE_LOOP);
    glVertex3fv(a);
    glVertex3fv(b);
    glVertex3fv(c);
  glEnd();
}
```

---

3. The regular icosahedron is composed of 20 equilateral triangles; it makes a nice starting point for generating spheres; see [Ope04a].

The tetrahedron can be drawn by

```
void tetrahedron()
{
    triangle(v[0], v[1], v[2] );
    triangle(v[3], v[2], v[1] );
    triangle(v[0], v[3], v[1] );
    triangle(v[0], v[2], v[3] );
}
```

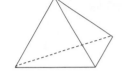

FIGURE 6.32   Tetrahedron.

The order of vertices obeys the right-hand rule, so we can convert the code to draw shaded polygons with little difficulty. If we add the usual code for initialization, our program will generate an image such as that in Figure 6.32: a simple regular polyhedron, but a poor approximation to a sphere.

We can get a closer approximation to the sphere by subdividing each facet of the tetrahedron into smaller triangles. Subdividing into triangles will ensure that all the new facets will be flat. There are at least three ways to do the subdivision, as shown in Figure 6.33. We can bisect each of the angles of the triangle and draw the three bisectors, which meet at a common point, thus generating three new triangles. We can also compute the center of mass (centrum) of the vertices by simply averaging them and then draw lines from this point to the three vertices, again generating three triangles. However, these techniques do not preserve the equilateral triangles that make up the regular tetrahedron. Instead—recalling a construction for the Sierpinski gasket of Chapter 2—we can connect the bisectors of the sides of the triangle, forming four equilateral triangles, as shown in Figure 6.33(c). We use this technique for our example.

After we have subdivided a facet as just described, the four new triangles will still be in the same plane as the original triangle. We can move the new vertices that we created by bisection to the unit sphere by normalizing each bisected vertex, using a simple normalization function such as

```
void normalize(GLfloat *p)
{
    double d=0.0;
    int i;
    for(i=0; i<3; i++) d+=p[i]*p[i];
```

(a)   (b)   (c)

FIGURE 6.33   Subdivision of a triangle by (a) bisecting angles, (b) computing the centrum, and (c) bisecting sides.

```
  d=sqrt(d);
  if(d > 0.0) for(i=0; i<3; i++) p[i]/=d;
}
```

We can now subdivide a single triangle, defined by the vertices numbered a, b, and c, by the code

```
GLfloat v1[3], v2[3], v3[3];
int j;
for(j=0; j<3; j++) v1[j]=v[a][j]+v[b][j];
normalize(v1);
for(j=0; j<3; j++) v2[j]=v[a][j]+v[c][j];
normalize(v2);
for(j=0; j<3; j++) v3[j]=v[c][j]+v[b][j];
normalize(v3);
triangle(v[a], v2, v1);
triangle(v[c], v3, v2);
triangle(v[b], v1, v3);
triangle(v1, v2, v3);
```

We can use this code in our tetrahedron routine to generate 16 triangles rather than four, but we would rather be able to repeat the subdivision process *n* times to generate successively closer approximations to the sphere. By calling the subdivision routine recursively, we can control the number of subdivisions.

First, we make the tetrahedron routine depend on the depth of recursion by adding an argument n:

```
void tetrahedron(int n)
{
   divide_triangle(v[0], v[1], v[2] , n);
   divide_triangle(v[3], v[2], v[1], n );
   divide_triangle(v[0], v[3], v[1], n );
   divide_triangle(v[0], v[2], v[3], n );
}
```

The divide_triangle function calls itself to subdivide further if n is greater than zero but generates triangles if n has been reduced to zero. Here is the code:

```
divide_triangle(GLfloat *a, GLfloat *b, GLfloat *c, int n)
{
 GLfloat v1[3], v2[3], v3[3];
 int j;
 if(n>0)
 {
   for(j=0; j<3; j++) v1[j]=a[j]+b[j];
   normalize(v1);
   for(j=0; j<3; j++) v2[j]=a[j]+c[j];
   normalize(v2);
```

```
for(j=0; j<3; j++) v3[j]=c[j]+b[j];
normalize(v3);
divide_triangle(a ,v2, v1, n-1);
divide_triangle(c ,v3, v2, n-1);
divide_triangle(b ,v1, v3, n-1);
divide_triangle(v1 ,v2, v3, n-1);
}
else triangle(a, b, c);
}
```

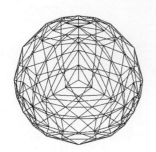

FIGURE 6.34 Sphere approximations using subdivision.

Figure 6.34 shows an approximation to the sphere drawn with this code. We now turn to adding lighting and shading to our sphere approximation. As a first step, we must examine how lighting and shading are handled by the OpenGL API.

6.7 Light Sources in OpenGL

OpenGL supports the four types of light sources that we just described and allows at least eight light sources in a program. Each must be individually specified and enabled. Although there are many parameters that must be specified, they are exactly the parameters required by the Phong model. The OpenGL functions

```
glLightfv(GLenum source, GLenum parameter, GLfloat *pointer_to_array)
glLightf(GLenum source, GLenum parameter, GLfloat value)
```

allow us to set the required vector and scalar parameters, respectively. There are four vector parameters that we can set: the position (or direction) of the light source and the amount of ambient, diffuse, and specular light associated with the source.

For example, suppose that we wish to specify the first source GL_LIGHT0 and to locate it at the point $(1.0, 2.0, 3.0)$. We store its position as a point in homogeneous coordinates:

```
GLfloat light0_pos[]={1.0, 2.0, 3.0, 1.0};
```

With the fourth component set to zero, the point source becomes a distant source with direction vector

```
GLfloat light0_dir[]={1.0, 2.0, 3.0, 0.0};
```

For our single light source, if we want a white specular component and red ambient and diffuse components, we can use the code

```
GLfloat diffuse0[]={1.0, 0.0, 0.0, 1.0};
GLfloat ambient0[]={1.0, 0.0, 0.0, 1.0};
GLfloat specular0[]={1.0, 1.0, 1.0, 1.0};
```

```
glEnable(GL_LIGHTING);
glEnable(GL_LIGHT0);

glLightfv(GL_LIGHT0, GL_POSITION, light0_pos);
glLightfv(GL_LIGHT0, GL_AMBIENT, ambient0);
glLightfv(GL_LIGHT0, GL_DIFFUSE, diffuse0);
glLightfv(GL_LIGHT0, GL_SPECULAR, specular0);
```

Note that we must enable both lighting and the particular source.

We can also add a global ambient term that is independent of any of the sources. For example, if we want a small amount of white light, we can use the code

```
GLfloat global_ambient[]={0.1, 0.1, 0.1, 1.0};
glLightModelfv(GL_LIGHT_MODEL_AMBIENT, global_ambient);
```

The distance terms are based on the distance-attenuation model,

$$f(d) = \frac{1}{a + bd + cd^2},$$

which contains constant, linear, and quadratic terms. These terms are set individually via glLightf; for example, the default values are equivalent to the code

```
glLightf(GL_LIGHT0, GL_CONSTANT_ATTENUATION, 1.0);
glLightf(GL_LIGHT0, GL_LINEAR_ATTENUATION, 0.0);
glLightf(GL_LIGHT0, GL_QUADRATIC_ATTENUATION, 0.0);
```

that gives a constant distance term.

We can convert a positional source to a spotlight by choosing the spotlight direction (GL_SPOT_DIRECTION), the exponent (GL_SPOT_EXPONENT), and the angle (GL_SPOT_CUTOFF). All three are specified by glLightf or glLightfv.

There are two other light parameters provided by OpenGL that we should mention: GL_LIGHT_MODEL_LOCAL_VIEWER and GL_LIGHT_MODEL_TWO_SIDE. Lighting calculations can be time-consuming. If the viewer is assumed to be an infinite distance from the scene, then the calculation of reflections is easier, because the direction to the viewer from any point in the scene is unchanged. The default in OpenGL is to make this approximation because its effect on many scenes is minimal. If you prefer that the full light calculation be made, using the true position of the viewer, you can change the model by using

```
glLightModeli(GL_LIGHT_MODEL_LOCAL_VIEWER, GL_TRUE);
```

In Chapter 4, we saw that a surface has both a front face and a back face. For polygons, we determine front and back by the order in which the vertices are specified, using the right-hand rule. For most objects, we see only the front faces, so we are not concerned with how OpenGL shades the back-facing surfaces. For

FIGURE 6.35   Shading of convex objects.

FIGURE 6.36   Visible back surfaces.

example, for convex objects, such as a sphere or a parallelepiped (Figure 6.35), the viewer can never see a back face, regardless of where she is positioned. However, if we remove a side from a cube or slice the sphere, as shown in Figure 6.36, a properly placed viewer may see a back face; thus, we must shade both the front and back faces correctly. We can ensure that OpenGL handles both faces correctly by invoking the function

```
glLightModeli(GL_LIGHT_MODEL_TWO_SIDED, GL_TRUE);
```

Light sources are special types of geometric objects and have geometric attributes, such as position, just like polygons and points. Hence, light sources are affected by the OpenGL model-view transformation. We can define them at the desired position or define them in a convenient position and move them to the desired position by the model-view transformation. The basic rule governing object placement is that vertices are converted to eye coordinates by the model-view transformation in effect at the time the vertices are defined. Thus, by careful placement of the light-source specifications relative to the definition of other geometric objects, we can create light sources that remain stationary while the objects move, light sources that move while objects remain stationary, and light sources that move with the objects.

6.8   Specification of Materials in OpenGL

Material properties in OpenGL match up directly with the supported light sources and with the Phong reflection model. We can also specify different material properties for the front and back faces of a surface. All our reflection parameters are specified through the functions

```
glMaterialfv(GLenum face, GLenum type, GLfloat * pointer_to_array)
glMaterialf(GLenum face, GLenum type, GLfloat value)
```

For example, we might define ambient, diffuse, and specular reflectivity coefficients (k_a, k_d, k_s) for each primary color through three arrays:

```
GLfloat ambient[] = {0.2, 0.2, 0.2, 1.0};
GLfloat diffuse[] = {1.0, 0.8, 0.0, 1.0};
GLfloat specular[]={1.0, 1.0, 1.0, 1.0};
```

Here we have defined a small amount of white ambient reflectivity, yellow diffuse properties, and white specular reflections. We set the material properties for the front and back faces by the calls

```
glMaterialfv(GL_FRONT_AND_BACK, GL_AMBIENT, ambient);
glMaterialfv(GL_FRONT_AND_BACK, GL_DIFFUSE, diffuse);
glMaterialfv(GL_FRONT_AND_BACK, GL_SPECULAR, specular);
```

If both the specular and diffuse coefficients are the same (as is often the case), we can specify both by using GL_DIFFUSE_AND_SPECULAR for the type parameter. To specify different front- and back-face properties, we use GL_FRONT and GL_ BACK. The shininess of a surface—the exponent in the specular-reflection term—is specified by glMaterialf; for example,

```
glMaterialf(GL_FRONT_AND_BACK, GL_SHININESS, 100.0);
```

OpenGL also allows us to define surfaces that have an emissive component that characterizes self-luminous sources. This method is useful if you want a light source to appear in your image. This term is unaffected by any of the light sources, and it does not affect any other surfaces. It adds a fixed color to the surfaces and is specified in a manner similar to other material properties. For example,

```
GLfloat emission[]={0.0, 0.3, 0.3, 1.0};
```

```
glMaterialfv(GL_FRONT_AND_BACK, GL_EMISSION, emission);
```

defines a small amount of blue-green (cyan) emission.

Material properties are also are part of the OpenGL state. Their values remain the same until changed and, when changed, affect only surfaces defined after the change. If we are using multiple materials, we can incur significant overhead if we have to change material properties each time we begin a new polygon. OpenGL contains a method, glColorMaterial, that you can use to change a single material property. It is more efficient for changing a single color material property but is less general than the method using glMaterial.

From an application programmer's perspective, we would like to have material properties that we can specify with a single function call, rather than having to make a series of calls to glMaterial for each polygon. We can achieve this goal by defining material objects in the application using structs or classes. For example, consider the typedef

```
typedef struct materialStruct
    GLfloat ambient[4];
    GLfloat diffuse[4];
    GLfloat specular[4];
    GLfloat shininess;
 materialStruct;
```

We can now define materials by code such as

```
materialStruct brassMaterials =
{
    0.33, 0.22, 0.03, 1.0,
    0.78, 0.57, 0.11, 1.0,
    0.99, 0.91, 0.81, 1.0,
    27.8
};
```

and access this code through a pointer,

```
currentMaterial=&brassMaterials;
```

which allows us to set material properties through a function,

```
void materials( materialStruct *materials)
{
    glMaterialfv(GL_FRONT, GL_AMBIENT, currentMaterial->ambient);
    glMaterialfv(GL_FRONT, GL_DIFFUSE, currentMaterial->diffuse);
    glMaterialfv(GL_FRONT, GL_SPECULAR, currentMaterial->specular);
    glMaterialf(GL_FRONT, GL_SHININESS, currentMaterial->shininess);
}
```

6.9 Shading of the Sphere Model

We can now shade our spheres. Here we omit our standard OpenGL initialization; the complete program is given in Appendix A.

If we are to shade our approximate spheres with OpenGL's shading model, we must assign normals. One simple, but illustrative choice is to flat shade each triangle, using the three vertices to determine a normal, then assign this normal to the first vertex. Following our approach of Section 6.6, we use the cross product and then normalize the result. A cross product function is

```
cross(GLfloat *a, GLfloat *b, GLfloat *c, GLfloat *d);
{
    d[0]=(b[1]-a[1])*(c[2]-a[2])-(b[2]-a[2])*(c[1]-a[1]);
    d[1]=(b[2]-a[2])*(c[0]-a[0])-(b[0]-a[0])*(c[2]-a[2]);
    d[2]=(b[0]-a[0])*(c[1]-a[1])-(b[1]-a[1])*(c[0]-a[0]);
    normalize(d);
}
```

Assuming that light sources have been defined and enabled, we can change the `triangle` routine to produce shaded spheres:

```
void triangle(GLfloat *a, GLfloat *b, GLfloat *c)
{
    GLfloat n[3];
    cross(a, b, c, n);
    glBegin(GL_POLYGON);
        glNormal3fv(n);
        glVertex3fv(a);
        glVertex3fv(b);
        glVertex3fv(c);
    glEnd();
}
```

The result of flat shading our spheres is shown in Figure 6.37. Note that even as we increase the number of subdivisions so that the interiors of the spheres appear smooth, we can still see edges of polygons around the outside of the sphere image. This type of outline is called a **silhouette edge**.

We can easily apply interpolative shading to the sphere models because we know that the normal at each point **p** on the surface is in the direction from the origin to **p**. We can then assign the true normal to each vertex, and OpenGL will interpolate the shades at these vertices across each triangle. Thus, we change triangle to

FIGURE 6.37   Flat-shaded sphere.

```
void triangle(GLfloat *a, GLfloat *b, GLfloat *c)
{
    GLfloat n[3];
    int i;
    glBegin(GL_POLYGON);
        for(i=0;i<3;i++) n[i]=a[i];
        normalize(n);
        glNormal3fv(n);
        glVertex3fv(a);
        for(i=0;i<3;i++) n[i]=b[i];
        normalize(n);
        glNormal3fv(n);
        glVertex3fv(b);
        for(i=0;i<3;i++) n[i]=c[i];
        normalize(n);
        glNormal3fv(n);
        glVertex3fv(c);
    glEnd();
}
```

The results of this definition of the normals are shown in Figure 6.38 and in Back Plate 2.

Although using the true normals produces a rendering more realistic than flat shading, the example is not a general one because we have used normals that are known analytically. We also have not provided a true Gouraud-shaded image. Suppose we want a Gouraud-shaded image of our approximate sphere. At each vertex, we need to know the normals of all polygons incident at the vertex. Our code does not have a data structure that contains the required information. Try Exercises 6.9 and 6.10, in which you construct such a structure. Note that six polygons meet at a vertex created by subdivision, whereas only three polygons meet at the original vertices of the tetrahedron.

FIGURE 6.38   Shading of the sphere with the true normals.

6.10   Global Illumination

There are limitations imposed by the local lighting model that we have used. Consider, for example, an array of spheres illuminated by a distant source, as

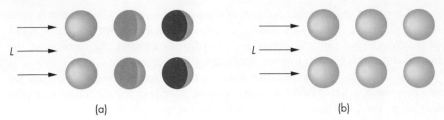

(a)   (b)

FIGURE 6.39   Array of shaded spheres. (a) Global lighting model. (b) Local lighting model.

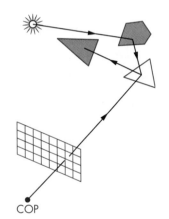

FIGURE 6.40   Polygon blocked from light source.

shown in Figure 6.39(a). The spheres close to the source block some of the light from the source from reaching the other spheres. However, if we use our local model, each sphere is shaded independently; all appear the same to the viewer (Figure 6.39(b)). In addition, if these spheres are specular, some light is scattered among spheres. Thus, if the spheres were very shiny, we should see the reflection of multiple spheres in some of the spheres and possibly even the multiple reflections of some spheres in themselves. Our lighting model cannot handle this situation. Nor can it produce shadows, except by using the tricks for some special cases, as we saw in Chapter 5.

All of these phenomena—shadows, reflections, blockage of light—are global effects and require a global lighting model. Although such models exist and can be quite elegant, in practice they are incompatible with the pipeline model. With the pipeline model, we must render each polygon independently of the other polygons, and we want our image to be the same regardless of the order in which the application produces the polygons. Although this restriction limits the lighting effects that we can simulate, we can render scenes very rapidly.

There are two alternative rendering strategies—ray tracing and radiosity—that can handle global effects. Each is best at different lighting conditions. Ray tracing starts with the synthetic-camera model but determines for each projector that strikes a polygon if that point is indeed illuminated by one or more sources before computing the local shading at each point. Thus, in Figure 6.40, we see three polygons and a light source. The projector shown intersects one of the polygons. A local renderer would use the Phong model to compute the shade at the point of intersection. The ray tracer would find that the light source cannot strike the point of intersection directly but that light from the source is reflected from the third polygon and this reflected light illuminates the point of intersection. In Chapter 12, we shall show how to find this information and make the required calculations.

A radiosity renderer is based upon energy considerations. From a physical point of view, all the light energy in a scene is conserved. Consequently, there is an energy balance that accounts for all the light that radiates from sources and is reflected by various surfaces in the scene. A radiosity calculation thus requires the solution of a large set of equations involving all the surfaces. As we shall see in Chapter 12, a ray tracer is best suited to a scene consisting of highly reflective surfaces, whereas a radiosity renderer is best suited for a scene in which all the surfaces are perfectly diffuse.

Although a pipeline renderer cannot take into account many global phenomena exactly, this observation does not mean we cannot produce realistic imagery with OpenGL or another API that is based upon a pipeline architecture. What we can do is use our knowledge of OpenGL and of the effects that global lighting produces to approximate what a global renderer would do. For example, our use of projective shadows in Chapter 5 shows that we can produce simple shadows. Many of the most exciting advances in computer graphics over the past few years have been in the use of pipeline renderers for global effects. We shall study many such techniques in the next few chapters, including mapping methods, multipass rendering, and transparency.

Summary and Notes

We have developed a lighting model that fits well with our pipeline approach to graphics. With it, we can create a variety of lighting effects, and we can employ different types of light sources. Although we cannot create the global effects of a ray tracer, a typical graphics workstation can render a polygonal scene using the modified Phong reflection model and smooth shading in the same amount of time as it can render a scene without shading. From the perspective of a user program, adding shading requires only setting parameters that describe the light sources and materials. In spite of the limitations of the local lighting model that we have introduced, our simple renderer performs remarkably well; it is the basis of the reflection model supported by most APIs, including OpenGL.

Programmable shaders, which we consider in Chapter 9, have changed the picture considerably. Not only can we create new methods of shading each vertex, we can use fragment shaders to do the lighting calculation for each fragment, thus avoiding the need to interpolate colors across each polygon. Methods such as Phong shading that were not possible within the standard pipeline can now be programmed by the user and will execute in about the same amount of time as the modified Phong shader. It is also possible to create a myriad of new shading effects.

The recursive-subdivision technique that we used to generate an approximation to a sphere is a powerful one that will reappear in various guises in Chapter 11, where we use variants of this technique to render curves and surfaces. It will also arise when we introduce modeling techniques that rely on the self-similarity of many natural objects.

This chapter concludes our development of polygonal-based graphics. You should now be able to generate scenes with lighting and shading. Techniques for creating even more sophisticated images, such as texture mapping and compositing, involve using the pixel-level capabilities of graphics systems—topics that we consider in Chapter 8.

Now is a good time for you to write an application program. Experiment with various lighting and shading parameters. Try to create light sources that move, either independently or with the objects in the scene. You will probably face difficulties in producing shaded images that do not have small defects, such as cracks between polygons through which light can enter. Many of these problems are artifacts of small numerical errors in rendering calculations. There are many tricks of the trade for mitigating the effects of these errors. Some you will discover on your own; others are given in the Suggested Readings for this chapter.

We turn to rasterization issues in Chapter 7. Although we have seen some of the ways in which the different modules in the rendering pipeline function, we have not yet seen the details. As we develop these details you will see how the pieces fit together such that each successive step in the pipeline requires only a small increment of work.

Suggested Readings

The use of lighting and reflection in computer graphics has followed two parallel paths: the physical and the computational. From the physical perspective, Kajiya's rendering equation [Kaj86] describes the overall energy balance in an environment and requires knowledge of the reflectivity function for each surface. Reflection models, such as the Torrance-Sparrow model [Tor67] and Cook-Torrance model [Coo82], are based on modeling a surface with small planar facets. See Hall [Hal89] and Foley [Fol90] for discussions of such models.

Phong [Pho75] is credited with putting together a computational model that included ambient, diffuse, and specular terms. The use of the halfway vector was first suggested by Blinn [Bli77]. The basic model of transmitted light was used by Whitted [Whi80]. It was later modified by Heckbert and Hanrahan [Hec84]. Gouraud [Gou71] introduced interpolative shading.

The *OpenGL Programming Guide* [Ope04a] contains many good hints on effective use of OpenGL's rendering capabilities.

Exercises

6.1   Most graphics systems and APIs use the simple lighting and reflection models that we introduced for polygon rendering. Describe the ways in which each of these models is incorrect. For each defect, give an example of a scene in which you would notice the problem.

6.2   Often, when a large polygon that we expect to have relatively uniform shading is shaded by OpenGL, it is rendered brightly in one area and more dimly in others. Explain why the image is uneven. Describe how you can avoid this problem.

6.3   In the development of the Phong reflection model, why do we not consider light sources being obscured from the surface by other surfaces in our reflection model?

6.4   How should the distance between the viewer and the surface enter the rendering calculations?

6.5   We have postulated an RGB model for the material properties of surfaces. Give an argument for using a subtractive color model instead.

6.6   Find four points equidistant from one another on a unit sphere. These points determine a tetrahedron. *Hint:* You can arbitrarily let one of the points be at $(0, 1, 0)$ and let the other three be in the plane $y = -d$ for some positive value of d.

6.7   Show that if $\mathbf{v}$ lies in the same plane as $\mathbf{l}$, $\mathbf{n}$, and $\mathbf{r}$, then the halfway angle satisfies

$$2\psi = \phi.$$

What relationship is there between the angles if $\mathbf{v}$ is not coplanar with the other vectors?

6.8   Consider all the combinations of near or far viewers, near or far light sources, flat or curved surfaces, and diffuse and specular reflections. For which cases can you simplify the shading calculations? In which cases does the use of the halfway vector help? Explain your answers.

6.9   Construct a data structure for representing the subdivided tetrahedron. Traverse the data structure such that you can Gouraud-shade the approximation to the sphere based on subdividing the tetrahedron.

6.10   Repeat Exercise 6.9 but start with an icosahedron instead of a tetrahedron.

6.11   Construct a data structure for representing meshes of quadrilaterals. Write a program to shade the meshes represented by your data structure.

6.12   Write a program that does recursive subdivisions on quadrilaterals and quadrilateral meshes.

6.13   Consider two materials that meet along a planar boundary. Suppose that the speed of light in the two materials is v_1 and v_2. Show that Snell's law is a statement that light travels from a point in one material to a point in the second material in the minimum time.

6.14   Show that the halfway vector $\mathbf{h}$ is at the angle at which a surface must be oriented so that the maximum amount of reflected light reaches the viewer.

6.15   Although we have yet to discuss frame-buffer operations, you can start constructing a ray tracer using a single routine of the form write_pixel(x, y, color) that places the value of color (either an RGB color or an intensity) at the pixel located at (x, y) in the frame buffer. Write a pseudocode routine ray that recursively traces a cast ray. You can assume that you have a function available that will intersect a ray with an object. Consider how to limit how far the original ray will be traced.

6.16 If you have a pixel-writing routine available on your system, write a ray tracer that will ray-trace a scene composed of only spheres. Use the mathematical equations for the spheres rather than a polygonal approximation.

6.17 Add light sources and shading to the maze program in Exercise 5.13.

6.18 Using the sphere-generation program in Appendix A as a starting point, construct an interactive program that will allow you to position one or more light sources and to alter material properties. Use your program to try to generate images of surfaces that match familiar materials, such as various metals, plastic, and carbon.

6.19 As geometric data pass through the viewing pipeline, a sequence of rotations, translations, scalings, and a projection transformation is applied to the vectors that determine the cosine terms in the Phong reflection model. Which, if any, of these operations preserve(s) the angles between the vectors? What are the implications of your answer for implementation of shading?

6.20 Estimate the amount of extra calculations required for Phong shading as compared to Gouraud shading. Take into account the results of Exercise 6.19.

6.21 Generalize the shadow-generation algorithm (Section 5.10) to handle flat surfaces at arbitrary orientations.

6.22 Convert the shadow-generation algorithm (Section 5.10) to an algorithm for distant sources. *Hint:* The perspective projection should become a parallel projection.

6.23 Compare the shadow-generation algorithm of Section 5.10 to the generation of shadows by a global-rendering method. What types of shadows can be generated by one method but not the other?

6.24 Consider a highly reflective sphere centered at the origin with a unit radius. If a viewer is located at **p**, describe the points she would see reflected in the sphere at a point on its surface.

FROM VERTICES TO FRAGMENTS

We now turn to the next steps in the pipeline: clipping, rasterization, and hidden-surface removal. Although we have yet to consider some major parts of OpenGL that are available to the application programmer, including discrete primitives, texture mapping, and curves and surfaces, there are several reasons for considering these topics at this point. First, you may be wondering how your programs are processed by the system that you are using: how lines are drawn on the screen, how polygons are filled, and what happens to primitives that lie outside the viewing volumes defined in your program. Second, our contention is that if we are to use a graphics system efficiently, we need to have a deeper understanding of the implementation process: which steps are easy, and which tax our hardware and software. Third, our discussion of implementation will open the door to new capabilities that are supported by the latest hardware.

Learning implementation involves studying algorithms. As when we study any algorithm, we must be careful to consider such issues as theoretical versus practical performance, hardware versus software implementations, and the specific characteristics of an application. Although we can test whether an OpenGL implementation works correctly in the sense that it produces the correct pixels on the screen, there are many choices for the algorithms employed. We focus on the basic operations that are both necessary to implement a standard API and required whether the rendering is done by a pipeline architecture or by another method, such as ray tracing. Consequently, we present a variety of the basic algorithms for each of the principal tasks in an implementation.

In this chapter, we are concerned with the basic algorithms that are used to implement the rendering pipeline employed by OpenGL. We shall focus on three issues: clipping, rasterization, and hidden-surface removal. Clipping involves eliminating objects that lie outside the viewing volume and thus cannot be visible in the image. Rasterization produces fragments from the remaining objects. These fragments can contribute to the final image. Hidden-surface removal determines which fragments correspond to objects that are visible, namely, those that are in the view volume and are not blocked from view by other objects closer to the camera.

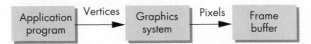

FIGURE 7.1   High-level view of the graphics process.

7.1   Basic Implementation Strategies

Let us begin with a high-level view of the implementation process. In computer graphics, we start with an application program, and we end with an image. We can again consider this process as a black box (Figure 7.1) whose inputs are the vertices and states defined in the program—geometric objects, attributes, camera specifications—and whose output is an array of colored pixels in the frame buffer.

Within the black box, we must do many tasks, including transformations, clipping, shading, hidden-surface removal, and rasterization of the primitives that can appear on the display. These tasks can be organized in a variety of ways, but regardless of the strategy that we adopt, we must always do two things: We must pass every geometric object through the system, and we must assign a color to every pixel in the color buffer that is displayed.

Suppose that we think of what goes into the black box in terms of a single program that carries out the entire process. This program takes as input a set of vertices specifying geometric objects and produces as output pixels in the frame buffer. Because this program must assign a value to every pixel and must process every geometric primitive (and every light source), we expect this program to contain at least two loops that iterate over these basic variables.

If we wish to write such a program, then we must immediately address the question, Which variable controls the outer loop? The answer we choose determines the flow of the entire implementation process. There are two fundamental strategies, often called the **image-oriented** and the **object-oriented** approaches.

In the object-oriented approach, the outer loop is over the objects. We can think of the program as controlled by a loop of this form:

```
for(each_object) render(object);
```

A pipeline renderer fits this description. Vertices are defined by the program and flow through a sequence of modules that transforms them, colors them, and determines whether they are visible. A polygon might flow through the steps illustrated in Figure 7.2. Note that after a polygon passes through geometric processing, the rasterization of this polygon can potentially affect any pixels in the frame buffer. Most implementations that follow this approach are based on construction of a rendering pipeline containing hardware or software modules for each of the tasks. Data (vertices) flow forward through the system.

In the past, the major limitations of the object-oriented approach were the large amount of memory required and the high cost of processing each object independently. Any geometric primitive that emerges from the geometric pro-

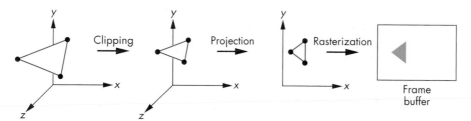

FIGURE 7.2   Object-oriented approach.

cessing can potentially affect any set of pixels in the frame buffer; thus, the entire color buffer—and various other buffers, such as the depth buffer used for hidden-surface removal—must be of the size of the display and must be available at all times. Before memory became both inexpensive and dense, this requirement was considered to be a serious problem. Now various pipelined geometric processors are available that can process tens of millions of polygons per second. In fact, precisely because we are doing the same operations on every primitive, the hardware to build an object-based system is fast and relatively cheap, with many of the functions implemented with special-purpose chips.

Today, the main limitation of object-oriented implementations is that they cannot handle most global calculations. Because each geometric primitive is processed independently—and in an arbitrary order—complex shading effects that involve multiple geometric objects, such as reflections, cannot be handled except by approximate methods. The major exception is hidden-surface removal, where the z buffer is used to store global information.

Image-oriented approaches loop over pixels, or rows of pixels called **scanlines**, that constitute the frame buffer. In pseudocode, the outer loop of such a program is of the following form:

```
for(each_pixel) assign_a_color(pixel);
```

For each pixel, we work backward, trying to determine which geometric primitives can contribute to its color. The advantages of this approach are that we need only limited display memory at any time and that we can hope to generate pixels at the rate and in the order required to refresh the display. Because the results of most calculations do not differ greatly from pixel to pixel (or scanline to scanline), we can use this coherence in our algorithms by developing incremental forms for many of the steps in the implementation. The main disadvantage of this approach is that, unless we first build a data structure from the geometric data, we do not know which primitives affect which pixels. Such a data structure can be complex and may imply that all the geometric data must be available at all times during the rendering process. For problems with very large databases, even having a good data representation may not avoid memory problems. However, because image-space approaches have access to all objects for each pixel, they are well suited to handle global effects such as shadows and reflections. Ray tracing (Chapter 12) is an example of the image-based approach.

We lean toward the object-based approach, although we look at examples of algorithms suited for both approaches.

7.2 Four Major Tasks

We start by reviewing the blocks in the pipeline, focusing on those blocks that we have yet to discuss in detail. There are four major tasks that any graphics system must perform to render a geometric entity, such as a three-dimensional polygon, as that entity passes from definition in a user program to possible display on an output device:

1. Modeling
2. Geometry processing
3. Rasterization
4. Fragment processing

Figure 7.3 shows how these tasks might be organized in a pipeline implementation. Regardless of the approach, all four tasks must be carried out.

7.2.1 Modeling

The usual results of the modeling process are sets of vertices that specify a group of geometric objects supported by the rest of the system. We have seen a few examples that required some modeling by the user, such as the approximation of spheres in Chapter 6. In Chapters 10 and 11, we explore other modeling techniques.

We can look at the modeler as a black box that produces geometric objects and is usually a user program. Yet, there are other tasks that the modeler might perform. Consider, for example, clipping: the process of eliminating parts of objects that cannot appear on the display because they lie outside the viewing volume. A user can generate geometric objects in her program, and she can hope that the rest of the system can process these objects at the rate at which they are produced; or the modeler can attempt to ease the burden on the rest of the system by minimizing the number of objects that it passes on. The latter approach often means that the modeler may do some of the same jobs as the rest of the system, albeit with different algorithms. In the case of clipping, the modeler, knowing more about the specifics of the application, can often use a

FIGURE 7.3 Implementation tasks.

good heuristic to eliminate many, if not most, primitives before they are sent on through the standard viewing process.

7.2.2 Geometry Processing

Geometry processing works with vertices. The goals of the geometry processor are to determine which geometric objects can appear on the display and to assign shades or colors to the vertices of these objects. Four processes are required: projection, primitive assembly, clipping, and shading.

Usually, the first step in geometry processing is to change representations from object coordinates to camera or eye coordinates using the model-view transformation. As we saw in Chapter 5, the conversion to camera coordinates is only the first part of the viewing process. The second step is to transform vertices using the projection transformation to a normalized view volume in which objects that might be visible are contained in a cube centered at the origin. Vertices are now represented in clip coordinates. Not only does this normalization convert both parallel and orthographic projections to a simple orthographic projection in a simple volume but, in addition, we simplify the clipping process, as we shall see in Section 7.7.

Geometric objects are transformed by a sequence of transformations that may reshape and move them (modeling) or may change their representations (viewing). Eventually, only those primitives that fit within a specified volume, the **view volume**, can appear on the display after rasterization. We cannot, however, simply allow all objects to be rasterized, hoping that the hardware will take care of primitives that lie wholly or partially outside the view volume. The implementation must carry out this task before rasterization. One reason is that rasterizing objects that lie outside the view volume is inefficient because such objects cannot be visible. Another reason is that when vertices reach the rasterizer, they can no longer be processed individually and first must be assembled into primitives. Primitives that lie partially in the viewing volume can generate new primitives with new vertices for which we must carry out shading calculations. Before clipping can take place, vertices must be grouped into objects, a process known as **primitive assembly**.

Note that even though an object lies inside the view volume, it will not be visible if it is obscured by other objects. Algorithms for **hidden-surface removal** (or **visible-surface determination**) are based on the three-dimensional spatial relationships among objects. This step is normally carried out as part of fragment processing.

Colors must be assigned to each vertex. These colors are either determined by the current color or, if lighting is enabled, vertex colors are computed using the modified Phong model.

After clipping takes place, the remaining vertices are still in four-dimensional homogeneous coordinates. Perspective division converts them to three-dimensional representation in normalized device coordinates.

Collectively, these operations constitute what has been called **front-end processing**. All involve three-dimensional calculations, and all require floating-point arithmetic. All generate similar hardware and software requirements. All are carried out on a vertex-by-vertex basis. We will discuss clipping, the only geometric step that we have yet to discuss, in Section 7.3.

7.2.3 Rasterization

Even after geometric processing has taken place, we still need to retain depth information for hidden-surface removal. However, only the x, y values of the vertices are needed to determine which pixels in the frame buffer can be affected by the primtive. For example, after perspective division, a line segment that was defined originally in three dimensions by two vertices becomes a line segment defined by a pair of three-dimensional vertices in normalized device coordinates. To generate a set of fragments that give the locations of the pixels in the frame buffer corresponding to these vertices, we only need their x, y components or, equivalently, the results of the orthogonal projection of these vertices. We determine these fragments through a process called **rasterization** or **scan conversion**. For line segments, rasterization determines which fragments should be used to approximate a line segment between the projected vertices. For polygons, rasterization determines which pixels lie inside the two-dimensional polygon determined by the projected vertices.

The colors that we assign to these fragments can be determined by the color attributes or obtained by interpolating the shades at the vertices that are computed, as in Chapter 6. Objects more complex than line segments and polygons are usually approximated by multiple line segments and polygons, and thus most graphics systems do not have special rasterization algorithms for them. We shall see exceptions to this rule for some special curves and surfaces in Chapter 11.

The rasterizer starts with vertices in normalized device coordinates but outputs fragments whose locations are in units of the display—**window coordinates**. As we saw in Chapters 2 and 5, the projection of the clipping volume must appear in the assigned viewport. In OpenGL, this final transformation is done after projection and is two-dimensional. The preceding transformations have normalized the view volume such that its sides are of length 2 and line up with the sides of the viewport (Figure 7.4), so this transformation is simply

$$x_v = x_{vmin} + \frac{x + 1.0}{2.0}(x_{vmax} - x_{vmin}),$$

$$y_v = y_{vmin} + \frac{y + 1.0}{2.0}(y_{vmax} - y_{vmin}),$$

$$z_v = z_{vmin} + \frac{z + 1.0}{2.0}(z_{vmax} - z_{vmin}).$$

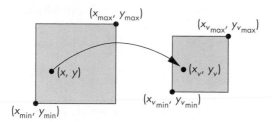

FIGURE 7.4 Viewport transformation.

Recall that for perspective viewing, these z values have been scaled nonlinearly by perspective normalization. However, they retain their original depth order, so they can be used for hidden-surface removal. We shall use the term **screen coordinates** to refer to the the two-dimensional system that is the same as window coordinates but lacks the depth coordinate.

7.2.4 Fragment Processing

In the simplest situations, fragments are assigned colors by the rasterizer and these colors are the ones that are placed in the frame buffer at the locations corresponding to the fragments' locations. However, there are many other possibilities.

The separate pixel pipeline (Chapter 8), supported by architectures such as OpenGL, merges with the results of the geometric pipeline at the rasterization stage. Consider what happens when a shaded and texture-mapped polygon is processed. Vertex lighting is computed as part of the geometric processing. The texture values are not needed until after rasterization when the renderer has generated fragments that correspond to locations inside a polygon. At this point, interpolation of per-vertex colors and texture coordinates takes place, and the texture parameters determine how to combine texture colors and fragment colors to determine final colors in the color buffer.

As we have noted, objects that are in the view volume will not be visible if they are blocked by any opaque objects closer to the viewer. The required hidden-surface removal process is typically carried out on a fragment-by-fragment basis.

Until now, we have assumed that all objects are opaque and thus an object located behind another object is not visible. We can also assume that objects are **translucent** and allow some light to pass through. In this case, fragment colors may have to be blended with the colors of pixels already in the color buffer. We consider this possibility in Chapter 8.

In most displays, the process of taking the image from the frame buffer and displaying it on a monitor happens automatically and is not of concern to the application program. However, there are numerous problems with the quality of display, such as the jaggedness associated with images on raster displays. In

Chapter 8, we introduce algorithms for reducing this jaggedness, or **aliasing**, and we discuss problems with color reproduction on displays.

7.3   Clipping

We can now turn to clipping, the process of determining which primitives, or parts of primitives, fit within the clipping or view volume defined by the application program. Clipping is done before the perspective division that is necessary if the w component of a clipped vertex is not equal to 1. The portions of all primitives that can possibly be displayed—we have yet to apply hidden-surface removal—lie within the cube

$$-w \leq x \leq w,$$
$$-w \leq y \leq w,$$
$$-w \leq z \leq w.$$

This coordinate system is called **normalized device coordinates** because it depends on neither the original application units nor the particulars of the display device, although the information to produce the correct image is retained in this coordinate system. Note also that projection has been carried out only partially. We still must do the perspective division and the final orthographic projection.

We shall concentrate on clipping of line segments and polygons because they are the most common primitives to pass down the pipeline. Although the OpenGL pipeline does clipping on three-dimensional objects, there are other systems in which the objects are first projected into the x, y plane. Fortunately, many of the most efficient algorithms are almost identical in two and three dimensions and we will focus on these algorithms.

7.4   Line-Segment Clipping

A **clipper** decides which primitives, or parts of primitives, can possibly appear on the display and be passed on to the rasterizer. Primitives that fit within the specified view volume pass through the clipper, or are **accepted**. Primitives that cannot appear on the display are eliminated, or **rejected** or **culled**. Primitives that are only partially within the view volume must be clipped such that any part lying outside the volume is removed.

Clipping can occur at one or more places in the viewing pipeline. The modeler may clip to limit the primitives that the hardware must handle. The primitives may be clipped after they have been projected from three- to two-dimensional objects. In OpenGL, primitives are clipped against a three-dimensional view volume before rasterization. We shall develop a sequence of clippers. For both pedagogic and historic reasons, we start with two two-dimensional line-segment clippers. Both extend directly to three dimensions and to clipping of polygons.

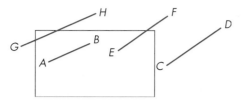

FIGURE 7.5 Two-dimensional clipping.

7.4.1 Cohen-Sutherland Clipping

The two-dimensional clipping problem for line segments is shown in Figure 7.5. We can assume for now that this problem arises after three-dimensional line segments have been projected onto the projection plane and that the window is part of the projection plane mapped to the viewport on the display. All values are specified as real numbers. We can see that the entire line segment AB appears on the display, whereas none of CD appears. EF and GH have to be shortened before being displayed. Although a line segment is completely determined by its endpoints, GH shows that, even if both endpoints lie outside the clipping window, part of the line segment may still appear on the display.

We could compute the intersections of the lines (of which the segments are parts) with the sides of the window and could thus determine the necessary information for clipping. However, we want to avoid intersection calculations, if possible, because each intersection requires a floating-point division. The Cohen-Sutherland algorithm was the first to seek to replace most of the expensive floating-point multiplications and divisions with a combination of floating-point subtractions and bit operations.

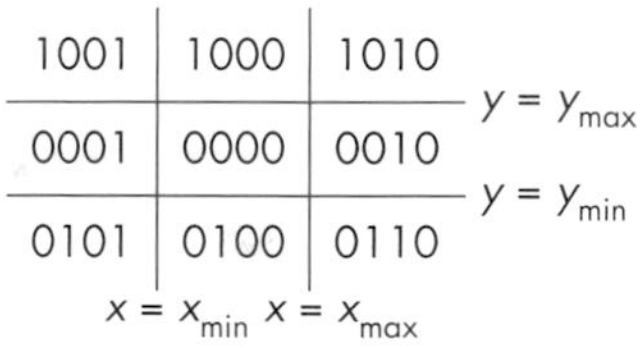

The algorithm starts by extending the sides of the window to infinity, thus breaking up space into the nine regions shown in Figure 7.6. Each region can be assigned a unique 4-bit binary number, or **outcode**, $b_0 b_1 b_2 b_3$, as follows. Suppose that (x, y) is a point in the region; then

$$
b_0 = \begin{cases} 1 & \text{if } y > y_{max}, \\ 0 & \text{otherwise.} \end{cases}
$$

Likewise, b_1 is 1 if $y < y_{min}$, and b_2 and b_3 are determined by the relationship between x and the left and right sides of the window. The resulting codes are indicated in Figure 7.7. For each endpoint of a line segment, we first compute the endpoint's outcode, a step that can require eight floating-point subtractions per line segment.

Consider a line segment whose outcodes are given by $o_1 = outcode(x_1, y_1)$ and $o_2 = outcode(x_2, y_2)$. We can now reason on the basis of these outcodes. There are four cases:

1001	1000	1010
0001	0000	0010
0101	0100	0110

$y = y_{max}$
$y = y_{min}$

$x = x_{min} \quad x = x_{max}$

FIGURE 7.6 Breaking up of space and outcodes.

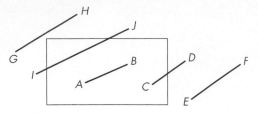

FIGURE 7.7 Cases of outcodes in Cohen-Sutherland algorithm.

1. ($o_1 = o_2 = 0$). Both endpoints are inside the clipping window, as is true for segment *AB* in Figure 7.7. The entire line segment is inside, and the segment can be sent on to be rasterized.
2. ($o_1 \neq 0, o_2 = 0$; or vice versa). One endpoint is inside the clipping window; one is outside (see segment *CD* in Figure 7.7). The line segment must be shortened. The nonzero outcode indicates which edge or edges of the window are crossed by the segment. One or two intersections must be computed. Note that after one intersection is computed, we can compute the outcode of the point of intersection to determine whether another intersection calculation is required.
3. ($o_1 \& o_2 \neq 0$). By taking the bitwise AND of the outcodes, we determine whether or not the two endpoints lie on the same outside side of the window. If so, the line segment can be discarded (see segment *EF* in Figure 7.7).
4. ($o_1 \& o_2 = 0$). Both endpoints are outside, but they are on the outside of different edges of the window. As we can see from segments *GH* and *IJ* in Figure 7.7, we cannot tell from just the outcodes whether the segment can be discarded or must be shortened. The best we can do is to intersect with one of the sides of the window and to check the outcode of the resulting point.

All our checking of outcodes requires only Boolean operations. We do intersection calculations only when they are needed, as in the second case, or where the outcodes did not contain enough information, as in the fourth case.

The Cohen-Sutherland algorithm works best when there are many line segments but few are actually displayed. In this case, most of the line segments lie fully outside one or two of the extended sides of the clipping rectangle and can thus be eliminated on the basis of their outcodes. The other advantage is that this algorithm can be extended to three dimensions. The main disadvantage of the algorithm is that it must be used recursively. Consider line segment GH in Figure 7.8. It must be clipped against both the left and top sides of the clipping window. Generally, the simplest way to do so is to use the initial outcodes to determine the first side of the clipping window to clip against. After this first shortening of the original line segment, a new outcode is computed for the new endpoint created by shortening, and the algorithm is reexecuted.

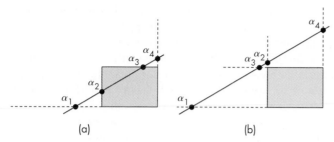

FIGURE 7.8 Two cases of a parametric line and a clipping window.

We have not discussed how to compute any required intersections. The form this calculation takes depends on how we choose to represent the line segment, although only a single division should be required in any case. If we use the standard explicit form of a line,

$$y = mx + h,$$

where m is the slope of the line and h is the line's y intercept, then we can compute m and h from the endpoints. However, vertical lines cannot be represented in this form—a critical weakness of the explicit form. If we were interested in only the Cohen-Sutherland algorithm, it would be fairly simple to program all cases directly because the sides of the clipping rectangle are parallel to the axes. However, we are interested in more than just clipping; consequently, other representations of the line and line segment are of importance. In particular, parametric representations are almost always used in computer graphics. We have already seen the parametric form of the line in Chapter 4; the parametric representation of other types of curves is considered in Chapter 11.

7.4.2 Liang-Barsky Clipping

If we use the parametric form for lines, we can approach the clipping of line segments in a different—and ultimately more efficient—manner. Suppose that we have a line segment defined by the two endpoints $\mathbf{p}_1 = [x_1, y_1]^T$ and $\mathbf{p}_2 = [x_2, y_2]^T$. We can use these endpoints to define a unique line that we can express parametrically, either in matrix form,

$$\mathbf{p}(\alpha) = (1 - \alpha)\mathbf{p}_1 + \alpha\mathbf{p}_2,$$

or as two scalar equations,

$$x(\alpha) = (1 - \alpha)x_1 + \alpha x_2,$$

$$y(\alpha) = (1 - \alpha)y_1 + \alpha y_2.$$

Note that this form is robust and needs no changes for horizontal or vertical lines. As the parameter α varies from 0 to 1, we move along the segment from $\mathbf{p}_1$

to $\mathbf{p}_2$. Negative values of α yield points on the line on the other side of $\mathbf{p}_1$ from $\mathbf{p}_2$. Similarly, values of $\alpha > 1$ give points on the line past $\mathbf{p}_2$ going off to infinity.

Consider a line segment and the line of which it is part, as shown in Figure 7.8(a). As long as the line is not parallel to a side of the window (if it is, we can handle that situation with ease), there are four points where the line intersects the extended sides of the window. These points correspond to the four values of the parameter: α_1, α_2, α_3, and α_4. One of these values corresponds to the line entering the window; another corresponds to the line leaving the window. Leaving aside, for the moment, how we compute these intersections, we can order them and determine which correspond to intersections that we need for clipping. For the given example,

$$1 > \alpha_4 > \alpha_3 > \alpha_2 > \alpha_1 > 0.$$

Hence, all four intersections are inside the original line segment, with the two innermost (α_2 and α_3) determining the clipped line segment. We can distinguish this case from the case in Figure 7.8(b), which also has the four intersections between the endpoints of the line segment, by noting that the order for this case is

$$1 > \alpha_4 > \alpha_2 > \alpha_3 > \alpha_1 > 0.$$

The line intersects both the top and the bottom of the window before it intersects either the left or the right; thus, the entire line segment must be rejected. Other cases of the ordering of the points of intersection can be argued in a similar way.

Efficient implementation of this strategy requires that we avoid computing intersections until they are needed. Many lines can be rejected before all four intersections are known. We also want to avoid floating-point divisions where possible. If we use the parametric form to determine the intersection with the top of the window, we find the intersection at the value

$$\alpha = \frac{y_{max} - y_1}{y_2 - y_1}.$$

Similar equations hold for the other three sides of the window. Rather than computing these intersections, at the cost of a division for each, we instead write the equation as

$$\alpha(y_2 - y_1) = \alpha \Delta y = y_{max} - y_1 = \Delta y_{max}.$$

All the tests required by the algorithm can be restated in terms of Δy_{max}, Δy, and similar terms can be computed for the other sides of the windows. Thus, all decisions about clipping can be made without floating-point division. Only if an intersection is needed (because a segment has to be shortened) is the division done. The efficiency of this approach, compared to that of the Cohen-Sutherland algorithm, is that we avoid multiple shortening of line segments and the related reexecutions of the clipping algorithm. We forgo discussion of other efficient two-dimensional, line-clipping algorithms because, unlike the Cohen-Sutherland and Liang-Barsky algorithms, these algorithms do not extend to three dimensions.

7.5 Polygon Clipping

Polygon clipping arises in a number of ways. Certainly, we want to be able to clip polygons against rectangular windows for display. However, we may at times want windows that are not rectangular. Other parts of an implementation, such as shadow generation and hidden-surface removal, can require clipping of polygons against other polygons. For example, Figure 7.9 shows the shadow of a polygon that we create by clipping a polygon that is closer to the light source against polygons that are farther away. Many antialiasing methods rely on our ability to clip polygons against other polygons.

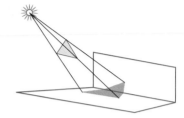

FIGURE 7.9 Polygon clipping in shadow generation.

We can generate polygon-clipping algorithms directly from line-clipping algorithms by clipping the edges of the polygon successively. However, we must be careful to remember that a polygon is a two-dimensional object with an interior, and depending on the form of the polygon, we can generate more than one polygonal object by clipping. Consider the nonconvex (or **concave**) polygon in Figure 7.10(a). If we clip it against a rectangular window, we get the result shown in Figure 7.10(b). Most viewers looking at this figure would conclude that we have generated three polygons by clipping. Unfortunately, implementing a clipper that can increase the number of objects can be a problem. We could treat the result of the clipper as a single polygon, as shown in Figure 7.11, with edges that overlap along the sides of the window, but this choice might cause difficulties in other parts of the implementation.

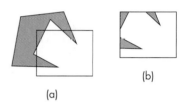

FIGURE 7.10 Clipping of a concave polygon. (a) Before clipping. (b) After clipping.

Convex polygons do not present such problems. Clipping a convex polygon against a rectangular window can leave at most a single convex polygon (see Exercise 7.3). A graphics system might then either forbid the use of concave polygons or divide (tessellate) a given polygon into a set of convex polygons, as shown in Figure 7.12.[1]

For rectangular clipping regions, both the Cohen-Sutherland and the Liang-Barsky algorithms can be applied to polygons on an edge-by-edge basis. There is another approach, developed by Sutherland and Hodgeman, that fits well with the pipeline architectures that we have discussed.

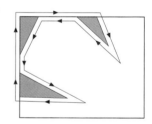

FIGURE 7.11 Creation of a single polygon.

A line-segment clipper can be envisioned as a black box (Figure 7.13) whose input is the pair of vertices from the segment to be tested and clipped and whose output either is a pair of vertices corresponding to the clipped line segment or is nothing if the input line segment lies outside the window.

---

1. OpenGL includes tessellation functions in the GLU library.

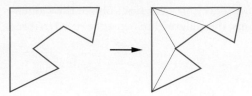

FIGURE 7.12   Tessellation of a concave polygon.

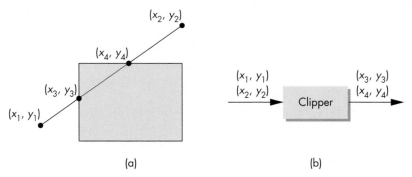

(a)   (b)

FIGURE 7.13   Two views of clipping. (a) Clipping against a rectangle. (b) Clipper as a black box.

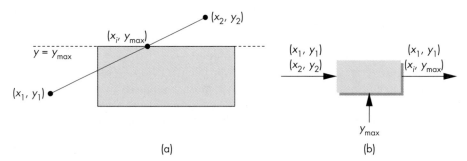

(a)   (b)

FIGURE 7.14   Clipping against top. (a) Graphically. (b) Black-box view.

Rather than considering the clipping window as four line segments, we can consider it as the object created by the intersection of four infinite lines that determine the top, bottom, right, and left sides of the window. We can then subdivide our clipper into a pipeline of simpler clippers, each of which clips against a single line that is the extension of an edge of the window. We can use the black-box view on each of the individual clippers.

Suppose that we consider clipping against only the top of the window. We can think of this operation as a black box (Figure 7.14) whose input and output are pairs of vertices, with the value of y_{max} as a parameter known to the clipper.

Using the similar triangles in Figure 7.15, we see that if there is an intersection, it lies at

$$x_3 = x_1 + (y_{max} - y_1)\frac{x_2 - x_1}{y_2 - y_1},$$

$$y_3 = y_{max}.$$

Thus, the clipper returns one of three pairs: $\{(x_1, y_1), (x_2, y_2)\}$; $\{(x_1, y_1), (x_i, y_{max})\}$; or $\{(x_i, y_{max}), (x_2, y_2)\}$. We can clip against the bottom, right, and left lines independently, using the same equations, with the roles of x and y exchanged as necessary and the values for the sides of the window inserted. The four clippers can now be arranged in the pipeline of Figure 7.16. If we build this configuration in hardware, we have a clipper that is working on four vertices concurrently. Figure 7.17 shows a simple example of the effect of successive clippers on a polygon.

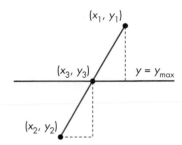

FIGURE 7.15 Intersection with the top of the window.

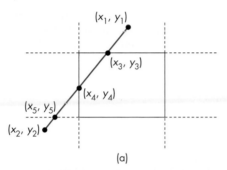

(a)

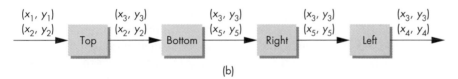

(b)

FIGURE 7.16 Pipeline clipping. (a) Clipping problem. (b) Pipeline clippers.

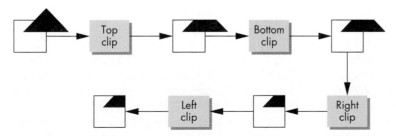

FIGURE 7.17 Example of pipeline clipping.

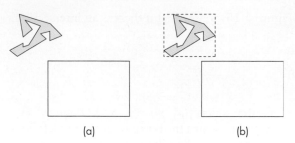

(a)   (b)

FIGURE 7.18 Using bounding boxes. (a) Polygon and clipping window. (b) Polygon, bounding box, and clipping window.

7.6   Clipping of Other Primitives

Our emphasis in Chapters 1 through 6 was on writing programs in which the objects are built from line segments and flat polygons. We often render the curved objects that we discuss in Chapter 11 by subdividing them into small, approximately flat polygons. In pipeline architectures, we usually find some variant of the clippers that we have presented. Nevertheless, there are situations in which we want either to clip objects before they reach the hardware or to employ algorithms optimized for other primitives.

7.6.1   Bounding Boxes and Volumes

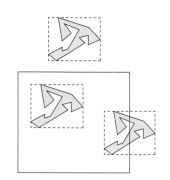

FIGURE 7.19 Clipping with bounding boxes.

Suppose that we have a many-sided polygon, as shown in Figure 7.18(a). We could apply one of our clipping algorithms, which would clip the polygon by individually clipping all that polygon's edges. However, we can see that the entire polygon lies outside the clipping window. We can exploit this observation through the use of the axis-aligned bounding box or the extent of the polygon (Figure 7.18(b)): the smallest rectangle, aligned with the window, that contains the polygon. Calculating the bounding box requires merely going through the vertices of the polygon to find the minimum and maximum of both the x and y values.

Once we have the bounding box, we can often avoid detailed clipping. Consider the three cases in Figure 7.19. For the polygon above the window, no clipping is necessary, because the minimum y for the bounding box is above the top of the window. For the polygon inside the window, we can determine that it is inside by comparing the bounding box with the window. Only when we discover that the bounding box straddles the window do we have to carry out detailed clipping, using all the edges of the polygon. The use of extents is such a powerful technique—in both two and three dimensions—that modeling systems often compute a bounding box for each object automatically and store the bounding box with the object.

Axis-aligned bounding boxes work in both two and three dimensions. In three dimensions, they can be used in the application to perform clipping to reduce the burden on the pipeline. Other volumes, such as spheres, can also work well. One of the other applications of bounding volumes is in collision detection (Chapter 10). One of the fundamental operations in animating computer games is to determine if two moving entities have collided. For example, consider two animated characters moving in a sequence of images. We need to know when they collide so that we can alter their paths. This problem has many similarities to the clipping problem because we want to determine when the volume of one intersects the volume of the other. The complexity of the objects and the need to do these calculations very quickly make this problem difficult. A common approach is to place each object in a bounding volume, either an axis-aligned bounding box or a sphere, and to determine if the volumes intersect. If they do, then detailed calculations can be done.

7.6.2 Curves, Surfaces, and Text

The variety of curves and surfaces that we can define mathematically makes it difficult to find general algorithms for processing these objects. The potential difficulties can be seen from the two-dimensional curves in Figure 7.20. For a simple curve, such as a quadric, we can compute intersections, although at a cost higher than that for lines. For more complex curves, such as the spiral, not only must intersection calculations be computed with numerical techniques, but even determining how many intersections we must compute may be difficult. We can avoid such problems by approximating curves with line segments and surfaces with planar polygons. The use of bounding boxes can also prove helpful, especially in cases such as quadratics, where we can compute intersections exactly but would prefer to make sure that the calculation is necessary before carrying it out.

The handling of text differs from API to API, with many APIs allowing the user to specify how detailed a rendering of text is required. There are two extremes. On one end, text is stored as bit patterns and is rendered directly by the hardware without any geometric processing. Any required clipping is done in the frame buffer. At the other extreme, text is defined like any other geometric object and is then processed through the standard viewing pipeline. OpenGL allows both these cases by not having a separate text primitive. The user can

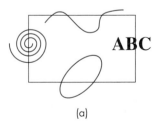
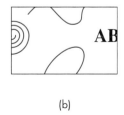

(a)   (b)

FIGURE 7.20 Curve clipping.

choose which mode she prefers by defining either bitmapped characters, using pixel operations, or stroke characters, using the standard primitives.

7.6.3 Clipping in the Frame Buffer

We might also consider delaying clipping until after objects have been projected and converted into screen coordinates. Clipping can be done in the frame buffer through a technique called **scissoring**. However, it is usually better to clip geometric entities before the vertices reach the frame buffer; thus, clipping within the frame buffer generally is required only for raster objects, such as blocks of pixels.

7.7 Clipping in Three Dimensions

In three dimensions, we clip against a bounded volume rather than against a bounded region in the plane. The simplest extension of two-dimensional clipping to three dimensions is for the right parallelepiped clipping region (Figure 7.21):

$$x_{min} \leq x \leq x_{max},$$
$$y_{min} \leq y \leq y_{max},$$
$$z_{min} \leq z \leq z_{max}$$

or in clip space

$$-w \leq x \leq w,$$
$$-w \leq y \leq w,$$
$$-w \leq z \leq w.$$

Our three clipping algorithms (Cohen-Sutherland, Liang-Barsky, and Sutherland-Hodgeman) and the use of extents can be extended to three di-

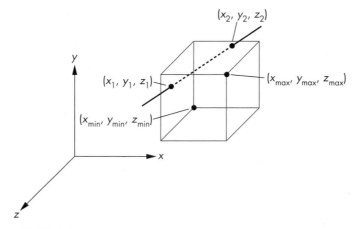

FIGURE 7.21   Three-dimensional clipping against a right parallelepiped.

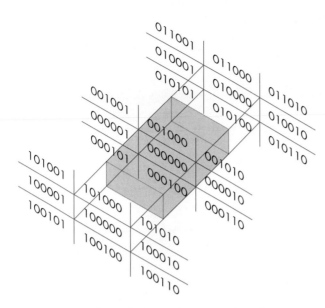

FIGURE 7.22   Cohen-Sutherland regions in three dimensions.

mensions. For the Cohen–Sutherland algorithm, we replace the 4-bit outcode with a 6-bit outcode. The additional 2 bits are set if the point lies either in front of or behind the clipping volume (Figure 7.22). The testing strategy is virtually identical for the two- and three-dimensional cases.

For the Liang-Barsky algorithm, we add the equation

$$z(\alpha) = (1 - \alpha)z_1 + \alpha z_2$$

to obtain a three-dimensional parametric representation of the line segment. We have to consider six intersections with the surfaces that form the clipping volume, but we can use the same logic as we did in the two-dimensional case. Pipeline clippers add two modules to clip against the front and back of the clipping volume.

The major difference between two- and three-dimensional clippers is that in three dimensions we are clipping either lines against planes or polygons against planes instead of clipping lines against lines as we do in two dimensions. Consequently, our intersection calculations must be changed. A typical intersection calculation can be posed in terms of a parametric line in three dimensions intersecting a plane (Figure 7.23). If we write the line and plane equations in matrix form (where $\mathbf{n}$ is the normal to the plane and $\mathbf{p}_0$ is a point on the plane), we must solve the equations

$$\mathbf{p}(\alpha) = (1 - \alpha)\mathbf{p}_1 + \alpha\mathbf{p}_2,$$
$$\mathbf{n} \cdot (\mathbf{p}(\alpha) - \mathbf{p}_0) = 0$$

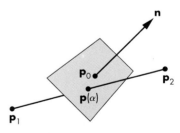

FIGURE 7.23   Plane–line intersection.

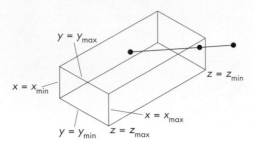

FIGURE 7.24   Clipping for orthographic viewing.

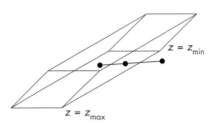

FIGURE 7.25   Clipping for oblique viewing.

for the α corresponding to the point of intersection. This value is

$$\alpha = \frac{\mathbf{n} \cdot (\mathbf{p}_0 - \mathbf{p}_1)}{\mathbf{n} \cdot (\mathbf{p}_2 - \mathbf{p}_1)},$$

and computation of an intersection requires six multiplications and a division. However, if we look at the standard viewing volumes, we see that simplifications are possible. For orthographic viewing (Figure 7.24), the view volume is a right parallelepiped, and each intersection calculation reduces to a single division, as it did for two-dimensional clipping.

When we consider an oblique view (Figure 7.25), we see that the clipping volume no longer is a right parallelepiped. Although you might think that we have to compute dot products to clip against the sides of the volume, here is where the normalization process that we introduced in Chapter 5 pays dividends. We showed that an oblique projection is equivalent to a shearing of the data followed by an orthographic projection. Although the shear transformation distorts objects, they are distorted such that they project correctly by an orthographic projection. The shear also distorts the clipping volume from a general parallelepiped to a right parallelepiped. Figure 7.26(a) shows a top view of an oblique volume with a cube inside the volume. Figure 7.26(b) shows the volume and object after they have been distorted by the shear. As far as projection is concerned, carrying out the oblique transformation directly or replacing it by a shear transformation and an orthographic projection requires the same amount

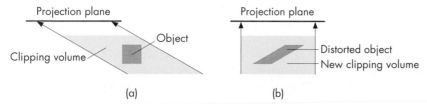

FIGURE 7.26 Distortion of view volume by shear. (a) Top view before shear. (b) Top view after shear.

of computation. When we add in clipping, it is clear that the second approach has a definite advantage because we can clip against a right parallelepiped. This example illustrates the importance of considering the incremental nature of the steps in an implementation. Analysis of either projection or clipping in isolation fails to show the importance of the normalization process.

For perspective projections, the argument for normalization is just as strong. By carrying out the perspective-normalization transformation from Chapter 5, but not the orthographic projection, we again create a rectangular clipping volume and simplify all subsequent intersection calculations.

OpenGL supports additional clipping planes that can be oriented arbitrarily. Hence, if this feature is used in a user program, the implementation may be able to carry out clipping against these planes only in software, at a performance cost.

7.8 Rasterization

We are now ready to take the final step in the journey from the specification of geometric entities in an application program to the formation of fragments: rasterization of primitives. In this chapter, we are concerned with only line segments and polygons, both of which are defined by vertices. We can assume that we have clipped the primitives such that each remaining primitive is inside the view volume.

Fragments are potential pixels. Each fragment has a color attribute and a location in screen coordinates that corresponds to a location in the color buffer. Fragments also carry depth information that can be used for hidden-surface removal. To clarify the discussion, we shall ignore hidden-surface removal until Section 7.12 and thus we can work directly in screen coordinates. Because we are not considering hidden-surface removal, translucent fragments, or antialiasing, we can develop rasterization algorithms in terms of the pixels that they color.

We further assume that the color buffer is an $n \times m$ array of pixels, with $(0, 0)$ corresponding to the lower-left corner. Pixels can be set to a given color by a single function inside the graphics implementation of the form

```
write_pixel(int ix,int iy, int value);
```

The argument value can be either an index, in color-index mode, or a pointer to an RGBA color. On the one hand, a color buffer is inherently discrete; it does not make sense to talk about pixels located at places other than integer values of ix and iy. On the other hand, screen coordinates, which range over the same values as do ix and iy, are real numbers. For example, we can compute a fragment location such as $(63.4, 157.9)$ in screen coordinates but must realize that the nearest pixel is centered either at $(63, 158)$ or at $(63.5, 157.5)$, depending on whether pixels are considered to be centered at whole or half integer values.

Pixels have attributes that are colors in the color buffer. Pixels can be displayed in multiple shapes and sizes that depend on the characteristics of the display. We address this matter in Section 7.13. For now, we can assume that a pixel is displayed as a square, whose center is at the location associated with the pixel and whose side is equal to the distance between pixels. In OpenGL, the centers of pixels are located at values halfway between integers. There are some advantages to this choice (see Exercise 7.19). We also assume that a concurrent process reads the contents of the color buffer and creates the display at the required rate. This assumption, which holds in many systems that have dual-ported memory, allows us to treat the rasterization process independently of the display of the contents of the frame buffer.

The simplest scan-conversion algorithm for line segments has become known as the **DDA algorithm**, after the digital differential analyzer, an early electromechanical device for digital simulation of differential equations. Because a line satisfies the differential equation $dy/dx = m$, where m is the slope, generating a line segment is equivalent to solving a simple differential equation numerically.

Suppose that we have a line segment defined by the endpoints (x_1, y_1) and (x_2, y_2). We assume that, because we are working in a color buffer, these values have been rounded to have integer values, so the line segment starts and ends at a known pixel.[2] The slope is given by

$$m = \frac{y_2 - y_1}{x_2 - x_1} = \frac{\Delta y}{\Delta x}.$$

We assume that

$$0 \le m \le 1.$$

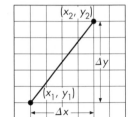

FIGURE 7.27 Line segment in window coordinates.

We can handle other values of m using symmetry. Our algorithm is based on writing a pixel for each value of ix in write_pixel as x goes from x_1 to x_2. If we are on the line segment, as shown in Figure 7.27, for any change in x equal to Δx, the corresponding changes in y must be

$$\Delta y = m \Delta x.$$

---

2. This assumption is not necessary to derive an algorithm. If we use a fixed-point representation for the endpoints and do our calculations using fixed-point arithmetic, then we retain the computational advantages of the algorithm and produce a more accurate rasterization.

As we move from x_1 to x_2, we increase x by 1 in each iteration; thus, we must increase y by

$$\Delta y = m.$$

Although each x is an integer, each y is not, because m is a floating-point number and we must round it to find the appropriate pixel, as shown in Figure 7.28. Our algorithm, in pseudocode, is

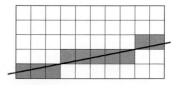

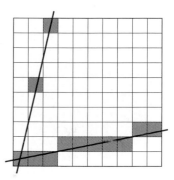

FIGURE 7.28 Pixels generated by DDA algorithm.

```
for(ix=x1; ix <= x2; ix++)
{
    y+=m;
    write_pixel(x, round(y), line_color);
}
```

where round is a function that rounds a real number to an integer. The reason that we limited the maximum slope to 1 can be seen from Figure 7.29. Our algorithm is of this form: For each x, find the best y. For large slopes, the separation between pixels that are colored can be large, generating an unacceptable approximation to the line segment. If, however, for slopes greater than 1, we swap the roles of x and y, the algorithm becomes this: For each y, find the best x. For the same line segments, we get the approximations in Figure 7.30. Note that the use of symmetry removes any potential problems from either vertical or horizontal line segments. You may want to derive the parts of the algorithm for negative slopes.

FIGURE 7.29 Pixels generated by high- and low-slope lines.

Because line segments are determined by vertices, we can use interpolation to assign a different color to each pixel that we generate. We can also generate various dash and dot patterns by changing the color that we use as we generate pixels. Neither of these effects has much to do with the basic rasterization

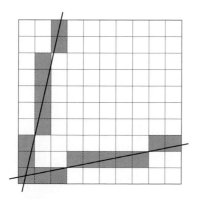

FIGURE 7.30 Pixels generated by revised DDA algorithm.

algorithm, as the latter's job is to determine only which pixels to color rather than to determine the color that is used.

7.9 Bresenham's Algorithm

The DDA algorithm appears efficient. Certainly it can be coded easily, but it requires a floating-point addition for each pixel generated. Bresenham derived a line-rasterization algorithm that, remarkably, avoids all floating-point calculations and has become the standard algorithm used in hardware and software rasterizers.

We assume, as we did with the DDA algorithm, that the line segment goes between the integer points (x_1, y_1) and (x_2, y_2) and that the slope satisfies

$$0 \leq m \leq 1.$$

This slope condition is crucial for the algorithm, as we can see with the aid of Figure 7.31. Suppose that we are somewhere in the middle of the scan conversion of our line segment and have just placed a pixel at $(i + \frac{1}{2}, j + \frac{1}{2})$. We know that the line of which the segment is part can be represented as

$$y = mx + h.$$

At $x = i + \frac{1}{2}$, this line must pass within one-half the length of the pixel at $(i + \frac{1}{2}, j + \frac{1}{2})$;[3] otherwise, the rounding operation would not have generated this pixel. If we move ahead to $x = i + \frac{3}{2}$, the slope condition indicates that we must set the color of one of only two possible pixels: either the pixel at $(i + \frac{3}{2}, j + \frac{1}{2})$ or the pixel at $(i + \frac{3}{2}, j + \frac{3}{2})$. Having reduced our choices to two pixels, we can pose the problem anew in terms of the **decision variable** $d = a - b$, where a and b are the distances between the line and the upper and lower candidate pixels at $x = i + \frac{3}{2}$, as shown in Figure 7.32. If d is positive, the line passes closer to the lower pixel, so we choose the pixel at $(i + \frac{3}{2}, j + \frac{1}{2})$; otherwise, we choose the pixel at $(i + \frac{3}{2}, j + \frac{3}{2})$. Although we could compute d by computing $y = mx + b$, we hesitate to do so because m is a floating-point number.

We obtain the computational advantages of Bresenham's algorithm through two further steps. First, we replace floating-point operations with fixed-point operations. Second, we apply the algorithm incrementally. We start by replacing d with the new decision variable

$$d = (x_2 - x_1)(a - b) = \Delta x(a - b),$$

---

3. We are assuming that the pixels' centers are located halfway between integers.

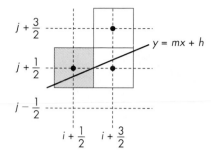

FIGURE 7.31 Conditions for Bresenham's algorithm.

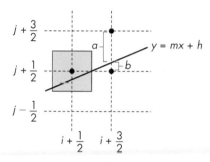

FIGURE 7.32 Decision variable for Bresenham's algorithm.

a change that cannot affect which pixels are drawn, because it is only the sign of the decision variable that matters. If we substitute for a and b, using the equation of the line and noting that

$$m = \frac{y_2 - y_1}{x_2 - x_1} = \frac{\Delta y}{\Delta x},$$

$$h = y_2 - mx_2,$$

then we can see that d is an integer. We have eliminated floating-point calculations, but the direct computation of d requires a fair amount of fixed-point arithmetic.

Let us take a slightly different approach. Suppose that d_k is the value of d at $x = k + \frac{1}{2}$. We would like to compute d_{k+1} incrementally from d_k. There are two situations, depending on whether or not we incremented the y location of the pixel at the previous step; these situations are shown in Figure 7.33. By observing that a is the distance between the location of the upper candidate location and the line, we see that a increases by m only if x was increased by the previous decision; otherwise, it decreases by $m - 1$. Likewise, b either decreases by $-m$ or increases by $1 - m$ when we increment x. Multiplying by Δx, we find that the

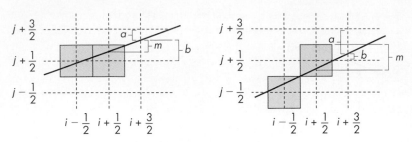

FIGURE 7.33 Incrementing of the values of a and b.

possible changes in d are either $-2\Delta y$ or $2(\Delta x - \Delta y)$. We can state this result in the form

$$d_{k+1} = d_k - \begin{cases} 2\Delta y & \text{if } d_k > 0; \\ 2(\Delta y - \Delta x) & \text{otherwise.} \end{cases}$$

The calculation of each successive pixel in the color buffer requires only an addition and a sign test. This algorithm is so efficient that it has been incorporated as a single instruction on graphics chips. See Exercise 7.14 for calculation of the initial value d_0.

7.10 Polygon Rasterization

One of the major advantages that the first raster systems brought to users was the ability to display filled polygons. At that time, coloring each point in the interior of a polygon with a different shade was not possible in real time, and the phrases *rasterizing polygons* and *polygon scan conversion* came to mean filling a polygon with a single color. Unlike rasterization of lines, where a single algorithm dominates, there are many viable methods for rasterizing polygons. The choice depends heavily on the implementation architecture. We concentrate on methods that fit with our pipeline approach and can also support shading. In Sections 7.10.4 through 7.10.6, we survey a number of other approaches.

7.10.1 Inside–Outside Testing

Flat simple polygons have well-defined interiors. If they are also convex, they are guaranteed to be rendered correctly by OpenGL and by other graphics systems. More general polygons arise in practice, however, and we can render them in multiple ways. For nonflat polygons,[4] we can work with their projections

---

4. Strictly speaking, there is no such thing as a nonflat polygon because the interior is not defined unless it is flat. However, from a programming perspective, we can *define* a polygon by simply giving a list of vertices, regardless of whether or not they lie in the same plane.

(Section 7.10.2), or we can use the first three vertices to determine a plane to use for the interior. For flat nonsimple polygons, we must decide how to determine whether a given point is inside or outside of the polygon. Conceptually, the process of filling the inside of a polygon with a color or pattern is equivalent to deciding which points in the plane of the polygon are interior (inside) points.

The **crossing** or **odd–even test** is the most widely used test for making inside–outside decisions. Suppose that **p** is a point inside a polygon. Any ray emanating from **p** and going off to infinity must cross an odd number of edges. Any ray emanating from a point outside the polygon and entering the polygon crosses an even number of edges before reaching infinity. Hence, a point can be defined as being inside if after drawing a line through it and following this line, starting on the outside, we cross an odd number of edges before reaching it. For the star-shaped polygon in Figure 7.34, we obtain the inside coloring shown. Odd–even testing is easy to implement and integrates well with the standard rendering algorithms. Usually, we replace rays through points with scanlines, and we count the crossing of polygon edges to determine inside and outside.

FIGURE 7.34 Filling with the odd-even test.

However, we might want our fill algorithm to color the star polygon as shown in Figure 7.35 rather than as shown in Figure 7.34. The **winding** test allows us to make that happen. This test considers the polygon as a knot being wrapped around a point or a line. To implement the test, we consider traversing the edges of the polygon from any starting vertex and going around the edge in a particular direction (which direction does not matter) until we reach the starting point. We illustrate the path by labeling the edges, as shown in Figure 7.35(b). Next we consider an arbitrary point. The **winding number** for this point is the number of times it is encircled by the edges of the polygon. We count clockwise encirclements as positive and counterclockwise encirclements as negative (or vice versa). Thus, points outside the star in Figure 7.35 are not encircled and have a winding number of 0; points that were filled in Figure 7.34 all have a winding number of 1; and points in the center that were not filled by the odd–even test have a winding number of 2. If we change our fill rule to be that a point is

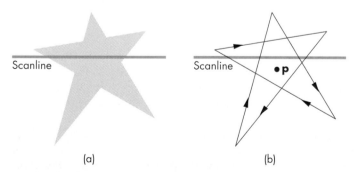

(a)   (b)

FIGURE 7.35 Fill using the winding number test.

FIGURE 7.36   S-shaped curve.

inside the polygon if its winding number is not zero, then we fill the inside of the polygon as shown in Figure 7.35(a).

There are several problems with our definition of the winding number. Consider the S-shaped curve in Figure 7.36, which we might approximate with a polygon containing many vertices. It is not clear how we should define encirclements for points inside the curve. With a little care, we can modify our odd–even definition to improve the definition for the winding number and to obtain a way of measuring the winding number for an arbitrary point. Consider any line through an interior point **p** that cuts through the polygon completely, as shown in Figure 7.35(b), and that is not parallel to an edge of the polygon. The winding number for this point is the number of edges that cross our line in the downward direction minus the number of edges that cross our line in the upward direction. If the winding number is not zero, the point is inside the polygon. Note that for this test, it does not matter how we define *up* and *down*.

7.10.2   OpenGL and Concave Polygons

Because OpenGL guarantees correct rendering of polygons only if they are convex, we still have the problem of what to do with more general polygons. One approach is to work with the application to ensure that all polygons obey these restrictions. Another is to provide software that can tessellate a given polygon into flat convex polygons, usually triangles. There are many ways to divide a given polygon into triangles. A good tessellation should not produce triangles that are long and thin; it should, if possible, produce sets of triangles that can use supported features, such as triangle strips and triangle fans. There is a tessellator in the GLU library. For a simple polygon without holes, we start by declaring a **tessellator object** and giving it the vertices of the polygons:

```
GLUtesslator *mytess;
mytess = gluNewTess();

gluTessBeginPolygon(mytess, NULL);
gluTessBeginContour(mytess);
for(i=0;i<nvertices;i++)
   glTessVertex(mytess,vertex[i],vertex[i]);
gluTessEndContour();
gluTessEndPolygon(mytess);
```

Although there are many parameters that can be set, the basic idea is that we have described a contour, and the tessellating software generates the required triangles and sends them off to be rendered based on the present tessellation parameters.

The use of the winding number is important in OpenGL tessellation algorithms and in trimmed NURBS surfaces (Chapter 11). Here the direction of encirclement of a point by the contours inside the polygon can cause—based on the tessellation parameters—a variety of possible renderings, as in Figure 7.37.

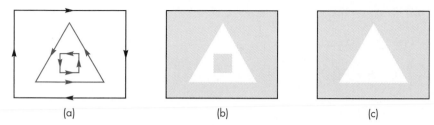

(a)   (b)   (c)

FIGURE 7.37   Polygon tessellations. (a) Polygon with edges and directions of contours. (b) Tessellation 1. (c) Tessellation 2.

The references in Suggested Readings give details of the various tessellation algorithms. From an OpenGL perspective, if tessellators are used, all rendering is done to convex polygons.

7.10.3   Fill and Sort

A different approach to rasterization of polygons starts with the idea of a polygon processor: a black box whose inputs are the vertices for a set of two-dimensional polygons and whose output is a frame buffer with the correct pixels set. Suppose that we consider filling each polygon with a constant color—a choice we make only to clarify the discussion. First, consider a single polygon. The basic rule for filling a polygon is as follows: *If a point is inside the polygon, color it with the inside (fill) color.* This conceptual algorithm indicates that polygon fill is a sorting problem, where we sort all the pixels in the frame buffer into those that are inside the polygon and those that are not. From this perspective, we obtain different polygon-fill algorithms using different ways of sorting the points. We introduce three possibilities:

- Flood fill
- Scanline fill
- Odd–Even fill

7.10.4   Flood Fill

We can display an unfilled polygon by rasterizing its edges into the frame buffer using Bresenham's algorithm. Suppose that we have only two colors: a background color (white) and a foreground, or drawing, color (black). We can use the foreground color to rasterize the edges, resulting in a frame buffer colored as shown in Figure 7.38 for a simple polygon. If we can find an initial point (x, y) inside the polygon—a **seed point**—then we can look at its neighbors recursively, coloring them with the foreground color if they are not edge points. The **flood-fill algorithm** can be expressed in pseudocode, assuming that there is a function read_pixel that returns the color of a pixel:

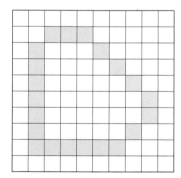

FIGURE 7.38   Polygon displayed by edges.

```
flood_fill(int x, int y)
{
    if(read_pixel(x,y)==WHITE)
    {
        write_pixel(x,y,BLACK);
        flood_fill(x-1,y);
        flood_fill(x+1,y);
        flood_fill(x,y-1);
        flood_fill(x,y+1);
    }
}
```

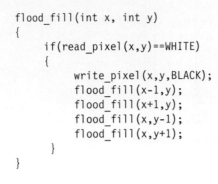

(a)

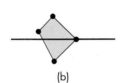

(b)

FIGURE 7.39   Singularities. (a) Zero or two edge crossings. (b) One edge crossing.

We can obtain a number of variants of flood fill by removing the recursion. One way to do so is to work one scanline at a time.

7.10.5   Singularities

We can extend most polygon-fill algorithms to other shapes if we use care (see Exercise 7.17). Polygons have the distinct advantage that the locations of their edges are known exactly. Even polygons can present problems, however, when vertices lie on scanlines. Consider the two cases in Figure 7.39. If we are using an odd–even fill definition, we have to treat these two cases differently. For case (a), we can count the intersection of the scanline with the vertex as either zero or two edge crossings; for case (b), the vertex–scanline intersection must be counted as one edge crossing.

We can fix our algorithm in one of two ways. We can check to see which of the two situations we have and then count the edge crossings appropriately. Or we can prevent the special case of a vertex lying on an edge—a **singularity**—from ever arising. We rule it out by ensuring that no vertex has an integer y value. If we find one that does, we perturb its location slightly. Another method—one that is especially valuable if we are working in the frame buffer—is to consider a virtual frame buffer of twice the resolution of the real frame buffer. In the virtual frame buffer, pixels are located only at even values of y, and all vertices are located only at odd values of y. Placing pixel centers halfway between integers, as OpenGL does, is equivalent to using this approach.

7.11   Hidden-Surface Removal

Although every fragment generated by rasterization corresponds to a location in a color buffer, we do not want to display the fragment by coloring the corresponding pixel if the fragment is from an object behind another opaque object. Hidden-surface removal (or visible-surface determination) is done to discover what part, if any, of each object in the view volume is visible to the viewer or is obscured from the viewer by other objects. We describe a number of techniques for a scene composed purely of planar polygons. Because most renderers will have subdivided surfaces into polygons at this point, this choice is appropriate. Line segments can be handled by slight modifications (see Exercise 7.7).

7.11.1 Object-Space and Image-Space Approaches

The study of hidden-surface–removal algorithms clearly illustrates the variety of available algorithms, the differences between working with objects and working with images, and the importance of evaluating the incremental effects of successive algorithms in the implementation process.

Consider a scene composed of k three-dimensional opaque flat polygons, each of which we can consider to be an individual object. We can derive a generic **object-space approach** by considering the objects pairwise, as seen from the center of projection. Consider two such polygons, A and B. There are four possibilities (Figure 7.40):

1. A completely obscures B from the camera; we display only A.
2. B obscures A; we display only B.
3. A and B both are completely visible; we display both A and B.
4. A and B partially obscure each other; we must calculate the visible parts of each polygon.

For complexity considerations, we can regard the determination of which case we have and any required calculation of the visible part of a polygon as a single operation. We proceed iteratively. We pick one of the k polygons and compare it pairwise with the remaining $k - 1$ polygons. After this procedure, we know which part (if any) of this polygon is visible, and we render the visible part. We are now done with this polygon, so we repeat the process with any of the other $k - 1$ polygons. Each step involves comparing one polygon, pairwise, with the other remaining polygons until we have only two polygons remaining, and we compare these to each other. We can easily determine that the complexity of this calculation is $O(k^2)$. Thus, without deriving any of the details of any particular object-space algorithm, we should suspect that the object-space approach works best for scenes that contain relatively few polygons.

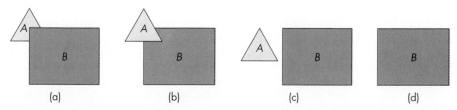

FIGURE 7.40   Two polygons. (a) B partially obscures A. (b) A partially obscures B. (c) Both A and B are visible. (d) B totally obscures A.

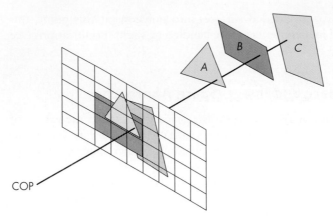

FIGURE 7.41   Image-space hidden-surface removal.

The **image-space approach** follows our viewing and ray-casting model, as shown in Figure 7.41. Consider a ray that leaves the center of projection and passes through a pixel. We can intersect this ray with each of the planes determined by our k polygons; determine for which planes the ray passes through a polygon; and finally, for those rays, find the intersection closest to the center of projection. We color this pixel with the shade of the polygon at the point of intersection. Our fundamental operation is the intersection of rays with polygons. For an $n \times m$ display, we have to carry out this operation nmk times, giving $O(k)$ complexity.[5] Again, without looking at the details of the operations, we were able to get an upper bound. In general, the $O(k)$ bound accounts for the dominance of image-space methods. The $O(k)$ bound is a worst-case bound. In practice, image-space algorithms perform much better (see Exercise 7.9). However, because image-space approaches work at the fragment or pixel level, their accuracy is limited by the resolution of the frame buffer.

7.11.2   Sorting and Hidden-Surface Removal

The $O(k^2)$ upper bound for object-oriented hidden-surface removal might remind you of the poorer sorting algorithms, such as bubble sort. Any method that involves brute-force comparison of objects by pairs has $O(k^2)$ complexity. But there is a more direct connection, which we exploited in the object-oriented sorting algorithms in Section 7.8.5. If we could organize objects by their distances from the camera, we should be able to come up with a direct method of rendering them.

---

5. We can use more than one ray for each pixel to increase the accuracy of the rendering.

But if we follow the analogy, we know that the complexity of good sorting algorithms is $O(k \log k)$. We should expect the same to be true for object-oriented hidden-surface removal and, in fact, such is the case. As with sorting, there are multiple algorithms that meet these bounds. In addition, there are related problems involving comparison of objects, such as collision detection, that start off looking as if they are $O(k^2)$ when, in fact, they can be reduced to $O(k \log k)$.

7.11.3 Scanline Algorithms

The attraction of a **scanline algorithm** is that such a method has the potential to generate pixels as they are displayed. Consider the polygon in Figure 7.42, with one scanline shown. If we use our odd–even rule for defining the inside of the polygon, we can see three groups of pixels, or **spans**, on this scanline that are inside the polygon. Note that each span can be processed independently for lighting or depth calculations, a strategy that has been employed in some hardware that has parallel span processors. For our simple example of constant fill, after we have identified the spans, we can color the interior pixels of each span with the fill color.

The spans are determined by the set of intersections of polygons with scanlines. The vertices contain all the information that we need to determine these intersections, but the method that we use to represent the polygon determines the order in which these intersections are generated. For example, consider the polygon in Figure 7.43, which has been represented by an ordered list of vertices. The most obvious way to generate scanline–edge intersections is to process edges defined by successive vertices. Figure 7.43 shows these intersections, indexed in the order in which this method would generate them. Note that this calculation can be done incrementally (see Exercise 7.18). However, as far as fill is concerned, this order is far from the one we want. If we are to fill one scanline at a time, we would like the intersections sorted, first by scanlines and then by order of x on each scanline, as shown in Figure 7.44. A brute-force approach might be to sort all the intersections into the desired order. However, a large or jagged polygon might intersect so many edges that the n intersections can be large enough that the $O(n \log n)$ complexity of the sort makes the calculation too slow for real-time implementations; consider, for example, a polygon that spans one-half of the scan lines.

A number of methods avoid the general search. One, originally known as the *y–x* **algorithm**, creates a bucket for each scanline. As edges are processed, the intersections with scanlines are placed in the proper buckets. Within each bucket, an insertion sort orders the x values along each scanline. The data structure is shown in Figure 7.45. Once again, we see that a properly chosen data structure can speed up the algorithm. We can go even further by reconsidering how to represent polygons. If we do so, we arrive at the scanline method that was introduced in Section 7.8.

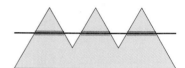

FIGURE 7.42 Polygon with spans.

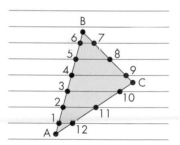

FIGURE 7.43 Polygon generated by vertex list.

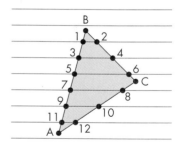

FIGURE 7.44 Desired order of vertices.

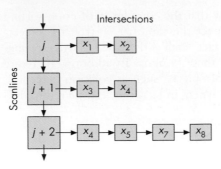

FIGURE 7.45   Data structure for $y-x$ algorithm.

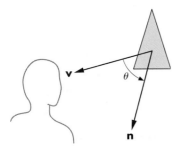

FIGURE 7.46   Back-face test.

7.11.4 Back-Face Removal

In Chapter 6, we noted that in OpenGL we can choose to render only front-facing polygons. For situations where we cannot see back faces, such as scenes composed of convex polyhedra, we can reduce the work required for hidden-surface removal by eliminating all back-facing polygons before we apply any other hidden-surface–removal algorithm. The test for **culling** a back-facing polygon can be derived from Figure 7.46. We see the front of a polygon if the normal, which comes out of the front face, is pointed toward the viewer. If θ is the angle between the normal and the viewer, then the polygon is facing forward if and only if

$$-90 \le \theta \le 90$$

or, equivalently,

$$\cos \theta \ge 0.$$

The second condition is much easier to test because, instead of computing the cosine, we can use the dot product:

$$\mathbf{n} \cdot \mathbf{v} \ge 0.$$

We can simplify this test even further if we note that usually it is applied after transformation to normalized device coordinates. In this system, all views are orthographic, with the direction of projection along the z-axis. Hence, in homogeneous coordinates,

$$\mathbf{v} = \begin{bmatrix} 0 \\ 0 \\ 1 \\ 0 \end{bmatrix}.$$

Thus, if the polygon is on the surface

$$ax + by + cz + d = 0$$

in normalized device coordinates, we need only to check the sign of c to determine whether we have a front- or back-facing polygon. This test can be implemented easily in either hardware or software; we must simply be careful to ensure that removing back-facing polygons is correct for our application.

In OpenGL, the function `glCullFace` allows us to turn on back-face elimination. OpenGL takes a slightly different approach to back-face determination. The algorithm is based on computing the area of the polygon in screen coordinates. A negative area indicates a back-facing polygon.

7.11.5 The z-Buffer Algorithm

The z-**buffer algorithm** is the most widely used hidden-surface–removal algorithm. It has the advantages of being easy to implement, in either hardware or software, and of being compatible with pipeline architectures, where it can execute at the speed at which fragments are passing through the pipeline. Although the algorithm works in image space, it loops over the polygons rather than over pixels and can be regarded as part of the scan-conversion process that we discussed in Section 7.10.

Suppose that we are in the process of rasterizing one of the two polygons shown in Figure 7.47. We can compute a color for each point of intersection between a ray from the center of projection and a pixel, using interpolated values of the vertex shades computed as in Chapter 6. In addition, we must check whether this point is visible. It will be visible if it is the closest point of intersection along the ray. Hence, if we are rasterizing B, its shade will appear on the screen if the distance z_2 is less than the distance z_1 to polygon A. Conversely, if we are rasterizing A, the pixel that corresponds to the point of intersection will not appear on the display. Because we are proceeding polygon by polygon, however, we do not have the information on all other polygons as we rasterize any given polygon. However, if we keep depth information with each fragment,

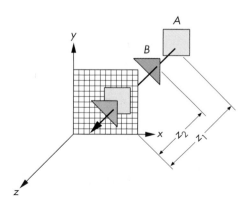

FIGURE 7.47   The z-buffer algorithm.

then we can store and update depth information for each location in the frame buffer as fragments are processed.

Suppose that we have a buffer, the z buffer, with the same resolution as the frame buffer and with depth consistent with the resolution that we wish to use for distance. For example, if we have a 1024×1280 display and we use standard integers for the depth calculation, we can use a 1024×1280 z buffer with 32-bit elements. Initially, each element in the depth buffer is initialized to a depth crresponding to the maximum distance away from the center of projection.[6] The color buffer is initialized to the background color. At any time during rasterization and fragment processing, each location in the z buffer contains the distance along the ray corresponding to this location of the closest intersection point on any polygon found so far.

The calculation proceeds as follows. We rasterize, polygon by polygon, using one of the methods from Section 7.10. For each fragment on the polygon corresponding to the intersection of the polygon with a ray through a pixel, we compute the depth from the center of projection. We compare this depth to the value in the z buffer corresponding to this fragment. If this depth is greater than the depth in the z buffer, then we have already processed a polygon with a corresponding fragment closer to the viewer, and this fragment is not visible. If the depth is less than the depth in the z buffer,[7] then we have found a fragment closer to the viewer. We update the depth in the z buffer and place the shade computed for this fragment at the corresponding location in the color buffer. Note that for perspective views, the depth we are using in the z-buffer algorithm is the distance that has been altered by the normalization transformation that we discussed in Chapter 5. Although this transformation is nonlinear, it preserves relative distances. However, this nonlinearity can introduce numerical inaccuracies, especially when the distance to the near clipping plane is small.

Unlike other aspects of rendering where the particular implementation algorithms may be unknown to the user, for hidden-surface removal, OpenGL uses the z-buffer algorithm. This exception arises because the application program must initialize the z buffer explicitly every time a new image is to be generated.

The z-buffer algorithm works well with image-oriented approaches to implementation because the amount of incremental work is small. Suppose that we are rasterizing a polygon, scanline by scanline—an option we examined in Section 7.9. The polygon is part of a plane (Figure 7.48) that can be represented as

$$ax + by + cz + d = 0.$$

6. If we have already done perspective normalization, we should replace the center of projection with the direction of projection because all rays are parallel. However, this change does not affect the z-buffer algorithm, because we can measure distances from any arbitrary plane, such as the plane $z = 0$, rather than from the COP.
7. In OpenGL, we can use the function `glDepthFunc` to decide what do when the distances are equal.

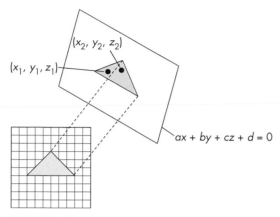

FIGURE 7.48   Incremental z-buffer algorithm.

Suppose that (x_1, y_1, z_1) and (x_2, y_2, z_2) are two points on the polygon (and the plane). If

$$\Delta x = x_2 - x_1,$$

$$\Delta y = y_2 - y_1,$$

$$\Delta z = z_2 - z_1,$$

then the equation for the plane can be written in differential form as

$$a\Delta x + b\Delta y + c\Delta z = 0.$$

This equation is in window coordinates, so each scanline corresponds to a line of constant y and $\Delta y = 0$ as we move across a scanline. On a scanline, we increase x in unit steps, corresponding to moving one pixel in the frame buffer, and Δx is constant. Thus, as we move from point to point across a scanline,

$$\Delta z = -\frac{a}{c}\Delta x.$$

This value is a constant that needs to be computed only once for each polygon.

Although the worst case performance of an image-space algorithm is proportional to the number of primitives, the performance of the z-buffer algorithm is proportional to the number of fragments generated by rasterization, which depends on the area of the rasterized polygons.

7.11.6   Scan Conversion with the z-Buffer

We have already presented most of the essentials of polygon rasterization. In Section 7.10.1, we discussed the odd–even and winding tests for determining whether a point is inside a polygon. In Chapter 6, we learned to shade polygons

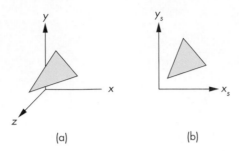

FIGURE 7.49   Dual representations of a polygon. (a) Normalized device coordinates. (b) Screen coordinates.

by interpolation. Here we have only to put together the pieces and to consider efficiency.

Suppose that we follow the pipeline once more, concentrating on what happens to a single polygon. The vertices and normals pass through the geometric transformations one at a time. The vertices must be assembled into a polygon before the clipping stage. If our polygon is not clipped out, its vertices and normals can be passed on for shading and hidden-surface removal. At this point, although projection normalization has taken place, we still have depth information. If we wish to use an interpolative shading method, we can compute the lighting at each vertex.

Three tasks remain: computation of the final orthographic projection, hidden-surface removal, and shading. Careful use of the z-buffer algorithm can accomplish all three tasks simultaneously. Consider the dual representations of a polygon illustrated in Figure 7.49. In (a) the polygon is represented in three-dimensional normalized device coordinates; in (b) it is shown after projection in screen coordinates.

The strategy is to process each polygon, one scanline at a time. If we work again in terms of these dual representations, we can see that a scanline, projected backward from screen coordinates, corresponds to a line of constant y in normalized device coordinates (Figure 7.50). Suppose that we simultaneously march across this scanline and its back projection. For the scanline in screen coordinates, we move one pixel width with each step. We use the normalized-device-coordinate line to determine depths incrementally and to see whether or not the pixel in screen coordinates corresponds to a visible point on the polygon. Having computed shading for the vertices of the original polygon, we can use bilinear interpolation to obtain the correct color for visible pixels.[8] This process requires little extra effort over the individual steps that we have already discussed. It is controlled, and thus limited, by the rate at which we can send polygons

---

8. Modern graphics processors carry out interpolation in a perspectively correct manner.

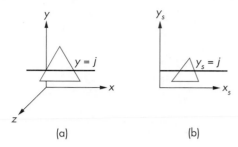

FIGURE 7.50 Dual representations of a scanline. (a) In normalized device coordinates. (b) In screen coordinates.

through the pipeline. Modifications such as applying bit patterns, called stipple patterns, or texture to polygons require only slight changes.

7.11.7   Depth Sort and the Painter's Algorithm

Although image-space methods are dominant in hardware due to the efficiency and ease of implementation of the z-buffer algorithm, often object-space methods are used within the application to lower the polygon count. **Depth sort** is a direct implementation of the object-space approach to hidden-surface removal. We present the algorithm for a scene composed of planar polygons; extensions to other classes of objects are possible. Depth sort is a variant of an even simpler algorithm known as the **painter's algorithm**.

Suppose that we have a collection of polygons that is sorted based on how far from the viewer the polygons are. For the example in Figure 7.51(a), we have two polygons. To a viewer, they appear as shown in Figure 7.51(b), with the polygon in front partially obscuring the other. To render the scene correctly, we could find the part of the rear polygon that is visible and render that part into the frame buffer—a calculation that requires clipping one polygon against the other. Or we could use another approach analogous to the way a painter might render the scene. She probably would paint the rear polygon in its entirety and then the front polygon, painting over that part of the rear polygon not visible to the viewer in the process. Both polygons would be rendered completely, with the hidden-surface removal being done as a consequence of the **back-to-front rendering** of the polygons.[9] The two questions related to this algorithm are how to do the sort and what to do if polygons overlap. Depth sort addresses both, although in many applications more efficiencies can be found (see, for example, Exercise 7.10).

---

9. Certain application problems can be solved more efficiently with *front-to-back rendering* of polygons.

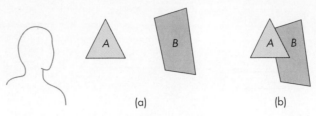

FIGURE 7.51 Painter's algorithm. (a) Two polygons and a viewer are shown. (b) Polygon A partially obscures B when viewed.

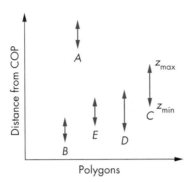

FIGURE 7.52 The z extents of sorted polygons.

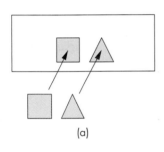

(a)

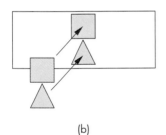

(b)

FIGURE 7.53 Test for overlap in x and y extents. (a) Nonoverlapping x extents. (b) Nonoverlapping y extents.

Suppose we have already computed the extent of each polygon. The next step of depth sort is to order all the polygons by how far away from the viewer their maximum z value is. This step gives the algorithm the name *depth sort*. Suppose that the order is as shown in Figure 7.52, which depicts the z extents of the polygons after the sort. If the minimum depth—the z value—of a given polygon is greater than the maximum depth of the polygon behind the one of interest, we can paint the polygons back to front and we are done. For example, polygon A in Figure 7.52 is behind all the other polygons and can be painted first. However, the others cannot be painted based solely on the z extents.

If the z extents of two polygons overlap, we still may be able to find an order to paint (render) the polygons individually and yield the correct image. The depth-sort algorithm runs a number of increasingly more difficult tests, attempting to find such an ordering. Consider a pair of polygons whose z extents overlap. The simplest test is to check their x and y extents (Figure 7.53). If either of the x or y extents do not overlap,[10] neither polygon can obscure the other and they can be

---

10. The x- and y-extent tests apply to only a parallel view. Here is another example of the advantage of working in normalized device coordinates *after* perspective normalization.

painted in either order. Even if these tests fail, it may still be possible to find an order in which we can paint the polygons individually. Figure 7.54 shows such a case. All the vertices of one polygon lie on the same side of the plane determined by the other. We can process the vertices (see Exercise 7.12) of the two polygons to determine whether this case exists.

Two troublesome situations remain. If three or more polygons overlap cyclically, as shown in Figure 7.55, there is no correct order for painting. The best we can do is to divide at least one of the polygons into two parts and attempt to find an order to paint the new set of polygons. The second problematic case arises if a polygon can pierce another polygon, as shown in Figure 7.56. If we want to continue with depth sort, we must derive the details of the intersection—a calculation equivalent to clipping one polygon against the other. If the intersecting polygons have many vertices, we may want to try another algorithm that requires less computation. A performance analysis of depth sort is difficult because the particulars of the application determine how often the more difficult cases arise. For example, if we are working with polygons that describe the surfaces of solid objects, then no two polygons can intersect. Nevertheless, it should be clear that, because of the initial sort, the complexity must be at least $O(k \log k)$, where k is the number of objects.

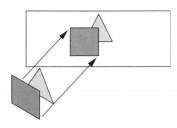

FIGURE 7.54 Polygons with overlapping extents.

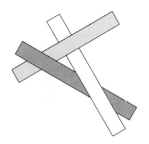

FIGURE 7.55 Cyclic overlap.

7.12 Antialiasing

Rasterized line segments and edges of polygons look jagged. Even on a display device that has a resolution as high as 1024×1280, we can notice these defects in the display. This type of error arises whenever we attempt to go from the continuous representation of an object, which has infinite resolution, to a sampled approximation, which has limited resolution. The name **aliasing** has been given to this effect because of the tie with aliasing in digital signal processing.

Aliasing errors are caused by three related problems with the discrete nature of the frame buffer. First, if we have an $n \times m$ frame buffer, the number of pixels is fixed, and we can generate only certain patterns to approximate a line segment. Many different continuous line segments may be approximated by the same pattern of pixels. We can say that all these segments are **aliased** as the same sequence of pixels. Given the sequence of pixels, we cannot tell which line segment generated the sequence. Second, pixel locations are fixed on a uniform grid; regardless of where we would like to place pixels, we cannot place them at other than evenly spaced locations. Third, pixels have a fixed size and shape.

At first glance, it might appear that there is little we can do about such problems. Algorithms such as Bresenham's algorithm are optimal in that they choose the closest set of pixels to approximate lines and polygons. However, if we have a display that supports more than two colors, there are other possibilities. Although mathematical lines are one-dimensional entities that have length but not width, rasterized lines must have a width in order to be visible. Suppose that

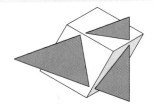

FIGURE 7.56 Piercing polygons.

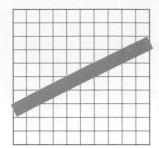

FIGURE 7.57   Ideal raster line.

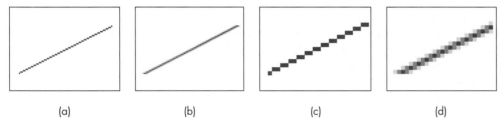

(a)   (b)   (c)   (d)

FIGURE 7.58   Aliased versus antialiased line segments. (a) Aliased line segment. (b) Antialiased line segment. (c) Magnified aliased line segment. (d) Magnified antialiased line segment.

each pixel is displayed as a square of width 1 unit and can occupy a box of 1-unit height and width on the display. Our basic frame buffer can work only in multiples of one pixel;[11] we can think of an idealized line segment in the frame buffer as being one pixel wide, as shown in Figure 7.57. Of course, we cannot draw this line, because it does not consist of our square pixels. We can view Bresenham's algorithm as a method for approximating the ideal one-pixel-wide line with our real pixels. If we look at the ideal one-pixel-wide line, we can see that it partially covers many pixel-sized boxes. It is our scan-conversion algorithm that forces us, for lines of slope less than 1, to choose exactly one pixel value for each value of x. If, instead, we shade each box by the percentage of the ideal line that crosses it, we get the smoother appearing image shown in Figure 7.58(b). This technique is known as **antialiasing by area averaging**. The calculation is similar to polygon clipping. There are other approaches to antialiasing, as well as antialiasing algorithms that can be applied to other primitives, such as polygons. Color Plate 8 shows aliased and antialiased versions of a small area of the object in Color Plate 1.

---

11. Some frame buffers permit operations in units of less than one pixel through multisampling methods.

A related problem arises because of the simple way that we are using the z-buffer algorithm. As we have specified that algorithm, the color of a given pixel is determined by the shade of a single primitive. Consider the pixel shared by the three polygons shown in Figure 7.59. If each polygon has a different color, the color assigned to the pixel is the one associated with the polygon closest to the viewer. We could obtain a much more accurate image if we could assign a color based on an area-weighted average of the colors of the three triangles. The accumulation buffer that we introduce in Chapter 8 will allow us to implement such techniques.

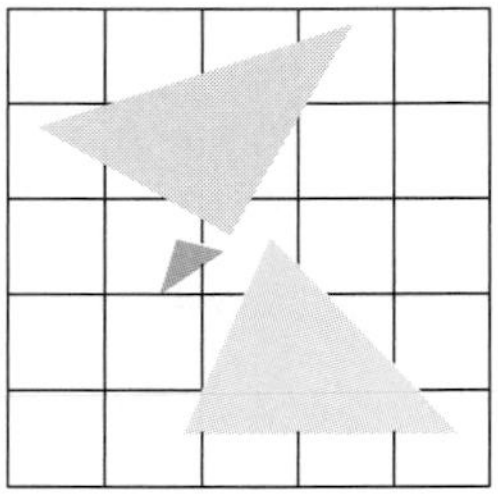

We have discussed only one type of aliasing: **spatial-domain aliasing**. When we generate sequences of images, such as for animations, we also must be concerned with **time-domain aliasing**. Consider a small object moving in front of the projection plane that has been ruled into pixel-sized units, as shown in Figure 7.60. If our rendering process sends a ray through the center of each pixel and determines what it hits, then sometimes we intersect the object and sometimes, if the projection of the object is small, we miss the object. The viewer will have the unpleasant experience of seeing the object flash on and off the display as the animation progresses. There are several ways to deal with this problem. For example, we can use more than one ray per pixel—a technique common in ray tracing. What is common to all antialiasing techniques is that they require considerably more computation than does rendering without antialiasing. In practice, for high-resolution images, antialiasing is done off-line and only when a final image is needed.

7.13 Display Considerations

In most interactive applications, the application programmer need not worry about how the contents of the frame buffer are displayed. From the application programmer's perspective, as long as she uses double buffering, the process of writing into the frame buffer is decoupled from the process of reading the frame buffer's contents for display. The hardware redisplays the present contents of

FIGURE 7.59 Polygons that share a pixel.

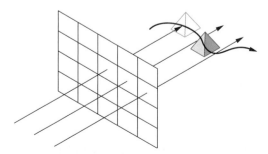

FIGURE 7.60 Time-domain aliasing.

the frame buffer at a rate sufficient to avoid flicker—usually 60 to 85 Hz—and the application programmer worries only about whether or not her program can execute and fill the frame buffer fast enough. As we saw in Chapter 3, the use of double buffering allows the display to change smoothly, even if we cannot push our primitives through the system as fast as we would like.

Numerous other problems affect the quality of the display and often cause users to be unhappy with the output of their programs. For example, the displays of two monitors may have the same nominal resolution but may display pixels of different sizes (see Exercises 7.22 and 7.23).

Perhaps the greatest source of problems with displays concerns the basic physical properties of displays: the range of colors they can display and how they map software-defined colors to the values of the primaries for the display. The color gamuts of different displays can differ greatly. In addition, because the primaries on different systems are different, even when two different monitors can produce the same visible color, they may require different values of the primaries to be sent to the displays from the graphics system. In addition, the mapping between brightness values defined by the program and what is displayed is nonlinear.

OpenGL does not address these issues directly because colors are specified as RGB values that are independent of any display properties. In addition, because RGB primaries are limited to the range from 0.0 to 1.0, it is often difficult to account for the full range of color and brightness detectable by the human visual system. However, if we expand on our discussion of color and the human visual system from Chapter 2, we can gain some additional control over color in OpenGL.

7.13.1   Color Systems

Our basic assumption about color, supported by the three-color theory of human vision, is that the three color values that we determine for each pixel correspond to the tristimulus values that we introduced in Chapter 2. Thus, a given color is a point in a color cube, as in Figure 7.61, and can be written symbolically as

$$C = T_1 \mathbf{R} + T_2 \mathbf{G} + T_3 \mathbf{B}.$$

However, there are significant differences across RGB systems. For example, suppose that we have a yellow color that OpenGL has represented with the RGB triplet (0.8, 0.6, 0.0). If we use these values to drive both a CRT and a film-image recorder, we will see different colors, even though in both cases the red is 80 percent of maximum, the green is 60 percent of maximum, and there is no blue. The reason is that the film dyes and the CRT phosphors have different color distributions. Consequently, the range of displayable colors (or the color **gamut**) is different for each.

The emphasis in the graphics community has been on device-independent graphics; consequently, the real differences among display properties are not

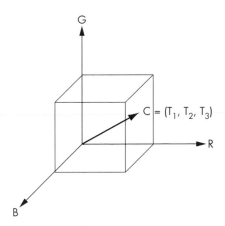

FIGURE 7.61   Color cube.

addressed by most APIs. Fortunately, the colorimetry literature contains the information we need. The standards for many of the common color systems exist. For example, CRTs are based on the National Television Systems Committee (NTSC) RGB system. We can look at differences in color systems as being equivalent to different coordinate systems for representing our tristimulus values. If $\mathbf{C}_1 - [R_1, G_1, B_1]^T$ and $\mathbf{C}_2 = [R_2, G_2, B_2]^T$ are the representations of the same color in two different systems, there is a 3×3 color-conversion matrix $\mathbf{M}$ such that

$$\mathbf{C}_2 = \mathbf{MC}_1.$$

Whether we determine this matrix from the literature or by experimentation, it allows us to produce similar displays on different output devices.

There are numerous potential problems even with this approach. The color gamuts of the two systems may not be the same. Hence, even after the conversion of tristimulus values, a color may not be producible on one of the systems. Second, the printing and graphic arts industries use a four-color subtractive system (CMYK) that adds black (K) as a fourth primary. Conversion between RGB and CMYK often requires a great deal of human expertise. Third, there are limitations to our linear color theory. The distance between colors in the color cube is not a measure of how far apart the colors are perceptually. For example, humans are particularly sensitive to color shifts in blue. Color systems such as YUV and CIE Lab have been created to address such issues.

Most RGB color systems are based on the primaries in real systems, such as CRT phosphors and film dyes. None can produce all the colors that we can see. Most color standards are based on a theoretical three-primary system called the **XYZ color system**. Here the Y primary is the luminance of the color. In the XYZ system, all colors can be specified with positive tristimulus values. We use 3×3 matrices to convert from an XYZ color representation to representations in the standard systems. Color specialists often prefer to work with **chromaticity coordinates** rather than tristimulus values. The chromaticity of a color consists of the three fractions of the color in the three primaries. Thus, if we have the tristimulus values, T_1, T_2, and T_3, for a particular RGB color, its chromaticity coordinates are

$$t_1 = \frac{T_1}{T_1 + T_2 + T_3},$$

$$t_2 = \frac{T_2}{T_1 + T_2 + T_3},$$

$$t_3 = \frac{T_3}{T_1 + T_2 + T_3}.$$

Adding the three equations, we have

$$t_1 + t_2 + t_3 = 1,$$

and thus we can work in the two-dimensional t_1, t_2 space, finding t_3 only when its value is needed. The information that is missing from chromaticity coordinates, which was contained in the original tristimulus values, is the sum $T_1 + T_2 + T_3$, a value related to the intensity of the color. When working with color systems, this intensity is often not important to issues related to producing colors or matching colors across different systems.

Because each color fraction must be nonnegative, the chromaticity values are limited by

$$1 \geq t_i \geq 0.$$

All producible colors must lie inside the triangle in Figure 7.62. Figure 7.63 shows this triangle for the XYZ system and a curve of the representation for each visible spectral line. For the XYZ system, this curve must lie inside the triangle.

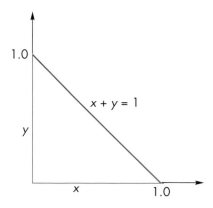

FIGURE 7.62   Triangle of producible colors in chromaticity coordinates.

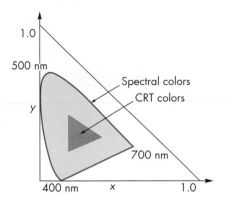

FIGURE 7.63 Visible colors and color gamut of a display.

Figure 7.63 also shows the range of colors (in x, y chromaticity coordinates) that are producible on a typical color printer or CRT. If we compare the two figures, we see that the colors inside the curve of pure spectral lines but outside the gamut of the physical display cannot be displayed on the physical device.

One defect of our development of color is that RGB color is based on how color is produced and measured rather than on how we perceive a color. When we see a given color, we describe it not by three primaries but based on other properties, such as the name we give the color and how bright a shade we see. The hue–saturation–lightness (HLS) system is used by artists and some display manufacturers. The **hue** is the name we give to a color: red, yellow, gold. The **lightness** is how bright the color appears. **Saturation** is the color attribute that distinguishes a pure shade of a color from the a shade of the same hue that has been mixed with white, forming a pastel shade. We can relate these attributes to a typical RGB color as shown in Figure 7.64(a). Given a color in the color cube, the lightness is a measure of how far the point is from the origin (black). If we note that all the colors on the principal diagonal of the cube, going from black to white, are shades of gray and are totally unsaturated, then the saturation is a measure of how far the given color is from this diagonal. Finally, the hue is a measure of where the color vector is pointing. HLS colors are usually described in terms of a color cone, as shown in Figure 7.64(b), or a double cone that also converges at the top. From our perspective, we can look at the HLS system as providing a representation of an RGB color in polar coordinates.

7.13.2 The Color Matrix

OpenGL provides a color matrix as part of the imaging subset supported by recent hardware. This matrix simplifies conversion between different color systems. The color matrix is a 4×4 matrix stored as a 16-element array by columns. It operates on RGBA color representations and can be looked at as part of the pipeline that converts a color, $rgba$, to a new color, $r'g'b'a'$, by the matrix multiplication

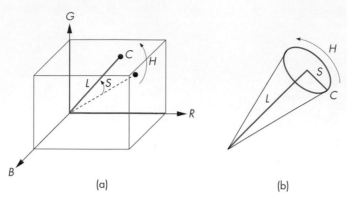

FIGURE 7.64   Hue–lightness–saturation color. (a) Using the RGB color cube. (b) Using a single cone.

$$\begin{bmatrix} r' \\ g' \\ b' \\ a' \end{bmatrix} = \mathbf{C} \begin{bmatrix} r \\ g \\ b \\ a \end{bmatrix}.$$

Thus, if we are dealing with opaque surfaces for which $A = 1$, the matrix

$$\mathbf{C} = \begin{bmatrix} -1 & 0 & 0 & 1 \\ 0 & -1 & 0 & 1 \\ 0 & 0 & -1 & 1 \\ 0 & 0 & 0 & 1 \end{bmatrix}$$

converts the additive representation of a color to its subtractive representation. We set this matrix as other OpenGL matrices by setting the matrix mode

```
glMatrixMode(GL_COLOR);
```

and then forming the matrix in the application.

7.13.3 Gamma Correction

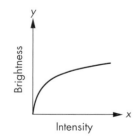

FIGURE 7.65   Logarithmic brightness.

In Chapter 2, we defined brightness as perceived intensity and observed that the human visual system perceives intensity in a logarithmic manner, as depicted in Figure 7.65. One consequence of this property is that if we want the brightness steps to appear to be uniformly spaced, the intensities that we assign to pixels should increase exponentially. These steps can be calculated from the measured minimum and maximum intensities that a display can generate.

In addition, the intensity I of a CRT is related to the voltage V applied by

$$I \propto V^{\gamma}$$

or

$$\log I = c_0 + \gamma \log V,$$

where the constants γ and c_0 are properties of the particular CRT. One implication of these two results is that two monitors may generate different brightnesses for the same values in the frame buffer. One way to correct for this problem is to have a lookup table in the display whose values can be adjusted for the particular characteristics of the monitor—the **gamma correction**.

There is an additional problem with CRTs. It is not possible to have a CRT whose display is totally black when no signal is applied. The minimum displayed intensity is called the **dark field** value and can be problematic, especially when CRT technology is used to project images. The contrast ratio of a display is the ratio of the maximum to minimum brightness. Newer display technologies have contrast ratios in the thousands.

7.13.4 Dithering and Halftoning

We have specified a color buffer by its spatial resolution (the number of pixels) and by its precision (the number of colors it can display). If we view these separate numbers as fixed, we say that a high-resolution, black-and-white laser printer can display only 1-bit pixels. This argument also seems to imply that any black-and-white medium, such as a book, cannot display images with multiple shades. We know from experience that that is not the case; the trick is to trade spatial resolution for grayscale or color precision. **Halftoning** techniques in the printing industry use photographic means to simulate gray levels by creating patterns of black dots of varying size. The human visual system tends to merge small dots together and sees not the dots, but rather an intensity proportional to the ratio of white to black in a small area.

Digital halftones differ because the size and location of displayed pixels are fixed. Consider a 4×4 group of 1-bit pixels, as shown in Figure 7.66. If we look at this pattern from far away, we see not the individual pixels, but rather a gray level based on the number of black pixels. For our 4×4 example, although there are 2^{16} different patterns of black and white pixels, there are only 17 possible shades, corresponding to 0 to 16 black pixels in the array. There are many algorithms for generating halftone, or **dither**, patterns. The simplest picks 17 patterns (for our example) and uses them to create a display with 17 rather than two gray levels, although at the cost of decreasing the spatial resolution by a factor of 4.

The simple algorithm—always using the same array to simulate a shade—can generate beat, or moiré, patterns when displaying anything regular. Such patterns

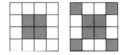

FIGURE 7.66 Digital halftone patterns.

arise whenever we image two regular phenomena, because we see the sum and differences of their frequencies. Such effects are closely related to the aliasing problems we shall discuss in Chapter 8.

Many dithering techniques are based on simply randomizing the least significant bit of the luminance or of each color component. More sophisticated dither algorithms use randomization to create patterns with the correct average properties but avoid the repetition that can lead to moiré effects (see Exercise 7.26).

Halftoning (or dithering) is often used with color, especially with hard-copy displays, such as ink-jet printers, that can produce only fully on or off colors. Each primary can be dithered to produce more visual colors. OpenGL supports such displays and allows the user to enable dithering (`glEnable(GL_DITHER)`). Color dithering allows color monitors to produce smooth color displays, and normally dithering is enabled. Because dithering is so effective, displays can work well with a limited number of bits per color, allowing frame buffers to have a limited amount of memory. In many applications we need to use the OpenGL query function `glGetIntegerv` to find out how many bits are being used for each color since this information is important when we use some of the techniques from Chapter 8 that read pixels from the frame buffer. If dithering is enabled and we read pixels out of the frame buffer, pixels that were written with the same RGB values may return different values when read. If these small differences are important, dithering should be disabled before reading from the frame buffer.

Summary and Notes

We have presented an overview of the implementation process, including a sampling of the most important algorithms. Regardless of what the particulars of an implementation are—whether the tasks are done primarily in hardware or in software, whether we are working with a special-purpose graphics workstation or with a simple graphics terminal, and what the API is—the same tasks must be done. These tasks include implementation of geometric transformations, clipping, and rasterization. The relationship among hardware, software, and APIs is an interesting one.

The Geometry Engine that was the basis of many Silicon Graphics workstations is a VLSI chip that performed geometric transformations and clipping through a hardware pipeline. GL, the predecessor of OpenGL, was developed as an API for users of these workstations. Much of the OpenGL literature also follows the pipeline approach. We should keep in mind, however, that OpenGL is an API: It does not say anything about the underlying implementation. In principle, an image defined by an OpenGL program could be obtained from a ray tracer. We should carry away two lessons from our emphasis on pipeline architectures. First, this architecture provides an aid to the applications programmer in understanding the process of creating images. Second, at present, the pipeline view can lead to efficient hardware and software implementations.

The example of the z-buffer algorithm is illustrative of the relationship between hardware and software. Fifteen years ago, many hidden-surface–removal algorithms were used, of which the z-buffer algorithm was only one. The availability of fast, dense, inexpensive memory has made the z-buffer algorithm the dominant method for hidden-surface removal.

A related example is that of workstation architectures, where special-purpose graphics chips have made remarkable advances in just the past few years. Not only has graphics performance increased at a rate that exceeds Moore's law, but many new features have become available in the graphics processors. As we shall see in Chapter 9, the new programmable architectures open up many new possibilities.

So what does the future hold? Certainly, graphics systems will get faster and cheaper. More than any other factor, advances in hardware probably will dictate what future graphics systems will look like. At the present, hardware development is being driven by the game industry. For less than $200, we can purchase a graphics card that exceeds the performance of graphics workstations that a few years ago would have cost more than $100,000. The features and performance of these cards are optimized for the needs of the computer game industry. Thus, we do not see uniform speedups in the various graphics functions that we have presented. In addition, new hardware features are appearing far faster than they can be incorporated into standard APIs. However, the speed at which these processors operate have challenged both the graphics and scientific communities to discover new algorithms to solve problems that until now had always been solved using conventional architectures.

On the software side, the low cost and speed of recent hardware has enabled software developers to produce rendering software that allows users to balance rendering time and quality of rendering. Hence, a user can add some ray-traced objects to a scene, the number depending on how long she is willing to wait for the rendering. The future of standard APIs is much less clear. On one hand, users in the scientific community prefer stable APIs, such as OpenGL, so that application code will have a long lifetime. On the other hand, users want to exploit new hardware features that are not supported on all systems.

Numerous advanced architectures under exploration use massive parallelism. How parallelism can be exploited most effectively for computer graphics is still an open issue. Our two approaches to rendering—object-oriented and image-oriented—lead to two entirely different ways to develop a parallel renderer, which we shall explore further in Chapter 12.

We have barely scratched the surface of implementation. The literature is rich with algorithms for every aspect of the implementation process. The references should help you to explore this topic further.

Suggested Readings

The books by Rogers [Rog85] and by Foley and colleagues [Fol90] contain many more algorithms than we can present here. Also see the series *Graphic*

Gems [Gra90, Gra91, Gra92, Gra94, Gra95]. Books such as Möller and Haines [Mol02] and Eberly [Ebe01] cover the influence of recent advances in hardware.

The Cohen-Sutherland [Sut63] clipping algorithm goes back to the early years of computer graphics, as does Bresenham's algorithm [Bre63, Bre87], which was originally proposed for pen plotters. See [Lia84] and [Sut74a] for the Liang-Barsky and Sutherland-Hogman clippers.

The z-buffer algorithm was developed by Catmull [Cat75]. See Sutherland [Sut74b] for a discussion of various approaches to hidden-surface removal.

Our decision to avoid details of the hardware does not imply that the hardware is either simple or uninteresting. The rate at which a modern graphics processor can display graphical entities requires sophisticated and clever hardware designs [Cla82, Ake88, Ake93]. The discussion by Molnar and Fuchs in [Fol90] shows a variety of approaches.

Pratt [Pra78] provides matrices to convert among various color systems. Halftone and dithering are discussed by Jarvis [Jar76] and by Knuth [Knu87].

Exercises

7.1   Consider two line segments represented in parametric form:

$$\mathbf{p}(\alpha) = (1 - \alpha)\mathbf{p}_1 + \alpha\mathbf{p}_2,$$

$$\mathbf{q}(\beta) = (1 - \beta)\mathbf{q}_1 + \beta\mathbf{q}_2.$$

Find a procedure for determining whether the segments intersect and, if they do, for finding the point of intersection.

7.2   Extend the argument of Exercise 8.1 to find a method for determining whether two flat polygons intersect.

7.3   Prove that clipping a convex object against another convex object results in at most one convex object.

7.4   In what ways can you parallelize the image- and object-oriented approaches to implementation?

7.5   Because both normals and vertices can be represented in homogeneous coordinates, both can be operated on by the model-view transformation. Show that normals may not be preserved by the transformation.

7.6   Derive the viewport transformation. Express it in terms of the three-dimensional scaling and translation matrices used to represent affine transformations in two dimensions.

7.7   Pre–raster-graphics systems were able to display only lines. Programmers produced three-dimensional images using hidden-line–removal techniques. Many current APIs allow us to produce wireframe images, composed of only lines, in which the hidden lines that define nonvisible surfaces have been removed. How does this problem differ from that of the polygon hidden-surface removal that we have considered? Derive a hidden-line–removal algorithm for objects that consist of the edges of planar polygons.

7.8   Often we display functions of the form $y = f(x, z)$ by displaying a rectangular mesh generated by the set of values $\{f(x_i, z_j)\}$ evaluated at regular intervals in x and z. Hidden-surface removal should be applied because parts of the surface can be obscured from view by other parts. Derive two algorithms, one using hidden-surface removal and the other using hidden-line removal, to display such a mesh.

7.9   Although we argued that the complexity of the image-space approach to hidden-surface removal is proportional to the number of polygons, performance studies have shown almost constant performance. Explain this result.

7.10   Consider a scene composed of only solid, three-dimensional polyhedra. Can you devise an object-space, hidden-surface–removal algorithm for this case? How much does it help if you know that all the polyhedra are convex?

7.11   We can look at object-space approaches to hidden-surface removal as analogous to sorting algorithms. However, we argued that the former's complexity is $O(k^2)$. We know that only the worst-performing sorting algorithms have such poor performance, and most are $O(k \log k)$. Does it follow that object-space, hidden-surface–removal algorithms have similar complexity? Explain your answer.

7.12   Devise a method for testing whether one planar polygon is fully on one side of another planar polygon.

7.13   What are the differences between our image-space approaches to hidden-surface removal and to ray tracing? Can we use ray tracing as an alternate technique to hidden-surface removal? What are the advantages and disadvantages of such an approach?

7.14   Write a program to generate the locations of pixels along a rasterized line segment using Bresenham's algorithm. Check that your program works for all slopes and all possible locations of the endpoints. What is the initial value of the decision variable?

7.15   Bresenham's algorithm can be extended to circles. Convince yourself of this statement by considering a circle centered at the origin. Which parts of the circle must be generated by an algorithm and which parts can be found by symmetry? Can you find a part of the circle such that if we know a point generated by a scan-conversion algorithm, we can reduce the number of candidates for the next pixel?

7.16 Show how to use flood fill to generate a maze like the one you created in Exercise 2.7.

7.17 Suppose that you try to extend flood fill to arbitrary closed curves by scan-converting the curve and then applying the same fill algorithm that we used for polygons. What problems can arise if you use this approach?

7.18 Consider the edge of a polygon between vertices at (x_1, y_1) and (x_2, y_2). Derive an efficient algorithm for computing the intersection of all scan lines with this edge. Assume that you are working in window coordinates.

7.19 Vertical and horizontal edges are potentially problematic for polygon-fill algorithms. How would you handle these cases for the algorithms that we have presented?

7.20 In two-dimensional graphics, if two polygons overlap, we can ensure that they are rendered in the same order by all implementations by associating a priority attribute with each polygon. Polygons are rendered in reverse-priority order; that is, the highest-priority polygon is rendered last. How should we modify our polygon-fill algorithms to take priority into account?

7.21 A standard antialiasing technique used in ray tracing is to cast rays not only through the center of each pixel but also through the pixel's four corners. What is the increase in work compared to casting a single ray through the center?

7.22 Although an ideal pixel is a square of 1 unit per side, most CRT systems generate round pixels that can be approximated as circles of uniform intensity. If a completely full unit square has intensity 1.0 and an empty square has intensity 0.0, how does the intensity of a displayed pixel vary with the radius of the circle?

7.23 Consider a bilevel display with round pixels. Do you think it is wiser to use small circles or large circles for foreground-colored pixels? Explain your answer.

7.24 Why is defocusing the beam of a CRT sometimes called "the poor person's antialiasing"?

7.25 Suppose that a monochrome display has a minimum intensity output of I_{min}—a CRT display is never completely black—and a maximum output of I_{max}. Given that we perceive intensities in a logarithmic manner, how should we assign k intensity levels such that the steps appear uniform?

7.26 Generate a halftone algorithm based on the following idea. Suppose that gray levels vary from 0.0 to 1.0 and that we have a random-number generator that produces random numbers that are uniformly distributed over this interval. If we pick a gray level g, $g/100$ percent of the random numbers generated will be less than g.

7.27 Images produced on displays that support only a few colors or gray levels tend to show contour effects because the viewer can detect the differences between adjacent shades. One technique for avoiding this visual effect is to add a little noise (jitter) to the pixel values. Why does this technique work? How much noise should you add? Does it make sense to conclude that the degraded image created by the addition of noise is of quality higher than that of the original image?

DISCRETE TECHNIQUES

For many years, computer graphics dealt exclusively with geometric objects, such as lines, polygons, and polyhedra. Raster systems have been in existence for more than 30 years, but until recently, application programmers have had only indirect access to pixels in the frame buffer. Although lines and polygons were rasterized into the frame buffer, application programmers had no functions in the API that would allow them to read or write individual pixels. Many of the most exciting methods that have evolved over the past decade rely on interactions among the various buffers that make up the frame buffer. Texture mapping, antialiasing, compositing, and alpha blending are only a few of the techniques that become possible when the API allows us to work with discrete buffers. This chapter introduces these techniques, focusing on those that are supported by OpenGL and by similar APIs.

We start by looking at the frame buffer in more detail and how we can read and write to it. We shall learn to work with arrays of pixels that form digital images. We then consider mapping methods. These techniques are applied during the rendering process, and they enable us to give the illusion of a surface of great complexity, although the surface might be a single polygon. All these techniques use arrays of pixels to define how the rendering process that we studied in Chapter 7 is modified to create these illusions. We shall then look at some of the other buffers that are supported by the OpenGL API and how these buffers can be used for new applications. In particular, we examine techniques for combining, or compositing, images. Here we use the fourth "color" in RGBA mode, and we shall see that we can use this channel to blend images and to create effects such as transparency. We conclude with a discussion of the aliasing problems that arise whenever we work with discrete elements.

8.1 Buffers

We have already used two types of standard buffers: color buffers and depth buffers. Later, we introduce others. What all buffers have in common is that they are inherently discrete: They have limited resolution, both spatially and in

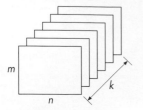

FIGURE 8.1 Buffer.

depth. We can define a (two-dimensional)[1] **buffer** as a block of memory with $n \times m$ k-bit elements (Figure 8.1).

As we have seen, OpenGL defines the frame buffer as consisting of a variety of buffers, including the front and back color buffers, the depth buffer, and other buffers that we shall introduce in this chapter. Thus at a given spatial location, the k bits in the frame buffer can include bits for an index, such as an 8-bit pointer into a color table, 32-bit RGBA colors, integers representing depths, or even floating-point numbers. Figure 8.2 shows the OpenGL frame buffer and some of its constituent parts. If we consider the whole frame buffer, the resolution of the frame buffer, n and m, matches the spatial resolution of the display. The depth of the frame buffer—the value of k—can exceed a few hundred bits. Even for the simple cases that we have seen so far, we have 64 bits for the front and back color buffers and 32 bits for the depth buffer. The numerical accuracy or **precision** of a given buffer is determined by its depth. Thus, if a frame buffer has 32 bits each for its front and back color buffers, each RGBA color component is stored with a precision of 8 bits.

When we work with the frame buffer, we usually work with one constituent buffer at a time. Accordingly, we shall use the term *buffer* in what follows to mean a particular buffer within the frame buffer. Each of these buffers is $n \times m$ and is k bits deep. However, k can be different for different buffers. For a color buffer, its k is determined by how many colors the system can display, usually 24 for RGB displays and 32 for RGBA displays. For the depth buffer, its k is determined by the depth precision that the system can support, often 32 bits to match the size of a floating-point number or an integer. We use the term **bitplane** to refer to any of the k $n \times m$ planes in a buffer, and **pixel** to refer to all k of the bits at a particular spatial location. With this definition, a pixel can be a byte, an integer, or even a floating-point number, depending on which buffer is used and how data are stored in the buffer.

The applications programmer generally will not know how information is stored in the frame buffer because the frame buffer is inside the implementation, which the programmer sees as a black box. Thus, the application program sends (writes or draws) information into the frame buffer or obtains (reads) information from the frame buffer through OpenGL functions. When the application program reads or writes pixels, not only are data transferred between ordinary processor memory and graphics memory on the graphics card, but usually these data must be reformatted to be compatible with the frame buffer. Consequently, what are ordinarily thought of as digital images, for example JPEG-, GIF-, or TIFF-formatted images, exist only on the application side of the process. Not only must the application programmer worry how to decode particular formats so they can be sent to the frame buffer through OpenGL functions, but the programmer also must be aware of the time that is spent in the movement of

1. We can also have one-, three-, and four-dimensional buffers.

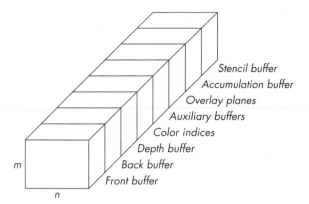

Stencil buffer
Accumulation buffer
Overlay planes
Auxiliary buffers
Color indices
Depth buffer
Back buffer
Front buffer

m

n

FIGURE 8.2 OpenGL frame buffer.

digital data between processor memory and the frame buffer. If the application programmer also knows the internal format of how data are stored in any of the buffers, she can often write application programs that execute more efficiently.

8.2 Digital Images

Before we look at how the graphics system can work with digital images through pixel and bit operations, let's first examine what we mean by a digital image.[2] Within our programs, we generally work with images that are arrays of pixels. These images can be of a variety of sizes and data types, depending on the type of image with which we are working. For example, if we are working with RGB images, we usually represent each of the color components with one byte whose values range from 0 to 255. Thus, we might define a 512×512 image in our application program as

```
GLubyte myimage[512][512][3];
```

If we are working with monochromatic or **luminance** images, each pixel represents a gray level from black (0) to white (255), so we would use

```
GLubyte myimage[512][512];
```

---

2. Most references often use the term *image* instead of *digital image*. This terminology can be confused with using the term *image* to refer to the result of combining geometric objects and a camera, through the projection process, to obtain what we have called an image. In this chapter, the context should be clear so there should be no confusion.

If we are working with color-index mode images, each pixel is a pointer into a table of colors, so we might use unsigned bytes for the image plus three color tables

```
GLubyte myimage[512][512], red[256], green[256], blue[256];
```

Thus, for example, the red for a given index is red[myimage[i][j]]. One way to form digital images is through code in the application program. For example, suppose that we want to create a 512×512 image that consists of an 8×8 checkerboard of alternating red and black squares, such as we might use for a game. The following code will work:

```
GLubyte check[512][512][3];
int i,j;
for (i=0; i<512; i++)
   for(j=0; j<512; j++)
   {
   for(k=0;k<3;k++)
      if((8*i+j/64)%64) check[i][j][0]=255;
         else check[i][j][k]=0;
   }
```

Usually, writing code to form images is limited to images that contain regular patterns. More often, we obtain images directly from data. For example, if we have an array of real numbers that we have obtained from an experiment or a simulation, we can scale them to go over the range 0 to 255 and then convert these data to unsigned bytes to form a luminance image.

There is a third method of obtaining images that has become much more prevalent because of the influence of the Internet. Images are produced by scanning continuous images, such as photographs, or produced directly using digital cameras. Each image is in one of many possible "standard" formats. Some of the most popular formats are GIF, TIFF, PS, EPS, and JPEG. These formats include direct coding of the values in some order, compressed but lossless coding, and compressed lossy coding. Each format arose from the particular needs of a group of applications. For example, PostScript (PS) images are defined by the PostScript language used to control printers. These images are an exact encoding of the image data—either RGB or luminance—into the 7-bit ASCII character set. Consequently, PostScript images can be understood by a large class of printers and other devices but tend to be very large. Encapsulated PostScript (EPS) images are similar but include additional information that is useful for previewing images. GIF images are color index images and thus store a color table and an array of indices for the image.

TIFF images can have two forms. In one form, all the image data are coded directly. A header describes how the data are arranged. In the second form, the data are compressed. Compression is possible because most images contain much redundant data. For example, large areas of most images show very little variation in color or intensity. This redundancy can be removed by algorithms that result in a compressed version of the original image that requires less storage. Compressed TIFF images are formed by the Lempel-Ziv algorithm, which provides optimal lossless compression that allows the original image to be compressed and recovered exactly. JPEG images are compressed by an algorithm that allows small errors in the compression and reconstruction of the image. Consequently, JPEG images have very high **compression ratios**, that is, the ratio of the number of bits in the original file to the number of bits in the compressed data file, with little or no visible distortion. Figure 8.3 shows three versions of a single 1200×1200 luminance image: uncompressed, as a TIFF image (a); and as two JPEG images, compressed with different ratios (b and c). The corresponding file sizes are 1,440,198; 80,109; and 38,962 bytes, respectively. Thus, the TIFF image has one byte for each pixel plus 198 bytes of header and trailer information.

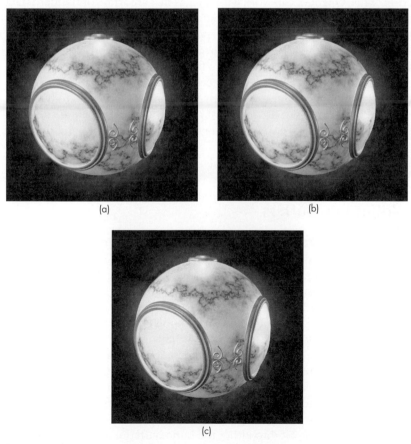

(a)

(b)

(c)

FIGURE 8.3 (a) Original TIFF luminance image. (b) JPEG image compressed by a factor of 18. (c) JPEG image compressed by a factor of 37.

For the JPEG images, the compression ratios are approximately 18 and 37. Even with the higher compression ratio, there is little visible distortion in the image. If we store the original image as a PostScript image, the file will be approximately twice as large as the TIFF image because each byte will be converted into two 7-bit ASCII characters, each pair requiring 2 bytes of storage. If we store the image as a compressed TIFF file, we need only about one-half of the storage. Using a zip file—a popular format used for compressing arbitrary files—would give about the same result. This amount of compression is image-dependent. Although this compression method is lossless, the compression ratio is far worse than is obtainable with lossy JPEG images, which are visibly almost indistinguishable from the original. This closeness accounts for the popularity of the JPEG format for sending images over the Internet.

The large number of image formats poses problems for a graphics API. Although some image formats are simple, others are quite complex. The OpenGL API avoids the problem by not including any image formats. As we shall see in the next section, while OpenGL can work with images that are arrays of standard data types in memory, it is the application programmer's responsibility to read any formatted images into processor memory and write them out as formatted files. We shall not deal with these issues here, because any discussion would require us to discuss the details of particular image formats. The necessary information can be found in the references in Suggested Readings.

We can also obtain digital images directly from our graphics system by forming images of three-dimensional scenes using the geometric pipeline and then reading these images back. We shall see how to do the required operations later in the chapter.

8.3 Writing into Buffers

In a modern graphics system, a user program can both write into and read from the buffers. There are two factors that make these operations different from the usual reading and writing into computer memory. First, we only occasionally want to read or write a single pixel or bit. Rather, we tend to read and write rectangular blocks of pixels (or bits), known as **bit blocks**. For example, we rasterize an entire scanline at a time when we fill a polygon; we write a small block of pixels when we display a raster character; we change the values of all pixels in a buffer when we do a clear operation. Hence, it is important to have both the hardware and software support a set of operations that work on rectangular blocks of pixels, known as **bit-block transfer** (**bitblt**) operations, as efficiently as possible. These operations are also known as **raster operations** (**raster-ops**).

Suppose that we want to take an $n \times m$ block of pixels from one of our buffers, the **source buffer**, and copy it into either the same buffer or another buffer, the **destination buffer**. This transfer is shown in Figure 8.4. A typical form for a bitblt write operation is

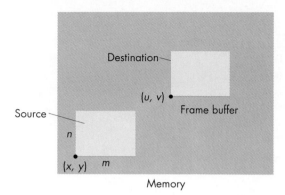

FIGURE 8.4 Writing a block.

```
write_block(source, n, m, x, y, destination, u, v);
```

where `source` and `destination` are the buffers. The operation writes an n × m source block whose lower-left corner is at (x,y) to the destination buffer starting at a location (u,v). Although there are numerous details that we must consider, such as what happens if the source block goes over the boundary of the destination block, the essence of bitblt is that a single function call alters the entire destination block. Note that from the hardware perspective, the type of processing involved has none of the characteristics of the processing of geometric objects. Consequently, the hardware that optimizes bitblt operations has a completely different architecture from the pipeline hardware that we use for geometric operations. Thus, the OpenGL architecture contains both a geometry pipeline and a pixel pipeline, each of which is usually implemented separately.

8.3.1 Writing Modes

A second difference between normal writing into memory and bitblt operations is the variety of ways we can write into the buffers. In Chapter 3, we introduced logic operations so that we could use the XOR write mode to draw rubberband lines. OpenGL supports 16 different modes. To understand the full range of possibilities, let's consider how we might write into a buffer.

The usual concept of a write to memory is replacement. The execution of a statement in a C program such as

```
y=x;
```

results in the value at the location where y is stored being replaced with the value at the location of x.

There are other possibilities. Suppose that we can work 1 bit at a time in our buffers. Consider the writing model in Figure 8.5. The bit that we wish to place in memory, perhaps in an altered form, is called the **source bit**, s; the place

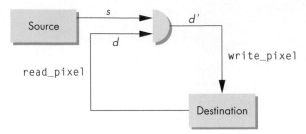

FIGURE 8.5   Writing model.

s	d	0	1	2	3	4	5	6	7	8	9	10	11	12	13	14	15
0	0	0	0	0	0	0	0	0	0	1	1	1	1	1	1	1	1
0	1	0	0	0	0	1	1	1	1	0	0	0	0	1	1	1	1
1	0	0	0	1	1	0	0	1	1	0	0	1	1	0	0	1	1
1	1	0	1	0	1	0	1	0	1	0	1	0	1	0	1	0	1

FIGURE 8.6   Writing modes.

in memory where we want to put it is called the **destination bit, d**. If, as in Chapter 3, we are allowed to read before writing, as depicted in Figure 8.5, then writing can be described by a replacement function f such that

$$d \leftarrow f(d, s).$$

For a 1-bit source and destination, there are only 16 possible ways to define the function f—namely, the 16 logical operations between two bits. These operations are shown in Figure 8.6, where each of the 16 columns on the right corresponds to one possible f. We can use the binary number represented by each column to denote a **writing mode**; equivalently, we can denote writing modes by the logical operation defined by the column. Suppose that we think of the logical value "1" as corresponding to a background color (say, white) and "0" as corresponding to a foreground color (say, black). We can examine the effects of various choices of f. Writing modes 0 and 15 are clear operations that change the value of the destination to either the foreground or the background color. The new value of the destination bit is independent of both the source and the destination values. Modes 3 and 7 are the normal writing modes. Mode 3 is the function

$$d \leftarrow s.$$

Color Plate 1 Image of sun object created using NURBS surfaces and rendered with bump mapping.

(Courtesy of Full Dome Project, University of New Mexico.)

Color Plate 2 Wire-frame representation of sun object surfaces.

(Courtesy of Full Dome Project, University of New Mexico.)

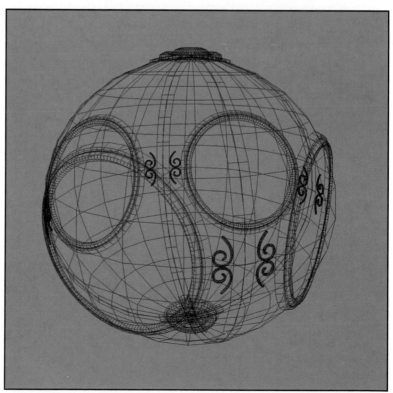

Color Plate 3 Flat-shaded polygonal rendering of sun object.

(Courtesy of Full Dome Project, University of New Mexico.)

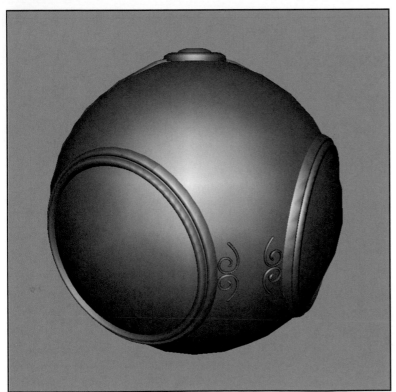

Color Plate 4 Smooth-shaded polygonal rendering of sun object.

(Courtesy of Full Dome Project, University of New Mexico.)

Color Plate 5 Wire-frame of NURBS representation of sun object showing the high number of polygons used in rendering the NURBS surfaces.

(Courtesy of Full Dome Project, University of New Mexico.)

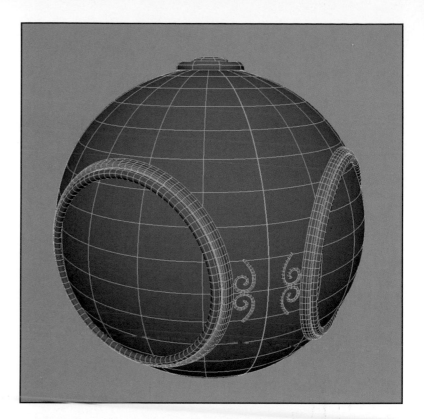

Color Plate 6 Rendering of sun object showing bump map.

(Courtesy of Full Dome Project, University of New Mexico.)

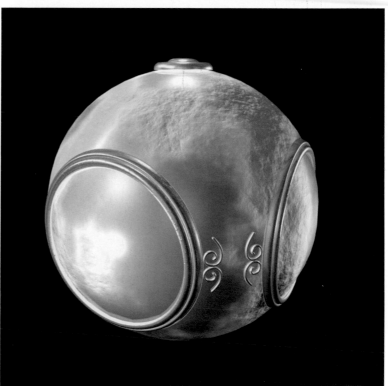

Color Plate 7 Rendering of sun object with an environment map.

(Courtesy of Full Dome Project, University of New Mexico.)

Color Plate 8 Rendering of a small part of the sun object with an environment map.

(Courtesy of Full Dome Project, University of New Mexico.)

(a) Without antialiasing

(b) With antialiasing

Color Plate 11 Factory environment from video, "I Thought, Therefore I Was."

(Courtesy of James Pinkerton, Thomas Keller, Brian Jones, John Bell, University of New Mexico and Sandia National Laboratories.)

Color Plate 12 Robot "Ed" from video, "I Thought, Therefore I Was."

(Courtesy of James Pinkerton, Thomas Keller, Brian Jones, John Bell, University of New Mexico and Sandia National Laboratories.)

Color Plate 13 Welding scene from video, "I Thought, Therefore I Was."

(Courtesy of James Pinkerton, Thomas Keller, Brian Jones, John Bell, University of New Mexico and Sandia National Laboratories.)

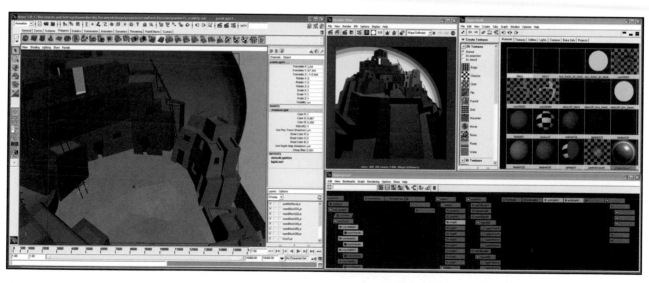

Color Plate 14
Interface for Animation using Maya

(Courtesy of Hue Walker, Arts Technology Center, University of New Mexico.)

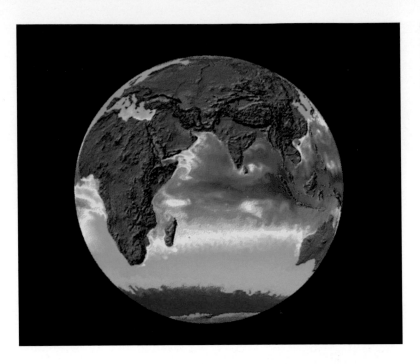

Color Plate 15 Ocean temperature distribution during El Niño. Data texture mapped to earth model.

(Courtesy of Allen McPherson, Advanced Computing Laboratory, Los Alamos National Laboratory.)

Color Plate 16 Physical robot and its graphical model. The graphical model is used for design, path planning, and simulation.

(Courtesy of Sandia National Laboratories.)

Color Plate 17 (a) NURBS surface representing surface of water and particles used to pull the NURBS control points to create successive images of moving water.

(Courtesy of Saty Raghavachary, DreamWorks Feature Animation.)

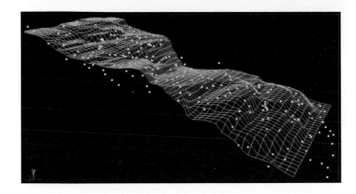

(b) Rendering of NURBS surface showing static water surface.

(Courtesy of Saty Raghavachary, DreamWorks Feature Animation.)

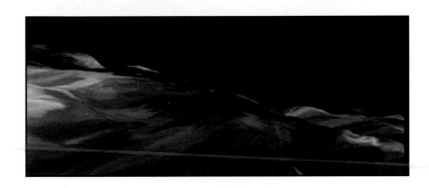

Color Plate 18 Rendering using particles showing moving water from "Spirit-Stallion of the Cimarron."

(Courtesy of Saty Raghavachary, DreamWorks Feature Animation.)

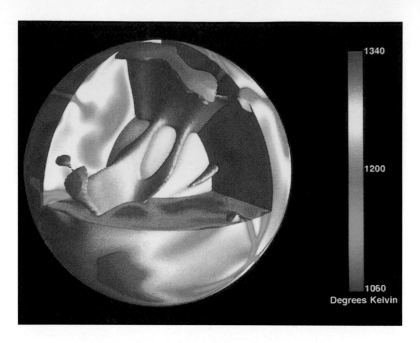

Color Plate 19 Fluid dynamics of the mantle of the Earth. Pseudocolor mapping of temperatures and isotemperature surface.

(Courtesy of James Painter,
Advanced Computing Laboratory,
Los Alamos National Laboratory.)

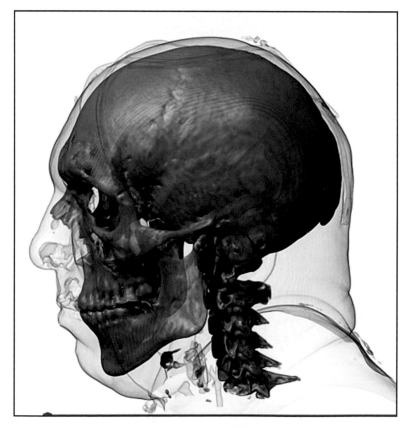

Color Plate 20 Volume Rendering of CT Data.

(Courtesy of J. Kniss, G. Kindlmann, C. Hansen,
Scientific Computing and Imaging Institute,
University of Utah.)

Color Plate 21 RGB color cube.

(Courtesy of University of New Mexico.)

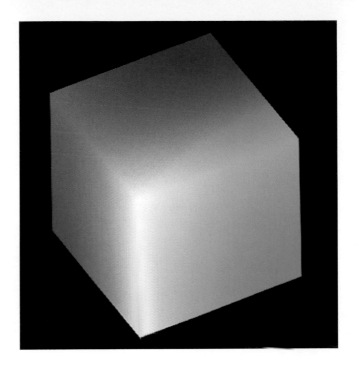

Color Plate 22 Avatar representing a patient who is being diagnosed and treated by a remotely located health professional (inset).

(Courtesy of Tom Caudell, Visualization Laboratory, Albuquerque High Performance Computing Center, University of New Mexico.)

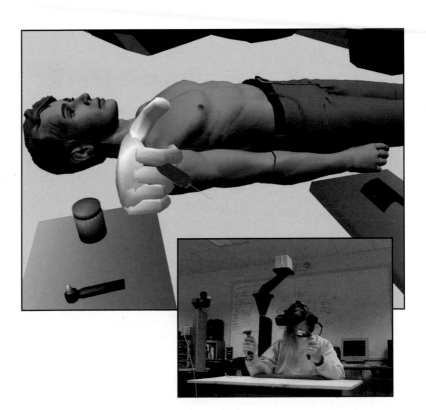

Color Plate 23 Rendering using ray tracer.

(Courtesy of Patrick McCormick, University of New Mexico
and Los Alamos National Laboratory.)

Color Plate 24 Radiosity rendering showing
soft shadows and diffuse-diffuse reflections.

(Courtesy of A. Van Pernis, K. Rasche,
R. Geist, Clemson University.)

Color Plate 25 Array of Utah teapots with different material properties.

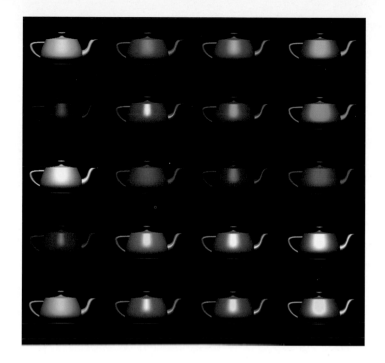

Color Plate 26 Phong shaded teapot

(a) Using a vertex shader

(b) Using a fragment shader

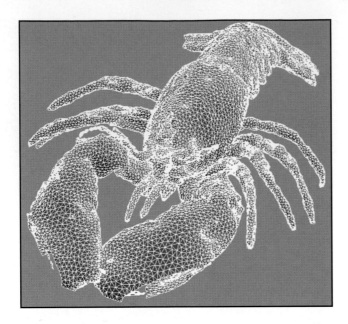

Color Plate 27 Isosurface mesh for lobster data set computed by a particle system of 40,000 particles.

(Courtesy of Patricia Crossno, University of New Mexico and Sandia National Laboratories.)

Color Plate 28 Interactively modeled and rendered volumetric procedural cloud.

(Courtesy of Joshua Schpok and David S. Ebert, Purdue University Rendering and Perceptualization Lab.)

Color Plate 29 One frame from Pixar's "Geri's Game" showing refraction through reflections on Geri's glasses.

(Courtesy of Pixar Animation Studios.)

Color Plate 30 Reflection map from environment computed from the center of the lens on Geri's glasses. The reflection map is then mapped to the glasses as part of the rendering process.

(Courtesy of Pixar Animation Studios.)

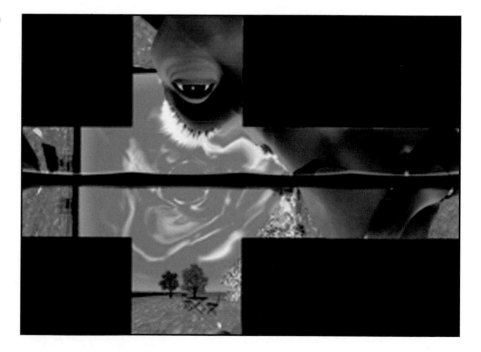

(a) Mesh of particles

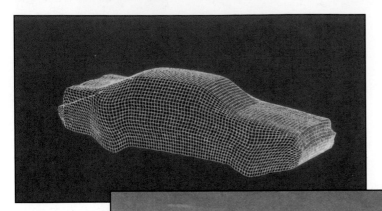

(b) Model of Lexus with surface

(c) Wind blowing mesh off Lexus

(d) Mesh blown away from Lexus

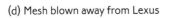

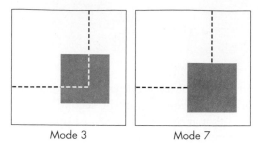

Mode 3   Mode 7

FIGURE 8.7   Writing in modes 3 and 7.

It simply replaces the value of the destination bit with the source. Mode 7 is the logical OR operation:

$$d \leftarrow s + d.$$

Figure 8.7 shows that these two writing modes can have different effects on the contents of the frame buffer. In this example, we write a dashed line into a frame buffer that already had a black (foreground colored) rectangle rendered into it. Both modes write the foreground color over the background color, but they differ if we try to write the background color over the foreground color. Which mode should be used depends on what effect the application programmer wishes to create.

8.3.2   Writing with XOR

Mode 6 is the exclusive-or operation XOR, denoted by $\oplus$; it is the most interesting of the writing modes. Unlike modes 3 and 7, mode 6 cannot be implemented without a read of the destination bit. The power of the XOR write mode comes from the property that, if s and d are binary variables, then

$$d = (d \oplus s) \oplus s.$$

Thus, if we apply XOR twice to a bit, we return that bit to its original state.

The most important applications of this mode involve interaction. In Chapter 3, we used XOR mode for rubberbanding. We can also use this mode to implement other operations that require the redrawing of parts of the display.

Consider what happens when we use menus in an interactive application, such as in our painting program from Chapter 3. In response to a mouse click, a menu appears, covering a portion of the screen. After the user indicates an action from the menu, the menu disappears, and the area of the screen that it covered is returned to that area's original state. What has transpired involves the use of off-screen memory, known as **backing store**. Suppose that the menu has been stored off-screen as an array of bits, M, and that the area of the screen where the menu appears is an array of bits, S. Consider the sequence of operations

$$S \leftarrow S \oplus M,$$

$$M \leftarrow S \oplus M,$$

$$S \leftarrow S \oplus M,$$

where we assume that the XOR operation is applied to corresponding bits in S and M. If we substitute the result of the first equation in the second and the result of the second in the third, we find that at the end of the three operations, the menu appears on the screen. The original contents of the screen, where the menu is now located, are now off-screen, where the menu was originally. We have swapped the menu with an area of the screen using three bitblt operations. This method of swapping is considerably different from the normal mode of swapping, which uses replacement-mode writing but requires temporary storage to effect the swap.

There are numerous variants of this technique. One is to move a cursor around the screen without affecting the area under it. Another is filling polygons with a solid color as part of scan conversion. Note that because many APIs trace their backgrounds to the days before raster displays became the norm, the XOR-write mode is not always available.

8.4 Bit and Pixel Operations in OpenGL

Digital images consist of k-bit pixels, where k can be any number from 1, for binary images, to 32, for RGBA images, to even greater numbers, for high-resolution color applications. Although, in principle, a 1-bit image, or **bitmap**, is the same type of entity as an 8-bit (1-byte) or 24-bit (3-byte) image, hardware and software often treat them differently. From the hardware perspective, bitmaps involve implementation of only logical operations, and they work one plane at a time in a buffer. From the software perspective, bitmaps are used differently from multibit images, even though both might use the same physical memory. Typically, bitmaps are used for fonts, masks, and patterns. OpenGL allows the user to work with either bitmaps or images of multibit pixels through two different sets of operations.

Bitblt operations make sense when we are working with 1-bit pixels, such as those used for fonts and cursors. It is less clear how to use these operations for multibit pixels and colors, because the bitwise result of the 16 operations does not usually translate into a visually sensible image, even though OpenGL allows us to use logic operations with any primitives. OpenGL supports logic operations through the `glLogicOp` functionality that we saw in Chapter 3.

Not only does OpenGL support a separate pixel pipeline and a variety of buffers, but also data can be moved among these buffers and between buffers and the processor memory. Depending on which buffer we are using, we can store information ranging from indices to color components to depths. In addition, we can store information in the processor memory in the standard data types

(bytes, integers, and floats). This plethora of formats and types can make writing efficient code for dealing with bits and pixels a difficult task. We shall not discuss all that here but instead shall look at what capabilities are supported.

8.4.1 OpenGL Buffers and the Pixel Pipeline

OpenGL can support various buffers, including the following:

- Color buffers
- Depth buffer
- Accumulation buffer
- Stencil buffer

The color buffers include the buffer whose contents are displayed on our output device, but as we saw in our discussion of double buffering in Chapter 3, the color buffers can include separate buffers for reading and writing. In double buffering, these color buffers are referred to as the **front** and **back buffers**. We may also want to produce stereo pairs of images, using **right** and **left buffers**, that contain the image as seen by the right and left eyes, respectively. For stereoscopic animations, we may want to employ four color buffers. Generally, we render geometric objects into the color buffers but we can also write pixels directly into, and can read pixels from, the buffers. Only color buffers can be made visible.

The depth buffer normally is used for hidden-surface removal, but we can also read data from it and write data to it. In Section 8.10, we show how the accumulation buffer can be used for a variety of operations that involve combining multiple images. The stencil buffer often is used for masking operations. For example, we can use the values in this buffer as a mask to determine whether a pixel in the color buffer should be written to the screen.

For now, we assume that we are working with a color buffer—typically the back buffer—although many of these operations can be applied to other buffers. Note that a given implementation may support only some of these buffers, and that the depth of a buffer is implementation-dependent.

OpenGL maintains a **raster position**. We can think of this position as defining an internal cursor, in screen coordinates, from which writing of raster primitives is measured. The raster position can be set by the variants of the function glRasterPos. For example, the function

```
glRasterPos3f(x, y, z);
```

describes a position by three floats that is subject to both the model-view and projection transformations before conversion to screen coordinates. This position is stored, like any other geometric entity, in four-dimensional homogeneous coordinates. However, once this position is transformed by the viewing pipeline to a position in screen coordinates, writing of pixels or bits takes place in raster units (integers), with the pixel centers located halfway between integers. Note

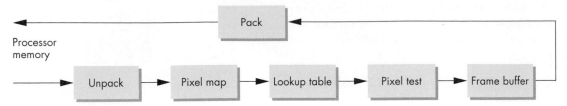

FIGURE 8.8   The OpenGL pixel pipeline.

that if the raster position is not inside the view volume, no drawing of pixels can take place; the entire bitmap or pixel rectangle is clipped out.

In OpenGL there is a **current drawing buffer** where pixel data from the user program are placed by draw operations and a **current read buffer** from which any pixel-read operation gets its data. Either could be any of the supported buffers. By default, they are both the back buffer in double buffer mode but can be changed by the glDrawBuffer and glReadBuffer functions.

As pixels make their way from processor memory—where they have been generated by the application—to one of the buffers in the frame buffer, a sequence of operations takes place. This sequence defines the pixel pipeline described in Figure 8.8. Although it may seem that pixels defined in the application should be able to go directly into an OpenGL buffer, in fact, they first go through the rasterizer and generate fragments, as do geometric primitives. This architecture allows for the uniform processing of geometric and discrete primitives, which is an advantage in applications that use both types.

The first operation, **unpacking**, converts pixels from the format in the user program to the format used internally by OpenGL. These new pixels can also be mapped into new values through user-defined lookup tables. The resulting pixels then pass through a series of tests that determine whether the pixel should be written into the frame buffer and, if it should be written, how it should be written. For example, we can mask out regions where no drawing will take place and use our logic operations to determine how to combine pixels with what is already in the buffer. If we read information from a buffer back to processor memory, we must convert (**pack**) the data from OpenGL's internal format to whatever format we want to use in our application.

8.4.2 Bitmaps

OpenGL treats arrays of 1-bit pixels (bitmaps) differently from multibit pixels (pixel maps) and provides different programming interfaces for the two cases. Bitmaps are used for fonts and for displaying cursors, often making use of the XOR writing mode. Both of these examples rely on the use of the present raster position to position the bitmap. Thus, once the bitmap is located in the present buffer, each bit in the bitmap corresponds to a pixel in this buffer. The bits in the bitmap are used as **masks** that determine whether the color of the pixel at that

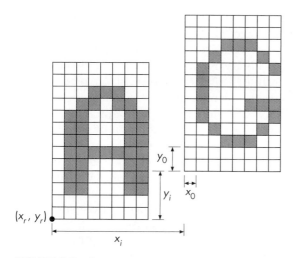

FIGURE 8.9 Outputting a bitmap.

location is to be altered. If a bit is 0, then the pixel is unchanged. If it is 1, then the pixel is changed based on the current **raster color** and the drawing mode. The raster color is set by glColor and is the same as the drawing color used for geometric primitives, except that the raster color is fixed by the last invocation of glRasterPos. Thus, suppose that a bit is positioned over a pixel that is red and the present raster color is green. If the bit has a value of 0, the pixel will remain red. If the bit has a value of 1 and we are in the default replacement write mode, then the red pixel will be changed to green. If, however, we were in XOR write mode, the new pixel color would be yellow, which is the result of the bitwise XOR between the 24-bit representations of the RGB colors red and green.

We place an array bitmap at the current raster position (assuming that this position is a valid location in the buffer) with the function

```
glBitmap(width, height, xo, yo, xi,yi, bitmap);
```

The width and height are in bits. The floating-point numbers xo and yo give an offset relative to the current raster position and give the position where the lower-left corner of the bitmap is to start (Figure 8.9); xi and yi are floating-point numbers used to move the raster position after the bitmap is drawn.

8.4.3 Raster Fonts

Raster fonts demonstrate the use of the raster position. In Chapter 3, we observed that raster text is much faster to render than is stroke text. In general, a **font**, or **typeface**, defines a set of characters of a particular family, such as Times, Courier,

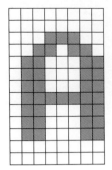

FIGURE 8.10 Definition of a character.

or Computer Modern. Each font can have various sizes, such as 10-point or 24-point,[3] and styles, such as bold or italic. However, we use the term *font* with *raster* to denote a set of characters of a particular size and style. Hence, an 8 × 13 font, as provided by the GLUT library, is denoted by GLUT_BITMAP_8_BY_13; a 10-point proportional font[4] is GLUT_BITMAP_TIMES_ROMAN_10. A typical font has 128 or 256 characters. Each character in a raster font is defined by a pattern of bits, as shown in Figure 8.10. Note that when we define a font as a pattern of bits, the size of text on the screen depends on the resolution of the screen—a relation that does not hold for the rendering of geometric objects.

Bitmapped fonts are designed both to fit in a certain space and to be readable. Thus, as we can see from Figure 8.10, in all but the smallest fonts, we must allow for vertical and horizontal spacing between characters; for room for descenders, as in the lowercase letters g and y; and for the size differences between uppercase and lowercase letters. Once we have designed a font, we can store it in an array as bits. For example, if we wish to define a 128-character 8 × 13 font, we can use an array

```
GLubyte my_font[128][13];
```

As we did in Chapter 3 (see Section 3.4), we can define a font using a display list for each character. Assuming that the array my_font has been defined, these display lists can be generated by the code [5]

```
base=glGenLists(128);
for(i=0; i<128; i++)
{
    glNewList(base+i, GL_COMPILE);
    glBitMap(8, 13, 0.0, 2.0, 10.0, 0.0, my_font[i]);
    glEndList();
}
```

In this example, note that each character is started 2 bits up from the current raster position, and the raster position is shifted 2 additional bits after the character is drawn, leaving a 2-bit horizontal and vertical separation between characters.

---

3. There are 72 points to 1 inch.
4. A *proportional font* is a font in which not all characters have the same width. In a *monotype font*, all characters have the same width.
5. We are, perhaps, wasting space by allocating memory for the first 32 ASCII characters. These characters are usually nonprinting characters, used only for control, and do not generate any visible output.

8.4.4   Pixels and Images

So that we can accommodate different types of images, in OpenGL, pixels can be handled as groups of 8-bit bytes in a variety of formats. For example, we can work with RGB images, where the value of each color component is stored as a single byte, or we can work with a monochrome (luminance) image, in which each pixel is a single floating-point number.

There are three functions for moving images in OpenGL:

```
glReadPixels(GLint x, GLint y, GLsizei width, GLsizei height,
             GLenum format, GLenum type, GLvoid *image)
glDrawPixels(GLsizei width, GLsizei height, GLenum format,
             GLenum type, GLvoid *image)
glCopyPixels(GLint x,GLint y, GLsizei width, GLsizei height, GLenum buffer)
```

The functions glReadPixels and glDrawPixels read and write rectangles of pixels between an OpenGL buffer and an array image in processor memory, whereas glCopyPixels reads a block of pixels starting with the lower-left corner at (x, y) from the frame buffer and copies them back into the frame buffer, starting at the current raster position. In glReadPixels, we can specify an offset (x, y) in the frame buffer where reading of the block of dimensions width and height should begin. Although, in most applications, we use the back color buffer, which is selected by default, we can use the functions glReadBuffer and glDrawBuffer to select any of OpenGL's buffers for reading and writing.

The format and type parameters describe the image in processor memory. Its format describes the kind of image (RGB, RBGA, color index), and its type is the data type used by the application (int, float). Thus, for the image we defined in Section 8.2, we had

```
GLubyte myimage[512][512][3]
```

to describe an RGB image. We could write this image into the present draw buffer by first setting the raster position

```
glRasterPos2i(startx, starty);
```

and then drawing the array

```
glDrawPixels(512, 512, GL_RGB, GL_UNSIGNED_BYTE, myimage);
```

There is another vexing problem that you may encounter. Different processors often have different methods for arranging information in memory. For example, processors differ as to which byte in a multibyte data type, such as an int, is the most significant byte. Some processors allow information to begin only on 4-byte boundaries. Consequently, the storage of an array such as myimage might differ on different computers. Such system-dependent features can affect

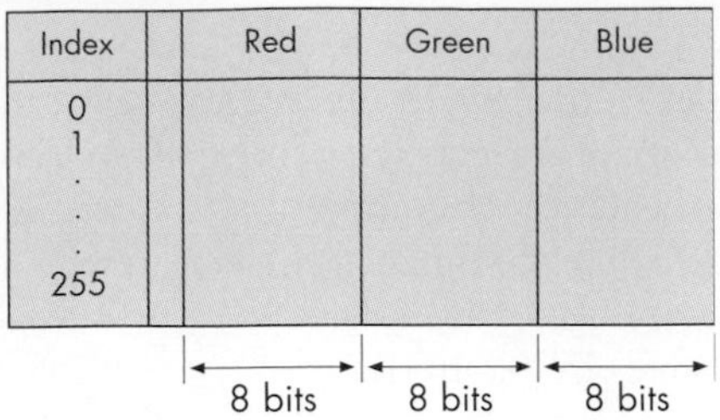

FIGURE 8.11   Lookup table for RGB.

OpenGL programs, especially when reading and writing pixels. OpenGL provides a function, `glPixelStore`, that allows the application program to describe how data should be packed and unpacked. Normally, the defaults in a system are set so that you will not need this function, but that is not always the case.

8.4.5 Lookup Tables

In OpenGL, all colors can be modified by lookup tables as they are placed into buffers. Suppose that a buffer contains 8-bit components. Then each component can have 256 possible values, and we can regard each of these values as an index into a 256-entry lookup table, as shown in Figure 8.11. If each value in the table is also 8 bits, then the index into the table selects a new value for the component. The tables are defaulted to provide an identity mapping of input values to output values. The function `glPixelMap` allows us to load user-defined maps.

These maps are essentially the same as the color lookup tables that we introduced in Chapter 2. If we make a correspondence between the color indices and the gray levels of a monochromatic (luminance) image, we can use these maps to enhance a display by converting gray levels to colors. An image colored in such a manner is called a **pseudocolor** image.

The major problem for the user is how to select the palette of 256 colors from the (typically) 2^{24} available RGB colors. One popular choice is based on a thermal scale, using hot colors (red, white, and yellow) for important values and cool colors (blues and greens) for unimportant values. For example, suppose that our grayscale image is such that the low values are least important and the high values are most important. Figure 8.12 shows a possible map of the gray levels to RGB that forms such a thermal scale. Color Plate 19 shows the use of a thermal scale in a scientific visualization. Here the colors represent temperatures in the mantle of the earth as generated by a computer model.

Another use of lookup tables is for color conversion and brightness adjustments. For example, the shading models that we use in computer graphics often generate images that are dark and lack contrast. If we were to plot the distribution of luminance values as a graph called a **histogram**, we might see a plot like

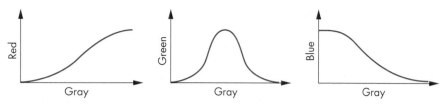

FIGURE 8.12   Thermal color map.

the one shown in Figure 8.13, which shows that the majority of the values are in the lower ranges. If we apply the lookup table in Figure 8.14 to each color, we map lower gray levels to higher (brighter) values and lighten the image. The distribution of levels for the resulting image is more uniform yet still spans the full range of luminance values, thus improving the contrast of the original image.

We can also use these tables for color conversion. As we discussed in Chapter 7, in most APIs, including OpenGL, the RGB values do not refer to any particular system. Often, if we photograph the image that is on the screen of a CRT, the resulting photographic print may look noticeably different from the image on the screen, due to the differences in the color properties of the film, the photographic paper, and the CRT and the perceptual characteristics of the viewer. We can use a lookup table for each of the R, G, and B components to make color adjustments, called **color balancing**, before we take the photograph. The lookup tables thus provide a method of color conversion across different RGB systems.

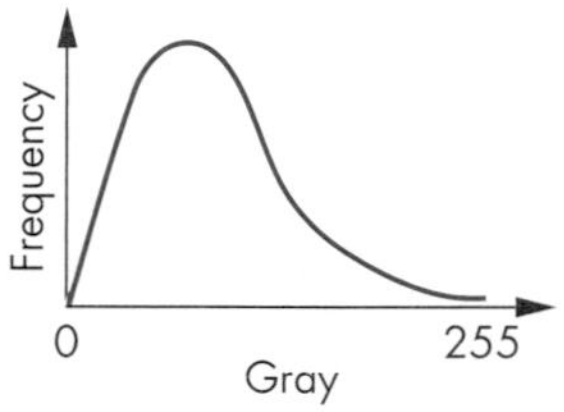

Operations such as histogram evaluation and using tables for color changes are core to the field of **image processing**. In Section 8.11, we shall investigate these and other imaging operations further and discuss how they can be supported within the OpenGL architecture.

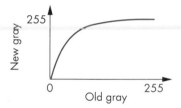

FIGURE 8.13   Histogram of a dark image.

FIGURE 8.14   Lookup table for lightening of an image.

8.5   Examples

We now consider three examples of writing pixels. The first, the construction of the Mandelbrot set, illustrates the use of lookup tables for displaying a luminance image. The second example will give you a simple method for testing algorithms, such as we developed in Chapter 7 by constructing a pseudo color buffer. The final example shows how buffers provide a simple alternative to the picking by selection approach that we introduced in Chapter 3.

8.5.1   The Mandelbrot Set

The famous Mandelbrot set is an interesting example of fractal geometry that can be generated easily with OpenGL's pixel drawing functionality. Although the Mandelbrot set is easy to generate, it shows infinite complexity in the patterns it generates. It also provides a good example of generating images and using color

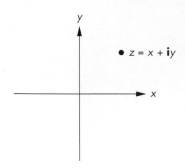

FIGURE 8.15 Complex plane.

lookup tables. In this discussion, we assume that you have a basic familiarity with complex arithmetic.

We denote a point in the complex plane as

$$\mathbf{z} = x + iy,$$

where x is the real part and y is the imaginary part of $\mathbf{z}$ (Figure 8.15). If $\mathbf{z}_1 = x_1 + iy_1$ and $\mathbf{z}_2 = x_2 + iy_2$ are two complex numbers, complex addition and multiplication are defined by

$$\mathbf{z}_1 + \mathbf{z}_2 = x_1 + x_1 + i(y_1 + y_2),$$
$$\mathbf{z}_1 \mathbf{z}_2 = x_1 x_2 - y_1 y_2 + i(x_1 y_2 + x_2 y_1).$$

The pure imaginary number $\mathbf{i}$ has the property that $\mathbf{i}^2 = -1$. A complex number $\mathbf{z}$ has magnitude given by

$$|\mathbf{z}|^2 = x^2 + y^2.$$

In the complex plane, a function

$$\mathbf{w} = F(\mathbf{z})$$

maps complex points into complex points. We can use such a function to define a complex recurrence of the form

$$\mathbf{z}_{k+1} = F(\mathbf{z}_k),$$

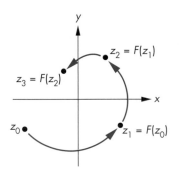

FIGURE 8.16 Paths from complex recurrence.

where $\mathbf{z}_0 = \mathbf{c}$ is a given initial point. If we plot the locations of $\mathbf{z}_k$ for particular starting points, we can see one of several possibilities in Figure 8.16. For a particular function F, some initial values generate sequences that go off to infinity. Others may repeat periodically, and still other sequences converge to points called **attractors**. For example, consider the function

$$\mathbf{z}_{k+1} = \mathbf{z}_k^2,$$

where $\mathbf{z}_0 = \mathbf{c}$. If $\mathbf{c}$ lies outside a unit circle, the sequence $\{\mathbf{z}_k\}$ diverges; if $\mathbf{c}$ is inside the unit circle, $\{\mathbf{z}_k\}$ converges to an attractor at the origin; if $|\mathbf{c}| = 1$, each $\mathbf{z}_k$ is on the unit circle. If we consider the points for which $|\mathbf{c}| = 1$, we can see that, depending on the value of $\mathbf{c}$, we can generate either a finite number of points or all the points on the unit circle.

A more interesting example is the function

$$\mathbf{z}_{k+1} = \mathbf{z}_k^2 + \mathbf{c},$$

with $\mathbf{z}_0 = 0 + i0$. The point $\mathbf{c}$ is in the **Mandelbrot set** if and only if the points generated by this recurrence remain finite. Thus, we can break the complex plane into two groups of points: those that belong to the Mandelbrot set and those that do not. Graphically, we can take a rectangular region of the plane and color points black if they are in the set and white if they are not (Figure 8.17(a)). However,

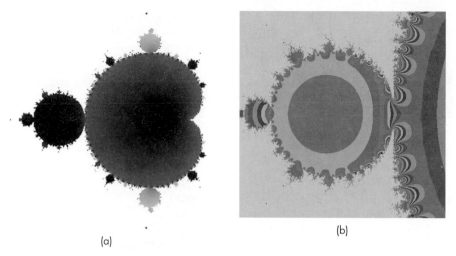

(a)   (b)

FIGURE 8.17   Mandelbrot set. (a) Black and white coloring. (b) Detail along edges.

it is the regions on the edges of the set that show the most complexity, so we often want to magnify these regions.

The computation of the Mandelbrot set can be time-consuming; there are a few tricks to speed it up. The area centered at $c = -0.5 + i0.0$ is of the most interest, although we probably want to be able to change both the size and the center of our window.

We can usually tell after a few iterations whether a point will go off to infinity. For example, if $|z_k| > 4$, successive values will be larger, and we can stop the iteration. It is more difficult to tell whether a point near the boundary will converge. Consequently, an approximation to the set is usually generated as follows. We fix a maximum number of iterations. If, for a given c, we can determine that the point diverges, we color white the point corresponding to c in our image. If after the maximum number of iterations, $|z_k|$ is less than some threshold, we decide that it is in the set and we color it black. For other values of $|z_k|$, we assign a unique color to the point corresponding to c. These colors are usually based on the value of $|z_k|$ after the last iteration.

Appendix A contains a program that generates an approximation to the set. The user can set the size and center of the rectangle and the number of iterations to be carried out. The magnitudes of the numbers z_k are scaled to be in the range of 0 to 255. We generate an $n \times m$ 1-byte array image by looping over all pixels up to the maximum number of iterations. The display consists of two parts. First, we define a color map in the initialization. The map shown uses a floating-point representation of the luminance values over the interval (0.0, 1.0). We define an intensity-to-red map that assigns no red to black (0.0), assigns full red to white (1.0), and linearly interpolates between these values for the other intensities. For blue, we go from full blue for zero intensity to no blue for full intensity. We assign the intensity-to-green values randomly. This green assignment enhances the detail in regions where there are slow changes in intensity (Figure 8.17(b)). The code is

```
for(i=0;i<256;i++)
{
    redmap[i]=i/255.;
    greenmap[i]=(rand()%256)/255.0; /* random number between 0.0 and 1.0 */
    bluemap[i]=1.0-i/255.;
}

glPixelMapfv(GL_PIXEL_MAP_I_TO_R, 256, redmap);
glPixelMapfv(GL_PIXEL_MAP_I_TO_G, 256, greenmap);
glPixelMapfv(GL_PIXEL_MAP_I_TO_B, 256, bluemap);
```

You should be able to implement other color maps with no difficulty. The display function requires only clearing of the screen and sending of the pixels to the frame buffer:

```
void display()
{
    glClear(GL_COLOR_BUFFER_BIT);
    glDrawPixels(n,m,GL_COLOR_INDEX, GL_UNSIGNED_BYTE, image);
}
```

8.5.2 Testing Algorithms

Another simple example of writing pixels is for testing some of the algorithms that we developed in Chapter 7. We can create a 500×500 window as part of our initialization and use the viewing settings

```
glMatrixMode(GL_PROJECTION);
glLoadIdentity;
gluOrtho2D(0.0, 500.0, 0.0, 500.0);
glViewport(0, 0, 500, 500);
```

Each execution of

```
GLubyte black[1][1][3]={0, 0, 0};
glRasterPos2i(ix, iy);
glDrawPixels(1, 1, GL_RGB, GL_UNSIGNED_BYTE, black);
```

will render a single black pixel at the specified location. Our draw_pixel function can be as simple as

```
void draw_pixel(int ix, int iy, int value)
{
    glRasterPos2i(ix, iy);
    glDrawPixels(1, 1, GL_RGB, GL_UNSIGNED_BYTE, value);
}
```

where `value` is a pointer into an array of RGB colors. Appendix A includes a program that uses Bresenham's algorithm in a 500×500 pseudo frame buffer.

8.5.3 Buffers for Picking

Buffers provide limitless opportunities for constructing and manipulating images. They can also be used interactively in ways that might not be apparent at first. Consider the problem of picking. In Chapter 3, we introduced the OpenGL mechanism that uses selection and hit lists to provide the information needed to identify objects on the display. This mechanism, although very general, required a fair amount of code to implement. If there are not too many distinct object identifiers, we can use buffers to provide an alternative picking mechanism, which is simpler to implement.

Suppose that we have no more than 256 identifiers (assuming 8-bit-deep buffers). As we render primitives, we place the identifier of the object being rendered into an extra buffer at a location corresponding to the location in the frame buffer where the fragment is rendered. Thus, the "colors" in this extra buffer are identifiers of objects located at corresponding pixels in the frame buffer. We can use OpenGL's pixel-reading functions to obtain these colors. Picking reduces to reading the value of this buffer at the pixel corresponding to the cursor location. This method will also work with 24-bit colors if we set up a table that maps the colors into object identifiers. If we combine this process with the z-buffer algorithm, then each pixel in this buffer has the identifier of the closest object to the camera along the ray through the pixel.

8.6 Mapping Methods

One of the most powerful uses of discrete data is for surface rendering. The process of modeling an object by a set of geometric primitives and then rendering these primitives has its limitations. Consider, for example, the task of creating a virtual orange by computer. Our first attempt might be to start with a sphere. From our discussion in Chapter 6, we know that we can build an approximation to a sphere out of triangles and can render these triangles using material properties that match those of a real orange. Unfortunately, such a rendering would be far too regular to look much like an orange. We could instead follow the path that we shall explore in Chapter 11: We could try to model the orange with some sort of curved surface, and then render the surface. This procedure would give us more control over the shape of our virtual orange, but the image produced still would not look right. Although it might have the correct overall properties, such as shape and color, it would lack the fine surface detail of a real orange. If we attempt to add this detail by adding more polygons to our model, even with hardware capable of rendering tens of millions of polygons per second, we can still overwhelm the pipeline.

An alternative is not to attempt to build increasingly more complex models but rather to build a simple model and add detail as part of the rendering process. As we saw in Chapter 7, as the implementation renders a surface—be it a polygon or a curved surface—it generates sets of fragments, each of which corresponds to a pixel in the frame buffer. Fragments carry color, depth, and other information that can be used to determine how they contribute to the pixels to which they correspond. As part of the rasterization process, we must assign a shade or color to each fragment. We started in Chapter 6 by using the modified Phong model to determine vertex colors that could be interpolated across surfaces. However, these colors can be modified during fragment processing after rasterization. The mapping algorithms can be thought of as either modifying the shading algorithm based on a two-dimensional array, the map, or as modifying the shading by using the map to alter surface parameters, such as material properties and normals. There are three major techniques:

- Texture mapping
- Bump mapping
- Environment mapping

Texture mapping uses a pattern (or texture) to determine the color of a fragment. These patterns could be determined by a fixed pattern, such as the regular patterns often used to fill polygons; by a procedural texture-generation method; or through a digitized image. In all cases, we can characterize the image produced by a mapping of a texture to the surface, as shown in Figure 8.18, as part of the rendering of the surface.

Whereas texture maps give detail by painting patterns onto smooth surfaces, **bump maps** distort the normal vectors during the shading process to make the surface appear to have small variations in shape, such as the bumps on a real orange. **Reflection maps**, or **environment maps**, allow us to create images that

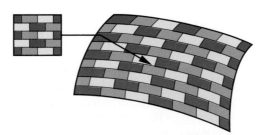

FIGURE 8.18   Texture-mapping a pattern to a surface.

have the appearance of ray-traced images without our having to trace reflected rays. In this case, an image of the environment is painted onto the surface as that surface is being rendered.

The three mapping methods have much in common. All three alter the shading of individual fragments as part of fragment processing. All rely on the map being stored as a one-, two-, or three-dimensional digital image. All keep the geometric complexity low while creating the illusion of complex geometry. However, all are also subject to aliasing errors.

There are various examples of two-dimensional mappings in the color plates. Color Plate 7 was created using an OpenGL environment map and shows how a single texture map can create the illusion of a highly reflective surface while avoiding global calculations. Color Plate 23 uses a texture map for the surface of the table; Color Plate 10 uses texture mapping to create a brick pattern. Much of the detail in Color Plate 15 is from a texture map. In these virtual reality and visualization simulations, real-time performance is required. When these simulations are executed on workstations with hardware texture mapping, texture mapping allows the detail to be added without significantly degrading the rendering time.

However, in terms of the standard fixed-function OpenGL pipeline, there are significant differences among the three techniques. Standard texture mapping is supported by the basic OpenGL pipeline and makes use of both the geometric and pixel pipelines. Environment maps are a special case of standard texture mapping but can be altered to create a variety of new effects if we can alter fragment processing, as we shall discuss in Chapter 9. Bump mapping requires us to process each fragment independently, so we shall delay discussion of this technique until Chapter 9.

8.7 Texture Mapping

Textures are patterns. They can range from regular patterns, such as stripes and checkerboards, to the complex patterns that characterize natural materials. In the real world, we can distinguish among objects of similar size and shape by their textures. Thus, if we want to create detailed virtual objects, we can extend our present capabilities by placing, or mapping, a texture to the objects that we create.

Textures can be one-, two-, three-, or four-dimensional. For example, a one-dimensional texture might be used to create a pattern for coloring a curve. A three-dimensional texture might describe a solid block of material from which we could sculpt an object. Because the use of surfaces is so important in computer graphics, mapping two-dimensional textures to surfaces is by far the most common use of texture mapping and will be the only form of texture mapping that we shall consider in detail. However, the processes by which we map these entities is much the same regardless of the dimensionality of the texture, and we lose little by concentrating on two-dimensional texture mapping.

8.7.1 Two-Dimensional Texture Mapping

Although there are multiple approaches to texture mapping, all require a sequence of steps that involve mappings among three or four different coordinate systems. At various stages in the process, we shall be working with window coordinates, where the final image is produced; object coordinates, where we describe the objects upon which the textures will be mapped; texture coordinates, which we use to locate positions in the texture; and parametric coordinates, which we use to help us define curved surfaces. Methods differ according to the types of surfaces we are using and the type of rendering architecture we have. Our approach will be to start with a fairly general discussion of texture, introducing the various mappings, and then to show how texture mapping is handled by a real-time pipeline architecture, such as that employed by OpenGL.

In most applications, textures start out as two-dimensional images of the sorts we introduced in Section 8.2. Thus, they might be formed by application programs or scanned in from a photograph, but regardless of their origin, they are eventually brought into processor memory as arrays. We call the elements of these arrays **texels**, or texture elements, rather than pixels to emphasize how they will be used. However, at this point, we prefer to think of this array as a continuous, rectangular, two-dimensional texture pattern $T(s, t)$. The independent variables s and t are known as **texture coordinates**.[6] With no loss of generality, we can scale our texture coordinates to vary over the interval $(0,1)$.

A **texture map** associates a texel with each point on a geometric object that is itself mapped to screen coordinates for display. If the object is represented in homogeneous or (x, y, z, w) coordinates, then there are functions such that

$$x = x(s, t),$$
$$y = y(s, t),$$
$$z = z(s, t),$$
$$w = w(s, t).$$

One of the difficulties we must confront is that although these functions exist conceptually, finding them may not be possible in practice. In addition, we are worried about the inverse problem: Having been given a point (x, y, z) or (x, y, z, w) on an object, how do we find the corresponding texture coordinates, or equivalently the "inverse" functions

$$s = s(x, y, z, w),$$
$$t = t(x, y, z, w),$$

to use to find the texel $T(s, t)$?

---

6. In four dimensions, the coordinates are in (s, t, r, q) space.

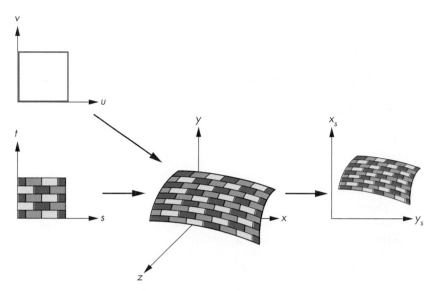

FIGURE 8.19 Texture maps for a parametric surface.

If we define the geometric object using parametric (u, v) surfaces, such as we did for the sphere in Section 6.4, there is an additional mapping function that gives object coordinate values, (x, y, z) or (x, y, z, w) in terms of u and v. Although this mapping is known for simple surfaces, such as spheres and triangles, and for the surfaces that we shall discuss in Chapter 11, we also need the mapping from parametric coordinates (u, v) to texture coordinates and sometimes the inverse mapping from texture coordinates to parametric coordinates.

We also have to consider the projection process that takes us from object coordinates to window coordinates. We can think of a function that takes a texture coordinate pair (s, t) and tells us where in the color buffer the corresponding value of $T(s, t)$ will make its contribution to the final image. Thus, there is a mapping of the form

$$x_s = x_s(s, t),$$
$$y_s = y_s(s, t)$$

into coordinates, where (x_s, y_s) is a location in the color buffer.

Depending on the algorithm and the rendering architecture, we might also want the function that takes us from a pixel in the color buffer to the texel that makes a contribution to the color of that pixel.

One way to think about texture mapping is in terms of two concurrent mappings (Figure 8.9): the first from texture coordinates to object coordinates, and the second from parametric coordinates to object coordinates. A third mapping takes us to screen coordinates.

Conceptually, the texture-mapping process is simple. A small area of the texture pattern maps to the area of the geometric surface, corresponding to a pixel in the final image. If we assume that the values of T are RGB color values, we can use these values either to modify the color of the surface or to assign a color to the surface based on only the texture value. This color assignment is carried out as part of the assignment of fragment colors.

On closer examination, we face a number of difficulties. First, we must determine the map from texture coordinates to object coordinates. A two-dimensional texture is usually defined over a rectangular region in texture space. The mapping from this rectangle to an arbitrary region in three-dimensional space may be a complex function or may have undesirable properties. For example, if we wish to map a rectangle to a sphere, we cannot do so without distortion of shapes and distances. Second, owing to the nature of the rendering process, which works on a pixel-by-pixel basis, we are more interested in the inverse map from window coordinates to texture coordinates. It is when we are determining the shade of a pixel that we must determine what point in the texture image to use—a calculation that requires us to go from window coordinates to texture coordinates. Third, because each pixel corresponds to a small rectangle on the display, we are interested in mapping not points to points but rather areas to areas. Here again is a potential aliasing problem that we must treat carefully if we are to avoid artifacts, such as wavy sinusoidal or moiré patterns.

Figure 8.20 shows several of the difficulties. Suppose that we are computing a color for the square pixel centered at screen coordinates (x_s, y_s). The center (x_s, y_s) corresponds to a point (x, y, z) in object space, but if the object is curved, the projection of the corners of the pixel backward into object space yields a curved **preimage** of the pixel. In terms of the texture image $T(s, t)$, projecting the pixel back yields a preimage in texture space that is the area of the texture that should contribute to the shading of the pixel.

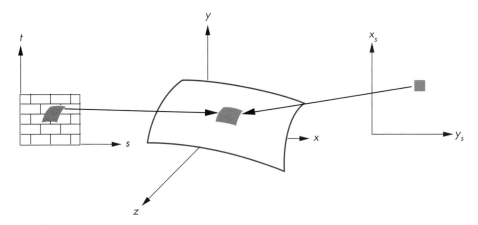

FIGURE 8.20   Preimages of a pixel.

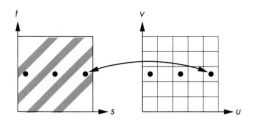

FIGURE 8.21   Aliasing in texture generation.

Let's put aside for a moment the problem of how we find the inverse map and look at the determination of colors. One possibility is to use the location that we get by back projection of the pixel center to find a texture value. Although this technique is simple, it is subject to serious aliasing problems, which are especially visible if the texture is periodic. Figure 8.21 illustrates the aliasing problem. Here we have a repeated texture and a flat surface. The back projection of the center of each pixel happens to fall in between the dark lines, and the texture value is always the lighter color. More generally, not taking into account the finite size of a pixel can lead to moiré patterns in the image. A better strategy—but one more difficult to implement—is to assign a texture value based on averaging the texture map over the preimage. Note that this method is imperfect too. For the example in Figure 8.21, we would assign an average shade, but we would still not get the striped pattern of the texture. Ultimately, we still have aliasing defects due to the limited resolution of both the frame buffer and the texture map. These problems are most visible when there are regular high-frequency components in the texture.

Now we can turn to the mapping problem. In computer graphics, most curved surfaces are represented parametrically. A point $\mathbf{p}$ on the surface is a function of two parameters u and v. For each pair of values, we generate the point

$$\mathbf{p}(u, v) = \begin{bmatrix} x(u, v) \\ y(u, v) \\ z(u, v) \end{bmatrix}.$$

In Chapter 11, we study in detail the derivation of such surfaces. Given a parametric surface, we can often map a point in the texture map $T(s, t)$ to a point on the surface $\mathbf{p}(u, v)$ by a linear map of the form

$$u = as + bt + c,$$
$$v = ds + et + f.$$

As long as $ae \neq bd$, this mapping is invertible. Linear mapping makes it easy to map a texture to a group of parametric surface patches. Looking at the example shown in Figure 8.22, if the patch determined by the corners (s_{min}, t_{min}) and (s_{max}, t_{max}) corresponds to the surface patch with corners (u_{min}, v_{min}) and (u_{max}, v_{max}), then the mapping is

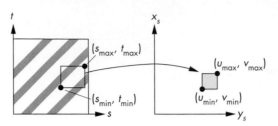

FIGURE 8.22   Linear texture mapping.

$$u = u_{min} + \frac{s - s_{min}}{s_{max} - s_{min}}(u_{max} - u_{min}),$$

$$v = v_{min} + \frac{t - t_{min}}{t_{max} - t_{min}}(v_{max} - v_{min}).$$

This mapping is easy to apply, but it does not take into account the curvature of the surface. Equal-sized texture patches must be stretched to fit over the surface patch.

Another approach to the mapping problem is to use a two-part mapping. The first step maps the texture to a simple three-dimensional intermediate surface, such as a sphere, cylinder, or cube. In the second step, the intermediate surface containing the mapped texture is mapped to the surface being rendered. This two-step mapping process can be applied to surfaces defined in either geometric or parametric coordinates. The following example is essentially the same in either system.

Suppose that our texture coordinates vary over the unit square and that we use the surface of a cylinder of height h and radius r as our intermediate object, as shown in Figure 8.23. Points on the cylinder are given by the parametric equations

$$x = r\cos(2\pi u),$$
$$y = r\sin(2\pi u),$$
$$z = v/h,$$

as u and v vary over $(0, 1)$. Hence, we can use the mapping

$$s = u,$$
$$t = v.$$

By using only the curved part of the cylinder and not the top and bottom, we were able to map the texture without distorting its shape. However, if we map to a closed object, such as a sphere, we must introduce shape distortion. This problem is similar to the problem of creating a two-dimensional image of the earth for a map. If you look at the various maps of the earth in an atlas, all distort shapes and distances. Both texture-mapping and map-design techniques must choose among a variety of representations, based on where we wish to

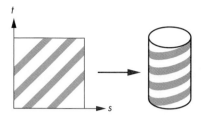

FIGURE 8.23   Texture mapping with a cylinder.

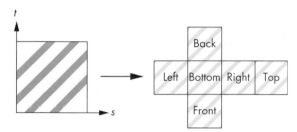

FIGURE 8.24   Texture mapping with a box.

place the distortion. For example, the familiar Mercator projection puts the most distortion at the poles. If we use a sphere of radius r as the intermediate surface, a possible mapping is

$$x = r \cos(2\pi u),$$
$$y = r \sin(2\pi u) \cos(2\pi v),$$
$$z = r \sin(2\pi u) \sin(2\pi v).$$

We can also use a rectangular box, as shown in Figure 8.24. Here we map the texture to a box that can be unraveled, like a cardboard packing box. This mapping is often used with environment maps (Section 8.10).

The second step is to map the texture values on the intermediate object to the desired surface. Figure 8.25 shows three possible strategies. In Figure 8.25(a), we take the texture value at a point on the intermediate object, go from this point in the direction of the normal until we intersect the object, and then place the texture value at the point of intersection. We could also reverse this method, starting at a point on the surface of the object and going in the direction of the normal at this point until we intersect the intermediate object, where we obtain the texture value, as shown in Figure 8.25(b). A third option, if we know the center of the object, is to draw a line from the center through a point on the object and calculate the intersection of this line with the intermediate surface, as shown in Figure 8.25(c). The texture at the point of intersection with the intermediate object is assigned to the corresponding point on the desired object.

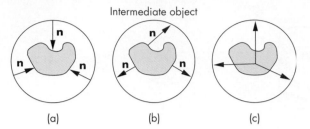

Intermediate object

(a) (b) (c)

FIGURE 8.25 Second mapping. (a) Using the normal from the intermediate surface. (b) Using the normal from the object surface. (c) Using the center of the object.

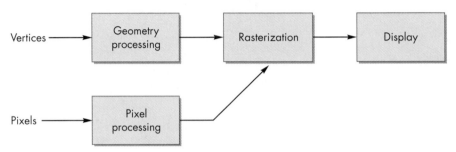

FIGURE 8.26 Pixel and geometry pipelines.

8.8 Texture Mapping in OpenGL

OpenGL supports a variety of texture-mapping options. The first version of OpenGL contained the functionality to map one- and two-dimensional textures to one- through four-dimensional graphical objects. Mapping of three-dimensional textures is now part of OpenGL and is supported by most hardware. Because of the many options and parameters, we focus on mapping two-dimensional textures to surfaces.

OpenGL's texture maps rely on its pipeline architecture. We have seen that there are actually two parallel pipelines: the geometric pipeline and the pixel pipeline. For the display of bitmaps and pixel rectangles, the pipelines merge during rasterization. For texture mapping, the pixel pipeline merges with fragment processing after rasterization, as shown in Figure 8.26. This architecture determines the type of texture mapping that is supported. In particular, texture mapping is done as fragments are colored. Each fragment generated is then tested for visibility with the z buffer. We can think of texture mapping as a part of the shading process, but a part that is done on a fragment-by-fragment basis. Texture coordinates are handled much like normals and colors. They are associated with vertices through the OpenGL state, and the required texture values can then be obtained by interpolating the texture coordinates at the vertices across polygons.

8.8.1   Two-Dimensional Texture Mapping

Two-dimensional texture mapping starts with an array of texels, which is the same as a two-dimensional pixel rectangle. Suppose that we have a 512×512 image my_texels that was generated by our program, or perhaps was read in from a file into an array

```
GLubyte my_texels[512][512][3];
```

We specify that this array is to be used as a two-dimensional texture (usually as part of our initialization) by

```
glTexImage2D(GL_TEXTURE_2D, 0, GL_RGB, 512, 512, 0,
          GL_RGB, GL_UNSIGNED_BYTE, my_texels);
```

More generally, two-dimensional textures are specified through the functions

```
glTexImage2D*(GLenum target, GLint level, GLint iformat,
          GLsizei width, GLsizei height, GLint border, GLenum format,
          GLenum type, GLvoid *tarray)
```

The texture pattern is stored in the width × height array tarray. The format of this image is described by the following two parameters. The value of iformat specifies the color components that we wish to store with the map. Many of these parameters are the same as the parameters we used to describe how pixel arrays are stored in processor memory for reading and writing with glReadPixels and glWritePixels. This similarity is expected because arrays of texels start in processor memory as arrays of pixels that are moved through the pixel pipeline. However, the pixels that move through the pixel pipeline as a result of the execution of the function glTexImage2D end up in texture memory, which is not part of the frame buffer. In modern graphics systems, the three types of memory—processor memory, the frame buffer, and texture memory—are often physically separate, each with its own characteristics and limitations.

The parameters level and border give us fine control over how texture is handled. We defer our discussion of these parameters. We must also enable texture mapping, as we do other options, through

```
glEnable(GL_TEXTURE_2D);
```

The second part of setting up a texture mapping is to specify how the texture is mapped onto a geometric object. OpenGL uses two coordinates, s and t, both of which range over the interval $(0.0, 1.0)$ over the texture image. For our example, the value $(0.0, 0.0)$ corresponds to the texel my_texels[0][0], and $(1.0, 1.0)$ corresponds to the texel my_texels[511][511], as shown in Figure 8.27. Any values of s and t in the unit interval correspond to a unique texel. OpenGL provides two options for how to deal with values outside the unit interval, which we shall discuss shortly.

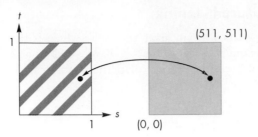

FIGURE 8.27   Mapping to texture coordinates.

OpenGL leaves the mapping of texture coordinates to vertices to the application by having the values of s and t as part of the OpenGL state. These values are assigned by the function

```
glTexCoord2f(s,t);
```

Thus, we use a mechanism similar to what we have used for colors and normal vectors. The renderer uses the present texture coordinates when processing a vertex. If we want to change the texture coordinate assigned to a vertex, we must set the texture coordinate before we specify the vertex. For example, if we want to assign our texture to a quadrilateral, then we use code such as

```
glBegin(GL_QUADS);
 glTexCoord2f(0.0,0.0);
 glVertex3f(x1, y1, z1);
 glTexCoord2f(1.0,0.0);
 glVertex3f(x2, y2, z2);
 glTexCoord2f(1.0,1.0);
 glVertex3f(x3, y3, z3);
 glTexCoord2f(0.0,1.0);
 glVertex3f(x4, y4, z4);
glEnd();
```

We also could set new normals or colors before we specify each vertex. OpenGL then uses interpolation to find the texture coordinates for the interior points of a polygon, just as it uses bilinear interpolation to determine interior colors from vertex colors.

In the example shown in Figure 8.28(a), we use the whole texture on a rectangle. If we used only part of the range of s and t, for example, $(0.0, 0.5)$, we would use only part of my_texels for the texture map, and would get an image like that in Figure 8.28(b). OpenGL interpolates s and t across the quadrilateral, then maps these values back to the appropriate texel in my_texels. The quadrilateral example is simple because there is an obvious mapping of texture coordinates to vertices. For general polygons, the application programmer must decide how to assign the texture coordinates. Figure 8.29 shows a few of the possibilities

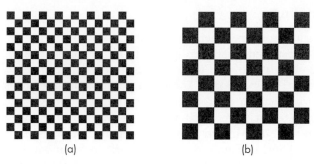

FIGURE 8.28 Mapping of a checkerboard texture to a quadrilateral. (a) Using the entire texel array. (b) Using part of the texel array.

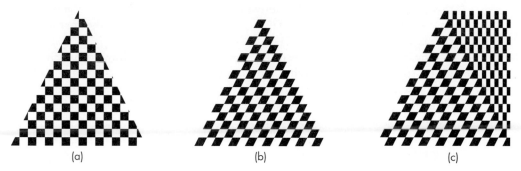

FIGURE 8.29 Mapping of texture to polygons. (a and b) Mapping of a checkerboard texture to a triangle. (c) Mapping of a checkerboard texture to a trapezoid.

with the same texture map. Figures 8.29(a) and (b) use the same triangle but different texture coordinates. Note the artifacts of the interpolation and how quadrilaterals are treated as two triangles as they are rendered in Figure 8.29(c).

The basics of OpenGL texture mapping are simple: Specify an array of colors for the texture values, then assign texture coordinates. Unfortunately, there are a few nasty details that we must discuss before we can use texture effectively. Solving the resulting problems involves making trade-offs between quality of the images and efficiency.

One problem is how to interpret a value of s or t outside of the range (0.0, 1.0). Generally, we want the texture either to repeat if we specify values outside this range or to clamp the values to 0.0 or 1.0—that is, we want to use the values at 0.0 and 1.0 for values below and above the interval (0.0, 1.0), respectively. For repeated textures, we set these parameters via

```
glTexParameteri(GL_TEXTURE_WRAP_S, GL_REPEAT);
```

For t, we use `GL_TEXTURE_WRAP_T`; for clamping, we use `GL_CLAMP`.

8.8.2 Texture Sampling

Aliasing of textures is a major problem. When we map texture coordinates to the array of texels, we rarely get a point that corresponds to the center of a texel. One option is to use the value of the texel that is closest to the one computed by the bilinear interpolation. This option is known as **point sampling** but is the one most subject to visible aliasing errors. A better strategy, although one that requires more work, is to use a weighted average of a group of texels in the neighborhood of the texel determined by point sampling. This option is known as **linear filtering**. Thus, in Figure 8.30, we see the location within a texel that is given by bilinear interpolation from the texture coordinates at the vertices and the four texels that would be used to obtain a smoother value. If we are using linear filtering, there is a problem at the edges of the texel array because we need additional texel values outside the array. We can get around this problem by adding a 1-texel-wide border around the texture and setting border in glTexImage2d to 1. Thus, if there is a border, then the texture array consists of $(2^m + 2) \times (2^n + 2)$ texels.

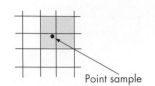

FIGURE 8.30 Texels used with linear filtering.

There is a further complication, however, in deciding how to use the texel values to obtain a texture value. The size of the pixel that we are trying to color on the screen may be smaller or larger than one texel, as shown in Figure 8.31.

In the first case, the texel is larger than one pixel (**magnification**); in the second, it is smaller (**minification**). In both cases, the fastest strategy is to use the value of the nearest point sampling. We can specify this option for both magnification and minification of textures by

```
glTexParameteri(GL_TEXTURE_2D, GL_TEXTURE_MAG_FILTER, GL_NEAREST);
glTexParameteri(GL_TEXTURE_2D, GL_TEXTURE_MIN_FILTER, GL_NEAREST);
```

Alternatively, we can use filtering to obtain a smoother, less aliased image if we specify GL_LINEAR instead of GL_NEAREST.

OpenGL has another way to deal with the minification problem; it is called **mipmapping**. For objects that project to an area of screen space that is small compared with the size of the texel array, we do not need the resolution of

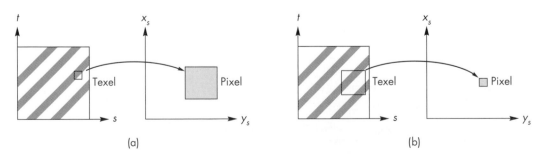

FIGURE 8.31 Mapping texels to pixels. (a) Magnification. (b) Minification.

the original texel array. OpenGL allows us to create a series of texture arrays at reduced sizes; it will then automatically use the appropriate size. For a 64×64 original array, we can set up 32×32, 16×16, 8×8, 4×4, 2×2, and 1×1 arrays through the GLU function:

```
gluBuild2DMipmaps(GL_TEXTURE_2D, GL_RGB, 64, 64, GL_RGB,
   GL_UNSIGNED_BYTE, my_texels);
```

We can also set up the maps directly using the level parameter in glTexImage2D. This parameter is the level in the mipmap hierarchy for the specified texture array. Thus, level 0 refers to the original image, level 1 to the image at half resolution, and so on. However, we can give a pointer to any image in different calls to glTexImage2D and thus can have entirely different images used at different levels of the mipmap hierarchy. These mipmaps are invoked automatically if we specify

```
glTexParameteri(GL_TEXTURE_2D,
   GL_TEXTURE_MIN_FILTER,GL_NEAREST_MIPMAP_NEAREST);
```

This option asks OpenGL to use point sampling with the best mipmap. We can also do filtering within the best mipmap (GL_NEAREST_MIPMAP_LINEAR), do point sampling using linear filtering between mipmaps (GL_LINEAR_MIPMAP_NEAREST), or use both filters (GL_LINEAR_MIPMAP_LINEAR). Figure 8.32 shows the differences in mapping a texture using the nearest texel, linear filtering, and mipmapping, both with use of the nearest texel and with linear filtering. The object is a quadrilateral that appears almost as a triangle when shown in perspective. The texture is a series of black and white lines applied so that the lines converge at the far side of the quadrilateral. Note that this texture map, because of its regularity, shows dramatic aliasing effects. The use of the nearest texel shows moiré patterns and jaggedness in the lines. Using linear filtering makes the lines smoother, but there are still clear moiré patterns. The texels between the black and white stripes are gray because of the filtering. Mipmapping also replaces many of the blacks and whites of the two-color patterns with grays that are the average of the two color values. For the parts of the object that are farthest from the viewer, the texels are gray and blend with the background. The mipmapped texture using the nearest texel in the proper mipmap still shows the jaggedness that is smoothed out when we use linear filtering with the mipmap. Advances in the speed of graphics processors (GPUs) and the inclusion of large amounts of texture memory in these GPUs often allows applications to use filtering and mipmapping without a performance penalty.

A final issue in using textures in OpenGL is the interaction between texture and shading. For RGB colors, there are multiple options. The texture can modulate the shade that we would have assigned without texture mapping by multiplying the color components of the texture by the color components from the shader. Modulation is the default mode; it can be set by

```
glTexEnvi(GL_TEX_ENV, GL_TEX_ENV_MODE, GL_MODULATE);
```

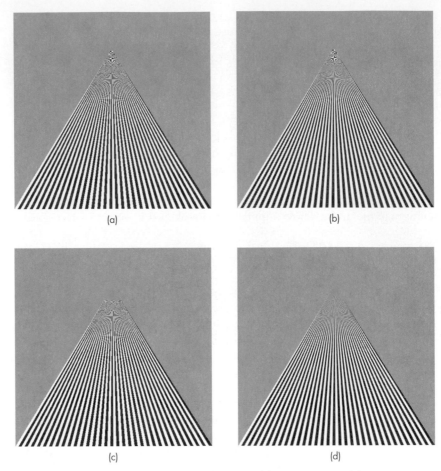

FIGURE 8.32   Texture mapping to a quadrilateral. (a) Point sampling. (b) Linear filtering. (c) Mipmapping point sampling. (d) Mipmapping linear filtering.

If we replace `GL_MODULATE` by `GL_DECAL`, the color of the texture determines the color of the object completely—a technique called **decaling**.

Proper texture mapping also depends on what type of projection is used. Normally, OpenGL uses bilinear interpolation in screen space to find a texture value. For orthogonal projections the bilinear map is correct, but it is not correct for perspective projections, because of the nonlinear depth scaling. We can ask OpenGL to employ a better interpolation scheme (if one is supported by the implementation) at a time penalty by

```
glHint(GL_PERSPECTIVE_CORRECTION, GL_NICEST);
```

With all recent graphics cards, correct perspective interpolation is the default and is supported by the GPU.

8.8.3 Working with Texture Coordinates

Our examples so far have assumed implicitly that we know how to assign texture coordinates. If we work with rectangular polygons of the same size, then it is fairly easy to assign coordinates. We can also use the fact that texture coordinates are stored as four-dimensional arrays, just as vertices are. The texture coordinates can be transformed by a 4×4 **texture matrix**. This matrix is initially set to an identity matrix and is manipulated in the same manner as the model-view and projection matrices. We use the texture matrix by first setting the current matrix mode by

```
glMatrixMode(GL_TEXTURE);
```

We can use this matrix to scale and orient textures and to create effects in which the texture moves with the object, the camera, or the lights.

However, if a set of polygons is an approximation to a curved object, then assigning texture coordinates is far more difficult. Consider the polygonal approximation of the Utah teapot[7] in Figure 8.33. Although the model uses only quadrilaterals, these quadrilaterals differ in size, with smaller quadrilaterals in areas where the object has higher curvature and larger quadrilaterals in flatter areas. Figure 8.34 shows our checkerboard texture mapped to the teapot without making any adjustment for the different sizes of the polygons. As we can see, by assigning the same set of texture coordinates to each polygon, the texture mapping processes adjusts to the individual sizes of the polygons by scaling the texture map as needed. Hence, in areas such as the handle, where many small polygons are needed to give a good approximation to the curved surface, the black and white boxes are small compared to those on the body of the teapot. In some applications, these patterns are acceptable. However, if all surfaces of the teapot were made from the same material, we would expect to see the same pattern on all its parts. In principle, we could use the texture matrix to scale texture coordinates to achieve the desired display. However, in practice, it is almost impossible to determine the necessary information from the model to form the matrix.

OpenGL provides some advanced texture features that can help with this problem. We can use the function glTexGen to generate texture coordinates automatically. We can have OpenGL compute texture coordinates for each vertex in terms of the distance from a plane in either eye coordinates or object coordinates. Mathematically, each texture coordinate is given as a linear combination of the homogeneous coordinate values. Thus, for s and t,

$$s = a_s x + b_s y + c_s z + d_s w,$$
$$t = a_t x + b_t y + c_t z + d_t w.$$

---

7. We shall discuss the Utah teapot in detail in Chapter 11.

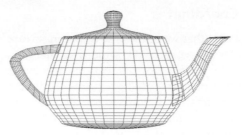

FIGURE 8.33   Polygonal model of Utah teapot.

FIGURE 8.34   Texture-mapped Utah teapot.

We specify the coefficients as arrays and then send them to OpenGL through glTexGen as follows:

```
GLfloat planes[] = {0.5, 0.0, 0.0, 0.5}; /* s = x/2+1/2 */
GLfloat planet[] = {0.0, 0.5, 0.0, 0.5}; /* t = y/2+1/2 */
glTexGeni(GL_S, GL_TEXTURE_GEN_MODE, GL_OBJECT_LINEAR);
glTexGeni(GL_T, GL_TEXTURE_GEN_MODE, GL_OBJECT_LINEAR);
glTexGenfv(GL_S, GL_OBJECT_LINEAR, planes);
glTexGenfv(GL_T, GL_OBJECT_LINEAR, planet);
```

The first two calls to TexGen identify the texture coordinate and the space to compute the distance. The second two calls provide the coefficients. We also have to enable automatic texture generation for each texture coordinate:

```
glEnable(GL_TEXTURE_GEN_S);
glEnable(GL_TEXTURE_GEN_T);
```

Figure 8.35(a) shows the teapot with automatic texture coordinate generation using GL_OBJECT_LINEAR. Figure 8.35(b) uses the same equations but with the calculations in eye space (GL_EYE_LINEAR). By doing the calculation in object space, the texture is fixed to the object and thus will rotate with the object. Using eye space, the texture pattern changes as we apply transformations to the object and give the illusion of the object moving through a texture field. One of the important applications of this technique is in terrain generation and mapping. We can map surface features as textures directly onto a three-dimensional mesh.

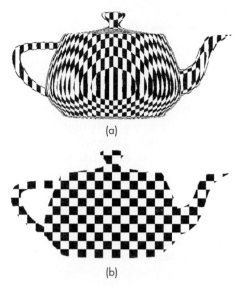

(a)

(b)

FIGURE 8.35 Teapot using automatic texture coordinate generation. (a) In object coordinates. (b) In eye coordinates.

8.8.4 Texture Objects

In OpenGL, there is a single *current texture* of each type (1D, 2D, 3D) that is part of the OpenGL state. Thus, if we need multiple textures—for example, if we want to apply different textures to different surfaces in the same scene—we can use glTexImage2D each time that another texture is used. This process is very inefficient. Each time glTexImage2D is executed, another texture image is loaded into texture memory, replacing the texels that were already there. Even if there is sufficient texture memory (and texture mapping can require a great deal of memory), this problem still exists.

OpenGL 1.1 introduced **texture objects** that allow the application program to define objects that consist of the texture array and the various texture parameters that control its application to surfaces. As long as there is sufficient memory to retain them, these objects reside in texture memory even though the present texture changes. If there is not sufficient texture memory, the application can prioritize the texture objects so as to control which ones are removed from memory first.

To create a two-dimensional texture object, we call the function glBindTexture first, as in the code

```
GLuint my_texture = 1;
glBindTexture(GL_TEXTURE_2D, my_texture);
```

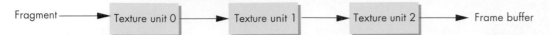

FIGURE 8.36   Sequence of texture units.

Subsequent texture functions define the texture image and its parameters. Another call to `glBindTexture` with a new name starts a new texture object. A later execution of `glBindTexture` with an existing name makes that texture object the current texture object. As with display lists, there are also functions to find unused names (`glGenTextures`) and to delete texture objects (`glDeleteTextures`).

8.8.5   Multitexturing

Thus far, we have looked at applying a single texture to an object. However, there are many surface rendering effects that can best be implemented by more than a single application of a texture. For example, suppose that we want to apply a shadow to an object whose surface shades are themselves determined by a texture map. We could use a texture map for the shadow, but if there were only a single texture application, this method would not work.

If, instead, we have multiple texture units, as in Figure 8.36, then we can accomplish this task. Each unit acts as an independent texturing stage starting with the results of the previous stage. This facility is supported in recent versions of OpenGL.

8.9   Texture Generation

One of the most powerful uses of texture mapping is to provide detail without generating numerous geometric objects. High-end graphics systems can do two-dimensional texture mapping in real time; for every frame, the texture is mapped to objects as part of the rendering process at almost the same rate as non–texture-mapped objects are processed. Graphics boards for personal computers now contain a significant amount of texture memory and allow game developers to use texture mapping to create complex animated environments.

If, for example, we want to simulate grass in a scene, we can texture-map an image of grass that we might have obtained, say, by scanning a photograph, faster than we can generate two- or three-dimensional objects that look like grass. In mapping applications, rather than generating realistic surface detail for terrain, we can digitize a real map and can paint it on a three-dimensional surface model by texture mapping.

We can also look for procedural methods for determining texture patterns. Of particular interest are patterns that we see in nature, such as the textures of sand, grass, or minerals. These textures show both structure (regular patterns) and considerable randomness. Most approaches to generating such textures

FIGURE 8.37 Texture generation.

algorithmically start with a random-number generator and process its output as shown in Figure 8.37. An ideal random-number generator produces a sequence of values that are statistically uncorrelated, or **white noise**. The algorithmic process correlates successive noise values. By carefully designing the procedural algorithm, we can simulate various patterns.

Researchers and application developers have applied such random techniques successfully to create three-dimensional textures. The generation of a three-dimensional texture field $T(s, t, r)$ is a direct extension of two-dimensional texture-generation techniques. There are some practical advantages to using three-dimensional textures. Most important is that by associating each (s, t, r) value directly with an (x, y, z) point, we can avoid the mapping problem entirely. The user needs only to define a function $T(s, t, r)$ with the desired properties. Conceptually, this process is similar to sculpting the three-dimensional object from a solid block whose volume is colored by the specified texture. This technique has been used to generate objects that look as if they were carved from solid rock. The texture-generation process defines a function $T(s, t, r)$ that displays the graininess we associate with materials such as marble and granite.

There are other advantages to using three-dimensional textures. Suppose that we have a two-dimensional texture that we obtained by photographing or modeling some natural material, such as stone. Now suppose that we want to create a cube that looks as if it were formed from this stone. If we use two-dimensional texture mapping, we have to map the same pattern to the six sides of the cube. To make the cube look real, we must try to make the texture map appear continuous at the edges of the cube, where two texture maps meet. When we work with natural patterns, it is virtually impossible to ensure that we can do this matching. Note that the problem is even more serious at the vertices of the cube, where three texture maps meet (see Exercise 8.24). Often we can use filtering and texture borders to give visually acceptable results. However, if we use three-dimensional textures, this problem does not arise.

8.10 Environment Maps

Highly reflective surfaces are characterized by specular reflections that mirror the environment. Consider, for example, a shiny metal ball in the middle of a room. We can see the contents of the room, in a distorted form, on the surface of the ball. Obviously, this effect requires global information, because we cannot shade the ball correctly without knowing about the rest of the scene. A physically based rendering method, such as a ray tracer, can produce this kind of image,

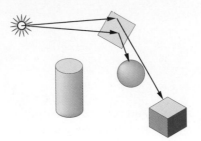

FIGURE 8.38   Scene with a mirror.

although in practice ray-tracing calculations usually are too time-consuming to be practical for real-time applications. We can, however, use variants of texture mapping that can give approximate results that are visually acceptable through the use of **environment** or **reflection maps**.

We shall break our discussion into two parts. Here, after introducing the basic ideas, we shall consider cube and sphere maps, the two forms that are supported by OpenGL's standard texture mapping. These maps are applied using the texture coordinates at each vertex. In Chapter 9, when we learn how to program fragment processing, we shall learn how to generate more accurate maps by working with fragments and more complex effects, such as bump mapping, that cannot be done with the fixed-function pipeline.

The basic idea is simple. Consider the mirror in Figure 8.38, which we can look at as a polygon whose surface is a highly specular material. From the point of view of a renderer, the position of the viewer and the normal to the polygon are known so that the angle of reflection is determined as in Chapter 6. If we follow along this angle until we intersect the environment, we obtain the shade that is reflected in the mirror. Of course, this shade is the result of a shading process that involves the light sources and materials in the scene. We can obtain an approximately correct value of this shade as part of a two-step rendering pass, similar in some respects to the two-step texture mapping process that we outlined in Section 8.7. In the first pass, we render the scene without the mirror polygon, with the camera placed at the center of the mirror pointed in the direction of the normal of the mirror. Thus, we obtain an image of the objects in the environment as "seen" by the mirror. This image is not quite correct (Exercise 8.3) but is usually good enough. We can then use this image to obtain the shades (texture values) to place on the mirror polygon for the second normal rendering with the mirror placed back in the scene.

There are two difficulties with this approach. First, the images that we obtain in the first pass are not quite correct, because they have been formed without one of the objects—the mirror—in the environment. Second, we must confront the mapping issue. Onto what surface should we project the scene in the first pass, and where should we place the camera? Potentially, we want *all* the information

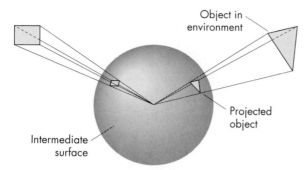

FIGURE 8.39   Mapping of the environment.

in the scene because we may want to do something like have our mirror move, in which case we should see different parts of the environment on successive frames; thus a simple projection will not suffice.

There have been a variety of approaches to this projection problem. The classic approach is to project the environment onto a sphere centered at the center of projection. In Figure 8.39, we see some polygons that are outside the sphere and their projections on the sphere. Note that a viewer located at the center of the sphere cannot tell whether she is seeing the polygons in their original positions or their projections on the sphere. This illusion is similar to what we see in a planetarium. The "stars" that appear to be an infinite distance away are actually the projection of lights onto the hemisphere that encloses the audience.

In the original version of environment mapping, the surface of the sphere was then converted to a rectangle using lines of longitude and latitude for the mapping. Although conceptually simple, there are problems at the poles where the shape distortion becomes infinite. Computationally, this mapping does not preserve areas very well and requires evaluating a large number of trigonometric functions.

OpenGL supports a variation of this method called **sphere mapping**. The application program supplies a circular image that is the orthographic projection of the sphere onto which the environment has been mapped. The advantage of this method is that the mapping from the reflection vector to two-dimensional texture coordinates on this circle is simple and can be implemented in either hardware or software. The difficult part is obtaining the required circular image. It can be approximated by taking a perspective projection with a very wide-angle lens or by remapping some other type of projection, such as the cube projection that we discuss next. We load the texture image in texture memory through glTexImage2D. We can generate texture coordinates ourselves, but it is usually easier to let OpenGL generate the texture coordinates automatically by

```
glTexGeni(GL_S, GL_TEXTURE_GEN_MODE, GL_SPHERE_MAP);
glTexGeni(GL_T, GL_TEXTURE_GEN_MODE, GL_SPHERE_MAP);

glEnable(GL_TEXTURE_GEN_S);
glEnable(GL_TEXTURE_GEN_T);
```

The equations for generating the texture coordinates can be understood with the help of Figure 8.40. It is probably easiest if we work backwards from the viewer to the image. Suppose that the texture map is in the plane $z = -d$, where d is positive and we project backwards orthogonally towards a unit sphere centered at the origin. Thus, if the texture coordinates in the plane are (s, t), then the projector intersects the sphere at $(s, t, \sqrt{(1.0 - s^2 - t^2)})$. For the unit sphere centered at the origin, the coordinates of any point on the sphere are also the components of the unit normal at that point. We can then compute the direction of reflection, as in Chapter 6, by

$$\mathbf{r} = 2(\mathbf{n} \cdot \mathbf{v})\mathbf{n} - \mathbf{v},$$

where

$$\mathbf{v} = \begin{bmatrix} s \\ t \\ 0 \end{bmatrix},$$

$$\mathbf{n} = \begin{bmatrix} s \\ t \\ \sqrt{1.0 - s^2 - t^2} \end{bmatrix}.$$

The vector $\mathbf{r}$ points into the environment. Thus, any object that $\mathbf{r}$ intersects has texture coordinates (s, t). However, this argument is backwards because we start with the object defined by vertices. Given $\mathbf{r}$, we can solve for s and t and find that if

$$\mathbf{r} = \begin{bmatrix} r_x \\ r_y \\ r_z \end{bmatrix},$$

then

$$s = \frac{r_x}{f} + \frac{1}{2},$$

$$t = \frac{r_y}{f} + \frac{1}{2},$$

where

$$f = 2\sqrt{r_x^2 + r_y^2 + (r_z + 1)^2}.$$

If we put everything into eye coordinates, we compute $\mathbf{r}$ using the unit vector from the origin to the vertex for $\mathbf{v}$ and the vertex normal for $\mathbf{n}$.

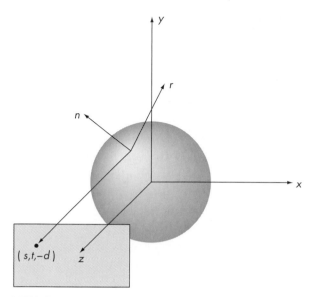

FIGURE 8.40   Reflection map.

This process reveals some issues that show that this method is only approximate. The reflection map is correct only for the vertex at the origin. In principle, each vertex should have its own reflection map. Actually, each point on the object should have its own map and not an approximate value computed by interpolation. The errors are most significant the farther the object is from the origin. Nevertheless, reflection mapping gives visually acceptable results in most situations, especially when there is animation as in films and games.

If we want to compute an environment map using the graphics system, we prefer to use the standard projections that are supported by the graphics systems. For an environment such as a room, the natural intermediate object is a box. We compute six projections, corresponding to the walls, floor, and ceiling, using six virtual cameras located at the center of the box, each pointing in a different direction. At this point, we can treat the six images as a single environment map and derive the textures from it as in Figure 8.41. Color Plate 29 shows one frame from Pixar Animation Studio's *Geri's Game*. A reflection map was computed on a box (Color Plate 30) and then mapped to Geri's glasses.

We could also compute the six images in our program and use them to compute the circular image required by OpenGL's spherical maps. Note that all these methods can suffer from geometric distortions and aliasing problems. In addition, unless the application recomputes the environment maps, they are not correct if the viewer moves.

Regardless of how the images are computing, once we have them, we can specify a cube map in OpenGL with six function calls, one for each face of a cube

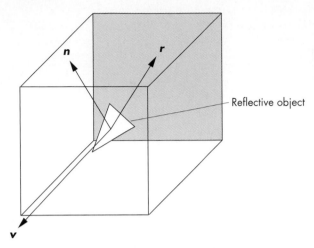

FIGURE 8.41   Reflective cube map.

centered at the origin. Thus, if we have a 512×512 RGBA image `imagexp` for the positive-x face, we have

```
glTexImage2D(GL_TEXTURE_CUBE_MAP_POSIITVE_X, 0, GL_RGBA, 512, 512,
        0, GL_RGBA, GL_UNSIGNED_BYTE, imagexp)'
```

For reflection maps, the calculation of texture coordinates can be done automatically. However, cube maps are fundamentally different from sphere maps, which are much like standard two-dimensional texture maps with special coordinate calculations. Here we must use three-dimensional texture coordinates and enable cube mapping:

```
glTexGeni(GL_S, GL_TEXTURE_GEN_MODE, GL_REFLECTION_MAP);
glTexGeni(GL_T, GL_TEXTURE_GEN_MODE, GL_REFLECTION_MAP);
glTexGeni(GL_R, GL_TEXTURE_GEN_MODE, GL_REFLECTION_MAP);
glEnable(GL_TEXTURE_GEN_S);
glEnable(GL_TEXTURE_GEN_T);
glEnable(GL_TEXTURE_GEN_R);
glEnable(GL_TEXTURE_CUBE_MAP);
```

Cube mapping has many other uses that we shall study in detail in Chapter 9. We can use the method to compute normals rapidly, to simulate more complex light–material phenomena, such as refraction, and for bump and displacement maps.

These techniques are examples of **multipass rendering** (or **multirendering**), where in order to compute a single image, we compute multiple images, each using the rendering pipeline. Multipass methods are becoming increasingly more important as the power of graphics cards has increased to the point that we can render a scene multiple times from different perspectives in less time than is needed for reasonable refresh rates. In Section 8.12, we shall introduce the accumulation buffer that supports multirendering and some techniques that use it.

8.11 Compositing Techniques

Thus far, we have assumed that we want to form a single image and that the objects that form this image have surfaces that are opaque. OpenGL provides a mechanism through **alpha (α) blending** that, among other effects, can create images with translucent objects. The **alpha channel** is the fourth color in RGBA (or RGBα) color mode. Like the other colors, the application program can control the value of A (or α) for each pixel. However, in RGBA mode, if blending is enabled, the value of α controls how the RGB values are written into the frame buffer. Because fragments from multiple objects can contribute to the color of the same pixel, we say that these objects are **blended**, or **composited**, together. We can use a similar mechanism to blend together images.

8.11.1 Opacity and Blending

The **opacity** of a surface is a measure of how much light penetrates through that surface. An opacity of 1 ($\alpha = 1$) corresponds to a completely opaque surface that blocks all light incident on it. A surface with an opacity of 0 is transparent: All light passes through it. The **transparency**, or **translucency**, of a surface with opacity α is given by $1 - \alpha$.

Consider the three uniformly lit polygons shown in Figure 8.42. Assume that the middle polygon is opaque and the front polygon, nearest to the viewer, is transparent. If the front polygon were perfectly transparent, the viewer would see only the middle polygon. However, if the front polygon is only partially opaque (partially transparent), similar to colored glass, the color the viewer sees is a blending of the colors of the front and middle polygons. Because the middle

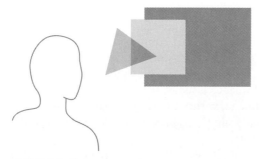

FIGURE 8.42 Translucent and opaque polygons.

polygon is opaque, the viewer does not see the back polygon. If the front polygon is red and the middle is blue, she sees magenta, due to the blending of the colors. If we let the middle polygon be only partially opaque, she sees the blending of the colors of all three polygons.

In computer graphics, we usually render polygons one at a time into the frame buffer. Consequently, if we want to use blending (or compositing), we need a way to apply opacity as part of fragment processing. We can use the notion of source and destination pixels, just as we used source and destination bits in Section 8.3. As a polygon is processed, pixel-sized fragments are computed and, if they are visible, are assigned colors based on the shading model in use. Until now, we have used the color of a fragment—as computed by the lighting model and by any mapping techniques—to determine the color of the pixel in the frame buffer at the location (in screen coordinates) of the fragment. If we regard the fragment as the source pixel and the frame-buffer pixel as the destination, we can combine these values in various ways. Using α values is one way of controlling the blending on a fragment-by-fragment basis. Combining the colors of polygons is similar to joining two pieces of colored glass into a single piece of glass that has a higher opacity and a color different from either of the original pieces.

If we represent the source and destination pixels with the four-element (RGBα) arrays

$$\mathbf{s} = [\; s_r \quad s_g \quad s_b \quad s_a \;],$$
$$\mathbf{d} = [\; d_r \quad d_g \quad d_b \quad d_a \;],$$

then a compositing operation replaces $\mathbf{d}$ with

$$\mathbf{d}' = [\; b_r s_r + c_r d_r \quad b_g s_g + c_g d_g \quad b_b s_b + c_b d_b \quad b_a s_a + c_a d_a \;].$$

The arrays of constants $\mathbf{b} = [\; b_r \quad b_g \quad b_b \quad b_a \;]$, $\mathbf{c} = [\; c_r \quad c_g \quad c_b \quad c_a \;]$ are the **source** and **destination blending factors**, respectively. As occurs with RGB colors, a value of α over 1.0 is limited or clamped to the maximum of 1.0, and negative values are clamped to 0.0. We can choose both the values of α and the method of combining source and destination values to achieve a variety of effects.

8.11.2 Image Compositing

The most straightforward use of α-blending is to combine and display several images that exist as pixel maps or, equivalently, as sets of data that have been rendered independently. In this case, we can regard each image as a radiant object that contributes equally to the final image. Usually, we wish to keep our RGB colors between 0 and 1 in the final image, without having to clamp those values greater than 1. Hence, we can either scale the values of each image or use the source and destination blending factors.

Suppose that we have n images that should contribute equally to the final display. At a given pixel, image i has components $\mathbf{C}_i \alpha_i$. Here we are using $\mathbf{C}_i$

to denote the color triplet (R_i, B_i, G_i). If we replace $\mathbf{C}_i$ by $\frac{1}{n}\mathbf{C}_i$ and α_i by $\frac{1}{n}$, then we can simply add each image into the frame buffer (assuming the frame buffer is initialized to black with an $\alpha = 0$). Alternately, we can use a source blending factor of $\frac{1}{n}$ by setting the α-value for each pixel in each image to be $\frac{1}{n}$ and using 1 for the destination blending factor and α for the source blending factor. Although these two methods produce the same image, if the hardware supports compositing, the second may be more efficient. Note that if n is large, blending factors of the form $\frac{1}{n}$ can lead to significant loss of color resolution. We address this problem in Section 8.12.

8.11.3 Blending and Compositing in OpenGL

The mechanics of blending in OpenGL are straightforward. We enable blending by

```
glEnable(GL_BLEND);
```

Then we set up the desired source and destination factors by

```
glBlendFunc(source_factor, destination factor);
```

OpenGL has a number of blending factors defined, including the values 1 (GL_ONE) and 0 (GL_ZERO), the source α and $1 - \alpha$ (GL_SRC_ALPHA and GL_ONE_MINUS_SRC_ALPHA), and the destination α and $1 - \alpha$ (GL_DST_ALPHA and GL_ONE_MINUS_DST_ALPHA). The application program specifies the desired options and then uses RGBA color.

The major difficulty with compositing is that for most choices of the blending factors, the order in which we render the polygons affects the final image. For example, many applications use the source α as the source blending factor and $1 - \alpha$ for the destination factor. The resulting color and opacity are

$$(R_{d'}, G_{d'}, B_{d'}, \alpha_{d'}) = (\alpha_s R_s + (1 - \alpha_s)R_d, \alpha_s G + (1 - \alpha_s)G_d, \alpha_s B_s$$
$$+ (1 - \alpha_s)B_d, \alpha_s \alpha_d + (1 - \alpha_s)\alpha_d).$$

This formula ensures that both transparent and opaque polygons are handled correctly and that neither colors nor opacities can saturate. However, the resulting color and α-values depend on the order in which the polygons are rendered. Consequently, unlike in most OpenGL programs, where the user does not have to worry about the order in which polygons are rasterized, to get a desired effect we must now control this order within the application.

A more subtle but visibly apparent problem occurs when we combine opaque and translucent objects in a scene. Normally, when we use blending, we do not enable hidden-surface removal, because polygons behind any polygon already rendered would not be rasterized and thus would not contribute to the final image. In a scene with both opaque and transparent polygons, any polygon behind an opaque polygon should not be rendered, but translucent polygons in front of opaque polygons should be composited. There is a simple solution to this problem that does not require the application program to order the polygons. We can enable hidden-surface removal as usual and can make the z buffer read-only for any polygon that is translucent. We do so by

```
glDepthMask(GL_FALSE);
```

When the depth buffer is read-only, a translucent polygon that lies behind any opaque polygon already rendered is discarded. A translucent polygon that lies in front of any polygon that has already been rendered is blended with the color of the polygons behind it. However, because the z buffer is read-only for this polygon, the depth values in the buffer are unchanged. Opaque polygons set the depth mask to true and are rendered normally. Note that because the result of compositing depends on the order in which we composite individual elements, we may notice defects in images in which we render translucent polygons in an arbitrary order. If we are willing to sort the translucent polygons, then we can render all the opaque polygons first and then render the translucent polygons in a back-to-front order with the z buffer in a read-only mode.

8.11.4 Antialiasing Revisited

One of the major uses of the α-channel is for antialiasing. Because a line must have a finite width to be visible, the default width of a line that is rendered should be one pixel wide. We cannot produce a thinner line. Unless the line is horizontal or vertical, such a line partially covers a number of pixels in the frame buffer, as shown in Figure 8.43. Suppose that, as part of the geometric-processing stage of the rendering process, as we process a fragment, we set the α-value for the corresponding pixel to be a number between 0 and 1 that is the fraction of that pixel covered by the fragment. We can then use this α-value to modulate the color as we render the fragment to the frame buffer. We can use a destination blending factor of $1 - \alpha$ and a source destination factor of α. However, if there is overlap of fragments within a pixel, then there are numerous possibilities, as we can see from Figure 8.44. In Figure 8.44(a), the fragments do not overlap; in Figure 8.44(b), they do overlap. Consider the problem from the perspective of a renderer that works one polygon at a time. For our simple example, suppose that we start with an opaque background and that the frame buffer starts with the background color $\mathbf{C}_0$. We can set $\alpha_0 = 0$ because no part of the pixel has yet been covered with fragments from polygons. The first polygon is rendered. The color of the destination pixel is set to

$$\mathbf{C}_d = (1 - \alpha_1)\mathbf{C}_0 + \alpha_1\mathbf{C}_1,$$

and its α-value is set to

$$\alpha_d = \alpha_1.$$

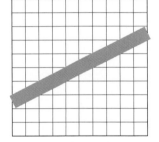

FIGURE 8.43 Raster line.

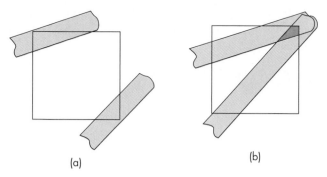

FIGURE 8.44 Fragments. (a) Nonoverlapping. (b) Overlapping.

Thus, a fragment that covers the entire pixel ($\alpha_1 = 1$) will have its color assigned to the destination pixel, and the destination pixel will be opaque. If the background is black, the destination color will be $\alpha_1 \mathbf{C}_1$. Now consider the fragment from the second polygon that subtends the same pixel. How we add in its color and α-value depends on how we wish to interpret the overlap. If there is no overlap, we can assign the new color by blending the color of the destination with the color of the fragment, resulting in the color and α:

$$\mathbf{C}_d = (1 - \alpha_2)((1 - \alpha_1)\mathbf{C}_0 + \alpha_1 \mathbf{C}_1) + \alpha_2 \mathbf{C}_2,$$
$$\alpha_d = \alpha_1 + \alpha_2.$$

This color is a blending of the two colors and does not need to be clamped. The resulting value of α represents the new fraction of the pixel that is covered. However, the resulting color is affected by the order in which the polygons are rendered. The more difficult questions are what to do if the fragments overlap and how to tell whether there is an overlap. One tactic is to take a probabilistic view. If fragment 1 occupies a fraction α_1 of the pixel, fragment 2 occupies a fraction α_2 of the same pixel, and we have no other information about the location of the fragments within the pixel, then the average area of overlap is $\alpha_1 \alpha_2$. We can represent the average case as shown in Figure 8.45. Hence, the new destination α should be

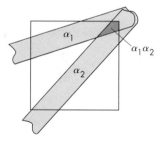

FIGURE 8.45 Average overlap.

$$\alpha_d = \alpha_1 + \alpha_2 - \alpha_1 \alpha_2.$$

How we should assign the color is a more complex problem because we have to decide whether the second fragment is in front of the first or the first is in front of the second, or even whether the two should be blended. We can define an appropriate blending for whichever assumption we wish to make. Note that in a pipeline renderer, polygons can be generated in an order that has nothing to do with their distances from the viewer. However, if we couple α-blending with hidden-surface removal, we can use the depth information to make front-versus-back decisions.

In OpenGL, we can invoke antialiasing without having the user program combine α-values explicitly if we enable blending and smoothing for points, lines, or polygons; for example, we can use

```
glEnable(GL_POINT_SMOOTH);
glEnable(GL_LINE_SMOOTH);
glEnable(GL_POLYGON_SMOOTH);
glEnable(GL_BLEND);
glBlendFunc(GL_SRC_ALPHA, GL_ONE_MINUS_SRC_ALPHA);
```

to enable all three. There may be a considerable performance penalty associated with antialiasing. Color Plate 8 shows OpenGL's antialiasing of polygons.

8.11.5   Back-to-Front and Front-to-Back Rendering

Although using the α-channel gives us a way of creating the appearance of translucency, it is difficult to handle transparency in a physically correct manner without taking into account how an object is lit and what happens to rays and projectors that pass through translucent objects. In Figure 8.46 we can see several of the difficulties. We ignore refraction of light through translucent surfaces—an effect that cannot be handled easily with a pipeline polygon renderer. Suppose that the rear polygon is opaque, but reflective, and that the two polygons closer to the viewer are translucent. By following various rays from the light source, we can see a number of possibilities. Some rays strike the rear polygon, and the corresponding pixels can be colored with the shade at the intersection of the projector and the polygon. For these rays, we should also distinguish between points illuminated directly by the light source and points for which the incident light passes through one or both translucent polygons. For rays that pass through only one translucent surface, we have to adjust the color based on the color and opacity of that polygon. We should also add a term that accounts for the light striking the front polygon that is reflected toward the viewer. For rays passing through both translucent polygons, we have to consider their combined effect.

For a pipeline renderer, the task is even more difficult—if not impossible—because we have to determine the contribution that each polygon makes as it is passed through the pipeline, rather than considering the contributions of all polygons to a given pixel at the same time. In applications where handling of

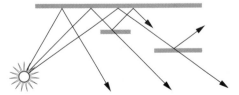

FIGURE 8.46   Scene with translucent objects.

translucency must be done in a consistent and realistic manner, we often must sort the polygons from front to back within the application. Then depending on the application, we can do a front-to-back or back-to-front rendering using OpenGL's blending functionality (see Exercise 8.27).

8.11.6 Depth Cueing and Fog

Depth cueing is one the oldest techniques in three-dimensional graphics. Before raster systems became available, graphics systems could draw only lines. We created the illusion of depth by drawing lines farther from the viewer dimmer than lines closer to the viewer, a technique known as **depth cueing**. We can extend this idea to create the illusion of partially translucent space between the object and the viewer by blending in a distance-dependent color as each fragment is processed.

Let f denote a **fog factor**, and let z be the distance between a fragment being rendered and the viewer. If the fragment has a color $\mathbf{C}_s$ and the fog is assigned a color $\mathbf{C}_f$, then we can use the color

$$\mathbf{C}_{s'} = f\mathbf{C}_s + (1 - f)\mathbf{C}_f$$

in the rendering. If f varies linearly between some minimum and maximum values, we have a depth-cueing effect. If this factor varies exponentially (Figure 8.47), then we get effects that look more like fog. OpenGL supports linear, exponential, and Gaussian fog densities. For example, in RGBA mode, we can set up a fog-density function $f = e^{-0.5z^2}$ by using the function calls

```
GLfloat fcolor[4] = {...};
glEnable(GL_FOG);
glFogf(GL_FOG_MODE, GL_EXP);
glFogf(GL_FOG_DENSITY, 0.5);
glFogfv(GL_FOG_COLOR, fcolor);
```

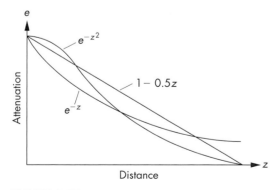

FIGURE 8.47 Fog density.

Note that the value of z is given in eye coordinates. Color Plate 11 uses fog to give the factory environment a more realistic (and gloomy) feel.

8.12   Multirendering and the Accumulation Buffer

There is one other buffer that, if present, is useful for many additional functions. Consider the problem of compositing a set of images each of whose color components is stored as 1 byte. If we simply add their RGB values into a typical 32-bit RGBA color buffer, many of the color components will overflow the values we can represent with a single byte. If the values in the buffer are clamped at their maximum value, then the resulting image will appear washed out as most of the colors in the composited image will tend toward white. If we try to avoid this problem by scaling the colors before they are added together, we will lose color resolution. Consider, for example, if we want to add together 64 images, each of which has 8 bits of resolution for each of its color components. To prevent limiting, we would have to scale each color component by a factor of 64 or, equivalently, lose 6 bits of accuracy on each color component.

A solution to this problem is to create a buffer, the **accumulation buffer**, that has the same spatial resolution as the frame buffer but greater depth resolution. We can think of it as a special type of color buffer whose components are stored as floating-point numbers.[8] We can use the additional resolution to render successive images into one location while retaining numerical accuracy. There are many possible applications.

In OpenGL, we can clear the accumulation buffer as we do any other buffer, and then we can use the function glAccum either to add or to multiply values from the frame buffer into the accumulation buffer or to copy the contents of the accumulation buffer back to a color buffer. For example, the code

```
glClear(GL_ACCUM_BUFFER_BIT);
for(i=0; i< num_mages; i++)
{
      glClear(GL_COLOR_BUFFER_BIT | GL_DEPTH_BUFFER_BIT);
      display_image(i);
      glAccum(GL_ACCUM, 1.0/ (float) num_images);
}
glAccum(GL_RETURN, 1.0);
```

employs the user's function display_images to generate a sequence of images into the write buffer. Each is added into or accumulated into the accumulation buffer, with a scale factor 1 over the number of images. At the end, the accumu-

---

8. In most implementations, the accumulation buffer is created in software.

lated image is copied back to the write buffer. Note that we could have attempted the same task using blending, but we would have been forced to scale the colors in a lower-resolution buffer to avoid clamping.[9]

8.12.1 Scene Antialiasing

One of the most important uses of the accumulation buffer is for antialiasing. Rather than antialiasing individual lines and polygons, as we discussed in Section 8.10.4, we can antialias an entire scene using the accumulation buffer. The idea is that if we regenerate the same scene with all the objects, or the viewer, shifted slightly (less than one pixel), then we generate different aliasing artifacts. If we can average together the resulting images, the aliasing effects are smoothed out. In general, it is easier to shift, or **jitter**, the viewer, as we have to change only the parameters in glPerspective or glOrtho. However, we have to do a calculation in the program to determine how a small change in screen coordinates converts to a corresponding change in camera coordinates. In terms of sampling theory (which we discuss in detail in Section 8.13.1), we have sampled the world at a finer resolution, or **supersampled** it, and have then used an averaging filter to reconstruct the world from these samples.

8.12.2 Bump Mapping and Embossing

In Chapter 9, we shall consider another mapping technique called bump mapping, which will allow us to render objects so that they appear to have fine details (bumps) that give the surface a rough appearance affected by the light position. Classically, bump mapping is done on a fragment by fragment basis. However, we can achieve a good approximation using the accumulation buffer.

A surface with bumps has an embossed appearance because we see shading differences due to the orientation of the bumps with respect to the light source. Surfaces that point toward the light source will appear brighter than surfaces pointing away from the light. The information to alter the surfaces is given by the relationship between the normal to the surface and the light vector. Although we could use the dot product between these two vectors, we can use the displacement matrix $\mathbf{D}$ in combination with the accumulation buffer.

Consider an image that is the difference between $\mathbf{D}$ and a version of it rotated in the direction of the light source. This image will have positive values where faces point toward the light source and negative values where faces point away from the light. We can use this idea as a part of the bump mapping process.

---

9. Recent GPUs provide floating-point frame buffers that allow us to do most accumulation buffer techniques using standard color buffers.

Suppose that we first render the scene into the accumulation buffer, using **D** as a texture map. Note that the texture will have a single color because each value of **D** has only one component. We then shift **D** in the direction of the light source and render the scene again with this rotated image as a texture, this time subtracting the results from the accumulation buffer. Finally, we render the image normally, that is without using **D**, and add the result to the accumulation buffer.

Note that to do the shift of **D** for the second pass, we need the direction of the light source relative to the surface. However, we have the information required to create a homogeneous coordinate matrix that can be applied to each vertex. We use the normal at the vertex—which is part of the state—and one of the two vectors that are used to define the orientation of the displacement function $d(u, v)$. These texture coordinates lie in the plane of the surface and are tangent to the normal. Thus, we can use either one of them and its crossproduct with the normal to obtain the three vectors that determine the required rotation matrix.

8.12.3   Image Processing

We can combine use of the accumulation buffer with pixel mapping to perform various image-processing operations. Suppose that we start with a discrete image. Perhaps this image was generated by a rendering, or perhaps we obtained it by digitizing a continuous image using a scanner. We can represent the image with an $N \times M$ matrix,

$$\mathbf{A} = [\, a_{ij} \,],$$

of scalar levels. If we process each color component of a color image independently, we can regard the entries in **A** as either individual color components or gray (luminance) levels. A **linear filter** produces a filtered matrix **B** whose elements are

$$b_{ij} = \sum_{k=-m}^{m} \sum_{l=-n}^{n} h_{kl}\, a_{i+k,j+l}.$$

We say that **B** is the result of **convolving A** with a filter matrix **H**. In general, the values of m and n are small, and we can represent **H** by a small $(2m + 1 \times 2n + 1)$ **convolution matrix**.

We can view the filtering operation as shown in Figure 8.48 for $m = n = 1$. For each pixel in **A**, we place the convolution matrix over a_{ij} and take a weighted average of the surrounding points. The values in the matrix are the weights. For example, for $n = m = 1$, we can average each pixel with its four surrounding neighbors using the 3×3 matrix

$$\mathbf{H} = \frac{1}{5} \begin{bmatrix} 0 & 1 & 0 \\ 1 & 1 & 1 \\ 0 & 1 & 0 \end{bmatrix}.$$

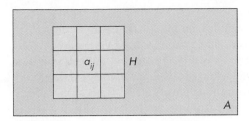

FIGURE 8.48   Filtering and convolution.

This filter can be used for antialiasing. We can use more points and can weight the center more heavily with

$$\mathbf{H} = \frac{1}{16} \begin{bmatrix} 1 & 2 & 1 \\ 2 & 4 & 2 \\ 1 & 2 & 1 \end{bmatrix}.$$

Note that we must define a border around $\mathbf{A}$ if we want $\mathbf{B}$ to have the same dimensions. Other operations are possible with small matrices. For example, we can use the matrix

$$\mathbf{H} = \begin{bmatrix} 0 & -1 & 0 \\ -1 & 4 & -1 \\ 0 & -1 & 0 \end{bmatrix}$$

to detect changes in value or edges in the image. If the matrix $\mathbf{H}$ is $k \times k$, we can implement a filter by accumulating k^2 images in the accumulation buffer, each time adding in a shifted version of $\mathbf{A}$ using a different filter coefficient in glAccum.

8.12.4   Imaging Extensions

Although we can implement many image-processing operations using the accumulation buffer, if we look closely at the process, we can detect a major efficiency issue. If we are going to be transferring images to and from the accumulation buffer, we will be moving large amounts of data among the processor memory, frame buffer, and texture memory. These transfers require packing and unpacking of the arrays, further slowing the process.

Our development of accumulation buffer techniques suggests two things. First, it should be fairly simple to add an API that supports standard image-processing operations. Second, it should not require large modifications to the graphics hardware to support imaging operations. In fact, both these issues have been addressed. From an OpenGL perspective, there is an **imaging subset** that defines an API for the most common image-processing operations. These operations are an **OpenGL extension** and are not required to be supported on all implementations. However, of all the OpenGL extensions, the imaging subset is the most commonly supported. Some of the facilities supported include histograms, convolutions (filters), color tables, and color transformations.

On the hardware side, we have seen that graphics hardware supports an imaging pipeline. Typically, this pipeline would be located within the graphics hardware, and this pipeline works on unpacked pixels. Hence, image data would need to be unpacked and transferred from the application only once. Operations such as table lookups, filtering, and color mapping can be accomplished without sending images back to processor memory until any sequence of imaging operations is complete.

8.12.5   Other Multipass Methods

We can also use the accumulation buffer for filtering in time and depth. For example, if we jitter an object and render it multiple times, leaving the positions of the other objects unchanged, we get dimmer copies of the jittered object in the final image. If the object is moved along a path, rather than randomly jittered, we see the trail of the object. This **motion-blur** effect is similar to the result of taking a photograph of a moving object using a long exposure time. We can adjust the constant in glAccum so as to render the final position of the object with greater opacity or to create the impression of speed differences.

We can use filtering in depth to create focusing effects. A real camera cannot produce an image with all objects in focus. Objects within a certain distance from the camera, the camera's **depth of field**, are in focus; objects outside this field are out of focus and appear blurred. Computer graphics produces images with an infinite depth of field because we do not have to worry about the limitations of real lenses. Occasionally, however, we want to create an image that looks as though it were produced by a real camera or to defocus part of a scene so as to emphasize the objects within a desired depth of field. Once more, we can use the accumulation buffer. This time, the trick is to move the viewer in a manner that leaves a particular plane fixed, as shown in Figure 8.49. Suppose that we wish to keep the plane at $z = z_f$ in focus and to leave the near ($z = z_{min}$) and far ($z = z_{max}$) clipping distances unchanged. If we use glFrustum, we specify the

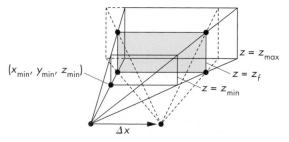

FIGURE 8.49   Depth-of-field jitter.

near clipping rectangle $(x_{min}, x_{max}, y_{min}, y_{max})$. If we move the viewer from the origin in the x direction by Δx, we must change x_{min} to

$$x'_{min} = x_{min} + \frac{\Delta x}{z_f}(z_f - z_{near}).$$

Similar equations hold for x_{max}, y_{min}, and y_{max}. As we increase Δx and Δy, we create a narrower depth of field.

8.13 Sampling and Aliasing

We have seen a variety of applications in which the conversion from a continuous representation of an entity to a discrete approximation of that entity leads to visible errors in the display. We have used the term *aliasing* to characterize these errors. When we work with buffers, we are always working with digital images, and if we are not careful, these errors can be extreme. In this section, we examine the nature of digital images and gather facts that will help us to understand where aliasing errors arise and how the effects of these errors can be mitigated.

We start with a continuous two-dimensional image $f(x, y)$. We can regard the value of f as either a gray level in a monochromatic image or the value of one of the primaries in a color image. In the computer, we work with a digital image that is an array of nm pixels arranged as n rows of m pixels. Each pixel has k bits. There are two processes involved in going from a continuous image to a discrete image. First, we must **sample** the continuous image at nm points on some grid to obtain a set of values $\{f_{ij}\}$. Each of these samples of the continuous image is the value of f measured over a small area in the continuous image. Then we must convert each of these samples into a k-bit pixel by a process known as **quantization.**

8.13.1 Sampling Theory

Suppose that we have a rectangular grid of locations where we wish to obtain our samples of f, as in Figure 8.50. If we assume that the grid is equally spaced, then an ideal sampler would produce a value

$$f_{ij} = f(x_0 + ih_x, y_0 + jh_y),$$

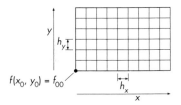

FIGURE 8.50 Sampling grid.

where h_x and h_y are the distances between the grid points in the x and y directions, respectively. Leaving aside for now the fact that no real sampler can make such a precise measurement, there are two important questions. First, what errors have we made in this idealized sampling process? That is, how much of the information in the original image is included in the sampled image? Second, can we go back from the digital image to a continuous image without incurring additional errors? This latter step is called **reconstruction** and describes display processes like those required in displaying the contents of a frame buffer on a monitor.

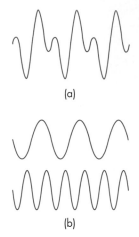

FIGURE 8.51 One-dimensional decomposition. (a) Function. (b) Components.

The mathematical analysis of these issues uses Fourier analysis, a branch of applied mathematics particularly well suited for explaining problems of digital signal processing. The essence of Fourier theory is that a function, of either space or time, can be decomposed into a set of sinusoids at possibly an infinite number of frequencies. This concept is most familiar with sound, where we routinely think of a particular sound in terms of its frequency components, or **spectrum**. We can think of a two-dimensional image as being composed of sinusoidal patterns in two spatial frequencies that when added together produce the image. Figure 8.51(a) shows a one-dimensional function; Figure 8.51(b) shows the two sinusoids that form it. Figure 8.52 shows two-dimensional periodic functions. Thus, every two-dimensional spatial function $f(x, y)$ has two equivalent representations. One is its spatial form $f(x, y)$; the other is a representation in terms of its spectrum—the frequency-domain representation $g(\xi, \eta)$. The value of g is the contribution to f at the two-dimensional spatial frequency (ξ, η). By using these alternate representations of functions, we find that many phenomena, including sampling, can be explained much more easily in the frequency domain.

We can explain the consequences of sampling without being overwhelmed by the mathematics if we accept, without proof, the fundamental theorem known as the **Nyquist sampling theorem**. There are two parts to the theorem: The first allows us to discuss sampling errors, whereas the second governs reconstruction. We examine the second in Section 8.13.2.

> **Nyquist sampling theorem (part 1):** The ideal samples of a continuous function contain all the information in the original function if and only if the continuous function is sampled at a frequency greater than twice the highest frequency in the function.

Thus, if we are to have any chance of not losing information, we must restrict ourselves to functions that are zero in the frequency domain except in a window of width less than the sampling frequency, centered at the origin. The lowest frequency that cannot be in the data so as to avoid aliasing—one-half of the sampling frequency—is called the **Nyquist frequency**. Functions whose spectra

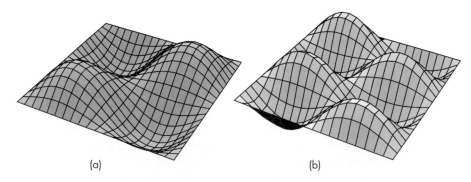

FIGURE 8.52 Two-dimensional periodic functions.

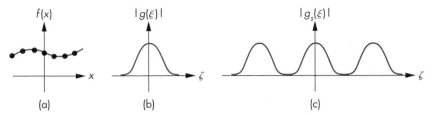

FIGURE 8.53 Band-limited function. (a) Function and its samples in the spatial domain. (b) Spectrum of the function. (c) Spectrum of the samples.

are zero outside of some window are known as **band-limited** functions. For a two-dimensional image, the sampling frequencies are determined by the spacing of a two-dimensional grid with x and y spacing of $1/h_x$ and $1/h_y$, respectively.

The theorem assumes an ideal sampling process that gathers an infinite number of samples, each of which is the exact value at the grid point. In practice, we can take only a finite number of samples—the number matching the resolution of our buffer. Consequently, we cannot produce a truly band-limited function. Although this result is a mathematical consequence of Fourier theory, we can observe that there will always be some ambiguity inherent in a finite collection of sampled points simply because we do not know the function outside the region from which we obtained the samples.[10]

The consequences of violating the Nyquist criteria are aliasing errors. We can see where the name *aliasing* derives by considering an ideal sampling process. Both the original function and its set of samples have frequency-domain representations. The spectral components of the sampled function are replicas of the spectrum of the original function, with their centers separated by the sampling frequency. Consider the one-dimensional function in Figure 8.53(a) with the samples indicated. Figure 8.53(b) shows its spectrum; in Figure 8.53(c) we have the spectrum of the sampled function, showing the replications of the spectrum in Figure 8.53(b).[11] Because we have sampled at a rate higher than the Nyquist frequency, there is a separation between the replicas.

Now consider the case in Figure 8.54. Here we have violated the Nyquist criterion and the replicas overlap. Consider the central part of the plot, which is magnified in Figure 8.55 and shows only the central replica, centered at the origin, and the replica to its right, centered at ξ_s. The frequency ξ_0 is above the Nyquist frequency $\xi_s/2$. There is, however, a replica of ξ_0, generated by the sampling process from the replica on the right, at $\xi_s - \xi_0$, a frequency less than the

---

10. This statement assumes no knowledge of the underlying function f other than a set of its samples. If we have additional information, such as knowledge that the function is periodic, knowledge of the function over a finite interval can be sufficient to determine the entire function.

11. We show the magnitude of the spectrum because the Fourier transform produces complex numbers for the frequency-domain components.

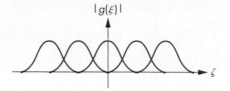

FIGURE 8.54   Overlapping replicas.

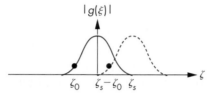

FIGURE 8.55   Aliasing.

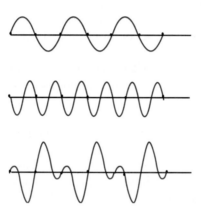

FIGURE 8.56   Aliasing of a sinusoid.

Nyquist frequency. The energy at this frequency can be heard, if we are dealing with digital sound, or seen, if we are considering two-dimensional images. We say that the frequency ξ_0 has an **alias** at $\xi_s - \xi_0$. Note that once aliasing has occurred, we cannot distinguish between information that was at a frequency in the original data and information that was placed at this frequency by the sampling process.

We can demonstrate aliasing and ambiguity without using Fourier analysis by looking at a single sinusoid, as shown in Figure 8.56. If we sample this sinusoid at twice its frequency, we can recover it from two samples. However, these same two samples are samples of a sinusoid of twice this frequency and can also be samples of sinusoids of other multiples of the basic frequency. All these frequencies are

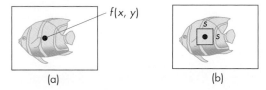

FIGURE 8.57 Scanning an image. (a) Point sampling. (b) Area averaging.

aliases of the same original frequency. If we know that the data were band limited, however, then the samples can describe only the original sinusoid.

If we were to do an analysis of the frequency content of real-world images, we would find that the spectral components of most images are concentrated in the lower frequencies. Consequently, although it is impossible to construct a finite-sized image that is band limited, the aliasing errors often are minimal because there is little content in frequencies above the Nyquist frequency, and little content is aliased into frequencies below the Nyquist frequency. The exceptions to this statement arise when there is regular (periodic) information in the continuous image. In the frequency representation, regularity places most of the information at a few frequencies. If any of these frequencies is above the Nyquist limit, the aliasing effect is noticeable as beat, or moiré, patterns. Examples that you might have noticed include the patterns that appear on video displays when people in the images wear striped shirts or plaid ties, and wavy patterns that arise both in printed (halftoned) figures derived from computer displays and in digital images of farmland with plowed fields.

Often, we can minimize aliasing by prefiltering before we scan an image or by controlling the area of the data that the scanner uses to measure a sample. Figure 8.57 shows two possible ways to scan an image. In Figure 8.57(a), we see an ideal scanner. It measures the value of a continuous image at a point, so the samples are given by

$$f_{ij} = f(x_i, y_i).$$

In Figure 8.57(b), we have a more realistic scanner that obtains samples by taking a weighted average over a small interval to produce samples of the form

$$f_{ij} = \int_{x_i-s/2}^{x_i+s/2} \int_{y_i-s/2}^{y_i+s/2} f(x, y) w(x, y) \, dy dx.$$

By selecting the size of the window s and the weighting function w, we can attenuate high-frequency components in the image, and thus we can reduce aliasing. Fortunately, real scanners must take measurements over a finite region, called the **sampling aperture**; thus, some antialiasing takes place even if the user has no understanding of the aliasing problem.

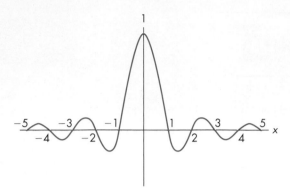

FIGURE 8.58   Sinc function.

8.13.2   Reconstruction

Suppose that we have an (infinite) set of samples, the members of which have been sampled at a rate greater than the Nyquist frequency. The reconstruction of a continuous function from the samples is based on part 2 of the Nyquist sampling theorem.

> **Nyquist sampling theorem (part 2):** We can reconstruct a continuous function $f(x)$ from its samples $\{f_i\}$ by the formula

$$f(x) = \sum_{i=-\infty}^{\infty} f_i \, \text{sinc}(x - x_i).$$

The function $\text{sinc}(x)$ shown in Figure 8.58 is defined as

$$\text{sinc}(x) = \frac{\sin \pi x}{\pi x}.$$

The two-dimensional version of the reconstruction formula for a function $f(x, y)$ with ideal samples $\{f_{ij}\}$ is

$$f(x, y) = \sum_{i=-\infty}^{\infty} \sum_{j=-\infty}^{\infty} f_{ij} \text{sinc}(x - x_i) \, \text{sinc}(y - y_j).$$

These formulas follow from the fact that we can recover an unaliased function in the frequency domain by using a filter that is zero except in the interval $(-\xi_s/2, \xi_s/2)$—a low-pass filter—to obtain a single replica from the infinite number of replicas generated by the sampling process shown in Figure 8.53. The reconstruction of a one-dimensional function is shown in Figure 8.59. In two dimensions, the reconstruction involves the use of a two-dimensional sinc, as shown in Figure 8.60. Unfortunately, the sinc function cannot be produced in a physical display, because of its negative side lobes. Consider the display problem for a CRT display. We start with a digital image that is a set of samples. For each sample, we can place a spot of light centered at a grid point on the

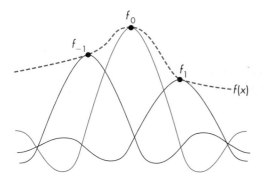

FIGURE 8.59 One-dimensional reconstruction.

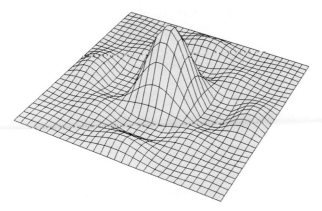

FIGURE 8.60 Two-dimensional sinc function.

display surface, as shown in Figure 8.61. The value of the sample controls the intensity of the spot, or modulates the beam. We can control the shape of the spot by using techniques such as focusing the beam. The reconstruction formula tells us that the beam should have the shape of a two-dimensional sinc, but because the beam puts out energy, the spot must be nonnegative at all points. Consequently, the display process must make errors. We can evaluate a real display by considering how well its spot approximates the desired sinc. Figure 8.62 shows the sinc and several one-dimensional approximations. The Gaussian-shaped spot corresponds to the shape of many CRT spots, whereas the rectangular spot might correspond to an LCD display with square pixels. Note that we can make either approximation wider or narrower. If we analyze the spot profiles in the frequency domain, we find that the wider spots are more accurate at low frequencies but are less accurate at higher frequencies. In practice, the spot size that we choose is a compromise. Visible differences across monitors often can be traced to different spot profiles.

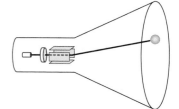

FIGURE 8.61 Display of a point on a CRT.

FIGURE 8.62 Display spots. (a) Ideal spot. (b) Rectangular approximation. (c) Piecewise-linear approximation. (d) Gaussian approximation.

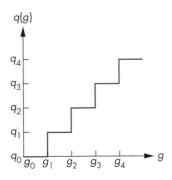

FIGURE 8.63 Quantizer.

8.13.3 Quantization

The mathematical analysis of sampling explains a number of important effects. However, we have not included the effect of each sample being quantized into k discrete levels. Given a scalar function g with values in the range

$$g_{min} \leq g \leq g_{max},$$

a **quantizer** is a function q such that if $g_i \leq g \leq g_{i+1}$, then

$$q(g) = q_i.$$

Thus, for each value of g, we assign it one of k values, as shown in Figure 8.63. In general, designing a quantizer involves choosing the $\{q_i\}$, the quantization levels, and the $\{g_i\}$, the threshold values. If we know the probability distribution for g, $p(g)$, we can solve for the values that minimize the mean square error:

$$e = \int (g - q(g))^2 p(g) dg.$$

However, we often design quantizers based on the perceptual issues that we discussed in Chapter 1. A simple rule of thumb is that we should not be able to detect one-level changes but should be able to detect all two-level changes. Given the threshold for the visual system to detect a change in luminance, we usually need at least 7 or 8 bits (or 128 to 256 levels). We should also consider the logarithmic intensity-brightness response of humans. To do so, we usually distribute the levels exponentially to give approximately equal perceptual errors as we go from one level to the next.

Summary and Notes

In the early days of computer graphics, people worked with only three-dimensional geometric objects, whereas those people who were involved with only two-dimensional images were considered to be working in image processing. Advances in hardware have made graphics and image-processing systems practically indistinguishable. For those people involved with synthesizing images—certainly a major part of computer graphics—this merging of fields has brought forth a multitude of new techniques. The idea that a two-dimensional image or texture can be mapped to a three-dimensional surface in no more time than it takes to render the surface with constant shading would have been unthinkable a few years ago. Now these techniques are routine.

Techniques such as texture mapping have had an enormous effect on real-time graphics. In fields such as animation, virtual reality, and scientific visualization, we use hardware texture mapping to add detail to images without burdening the geometric pipeline. The use of compositing techniques, through the accumulation buffer and the alpha channel, allows the application programmer to perform tasks, such as antialiasing, and to create effects, such as fog and depth of field, that until recently were done on different types of architectures after the graphics had been created.

Mapping methods provide some of the best examples of the interactions among graphics hardware, software, and applications. Consider texture mapping. Although it was first described and implemented purely as a software algorithm, once people saw its ability to create scenes with great visual complexity, hardware developers started putting large amounts of texture memory in graphics systems. Once texture mapping was implemented in hardware, texture mapping could be done in real time, a development that led to the redesign of many applications, notably computer games.

Recent advances in GLUs provide many new possibilities. One is that the pipeline is now programmable, the topic of Chapter 9. We shall see there that programmability of the fragment processor makes possible many new texture manipulation techniques while preserving interactive speeds. Second, the inclusion of large amounts of memory on the GPU removes one of the major bottlenecks in discrete methods, namely many of the transfers of image data between processor memory and the GPU. Third, GPU architectures are designed for rapid processing of discrete data by incorporating a high degree of parallelism for fragment processing. Finally, the availability of floating-point frame buffers eliminates many of the precision issues that plagued techniques that manipulated image data.

In this chapter, we have concentrated on techniques that are supported by recently available hardware and APIs. Many of the techniques introduced here are new; many more are just appearing in the literature; even more remain to be discovered.

Suggested Readings

Environment mapping was developed by Blinn and Newell [Bli76]. Texture mapping was first used by Catmull; see the review by Heckbert [Hec86]. Hardware support for texture mapping came with Silicon Graphics' Reality Engine; see Akeley [Ake93]. Perlin and Hoffert [Per89] designed a noise function to generate two- and three-dimensional texture maps. Many texture synthesis techniques are discussed in Ebert [Ebe02].

The aliasing problem in computer graphics has been of importance since the advent of raster graphics; see Crow [Cro81]. The first concerns were with rasterization of lines, but later other forms of aliasing arose with animations [Mag85] and ray tracing [Gla89]. The image-processing books [Pra78, Gon87, Cas96] provide an introduction to signal processing and aliasing in two dimensions. The books by Glassner [Gla95] and Watt and Policarpo [Wat98] are aimed at practitioners of computer graphics.

Many of the compositing techniques, including use of the α-channel, were suggested by Porter and Duff [Por84]. The *OpenGL Programming Guide* [Ope04a] contains many examples of how buffers can be used. The recent literature includes many new examples of the use of buffers. See the recent issues of the journals *Computer Graphics* and *IEEE Computer Graphics and Applications*.

Technical details on most of the standard image formats can be found in [Mia99, Mur94].

Exercises

8.1   Show how you can use the XOR writing mode to implement an odd–even fill algorithm.

8.2   What are the visual effects of using XOR to move a cursor around on the screen?

8.3   How is an image produced with an environment map different from a ray-traced image of the same scene?

8.4   In the movies and television, the wheels of cars and wagons often appear to be spinning in the wrong direction. What causes this effect? Can anything be done to fix this problem? Explain your answer.

8.5   We can attempt to display sampled data by simply plotting the points and letting the human visual system merge the points into shapes. Why is this technique dangerous if the data are close to the Nyquist limit?

8.6   Why do the patterns of striped shirts and ties change as an actor moves across the screen of your television?

8.7   Why should we do antialiasing by preprocessing the data rather than by postprocessing them?

8.8   Suppose that we have two translucent surfaces characterized by opacities α_1 and α_2. What is the opacity of the translucent material that we create by using the two in series? Give an expression for the transparency of the combined material.

8.9   Assume that we view translucent surfaces as filters of the light passing through them. Develop a blending model based on the complementary colors CMY.

8.10 In Section 8.9, we used $1 - \alpha$ and α for the destination and source blending factors, respectively. What would be the visual difference if we used 1 for the destination factor and kept α for the source factor?

8.11 Add paintbrushes that add color gradually to image in the paint program in Chapter 3. Also use blending to add erasers that gradually remove images from the screen.

8.12 Devise a method of using texture mapping for the display of arrays of three-dimensional pixels (voxels).

8.13 Show how to use the luminance histogram of an image to derive a lookup table that will make the altered image have a flat histogram.

8.14 When we supersample a scene using jitter, why should we use a random jitter pattern?

8.15 Suppose that a set of objects is texture mapped with regular patterns such as stripes and checkerboards. What is the difference in aliasing patterns that we would see when we switch from parallel to perspective views?

8.16 Consider a scene composed of simple objects, such as parallelepipeds, that are instanced at different sizes. Suppose that you have a single texture map and you are asked to map this texture to all the objects. How would you map the texture so that the pattern would be the same size on each face of each object?

8.17 Write a program using mipmaps in which each mipmap is constructed from a different image. Is there a practical application for such a program?

8.18 Using either your own image-processing code for convolution or the imaging extensions of OpenGL, implement a general 3×3 filtering program for luminance images.

8.19 Take an image from a digital camera or from some other source and apply 3×3 smoothing and sharpening filters repetitively. Pay special attention to what happens at the edges of the filtered images.

8.20 Repeat Exercise 8.19 but first add a small amount of random noise to the image. Describe the differences between the results of the two exercises.

8.21 If your system supports the imaging extensions, compare the performance of filtering using the extensions with filtering done by your own code using processor memory.

8.22 One of the most effective methods of altering the contrast of an image is to allow the user to design a lookup interactively. Consider a graph such as that in Figure 8.14 where the curve is approximated with three connected line segments. Write a program that displays an image, allows the user to specify the line segments interactively, and shows the image after it has been altered by the curve.

8.23 In a similar vein to Exercise 8.22, write an interactive program that allows users to design pseudocolor maps.

8.24 Devise a method to convert the values obtained from a cube map to values for a spherical map.

8.25 Write an interactive program that will return the colors of pixels on the display.

8.26 Suppose we want to create a cube that has a black and white checkerboard pattern texture mapped to its faces. Can we texture map the cube so that the colors alternate as we traverse the cube from face to face?

8.27 In what types of applications might you prefer a front-to-back rendering instead of a back-to-front rendering?

PROGRAMMABLE SHADERS

In developing the graphics pipeline, we assigned a fixed functionality to each box in the pipeline. Consequently, when we wanted to use light–material interactions to determine the colors of an object, we were limited to the modified Phong model because it was the only lighting model supported by the fixed-function pipeline defined in the OpenGL specification and, until recently, the only model supported by most hardware. In addition to having only one lighting model available, lighting calculations were done only for each vertex. The resulting vertex colors were then interpolated over the primitive by the fixed-function fragment processor. If we wanted to use some other lighting model, we usually had to resort to an off-line renderer.

Over the past few years, graphics processors have changed dramatically. Both the vertex processor and fragment processor are now user programmable. We can write programs called vertex shaders and fragment shaders to achieve complex visual effects at the same rate as the standard fixed-function pipeline.

In this chapter, we introduce the concept of programmable shaders. First, we review some of the efforts to develop languages to describe shaders. These efforts culminated in the **OpenGL Shading Language** (**GLSL**), which is now a standard part of OpenGL. We then use GLSL to develop a variety of vertex shaders that compute vertex properties, including their positions and colors. Finally, we develop fragment shaders that let us program the calculations performed on each fragment and ultimately determine the color of each pixel. Our discussion of fragment shaders will also introduce many new ways of using texture mapping.

9.1 Programmable Pipelines

When we developed the Phong and modified Phong lighting models in Chapter 6, we placed great emphasis on their efficiency but much less on how well they modeled physical light–material interactions. The modified Phong model is remarkable in that while it has a very loose coupling with physical reality, it yields images that are adequate for many purposes. Hence, as graphics hardware and especially pipeline architectures developed, it was natural that this model

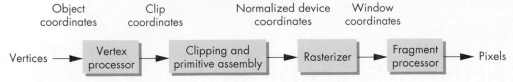

FIGURE 9.1 Pipeline architecture.

was built into the specification of OpenGL and was implemented in commodity hardware.

Often, however, we need a more physically realistic model. For example, specular reflections depend on the angle of the incident light, not just on the angle between the angle of reflection and the viewer (and certainly not just on the half-angle). When we work with translucent materials, we want to incorporate **refraction**, the bending of light as it passes through materials with different properties. We might also want to account for the fact that how light is bent by refraction is a function of the wavelength of the light.

In other situations, we want nonphotorealistic effects. For example, we might want to simulate the brush strokes of a painter or we might want to create cartoonlike shading effects. Many of these effects can be achieved only by working with fragments in ways that are not possible with a fixed-function pipeline. For example, in bump mapping, a topic that we consider in Section 9.12, we change the normal for each fragment to give the appearance of a surface with great complexity that appears correct as either the lights or the surface move. Many of these algorithms and effects were developed over 20 years ago but were only available through non–real-time renderers, such as RenderMan. Recent advances in graphics architectures have changed this situation dramatically.

Consider the pipeline architecture in Figure 9.1. This figure represents the same architecture we have been discussing starting with Chapter 1. First, we process vertices. Note that because both the model-view and projection transformations are applied during vertex processing, the representation of vertices in eye coordinates occurs only within the vertex processer. At the end of vertex processing, each vertex has been assigned a color, a position, and depending on which options are enabled, other attributes such as texture coordinates. Vertices are then assembled into primitives that are clipped. The potentially visible primitives that are not clipped out are rasterized, generating fragments. Ultimately, the fragments are processed to generate the final display. What has changed is that the vertex processor and the fragment processor are now programmable by application programs called **shaders**.

9.2 Shading Languages

Before we can develop a programming model for shaders, we need a method to express lighting models and shaders. An approach that was inspired by the

RenderMan shading language is to look at shaders as mathematical expressions. Mathematical expressions involve variables, constants, and operations among these entities. They can also be written in the form of tree data structures, and these trees can be traversed by a variety of algorithms that evaluate the expression represented by the tree. Hence, there is a direct relationship between languages that describe expressions and algorithms to evaluate these expressions.

9.2.1 Shade Trees

Consider the original Phong shading model from Chapter 6, without the distance term:

$$I = k_d L_d \mathbf{l} \cdot \mathbf{n} + k_s L_s (\mathbf{r} \cdot \mathbf{v})^\alpha + k_\alpha L_\alpha I_\alpha.$$

When a graphics system computes this expression[1] $\mathbf{n}$ and $\mathbf{l}$ are known from the OpenGL state, and $\mathbf{r}$ is computed by

$$\mathbf{r} = 2(\mathbf{l} \cdot \mathbf{n})\mathbf{n} - \mathbf{l}.$$

Both of these equations are expressions that involve both arithmetic operations, including exponentiation, and vector operations, such as the dot product. We can represent these equations using a tree data structure[2] as in Figure 9.2. Trees of this type are known as **expression trees**. Variables and constants appear at the terminal nodes and all internal nodes represent operations. Because all our operators are binary, the resulting tree is a binary tree in which all internal nodes have exactly two child nodes.

Evaluating an arithmetic expression is equivalent to traversing the corresponding tree, that is visiting every node and carrying out the requisite mathematical operations at the internal nodes. In this sense, trees and their associated traversal algorithms provide a means of both representing and implementing mathematical expressions, such as that for the Phong shader.

But the more interesting application of expression trees is in designing new shaders. Given a set of variables that might be available in a graphics system and operations that are supported by the system, we can form collections of trees, each of which defines a different method for shading a surface. This is the approach taken in the RenderMan shading language. Variables, such as normals and light source parameters, are assumed to be available from the environment and can be combined using a set of scalar and vector operations. From basic data structures, we know that arithmetic expressions and binary trees are equivalent. Thus, we can use standard tree-traversal algorithms for the evaluation of expressions that define shaders. Looked at slightly differently, shade

---

1. The computation actually uses $\max(0, \mathbf{l} \cdot \mathbf{n})$ and $\max(0, \mathbf{r} \cdot \mathbf{v})$ to guard against the effects of negative dot products.
2. We consider the use of trees in greater depth in Chapter 10.

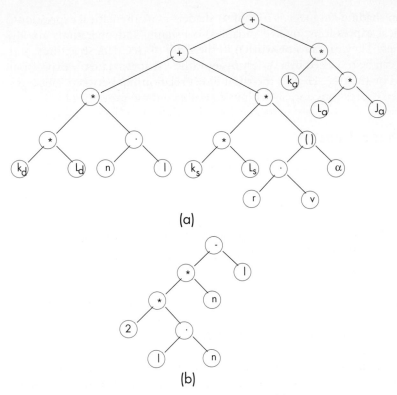

FIGURE 9.2   Expression trees. (a) For Phong shading. (b) For reflection vector.

trees can be translated to programs that can be executed by graphics processors. This approach to developing shaders is supported by the latest graphics cards through programmable pipelines.

9.3   Extending OpenGL

Before getting into the details of programmable shaders, which add a new level of complexity to OpenGL, we pause to examine the mechanisms by which OpenGL has evolved to incorporate advances in graphics hardware and software. Graphics APIs, such as OpenGL, developed as a way to provide application programmers with access to hardware features that were being provided by the latest graphics hardware. As more and more hardware features became available, processor speeds increased, and as more memory was provided on graphics processors, more complex graphics techniques became possible and even routine. It was only natural that application programmers would expect such techniques to be supported by graphics APIs.

The problem that API developers must confront is how to support such features through an existing API while not forcing programmers to replace existing code. One approach is to release new versions of the API even though they may not be compatible with earlier versions. Another approach is to add optional extensions to the API that allow application programs to access particular hardware features. OpenGL has used both these mechanisms. However, in order to access the new features of programmable graphics processors, entirely new programming tools are required.

9.3.1 OpenGL Versions and Extensions

One of the main features of OpenGL is that the API has been very stable. There were upgrades from OpenGL 1.0 through OpenGL 1.5 that were released over a 10-year period, each of which was compatible with previous releases. OpenGL 2.0, which was released in 2004, is a major upgrade but still retains code compatibility with earlier versions. Thus, any program written on an older version of OpenGL runs as expected on a later version. Changes to OpenGL reflect advances in hardware that became common to many graphics processors. For example, as hardware support for texture mapping increased, newer versions of OpenGL contained many new functions for using texture maps. Features such as texture objects, mipmapping, and three-dimensional textures were added to the early versions of OpenGL.

Whereas OpenGL versions represent a consensus of many users and hardware providers, a given graphics card or high-end workstation is likely to support features that are not generally available on other hardware. Such is especially the case with commodity cards that are used for computer games. Nevertheless, programmers who have access to a particular piece of hardware want to be able to access its features through OpenGL, even though these features are not general enough to be supported by the latest version of the API. One solution to this dilemma is to have an extension mechanism within OpenGL. Individual hardware providers can provide access to (or **expose**) hardware features through OpenGL-like function calls that may only work on a particular manufacturer's hardware. OpengGL extensions have names that identify the provider. For example, an extension with a name such as `glCommandSGI` identifies it as provided by Silicon Graphics, Inc. Other manufacturers could then implement the same extension. Extensions that have been widely used are approved by the OpenGL Architectural Review Board (ARB) and are designated as ARB extensions.

When programmable vertex shaders first became available, the ARB approved extensions for low-level vertex programs. Later extensions supported low-level fragment programs. However, the original interfaces to programmable hardware were somewhat unwieldy. The first software support for programmable hardware was much like assembly language interfaces for general purpose computers. Application programmers had to write moderately long programs that kept track of low-level details, such as register assignments in the graphics processor and moving data between registers and memory. The OpenGL extensions provided a mechanism for loading this assemblylike code into a programmable pipeline. Although this mechanism allowed users to work with programable shaders, it had all the faults of an assembly language program. As GPUs became more sophisticated, it became increasingly more difficult to program shaders using assembly language. In a manner similar to the development of standard programming languages, higher-level programming interfaces and compilers for shader code have now replaced assembly language programming for most users.

9.3.2   GLSL and Cg

The two high-level shading languages of most interest to us are the **OpenGL Shading Language** (**GLSL**) and **Cg**, which is an acronym for *C for Graphics*. They are similar but have different targeted users. Both are based on the C programming language and include most of its programming constructs but add language features and data types that make it easier to program shaders.

The main differences arise because Cg is designed to support both OpenGL and Microsoft's DirectX. Cg is virtually identical to Microsoft's High Level Shading Language (HLSL) and thus has the advantage for Window's developers that it allows them to develop shaders for both DirectX and OpenGL at the same time. However, the interface between OpenGL and Cg shaders is more complex than the interface between OpenGL and GLSL is. Furthermore, GLSL is part of OpenGL 2.0 and should be supported by multiple vendors and on multiple platforms. Hence, we shall focus on GLSL, understanding that the two approaches have far more similarities than differences.

9.4   The OpenGL Shading Language

The OpenGL Shading Language is a C-like language that allows the programmer to write both vertex and fragment shaders. It is incorporated into OpenGL 2.0. In GLSL, there is little distinction in the syntax between a vertex program and a fragment program, although the two are used in different contexts. Before we examine the GLSL language, we first examine the different tasks that these shaders must perform.

9.4.1   Vertex Shaders

A **vertex program**, or **vertex shader**, replaces the fixed-function operations performed by the vertex processor with operations defined by the shader. If a vertex shader is not provided by the application, a programmable vertex processor carries out the standard operations of the OpenGL fixed-function vertex processor. A vertex shader is executed on *each* vertex as it passes down the pipeline. Every vertex shader must output the information that the rasterizer needs to do its job. At a minimum, every vertex shader must output a vertex position for the rasterizer. For each vertex, the input to the vertex program can use the vertex position defined by the application program and most of the information that is in the OpenGL state, including the current color, texture coordinates, material properties, and transformation matrices. In addition, the application program can pass other application-specific information on a per-vertex basis to the vertex shader.

There are a few operations that virtually every vertex program must carry out. Recall that most application programs define vertex positions in object space, and the vertex processor transforms these positions first by the model-view matrix into eye coordinates and then by the projection matrix into clip coordinates. Because an application-supplied vertex shader replaces the fixed function vertex operations, one of the jobs that almost all vertex programs must carry out is to transform the input vertex position from object coordinates to clip coordinates. Because the vertex program can access the OpenGL state, it has access to the standard transformation matrices or it can compute its own transformations.

Here is a simple, but complete, vertex program:

```
/* pass through vertex shader */

void main(void)
{
    gl_Position = gl_ProjectionMatrix*gl_ModelViewMatrix*gl_Vertex;
}
```

This shader simply takes each vertex's position (`gl_Vertex`) in object coordinates and multiplies it by the model-view and projection matrices to obtain the position (`gl_Position`) in clip coordinates. The four variables in the shader are all part of the OpenGL state and thus do not have to be declared in the shader. Each execution of `glVertex` in an application triggers the execution of the shader. This shader is so simple that it does not even set a color or any other vertex attribute, leaving such matters to the fragment processor. Because this shader does nothing but send on the position of the vertex, it is sometimes called a *pass-through shader*.

A slightly more complex version that also assigns a red color to each vertex is

```
/* simple vertex shader */
const vec4 red = vec4(1.0, 0.0, 0.0, 1.0); /* C++ style constructor */

void main(void)
{
   gl_Position =  gl_ModelViewProjectionMatrx*gl_Vertex;
   gl_FrontColor = red;
}
```

This program does two things. It uses the model-view and projection matrices to convert the input vertex position (`gl_Vertex`) to a position in clip coordinates (`gl_Position`) and colors each vertex red. Because the conversion of a vertex's

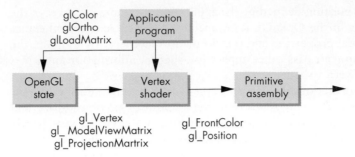

FIGURE 9.3   Vertex shader architecture.

position from object to clip coordinates is so common, GLSL provides the precomputed product of the model-view and projection matrices through the built-in variable gl_ModelViewProjectionMatrix. Note that names that begin with gl_ refer to variables that are part of the OpenGL state. Suppose that the application program that uses this vertex shader contains the code

```
glBegin(GL_POLYGON);
  glVertex3fv(v0);
  glVertex3fv(v1);
  glVertex3fv(v2);
glEnd();
```

where the vertices v0, v1, and v2 have been defined previously in the program. Each execution of glVertex invokes our shader with a new value of gl_Vertex, which is the internal four-dimensional representation of the vertex in glVertex. Each execution of the vertex program outputs a color (gl_FrontColor) and a new vertex position (gl_Position) that are passed on for primitive assembly. This process is illustrated in Figure 9.3. Note that a vertex shader has a main function designation and can call other functions written in GLSL. The same is true for fragment shaders.

GLSL includes new data types and the associated operations among them. Thus, the model-view and projection matrices are of type mat4, whereas the vertex position is a vec4 data type. The multiplication operator * is overloaded so that matrix-vector multiplications are defined as we would expect. Hence, the code in our simple vertex shader

```
gl_Position = gl_ModelViewProjectionMatrix*gl_Vertex;
```

yields the final position that is a vec4 data type.

Until now we have used the terms *column matrix* and *row matrix* rather than *vector* so as not to confuse the *vector* geometric type with its representation using row and column matrices. GLSL defines a *vector* data type that is a one-dimensional C-style array. GLSL reserves the *matrix* data type for square matrices that are two-dimensional C-style arrays. We shall use the GLSL terminology in this chapter.

In our example, we used built-in variables gl_FrontColor and gl_Position for the output of the vertex program. These values are available to either a fragment program or the fixed-function fragment processor. Note that the red color has a **const** qualifier and will be the same for each invocation of the program. In general, the output position and color can change with each invocation of the vertex program. Also note the use of a C++-style constructor to initialize the red color vector.

9.4.2 Fragment Shaders

Fragment shaders written in GLSL have the same syntax as vertex programs. However, fragment programs are executed after the rasterizer and thus operate on each fragment rather than on each vertex.

Consider our trivial example in which the front color is passed onto primitive assembly and clipping stages. If the vertex is not eliminated by clipping, it goes on to the rasterizer, which generates fragments that are then processed by the fragment processor using either fixed function fragment processing or an application-defined **fragment program**, or **fragment shader**. In the simplest case, vertex attributes, such as vertex colors and positions, are interpolated across a primitive to generate the corresponding fragment attributes. A minimal fragment program is

```
/* simple fragment program */
void main()
{
    gl_FragColor = gl_FrontColor;
}
```

As trivial as this program appears, there is a major difference between how it and a vertex program function. The values of gl_FrontColor are not the values produced by the vertex program. Rather, the values of gl_FrontColor in the fragment program have been produced by interpolating the vertex values of gl_FrontColor over the primitive to produce the values used in the fragment program. Thus, unless all the vertex colors are identical, each time the fragment program executes, it will use a different value of gl_FrontColor. The fragment color produced by the fragment program is then used to modify the color of a pixel in the frame buffer. This process is shown in Figure 9.4. We now present the main features of GLSL and then develop some more sophisticated shaders.

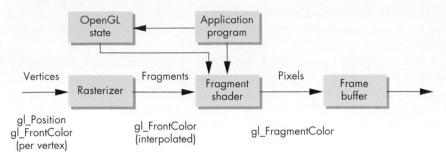

FIGURE 9.4   Fragment shader architecture.

9.5   The OpenGL Shading Language

The OpenGL Shading Language is based on the C programming language. GLSL has similar naming conventions, data types, and control structures. However, because vertex and fragment shaders execute in a very different environment than normal programs, including the OpenGL application that invokes them, there are some significant differences from C.

9.5.1   GLSL Execution

Let's consider what happens when a typical OpenGL application program executes. Most OpenGL functions change the OpenGL state but do not cause anything to flow down the pipeline. However, once we execute a glVertex function, the pipeline goes into action. With the fixed-function pipeline, various calculations are made in the pipeline to determine if the primitive to which the vertex belongs is visible and, if it is, to color the corresponding pixels in the frame buffer. These calculations generally do not change the OpenGL state. Subsequent executions of glVertex invoke the same calculations but use updated values of state variables if any state changes have been made in between the calls to glVertex.

   If we look at these calculations as the work of the software and hardware that implement the vertex processor, we see that there must be multiple types of variables involved in the execution of this code. Some variables will change as the vertex color is computed. Others, whose values are determined by the OpenGL state, cannot be changed by the calculation. Most internal variables must be initialized to their original values after each vertex is processed so that the calculation for the next vertex will be identical. Other variables must be computed and passed onto the next stage of the pipeline. Consequently, when we substitute a user-written vertex program for the fixed-function vertex processor, we must identify these different types of variables.

The same argument is true when we use a fragment program. The major difference is that the program will be executed on each fragment. Some values will be provided by the OpenGL state and thus cannot be changed. Others will be changed only on a vertex-by-vertex or primitive-by-primitive basis. Most shader variables must be initialized for each fragment.

A typical application will not only change state variables and entities such as texture maps, but it may also use multiple vertex and fragment shaders. Hence, we shall also examine how to load in shaders and change the current shader. However, this process is not part of GLSL but is accomplished using a set of functions that formerly were OpenGL extensions but are now part of OpenGL 2.0.

9.5.2 Data Types and Qualifiers

GLSL has basic data types that are similar to C and C++. The atomic types, however, are limited to a single floating-point type, `float`, a single integer type, `int`, and a boolean type, `bool`. Arrays and structures are declared in the standard C way. There are no pointer variables in GLSL.

GLSL introduces new vector and matrix types for working with the two-, three-, and four-dimensional matrices that we use in computer graphics. Vectors are special one-dimensional arrays. We can use floating-point (`vec2`, `vec3`, `vec4`), integer (`ivec2`, `ivec3`, `ivec4`), or Boolean (`bvec2`, `bvec3`, `bvec4`) types. Because the vector types can be used to store vertex positions, colors, or texture coordinates, the elements can be indexed by position (x, y, z, w), color (r, g, b, a), or texture coordinates (s, t, p, q). Thus, if c is a vector, then `c[1]`, `c.y`, `c.g`, and `c.t` all refer to the second element of c. Note that this flexibility is there only to create more readable code and carries no semantic information. Hence, there is no reason that `c.y` cannot contain color or texture information.

Matrices in GLSL are always square and floating point (`mat2`, `mat3`, `mat4`). As with other OpenGL matrices, storage is by *columns*. However, the usual C/C++ referencing applies. If m is a matrix, `m[1]` is its second row and `m[1][2]` is the element in row 2, column 3.

GLSL uses C++-style constructors to initialize the vectors and matrix types, for example,

```
vec3 a = vec3(1.0, -2.0, 5.0);
```

Constructors also can be used for conversion between types as in

```
vec2 b = vec2(a);
```

which uses the first two components of the `vec3` variable a to form b.

Variables can be qualified in different ways. Ordinary (nonlocal) variables, those that are not function parameters or function temporaries, can be qualified as `attribute`, `uniform`, `varying`, or `const`. The **const** qualifier is the same as in C and makes the variable unchangeable by the shader. Thus, we can create a constant scalar and vector as

```
const float one = 1.0;
const vec3 origin = vec2(1.0, 2.0, 3.0);
```

Attribute-qualified variables are used by vertex shaders for variables that change at most once per vertex in the vertex shader. There are two types of attribute-qualified variables. The first type includes the OpenGL state variables that we associate with a vertex, such as its color, position, texture coordinates, and normal. These are known as **built-in** variables. In our simple example, the state variables `gl_Vertex` and `gl_FrontColor` are built-in attribute-qualified variables. Built-in variables need not be declared in shaders. GLSL allows additional vertex attributes to be defined in the application program so that it can convey other information on a per-vertex basis to the shader. For example, in a scientific visualization application, we might want to associate a scalar temperature or a flow velocity vector with each vertex. Only floating-point types can be attribute qualified. User-defined attribute-qualified variables are declared as in the code

```
attribute float temperature;
attribute vec3 velocity;
```

Because they vary on a vertex-by-vertex basis, vertex attributes cannot be declared in a fragment shader.

Uniform qualifiers are used for variables that are set in the application program for an entire primitive, that is variables whose values are assigned outside the scope of a `glBegin` and a `glEnd`. Because the names of uniform variables are common to the OpenGL program and the shaders, uniform variables provide a mechanism for sharing data among an application program, vertex shaders, and fragment shaders. However, uniform variables cannot be changed in a shader. Hence, we use uniform variables to pass information into shaders. For example, we might want to compute the bounding box of a set of vertices that define a primitive in the application and send this information to a shader to simplify its calculations.

Although naming a variable as a *varying variable* may seem a bit strange at first, **varying**-qualified variables provide the mechanism for conveying data from a vertex shader to a fragment shader. These variables are defined on a per-vertex basis but are interpolated over the primitive by the fragment shader. As with attribute-qualified variables, varying variables can be either built-in or user defined.

Consider, for example, how colors are determined in the fixed-function pipeline. The vertex processor computes a color for each vertex. The color of a fragment is determined by interpolating the vertex colors. Likewise, texture coordinates for each fragment are determined by interpolating texture coordinates at the vertices. Both vertex colors and texture coordinates are varying variables. In our simple vertex shader, gl_FrontColor is a built-in varying variable. If we created a more complex vertex shader that computed a different color for each vertex, using the varying-qualified variable gl_FrontColor would ensure that there is an interpolated color for each fragment, whether or not we write our own fragment program.

With a few exceptions[3], user-defined varying variables that are set in the vertex program are automatically interpolated by the fragment program. It does not make sense to define a varying variable in a vertex shader and not use it in a fragment shader. Hence, a user-defined varying variable must appear in both the vertex and fragment shaders. Consequently, if we use such a variable in the vertex shader, we must write a corresponding fragment shader. Thus, while our simple vertex shader did not need the simple fragment shader, the equivalent vertex shader

```
const vec4 red = vec4(1.0, 0.0, 0.0, 1.0);

varying vec3 color_out; /* varying variable */

void main(void)
{

    gl_Position =  gl_ModelViewProjectionMatrix*gl_Vertex;
    color_out = red;
}
```

requires at a minimum the pass-through fragment shader

```
varying vec3 color_out;

void main()
{
    gl_FragColor = color_out;
}
```

Variables that are function parameters necessitate a few additional options. Because of the nature of execution of vertex and fragment shaders and the lack of pointers, GLSL uses a mechanism known as **call by value-return**. Function parameters are qualified as **in** (the default), **out**, or **inout**. GLSL functions have return types. Returned variables are copied back to the calling function. Input parameters are copied from the calling program. If a variable is qualified as in, it is copied in but is not copied out, even though its value may be changed within the function. A function parameter that is qualified as out is undefined on entry

---

3. For example, there is no need for interpolating colors if the shading model has been set to GL_FLAT.

to the function but can be set in the function and is copied back to the calling function. A parameter that is inout-qualified is copied in and also copied out.

Note that because there are no pointers, we cannot return arrays as we would normally with C, but we can use arrays as structure members and thus have them copied back from a function. Because vectors and matrices are basic types, they can be copied into and copied from functions.

9.5.3 Operators and Functions

For the most part, the operators are as in C with the same precedence rules. However, because the internal format of the float and integer types is not specified by GLSL, bit operations are not allowed.

The operations among the usual C types and the vector and matrix types are overloaded so that matrix-vector operators can be used as we would expect. For example, the code

```
mat4 a;
vec4 b, c, d;

c = b*a;
d = a*b;
```

makes sense. In the first case, GLSL computes c treating b as a row matrix, whereas d is computed treating b as a column matrix. Hence, although c and d are the same type, they will have different values.

GLSL has a **swizzling** operator that is a variant of the C selection operator (.). Swizzling allows us to select multiple components from the matrix and vector types. We can use swizzling and write masking to select and rearrange elements of vectors and matrices. For example, we can change selected elements as in

```
vec4 a =  vec4(1.0, 2.0, 3.0, 1.0);

a.x = 2.0;
a.yz = vec2(-1.0, 4.0);
```

or swap elements, as in the code

```
a.xy =  a.yx;
```

Note that we can use any of the formats (x, y, z, w; r, g, b, a; s, t, p, q) as long as we do not mix them in single selection.

GLSL has many built-in functions including the trigonometric functions (sin, cos, tan), inverse trigonometric functions (asin, acos, atan), and mathematical functions (pow, log2, sqrt, abs, max, min). Of particular importance are functions that help with geometric calculations involving vectors that are required in computer graphics. Hence, there is a length function, a distance function, a dot product function, a `normalize` function, and a `reflect` function. Most of these functions are overloaded so that they work with both floats and vectors. We shall see examples of these and other built-in functions in the examples. We shall delay our discussion of the texture functions until Section 9.10.

9.6 Linking Shaders with OpenGL Programs

With GLSL, we can write shaders independent of any OpenGL application. There exist various development environments that let users write and test shaders. However, at some point, we have to link the shaders with the OpenGL application.

There is a set of OpenGL functions that deal with how to create vertex and shader objects, link them with an OpenGL application, and enable passing of variables among the OpenGL program and the shaders. Originally, these functions were in three OpenGL extensions (`ARB_shader_objects`, `ARB_vertex_shader`, and `ARB_fragment_shader`). Although these extensions still exist, their functionality has been incorporated into OpenGL 2.0. Because the functions are now part of OpenGL 2.0, the function names do not need extension suffixes[4].

Generally, we start by declaring a **program object** and getting an identifier for it:

```
GLunit myProgObj;
myProgObj = glCreateProgram();
```

The program object is a container that can hold multiple shaders and other GLSL functions. Suppose that we have written a vertex shader and stored it in a file named `my_vertex_shader`. We can add this shader to our program object as follows. We create a **shader object**, identify where the source code for the shader is located, compile the shader, and finally attach it to the program object, as in the following code:

```
GLchar vertexProg[] = "my_vertex_shader";
GLunit myVertexObj;

myVertexObj = glCreateShader(GL_VERTEX_SHADER);
glShaderSource(myVertexObj, 1, vertexProg, NULL);
glCompileShader(myVertexObj);
glAttachObject(myProgObj, myVertexObj);
```

This code is pretty minimal. A more polished version is in Appendix A. We should do various checks, such as whether the specified shader file exists and whether

---

4. There are also a few changes to variable types and function names when going from the extensions to OpenGL 2.0.

the shader compiled successfully. Note that we have used only a single shader here. We can load multiple shaders from a single file or load them one at a time into a single program object.

Because we can create multiple program objects, we must identify which one to use. For the program object that we just created, we execute the function

```
glUseProgram(myProgObj);
```

Now we can link everything together:

```
glLinkProgram(myProgObj);
```

The next step is aligning the variables in the shaders with variables in the program. Vertex attributes in the shader are indexed in the main program through tables that are set up during linking. We obtain the needed indices through the function glGetAttribLocation. These indices are used later to obtain values computed in the shader using the various forms of the function glVertexAttrib. For example, suppose that we set an RGBA color in the shader in a variable named myColor. We get its index by

```
GLint colorAttr;
colorAttr = glGetAttribLocation(myProgObj, "myColor");
```

Later, we can use its value in the OpenGL program as

```
GLfloat color[4];
glVertexAttrib4fv(colorAttrib, color);
```

A similar process holds for uniform variables. Suppose that we compute a uniform variable angle in the application and want to send it to the shader. We get an index

```
GLint angleParam;
angleParam = glGetUniformLocation(myProgObj, "angle");
```

and later can compute a value in the application program

```
GLfloat my_angle;

my_angle = 5.0 /* or some other value */
```

and send it to the the shaders by

```
glUniform1f(myProgObj, angleParam, my_angle);
```

The function glUniform has one- to four-dimensional forms and a pointer (v) version and can be used to set scalar and vector values. For example, the code

```
GLfloat red[4] = {1.0, 0.0, 0.0, 1.0};
GLint ColorParam;

colorParam = glGetUniformLocation(myProgObj, "redColor")
glUniform4fv(myProgObj, colorParam, red)
```

sets the uniform shader variable `redColor`. The various forms of the function `glMatrixUniform` are used to set uniform matrices in shaders.

If we want to get the value of the uniform variable from a shader, we use the function `glGetUniform`. However, because we rarely need to get uniform values from shaders, we shall not discuss these functions, which closely match the functions for sending values to shaders.

Although there is a fair number of functions here, as with most OpenGL programs, most of them are used during initialization and do not change much from application to application. If we look at what we have to do each time, there are two basic parts. First, we set up various shaders and then link them to program objects. This part can be put in an initialization function in the OpenGL program. Second, within the body of the OpenGL program, we either get values from shaders or send values to shaders. Usually, we do these operations where we would normally set values for colors, texture coordinates, normals, and other program variables with an application that uses the fixed-function pipeline.

Although we have not said much about fragment programs, the mechanism for creating and linking fragment programs is much the same as for vertex programs and we shall see it in more detail soon. Appendix A contains a full program with a basic vertex shader and a basic fragment shader. Next, we focus on what we can do with vertex shaders.

9.7 Moving Vertices

We now develop some examples of vertex shaders. The first examples involve moving vertices, something that is part of many animation strategies. In each case, we must generate an initial vertex position in the OpenGL program because the execution of the function `glVertex` initiates the vertex shader. In these first examples, the work done by the vertex shaders could have been done in your application program. However, we often want to do this work in the vertex shader because it frees up the CPU for other tasks. The second set of examples involves determining vertex colors. In these examples, we have no choice other than replacing the fixed-function vertex processing with a vertex shader.

9.7.1 Scaling Vertex Positions

One of the simplest examples of a vertex shader is a program that changes the location of each vertex that triggers the shader. However, we must remember that once we use a vertex program of our own, we must do all the functions of the fixed-function vertex processor. In particular, we are responsible for converting vertex locations from object coordinates to clip coordinates. In our simplest examples, we can do this operation by using the model-view and projection matrices that are part of the OpenGL state. Alternately, we could compute the clip space position of each vertex in the shader without using the built-in matrices.

In our first example, we scale each vertex so that the object appears to expand and contract. The scale factor varies sinusoidally, based on a time parameter that is passed in as a uniform variable from the OpenGL program.

```
/* vertex shader that moves vertex locations sinusoidally */

uniform float time; /* value provided by application program */

void main()
{
  float s;
  s = 1.0 + 0.5*sin(time);
  gl_Position =  vec4(s, s, s, 1.0)*gl_ModelViewProjectionMatrix*gl_Vertex;
}
```

Note that we use the product of the model-view and projection matrices from the OpenGL state and that we apply the scale factor only to the first three components of the vector (see Exercise 9.18).

We can make the example somewhat more interesting if we let the variation depend on the position of each vertex. Suppose that we start with a height field in which the y value of each vertex is the height and we change only this value. Consider the code

```
/* vertex program for varying a height field */

uniform float time;
uniform float xs, zs;

void main()
{
   float s;
   s = 1.0 + 0.1*sin(xs*time)*sin(zs*time);
   gl_Position =  gl_ModelViewProjectionMatrix*gl_Vertex;
   gl_Position.y = s*gl_Position.y;
}
```

We now create a wave effect as the time is incremented in the OpenGL program. The form of the wave can be controlled by setting the uniform variables xs and zs in the OpenGL program.

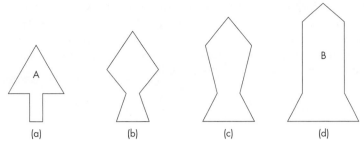

FIGURE 9.5   Morphing. (a) Object A. (b) A 1/3 morphed to B. (c) A 2/3 morphed to B. (d) Object B.

9.7.2 Morphing

One of the standard techniques in animation is known as **key framing**. In this technique, we define the positions of objects in our scene at a set of times or in a set of positions, thus defining the key frames. We then interpolate between successive frames or positions to get the **in-between** frames or positions. We shall see this topic again in Chapter 10.

One variant of this idea is **morphing**, a technique in which we smoothly change one object into another. Suppose that we have two sets of vertices that define our initial and final shapes. We assume that for each object that we want to morph, we have a set of ordered vertices stored in an array. If we want to morph object A into object B, we assume that they have the same number of vertices and that corresponding vertices are matched. Thus vertex k in the first array of vertices should morph into vertex k in the second array. In general, these sets are formed by the animator with the aid of software that can create extra vertices to ensure that the two-sets are of the same size with matching vertices. Figure 9.5 shows a two-dimensional polygon morphing into another two-dimensional polygon.

The vertex shader needs to output a single vertex that is constructed by interpolating between two vertices provided by the OpenGL program. The main problem is that we can pass in only a single vertex through the built-in uniform variable gl_Vertex. However, we can pass in the corresponding vertex using an application-defined vertex attribute. We also pass in a uniform variable that determines how much of each vertex's location we should use in the interpolation. Here is the vertex shader:

```
uniform float blend;
attribute vec4 second_vertex;
void main()
{
    gl_Position = gl_ModelViewProjectionMatrix*mix(gl_Vertex, second_vertex,
                                              blend);
}
```

The GLSL function `mix` forms the affine combination of the two vertices. Thus, for example, the first component of `mix(gl_Vertex, second_vertex, blend)` is `(1-blend)*gl_Vertex.x + blend*second_vertex.x`. On the OpenGL side, we have to define the required vertex attribute and uniform parameter `blend`. Within the display callback, we should see code something like

```
#define N 50 /*number of vertices*/
GLfloat vertices_two[N][3], vertices[N][3];

void mydisplay()
{
  blend = .....; /* set value of blend */

  glBeginGL_POLYGON
     for(i = 0; i< N; i++)
     {
        glUniform(blendLocation, blend);
        glAttrib3fv(vertices_two_location, 3, &vertices_two[i]);
        glVertex3fv(vertices[i]);
     }
  glEnd();

  glutSwapBuffers();
}
```

In this code, the locations `blendLocation` and `vertices_two_location` were obtained using `glGetUniformLocation` and `glGetAttributeLocation` during the initialization of the application program. We probably want to embellish this program quite a bit by blending colors, texture coordinates, and other vertex attributes (see Exercise 9.1).

9.7.3   Particle Systems

One of the most important approaches to simulating complex real-world objects, such as clouds, trees, water, and hair, is through **particle systems**. Particle systems are one of many procedural methods used in computer graphics, a topic to which we shall return in Chapter 10. The basic idea in all particle systems is that we can model the motion of points in space either using realistic physics or by creating our own physics. For each time step, we determine a new location for each particle. We can then display any object that we desire at these locations. For example, if want to create clouds, we might use a collection of translucent polygons, each of which would be centered at the location of a particle. For a piece of cloth, we can start with an array of locations that determine a mesh, each of whose vertices is a particle whose location changes with time.

Vertex shaders work well for particle systems. One reason is that we can have the shader do much of the work involved in positioning each particle much faster than the CPU can. Because shaders cannot create new vertices, at a minimum, the OpenGL program must generate each particle as a vertex so as to trigger the vertex shader. A particularly simple example, but one that can be extended easily (Exercise 9.2), is to generate particles that are subject only to the forces of gravity.

Consider an ideal point subject to Newton's laws. Suppose that it has a mass m, an initial position (x_0, y_0, z_0), and an initial velocity (v_x, v_y, v_z). If we ignore effects such as friction, using the gravitational constant g, its position at time t is given by

$$x(t) = x_0 + v_x t,$$

$$y(t) = y_0 + v_y t + \frac{g}{2m} t^2,$$

$$z(t) = y_0 + v_z t.$$

Thus, we can pass the time and each particle's initial velocity to the shader as uniform variable and pass in the particles's initial position through gl_Vertex. Each time that the vertex program is executed, it then computes the present position of the vertex. Because the time variable is updated by the application, each time through the display callback, the vertex shader computes new vertex positions. Here is a simple vertex shader for such a particle system:

```
uniform vec3 init_vel;
uniform float g, m, t;
void main()
{
    vec3 object_pos;
    object_pos.x = gl_Vertex.x + vel.x*t;
    object_pos.y = gl_Vertex.y + vel.y*t + g/(2.0*m)*t*t;
    object_pos.z = gl_Vertex.z + vel.z*t;
    gl_Position =  gl_ModelViewProjectionMatrix*vec4(object_pos,1);
}
```

One simple application that we can create with this shader is to simulate fireworks by having each vertex render as a point and sending each vertex to the shader with the same initial position for each particle but giving each vertex a slightly different initial velocity. In addition, we can change the color as time progresses and even make particles disappear (see Exercise 9.3).

If the vertices are part of a more complex object than a point, the entire object is now subject to gravity. One interesting variant is to create a bouncing effect by using the reflect function to change the velocity when the vertex location hits the ground (see Exercise 9.5).

9.8   Lighting with Shaders

Perhaps the most important use of vertex shaders, at least without a corresponding fragment shader, is to replace the modified Phong lighting model that is used by the fixed-function pipeline. We start by writing both the Phong and modified Phong models as independent vertex shaders. We do so primarily to introduce the structure and functions used to compute lighting with a vertex shader. Then we shall examine alternate shading methods.

9.8.1   Phong Shading

The Phong lighting model that we developed in Chapter 6 can be written, without the distance terms, as

$$I = k_d L_d \mathbf{l} \cdot \mathbf{n} + k_s L_s (\mathbf{r} \cdot \mathbf{v})^\alpha + k_\alpha L_\alpha I_\alpha.$$

Recall that this expression is for any component of an RGB color. Hence, all the constants for the diffuse, specular, and ambient reflection coefficients are arrays of three elements, as are the corresponding components for the light sources.

When we write shaders that determine the color of a vertex, we must be careful to keep track of which frame we are working in. We know that we must transform vertex locations to clip coordinates. However, when we work with normals, lights, and texture coordinates, we have multiple coordinate systems and we often have choices as to which frame we wish to do our calculations in. For example, whereas the vertex location is transformed by the product of the model-view and projection matrices with `gl_ModelViewProjectionMatrix`, the position of a light source should be transformed only into eye coordinates with the model-view matrix (`gl_ModelViewMatrix`) in the shader.

To keep our first example simple, we assume that a single light source (`GL_LIGHT0`) has been defined in the OpenGL program, as well as the material properties.

Let's examine the basics piece by piece. First, we must convert the vertex location to clip coordinates for use by the fragment shader:

```
gl_Position = gl_ModelViewProjectionMatrix*gl_Vertex;
```

The normal vector, `gl_Normal`, is also a built-in uniform variable, but we must ensure that it has unit length and has been transformed into eye coordinates. However, recall from Chapter 6 that because we must preserve the angle between the normal and the light source, we must transform the normal in object coordinates by the inverse transpose of the 3×3, upper-left part of the model-view matrix. The matrix is called the **normal matrix** and is provided by the built-in uniform variable `gl_NormalMartrix`. We must also ensure that the resulting vector has unit length. We can accomplish both tasks using the single line of code

```
vec3 norm = normalize(gl_NormalMatrix*gl_Normal);
```

All the light parameters for light source i are available as built-in uniform variables through the built-in structure gl_LightSource[i]. We need the light position to compute the light source vector

```
vec3 lightv = normalize(vec3(gl_LightSource[0].position
                      - gl_ModelViewMatrix*gl_Vertex));
```

and the reflection vector

```
vec3 reflectv = reflect( lightv, norm);
```

We can get the view vector in eye coordinates from the position in eye coordinates as

```
vec3 viewv = normalize(gl_ModelViewMatrix*gl_Vertex);
```

We now have all the information that we need to compute a vertex color using either the Phong or modified Phong model. The material values for the front face are in the built-in structure gl_FrontMaterial. Neglecting the distance term, the diffuse component of the color is given by

```
vec4 diffuse = max(0, dot(lightv, viewv)*gl_FrontMaterial.diffuse
            *gl_LightSource[0].diffuse);
```

Note that the product of two variables of type vec3 is done component by component, thus avoiding having to loop over the color components in our code. Also, we use the max function to take care of cases when the dot product is negative. The ambient color is given by

```
vec4 ambient = gl_FrontMaterial.ambient*gl_LightSource[0].ambient;
```

The diffuse and ambient contributions for the vertex color are the same in the Phong and modified Phong models. For the modified Phong model, we can compute the specular component by first computing the half-angle vector

```
vec3 halfv = normalize(lightv + norm);
vec4 specular = f*pow(max(0, dot( norm, halfv)),gl_FrontMaterial.shininess)
     *gl_FrontMaterial.specular*gl_LightSource[0].specular);
```

The factor f is either 0 or 1, depending on the sign of the dot product between the light vector and the normal:

```
float f;

if(dot(lightv, norm) > 0.0) f = 1.0;
  else f = 0.0;
```

For the Phong model, we use the dot product of the reflection vector and the view vector. However, if we want our Phong model and our modified Phong model to provide approximately the same result, we must alter the value of the shininess coefficient provided by the OpenGL state. We can approximate the value from the shininess coefficient in the OpenGL state for the modified Phong model (see Exercise 9.8) or simply take an approximate value such as

```
float shininess = gl_FrontMaterial.shininess*factor;
```

for some constant `factor` that can be supplied by the application. The corresponding specular term is

```
vec4 specular = f*pow(max(0, dot( reflectv, viewv)), shininess)
  *gl_FrontMaterial.specular*gl_LightSource[0].specular);
```

We can now add up the contributions as the color for the front face

```
gl_FrontColor = vec4(ambient + diffuse + specular, 1);
```

We have been using built-in uniform variables to obtain most of the required values from the OpenGL state. In other situations, we might pass in values through the function parameters or non–built-in uniform variables. If we are using a fragment program, we often will use varying variables to pass the results of the vertex program onward. We shall see more examples of this type when we consider texture mapping in Section 9.10.

Putting everything together, we have a vertex shader that computes the modified Phong shading for each vertex.

```
void main()

    /* modified Phong vertex shader (without distance term) */
{
    float f;

  /* compute normalized normal, light vector, view vector,
    half-angle vector in eye cordinates */

    vec3 norm = normalize(gl_NormalMatrix*gl_Normal);
    vec3 lightv = normalize(gl_LightSource[0].position
                            - gl_ModelViewMatrix*gl_Vertex);
    vec3 viewv = -normalize(gl_ModelViewMatrix*gl_Vertex);
    vec3 halfv = normalize(lightv + norm);

    if(dot(lightv, norm) > 0.0) f = 1.0;
        else f = 0.0;

    /* compute diffuse, ambient, and specular contributions */
```

```
vec4 diffuse = max(0, dot(lightv, norm))*gl_FrontMaterial.diffuse
              *LightSource[0].diffuse;
vec4 ambient = gl_FrontMaterial.ambient*LightSource[0].ambient;
vec4 specular = f*gl_FrontMaterial.specular*gl_LightSource[0].specular)
        *pow(max(0, dot( norm, halfv)), gl_FrontMaterial.shininess);
vec3 color = vec3(ambient + diffuse + specular)
gl_FrontColor = vec4(color, 1);
gl_Position = gl_ModelViewProjectionMatrix*gl_Vertex;
}
```

9.8.2 Nonphotorealistic Shading

Vertex shaders make it possible to incorporate more realistic lighting models in real time. In Section 9.11, we consider effects such as refraction and chromatic dispersion. However, many interesting applications of programmable shaders involve using shaders to create nonphotorealistic effects. Two interesting examples are the use of only a few colors and emphasizing the edges in objects. Both these effects are techniques that we might want to use to obtain a cartoonlike effect in an image.

Suppose that we define two colors in our shader:

```
const vec4 color1 = {1.0, 1.0, 0.0, 1.0}; /* yellow */
const vec4 color2 = {1.0, 0.0, 0.0, 1.0}; /* red */
```

We could then switch between the colors based, for example, on the magnitude of the diffuse color. Using the light and normal vectors, we could assign colors as

```
if(dot(lightv, norm)) > 0.5) gl_FrontColor = color1;
   else gl_FrontColor = color2;
```

Although we could have used two colors in simpler ways, by using the diffuse color to determine a threshold, the color of the object changes with its shape and the position of the light source.

We can also try to draw the silhouette edge of an object. One way to identify such edges is to look at sign changes in dot(lightv, norm). This value should be positive for any vertex facing the viewer and negative for a vertex pointed away from the viewer. Thus, we can test for small values of this value and assign a color such as black to the vertex:

```
vec3 color3 = {0.0, 0.0, 0.0, 1.0}; /* black */

if(abs(dot(viewv, norm) < 0.01) glFrontColor = color3;
```

9.9 Fragment Shaders

Whereas vertex shaders are part of the geometric processing at the front end of the graphics pipeline, fragment shaders work on individual fragments, each of which can contribute directly to the color of a pixel. Consequently, fragment shaders open up myriad possibilities for producing an image on a pixel-by-pixel basis.

One of the most interesting aspects of fragment shaders is that they enable us to work with texture maps in new ways. In particular, we shall see how to use cube maps to create effects such as refraction in environment maps and displacement maps. Fragment shaders allow many more possibilities than vertex shaders, some of which (such as normalization maps) can increase the efficiency of our programs.

Syntactically, fragment and vertex shaders in GLSL are almost identical. We have the same data types, most of the same qualifiers, and the same functions. However, fragment shaders execute in a fundamentally different manner. Let's review what the fragment processor does.

The rasterizer generates fragments for all primitives that have not been clipped out. Each fragment corresponds to a pixel in the frame buffer and has attributes including its color and position in the frame buffer. Other attributes are determined from vertex attributes by interpolating values at the vertices. Thus, even with a pass-through fragment shader such as

```
/* pass-through fragment shader */
void main(void)
{
    gl_FragColor = gl_FrontColor;
}
```

the color of each fragment is interpolated from the vertex colors, whether these colors were set by the application through the OpenGL state, computed in the fixed function pipeline, or computed with a vertex shader. Likewise, the texture coordinates of each fragment are interpolated from the texture coordinates of the vertices, regardless of how they were assigned. In addition, any varying variable output by the vertex shader will be interpolated automatically across each primitive.

9.10 Per-Vertex Versus Per-Fragment Phong Shading

Because virtually any quantity that is defined at a vertex can be interpolated across a primitive in a fragment shader, we can do lighting calculations on a fragment-by-fragment basis rather than on a vertex-by-vertex basis. Consider polygonal shading as discussed in Chapter 6. We discussed three methods for shading a single polygon. In the simplest, constant shading, we used a single color for the entire polygon. This color could either be set in the application or calculated in the pipeline using the modified Phong model at the first vertex. This option is specified in OpenGL by setting the shading model to GL_FLAT. The second method that we discussed is smooth shading, the default for the fixed-function pipeline. Here colors are computed for each vertex as part of vertex processing and then interpolated across the polygon by the fragment processor. This method works the same as the Phong vertex shader that we developed in Section 9.7. The fragment processor does not know how the vertex colors were produced and simply interpolates vertex colors across the polygon.

The third method, Phong shading,[5] is based on interpolating vertex positions and normals, rather than interpolating vertex colors across the polygon and then applying the shading model at each fragment using the interpolated normals. Until the advent of programmable fragment programs, per-fragment shading was only possible as an off-line process and thus incurred a considerable time penalty compared to using the standard modified Phong shader provided by the fixed-function pipeline. With a fragment shader, we can do the computation on a per-fragment basis. Given the speed of recent GPUs, even though the lighting calculations are done for each fragment, we can still process complex geometric models interactively.

Let's now write a fragment shader to do per-fragment, modified Phong shading with a single light source (GL_LIGHT0). Because we need to transfer data from the vertex shader to the fragment shader, we need to write both shaders. We shall use a slightly different approach from Section 9.7, one that makes use of varying variables.

In the vertex program, we compute the position and normal in eye coordinates and pass them to the fragment program. In this example, we assume that the vertex normal that the vertex program starts with is available from the OpenGL state. In the simplest case, this vertex normal will be unchanged for a given primitive. If the application program can compute a different vertex normal for each vertex using data from surrounding polygons, then our program will do true Gouraud shading without modifying either the vertex or fragment shaders. Here is a basic vertex program:

```
/* vertex shader for per-fragment Phong shading */

varying vec3 normale;
varying vec4 positione;

void main()
{
    normale = gl_NormalMatrixMatrix*gl_Normal;
```

---

5. Phong shading is often confused with the Phong lighting model. The latter models light–material interaction, the former how colors are interpolated across polygons.

```
    positione = gl_ModelViewMatrix*gl_Vertex;
    gl_Position = gl_ModelViewProjectionMatrix*gl_Vertex;
}
```

Note that to have a correct vertex program, we must compute gl_Position, even if we do not use it in the fragment program.

We can access all the light and material properties that we need in the fragment shader from the OpenGL state. Because the normal and position are passed in from the vertex shader and share the same name space, they will be interpolated across the primitive automatically. Consequently, the fragment shader looks very similar to the modified Phong vertex shader from Section 9.7.

```
varying vec3 normale;
varying vec4 positione;

void main()
{
    vec3 norm = normalize(normale);
    vec3 lightv = normalize(gl_LightSource[0].position-positione.xyz);
    vec3 viewv = normalize(positione);
    vec3 halfv = normalize(lightv + viewv);
    vec4 diffuse = max(0, dot(lightv, viewv))*gl_FrontMaterial.diffuse
            *gl_LightSource[0].diffuse;
    vec4 ambient = gl_FrontMaterial.ambient*gl_LightSource[0].ambient;
    int f;
    if(dot(lightv, viewv)> 0.0) f =1.0);
        else f = 0.0;
    vec3 specular = f*pow(max(0, dot(norm, halfv),
        gl_FrontMaterial.shininess)
      *gl_FrontMaterial.specular*gl_LightSource[0].specular);
    vec3 color = vec3(ambient + diffuse + specular);
    gl_FragColor = vec4(color, 1.0);
}
```

Figures 9.6 and 9.7 and Color Plate 26 show the difference between per-vertex and per-fragment shading on the teapot. Each was generated using the same material and light properties. Note the greater detail on the specular highlight with per-fragment shading.

9.11 Samplers

Although a part of texture mapping, namely, setting texture coordinates, is part of vertex processing, textures are not applied until fragment processing. Consequently, it is not surprising that many of the most interesting uses of programmable pipelines involve texture manipulation in fragment shaders.

Probably the greatest difficulty in dealing with textures is the large number of options that are available, including the wrapping mode, filtering, mipmapping,

FIGURE 9.6 Per-vertex Phong shading.

FIGURE 9.7 Per-fragment Phong shading.

the texture matrix, and packing parameters. In addition, because we can create multiple texture objects, there can be multiple textures available to the shader. If the implementation supports multiple texture units, the shader should be able to interact with any of them. GLSL helps us avoid getting buried in these options by allowing the program to access textures through a new type of variable called a **sampler**.

A *sampler* variable provides access to a particular texture object, including all its parameters. There are sampler types for the types of textures supported by OpenGL. In particular, there are samplers for one-dimensional (`sampler1D`), two-dimensional (`sampler2D`), three-dimensional (`sampler3D`), and cube-map (`samplerCube`) textures.

Suppose that we define a texture object as in Chapter 8. We can assign the name `myTexture` to a uniform sampler variable to make it known to the vertex and fragment programs by declaring

```
uniform sampler2D myTexture;
```

in these programs. Samplers are passed to the shader from the application using the function glUniform1f to align the sampler with a texture object and texture unit. In the application, we obtain the location of the sampler myTexture by

```
glGetUniformLocation(myProg, "myTexture");
```

after we have linked the shaders and application into the program object myProg. We can then associate texture unit 0 with the shader by

```
glUniform1iARB(texMapLocation, 0);
```

Note that texture unit 0 is the texture unit that is used by default for texture mapping if no other unit is specified. Thus, if we form a texture object as in Chapter 8 and do not specifically assign it to a texture unit, it will be associated with unit 0. Because a sampler must be a uniform variable, it cannot be altered by the vertex or fragment shaders. Once a sampler is defined, we can use it to provide a texture value using one of the texture functions texture1D, texture2D, texture3D, or textureCube. For example, we can obtain a value for the texture corresponding to the sampler myTexture by

```
vec2 texcoord;
```

```
vec4 texcolor = texture2D(myTexture, texcoord);
```

The texture coordinates can be specified as a vertex attribute in a vertex program or through the built-in vertex attribute glMultiTexCoord0. In this case, we can use code of the form

```
attribute vec2 vertexTexST;
varying vec2 texcoord;

texcoord = vertexTexST;
```

Here, we pass in the texture coordinates on a per-vertex basis and copy these values into a varying variable that will be interpolated automatically in the fragment program.

A second strategy allows us to use the texture coordinates that are defined for each texture unit in a system that supports multiple texture units. We can use the fact that in OpenGL, texture coordinates specified by glTexCoord are the same as coordinates specified for texture unit 0 by glMulitTexCoord in the application program. These coordinates are built-in through the GLSL variable gl_glMultTexCoord0 and can be passed on to the fragment program using gl_TexCoord[0] as follows:

```
gl_TexCoord[0] = gl_MultiTexCoord0;
```

In the following simple example, we apply a two-dimensional texture with contributions from diffuse and specular lighting. First, we consider the vertex program. It has little new in it; it must compute the various lighting parameters in eye coordinates and pass this information on to the fragment program.

```
/* vertex shader for texture mapping */

varying vec4 eyePos;
varying vec3 norme;
varying vec3 lightv;
varying vec3 viewv;
varying vec3 halfv;

void main()
{
    eyePos = gl_ModelViewMatrix*gl_Vertex;
    norme = normalize(gl_NormalMatrix*gl_Normal);
    viewv = normalize(vec3(gl_ModelViewMatrix*gl_Vertex));
    lightv = normalize(vec3(gl_LightSource[0].position
                        - gl_ModelView*gl_Vertex));
    gl_TexCoord[0] = gl_MultiTexCoord0;
    halfv = normalize(lightv + viewv);
}
```

In the fragment program, we compute the diffuse and specular components and combine them with the texture color that we get from a sampler.

```
/* fragment shader for combining a texture with diffuse and specular
lighting */

varying vec4 eyePos;
varying vec2 texCoord;
varying vec3 norme;
varying vec3 lightv;
varying vec3 viewv;
varying vec3 halfv


void main()
{
    uniform sampler2D myTexture;
    vec3 norm = normalize(norme);
    vec4 diffuse = max(0, dot(lightv, norm))*gl_FrontMaterial.diffuse
            *LightSource[0].diffuse;
    int f;
    if(dot(lightv, viewv)> 0.0) f =1.0);
        else f = 0.0;
```

```
    vec4 specular = f*pow(max(max(0, dot(norm, halfv)),
        gl_FrontMaterial.shininess)
        *gl_FrontMaterial.specular*gl_LightSource[0].specular);
    vec4 texColor = texture2D(myTexture, texCoord);
    vec3 color = vec3(diffuse + specular + texColor);
    gl_FragColor = vec4(color, 1);
}
```

This example has been fairly straightforward. The only major difference between it and the fixed-function pipeline is that we are computing the diffuse and specular components on a per-fragment basis. In the following two sections, we explore some applications of fragment shaders that we cannot even approximate with the fixed-function pipeline.

9.12   Cube Maps

In Chapter 8, we saw how to define a cube map texture from six two-dimensional images. With fragment shaders, we can use cube maps for a wide variety of applications. Once we have defined the cube texture and texture coordinates, we can apply the texture using the samplerCube variable with the textureCube function to do the lookup. Thus, if we define a cube texture myCube in the application, the fragment shader can obtain a texture value through the code

```
vec4 texColor = textureCube(myCube, texcoord);
```

Recall that the texture coordinates must be three-dimensional when we use a cube map.

9.12.1   Reflection Maps

The required computations for a reflection or environment map are shown in Figure 9.8. We assume that the environment has already been mapped to the cube. The difference between a reflection map and a simple cube texture map is that we use the reflection vector to access the texture for a reflection map rather than the view vector. We can compute the reflection vector at each vertex in our vertex program and then let the fragment program interpolate these values over the primitive.

However, we must be careful as to which frame we want to use in each part of the program. The difference between this example and previous ones is that the environment map usually is computed in world coordinates. Object positions and normals are specified in object coordinates and are brought into the world frame by modeling transformations in the application. We usually never see the world-coordinate representation of objects because the model-view transformation converts object coordinates directly to eye coordinates. In many applications, we define our objects directly without modeling transformations so that world

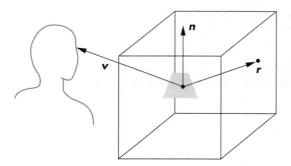

FIGURE 9.8 Reflection cube map.

and object coordinates are the same. However, we want to write our program in a manner that allows for modeling transformations when we do reflection mapping. One way to accomplish this task is to compute the modeling matrix in the application and pass it to the fragment program as a uniform variable. Here is a vertex shader that computes a reflection vector in world coordinates using such a matrix:

```
/* vertex shader for computing reflection vector
   for an environment map*/

varying vec3 reflectw;
uniform mat4 modelMat;
uniform mat3 invModelMat;
uniform vec4 eyew;

void main()
{

    vec4 positionw = modelMat*gl_Vertex;
    vec3 normw = normalize(gl_Normal*invModelMat.xyz);
    vec3 lightw = normalize(eyew.xyz-positionw.xyz);
    eyew = reflect(normw, eyew);
    gl_Position = gl_ModelViewProjectionMatrix*gl_Vertex;
}
```

Note that to keep the vertex program simple, we assume that the application passes in the eye position in world coordinates. Also note that we need the inverse transpose of the modeling matrix to transform the normal. However, if we pass in the inverse matrix as another uniform variable, we can postmultiply the normal to obtain the desired result. If we want the color to be determined only by the texture lookup, we are done with the vertex program. Otherwise, we can compute diffuse, specular, and ambient components in eye coordinates for each vertex and pass them on to the fragment program.

Let's assume that we have set up the cube map as myMap. A fragment shader for using the sampled texture to determine the fragment color is simply

```
/* fragment shader for reflection map */

varying vec3 reflectw;
uniform samplerCube MyMap;

void main()
{
    gl_FragColor =  textureCube(myMap, reflectw);
}
```

The interpolated reflection vector gives the desired texture coordinates.

We can extend this example in some interesting ways to create effects that cannot be done with the fixed-function pipeline by altering the direction of the vector into the cube map.

9.12.2 Refraction

Our discussion of environment and reflection maps thus far has assumed that the reflective object was opaque. We can also assume that the object is translucent, with part of the light we see on the surface determined by shading, part by reflecting the environment onto the surface, and part by transmission of light through the object so that we can see a contribution from the environment behind the object.

Before we can write the required programs, we need a model for how light passes through a translucent material. Consider a surface that transmits all the light that strikes it, as shown in Figure 9.9. If the speed of light differs in the two materials, the light is bent at the surface. Let η_l and η_t be the **indices of refraction**—a measure of the relative speed of light in the two materials on the two sides of the surface. **Snell's law** (see Exercise 9.13) states that

$$\frac{\sin \theta_l}{\sin \theta_t} = \frac{\eta_t}{\eta_l}.$$

We can find the direction of the transmitted light $\mathbf{t}$ as follows. We know $\cos \theta_l$ from $\mathbf{n}$ and $\mathbf{l}$; if they have been normalized, it is simply their dot product. Given $\cos \theta_l$, we can find $\sin \theta_l$, and from then $\sin \theta_t$. Letting $\eta = \eta_t/\eta_l$, we have

$$\cos \theta_t = \left(1 - \frac{1}{\eta^2}(1 - \cos^2 \theta_l)\right)^{\frac{1}{2}}.$$

Just as in the computation of the reflected light, the three vectors must be coplanar; thus,

$$\mathbf{t} = \alpha \mathbf{n} + \beta \mathbf{l}.$$

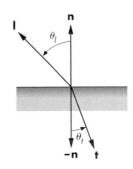

FIGURE 9.9 Perfect light transmission.

If we further impose the condition that **t** have unit length, we can do a derivation, similar to that for the reflected vector, to find

$$\mathbf{t} = -\frac{1}{\eta}\mathbf{l} - \left(\cos\theta_t - \frac{1}{\eta}\cos\theta_l\right)\mathbf{n}.$$

The first two negative signs in this equation are a consequence of **t** pointing away from the back side of the surface. The angle for which the square-root term in the expression for $\cos\theta_t$ becomes zero ($\sin\theta_l = \eta$) is known as the **critical angle**. If light strikes the surface at this angle, the transmitted light is in a direction along the surface. If θ_l is increased further, all light is reflected, and none is transmitted.

Suppose we have an object that is composed of a translucent material in which the speed of light is less than the speed of light in air. Thus, a light ray passing directly through it is bent and intersects points inside the object at a place determined by Snell's law. If we use a cube map for the environment, the program looks similar to the previous one, except for the calculation of the vector into the environmental map. The vertex program computes the transmitted vector for each vertex and passes it on to the fragment program.

```
/* vertex shader for refraction with
   an environment map */

varying vec3 transw;
uniform mat4 modelMat;
uniform mat3 invModelMat;
uniform vec4 eyew;
uniform float eta;

void main()
{
    vec4 positionw = modelMat*gl_Vertex;
    vec3 normw = normalize(gl_Normal*invModelMat);
    vec3 lightw = normalize(eyew.xyz-positionw.xyz);
    transw = trans(normw, lightw, eta);
    gl_Position = gl_ModelViewProjectionMatrix*gl_Vertex;
}
```

The fragment program is virtually identical to our fragment program for reflections. The only change we need make is to use the transmitted vector rather than the reflected vector in the sampler.

```
/* fragment shader for refraction with
   an environment map */
vec3 trans(vec3 normal, vec3 light, float ratio)
{
    float cosL = dot(light, normal);
    float d = 1-(1-cosL*cosL)/(ratio*ratio);
```

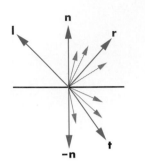

FIGURE 9.10 Light interaction at surface.

```
if(d <= 0.0) return 0.0;
float cosT = sqrt(d);
return -(1.0/ratio)*light-(cosT-(1.0/ratio)*cosL)*normal;
}
```

A more general expression for what happens at a transmitting surface corresponds to Figure 9.10. Some light is transmitted, some is reflected, and the rest is absorbed. Of the transmitted light, some is scattered in a manner similar to specular reflections, except that here the light is concentrated in the direction of $\mathbf{t}$. Thus, a transmission model might include a term proportional to $\mathbf{t} \cdot \mathbf{v}$ for viewers on the transmitted side of the surface. We can also use the analogy of a half-angle to simplify calculation of this term (see Exercise 9.14).

We can do a few more things with a simple fragment shader and our reflected and transmitted vectors to create more realistic effects. When light strikes a real translucent material, some of the light is absorbed, some is reflected, and some is refracted through the material. Unlike the simple lighting models that we have used so far, the fraction of light refracted and the amount reflected depend on the angle between the light and the normal. In addition, the relationship also depends on the wavelength and polarization of the light. The physical relationship is given by the **Fresnel equation**. Not only is discussion of the Fresnel equation beyond the scope of this book (see suggested Readings), its complexity is counter to the simplicity we want for efficiency of our programs. Consequently, we can use an approximation that can be computed on a fragment or vertex program.

Suppose that we have a reflected color, C_r, and a refracted color, C_t, that are colors we get from an environment map by following the reflected and refracted angles, respectively. The color that we will use is an affine combination of these two colors determined by a coefficient r. Thus, the fragment color is given by C_f:

$$C_f = rC_r + (1 - r)C_t.$$

The value of r should approximate the value we would obtain for the Fresnel term if we were able to compute it easily. If we let this term depend on the cosine of the angle between the light and the normal, we can use $\mathbf{l} \cdot \mathbf{n}$, the same easily computed term that we use for diffuse reflections; it ranges from 0 to 1 as the angle ranges from −90 degrees to 90 degrees. If we raise this term to a power, as we do with specular reflection term $\mathbf{r} \cdot \mathbf{v}$, we can make the range of values for which it is much greater than 0 as narrow as desired. Thus, we can use an approximation of the form

$$r = \max(0, (\mathbf{l} \cdot \mathbf{n})^p).$$

We can get some additional flexibility using the form

$$r = \max(0, \min(1, a + b(1 + \mathbf{l} \cdot \mathbf{n})^p),$$

and varying a and b in addition to p.

We can also try to simulate the effect of the coefficient of refraction's dependence on wavelength. Shorter wavelengths are refracted more than longer wavelengths when they enter a slower material. This effect accounts for the rainbows created by prisms. Because we use an RGB model and process only three components rather than all wavelengths, we can only approximate this effect, known as **chromatic dispersion**. If we use a different value of the refraction index for each color component (see Exercise 9.15), we would expect to see colored fringes at the edges of objects in our images.

Note that we have only considered what happens when light enters a material in which the speed of light is slower than the speed of light in air. If the material has a finite width, the light bends again as it leaves the material. See Exercise 9.20.

9.12.3 Normalization Maps

Cube maps can be used to look up values other than colors. Because the cube map stores RGBA colors, we can store up to four values at each position in the cube map. One clever example of extending our use of cube maps is for normalization. If we use the function normalize on a three-component vector, as in the code

```
vec3 a = {1.0, 2.0, 3.0};
vec3 b = normalize (a);
```

a typical implementation does three multiplications to square the components, two additions and a square root. If this operation is in a fragment program, we are requiring the GPU to do quite a bit of computation because it must carry out these arithmetic operations on every fragment.

Consider all points along a line from the origin. The vector between any two of these points and, in particular, the vector determined by any point on the line and the origin all normalize to the same vector. Suppose that we look at where such a vector intersects the cube map. What we can do is put the components of the normalized vector at these texture coordinates. Of course, we must precompute these values to form the cube map, but as we shall see, this computation is fairly easy.

Consider the cube map in Figure 9.11. The sides are determined by the six planes $x = \pm 1$, $y = \pm 1$, and $z = \pm 1$. If we place a given vector $\mathbf{v} = (a, b, c)$ with one end at the origin, the side of the cube that it intersects is determined by the magnitude and sign of the largest component. Thus, the vector $(1.0, 2.0, 3.0)$ intersects the side determined by the plane $z = 1$, whereas the vector $(1.0, -3.0, 2.0)$ intersects the side determined by the plane $y = -1$. In the first case, the point of intersection is $(0.33, 0.67, 1.0)$ and in the second, it is $(0.33, -1.0, 0.67)$.

The components of a normalized vector have a range of -1.0 to 1.0, whereas texture components are colors and range over 0.0 to 1.0. We can store normalized vectors as colors if we first compress the ranges of the components. The simple transformation function

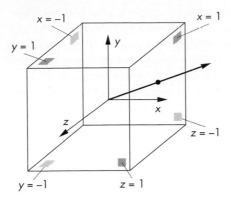

FIGURE 9.11 Cube map.

```
GLfloat compress(GLfloat color_component)
{
    return 0.5*color_component+0.5;
}
```

compresses values over $(-1.0, 1.0)$ to the range $(0.0, 1.0)$. The function

```
GLfloat uncompress(GLfloat texture_component)
{
    return 2.0*texture_component-1.0;
}
```

reverses the operation. Thus, the RGB value $(0.33, 0.67, 1.0)$ is compressed to $(0.66, .83, 1.0)$, and $(0.33, -1.0, 0.67)$ is compressed to $(0.66, 0.0, 0.83)$.

Hence, we can form a normalization map by using a cube map. For each texel on the six sides of the cube, the RGB values are the range-compressed values of the normalized vector from the origin through the texel. Thus, at the texel with s, t, r coordinates $(0.33, 0.67, 1.0)$, in the cube map, we find the RGB triplet $(0.63, 0.765, 0.90)$, which is the range-compressed representation of the normalized vector $(0.26, 0.53, 0.80)$. In terms of a fragment shader, we often see code of the form

```
vec3 normal;
vec3 texCoord;
samplerCube NormalMap;

normal = 2.0*textureCube(NormalMap, texCoord)-1.0;
```

The effort goes into computing the normalization map and we need space for it, but usually if we use 64×64 or 128×128 texture maps for the sides, the accuracy is sufficient for most applications and the storage requirements are minimal.

9.13 Bump Mapping

We conclude this chapter with some examples of bump mapping. We introduced bump mapping in Chapter 8 as a texture mapping technique that can give the appearance of great complexity in an image without increasing the geometric complexity. Unlike simple texture mapping, bump mapping will show changes in shading as the light source or object move, making the object appear to have variations in surface smoothness.

Let's start by returning to our example from Chapter 8 of creating an image of an orange. If we take a photograph of a real orange, we can apply this image as a texture map to a surface. However, if we move the lights or rotate the object, we immediately notice that we have the image of a model of an orange rather than the image of a real orange. The problem is that a real orange is characterized primarily by small variations in its surface rather than by variations in its color, and the former are not captured by texture mapping. The technique of **bump mapping** varies the apparent shape of the surface by perturbing the normal vectors as the surface is rendered; the colors that are generated by shading then show a variation in the surface properties.

9.13.1 Finding Bump Maps

We start with the observation that the normal at any point on a surface characterizes the orientation of the surface at that point. If we perturb the normal at each point on the surface by a small amount, then we create a surface with small variations in its shape. If this perturbation to the normal can be applied only during the shading process, we can use a smooth model of the surface, which must have a smooth normal, but we can shade it in a way that gives the appearance of a complex surface. Because the perturbations are to the normal vectors, the rendering calculations are correct for the altered surface, even though the more complex surface defined by the perturbed normals need never be created.

We can perturb the normals in many ways. The following procedure for parametric surfaces is an efficient one. Let $\mathbf{p}(u, v)$ be a point on a parametric surface. The unit normal at that point is given by the cross product of the partial derivative vectors:

$$\mathbf{n} = \frac{\mathbf{p}_u \times \mathbf{p}_v}{|\mathbf{p}_u \times \mathbf{p}_v|},$$

where

$$\mathbf{p}_u = \begin{bmatrix} \frac{\partial x}{\partial u} \\ \frac{\partial y}{\partial u} \\ \frac{\partial z}{\partial u} \end{bmatrix}, \qquad \mathbf{p}_v = \begin{bmatrix} \frac{\partial x}{\partial v} \\ \frac{\partial y}{\partial v} \\ \frac{\partial z}{\partial v} \end{bmatrix}.$$

Suppose that we displace the surface in the normal direction by a function called the **bump**, or **displacement, function**, $d(u, v)$, which we can assume is known and small ($|d(u, v)| << 1$). The displaced surface is given by

$$\mathbf{p}' = \mathbf{p} + d(u, v)\mathbf{n}.$$

We would prefer not to create the displaced surface because such a surface would have a higher geometric complexity than the undisplaced surface and would thus slow down the rendering process. We just want to make it look as though we have displaced it. We can achieve the desired look by altering the normal $\mathbf{n}$, instead of $\mathbf{p}$, and using the perturbed normal in our shading calculations.

The normal at the perturbed point $\mathbf{p}'$ is given by the cross product

$$\mathbf{n}' = \mathbf{p}'_u \times \mathbf{p}'_v.$$

We can compute the two partial derivatives by differentiating the equation for $\mathbf{p}'$, obtaining

$$\mathbf{p}'_u = \mathbf{p}_u + \frac{\partial d}{\partial u}\mathbf{n} + d(u, v)\mathbf{n}_u,$$

$$\mathbf{p}'_v = \mathbf{p}_v + \frac{\partial d}{\partial v}\mathbf{n} + d(u, v)\mathbf{n}_v.$$

If d is small, we can neglect the term on the right of these two equations and take their cross product, noting that $\mathbf{n} \times \mathbf{n} = 0$, to obtain the approximate perturbed normal:

$$\mathbf{n}' \approx \mathbf{n} + \frac{\partial d}{\partial u}\mathbf{n} \times \mathbf{p}_v + \frac{\partial d}{\partial v}\mathbf{n} \times \mathbf{p}_u.$$

The two terms on the right are the displacement, the difference between the original and perturbed normals. The cross product of two vectors is orthogonal to both of them. Consequently, both cross products yield vectors that lie in the tangent plane at $\mathbf{p}$ and their sum must also be in the tangent plane.

Although $\mathbf{p}'_u$ and $\mathbf{p}'_v$ lie in the tangent plane perpendicular to $\mathbf{n}'$, they are not necessarily orthogonal to each other. We can obtain an orthogonal basis and a corresponding rotation matrix using the cross product. First, we normalize $\mathbf{n}'$ and $\mathbf{p}'_u$, obtaining the vectors

$$\mathbf{m} = \frac{\mathbf{n}'}{|\mathbf{n}'|},$$

$$\mathbf{t} = \frac{\mathbf{p}'_u}{|\mathbf{p}'_u|}.$$

We obtain the third orthogonal vector $\mathbf{b}$ by

$$\mathbf{b} = \mathbf{m} \times \mathbf{t}.$$

The vector $\mathbf{t}$ is called the **tangent vector** and $\mathbf{b}$ is called the **binormal vector**. The matrix

$$\mathbf{M} = [\,\mathbf{t} \quad \mathbf{t} \quad \mathbf{m}\,]^T$$

is the rotation matrix that will convert representations in the original space to representations in terms of the three vectors. The new space is sometimes called **tangent space**.

To apply the bump map, we need two arrays that contain the values of $\partial d/\partial u$ and $\partial d/\partial v$. These arrays can be precomputed by methods similar to those used for texture generation. The normal can then be perturbed during the shading process. One method to obtain these perturbation arrays is to use an image processing method directly on the function $d(u, v)$. Suppose that we have a sampled version of $d(u, v)$ as an array of pixels $\mathbf{D} = [d_{ij}]$. The required partial derivatives are proportional to the difference between adjacent elements in the array

$$\frac{\partial d}{\partial u} \propto d_{ij} - d_{i-1,j},$$

$$\frac{\partial d}{\partial v} \propto d_{ij} - d_{i,j-1}.$$

These computations can be looked at as taking the differences between an image $\mathbf{D}$ and shifted versions of itself. Although we could do this calculation within the application, many graphics systems support these operations directly in hardware. This method works well for surfaces such as spheres and cylinders that have simple parametric representations.

9.13.2 Bump Mapping with Height Fields

When we work with polygonal models, a more common approach to bump mapping is to work directly in the model or object frames using height fields. Suppose we have a flat surface in the plane $z = 0$. We can think of the bumps as displacements represented by a function

$$z = d(x, y),$$

where the d is small. If we proceed as with the parametric case, where we replace u by x and v by y, we can take the differences in the x and y directions at sampled values of x and y to obtain approximations to $\frac{\partial d}{\partial x}$ and $\frac{\partial d}{\partial y}$ at the sampled points. If we denote these differences as Δ_x and Δ_y, then the perturbed normal at a sampled point is approximately

$$\mathbf{n}' = \begin{bmatrix} \Delta_x \\ \Delta_y \\ 1 \end{bmatrix}.$$

We generally precompute these values as an array, normalize each value, and store them in range-compressed form. The result is a valid two-dimensional texture called a **normal map**. Note that this texture is oriented with respect to the displacement function, not to the orientation of any polygon on our model.

We have, in essence, introduced a local frame for textures, that we can refer to as the **texture frame**.

9.13.3   Bump Mapping with Fragment Shaders

Because bump mapping involves manipulating the normal for each fragment, it is not a technique that can be implemented easily with a fixed-function pipeline. However, with a fragment shader, we can alter the normal at each fragment. Hence, fragment shaders provide a simple method of implementing bump mapping at interactive rates.

Bump mapping can be implemented in a variety of ways with programmable shaders. One method is through a fragment program that varies the normal by executing a function as it processes each fragment. Although this approach is conceptually simple, the computational cost can be high if we have to compute the perturbation to the normal for each fragment.

Alternately, we can precompute the perturbations and store them in texture maps. We must specify the perturbations in a coordinate system consistent with the normals to be perturbed. This requirement leaves us with some options as to which coordinate system we do the calculations in.

We are almost ready to write vertex and fragment shaders for bump mapping, but we have to deal with one additional issue. Our normal map was based on the the displacement function given as

$$z = d(x, y).$$

Hence, the displacements are correct only if the polygon is the plane $z = 0$.

The entities that we need for lighting—the surface normal, the light vector(s), the half-angle vector, the vertex location—are usually in eye or object coordinates at the point in the process when we do lighting. We can view the normal map as being in texture-space coordinates. For correct shading, we have to convert either the normal map to object-space coordinates or the object-space coordinates to texture-space coordinates. In general, the latter requires less work because it can be carried out on a per-vertex basis in the vertex shader rather than on a per-fragment basis. The matrix needed to convert from lighting-coordinate space to texture-coordinate space is precisely the matrix composed of the normal, tangent, and binormal. Generally, the object-space normal is available as `gl_Normal`. The application can provide a tangent vector as a vertex attribute. These two quantities can be computed for each polygon or each vertex. The binormal can then be computed in the shader using the cross product function.

9.13.4   Example

In this simple example, we do the calculations in texture space. Hence, we must transform both the light vector and eye vector to this space. The required transformation matrix is composed of the normal, tangent, and binormal vectors. The normal is available from the OpenGL state (`gl_Normal`). The tangent can be provided by the application by creating a vertex attribute (tangento) in the application. The binormal can then be computed by the cross product. The normal and tangent are specified in object coordinates, so they must first be multiplied by the normal matrix.

The view vector that is provided by the application through gl_Vertex must be converted to clip coordinates as usual and also to a representation in texture space. We can obtain the second representation by first converting to eye coordinates and then using the same matrix that we apply to the light vector. Here is the vertex shader:

```
/* bump map vertex shader */

varying vec3 lightv; /* light vector in texture-space coordinates */
varying vec3 viewv; /* view vector in texture-space coordinates */
attribute vec3 tangento; /* tangent vector in object coordinates */


void main()
{
    /* position in clip coordinates */
    gl_Position = gl_ModelViewProjectionMatrix*gl_Vertex;
    /* view vector in eye coordinates */
    vec3 viewe = vec3(gl_ModelViewMatrix*gl_Vertex);
    gl_TexCoord[0] = gl_MultiTexCoord0;
    /* light vector in eye coordinates */
    vec3 lighte = normalize(vec3(gl_LightSource[0].position)-viewe);

    vec3 normal = normalize(gl_NormalMatrix*gl_Normal);
    vec3 tangent  = normalize(gl_NormalMatrix*tangento);
    vec3 binormal = cross(normal, tangent);

    /* light vector in texture space */

    lightv.x = dot(tangent, lighte.xyz);
    lightv.y = dot(binormal, lighte.xyz);
    lightv.z = dot(normal, lighte.xyz);

    /* view vector in texture space */

    viewv.x = dot(tangent, viewe.xyz);
    viewv.y = dot(binormal, viewe.xyz);
    viewv.z = dot(normal, viewe.xyz);

    lightv = normalize(lightv);
    viewv = normalize(viewv);
}
```

Our simple fragment program computes only the bump map term, which is a diffuse illumination term. The dot product uses a normal that is provided by a normal map (`normalMap`), stored as a two-dimensional, range-compressed texture and a light vector that is the interpolated light vector from the vertex shader. The base colors are stored in another two-dimensional texture `texMap`. The fragment shader is given by the code

```
/* bump map fragment shader */

varying vec3 lightv;
varying vec3 viewv;
uniform sampler2D texMap;
uniform sampler2D normalMap;

void main()
{
    vec3 Light  = normalize(lightv);
    vec4 texColor = texture2D(texMap, gl_TexCoord[0].st);
    vec3 normal = 2 * (texture2D(normalMap, gl_TexCoord[0].st).rgb - 0.5);

    gl_FragColor = max(dot(Light, normal), 0.0) * texColor;
}
```

Note that this example does not use the texture-space view vectors computed in the vertex shader. These vectors would be necessary if we wanted to add a specular term (see Exercise 9.22).

Summary and Notes

The NVIDIA GForce 3 was the first programmable GPU. Although initially programmable GPUs supported only vertex programs, within a short time multiple venders, including NVIDIA, ATI, and 3DLabs, were producing GPUs that support both vertex and fragment programs.

Vertex programs, while interesting for some applications, are limited in what they can do. In particular, vertex programs can manipulate texture coordinates but cannot always work with the textures themselves. Now that fragment programs are supported, the door is open to many new techniques. Many involve using textures in both traditional and new ways. Concurrent with the development of programmable pipelines, GPUs became available with more texture memory, multiple texture units, and parallel fragment processors. Many techniques involve per-fragment lighting calculation. Not only can we use new models and interact with texture maps on a fragment by fragment basis, simply using the standard modified Phong model on a per-fragment basis improves the visual quality of our images. For graphics, the ability to carry out methods such as bump mapping in real time has had a major effect on application developers. For example, almost all video games make heavy use of bump mapping.

Recent developments in GPUs are opening up even more possibilities. Although both vertex and fragment shaders support floating-point data, until recently the frame buffers still stored color components with only 8-bit precision. The latest GPUs have floating-point frame buffers, which removes many of the precision issues with techniques such as compositing, or blending. If we step back and look at GPUs from the perspective of more general computing, we can observe that GPUs operate at speeds associated with supercomputers and cost only a few hundred dollars. The difficulty is that GPUs are organized far differently from standard CPUs and get much of their speed from how their components are organized and the parallelism that is built in for processing four-component entities. At present, there is considerable interest in general-purpose computing with GPUs (abbreviated GP-GPU). For a given application, we often have to rethink our standard algorithms and create new algorithms that can use the capabilities of the GPU. One simple example is the use of texture maps for function lookup, which we employed with normalization maps. Other applications of fragment programs for GP-GPU include signal processing and linear algebra.

Suggested Readings

For a discussion of the RenderMan shading language, see *The RenderMan Companion* [Ups89].

The standard reference for GLSL is *The OpenGL Shading Language* [Ros04]. Also see *The Cg Tutorial* [Fer03]. Although there are differences between GLSL and Cg, shaders written in one language can easily be converted to the other. Both books provide many examples of vertex and fragment shaders. The Web sites of NVIDIA (*www.nvidia.com/developer*), ATI (*www.ati.com/developer*), and 3DLabs (*www.3DLabs.com*) provide additional examples and documentation. The OpenGL Web site, *www.opengl.org*, provides access to the specifications of the various versions of OpenGL, in particular to the extensions that define the interface between an OpenGL program and programmable shaders.

The Fresnel term is discussed in some of the graphics texts, including [Fol90] and [Hil01]. The discussion of the approximation to the Fresnel equation follows *The Cg Tutorial* [Fern03].

Bump mapping was first suggested by Blinn [Bli77]. Many of the details needed to do correct bump mapping for different types of surfaces are presented in the *The Cg Tutorial*.

Many algorithms for GPUs are in [Fern04].

Exercises

9.1 Write a program that uses a vertex shader to morph one object into another. Besides morphing the vertices, morph other variables such as the colors of the vertices.

9.2 Implement a particle system for a cascade in which particles are generated by the application program with increasing numbers of new particles being created as time is increased. The particles should have their initial velocities and positions within a narrow range.

9.3 Write an application using a particle system and a vertex shader to generate a fireworks display. The colors of the particles should change with time and the particles should appear to have different lifetimes.

9.4 In many particle systems, particles interact with each other through attractive or repulsive forces. Can we create such systems with just a vertex program? Explain.

9.5 Write a vertex program that will bounce a ball whose initial velocity and position are provided by the application program. *Hint:* You can use the `reflect` function to compute the new direction of the ball after it hits the floor. Its vertical speed should be reduced by a constant value, the **coefficient of restitution**, each time that it hits the floor.

9.6 Create a model of the solar system using a vertex program to move the planets and any moons.

9.7 Add distance terms to the Phong and modified Phong vertex shaders.

9.8 Modify the modified Phong vertex shader to use multiple light sources.

9.9 In Chapter 6, we noted that if the light vector, normal, and reflection vector lie in the same plane, then the half-angle is half the angle between the view vector and the light vector. Use this observation to derive a shininess coefficient for the Phong model based on the shininess coefficient in the modified Phong model.

9.10 Programmable shaders can make for more efficient code by freeing up the CPU. However, because so much functionality is built into the GPU, many traditional assumptions about efficiency may no longer hold. Write OpenGL programs to shade objects of your choice using (a) the fixed-function pipeline, (b) a modified Phong shader through a vertex program, and (c) a Phong shader using a vertex program. Compare the efficiency of the three methods.

9.11 Redo the Phong shaders so that the computation is done in object rather than eye coordinates.

9.12 Write a fragment program that does Phong shading.

9.13 Write vertex and fragment programs to do environmental mapping using sphere maps.

9.14 Show that Snell's law can be derived from the assumption that light travels along the shortest path in time between two points.

9.15 Find an analogy of the halfway vector for use in calculating the contribution from transmitted light.

9.16 Redo the vertex and fragment programs for refraction to take into account chromatic dispersion by having the application supply three indices of refraction, one for each of the red, blue, and green color components.

9.17 Suppose that we bump-map a height map of the earth onto a sphere. How might you be able to see that the image was produced with a bump map rather than by altering the surface?

9.18 Write a program to apply a bump map $d(x, y)$ to a parametrically defined sphere.

9.19 In Section 9.6.1, what would happen if we used a scalar s rather than the vector [s, s, s, 1] to scale each vertex?

9.20 Consider the effect of light entering and leaving a thin material in which the speed of light is less than the speed of light in air. How would you alter the transmitted light calculations for a cube map?

9.21 How do you have to change the bump map shaders to work correctly with a polygonal mesh?

9.22 Add a specular term to the bump mapping example in Section 9.13.

MODELING

Models are abstractions of the world—both of the real world in which we live and of virtual worlds that we create through our programs. We are all familiar with mathematical models that are used in all areas of science and engineering. These models use equations to model the physical phenomena that we wish to study. In computer science, we use abstract data types to model organizations of objects; in computer graphics, we model our worlds with geometric objects. When we build a mathematical model, we choose carefully which type of mathematics fits the phenomena that we wish to model. Although ordinary differential equations may be appropriate for modeling the dynamic behavior of a system of springs and masses, we would probably use partial differential equations to model turbulent fluid flow. We go through analogous processes in computer graphics, choosing which primitives to use in our models and how to show relationships among them. Often, as is true of choosing a mathematical model, there are multiple approaches, so we seek models that can take advantage of the capabilities of our graphics systems.

In this chapter, we explore multiple approaches to developing and working with models of geometric objects. We consider models that use a set of simple geometric objects: either the primitives supported by our graphics systems or a set of user-defined objects built from these primitives. We extend the use of transformations from Chapter 4 to include hierarchical relationships among the objects. The techniques that we develop are appropriate for applications, such as robotics and figure animation, where the dynamic behavior of the objects is characterized by relationships among the parts of the model.

The notion of hierarchy is a powerful one and is an integral part of object-oriented methodologies. We extend our hierarchical models of objects to hierarchical models of whole scenes, including cameras, lights, and material properties. Such models allow us to extend our graphics APIs to more object-oriented systems and also give us insight into using graphics over networks and distributed environments, such as the World Wide Web.

We also consider some aspects of procedural modeling. In particular, we present the elements of particle systems. Each particle obeys a set of differential equations that can be based on physical models or on principles designed by animators. We can use systems of particles to model the behavior of multiple interacting objects.

10.1   Symbols and Instances

Our first concern is how we can store a model that may include many sophisticated objects. There are two immediate issues: how we define an object more complex than the ones we have dealt with until now and how we represent a collection of these objects. Most APIs take a minimalist attitude toward primitives: They contain only a few primitives, leaving it to the user to construct more complex objects from these primitives. Sometimes additional libraries, such as GLU and GLUT that we have used with OpenGL, provide objects built on top of the basic primitives. We assume that we have available a collection of basic three-dimensional objects provided by these options.

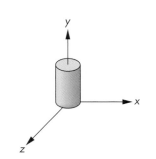

FIGURE 10.1   Cylinder symbol.

We can take a nonhierarchical approach to modeling by regarding these objects as **symbols** and by modeling our world as a collection of symbols. Symbols can include geometric objects, fonts, and application-specific sets of graphical objects. Symbols are usually represented at a convenient size and orientation. For example, a cylinder is usually oriented parallel to one of the axes, as shown in Figure 10.1, often with a unit height, a unit radius, and its bottom centered at the origin.

Most APIs, including OpenGL, make a distinction between the frame in which the symbol is defined, sometimes called the **object**, or **model, frame** (where we use **object coordinates**) and the **world frame**. This distinction can be helpful when the symbols are purely shapes, such as the symbols that we might use for circuit elements in a CAD application, and have no physical units associated with them. In OpenGL, we have to set up the appropriate transformation from the frame of the symbol to the world coordinate frame and to apply it to the model-view matrix before we execute the code for the symbol.

The instance transformation that we introduced in Chapter 4 allows us to place instances of each symbol in the model, at the desired size, orientation, and location. Thus, the instance transformation

$$\mathbf{M} = \mathbf{TRS}$$

is a concatenation of a translation, a rotation, and a scale (and possibly a shear), as shown in Figure 10.2. Consequently, OpenGL programs often contain repetitions of code in the form

```
glMatrixMode(GL_MODELVIEW);
glLoadIdentity();
glTranslatef(dx, dy, dz);
glRotatef(angle, rx, ry, rz);
glScalef(sx, sy, sz);
glutSolidCube(side); /* or some other symbol */
```

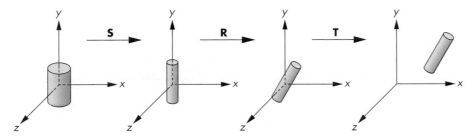

FIGURE 10.2   Instance transformation.

Symbol	Scale	Rotate	Translate
1	s_x, s_y, s_z	$\theta_x, \theta_y, \theta_z$	d_x, d_y, d_z
2			
3			
1			
1			
.			
.			
.			

FIGURE 10.3   Symbol–instance transformation table.

We can also think of such a model in the form of a table, as shown in Figure 10.3. Here each symbol is assumed to have a unique numerical identifier. The table shows that this modeling technique contains no information about relationships among objects. However, the table contains all the information that we require to draw the objects and is thus a simple data structure or model for a group of geometric objects. We could search the table for an object, change the instance transformation for an object, and add or delete objects. However, the flatness of the representation limits us.

10.2 Hierarchical Models

Suppose that we wish to build a model of an automobile that we can animate. We can compose the model from five parts—the chassis and the four wheels (Figure 10.4)—each of which we can describe by using our standard graphics primitives. Two frames of a simple animation of the model are shown in Figure 10.5. We could write a program to generate this animation by noting that if each wheel has a radius r, then a 360-degree rotation of a wheel must correspond to the car moving forward (or backward) a distance of $2\pi r$. The program could then contain one function to generate each wheel and another to generate the

FIGURE 10.4   Automobile model.

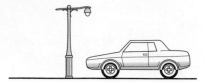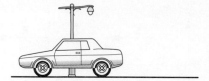

FIGURE 10.5   Two frames of animation.

chassis. All these functions could use the same input, such as the desired speed and direction of the automobile. In pseudocode, our program might look like this:

```
{
    float s; /* speed */
    float d[3] /* direction */

    /* determine speed and direction */

    draw_right_front_wheel(s,d);
    draw_left_front_wheel(s,d);
    draw_right_rear_wheel(s,d);
    draw_left_rear_wheel(s,d);
    draw_chassis(s,d);
}
```

This program is just the kind that we do *not* want to write. It is linear and it shows none of the relationships among the components of the automobile. There are two types of relationships that we would like to exploit. First, we cannot separate the movement of the car from the movement of the wheels. If the car moves forward, the wheels must turn.[1] Second, we would like to use the fact that all the wheels of the automobile are identical; they are merely located in different places, with different orientations.

We can represent the relationships among parts of the models, both abstractly and visually, with graphs. Mathematically, a **graph** consists of a set of **nodes** (or vertices) and a set of **edges**. Edges connect pairs of nodes or possibly connect a node to itself. Edges can have a direction associated with them; the graphs we use here are all **directed graphs**, which are graphs that have their edges leaving one node and entering another.

The most important type of graph we use is a tree. A (connected) **tree** is a directed graph without closed paths or loops. In addition, each node but one—the **root node**—has one edge entering it. Thus, every node except the root has

---

1. It is not clear whether we should say the wheels move the chassis or the chassis moves the wheels. From a graphics perspective, the latter view is probably more useful.

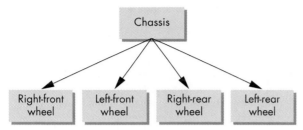

FIGURE 10.6 Tree structure for an automobile.

a **parent node**, the node from which an edge enters, and can have one or more **child nodes**, nodes to which edges are connected. A node without children is called a **terminal node**, or **leaf**. Figure 10.6 shows a tree that represents the relationships in our car model. The chassis is the root node, and all four wheels are its children. Although the mathematical graph is a collection of set elements, in practice, both the edges and nodes can contain additional information. For our car example, each node can contain information defining the geometric objects associated with it. The information about the location and orientation of the wheels can be stored either in their nodes or in the edges connecting them with their parent.

In most cars the four wheels are identical, so storing the same information on how to draw each one at four nodes is inefficient. We can use the ideas behind the instance transformation to allow us to use a single prototype wheel in our model. If we do so, we can replace the tree structure by the **directed acyclic graph (DAG)** in Figure 10.7. In a DAG, although there are loops, we cannot follow directed edges around the loop. Thus, if we follow any path of directed edges from a node, the path terminates at another node, and in practice, working with DAGs is no more difficult than working with trees. For our car, we can store the information that positions each instance of the single prototype wheel in the chassis node, in the wheel node, or with the edges.

Both forms—trees and DAGs—are **hierarchical** methods of expressing the relationships in the physical model. In each form, various elements of a model can be related to other parts—their parents and their children. We explore how to express these hierarchies in a graphics program.

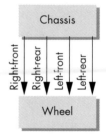

FIGURE 10.7 Directed-acyclic-graph (DAG) model of an automobile.

10.3 A Robot Arm

Robotics provides many opportunities for developing hierarchical models. Consider the simple robot arm in Figure 10.8(a). We can model it with three simple objects, or symbols, perhaps using only parallelepipeds and a cylinder. Each of the symbols can be built up from our basic primitives.

The robot arm consists of the three parts shown in Figure 10.8(b). The mechanism has three degrees of freedom, two of which can be described by

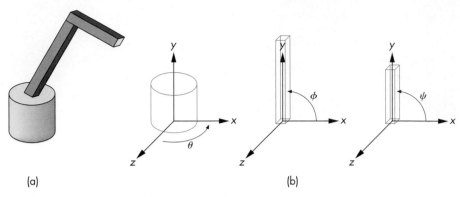

(a)   (b)

FIGURE 10.8   Robot arm. (a) Total model. (b) Components.

a **joint angle** between components and the third by an angle the base makes with respect to the ground. In our model, each joint angle determines how to position a component with respect to the component to which it is attached, or in the case of the base, the joint angle positions it relative to the surrounding environment. Each joint angle is measured in each component's own frame. We can rotate the base about its vertical axis by an angle θ. This angle is measured from the x-axis to some fixed point on the bottom of the base. The lower arm of the robot is attached to the base by a joint that allows the arm to rotate in the plane $z = 0$ in the arm's frame. This rotation is specified by an angle ϕ that is measured from the x-axis to the arm. The upper arm is attached to the lower arm by a similar joint, and it can rotate by an angle ψ, measured like that for the lower arm, in its own frame. As the angles vary, we can think of the frames of the upper and lower arms as moving relative to the base. By controlling the three angles, we can position the tip of the upper arm in three dimensions.

Suppose that we wish to write a program to animate our simple robot. Rather than defining each part of the robot and its motion independently, we take an incremental approach. The base of the robot can rotate about the y-axis in its frame by the angle θ. Thus, we can describe the motion of any point **p** on the base by applying a rotation matrix $\mathbf{R}_y(\theta)$ to it.

The lower arm is rotated about the z-axis in its own frame, but this frame must be shifted to the top of the base by a translation matrix $\mathbf{T}(0, h_1, 0)$, where h_1 is the height above the base to the point where the joint between the base and the lower arm is located. However, if the base has rotated, then we must also rotate the lower arm, using $\mathbf{R}_y(\theta)$. We can accomplish the positioning of the lower arm by applying $\mathbf{R}_y(\theta)\mathbf{T}(0, h_1, 0)\mathbf{R}_z(\phi)$ to the arm's vertices. We can interpret the matrix $\mathbf{R}_y(\theta)\mathbf{T}(0, h_1, 0)$ as the matrix that positions the lower arm *relative* to the world frame and $\mathbf{R}_z(\phi)$ as the matrix that positions the lower arm *relative* to the base. Equivalently, we can interpret these matrices as positioning the frames of the lower arm and base relative to some world frame, as shown in Figure 10.9.

When we apply similar reasoning to the upper arm, we find that this arm has to be translated by a matrix $\mathbf{T}(0, h_2, 0)$ relative to the lower arm and then rotated by $\mathbf{R}_z(\psi)$. The matrix that controls the upper arm is thus $\mathbf{R}_y(\theta)\mathbf{T}(0, h_1, 0)\mathbf{R}_z(\phi)\mathbf{T}(0, h_2, 0)\mathbf{R}_z(\psi)$. The form of the display function for an OpenGL program to display the robot as a function of the joint angles shows how we can alter the model-view matrix incrementally to display the various parts of the model efficiently:

```
display()
{
    glRotatef(theta, 0.0, 1.0, 0.0);
    base();
    glTranslatef(0.0, h1, 0.0);
    glRotatef(phi, 0.0, 0.0, 1.0);
    lower_arm();
    glTranslatef(0.0, h2, 0.0);
    glRotatef(psi, 0.0, 0.0, 1.0);
    upper_arm();
}
```

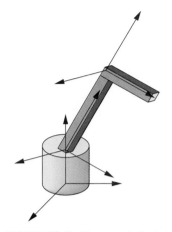

FIGURE 10.9 Movement of robot components and frames.

Note that we have described the positioning of the arm independently of the details of the individual parts. As long as the positions of the joints do not change, we can alter the form of the robot by changing only the functions that draw the three parts. This separation makes it possible to write separate programs to describe the components and to animate the robot. Figure 10.10 shows the relationships among the parts of the robot arm as a tree. The program robot.c in Appendix A implements the structure and allows you to animate the robot with the mouse through a menu. It uses a cylinder for the base and parallelepipeds for the arms.

Returning to the tree in Figure 10.10, we can look at it as a tree data structure of nodes and edges—as a graph. If we store all the necessary information in the nodes, rather than in the edges, then each node (Figure 10.11) must store at least three items:

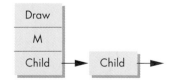

FIGURE 10.10 Tree structure for the robot arm in Figure 9.8.

1. A pointer to a function that draws the object represented by the node.
2. A homogeneous-coordinate matrix that positions, scales, and orients this node (and its children) relative to the node's parent.
3. Pointers to children of the node.

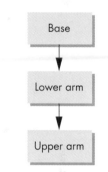

FIGURE 10.11 Node representation.

Certainly, we can include other information in a node, such as a set of attributes (color, texture, material properties) that applies to the node. Drawing an object described by such a tree requires performing a tree **traversal**. That is, we must visit every node; at each node, we must compute the matrix that applies to the primitives pointed to by the node and must display these primitives. Our OpenGL program shows an incremental approach to this traversal.

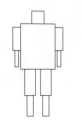

FIGURE 10.12   A humanoid figure.

This example is a simple one: There is only a single child for each of the parent nodes in the tree. The next example shows how we handle more complex models.

10.4   Trees and Traversal

Figure 10.12 shows a boxlike representation of a humanoid that might be used for a robot or in a virtual reality application. If we take the torso as the root element, we can represent this figure with a tree, as shown in Figure 10.13. Once we have positioned the torso, the position and orientation of the other parts of the model are determined by the set of joint angles. We can animate the figure by defining the motion of its joints. In a basic model, the knee and elbow joints might each have only a single degree of freedom, like the robot arm, whereas the joint at the neck might have two or three degrees of freedom.

Let us assume that we have functions, such as head and left_upper_arm, that draw the individual parts (symbols) in their own frames. We can now build a set of nodes for our tree by defining matrices that position each part relative to its parent, exactly as we did for the robot arm. If we assume that each body part has been defined at the desired size, each of these matrices is the concatenation of a translation matrix with a rotation matrix. We can show these matrices, as we do in Figure 10.14, by using the matrices to label the edges of the tree. Remember that each matrix represents the incremental change when we go from the parent to the child.

The interesting part of this example is how we do the traversal of the tree to draw the figure. In principle, we could use any tree-traversal algorithm, such as a depth-first or breadth-first search. Although, in many applications, it is insignificant which traversal algorithm is used, we shall see that there are good reasons for always using the same algorithm for traversing our graphs. We shall always traverse our trees left to right, depth first. That is, we start with the left branch, follow it to the left as deep as we can go, then go back up to the first

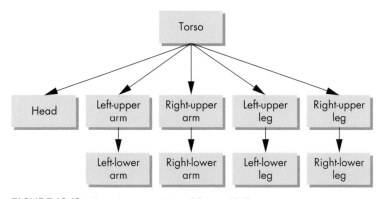

FIGURE 10.13   Tree representation of Figure 10.12.

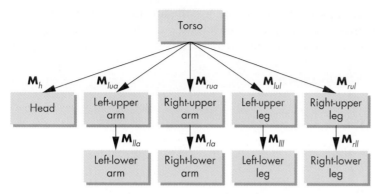

FIGURE 10.14 Tree with matrices.

right branch, and proceed recursively. This order of traversal is called a **pre-order traversal**.

We can write a tree-traversal function in one of two ways. We can do the traversal explicitly in the code, using stacks to store the required matrices and attributes as we move through the tree. We can also do the traversal recursively. In this second approach, the code is simpler as the storage of matrices and attributes is done implicitly. We develop both approaches because both are useful and because their development yields further insights into how we can build graphics systems.

10.4.1 A Stack-Based Traversal

Consider the drawing of the figure by a function `figure`. This function might be called from the display callback or from a mouse callback in an animation that uses the mouse to control the joint angles. The model-view matrix, $\mathbf{M}$, in effect when this function is invoked determines the position of the figure relative to the rest of the scene (and to the camera). The first node that we encounter results in the torso being drawn with $\mathbf{M}$ applied to all the torso's primitives. We then trace the leftmost branch of the tree to the node for the head. There we invoke the function `head` with the model-view matrix updated to $\mathbf{MM}_h$. Next, we back up to the torso node, then go down the subtree defining the left leg. This part looks just like the code for the robot arm; we draw the left-upper leg with the matrix $\mathbf{MM}_{lul}$ and the left-lower leg with matrix $\mathbf{MM}_{lul}\mathbf{M}_{lll}$. Then we move on to the right leg, left arm, and left leg. Each time we switch limbs, we must back up to the root and recover $\mathbf{M}$.

It is probably easiest to think in terms of the current transformation matrix of Chapter 4—the model-view matrix $\mathbf{C}$ that is applied to the primitives defined at a node. The matrix $\mathbf{C}$ starts out as $\mathbf{M}$, is updated to $\mathbf{MM}_h$ for the head, and later to $\mathbf{MM}_{lul}\mathbf{M}_{lll}$, and so on. The user program must manipulate $\mathbf{C}$ before each call to a function defining a part of the figure. In addition to the usual OpenGL functions for rotation, translation, and scaling, the functions `glPushMatrix` and `glPopMatrix` are particularly helpful for traversing our tree.

Consider the code (without parameter values) for the beginning of the function `figure`:

```
figure()
{
    glPushMatrix();
        torso();
        glTranslate();
        glRotate3():
        head();
    glPopMatrix();
    glPushMatrix();
        glTranslate();
        glRotate3();
        left_upper_leg();
        glTranslate();
        glRotate3();
        left_lower_leg();
    glPopMatrix();
    glPushMatrix();
        glTranslate();
        glRotate3();
        right_upper_leg();
    glPopMatrix();
    glPushMatrix();
        .
        .
        .
```

The first `glPushMatrix` duplicates the current model-view matrix (assuming that we have done a previous `glMatrixMode(GL_MODELVIEW)`), putting the copy on the top of the model-view–matrix stack. This method of pushing allows us to work immediately with the other transformations that alter the model-view matrix, knowing that we have preserved a copy on the stack. The following calls to `glTranslate` and `glRotate` determine $\mathbf{M}_h$ and concatenate it with the initial model-view matrix. We can then generate the primitives for the head. The subsequent `glPopMatrix` recovers the original model-view matrix. Note that we must do another `glPushMatrix` to leave a copy of the original model-view matrix that we can recover when we come back to draw the right leg. You should be able to complete this function by continuing in a similar manner.

The program `figure.c` in Appendix A implements this figure with a menu that will allow you to change the various joint angles. The individual parts are implemented using OpenGL quadrics—ellipses and cylinders—and the entire model is shaded as we discussed in Chapter 6.

We have not considered how attributes such as color and material properties are handled by our traversal of a hierarchical model. Attributes are state variables:

Once set, they remain in place until changed again. Hence, we must be careful as we traverse our tree. For example, suppose that within the code for torso, we set the color to red; then within the code for head, we set the color to blue. If there are no other color changes, the color will still be blue as we traverse the rest of the tree and may remain blue after we leave the code for figure. Here is an example in which the particular traversal algorithm can make a difference, because what will be affected by a change in attributes depends on the order in which the nodes are visited.

This situation may be disconcerting, but there is a solution. OpenGL has the functions glPushAttrib and glPopAttrib,[2] which allow us to deal with attributes in a manner similar to our use of the model-view matrix. If we push the attributes on the attribute stack on entrance to the function figure, and pop on exit, we have restored the attributes to their original state. Moreover, we can use additional pushes and pops within figure to control how attributes are handled in greater detail. OpenGL divides its state into groups and allows a user to push any set of these groups on the attribute stack. The user needs only to set the bits in a mask that is the parameter for glPushAttrib. Attribute groups include lighting, so we can push material properties and lights onto the stack, polygon, and line groups.

In a more complex model, we can apply these ideas recursively. If, for example, we want to use a more detailed model of the head—one incorporating eyes, ears, a nose, and a mouth—then we could model these parts separately. The head would then itself be modeled hierarchically, and its code would include the pushing and popping of matrices and attributes.

Although we have discussed only trees, if two or more nodes call the same function, we really have a DAG. Pushing and popping allow us to isolate the graphics state for different pieces of code. In OpenGL, display lists can call other display lists—so we have another method of creating trees and DAGs.

Color Plates 12, 16, and 22 show hierarchical models of robots and figures used in simulations. These objects were created with high-level interactive software that relies on our ability to traverse hierarchical structures to render the models.

The approach that we used to describe hierarchal objects is workable but has limitations. The code is explicit and relies on the application programmer to push and pop the required matrices and attributes. In reality, we implemented a stack-based representation of a tree. The code was hardwired for the particular example and thus would be difficult to extend or use dynamically. The code also does not make a clear distinction between building a model and rendering it. Although many application programmers write code in this form, we prefer to use it primarily to illustrate the flow of an OpenGL program that implements tree

---

2. Pushing and popping of matrices and attributes are slow operations. The alternative is to carefully manage state within the application program.

hierarchies. We now turn to a more general and powerful approach to working with tree-structured hierarchies.

10.5   Use of Tree Data Structures

Our second approach is to use a standard tree data structure to represent our hierarchy and then to render it with a traversal algorithm that is independent of the model. We use a **left-child, right-sibling** structure.

Consider the alternate representation of a tree in Figure 10.15. It is arranged such that all the elements at the same level are linked left to right. The children of a given node are represented as a second list arranged from the leftmost child to the rightmost. This second list points downward in Figure 10.15. This representation describes the structure of our hierarchical figure, but the structure still lacks the graphical information.

At each node we must store the information necessary to draw the object: a function that defines the object and the homogeneous coordinate matrix that positions the object relative to its parent. Consider the node structure

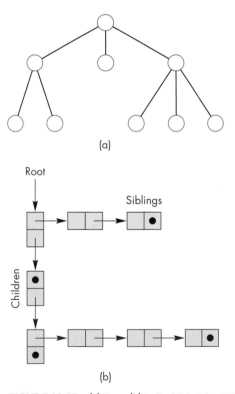

FIGURE 10.15   (a) Tree. (b) Left-child, right-sibling representation.

```
typedef struct treenode
{
   GLfloat m[16];
   void (*f)();
   struct treenode *sibling;
   struct treenode *child;
} treenode;
```

The array m stores a 4×4 homogeneous coordinate matrix by columns, as is standard in OpenGL. When we render the node, this matrix must first multiply the current model-view matrix; then the function f, which includes the graphics primitives, is rendered. We also store a pointer to the sibling node on the right and a pointer to the leftmost child. If one or the other does not exist, then we store the null pointer (NULL). For our figure, we define 10 nodes corresponding to the 10 parts of our model:

```
treenode torso_node, head_node, lua_node, rua_node, lll_node,
        rll_node, lla_node, rla_node, rul_node, lul_node;
```

We can define the nodes either in the main function or in myinit. For example, consider the root of the figure tree—the torso node. It can be oriented by a rotation about the y-axis. We can form the required rotation matrix element by element in our code, or we can use OpenGL to form the rotation matrix, then copy the matrix's elements to the m member of the node by the code

```
glLoadIdentity();
glRotatef(theta[0], 0.0, 1.0, 0.0);
glGetFloatv(GL_MODELVIEW_MATRIX,torso_node.m);
```

The function to be executed is the torso function that draws a cylinder. The torso node has no siblings, and its leftmost child is the head node, so the rest of torso node is given by

```
torso_node.f = torso;
torso_node.sibling = NULL;
torso_node.child = &head_node;
```

The code for the left-upper arm node is

```
glLoadIdentity();
glTranslatef(-(TORSO_RADIUS+UPPER_ARM_RADIUS),
   0.9*TORSO_HEIGHT, 0.0);
glRotatef(theta[3], 1.0, 0.0, 0.0);
glGetFloatv(GL_MODELVIEW_MATRIX,lua_node.m);
lua_node.f = left_upper_arm;
lua_node.sibling = &rua_node;
lua_node.child = &lla_node;
```

We determine the matrix for this node by shifting the arm's position relative to the torso and rotating about its joint angle. The translation parameters position the left-upper arm's pivot joint. This node's child is the left-lower arm, and its rightmost sibling is the right-upper arm. The other nodes are defined in a similar manner.

Traversing the tree in the same order (preorder traversal) as in Section 10.4 can be accomplished by the recursive code

```
void traverse(treenode* root)
{
  if(root==NULL) return;
  glPushMatrix();
    glMultMatrixf(root->m);
    root->f();
    if(root->child!=NULL) traverse(root->child);
  glPopMatrix();
  if(root->sibling!=NULL) traverse(root->sibling);
}
```

To render a nonnull node, we first save the graphics state (glPushMatrix). We then use the matrix at the node to modify the model-view matrix (assuming that we already are in the correct matrix mode). We then draw the objects at the node with the function pointed to by f. Finally, we traverse all the children recursively. Note that because we have multiplied the model-view matrix by the local matrix, we are passing this altered matrix to the children. For the siblings, however, we do not want to use this matrix, because each has its own local matrix. Hence, we must return to the original state (glPopMatrix) before traversing the children. If we are changing attributes within nodes, either we can push and pop attributes within the rendering functions, or we can push the attributes when we push the model-view matrix.

One of the nice aspects of this traversal method is that it is completely independent of the particular tree; thus, we can use a generic display callback such as

```
void display(void)
{
  glClear(GL_COLOR_BUFFER_BIT|GL_DEPTH_BUFFER_BIT);
  glLoadIdentity();
  traverse(&torso_node);
  glutSwapBuffers();
}
```

The complete code is given in figuretree.c. In this code, we again animate the figure by controlling individual joint angles, which are selected from a menu and are incremented and decremented through the mouse buttons. Thus, the dynamics of the program are in the mouse callback, which changes an angle, recomputes the appropriate node matrix, and then posts a redisplay:

```
void mouse(int btn, int state, int x, int y)
{
  if(btn==GLUT_LEFT_BUTTON && state == GLUT_DOWN)
  {
    theta[angle] += 5.0;
    if( theta[angle] > 360.0 ) theta[angle] -= 360.0;
  }
  if(btn==GLUT_RIGHT_BUTTON && state == GLUT_DOWN)
  {
    theta[angle] -= 5.0;
    if( theta[angle] < 360.0 ) theta[angle] += 360.0;
  }
  glPushMatrix();
  switch(angle)
  {
    case 0 :
      glLoadIdentity();
      glRotatef(theta[0], 0.0, 1.0, 0.0);
      glGetFloatv(GL_MODELVIEW_MATRIX,torso_node.m);
      break;

/* other cases */
  }
  glPopMatrix();
  glutPostRedisplay();
}
```

There is one more feature that we can add to show the flexibility of this approach. As the program executes, we can add or remove dynamic nodes rather than static nodes. We can create dynamic nodes with the C code[3]

```
typedef treenode* tree_ptr;
tree_ptr torso_ptr;
torso_ptr = (treenode*) malloc(sizeof(treenode));
```

Nodes are defined as before. For example,

```
glLoadIdentity();
glTranslatef(-(TORSO_RADIUS+UPPER_ARM_RADIUS),
   0.9*TORSO_HEIGHT, 0.0);
glRotatef(theta[3], 1.0, 0.0, 0.0);
glGetFloatv(GL_MODELVIEW_MATRIX,lua_ptr->m);
lua_ptr->f = left_upper_arm;
lua_ptr->sibling =  rua_ptr;
lua_ptr->child = lla_ptr;
```

---

3. We shall use C++ syntax for these types starting in Section 10.7 when we discuss objects.

with the traversal by

```
traverse(torso_ptr);
```

For our figure example, there is no particular advantage to the dynamic approach; in a more general setting, however, we can use the dynamic approach to create structures that change interactively. For example, we can use this form to write an application that will let us edit figures, adding and removing parts as desired. This type of implementation is the basis for the scene trees that we discuss in Section 10.8. Back Plate 1 shows one frame of an animation with the figure.

Note that as we have coded our examples, there is a fixed traversal order for the graph. If we had applied some other traversal algorithm, we could have produced a different image if we made any state changes within the graph such as changing transformations or attributes. We can avoid some of these potential problems if we are careful to isolate parts of our code by pushing and popping attributes and matrices in each node (although there is a performance penalty for doing so too often).

10.6 Animation

Our two examples—the robot and the figure—are **articulated**: The models consist of rigid parts connected by joints. We can make such models change their positions in time—animate them—by altering the values of a small set of parameters. Hierarchical models allow us to model the compound motions incorporating the physical relationships among the parts of the model. What we have not discussed is how to alter the parameters over time so as to achieve the desired motion.

Of the many approaches to animation, a few basic techniques are of particular importance when we work with articulated figures. These techniques arise both from traditional hand animation and from robotics.

In the case of our robot model, consider the problem of moving the tip of the upper arm from one position to another. The model has three degrees of freedom—the three angles that we can specify. Although each set of angles has a unique position for the tip, the converse is not true. Given a desired position of the tip of the arm, there may be no set of angles that place the tip as desired, a single set of angles that yields the specified position, or multiple sets of angles that place the tip at the desired position.

Studying **kinematics** involves describing the position of the parts of the model based on only the joint angles. We can use our hierarchical-modeling methods either to determine positions numerically or to find explicit equations that give the position of any desired set of points in the model in terms of the joint angles. Thus, if θ is an array of the joint angles and $\mathbf{p}$ is an array whose elements are the vertices in our model, a kinematic model is of the form

$$\mathbf{p} = f(\theta).$$

Likewise, if we specify the rates of change of the joint angles—the joint velocities—then we can obtain velocities of points on the model.

The kinematic model neglects matters such as the effects of inertia and friction. We could derive more complex differential equations that describe the dynamic behavior of the model in terms of applied forces—a topic that is studied in robotics.

Whereas both kinematics and dynamics are ways of describing the forward behavior of the model, in animation, we are more concerned with **inverse kinematics** and **inverse dynamics**: Given a desired state of the model, how can we adjust the joint angles so as to achieve this position? There are two major concerns. First, given an environment including the robot and other objects, we must determine whether there exists a sequence of angles that achieves the desired state. There may be no single-valued function of the form

$$\theta = g(\mathbf{p}).$$

Not only must we determine whether the final position corresponds to a set of joint angles, but we must also find a way to alter the joint angles so as not to hit any obstacles and not to violate any physical constraints. Although, for a model as simple as our robot, we might be able to find equations that give the joint angles in terms of the position, we cannot do so in general, because the forward equations do not have unique inverses. The figure model, which has 11 degrees of freedom, should give you an idea of how difficult this problem is to solve.

A basic approach to overcoming these difficulties comes from traditional hand-animation techniques. In **key-frame animation**, the animator positions the objects at a set of times—the key frames. In hand animation, animators then can fill in the remaining frames, a process called **in-betweening**. In computer graphics, we can automate in-betweening by interpolating the joint angles between the key frames or, equivalently, using simple approximations to obtain the required dynamic equations between key frames. As we saw in Chapter 9, much of the work required for in-betweening can now be automated as part of the pipeline, often using the programmability of recent GPUs. We can also use the spline curves that we develop in Chapter 11 to give smooth methods of going between key frames. Although we can develop code for the interpolation, both a skillful (human) animator and good interactive methods are crucial if we are to choose the key frames and the positions of objects in these frames.

10.7 Graphical Objects

Although we have introduced multiple graphics paradigms, our development has been heavily based on a pipeline implementation of the synthetic-camera model. We made this choice because we want to support interactive three-dimensional applications with currently available hardware and software. Consequently, we have emphasized immediate-mode graphics where primitives are rendered to the screen when the code defining them is executed in a user program. Once primitives are rendered, they leave no trace other than their images on the screen and the contents of the frame buffer. Any changes in attributes or positioning require that we reexecute code in the application program.

In addition, our desire to present the basics of implementation has led us to develop graphics in a manner that was never far from the details of the implementation. For all its benefits, this approach has not let us exploit many high-level alternatives to developing graphical applications.

Now we move to a higher level of abstraction and introduce two major concepts. First, we expand our notion of objects from geometric objects, such as polygons and vectors, to include most of the elements within a graphics program, such as viewers, lights, and material properties. Second, we focus on objects that exist even after their images have been drawn and even if we never display them. We have already seen that we can create such objects using display lists as in Chapter 3. Here we investigate other approaches, such as the use of classes in C++ or structures in C. Although the OpenGL API does not support this approach directly, we do not have to abandon OpenGL. We still use OpenGL for rendering, and we regard what we develop as a software layer on top of OpenGL.

10.7.1 Methods, Attributes, and Messages

Our programs manipulate data. The data may be in many forms, ranging from numbers to strings to the geometric entities that we build in our applications. In traditional imperative programming, the programmer writes code to manipulate the data, usually through functions. The data are passed to a function through the function's parameters. Data are returned in a similar manner. To manipulate the data sent to it, the function must be aware of how those data are organized. Consider, for example, the cube that we have used in many of our previous examples. We have seen that we can model it in various ways, including with vertex pointers, edge lists, and lists of polygon vertices. The application programmer may care little about which model is used and may prefer to regard the cube as an atomic entity or an *object*. In addition, she may care little about the details of how the cube is rendered to the screen: which shading model or which polygon-fill algorithm is used. She can assume that the cube "knows how to render itself" and that conceptually the rendering algorithm is tied to the object itself. In some ways, OpenGL supports this view by using the state of the graphics system to control rendering. For example, the color of the cube, its orientation, and the lights that are applied to its surfaces can all be part of the state of the graphics system and may not depend on how the cube is modeled.

However, if we are working with a physical cube, we might find this view a bit strange. The location of a physical cube is tied to the physical object, as are its color, size, and orientation. Although we could use OpenGL to tie some properties to a virtual cube—through pushing and popping various attributes and matrices—the underlying programming model does not support

FIGURE 10.16 Imperative programming paradigm.

FIGURE 10.17 Object-oriented paradigm.

these ideas well. For example, a function that transforms the cube other than by a homogeneous coordinate transformation would have to know exactly how the cube is represented and would work as shown in Figure 10.16.

The application programmer would write a function that would take as its inputs a pointer to the cube's data and the parameters of the transformation. It would then manipulate the data for the cube and return control to the application program (perhaps also returning some values).

Object-oriented design and object-oriented programming look at manipulation of objects in a fundamentally different manner. Even in the early days of object-oriented programming, languages such as Smalltalk recognized that computer graphics provides excellent examples of the power of the object-oriented approach. Recent trends within the software community indicate that we can combine our pipeline orientation with an object orientation to build even more expressive and high-performance graphics systems.

Object-oriented programming languages define **objects** as modules with which we build programs. These modules include the data that define the module, such as the vertices for our cube, properties of the module (**attributes**), and the functions (**methods**) that manipulate the module and its attributes. We send **messages** to objects to invoke a method. This model is shown in Figure 10.17.

The advantage to the writer of the application program is that she now does not need to know how the cube is represented; she needs to know only what functionality the cube object supports—what messages she can send to it.

Although the C struct has some of the properties of objects, the C language does not support the full power of an object-oriented approach. In C++, the struct is replaced with the class. C++ classes have two important properties that we can exploit to get the flavor of the object-oriented approach. C programmers should have no trouble understanding these concepts.

10.7.2 A Cube Object

Suppose that we wish to create a cube object in C that has a color attribute and a homogeneous coordinate transformation associated with it. In C, we could use a struct of the form

```
struct  cube
{
    float color[3];
    float matrix[4][4];

/* implementation goes here */

}
```

The implementation part of the structure contains the information on how a cube is actually represented. Typically, a user does not need this information and needs to change only the color or matrix associated with the cube.

Once the struct has been defined, **instances** of the cube object can be created as are other basic data types:

```
cube a, b;
```

Attributes that are part of the class definition can be changed for each instance of the cube. Thus, we can set the color of cube a to red by

```
a.color[0]=1.0;
a.color[1]=a.color[2]=0.0;
```

It should be clear how such a struct can be implemented within an OpenGL system. For example, within the implementation of the cube, we would expect to see a line of code like

```
glColor3fv(color);
```

Although we have created a retained cube object, we are limited in how we can manipulate it or render it. We could write a function that would render the cube through code such as

```
render_cube(a);
```

Or we could rotate the cube by

```
rotate_cube(a, theta, d);
```

where d is the vector about which we wish to rotate.

This approach is workable but has limitations. One is that we need separate rendering and rotation functions for each type of object. A second is that the implementation part of the code is accessible to application programs. C++ classes solve both of these problems. A C++ class can have public, private, and protected members. The **public members** are similar to the members of C struct and can be altered by any function. The **private members** neither are visible to nor can be altered by a function that uses the class. The **protected members** are visible to classes within the same hierarchy. A programmer can also declare classes to be **friends** to give access to specific classes. Thus, in C++, we define the cube as

```
class  cube
{
 public:
   float color[3];
   float matrix[4][4];
 private:

/* implementation goes here */

}
```

thereby protecting and hiding the details of the implementation. Furthermore, C++ classes allow us to have members that are functions or methods. Once we add such functions, the object-orientation becomes clearer. Suppose that we add member functions to the public part of the cube class, such as

```
void render();
void translate(float x, float y, float z);
void rotate(float theta, float axis_x, float axis_y,
            float axis_z);
```

Now an application program could create, translate, rotate, and render a cube through the code

```
cube a;
a.rotate(45.0, 1.0, 0.0, 0.0);
a.translate(1.0, 2.0, 3.0);
a.render();
```

Conceptually, this code assumes that an instance of the cube "knows" how to rotate itself and that by executing the code a.rotate, we are sending a message to a cube object that we would like it to carry out such a rotation. We could easily write an implementation of the rotation and translation methods that would issue the correct OpenGL transformation function calls.

It is less clear what a function call such as a.render really does or how our rotate function relates to the state of the graphics system. One way to understand what this change to an object orientation means is to note that we can no longer work with immediate-mode graphics. Each instance of an object persists and can be altered by further code in the program. OpenGL display lists might be useful as a way of implementing our instances as they continue to exist after the object has been displayed, but there are other possible implementations. What is most important is that we have created an object that continues to exist somewhere in our system in a form unknown to the application program. The attributes of the object are also in the system and can be altered by functions such as rotate. The render function causes the object to be redrawn using the object's rather than the system's present state. In an OpenGL setting, the render step probably involves either executing code such as

```
glBegin(GL_POLYGON);
    glVertex3f(...);
    .
    .
    glVertex3f(...);
glEnd();
```

where the necessary vertex information comes from the implementation part of the structure, or redisplaying a display list corresponding to the instance.

10.7.3 Implementing the Cube Object

As an example of the choices that go into developing the private part of an object, let us consider the cube. One basic implementation would simply use OpenGL polygons or, perhaps, quadrilaterals. Thus, we might base the implementation on a vertex implementation of the form

```
GLfloat vertices[6][3]

glBeginGL_POLYGON; /* begin first face */
    glVertex3fv(vertices[0]);
    glVertex3fv(vertices[1]);
    glVertex3fv(vertices[2]);
    glVertex3fv(vertices[3]);
glEnd(); /* end first face */
    /* next 5 faces */
```

But as we saw in Chapter 4, this implementation requires many more function calls than necessary in the rendering. We could instead use the vertex array data structure that we developed, or we could use OpenGL vertex arrays. We can also use other data structures that may be more efficient depending upon how we intend to use the objects.

We can do far better if we include more information in the implementation. Of particular interest is information that might help in the rendering. Thus, whereas OpenGL will do hidden-surface removal correctly through the z-buffer algorithm, we can often do much better by eliminating objects earlier through a separate visibility test, as we shall discuss in Section 10.10. To support this functionality, we might want to include information that determines a bounding volume for the object. For example, we can include the axis-aligned bounding box for objects within the private part of the code. For polygonal objects, we need simply save the minimum and maximum of the x, y, and z of the vertices (after they have been transformed by any transformation matrix stored with the object).

10.7.4 Objects and Hierarchy

One of the major advantages of object-oriented design is the ability to reuse code and to build more sophisticated objects from a small set of simple objects. As in Section 10.4, we can build a figure object from cylinders and have multiple instances of this new object, each with its own color, size, location, and orientation. A class for the humanoid figure could refer to the classes for arms and legs; the class for a car could refer to classes for wheels and a chassis. Thus, we would once more have treelike representations similar to those that we developed in Section 10.5.

Often in object-oriented design, we want the representations to show relationships more complex than the parent–child relationship that characterizes trees. As we have used trees, the structure is such that the highest level of complexity at the root and the relationship between a parent and child is a "has-a" relationship. Thus, the stick figure has two arms and two legs, whereas the car has four wheels and a chassis.

We can look at hierarchy in a different manner, with the simplest objects being the top of the hierarchy and the relationship between parents and children being an "is-a" relationship. This type of hierarchy is typical of taxonomies. A mammal is an animal. A human is a mammal. We used this relationship in describing projections. A parallel projection is a planar geometric projection; an oblique projection is a parallel projection. "Has-a" relationships allow us to define multiple complex objects from simpler objects and also allow the more complex object to inherit properties from the simpler object. Thus, if we write the code for a parallel projection, the oblique-projection code can use this code and refine only the parts that are necessary to convert the general parallel projection to an oblique one. For geometric objects, we can define base objects with a default set of properties such as their color and material properties. A user could then use these properties or change them in sub-objects. These concepts are supported by languages such as C++ that allow for subclasses and inheritance.

10.7.5 Geometric Objects

Suppose that we now want to build an object-oriented graphics system. What objects should we include? Although it is clear that we want to have objects such as points, vectors, polygons, rectangles, and triangles (possibly using subclasses), it is less clear how we should deal with attributes, light sources, and viewers. For example, should a material property be associated with an object such as a cube, or is it a separate object? The answer can be either or both. We could create a cube class in which there is a member for each of the ambient, diffuse, and specular material properties that we introduced with the Phong model in Chapter 6. We could also define a material class using code such as

```
class material
{
 public:
   float specular[3];
   float shininess;
   float diffuse[3];
   float ambient[3];
}
```

We could then assign the material to a geometric object through a member function of the cube class

```
cube a;
material b;
a.setMaterial(b);
```

Light sources are geometric objects—they have position and orientation among their features—and we can easily add a light source object:

```
class light
{
  public:
     boolean type;
     boolean near;
     float position[3];
     float orientation[3];
     float specular[3];
     float diffuse[3];
     float ambient[3];
}
```

Once we have built up a collection of geometric objects, we can use it to describe a scene. To take advantage of the hierarchical relationships that we have introduced, we develop a new tree structure called a **scene graph**.

10.8 Scene Graphs

If we think about what goes into describing a scene, we can see that in addition to our graphical primitives and geometric objects derived from these primitives, we have other objects, such as lights and a camera. These objects may also be defined by vertices and vectors and may have attributes, such as color, that are similar to the attributes associated with geometric primitives. It is the totality of these objects that describes a scene, and there may be hierarchical relationships among these objects. For example, when a primitive is defined in a program, the camera parameters that exist at that time are used to form the image. If we alter the camera lens between the definition of two geometric objects, we may produce an image in which each object is viewed differently. Although we cannot create such an image with a real camera, the example points out the power of our graphics systems. We can extend our use of tree data structures to describe these relationships among geometric objects, cameras, lights, and attributes.

Knowing that we can write a graphical application program to traverse a graph, we can expand our notion of the contents of a graph to describe an entire scene. One possibility is to use a tree data structure and to include various attributes at each node—in addition to the instance matrix and a pointer to the drawing function. Another possibility is to allow new types of nodes, such as attribute-definition nodes and matrix-transformation nodes. Consider the tree in Figure 10.18. Here we have set up individual nodes for the colors and for the model-view matrices. The place where there are branches at the top can be considered a special type of node, a **separator node** whose function is to isolate the two children. The separator node allows us to preserve the state that exists at the time that we enter a node and thus isolates the state of the subtree beginning at a separator node from the rest of the tree. Using our preorder traversal algorithm, the corresponding OpenGL code is of the form

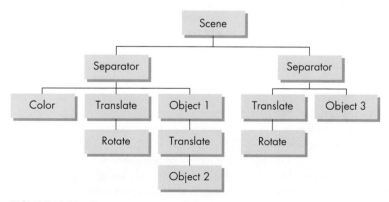

FIGURE 10.18 Scene tree.

```
glPushAttrib
glPushMatrix
    glColor
    glTranslate
    glRotate
    object1
    glTranslate
    object2
glPopMatrix
glPushMatrix
    glTranslate
    glRotate
    object3
glPopMatrix
glPopAttrib
```

The separator nodes correspond to the OpenGL push and pop functions. This code preserves and restores both the attributes and the model-view matrix before exiting. It sets a drawing color that applies to the rest of the tree and traverses the tree in a manner similar to the figure example.

We can go further and note that we can use the attribute and matrix stacks to store the viewing conditions; thus, we can create a camera node in the tree. Although we probably do not want a scene in which individual objects are viewed with different cameras, we may want to view the same set of objects with multiple cameras producing, for example, the multiview orthographic projections and isometric view that are used by architects and engineers. Such images can be created with a scene graph that has multiple cameras.

The scene graph we have just described is equivalent to an OpenGL program in the sense that we can use the tree to generate the program in a totally mechanical fashion. This approach is taken by Open Inventor, an object-oriented API that is built on top of OpenGL. An Inventor program builds, manipulates, and renders a scene graph. Execution of the program causes traversal of the scene graph, which in turn executes graphics functions that are written in OpenGL.

The notion of scene graphs couples nicely with the object-oriented paradigm introduced in Section 10.7. We can regard all primitives, attributes, and transformations as software objects, and we can define classes to manipulate these entities. From this perspective, we can make use of concepts such as data encapsulation to build up scenes of great complexity with simple programs that use predefined software objects. We can even support animations through software objects that appear as nodes in the scene graph but cause parameters to change and the scene to be redisplayed. Although, in Open Inventor, the software objects are typically written in OpenGL, the scene graph itself is a database that includes all the elements of the scene. OpenGL is the rendering engine that allows the database to be converted to an image but is not used in the specification of the scene.

Graphics software systems are evolving to the configuration shown in Figure 10.19. OpenGL is the rendering engine. It may sit on top of another layer such as Microsoft's DirectX or talk directly to the hardware. Above OpenGL is an object-oriented layer that supports scene graphs and a storage mechanism. User programs can be written for any of the layers, depending on what facilities are required by the application.

10.9 A Simple Scene Graph API

Although there are a few standard scene graph APIs available, including the Virtual Reality Modeling Language (VRML), Java3D, and Open Scene Graph, none have yet become dominant. Rather than discuss one of these, we opt instead to construct our own simple, but extensible, scene graph API. It will include the basics shared by more complex scene graph APIs and will be easy to extend. We start with the public interface that a user can use to define a scene graph and display it. Then we consider a possible implementation using the left-child, right-sibling data structure of Section 10.5.

Our design[4] employs two base classes: a node class and a viewer class. We shall use the node class to construct nodes for all our objects, including geometric objects, camera objects, material objects, and light source objects. These nodes can then be used to form a tree that is our scene graph. The viewer object provides a simple mechanism that will allow us to view the scene graph with an OpenGL program.

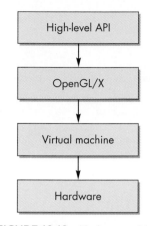

FIGURE 10.19 Modern graphics architecture.

10.9.1 The Node Class

Our fundamental node has the public interface

```
class Node
{
 public:
  Node();
  virtual ~Node();
  virtual void Render();
  void AddChild(Node *);

  friend class GLViewer;

  //private part goes here
};
```

---

4. This scene graph API and implementation started as a class project by Ye Cong at the University of New Mexico.

We have both a constructor and a destructor for creating and deleting nodes that will enable us to create dynamic scene graphs. We can define a tree hierarchy by having a single method, AddChild, for adding a child to a node. However, as we shall see when we discuss implementation, the order in which we add children can affect the image produced by the scene graph.

As we will have many types of nodes (geometry, camera, materials, lights), each node must have its own render method that will execute when the node is encountered as part of the traversal process.

We can invoke the rendering process from the viewer. The viewer will also let us take care of the standard OpenGL interface with the window system by using GLUT. Here is the public part of the viewer:

```
class GLViewer
{
public:
  GLViewer();
  ~GLViewer();

  void SetValue(Enum PName, Enum Type);
  void Init(int argc, char **argv);
  void Show(Node *N);
  int CreateWin(char *name, int width, int height);

  //private part goes here

};
```

We will be able to have multiple viewers so that we can, for example, display two different views using two different cameras in two OpenGL windows. We could also use different OpenGL windows to view different parts of the same scene graph by passing in different nodes to the Show method. The Show method initiates traversal of a scene graph.

Both the viewer and node classes have many parameters that are used to specify attributes, such as color, line style, and material properties, and rendering options, such as double buffering and hidden-surface removal. We take an approach similar to OpenGL and GLUT by specifying symbolic constants as an enumerated type:

```
enum Enum
 {
  PERSPECTIVE, ORTHO, POSITION, AIMAT, UPDIRECTION, ASPECT,
  NEAR, FAR, YANGLE, BLACK, WHITE, RED, GREEN, YELLOW, BLUE,
  MAGENTA, CYAN, GRAY, WIDTH, HEIGHT,DEPTH,
  AMBIENT, DIFFUSE, SPECULAR, SPOT_DIRECTION, DROPOFFRATE,
  CUTOFFANGLE, EMISSION, SHININESS, TRANSLATION, ROTATION, SCALE,
  BUFFER, SINGLE, DOUBLE, RADIUS, STYLE, POINTSIZE, LINEWIDTH,
  FILLED, LINE, POINT, BACKCOLOR
 };
```

The following code from a typical application sets up a window on the display and renders a scene graph:

```
GLViewer *MyViewer=new GLViewer;

MyViewer->Init(argc, argv);
MyViewer->SetValue(BACKCOLOR, GRAY);
MyViewer->SetValue(BUFFER, DOUBLE);
MyViewer->CreateWin("Working Hard", 500, 500);

MyViewer->Show(Root);
```

We have five major subclasses of our node class: geometry nodes, light nodes, camera nodes, attribute nodes, and transformation nodes. From the OpenGL perspective, there are two types of operations: those that generate primitives and those that change state. However, from the perspective of a scene graph, both types of operations can be initiated from within a node.

10.9.2 Geometry Nodes

Our scene graph allows for both basic objects, such as lines and polygons, and the more complex objects, including cubes, cylinders, triangles, and spheres. Geometry nodes have many properties in common, including color attributes, material properties, and instance matrices that can be applied to them. These properties can be set by a user program, and we have included set methods for them within the geometry class.

```
class Geometry: public Node
{
 public:
  Geometry();
  ~Geometry();

  void SetColor(Enum icolor);
  void SetColor(float red, float green, float blue);
  void SetColorv(float *color);
  void SetColor(Color *colorp);
  void SetMaterial(Enum type, float red, float green, float blue,
                   float alpha);
  void SetMaterialv(Enum type, float *materialv);
  void SetMaterial(Enum type, float materialv);
  void SetMaterial(Material *material);
  void SetTransform(Enum, float *transform, int order);
  void SetTransform(Enum type, float xparam, float yparam, float zparam,
                    int order);
  void SetTransform(Enum type, float angle, float xparam, float yparam,
                    float zparam, int order);
  void SetTransform(Transformation *transform);
  void SetStyle(Enum pname, Enum eparam);
```

```
void SetStyle(Enum pname, float fparam);
void SetStyle(DrawStyle *stylev);
virtual void Render();

private:
  //implementation
}
```

Note that a user can set an attribute, such as a color, by setting the attribute directly within a geometry node by using a set method whose parameters are the individual values

```
myObject->SetColor(red, green , blue);
```

or she can first define an attribute object and then attach this object to one or more geometry nodes, as in the code

```
Color *myColor = new Color;
myColor->SetValue(red, green, blue);
myObject->SetColor(myColor);
```

Now we can look at a few of the geometry nodes. The simplest is a line segment that allows us to set the endpoints, either directly or by a pointer to an array of two vertices. Note that in our simple system, we have included only three-dimensional vertices. It is a simple exercise to add two-dimensional vertices. Also note that we could use a single function SetVertices for all cases, as C++ permits overloading of functions.

```
class Line: public Geometry
{
 public:
  Line(){};
  void SetVertices(float *vert0, float *vert1);
  void SetVerticesv(float v[][3]);
  void Render();
 private:
   //implementation
};
```

Two other simple geometric objects are a sphere centered at the origin and a cylinder oriented along the y direction with its base lying in the x, z plane.

```
class Sphere: public Geometry
{
 public:
  Sphere(){};
  Sphere(float R);
```

```
  void SetValue(Enum Pname, float param);
  void Render();
private:
   //implementation
};


class Cylinder: public Geometry
{
public:
  Cylinder(){};
  void SetValue(Enum Pname, float param);
  void Render();
private:
   //implementation
};
```

We also allow for general polygons

```
class Polygon: public Geometry
{
 public:
  Polygon(){};
  void SetVerticesv(float v[][3], int);
  void Render();
 private:
   //implementation
};
```

10.9.3   Camera Class

The camera class needs only a very simple interface because most of the camera parameters can be specified through a set mechanism. The constructor parameter determines whether the camera is for perspective or orthogonal viewing. The camera orientation can be set by using the same parameters as the OpenGL Lookat function.

```
class Camera: public Node
{
 public:
  Camera(Enum CType);

  void Render();
  void SetValuev(Enum PName, float *v);
  void SetValue(Enum PName, float v1, float v2, float v3);
  void SetValue(Enum PName, float v);
 private:
   //implementation
};
```

Here is an example of specifying a perspective camera:

```
Camera *Camera1=new Camera(PERSPECTIVE);

Camera1->SetValue(POSITION, 2.2, 0.9, 3);
Camera1->SetValue(AIMAT, 0, 0, 0);
Camera1->SetValue(UPDIRECTION, 0, 1, 0);
Camera1->SetValue(ASPECT, 1);
Camera1->SetValue(NEAR, 1);
Camera1->SetValue(FAR, 20);
Camera1->SetValue(YANGLE, 50);
```

From an OpenGL perspective, some of these parameters affect the model-view matrix, whereas others affect the projection matrix. From an object-oriented perspective, these parameters simply describe a virtual camera.

10.9.4 Lights and Materials

Lights and materials have simple public interfaces that allow us to set the standard parameters in the Phong model. Because the scene graph can alter state variables as it is traversed, we want to be able to turn lights on and off within the scene graph. We handle this problem by having a switch object.

```
class Light: public Node
{
 public:
  Light();
  void Render();

  void SetValue(Enum PName, Enum color);
  void SetValue(Enum PName, float v1, float v2, float v3, float v4 );
  void SetValue(Enum PName, float v1, float v2, float v3);
  void SetValue(Enum PName, float f);
  void SetValuev(Enum PName, float *);
  void TurnOn();
  void TurnOff();

  friend class TurnOff;

 private:
   //implementation
};

class TurnOff: public Node
{
 public:
  TurnOff(Light *L);
  void Render();
```

```
private:
  //implementation
};
```

Thus, if we want to set a light and be able to turn it on and off, we must create both the light and switch object as in the code

```
Light *Light1=new Light;
TurnOff *Off1=new TurnOff(Light1);

Light1->SetValue(POSITION, -2, -3, 1.5, 1);
Light1->SetValue(SPOT_DIRECTION, 2, 3, -1.5);
Light1->SetValue(CUTOFFANGLE, 40.0);
Light1->TurnOn();
```

Material nodes are similar to light nodes and contain a render method and methods to set the standard material parameters.

```
class Material: public Node
{
 public:
  Material();
  void SetValuev(Enum Pname, float *);
  void SetValue(Enum Pname, float v1, float v2, float v3, float v4);
  void SetValue(Enum Pname, float Value);
  void Render();
 private:
   //implementation
};
```

Thus, we might set a material node as

```
Material *myMat = new Material;

myMat->SetValue(DIFFUSE, 0.0, 0.0, 1.0, 1.0);
myMat->SetValue(AMBIENT, 0.0, 0.0, 1.0, 1.0);
myMat->SetValue(SPECULAR, 1.0, 1.0, 1.0, 1.0);
myMat->SetValue(SHININESS, 100.0);
```

and then assign it to an object by

```
myObject->SetMaterial(myMat);
```

10.9.5 Transformations

Transformations include the standard rotation, translation, and scaling matrices whose parameters are set through SetValue methods. The Order member allows us to define a sequence of transformation matrices and the order in which they are multiplied.

```
class Transformation: public Node
{
 public:
  Transformation();
  void SetValuev(Enum Pname, float *, int Order);
  void SetValue(Enum Pname, float x, float y, float z, int Order);
  void SetValue(Enum Pname, float a, float x, float y, float z, int Order);
  void Render();
 private:
   //implementation
};
```

For any of the geometry nodes, we can use the SetTransform method to associate an instance transformation with the object, as in the code

```
Cylinder myCylinder = new Cylinder;
myCylinder->SetTransformation(SCALE, sx, sy, sz, 0);
myCylinder->SetTransformation(TRANSLATION, tx, ty, tz, 2);
myCylinder->SetTransformation(ROTATION, theta, rx, ry, rz, 1);
```

Thus, in the example, the order parameter forces the evaluation order to be scale first, followed by rotation, and then translation.

10.9.6 The Robot Figure

Before discussing the implementation, let us consider a simple example, the robot figure again. The full code is in Appendix A.

```
#include "Scene.h"

int main(int argc, char **argv)

{

  //define a light

  Light *Light1=new Light;
  TurnOff *Off1=new TurnOff(Light1);

  //set light parameters here

  //define a Camera

  Camera *Camera1=new Camera(PERSPECTIVE);

  //set camera parameters

  //define materials
```

```
Material *RobotMat=new Material;

//set material parameters

RobotMat->SetValue(DIFFUSE, 0.0, 0.0, 1.0, 1.0);
RobotMat->SetValue(AMBIENT, 0.0, 0.0, 1.0, 1.0);
RobotMat->SetValue(SPECULAR, 1.0, 1.0, 1.0, 1.0);
RobotMat->SetValue(SHININESS, 100.0);

//define other materials

//define robot geometry nodes

Sphere *Head=new Sphere;

Cylinder *Torso = new Cylinder;
Cylinder *UpperArmL=new Cylinder;
Cylinder *UpperArmR=new Cylinder;
Cylinder *LowerArmL=new Cylinder;
Cylinder *LowerArmR=new Cylinder;
Cylinder *UpperLegL=new Cylinder;
Cylinder *UpperLegR=new Cylinder;
Cylinder *LowerLegL=new Cylinder;
Cylinder *LowerLegR=new Cylinder;

Transformation *HeadTrans=new Transformation;
Transformation *UpArmLTrans=new Transformation;

//transformation for left upper arm

HeadTrans->SetValue(TRANSLATION, 0, 0, BaseLen+BaseRadius+BaseRadius/3, 0);
UpArmLTrans->SetValue(TRANSLATION, 0, 0, -UpLen, 0);
UpArmLTrans->SetValue(ROTATION, -45, 0, 1, 0, 1);
UpArmLTrans->SetValue(TRANSLATION, 0, BaseRadius+Radius, BaseLen, 2);

//set up other transformation matrices

UpperArmL->SetTransform(UpArmLTrans);
LowerArmL->SetTransform(LowArmTrans);

//assign transformations to nodes

//set relationship in robot:
RobotMat->AddChild(Light1);
Light1->AddChild(Base);

Torso->AddChild(Off1);

Torso->AddChild(UpperArmL);
```

```
UpperArmL->AddChild(LowerArmL);
Torso->AddChild(UpperArmR);
UpperArmR->AddChild(LowerArmR);
Torso->AddChild(UpperLegL);
UpperLegL->AddChild(LowerLegL);
Torso->AddChild(UpperLegR);
UpperLegR->AddChild(LowerLegR);

//transformation nodes for robot

Transformation *Trans1=new Transformation;

Trans1->SetValue(TRANSLATION, -0.5, 0, 0, 2);

Trans1->AddChild(RobotMat);

//root node:
Node *Root=new Node;

Root->AddChild(Trans1);
Root->AddChild(Camera1);

//set up viewer

GLViewer *MyViewer=new GLViewer;

//viewer parameters

//render

MyViewer->Show(Root);

    return 0;
}
```

10.9.7   Implementing the Viewer

Let us start our discussion of implementation with the viewer. It initiates the traversal process, and it must interact with the windowing system. We shall make our interface through GLUT so that the viewer will be compatible with everything else we have done. Here is the definition of the viewer, this time including the private members and methods used for its implementation:

```
class GLViewer
{
public:
 GLViewer();
 ~GLViewer();
```

```
void SetValue(Enum PName, Enum Type);
void Init(int argc, char **argv);
void Show(Node *N);
void CreateWin(char* name, int width, int height);

private:
 void GLInit();
 int ViewerIndex;
 char *WinName;
 float BackColor[3];

 static Node *Root[3];
 static int ViewerNum;
 static int BufType[3];
 static int WinWidth[3];
 static int WinHeight[3];
 static void Reshape0(int w, int h);
 static void Display0();
 static void Reshape1(int w, int h);
 static void Display1();
 static void Reshape2(int w, int h);
 static void Display2();

};
```

The viewer class has been implemented to allow for up to three independent viewers. The information about these viewers is stored as static members. Each viewer can have its own display and reshape callbacks. We must use a few tricks because we are using GLUT. For example, we must ensure that there is exactly one call to glutMainLoop. The array Root stores the root node for each viewer. The constructor sets up a default window.

```
GLViewer::GLViewer()
{
  int i;

  ViewerIndex=ViewerNum;
  ViewerNum++;

  WinName="";
  BufType[ViewerIndex]=GLUT_DOUBLE;
  Root[ViewerIndex]=NULL;
  for(i=0; i<3; i++)
    BackColor[i]=0.0;
}
```

We can set up a nondefault window with CreateWin and set parameters with SetValue.

```
GLViewer::~GLViewer()
{
  if(Root[ViewerIndex])
    {
      delete Root[ViewerIndex];
      Root[ViewerIndex]=NULL;
    }
}

void GLViewer::Init(int argc, char **argv)
{
  if(ViewerIndex==0)
    glutInit(&argc, argv);
}

void GLViewer::CreateWin(char *Name, int Width, int Height)
{
  WinName=Name;
  WinWidth[ViewerIndex]=Width;
  WinHeight[ViewerIndex]=Height;

}

void GLViewer::SetValue(Enum PName, Enum Type)
{
  switch(PName)
    {
    case BUFFER:
      if(Type==DOUBLE)
    BufType[ViewerIndex]=GLUT_DOUBLE;
      else if(Type==SINGLE)
    BufType[ViewerIndex]=GLUT_SINGLE;
      break;
    case BACKCOLOR:
      Root[ViewerIndex]->GetColor(Type, BackColor);
      break;
    default:
      break;
    }
}
```

Because we have done our implementation with OpenGL and GLUT, the traversal mechanism must be part of the display callback. Thus, each viewer has a display callback that starts the traversal at the root node associated with that viewer. The traverse method is a method of the node class.

```
void GLViewer::Show(Node *N)
{
  GLInit();
```

```
    Root[ViewerIndex]=N;
    if(ViewerIndex==(ViewerNum-1))
      glutMainLoop();
}

void GLViewer::GLInit()
{
  glutInitDisplayMode(BufType[ViewerIndex] | GLUT_RGB | GLUT_DEPTH);
  glutInitWindowSize(WinWidth[ViewerIndex], WinHeight[ViewerIndex]);
  glutCreateWindow(WinName);
  switch(ViewerIndex)
    {
    case 0:
      glutReshapeFunc(Reshape0);
      glutDisplayFunc(Display0);
      break;
    case 1:
      glutReshapeFunc(Reshape1);
      glutDisplayFunc(Display1);
      break;
    case 2:
      glutReshapeFunc(Reshape2);
      glutDisplayFunc(Display2);
      break;
    default:
      break;
    }

  glEnable(GL_DEPTH_TEST);
  glClearColor(BackColor[0], BackColor[1], BackColor[2], 1.0);
}

void GLViewer::Display0()
{
  glClear(GL_COLOR_BUFFER_BIT | GL_DEPTH_BUFFER_BIT);
  Root[0]->Traverse();
  if(BufType[0]==GLUT_DOUBLE)
    glutSwapBuffers();
  glFlush();
}

void GLViewer::Reshape0(int w, int h)
{
  glViewport(0, 0, (GLsizei)w, (GLsizei)h);
  WinWidth[0]=w;
  WinHeight[0]=h;
}

// similar code for other display and reshape functions
```

10.9.8   Implementing a Node

The private part of the node contains its implementation as a left-sibling, right-child tree. We have also included a traversal method that is similar to the one that we used for our robot, but we could use any standard traversal algorithm.

There is a protected member, KeepMatrix, that can be used to push the present model-view or projection matrix on the stack. This Boolean variable enables us to choose whether or not to pass the present matrix state onto a child and avoids the need for a separator node. Here is a basic traversal:

```
void Node::Traverse()
{
  if(!KeepMatrix)
    glPushMatrix();

  Render();
  if(LeftChild!=NULL)
    LeftChild->Traverse();
  if(!KeepMatrix)
    glPopMatrix();
  if(RightSibling!=NULL)
    RightSibling->Traverse();
}
```

Note that the use of the left-sibling, right-child structure implies that children and siblings will be encountered in a predetermined order as the tree is traversed.

What gets drawn on the display depends on each node's render method. These methods will be different for each type of node (geometry, light, material), but all will invoke OpenGL code. Let us look at a few examples. First, returning to the geometry node, we look at all its protected members and see that there are members to store the parameters that can be set by the public methods.

```
class Geometry: public Node
{
 public:
  //public members

 protected:
  Color *ColorNode;
  Material *MatNode;
  Transformation *TransNode;
  DrawStyle *StyleNode;
};
```

Many of the methods for a geometry node are common for all geometry nodes and are similar over the basic parameters. We can can create a geometry node through the constructor

```
Geometry::Geometry()
{
  ColorNode=NULL;
  MatNode=NULL;
  TransNode=NULL;
  StyleNode=NULL;
}
```

and delete through the destructor

```
Geometry::~Geometry()
{
  if(ColorNode)
    {
      delete ColorNode;
      ColorNode=NULL;
    }
// same for other types
```

All the methods for setting parameters are fairly similar. For example, for colors we have

```
void Geometry::SetColor(Enum C)
{
  if(ColorNode==NULL)
    ColorNode=new Color;

  ColorNode->SetValue(C);
}

void Geometry::SetColor(float v1, float v2, float v3)
{
  if(ColorNode==NULL)
    ColorNode=new Color;

  ColorNode->SetValue(v1, v2, v3);
}
```

However, to render each geometry node, we need to have a render method for the particular type. For example, for the polygon, we have the methods and members

```
class Polygon: public Geometry
{
 public:
  Polygon();
  void SetVerticesv(float v[][3], int);
  void Render();
```

```
private:
  float Vertices[1000][3];
  int Size;
};
```

and the simple implementation

```
void Polygon::SetVerticesv(float v[][3], int S)
{
  int i, j;
  Size=S;

  for(i=0; i<S; i++)
    for(j=0; j<3; j++)
      Vertices[i][j]=v[i][j];
}

void Polygon::Render()
{
  int i;

  glPushAttrib(GL_ALL_ATTRIB_BITS);

  if(ColorNode)
    ColorNode->Render();
  if(MatNode)
    MatNode->Render();
  if(TransNode)
    TransNode->Render();
  if(StyleNode)
    StyleNode->Render();

  glBegin(GL_POLYGON);
  for(i=0; i<Size; i++)
    glVertex3fv(Vertices[i]);
  glEnd();

  glPopAttrib();

}
```

Note the pushing and popping of attributes to isolate state changes made during the rendering of the internal nodes. The internal nodes use the rendering methods from their own classes. For example, color nodes have two private members:

```
class Color: public Node
{
 public:
  Color();
  void SetValuev(float *v);
  void SetValue(float v1, float v2, float v3);
  void SetValue(Enum Type);
  void Render();

 private:
  bool Changed;
  float Color3f[3];
};
```

The `Changed` flag is set whenever a color is set. Thus, the render method is simply

```
void Color::Render()
{
  if(Changed) glColor3fv(Color3f);
}
```

Although there is a fair amount of code required to implement all the nodes that we have described, the implementation is straightforward.

10.10 Other Tree Structures

Tree and DAG structures provide powerful tools to describe scenes; trees are used in a variety of other ways in computer graphics, of which we consider three. The first is the use of expression trees to describe an object hierarchy for solid objects; the other two describe spatial hierarchies that we can use to increase the efficiency of many rendering algorithms.

10.10.1 CSG Trees

The polygonal representation of objects that we have used has many strengths and a few weaknesses. The most serious weakness is that polygons describe only the surfaces that enclose the interior of a three-dimensional object, such as a polyhedron. In CAD applications, this limitation causes difficulties whenever we must employ any volumetric properties of the graphical object, such as its weight or its moment of inertia. In addition, because we display an object by drawing its edges or surfaces, there can be ambiguities in the display. For example, the wire frame in Figure 10.20 can be interpreted either as a cube with a hole through it created by removal of a cylinder or as a solid cube composed of two different materials.

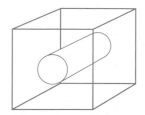

FIGURE 10.20 Wire frame that has two possible interpretations.

Constructive solid geometry (CSG) addresses these difficulties. Assume that we start with a set of atomic solid geometric entities, such as parallelepipeds, cylinders, and spheres. The attributes of these objects can include surface properties, such as color or reflectivity, but also volumetric properties, such as size and density. In describing scenes of such objects, we consider those points in space that constitute each object. Equivalently, each object is a set of points, and we can use set algebra to form new objects from these solid primitives.

CSG modeling uses three set operations: union, intersection, and set difference. The **union** of two sets A and B, written $A \cup B$, consists of all points that are either in A or in B. The **intersection** of A and B, $A \cap B$, is the set of all points that are in both A and B. The **set difference**, $A - B$, is the set of points that are in A and are not in B. Figure 10.21 shows two objects and possible objects created by the three set operations.

Objects are described by algebraic expressions. The expression $(A - B) \cap (C \cup D)$ might describe an object such as that in Figure 10.22.

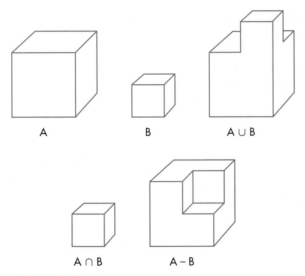

FIGURE 10.21   Set operations.

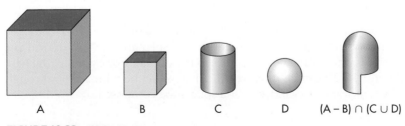

FIGURE 10.22   CSG object.

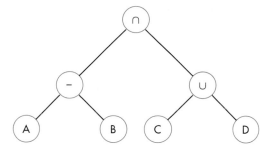

FIGURE 10.23   CSG tree.

Typically, we store and parse algebraic expressions using expression trees, where internal nodes store operations and terminal nodes store operands. For example, the tree in Figure 10.23 is a CSG tree that represents the object $(A - B) \cap (C \cup D)$ in Figure 10.22. We can evaluate or render the CSG tree by a **postorder** traversal; that is, we recursively evaluate the tree to the left of a node and the tree on the right of the node, and finally use these values to evaluate the node itself. Rendering of objects in CSG often is done with a variant of ray tracing; see Exercise 10.10 and Chapter 12.

10.10.2   BSP Trees

Scene graphs and CSG trees describe hierarchical relationships among the parts of an object. We can also use trees to describe the world object space and encapsulate the spatial relationships among groups of objects. These relationships can lead to fast methods of **visibility testing** to determine which objects might be seen by a camera, thus avoiding processing all objects with tests such as the z-buffer algorithm. These techniques have become very important in real-time animations for computer games.

One approach to spatial hierarchy starts with the observation that a plane divides or partitions three-dimensional space into two parts (half spaces). Successive planes subdivide space into increasingly smaller partitions. In two dimensions, we can use lines to partition space.

Consider the polygons in Figure 10.24, with the viewer located as indicated. Arguing as we did in Chapter 7, there is an order in which to paint these polygons so that the image will be correct. Rather than using a method such as depth sort each time we want to render these polygons, we can store the relative-positioning information in a tree. We start the construction of the tree using the plane of one polygon to separate groups of polygons that are in front of it from those that are behind it. For example, consider a simple world in which all the polygons are parallel and are oriented with their normals parallel to the z-axis. This assumption makes it easier to illustrate the algorithm but does not affect the algorithm as long as the plane of any polygon separates the other polygons into two groups. In this world, the view from the z-direction is as shown in Figure 10.25.

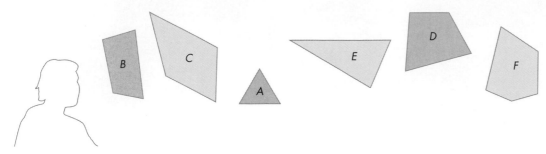

FIGURE 10.24   Collection of polygons and a viewer.

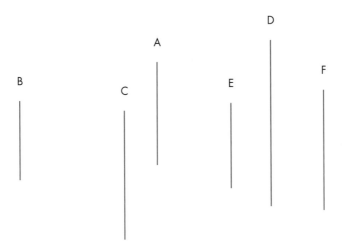

FIGURE 10.25   Top view of polygons.

Plane A separates the polygons into two groups, one containing B and C, which are in front of A, and the second containing D, E, and F, which are behind A. We use this plane to start a **binary spatial-partition tree** (**BSP tree**) that stores the separating planes and the order in which they are applied. Thus, in the BSP tree in Figure 10.26, A is at the root, B and C are in the left subtree, and D, E, and F are in the right subtree. Proceeding recursively, C is behind the plane of B, so we can complete the left subtree. The plane of D separates E and F, thus completing the right subtree. Note that for a given set of polygons, there are multiple possible BSP trees corresponding to the order in which we choose to make our partitions. In the general case, if a separating plane intersects a polygon, then we can break up the polygon into two polygons, one in front of the plane and one behind it, similar to what we did with overlapping polygons in the depth sort algorithm in Chapter 7.

We can use this tree to paint the polygons by doing a **backward in-order traversal**. That is, we traverse the tree recursively, drawing the right subtree

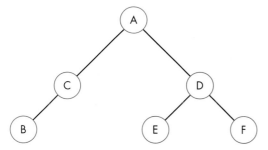

FIGURE 10.26   Binary spatial-partition (BSP) tree.

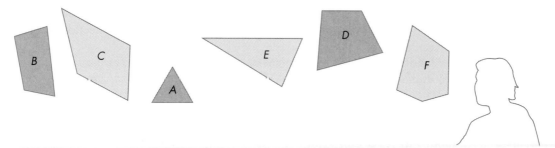

FIGURE 10.27   Movement of the viewer to back.

first, followed by the root, and finally by the left subtree. One of the advantages of BSP trees is that we can use the same tree even if the viewer moves by changing the traversal algorithm. If the viewer moves to the back, as in Figure 10.27, then we can paint the polygons using a standard in-order traversal—left subtree, root, right subtree. Also note that we can use the algorithm recursively wherever planes separate sets of polygons or other objects into groups, called **clusters**. Thus, we might group polygons into polyhedral objects, then group these polyhedra into clusters. We can then apply the algorithm within each cluster. In applications such as flight simulators, where the world model does not change but the viewer's position does, the use of BSP trees can be efficient for doing visible surface determination during rendering. The tree contains all the required information to paint the polygons; the viewer's position determines the traversal algorithm.

10.10.3 Quadtrees and Octrees

One limitation of BSP trees is that the planes that separate polygons can have an arbitrary orientation so that construction of the tree can be costly, involving ordering and often splitting of polygons. Octrees and quadtrees avoid this problem by using separating planes and lines parallel to the coordinate axes.

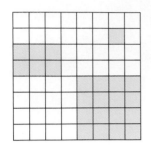

FIGURE 10.28 Two-dimensional space of pixels.

Consider the two-dimensional picture in Figure 10.28. We assume that this picture is composed of black and white pixels, perhaps formed by the rendering of a three-dimensional scene. If we wish to store the scene, we can save it as a binary array. But notice the great deal of coherence in the picture. Pixels of each color are clustered together. We can draw two lines as in Figure 10.29, dividing the region into quadrants. Noting that one quadrant is all white, we can assign a single color to it. For the other three, we can subdivide again and continue subdividing any quadrant that contains pixels of more than a single color. This information can be stored in a tree called a **quadtree**, in which each level corresponds to a subdivision and each node has four children. Thus, the quadtree for our original simple picture is as shown in Figure 10.30.

Because we construct the quadtree by subdividing space with lines parallel to the coordinate axes, formation and traversal of the tree are simpler than are the corresponding operations for a BSP tree. One of the most important advantages of quadtrees is that they can reduce the amount of memory needed to store images.

Quadtrees partition two-dimensional space. They can also be used to partition object space in a manner similar to BSP trees and thus can be traversed in an order depending on the position of the viewer so as to render correctly the objects in each region. In three dimensions, quadtrees extend to **octrees**. The partitioning is done by planes parallel to the coordinate axes, and each step of the partitioning subdivides space into eight octants, as shown in Figure 10.31.

Octrees are used for representing volume data sets that consist of volume elements called **voxels**, as shown in Figure 10.32. The arguments that have made for quadtrees and octrees can also be applied to the spatial partitioning of objects, rather than pixels or voxels. For example, we can use recursive subdivision of two- or three-dimensional space for clipping. After each subdivison, we compare the bounding box of each object with each subdivided rectangle or cube to determine if the object lies in that region of the subdivided space.

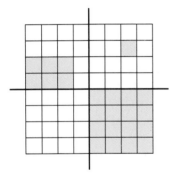

FIGURE 10.29 First subdivision of space.

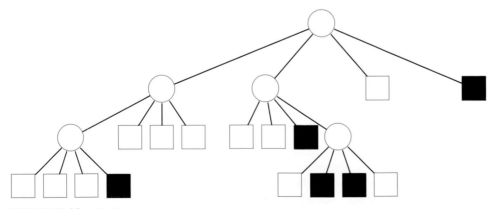

FIGURE 10.30 Quadtree.

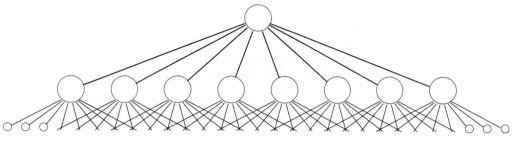

FIGURE 10.31 Octree.

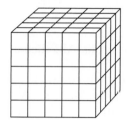

FIGURE 10.32 Volume data set.

10.11 Graphics and the Internet

The Internet has had an enormous effect on virtually all communications and computer applications. It allows us to communicate information in a multitude of forms and makes possible new methods of interaction. In order to use the Internet to its full potential, we need to move graphical information efficiently, to build applications that are viewable from many locations, and to access resources distributed over many sites. OpenGL and its extensions have had a major influence on the development of net-based, three-dimensional applications and standards. We shall take a graphics-oriented approach and see what extensions we need to develop Internet applications. Some of the concepts will be familiar. We use the client–server model to allow efficient rendering. We also look at how we can implement graphical applications that are independent of the API.

10.11.1 Networks and Protocols

When we discussed networks in the context of client–server graphics in Chapter 3, we were able to ignore the details of how the information was conveyed over the network. Most architectural models of networks are based on a multilevel model such as the one shown in Figure 10.33. The model shown is a simplified version of the standard International Standards Organization (ISO) model. At the lowest level are the physical media that convey the bits. Elements at this level include cables between computers, telephone lines, fiber-optic cables, and any

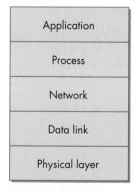

FIGURE 10.33 Protocol layers.

other hardware that can convey binary information between entities on the network. At the next level is a hierarchy of protocols for conveying bits between two entities in a reliable manner. Usually, what we find here is an addressing scheme that allows the information to be sent to and received at the correct location and an error-detection and error-correction method.

At the next level are protocols for sending information between a process on one computer and a process on another. Whereas the lower-level protocols are concerned with point-to-point communication, at the higher levels we are concerned with process-to-process communication, in which packets of information may travel through many entities before arriving at their destination. For the millions of computers that form the Internet, the key protocols are the Transmission Control Protocol and Internet Protocol (TCP/IP), both of which are used at this level. One definition of the Internet is that it is the loosely coupled network of computers that use the Internet Protocol. At the highest level, we have applications that communicate over the network. When we use an API such as OpenGL, we are working at this level.

Consider an application that uses the display lists that we discussed in Chapter 3. On one computer there will be a user (client) program that is using a remote graphics server to render graphical entities defined in the application but placed in display lists. At the lowest level, the computers might be connected by means of an Ethernet and use standard Ethernet protocols to communicate. At the middle levels, the two computers can communicate using the TCP/IP protocols. At the next level up, they can exchange graphical information using the X protocols with the OpenGL extensions. From the application program's perspective, we simply use display lists in our program. The levels of communication are illustrated in Figure 10.34.

Stacking protocols gives high-level applications a way to communicate over various standard networks. If we were to have all users write graphical applications in OpenGL, we could do a fair amount of graphics over the Web using client–server methods such as display lists. Not all users use the same API, however, and not all machines that support a given API have the same architecture. There are additional possibilities available. Let us leave aside graphics temporarily and consider a network from a difference perspective—that of gathering information from a variety of resources.

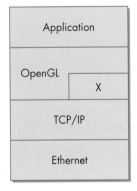

FIGURE 10.34 Protocols in OpenGL.

10.11.2 Hypermedia and HTML

As the Internet evolved, a series of standard high-level protocols became widely accepted for transferring mail, files, and other types of information. Systems such as the X Window system allowed users to open windows on remote systems and to transfer basic graphical information. As the Internet grew, however, more and more information became publicly available, and users needed more sophisticated methods to share information that was stored in a distributed way in diverse formats. There are three key elements necessary for sharing such information: (1) an addressing scheme that allows users to identify resources over the network, (2) a method of encoding information in addition to simple text such as pictures and references (or **links**) to other resources, and (3) a method of searching for resources interactively.

The first two needs were addressed by researchers at the European Particle Physics Center (CERN) who created the World Wide Web, which is essentially a networked hypertext system. Resources—files—are identified by a unique **Uniform Resource Locator** (**URL**) that consists of three parts: the protocol for transferring the document, the server where the document is located, and the location on the server where the document is to be found. For example, the URL for the programs in this text is *ftp://ftp.cs.unm.edu/pub/angel/BOOK*. The first part (*ftp*) indicates that the information will be transferred using the standard file-transfer protocol *ftp*; the second part (*ftp.cs.unm.edu*) identifies the server; and the final part indicates that the information is stored in the directory *pub/angel/BOOK*. The URL for the OpenGL Organization is *http://www.opengl.org*. This URL indicates that this document should be transferred with the hypertext transfer protocol (*http*) and is located at *www.opengl.org*. Because no document is indicated, a default document—the home page—will be returned.

The second contribution of CERN was the **Hypertext Markup Language** (**HTML**), which provided a simple way to describe a document consisting of text, references to other documents (links), and images. HTML documents are text documents, typically in ASCII code or one of the standard extended character sets.

The combination of URL addressing and HTML documents provided a way of making resources available. But until the National Center for SuperComputer Applications (NCSA) came up with its browser, Mosaic, it was not easy for a user to find resources and to search the Web. **Browsers** are interactive programs that allow the user to search for and download documents on the Web. Mosaic and later Netscape Navigator opened the door to "surfing" the Web.

10.11.3 Databases and VRML

HTML provides only limited resources for supporting interactive three-dimensional graphics over the Web. The main problem is that HTML recognizes images—arrays of pixels—in only two common formats (GIF and JPEG). HTML lacks any concept of a geometric object, even in two dimensions. This limitation was recognized by the user community, and various proposals for a new language were considered, resulting in the Virtual Reality Modeling Language, or VRML.

There are many ways to convey graphics over a network. We can simply send images as HTML does, but there are obvious limitations to this approach. A second method is to send source code in a common language such as OpenGL. There are clear advantages to this strategy, and they provide arguments in favor of graphics standards. However, using source code would force users to compile programs on the client end of the network—for example, in the browser. A third approach is to use the client–server model, as in OpenGL. However, we have to agree on a single API and on a common format to transmit display lists. Java uses this philosophy.

There is a fourth approach that gives us considerably more flexibility in how graphics are created, stored, and transmitted. We can create a database that describes a scene, including the geometric objects, lights, materials, and other properties. This database can be stored in a standard text format and then conveyed over a network easily. The receiver of the database can then render the scene with whatever hardware and software are available locally. VRML employs this approach.

The design of the database involves many of the same concerns that we discussed in Chapter 2 in relation to what functionality is supported by an API. Because many questions, such as which primitives to support, are the same, it made sense to choose database elements related to a commonly accepted API that was supported on a variety of architectures. OpenGL was an obvious candidate, but it lacked the object orientation necessary to describe complex scenes whose components could be distributed over the Web. VRML chose to start with the Open Inventor database. As we noted in Section 10.8, Open Inventor is built on top of OpenGL and adds, among other functions, scene graphs. Open Inventor allows the user to store scenes as text files. Once we add links to the database, we have most of what we need to describe three-dimensional scenes whose constituent parts can be located over a network.

VRML is tightly coupled to OpenGL. VRML gives us a way to describe distributed three-dimensional worlds, and a VRML browser can obtain the scene from the Web. The browser must also be able to render the scene for the viewer. Consequently, there is an intimate tie between OpenGL and VRML. Although, in principle, the browser could use a rendering engine based on any of our models—pipeline, ray tracing, or radiosity—the fact that the underlying database is based on Open Inventor biases the choice toward an OpenGL-based VRML browser.

10.11.4 Java and Applets

Interaction over the Web can be problematic when we use the models and tools that we have discussed. VRML databases are in text format and thus require that the client render whatever is in the database. Thus, a user cannot develop code on one end and know that the same code will be executed on the other, because the two machines may be entirely different.

Java solves a portion of this problem by creating a machine in software that can be implemented on any computer. Java programs are compiled into **byte code** that can be run on any Java machine, regardless of what the underlying hardware is. Thus, the client and server exchange byte code over the Web. Small programs in byte code, called **applets**, are understood by the standard Web browsers and have added a tremendous amount of dynamic behavior to the Web.

Java initially included only two-dimensional graphics. There is an extension, Java3D, that allows the creation and rendering of scene graphs, although it remains to be seen if it will realize its potential. Within the next few years, we hope to see a convergence of the various approaches. What we hope will emerge is a universal way of conveying graphics over the Web—one that can make use of the interactive and rendering capabilities of OpenGL and the object orientation of scene graphs.

10.12 Procedural Methods

We now turn to an entirely different approach to modeling. Thus far, we have assumed that the geometric objects that we wish to create can be described by their surfaces, and that these surfaces can be modeled (or approximated) by convex planar polygons. Our use of polygonal objects was dictated by the ease with which we could describe these objects and our ability to render them on existing systems. The success of computer graphics attests to the importance of such models.

Nevertheless, even as these models were being used in large CAD applications and for flight simulators, both users and developers recognized the limitations of these techniques. Physical objects such as clouds (see Color Plate 28), smoke, and water did not fit this style of modeling. Adding physical constraints and modeling complex behaviors of objects were not part of polygonal modeling. In response to such problems, researchers have developed procedural models that use algorithmic models to build representations of the underlying phenomena, generating polygons only as needed during the rendering process.

When we review the history of computer graphics, we see that the desire to create increasingly more realistic graphics has always outstripped advances in hardware. Although we can render more than 50 million polygons per second on existing hardware (including on personal computers), applications such as flight simulation, virtual reality, and computer games can demand rendering speeds greater than 500 million polygons per second. Furthermore, as rendering speeds have increased, database sizes also have increased dramatically. A single data set may contain more than 1 billion polygons.

Often, however, applications have such needs because they use existing software and modeling paradigms. Astute researchers and application programmers have suggested that we would not require as many polygons if we could render a model generating only those polygons that both are visible and project to an area at least the size of one pixel. We have seen examples of this idea in previous chapters, for example, when we considered culling polygons before they reached the rendering pipeline. Nevertheless, a more productive approach has been to reexamine the way in which we do our modeling and seek techniques, known as **procedural methods**, that generate geometrical objects in a different manner from what we have seen thus far. Procedural methods span a wide range of techniques. What they have in common is that they describe objects in an algorithmic manner and produce polygons only when needed as part of the rendering process.

In many ways, procedural models can be understood by an analogy with methods that we use to represent irrational numbers—such as square roots, sines, and cosines—in a computer. Consider, for example, three ways of representing $\sqrt{2}$. We can say that numerically

$$\sqrt{2} = 1.414\ldots,$$

filling in as many digits as we like; or, more abstractly, we can define the $\sqrt{2}$ as the positive number x such that

$$x^2 = 2.$$

However, within the computer, $\sqrt{2}$ might be the result of executing an algorithm. For example, consider Newton's method. Starting with an initial approximation $x_0 = 1$, we compute the recurrence

$$x_{k+1} = \frac{x_k}{2} + \frac{1}{x_k}.$$

Each successive value of x_k is a better approximation to the $\sqrt{2}$. From this perspective, $\sqrt{2}$ is defined by an algorithm; equivalently, it is defined through a program. For objects we deal with in computer graphics, we can take a similar approach. For example, a sphere centered at the origin can be defined as the mathematical object that satisfies the equation

$$x^2 + y^2 + z^2 = r^2.$$

It also is the result of the tetrahedron subdivision process that we developed in Chapter 6 and of our program for doing that subdivision. A potential benefit of the second view is that when we render spheres, we can render small spheres (in screen space) with fewer triangles than we would need for large spheres.

A second type of problem with polygonal modeling has been the difficulty of combining computer graphics with physical laws. Although we can build and animate polygonal models of real-world objects, it is far more difficult to make these graphical objects act as solids and not penetrate one another.

We introduce two of many possible approaches to procedural modeling. In the first, we work with particles that obey Newton's laws. We then design systems of particles that are capable of complex behaviors that arise from solving sets of differential equations—a routine numerical task for up to thousands of particles. The positions of the particles yield the locations at which to place our standard geometric objects in a world model.

The second approach—algorithmic models—enables us to control complexity by replacing polygonal models with language-based models, similar to those used for both natural and computer languages. With these models we can approximate many natural objects with a few rules that generate the required graphical entities.

Combined with fractal geometry, these models allow us to generate images using only the number of polygons required for display.

10.13   Physically Based Models and Particle Systems

One of the great strengths—and weaknesses—of modeling in computer graphics is that we can build models based on any principles we choose. The graphical objects that we create may have little connection with physical reality. Historically, the attitude was that if something looked right, that was sufficient for most purposes. Not being constrained by physical models, which were often either not known or too complex to simulate in real time, allows the creation of the special effects that we see in computer games and movies. In fields such as scientific visualization, this flexibility allows mathematicians to "see" shapes that do not exist in the usual three-dimensional space and to display information in new ways. Researchers and engineers can construct prototypes of objects that are not limited by our ability to construct them with present materials and equipment.

However, when we wish to simulate objects in the real world and to see the results of this simulation on our display, we can get into trouble. Often, it is easy to make a model for a group of objects moving through space, but it is far more difficult to keep track of when two objects collide and to have the graphics system react in a physically correct manner. Indeed, it is far easier in computer graphics to let a ball go directly through a wall than to model the ball bouncing off the surface, incorporating the correct elastic rebound.

Recently, researchers have become interested in **physically based modeling**, a style of modeling in which the graphical objects obey physical laws. Such modeling can follow either of two related paths. In one, we model the physics of the underlying process and use the physics to drive the graphics. For example, if we want a solid object to appear to tumble in space and to bounce from various surfaces, we can, at least in principle, use our knowledge of dynamics and continuum mechanics to derive the required equations. This approach is beyond the scope of a first course in computer graphics, and we shall not pursue it. The other approach is to use a combination of basic physics and mathematical constraints to control the dynamic behavior of our objects. We follow this approach for a group of particles.

Particle systems are collections of particles, typically point masses, in which the dynamic behavior of the particles can be determined by the solution of sets of coupled differential equations. Particle systems have been used to generate a wide variety of behaviors in a number of fields. In fluid dynamics, people use particle systems to model turbulent behavior. Rather than solving partial differential equations, we can simulate the behavior of the system by following a group of particles that is subject to a variety of forces and constraints. We can also use particles to model solid objects. For example, a deformable solid can be modeled as a three-dimensional array of particles that are held together by springs. When the object is subjected to external forces, the particles move and their positions approximate the shape of the solid object.

In computer graphics, people have used particles to model such diverse phenomena as fireworks, the flocking behavior of birds, and wave action. In these applications, the dynamics of the particle system gives the positions of the particles, but at each location we can place a graphical object, rather than a point.

In all these cases, we work with a group of particles, each member of which we can regard as a point mass. We use physical laws to write equations that we can solve numerically to obtain the state of these particles at each time step. As a final step, we can render each particle as a graphical object—perhaps as a colored point for a fireworks application or a cartoon character in an animation.

10.14   Newtonian Particles

We consider a set of particles that is subject to Newton's laws. Although there is no reason that we could not use other physical laws or construct a set of our own (virtual) physical laws, the advantage of starting with Newtonian particles is that we can obtain a wide range of behaviors using simple, well-understood physics. A Newtonian particle must obey Newton's second law, which states that the mass of the particle (m) times that particle's acceleration ($\mathbf{a}$) is equal to the sum of the forces ($\mathbf{f}$) acting on the particle, or symbolically,

$$m\mathbf{a} = \mathbf{f}.$$

Note that both the acceleration and force are vectors, usually in three dimensions. One consequence of Newton's laws is that for an ideal point-mass particle—one whose total mass is concentrated at a single point—its state is completely determined by its position and velocity. Thus, in three-dimensional space, an ideal particle has 6 degrees of freedom, and a system of n particles has $6n$ state variables—the positions and velocities of all the particles. Within some reference frame, the state of the ith particle is given by two three-element column matrices,[5] a position matrix

$$\mathbf{p}_i = \begin{bmatrix} x_i \\ y_i \\ z_i \end{bmatrix},$$

and a velocity matrix

$$\mathbf{v}_i = \begin{bmatrix} \dot{x}_i \\ \dot{y}_i \\ \dot{z}_i \end{bmatrix} = \begin{bmatrix} \frac{dx}{dt} \\ \frac{dy}{dt} \\ \frac{dz}{dt} \end{bmatrix}.$$

5. We have chosen to use three-dimensional arrays here, rather than homogeneous coordinate representations, both to be consistent with the way these equations are usually written in the physics literature and to simplify the resulting differential equations.

Knowing that acceleration is the derivative of velocity and that velocity is the derivative of position, we can write Newton's second law for a particle as the six coupled, first-order differential equations

$$\dot{\mathbf{p}}_i = \mathbf{v}_i,$$

$$\dot{\mathbf{v}}_i = \frac{1}{m_i}\mathbf{f}_i(t).$$

Hence, the dynamics of a system of n particles is governed by a set of $6n$ coupled, ordinary differential equations.

In addition to its state, each particle may have a number of attributes, including its mass (m_i), and a set of properties that can alter what its behavior is and how it is displayed. For example, some attributes govern how we render the particle and determine its color, shape, and surface properties. Note that although the dynamics of a simple particle system is based on each particle being treated as a point mass, the user can specify how each particle should be rendered. For example, each particle may represent a person in a crowd scene, or a molecule in a chemical-synthesis application, or a piece of cloth in the simulation of a flag blowing in the wind. In each case, the underlying particle system governs the location and the velocity of the center of mass of the particle. Once we have the location of a particle, we can place the desired object at this location.

The set of forces on the particles, $\{\mathbf{f}_i\}$, determines the behavior of the system. These forces are based on the state of the particle system and can change with time. We can base these forces on simple physical principles, such as spring forces, or on physical constraints that we wish to impose on the system; or we can base them on external forces, such as gravity, that we wish to apply to the system. By designing the forces carefully, we can obtain the desired system behavior.

The dynamic state of the system is obtained by numerical methods that involve stepping through approximations to the set of differential equations. A typical time step is based on computing the forces that apply to the n particles through a user-defined function, using these forces to update the state through a numerical differential-equation solver, and finally using the new positions of the particles and their attributes to render whatever graphical objects we wish to place at the particles' locations. Thus, in pseudocode, we have a loop of the form

```
float time, delta; float state[6n], force[3n];
state=get_initial_state();
for(time=t0; time<time_final; time+=delta)
 {
 /* compute forces */
    force=force_function(state, time);

 /* apply standard differential equation solver */
    state=ode(force, state, time, delta);

 /* display result */
    render(state, time);
}
```

The main component that we must design in a given application is the function that computes the forces on each particle.

10.14.1 Independent Particles

There are numerous simple ways that particles can interact and determine the forces that act on each particle. If the forces that act on a given particle are independent of other particles, the force on the ith particle can be described by the equation

$$\mathbf{f}_i = \mathbf{f}_i(\mathbf{p}_i, \mathbf{v}_i).$$

A simple case occurs where each particle is subject only to a constant gravitational force

$$\mathbf{f}_i = \mathbf{g}.$$

If this force points down, then

$$\mathbf{g} = \begin{bmatrix} 0 \\ -g \\ 0 \end{bmatrix},$$

where g is positive, and each particle will trace out a parabolic arc. If we add a term proportional to the velocity, we can have the particle subject to frictional forces, such as drag. If some of the attributes, such as color, change with time and if we give each particle a (random) lifetime, then we can simulate phenomena such as fireworks. More generally, external forces are applied independently to each point. If we allow the particles to drift randomly and render each as a large object, rather than as a point, we can model clouds or flows with independent particles.

Color Plate 13 shows the use of independent particles to model the sparks generated by welding. Each particle is independent of the others, is subject to gravity, and has a random lifetime.

10.14.2 Spring Forces

If in a system of n particles, all particles are independent, then the force calculation is $O(n)$. In the most general case, the computation of the forces on a given particle may involve contributions due to pairwise interactions with all the other particles, an $O(n^2)$ computation. For large particle systems, an $O(n^2)$ can slow the computation significantly. Often, we can reduce this complexity by having a particle interact with only those particles that are close to it.

Consider the example of using particles to create a surface whose shape varies over time, such as a curtain or a flag blowing in the wind. We can use the location of each particle as a vertex for a rectangular mesh, as shown in Figure 10.35. The shape of the mesh changes over time, as a result both of external forces that act on each particle, such as gravity or wind, and of forces between particles that

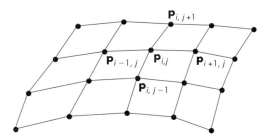

FIGURE 10.35 Mesh of particles.

give the mesh the appearance of being a solid surface. We can approximate this second type of force by considering the forces between a particle and the latter's closest neighbors. Thus, if $\mathbf{p}_{ij}$ is the location of the particle at row i, column j of the mesh, the force calculation for $\mathbf{p}_{ij}$ needs to consider only the forces between $\mathbf{p}_{i,j}$ and $\mathbf{p}_{i+1,j}$, $\mathbf{p}_{i-1,j}$, $\mathbf{p}_{i,j+1}$, and $\mathbf{p}_{i,j-1}$—an $O(n)$ calculation.

One method to model the forces among particles is to consider adjacent particles as connected by a spring. Consider two adjacent particles, located at $\mathbf{p}$ and $\mathbf{q}$, connected by a spring, as shown in Figure 10.36. Let $\mathbf{f}$ denote the force acting on $\mathbf{p}$ from $\mathbf{q}$. A force $-\mathbf{f}$ acts on $\mathbf{q}$ from $\mathbf{p}$. The spring has a resting length s, which is the distance between particles if the system is not subject to external forces and is allowed to come to rest. When the spring is stretched, the force acts in the direction $\mathbf{d} = \mathbf{p} - \mathbf{q}$; that is, it acts along the line between the points. This force obeys **Hooke's law**:

FIGURE 10.36 Particles connected by a spring.

$$\mathbf{f} = -k_s(|\mathbf{d}| - s)\frac{\mathbf{d}}{|\mathbf{d}|},$$

where k_s is the spring constant and s is the length of the spring when it is at rest. This law shows that the farther apart the two particles are stretched, the stronger is the force attracting them back to the resting position. Conversely, when the ends of the spring are pushed together, the force pulls them back such that their positions move to a separation by the resting length. As we have stated Hooke's law, however, there is no damping (or friction) in the system. A system of masses and springs defined in such a manner will oscillate forever when perturbed. We can include a **drag**, or **damping term**, in Hooke's law. The damping force operates in the same direction as the spring force, but depends on the velocity between the particles. The fraction of the velocity that contributes to damping is proportional to the projection of the velocity vector onto the vector defined by the two points as shown in Figure 10.37. Mathematically, Hooke's law with the damping term is given by

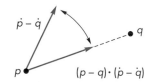

FIGURE 10.37 Computation of the spring damping force.

$$\mathbf{f} = -\left(k_s(|\mathbf{d}| - s) + k_d\frac{\dot{\mathbf{d}} \cdot \mathbf{d}}{|\mathbf{d}|}\right)\frac{\mathbf{d}}{|\mathbf{d}|}.$$

Here, k_d is the damping constant, and

$$\dot{\mathbf{d}} = \dot{\mathbf{p}} - \dot{\mathbf{q}}.$$

A system of masses and springs with damping that is not subjected to external forces will eventually come to rest.

The four images in Color Plate 31 show a mesh that is generated from the locations of a set of particles. Each interior particle is connected to its four neighbors by springs. The particles are also subject to external forces—the wind. At each time step, once the positions of the particles are determined, we can render the mesh using techniques such as texture mapping (Section 7.5) to create the detailed appearance of the surface.

10.14.3   Attractive and Repulsive Forces

Whereas spring forces are used to keep a group of particles together, repulsive forces push particles away from one another and attractive forces pull particles toward one another. We could use repulsive forces to distribute particles over a surface, or if the particles represent locations of objects, to keep objects from hitting one another. We could use attractive forces to build a model of the solar system or to create applications that model satellites revolving about the earth. The equations for attraction and repulsion are essentially the same except for a sign.

For a pair of particles, located at $\mathbf{p}$ and $\mathbf{q}$, the repulsive force acts in the direction $\mathbf{d} = \mathbf{p} - \mathbf{q}$ and is inversely proportional to the particles' distance from each other. For example, we could use the expression

$$\mathbf{f} = -k_r \frac{\mathbf{d}}{|\mathbf{d}|^3}$$

for an inverse-square-law term. Changing the minus sign to a positive sign and replacing k_r by $(m_a m_b)/g$ gives us the attractive force between two particles of mass m_a and m_b, where g is the gravitational constant.

In the general case, where each particle is subject to forces from all other particles, the computation of attractive and repulsive forces is $O(n^2)$. Unlike meshes of particles connected by springs, where we attempt to keep the particles in the same topological arrangement, particles subject to attractive and repulsive forces usually change their positions among themselves. Hence, strategies to avoid the $O(n^2)$ force calculation are more complex. One approach is to divide space into three-dimensional cells, each of which can contain multiple particles or even no particles, as shown in Figure 10.38.

For forces that are inversely proportional to distance, we can choose a cell size such that the forces on a particle from particles in other than its own or adjacent cells are negligible. If this partitioning is possible, then the $O(n^2)$ calculation is reduced to $O(n)$. However, there is a cost to partitioning, and particles can

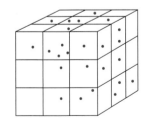

FIGURE 10.38 Division of space into cells.

move from one cell to another. The difficulty of the first problem depends on the particular application, because we can often obtain an initial particle distribution with little effort, but at other times we might have to do a sort. We can solve the second problem by looking at the particle positions after each time step and redistributing the particles or, perhaps, changing the cells. We can use various data structures to store the particles and cell information.

One other approach that is often used is to replace interactions among particles by interactions between particles and a force field. For example, when we compute the gravitational force on a point mass on the surface of the earth, we use the value of the gravitational field rather than the point-to-point force between the point mass of the particle and a second large point mass at the center of the earth. If we were concerned with only the mass of the earth and our point on the surface, the two approaches would require about the same amount of work. However, if we were to also include the force from the moon, the situation would be more complex. If we used point masses, we would have two point-to-point forces to compute for our mass on the surface, but if we knew the gravitational field, the calculation would be the same as before. Of course, the calculation of the field is more complex when we consider the moon; for particle systems, however, we can often neglect distant particles, so the particle-field method may be more efficient. We can often compute the approximate field on a grid, then use the value at the nearest grid points to give the forces on each particle. After the new state of each particle has been computed, we can update the field. Both of these strategies can often reduce the $O(n^2)$ calculation of forces to $O(n \log n)$.

10.15 Solving Particle Systems

Consider a particle system of n particles. If we restrict ourselves to the simple forces that we just described, the entire particle system can be described by $6n$ ordinary differential equations of the form

$$\dot{\mathbf{u}} = \mathbf{g}(\mathbf{u}, t),$$

where $\mathbf{u}$ is an array of the $6n$ position and velocity components of our n particles, and $\mathbf{g}$ includes any external forces applied to the particles. Thus, if we have two particles $\mathbf{a}$ and $\mathbf{b}$ connected by a spring without damping, we might have

$$\mathbf{u}^T = [\, u_0 \quad u_1 \quad u_2 \quad u_3 \quad u_4 \quad u_5 \quad u_6 \quad u_7 \quad u_8 \quad u_9 \quad u_{10} \quad u_{11} \,]$$
$$= [\, a_x \quad a_y \quad a_z \quad \dot{a}_x \quad \dot{a}_y \quad \dot{a}_z \quad b_x \quad b_y \quad b_z \quad \dot{b}_x \quad \dot{b}_y \quad \dot{b}_z \,].$$

Given the external forces and the state of the particle system $\mathbf{u}$ at any time t, we can evaluate

$$\mathbf{g}^T = \left[\, u_3 \quad u_4 \quad u_5 \quad -kd_x \quad -kd_y \quad -kd_z \quad u_9 \quad u_{10} \quad u_{11} \quad kd_x \quad kd_y \quad kd_z \,\right].$$

Here k is the spring constant and d_x, d_y, and d_z are the components of the normalized vector d between $\mathbf{a}$ and $\mathbf{b}$. Thus, we must first compute

$$\mathbf{d} = \frac{1}{\sqrt{(u_0 - u_5)^2 + (u_1 - u_6)^2 + (u_2 - u_7)^2}} \begin{bmatrix} u_0 - u_6 \\ u_1 - u_7 \\ u_2 - u_8 \end{bmatrix}.$$

Numerical ordinary differential equation solvers rely on our ability to evaluate $\mathbf{g}$ to approximate $\mathbf{u}$ at future times. We can develop a family of differential equation solvers based upon Taylor's theorem. The simplest is known as Euler's method. Suppose that we integrate the expression

$$\dot{\mathbf{u}} = \mathbf{g}(\mathbf{u}, t)$$

over a short time h:

$$\int_t^{t+h} \dot{\mathbf{u}} d\tau = \mathbf{u}(t + h) - \mathbf{u}(t) = \int_t^{t+h} \mathbf{g}(\mathbf{u}, \tau) d\tau.$$

If h is small, we can approximate the value of $\mathbf{g}$ over the interval $[t, t + h]$ by the value of $\mathbf{g}$ at t; thus,

$$\mathbf{u}(t + h) \approx \mathbf{u}(t) + h\mathbf{g}(\mathbf{u}(t), t).$$

This expression shows that we can use the value of the derivative at t to get us to an approximate value of $\mathbf{u}(t + h)$, as shown in Figure 10.39.

This expression matches the first two terms of the Taylor expansion; we can write it as

$$\mathbf{u}(t + h) = \mathbf{u}(t) + h\dot{\mathbf{u}}(t) + O(h^2) = \mathbf{u}(t) + h\mathbf{g}(\mathbf{u}(t), t) + O(h^2),$$

showing that the error we incur in making the approximation is proportional to the square of the step size.

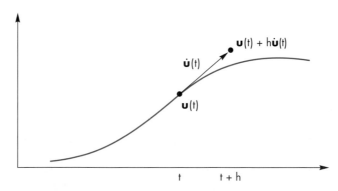

FIGURE 10.39   Approximation of the solution of a differential equation.

This method is particularly easy to implement. We evaluate the forces (both external and among particles) at time t, compute $\mathbf{g}$, multiply it by h, and add it to the present state. We can apply this method iteratively to compute further values at $t + 2h, t + 3h, \ldots$. The work involved is one calculation of the forces for each time step.

There are two potential problems with Euler's method: accuracy and stability. Both are affected by the step size. The accuracy of Euler's method is proportional to the square of the step size. Consequently, to increase the accuracy we must cut the step size, thus increasing the time it takes to solve the system. A potentially more serious problem concerns stability. As we go from step to step, the per-step errors that we make come from two sources: the approximation error that we made by using the Taylor series approximation and the numerical errors that we make in computing the functions. These errors can either cancel themselves out as we compute further states, or they can accumulate and give us unacceptably large errors that mask the true solution. Such behavior is called **numerical instability**. Fortunately, for the standard types of forces that we have used, if we make the step size small enough, we can guarantee stability. Unfortunately, the required step size for stability may be so small that we cannot solve the equations numerically in a reasonable amount of time. This unstable behavior is most pronounced for spring–mass systems, where the spring constant determines the stiffness of the system and leads to what are called **stiff** sets of differential equations.

There are two general approaches to this problem. One is to seek another type of ordinary differential equation solver, called a stiff equation solver—a topic that is beyond the scope of this book. Another is to find other differential equation solvers similar in philosophy to Euler's method but with a higher per-step accuracy. We derive one such method because it gives us insight into the family of such methods. References to both approaches are given at the end of the chapter.

Suppose that we start as before by integrating the differential equations over a short time interval to obtain

$$\mathbf{u}(t + h) = \mathbf{u}(t) + \int_t^{t+h} \mathbf{g}(\mathbf{u}, \tau) d\tau.$$

This time, we approximate the integral by an average value over the interval $[t, t + h]$:

$$\int_t^{t+h} \mathbf{g}(\mathbf{u}, \tau) d\tau \approx \frac{h}{2}(\mathbf{g}(\mathbf{u}(t), t) + \mathbf{g}(\mathbf{u}(t + h), t + h)).$$

The problem now is we do not have $\mathbf{g}(\mathbf{u}(t + h), t + h)$; we have only $\mathbf{g}(\mathbf{u}(t), t)$. We can use Euler's method to approximate $\mathbf{g}(\mathbf{u}(t + h), t + h)$; that is, we can use

$$\mathbf{g}(\mathbf{u}(t + h), t + h) \approx \mathbf{g}(\mathbf{u}(t) + h\mathbf{g}(\mathbf{u}(t), t), t + h).$$

This method is known as the **improved Euler method** or the **Runge–Kutta method of order 2**. Note that to go from t to $t + h$, we must evaluate **g** twice. However, if we were to use Taylor's theorem to evaluate the per-step error, we would find that it is now $O(h^3)$. Thus, even though we are doing more work per step, we can use larger step sizes, and the method is stable for step sizes larger than those for which Euler's method was stable. In general, we can use increasingly more accurate per-step formulas and derive a set of methods called the Runge–Kutta formulas. The most popular is the fourth-order method that has a per-step error of $O(h^4)$ and requires four function evaluations per step. In practice, we can do even better with this number of function evaluations, achieving errors of $O(h^5)$. More important, good solvers adjust their own step size so as to ensure stability.

10.16   Constraints

Simply allowing a group of particles to change state according to a set of differential equations often is insufficient to model real-world behavior such as collisions. Although the impact of an object hitting a wall is subject to Newton's laws, if we were to model the object as a collection of particles, the resulting system would be too complex for most purposes. Instead, we regard conditions such as the one in which two solid objects cannot penetrate each other as constraints that can be stated separately from the laws governing individual particle behavior.

There are two types of constraints that we can impose on particles. **Hard constraints** are those that must be adhered to exactly. For example, a ball must bounce off a wall; it cannot penetrate the wall and emerge from the other side. Nor can we allow the ball just to come close and then go off in another direction. **Soft constraints** are those that we need only come close to satisfying. For example, we might want two particles to be separated approximately by a specified distance, as in a particle mesh.

10.16.1   Collisions

Although, in general, hard constraints can be difficult to impose, there are a few situations that can be dealt with directly for ideal point particles. Consider the problem of collisions. We can separate the problem into two parts: detection and reaction. Suppose that we have a collection of particles and other geometric objects and the particles repel one another. We therefore need to consider only collisions between each particle and the other objects. If there are n particles and m polygons that define the geometric objects, at each time step we can check whether any particle has gone through any of the polygons.

Suppose that one of the particles has penetrated a polygon, as shown in Figure 10.40. We can detect this collision by inserting the position of the particle into the equation of the plane of the polygon. If the time step of our differential

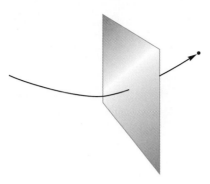

FIGURE 10.40   Particle penetrating a polygon.

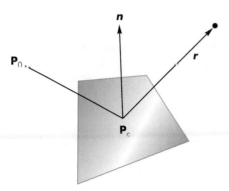

FIGURE 10.41   Particle reflection.

equation solver is small, we can assume that the velocity between time steps is constant, and we can use linear interpolation to find the time at which the particle actually hit the polygon.

What happens to the particle after a collision is similar to what happens when light reflects from a surface. If there is an **inelastic collision**, the particle loses none of its energy, so its speed is unchanged. However, its direction after the collision is in the direction of a perfect reflection. Thus, given the normal at the point of collision P_c and the previous position of the particle P_0, we can compute the direction of a perfect reflection, as we did in Chapter 6, using the vector from the particle to the surface and the normal at the surface, as shown in Figure 10.41:

$$\mathbf{r} = 2(\mathbf{p}_0 - \mathbf{p}_c) \cdot \mathbf{n} \ \mathbf{n} - (\mathbf{P}_0 - \mathbf{P}_c).$$

The particle will be a distance along this reflector equal to the distance it would have penetrated the polygon in the absence of collision detection, as shown in Figure 10.42.

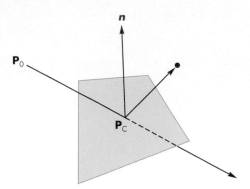

FIGURE 10.42   Position after collision.

The velocity is changed to be along the direction of reflection, with the same magnitude. Equivalently, the tangential component of the velocity—the part in the plane of the polygon—is unchanged, whereas the direction of the normal component is reversed.

A slightly more complex calculation is required for an **elastic collision** in which the particle loses some of its energy when it collides with another object. The **coefficient of restitution** of a particle is the fraction of the normal velocity retained after the collision. Thus, the angle of reflection is computed as for the inelastic collision, and the normal component of the velocity is reduced by the coefficient of restitution.

The major cost of dealing with collisions is the complexity of detection. In applications such as games, approximate detection often is sufficient. In this case, we can replace complex objects consisting of many polygons by simple objects, such as their bounding rectangles or parallelepipeds, for which collision detection is simpler.

Note that use of particles avoids the complex calculations necessary for objects with finite sizes. In many ways, solving the collision problem is similar to clipping arbitrary objects against each other; the calculation is conceptually simple but is in practice time-consuming and messy. In addition, if we have objects with finite size, we have to consider inertial forces, thereby increasing the dimension of the system of equations that we must solve. Consequently, in computer graphics, we are usually willing to accept an approximate solution using ideal point particles, and we obtain an acceptable rendering by placing objects at the location of the particle.

There is another case of hard constraints that arises often and can be handled correctly: contact forces. Suppose that we have a particle that is subject to a force pushing it along a surface, as shown in Figure 10.43. The particle cannot penetrate the surface, and it cannot bounce from the surface because of the force being applied to it. We can argue that the particle is subject to the tangential

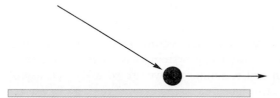

FIGURE 10.43   Contact force.

component of the applied force—that is, the part of the applied force along the surface. We can also apply frictional terms in this direction.

Note that collision detection, as opposed to how we deal with a collision once it has been detected, is often another $O(n^2)$ calculation. Consider, for example, a game such as pool, in which balls are moving around a table, or a simulation of molecules moving within a bounded volume. As any pair of particles can collide, a brute force approach would be to check all pairs of particles at each time step. Faster approaches involve bounding-box methods and hardware support for collision detection.

10.16.2   Soft Constraints

Most hard constraints are difficult to enforce. For example, if we want to ensure that a particle's velocity is less than a maximum velocity or that all the particles have a constant amount of energy, then the resulting mathematics is far more difficult than what we have already seen, and such constraints do not always lead to a simple set of ordinary differential equations.

In many situations, we can work with soft constraints: constraints that we need to come only close to satisfying. For example, if we want a particle whose location is $\mathbf{p}$ to remain near the position $\mathbf{p}_0$, we can consider the **penalty function** $|\mathbf{p} - \mathbf{p}_0|^2$. The smaller this function is, the closer we are to obeying the constraint. This function is one example of an **energy function** whose value represents the amount of some type of energy stored in the system. In physics, such functions can represent quantities, such as the potential or kinetic energy in the system. Physical laws can be written either as differential equations, like those we used for our particles, or in terms of the minimization of expressions involving energy terms. One advantage of the latter form is that we can express constraints or desired behavior of a system directly in terms of potential or energy functions. Conversion of these expressions to force laws is a mechanical process, but its mathematical details are beyond the scope of this book.

Color Plate 27 shows the use of a particle system for scientific visualization. In this example, particles were injected into a three-dimensional data set, and each particle sought to find a surface of constant value—an isosurface. Constraints made the particles seek the desired surfaces, whereas repulsive forces kept the particles separated once they found a surface.

Summary and Notes

The speed at which modern hardware can render geometric objects has opened up the possibilities of a variety of modeling systems. As users of computer graphics, we need a large arsenal of techniques if we are to make full use of our graphics systems. We have introduced hierarchical modeling. Not only are there the many other forms that we investigate in this chapter and the next, but we can also combine these techniques to generate new ones. The Suggested Readings will help you to explore modeling methods.

We have presented basic themes that apply to most approaches to modeling. One is the use of hierarchy to incorporate relationships among objects in a scene. We have seen that we can use fundamental data structures, such as trees and DAGs, to represent such relationships; traversing these data structures becomes part of the rendering process. The use of scene graphs in Open Inventor, VRML, and Java3D allows the user to build complex animated scenes from a combination of predefined and user-defined software modules. As we saw in Chapter 9, tree-structured models are also used to describe complex shaders that involve the interaction of light sources, material properties, atmospheric effects, and a variety of local reflection models. These could be implemented with RenderMan, Cg, or GLSL.

Object-oriented approaches are standard for complex applications and for applications that are distributed over networks. Unfortunately, there has not been agreement on a single object-oriented API. However, the actual rendering in most high-end systems is done at the OpenGL level because the closeness of this API to the hardware makes for efficient use of the hardware. Consequently, both application programmers and system developers need to be familiar with multiple levels of APIs.

Procedural methods have advantages in that we can control how many primitives we produce and at which point in the process these primitives are generated. Equally important is that procedural graphics provides an object-oriented approach to building models—an approach that should be of increasing importance in the future.

Combining physics with computer graphics provides a set of techniques that has the promise of generating physically correct animations and of providing new modeling techniques. Particle systems are but one example of physically based modeling, but they represent a technique that has wide applicability. One of the most interesting and informative exercises that you can undertake at this point is to build a particle system.

Particle methods are used routinely in commercial animations, both for simulation of physical phenomena, such as fire, clouds, and moving water, and in determining the positions of animated characters. Particle systems have also become a standard approach to simulating physical phenomena, often replace complex partial differential equation models, and are used even if a graphical result is not needed.

Suggested Readings

Hierarchical transformations through the use of a matrix stack were described in the graphics literature almost 30 years ago [New73]. The PHIGS API [ANSI88] was the first to incorporate them as part of a standard package. See Watt [Wat92] for an introduction to the use of articulated figures in animation. The paper by Lassiter [Las87] shows the relationship between traditional animation techniques as practiced in the movie industry and animation in computer graphics.

BSP trees were first proposed by Fuchs, Kedem, and Naylor [Fuc80] for use in visibility testing and were later used in many other applications, such as CSG. See [Mol02] for additional applications.

Scene graphs are the heart of Open Inventor [Wer94]. The Open Inventor database format was the basis of VRML [Har96]. Most recent APIs, such as Java3D [Swo00] and DirectX [Kov97], are object oriented. For a discussion of Java and applets, see the books [Cha98] and [Arn96]. Trees are integral to the RenderMan Shading Language [Ups89], where they are used to construct shaders. Modeling systems, such as Maya, allow the user to specify different shaders and rendering algorithms for different objects.

Many applications of visibility testing can be found in [Mol02].

Particle systems were introduced in computer graphics by Reeves [Ree83]. Since then, they have been used for a variety of phenomena, including flocking of birds [Rey87], fluid flow, modeling of grass, and display of surfaces [Wit94a]. Our approach follows Witkin [Wit94b].

Exercises

10.1 For our simple robot model, describe the set of points that can be reached by the tip of the upper arm.

10.2 Find equations for the position of any point on the simple robot in terms of the joint angles. Can you determine the joint angles from the position of the tip of the upper arm? Explain your answer.

10.3 Given two points in space that are reachable by the robot, describe a path between them in terms of the joint angles.

10.4 Write a simple circuit-layout program in terms of a symbol–instance transformation table. Your symbols should include the shapes for circuit elements—such as resistors, capacitors, and inductors for electrical circuits—or the shapes for various gates (AND, OR, NOT) for logical circuits.

10.5 We can write a description of a binary tree, such as we might use for a search, as a list of nodes with pointers to its children. Write an OpenGL program that will take such a description and display the tree graphically.

10.6   Robotics is only one example in which the parts of the scene show compound motion, where the movement of some objects depends on the movement of other objects. Other examples include bicycles (with wheels), airplanes (with propellers), and merry-go-rounds (with horses). Pick an example of compound motion. Write a graphics program to simulate your selection.

10.7   Given two polygons with the same number of vertices, write a program that will generate a sequence of images that converts one polygon into the other.

10.8   Starting with the tree node in Section 9.5, add an attribute to the node and make any required changes to the traversal algorithm.

10.9   Build a simple scene graph system that includes polygons, materials, a viewer, and light sources.

10.10   Why is ray tracing or ray casting a good strategy for rendering a scene described by a CSG tree?

10.11   Show how quadtrees can be used to draw an image at different resolutions.

10.12   Write a program that will allow the user to construct simple articulated figures from a small collection of basic shapes. Your program should allow the user to place the joints, and it should animate the resulting figures.

10.13   Is it possible to design a scene graph structure that is independent of the traversal algorithm?

10.14   Using the scene graph we developed in this chapter, add the ability to store scene graphs in text format and to read them in from files.

10.15   Add the ability to animate objects to our scene graph.

10.16   Starting with the robot in Section 9.3, add a hand or "gripper" to the end of the arm.

10.17   Add wheels to the robot of Section 9.3 and thus the ability to have it move over a flat surface.

10.18   BSP trees can be made more efficient if they are used hierarchically with objects grouped in clusters. Visibility checking is then done using the bounding volumes of the clusters. Implement such an algorithm and use it with a scene graph renderer.

10.19   Write a particle system that simulates the sparks that are generated by welding or by fireworks.

10.20   In the Lennard-Jones particle system, particles are attracted to each other by a force proportional to the inverse of the distance between them raised to the 12th power but are repelled by another force proportional to the inverse of the same distance raised to the 24th power. Simulate such a system in a box. To make the simulation easier, you can assume that a particle that leaves the box reenters the box from the opposite side.

10.21 Create a particle system in which the region of interest is subdivided into cubes of the same size. A particle can only interact with particles in its own cube and the cubes adjacent to it.

10.22 In animations, particle systems are used to give the positions of the characters. Once the positions are determined, two-dimensional images of the characters can be texture-mapped onto polygons at these positions. Build such a system for moving characters subject to both external forces that move them in the desired direction and repulsive forces that keep them from colliding. How can you keep the polygons facing the camera?

CURVES AND SURFACES

The world around us is full of objects of remarkable shapes. Nevertheless, in computer graphics, we continue to populate our virtual worlds with flat objects. We have a good reason for such persistence. Graphics systems can render flat three-dimensional polygons at high rates, including doing hidden-surface removal, shading, and texture mapping. We could take the approach that we took with our sphere model and define curved objects that are, in (virtual) reality, collections of flat polygons. Alternatively, and as we shall do here, we can provide the user with the means to work with curved objects in her program, leaving the eventual rendering of these objects to the implementation.

We introduce three ways to model curves and surfaces, paying most attention to the parametric polynomial forms. We also discuss how curves and surfaces can be rendered on current graphics systems, a process that usually involves subdividing the curved objects into collections of flat primitives. From the application programmer's perspective, this process is transparent because it is part of the implementation. It is important to understand the work involved, however, so that we can appreciate the practical limitations we face in using curves and surfaces.

11.1 Representation of Curves and Surfaces

Before proceeding to our development of parametric polynomial curves and surfaces, we pause to summarize our knowledge of the three major types of object representation—explicit, implicit, and parametric—and to observe the advantages and disadvantages of each form. We can illustrate the salient points using only lines, circles, planes, and spheres.

11.1.1 Explicit Representation

The **explicit form** of a curve in two dimensions gives the value of one variable, the **dependent variable**, in terms of the other, the **independent variable**. In x, y space, we might write

$y = f(x),$

or if we are fortunate, we might be able to invert the relationship and express x as a function of y:

$$x = g(y).$$

There is no guarantee that either form exists for a given curve. For the line, we usually write the equation

$$y = mx + h,$$

in terms of its slope m and y-intercept h, even though we know that this equation does not hold for vertical lines. This problem is one of many coordinate-system–dependent effects that cause problems for graphics systems and, more generally, for all fields where we work with design and manipulation of curves and surfaces. Lines and circles exist independently of any representation, and any representation that fails for certain orientations, such as vertical lines, has serious deficiencies.

Circles provide an even more illustrative example. Consider a circle of radius r centered at the origin. A circle has constant **curvature**—a measure of how rapidly a curve is bending at a point. No closed two-dimensional curve can be more symmetric than the circle. However, the best we can do, using an explicit representation, is to write one equation for half of it,

$$y = \sqrt{r^2 - x^2},$$

and a second equation,

$$y = -\sqrt{r^2 - x^2},$$

for the other half. In addition, we must also specify that these equations hold only if

$$0 \le |x| \le r.$$

In three dimensions, the explicit representation of a curve requires two equations. For example, if x is again the independent variable, we have two dependent variables:

$$y = f(x),$$

$$z = g(x).$$

A surface requires two independent variables, and a representation might take the form

$$z = f(x, y).$$

As is true in two dimensions, a curve or surface may not have an explicit representation. For example, the equations

$$y = ax + b,$$

$$z = cx + d$$

describe a line in three dimensions, but these equations cannot represent a line in a plane of constant x. Likewise, a surface represented by an equation of the form $z = f(x, y)$ cannot represent a sphere, because a given x and y can generate zero, one, or two points on the sphere.

11.1.2 Implicit Representations

Most of the curves and surfaces with which we work have implicit representations. In two dimensions, an **implicit curve** can be represented by the equation

$$f(x, y) = 0.$$

Our two examples—the line and the circle centered at the origin—have the respective representations

$$ax + by + c = 0,$$
$$x^2 + y^2 - r^2 = 0.$$

The function f, however, is really a testing, or **membership**, function that divides space into those points that belong to the curve and those that do not. It allows us to take an x, y pair and to evaluate f to determine whether this point lies on the curve. In general, however, it gives us no analytic way to find a value y on the curve that corresponds to a given x, or vice versa. The implicit form is less coordinate-system–dependent than is the explicit form, however, in that it does represent all lines and circles.

In three dimensions, the implicit form

$$f(x, y, z) = 0$$

describes a surface. For example, any plane can be written as

$$ax + by + cz + d = 0$$

for constants a, b, c, and d, and a sphere of radius r centered at the origin can be described by

$$x^2 + y^2 + z^2 - r^2 = 0.$$

Curves in three dimensions are not as easily represented in implicit form. We can represent a curve as the intersection, if it exists, of the two surfaces:

$$f(x, y, z) = 0,$$
$$g(x, y, z) = 0.$$

Thus, if we test a point (x, y, z) and it is on both surfaces, then it must lie on their intersection curve. In general, most of the curves and surfaces that arise in real applications have implicit representations. Their use is limited by the difficulty in obtaining points on them.

Algebraic surfaces are those for which the function $f(x, y, z)$ is the sum of polynomials in the three variables. Of particular importance are the **quadric** surfaces, where each term in f can have degree up to 2.[1] Quadrics are of interest not only because they include useful objects (such as spheres, disks, and cones) but also because when we intersect these objects with lines, at most two intersection points are generated. We shall use this characteristic to render quadrics in Section 11.9 and for use in ray tracing in Chapter 12.

11.1.3 Parametric Form

The **parametric form** of a curve expresses the value of each spatial variable for points on the curve in terms of an independent variable, u, the **parameter**. In three dimensions, we have three explicit functions:

$$x = x(u),$$
$$y = y(u),$$
$$z = z(u).$$

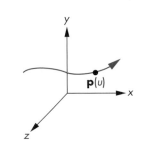

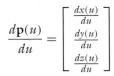

FIGURE 11.1 Parametric curve.

One of the advantages of the parametric form is that it is the same in two and three dimensions. In the former case, we simply drop the equation for z. A useful interpretation of the parametric form is to visualize the locus of points $\mathbf{p}(u) = [\; x(u) \quad y(u) \quad z(u) \;]^T$ being drawn as u varies, as shown in Figure 11.1. We can think of the derivative

$$\frac{d\mathbf{p}(u)}{du} = \begin{bmatrix} \frac{dx(u)}{du} \\ \frac{dy(u)}{du} \\ \frac{dz(u)}{du} \end{bmatrix}$$

as the velocity with which the curve is traced out and points in the direction tangent to the curve.

Parametric surfaces require two parameters. We can describe a surface by three equations of the form

$$x = x(u, v),$$
$$y = y(u, v),$$
$$z = z(u, v),$$

or we can use the column matrix

$$\mathbf{p}(u, v) = \begin{bmatrix} x(u, v) \\ y(u, v) \\ z(u, v) \end{bmatrix}.$$

---

1. Degree is measured as the sum of the powers of the individual terms, so x, yz, or z^2 can be in a quadric, but xy^2 cannot.

As u and v vary over some interval, we generate all the points $\mathbf{p}(u, v)$ on the surface. As we saw with our sphere example in Chapter 6, the vectors given by the column matrices

$$\frac{\partial \mathbf{p}}{\partial u} = \begin{bmatrix} \frac{\partial x(u, v)}{\partial u} \\ \frac{\partial y(u, v)}{\partial u} \\ \frac{\partial z(u, v)}{\partial u} \end{bmatrix}$$

and

$$\frac{\partial \mathbf{p}}{\partial v} = \begin{bmatrix} \frac{\partial x(u, v)}{\partial v} \\ \frac{\partial y(u, v)}{\partial v} \\ \frac{\partial z(u, v)}{\partial v} \end{bmatrix}$$

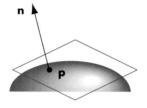

determine the tangent plane at each point on the surface. In addition, as long as these vectors are not parallel, their cross product gives the normal (Figure 11.2) at each point; that is,

$$\mathbf{n} = \partial \mathbf{p}/\partial u \times \partial \mathbf{p}/\partial v.$$

FIGURE 11.2   Tangent plane and normal at a point on a parametric surface.

The parametric form of curves and surfaces is the most flexible and robust for computer graphics. We could still argue that we have not fully removed all dependencies on a particular coordinate system or frame, because we are still using the x, y, and z for a particular representation. It is possible to develop a system solely on the basis of $\mathbf{p}(u)$ for curves and $\mathbf{p}(u, v)$ for surfaces. For example, the **Frenet frame** is often used for describing curves in three-dimensional space, and it is defined starting with the tangent and the normal at each point on the curve. As in our discussion of bump mapping in Chapter 9, we can compute a binormal for the third direction. However, this frame changes for each point on the curve. For our purposes, the parametric form for x, y, z within a particular frame is sufficiently robust.

11.1.4 Parametric Polynomial Curves

Parametric forms are not unique. A given curve or surface can be represented in many ways, but we shall find that parametric forms in which the functions are polynomials in u for curves and polynomials in u and v for surfaces are of most use in computer graphics. Many of the reasons will be summarized in Section 11.2.

Consider a curve of the form[2]

$$\mathbf{p}(u) = \begin{bmatrix} x(u) \\ y(u) \\ z(u) \end{bmatrix}.$$

2. At this point there is no need to work in homogeneous coordinates; in Section 11.8 we shall work in them to derive NURBS curves.

A polynomial parametric curve of degree[3] n is of the form

$$\mathbf{p}(u) = \sum_{k=0}^{n} u^k \mathbf{c}_k,$$

where each $\mathbf{c}_k$ has independent x, y, and z components; that is,

$$\mathbf{c}_k = \begin{bmatrix} c_{xk} \\ c_{yk} \\ c_{zk} \end{bmatrix}.$$

The $n+1$ column matrices $\{\mathbf{c}_k\}$ are the coefficients of $\mathbf{p}$; they give us $3(n+1)$ degrees of freedom in how we choose the coefficients of a particular $\mathbf{p}$. There is no coupling, however, among the x, y, and z components, so we can work with three independent equations, each of the form

$$p(u) = \sum_{k=0}^{n} u^k c_k,$$

where p is any one of x, y, or z. There are $n+1$ degrees of freedom in $p(u)$. We can define our curves for any range interval of u:

$$u_{min} \le u \le u_{max};$$

but with no loss of generality (see Exercise 11.3), we can assume that $0 \le u \le 1$. As the value of u varies over its range, we define a **curve segment**, as shown in Figure 11.3.

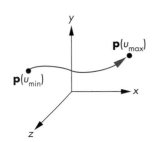

FIGURE 11.3   Curve segment.

11.1.5   Parametric Polynomial Surfaces

We can define a parametric polynomial surface as

$$\mathbf{p}(u, v) = \begin{bmatrix} x(u, v) \\ y(u, v) \\ z(u, v) \end{bmatrix} = \sum_{i=0}^{n} \sum_{j=0}^{m} \mathbf{c}_{ij} u^i v^j.$$

We must specify $3(n+1)(m+1)$ coefficients to determine a particular surface $\mathbf{p}(u, v)$. We shall always take $n = m$, and let u and v vary over the rectangle $0 \le u, v \le 1$, defining a **surface patch**, as shown in Figure 11.4. Note that any surface patch can be viewed as the limit of a collection of curves that we generate by holding either u or v constant and varying the other. Our strategy shall be to define parametric polynomial curves and to use the curves to generate surfaces with similar characteristics.

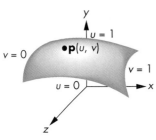

FIGURE 11.4   Surface patch.

---

3. OpenGL often uses the term *order* to mean 1 greater than the degree.

11.2 Design Criteria

The way curves and surfaces are used in computer graphics and computer-aided design is often different from the way they are used in other fields and from the way you may have seen them used previously. There are many considerations that determine why we prefer to use parametric polynomials of low degree, including

- Local control of shape
- Smoothness and continuity
- Ability to evaluate derivatives
- Stability
- Ease of rendering

FIGURE 11.5   Model airplane.

We can understand these criteria with the aid of a simple example. Suppose that we want to build a model airplane, using flexible strips of wood for the structure. We can build the body of the model by constructing a set of cross sections and then connecting them with longer pieces, as shown in Figure 11.5. To design our cross sections, we might start with a picture of a real airplane or sketch a desired curve. One such cross section might be like that shown in Figure 11.6. We could try to get a single global description of this cross section, but that description probably would not be what we want. Each strip of wood can be bent to only a certain shape before breaking and can bend in only a smooth way. Hence, we can regard the curve in Figure 11.6 as only an approximation to what we actually build, which might be more like Figure 11.7. In practice, we probably will make our cross section out of a number of wood strips, each of which will become a curve segment for the cross section. Thus, not only will each segment have to be smooth, but also we want a degree of smoothness where the segments meet at **join points**.

FIGURE 11.6   Cross-section curve.

Note that, although we might be able ensure that a curve segment is smooth, we have to be particularly careful at the join points. Figure 11.8 shows an example in which, although the two curve segments are smooth, at the join point the derivative is discontinuous. The usual definition of **smoothness** is given in terms of the derivatives along the curve. A curve with discontinuities is of little interest to us. Generally, a curve with a continuous first derivative is smoother than a curve whose first derivative has discontinuities (and so on for the higher derivatives). These notions become more precise in Section 11.3. For now, it should be clear that, for a polynomial curve

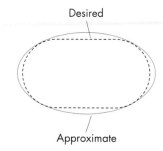

FIGURE 11.7   Approximation of cross-section curve.

$$\mathbf{p}(u) = \sum_{k=0}^{n} \mathbf{c}_k u^k,$$

all derivatives exist and can be computed analytically. Consequently, the only places where we can encounter continuity difficulties are at the join points.

We would like to design each segment individually, rather than designing all the segments by a single global calculation. One reason for this desire is that we would like to work interactively with the shape, carefully molding it to meet

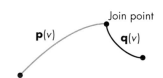

FIGURE 11.8   Derivative discontinuity at join point.

our specifications. When we make a change, this change will affect the shape in only the area where we are working. This sort of local control is but one aspect of a more general stability principle: *Small changes in the values of input parameters should cause only small changes in output variables.* Another statement of this principle is: *Small changes in independent variables should cause only small changes in dependent variables.*

Working with our piece of wood, we might be able to bend it to approximate the desired shape by comparing it to the entire curve. More likely, we would consider data at a small number of **control**, or **data, points** and would use only those data to design our shape. Figure 11.9 shows a possible curve segment and a collection of control points. Note that the curve passes through, or **interpolates**, some of the control points but only comes close to others. As we shall see throughout this chapter, in computer graphics and CAD, we are usually satisfied if the curve passes close to the control-point data, as long as it is smooth.

This example shows many of the reasons for working with polynomial parametric curves. In fact, the spline curves that we discuss in Sections 11.7 and 11.8 derive their name from a flexible wood or metal device that shipbuilders used to design the shape of hulls. Each spline was held in place by pegs, and the bending properties of the material gave the curve segment a polynomial shape.

Returning to computer graphics, remember that we need methods for rendering curves (and surfaces). A good mathematical representation may be of limited value if we cannot display the resulting curves and surfaces easily. We would like to display whatever curves and surfaces we choose with techniques similar to those used for flat objects, including color, shading, and texture mapping.

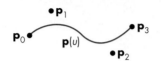

FIGURE 11.9 Curve segment and control points.

11.3 Parametric Cubic Polynomial Curves

Once we have decided to use parametric polynomial curves, we must choose the degree of the curve. On one hand, if we choose a high degree, we will have many parameters that we can set to form the desired shape, but evaluation of points on the curve will be costly. In addition, as the degree of a polynomial curve becomes higher, there is more danger that the curve will become rougher. On the other hand, if we pick too low a degree, we may not have enough parameters with which to work. However, if we design each curve segment over a short interval, we can achieve many of our purposes with low-degree curves. Although there may be only a few degrees of freedom, these few may be sufficient to allow us to produce the desired shape in a small region. For this reason, most designers, at least initially, work with cubic polynomial curves.

We can write a cubic parametric polynomial using a row and column matrix as

$$\mathbf{p}(u) = \mathbf{c}_0 + \mathbf{c}_1 u + \mathbf{c}_2 u^2 + \mathbf{c}_3 u^3 = \sum_{k=0}^{3} \mathbf{c}_k u^k = \mathbf{u}^T \mathbf{c},$$

where

$$\mathbf{c} = \begin{bmatrix} \mathbf{c}_0 \\ \mathbf{c}_1 \\ \mathbf{c}_2 \\ \mathbf{c}_3 \end{bmatrix}, \qquad \mathbf{u} = \begin{bmatrix} 1 \\ u \\ u^2 \\ u^3 \end{bmatrix}, \qquad \mathbf{c}_k = \begin{bmatrix} c_{kx} \\ c_{ky} \\ c_{kz} \end{bmatrix}.$$

Thus, $\mathbf{c}$ is a column matrix containing the coefficients of the polynomial; it is what we wish to determine from the control-point data. We shall derive a number of types of cubic curves. The types will differ in how they use the control-point data. We seek to find 12 equations in 12 unknowns for each type, but because x, y, and z are independent, we can group these equations into three independent sets of four equations in four unknowns. When we discuss NURBS in Section 11.8.4, we shall be working in homogeneous coordinates so will have to use the w coordinate and thus will have four sets of four equations in four unknowns.

The design of a particular type of cubic will be based on data given at some values of the parameter u. These data might take the form of interpolating conditions in which the polynomial must agree with the data at some points. The data may also require the polynomial to interpolate some derivatives at certain values of the parameter. We might also have smoothness conditions that enforce various continuity conditions at the join points that are shared by two curve segments. Finally, we may have conditions that are not as strict, requiring only that the curve pass close to several known data points. Each type of condition will define a different type of curve, and depending on how we use some given data, the same data can define more than a single curve.

11.4 Interpolation

Our first example of a cubic parametric polynomial is the cubic **interpolating polynomial**. Although we rarely use interpolating polynomials in computer graphics, the derivation of this familiar polynomial illustrates the steps we must follow for our other types, and the analysis of the interpolating polynomial illustrates many of the important features by which we evaluate a particular curve or surface.

Suppose that we have four control points in three dimensions: $\mathbf{p}_0$, $\mathbf{p}_1$, $\mathbf{p}_2$, and $\mathbf{p}_3$. Each is of the form

$$\mathbf{p}_k = \begin{bmatrix} x_k \\ y_k \\ z_k \end{bmatrix}.$$

We seek the coefficients $\mathbf{c}$ such that the polynomial $\mathbf{p}(u) = \mathbf{u}^T \mathbf{c}$ passes through, or interpolates, the four control points. The derivation should be easy. We have four three-dimensional interpolating points; hence, we have 12 conditions and 12 unknowns. First, however, we have to decide at which values of the parameter

u the interpolation takes place. Lacking any other information, we can take these values to be the equally spaced values $u = 0, \frac{1}{3}, \frac{2}{3}, 1$—remember that we have decided to let u always vary over the interval $[0, 1]$. The four conditions are thus

$$\mathbf{p}_0 = \mathbf{p}(0) = \mathbf{c}_0,$$

$$\mathbf{p}_1 = \mathbf{p}\left(\frac{1}{3}\right) = \mathbf{c}_0 + \frac{1}{3}\mathbf{c}_1 + \left(\frac{1}{3}\right)^2 \mathbf{c}_2 + \left(\frac{1}{3}\right)^3 \mathbf{c}_3,$$

$$\mathbf{p}_2 = \mathbf{p}\left(\frac{2}{3}\right) = \mathbf{c}_0 + \frac{2}{3}\mathbf{c}_1 + \left(\frac{2}{3}\right)^2 \mathbf{c}_2 + \left(\frac{2}{3}\right)^3 \mathbf{c}_3,$$

$$\mathbf{p}_3 = \mathbf{p}(1) = \mathbf{c}_0 + \mathbf{c}_1 + \mathbf{c}_2 + \mathbf{c}_3.$$

We can write these equations in matrix form as

$$\mathbf{p} = \mathbf{Ac},$$

where

$$\mathbf{p} = \begin{bmatrix} \mathbf{p}_0 \\ \mathbf{p}_1 \\ \mathbf{p}_2 \\ \mathbf{p}_3 \end{bmatrix}$$

and

$$\mathbf{A} = \begin{bmatrix} 1 & 0 & 0 & 0 \\ 1 & \frac{1}{3} & \left(\frac{1}{3}\right)^2 & \left(\frac{1}{3}\right)^3 \\ 1 & \frac{2}{3} & \left(\frac{2}{3}\right)^2 & \left(\frac{2}{3}\right)^3 \\ 1 & 1 & 1 & 1 \end{bmatrix}.$$

The matrix form here has to be interpreted carefully. If we interpret $\mathbf{p}$ and $\mathbf{c}$ as column matrices of 12 elements, the rules of matrix multiplication are violated. Instead, we view $\mathbf{p}$ and $\mathbf{c}$ each as a four-element column matrix whose elements are three-element row matrices. Hence, multiplication of an element of $\mathbf{A}$, a scalar, by an element of $\mathbf{c}$, a three-element column matrix, yields a three-element column matrix, which is the same type as an element of $\mathbf{p}$.[4] We can show that $\mathbf{A}$ is nonsingular, and can invert it to obtain the **interpolating geometry matrix**

$$\mathbf{M}_I = \mathbf{A}^{-1} = \begin{bmatrix} 1 & 0 & 0 & 0 \\ -5.5 & 9 & -4.5 & 1 \\ 9 & -22.5 & 18 & -4.5 \\ -4.5 & 13.5 & -13.5 & 4.5 \end{bmatrix}$$

---

4. We could use row matrices for the elements of $\mathbf{p}$ and $\mathbf{c}$: In that case, ordinary matrix multiplications would work, because we would have a 4×4 matrix multiplying a 4×3 matrix. However, this method would fail for surfaces. The real difficulty is that we should be using *tensors* to carry out the mathematics—a topic beyond the scope of this book.

FIGURE 11.10 Joining of interpolating segments.

and the desired coefficients

$$\mathbf{c} = \mathbf{M}_I \mathbf{p}.$$

Suppose that we have a sequence of control points $\mathbf{p}_0, \mathbf{p}_1, \ldots, \mathbf{p}_m$. Rather than defining a single interpolating curve of degree m for all the points—a calculation we could do by following a similar derivation to the one for cubic polynomials— we can define a set of cubic interpolating curves, each defined by a group of four control points, and each valid over a short interval in u. We can achieve continuity at the join points by using the control point defining the right side of one segment as the first point for the next segment (Figure 11.10). Thus, we use $\mathbf{p}_0, \mathbf{p}_1, \mathbf{p}_2, \mathbf{p}_3$ to define the first segment; we use $\mathbf{p}_3, \mathbf{p}_4, \mathbf{p}_5, \mathbf{p}_6$, for the second; and so on. Note that if each segment is defined for the parameter u varying over the interval $(0, 1)$, then the matrix $\mathbf{M}_I$ is the same for each segment. Although we have achieved continuity for the sequence of segments, derivatives at the join points will not be continuous.

11.4.1 Blending Functions

We can obtain additional insights into the smoothness of the interpolating polynomial curves by rewriting our equations in a slightly different form. We can substitute the interpolating coefficients into our polynomial; we obtain

$$\mathbf{p}(u) = \mathbf{u}^T \mathbf{c} = \mathbf{u}^T \mathbf{M}_I \mathbf{p},$$

which we can write as

$$\mathbf{p}(u) = \mathbf{b}(u)^T \mathbf{p},$$

where

$$\mathbf{b}(u) = \mathbf{M}_I^T \mathbf{u}$$

is a column matrix of the four **blending polynomials**

$$\mathbf{b}(u) = \begin{bmatrix} b_0(u) \\ b_1(u) \\ b_2(u) \\ b_3(u) \end{bmatrix}.$$

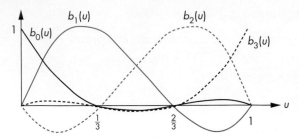

FIGURE 11.11   Blending polynomials for interpolation.

Each blending polynomial is a cubic. If we express $\mathbf{p}(u)$ in terms of these blending polynomials as

$$\mathbf{p}(u) = b_0(u)\mathbf{p}_0 + b_1(u)\mathbf{p}_1 + b_2(u)\mathbf{p}_2 + b_3(u)\mathbf{p}_3 = \sum_{i=0}^{3} b_i(u)\mathbf{p}_i,$$

then we can see that the polynomials blend together the individual contributions of each control point and enable us to see the effect of a given control point on the entire curve. These blending functions for the cubic interpolating polynomial are shown in Figure 11.11 and are given by the equations

$$b_0(u) = -\frac{9}{2}\left(u - \frac{1}{3}\right)\left(u - \frac{2}{3}\right)(u - 1),$$

$$b_1(u) = \frac{27}{2}u\left(u - \frac{2}{3}\right)(u - 1),$$

$$b_2(u) = -\frac{27}{2}u\left(u - \frac{1}{3}\right)(u - 1),$$

$$b_3(u) = \frac{9}{2}u\left(u - \frac{1}{3}\right)\left(u - \frac{2}{3}\right).$$

Because all the zeros of the blending functions lie in the closed interval [0, 1], the blending functions must vary substantially over this interval and are not particularly smooth. This lack of smoothness is a consequence of the interpolating requirement that the curve must pass through the control points, rather than just come close to them. This characteristic is even more pronounced for interpolating polynomials of higher degree. This problem and the lack of derivative continuity at the join points account for limited use of the interpolating polynomial in computer graphics. However, the same derivation and analysis process will allow us to find smoother types of cubic curves.

11.4.2 The Cubic Interpolating Patch

There is a natural extension of the interpolating curve to an interpolating patch. A **bicubic surface patch** can be written in the form

$$\mathbf{p}(u, v) = \sum_{i=0}^{3} \sum_{j=0}^{3} u^i v^j \mathbf{c}_{ij},$$

where $\mathbf{c}_{ij}$ is a three-element column matrix of the x, y, and z coefficients for the ijth term in the polynomial. If we define a 4×4 matrix whose elements are three-element column matrices,

$$\mathbf{C} = [\, \mathbf{c}_{ij} \,],$$

then we can write the surface patch as

$$\mathbf{p}(u, v) = \mathbf{u}^T \mathbf{C} \mathbf{v},$$

where

$$\mathbf{v} = \begin{bmatrix} 1 \\ v \\ v^2 \\ v^3 \end{bmatrix}.$$

A particular bicubic polynomial patch is defined by the 48 elements of $\mathbf{C}$—that is, 16 three-element vectors.

Suppose that we have 16 three-dimensional control points $\mathbf{p}_{ij}$, $i = 0, \ldots, 3$, $j = 0, \ldots, 3$. We can use these points to define an interpolating surface patch, as shown in Figure 11.12. If we assume that these data are used for interpolation

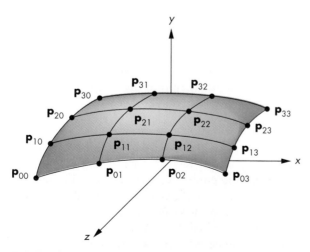

FIGURE 11.12 Interpolating surface patch.

at the equally spaced values of both u and v of 0, $\frac{1}{3}$, $\frac{2}{3}$, and 1, then we get three sets of 16 equations in 16 unknowns. For example, for $u = v = 0$, we get the three independent equations

$$\mathbf{p}_{00} = [\,1 \quad 0 \quad 0 \quad 0\,]\,\mathbf{C}\begin{bmatrix} 1 \\ 0 \\ 0 \\ 0 \end{bmatrix} = \mathbf{c}_{00}.$$

Rather than writing down and solving all these equations, we can proceed in a more direct fashion. If we consider $v = 0$, we get a curve in u that must interpolate $\mathbf{p}_{00}$, $\mathbf{p}_{10}$, $\mathbf{p}_{20}$, and $\mathbf{p}_{30}$. Using our results on interpolating curves, we write this curve as

$$\mathbf{p}(u, 0) = \mathbf{u}^T \mathbf{M}_I \begin{bmatrix} \mathbf{p}_{00} \\ \mathbf{p}_{10} \\ \mathbf{p}_{20} \\ \mathbf{p}_{30} \end{bmatrix} = \mathbf{u}^T \mathbf{C} \begin{bmatrix} 1 \\ 0 \\ 0 \\ 0 \end{bmatrix}.$$

Likewise, the values of $v = \frac{1}{3}$, $\frac{2}{3}$, 1 define three other interpolating curves, each of which has a similar form. Putting these curves together, we can write all 16 equations as

$$\mathbf{u}^T \mathbf{M}_I \mathbf{P} = \mathbf{u}^T \mathbf{C} \mathbf{A}^T,$$

where $\mathbf{A}$ is the inverse of $\mathbf{M}_I$. We can solve this equation for the desired coefficient matrix

$$\mathbf{C} = \mathbf{M}_I \mathbf{P} \mathbf{M}_I^T,$$

and substituting into the equation for the surface, we have

$$\mathbf{p}(u, v) = \mathbf{u}^T \mathbf{M}_I \mathbf{P} \mathbf{M}_I^T \mathbf{v}.$$

We can interpret this result in several ways. First, the interpolating surface can be derived from our understanding of interpolating curves—a technique that will enable us to extend other types of curves to surfaces. Second, we can extend our use of blending polynomials to surfaces. By noting that $\mathbf{M}_I^T \mathbf{u}$ describes the interpolating blending functions, we can rewrite our surface patch as

$$\mathbf{p}(u, v) = \sum_{i=0}^{3} \sum_{j=0}^{3} b_i(u) b_j(v) \mathbf{p}_{ij}.$$

Each term $b_i(u)b_j(v)$ describes a **blending patch**. We form a surface by blending together 16 simple patches, each weighted by the data at a control point. The basic properties of the blending patches are determined by the same blending polynomials that arose for interpolating curves; thus, most of the characteristics of surfaces are similar to those of the curves. In particular, the blending patches are not particularly smooth, because the zeros of the functions $b_i(u)b_j(v)$ lie inside the unit square in u, v space. Surfaces formed from curves using this technique are known as **tensor-product surfaces**. Bicubic tensor-product surfaces are a subset of all surface patches that contain up to cubic terms in both parameters. They are an example of **separable surfaces**, which can be written as

$$\mathbf{p}(u, v) = \mathbf{f}(\mathbf{u})\mathbf{g}(v),$$

where $\mathbf{f}$ and $\mathbf{g}$ are suitably chosen row and column matrices, respectively. The advantage of such surfaces is that they allow us to work with functions in u and v independently.

11.5 Hermite Curves and Surfaces

We can use the techniques that we developed for interpolating curves and surfaces to generate various other types of curves and surfaces. The major difference is in the way we use the data at control points.

11.5.1 The Hermite Form

Suppose that we start with only the control points $\mathbf{p}_0$ and $\mathbf{p}_3$,[5] and again, we insist that our curve interpolate these points at the parameter values $u = 0$ and $u = 1$, respectively. Using our previous notation, we have the two conditions

$$\mathbf{p}(0) = \mathbf{p}_0 = \mathbf{c}_0,$$

$$\mathbf{p}(1) = \mathbf{p}_3 = \mathbf{c}_0 + \mathbf{c}_1 + \mathbf{c}_2 + \mathbf{c}_3.$$

We can get two other conditions if we assume that we know the derivatives of the function at $u = 0$ and $u = 1$. The derivative of the polynomial is simply the parametric quadratic polynomial

$$\mathbf{p}'(u) = \begin{bmatrix} \frac{dx}{du} \\ \frac{dy}{du} \\ \frac{dz}{du} \end{bmatrix} = \mathbf{c}_1 + 2u\mathbf{c}_2 + 3u^2\mathbf{c}_3.$$

If we denote the given values of the two derivatives as $\mathbf{p}_0'$ and $\mathbf{p}_3'$, then our two additional conditions (Figure 11.13) are

$$\mathbf{p}_0' = \mathbf{p}'(0) = \mathbf{c}_1,$$

$$\mathbf{p}_3' = \mathbf{p}'(1) = \mathbf{c}_1 + 2\mathbf{c}_2 + 3\mathbf{c}_3.$$

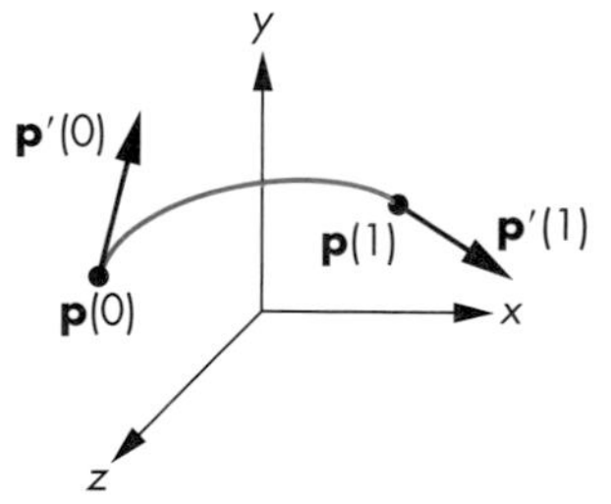

FIGURE 11.13 Definition of the Hermite cubic.

---

5. We use this numbering to be consistent with our interpolation notation, as well as with the numbering that we use for Bézier curves in Section 11.6.

We can write these equations in matrix form as

$$
\begin{bmatrix} \mathbf{p}_0 \\ \mathbf{p}_3 \\ \mathbf{p}_0' \\ \mathbf{p}_3' \end{bmatrix} = \begin{bmatrix} 1 & 0 & 0 & 0 \\ 1 & 1 & 1 & 1 \\ 0 & 1 & 0 & 0 \\ 0 & 1 & 2 & 3 \end{bmatrix} \mathbf{c}.
$$

Letting $\mathbf{q}$ denote the data matrix

$$
\mathbf{q} = \begin{bmatrix} \mathbf{p}_0 \\ \mathbf{p}_3 \\ \mathbf{p}_0' \\ \mathbf{p}_3' \end{bmatrix},
$$

we can solve the equations to find

$$
\mathbf{c} = \mathbf{M}_H \mathbf{q},
$$

where $\mathbf{M}_H$ is the **Hermite geometry** matrix

$$
\mathbf{M}_H = \begin{bmatrix} 1 & 0 & 0 & 0 \\ 0 & 0 & 1 & 0 \\ -3 & 3 & -2 & -1 \\ 2 & -2 & 1 & 1 \end{bmatrix}.
$$

The resulting polynomial is given by

$$
\mathbf{p}(u) = \mathbf{u}^T \mathbf{M}_H \mathbf{q}.
$$

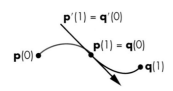

FIGURE 11.14 Hermite form at join point.

We use this method as shown in Figure 11.14, where both the interpolated value and the derivative are shared by the curve segments on the two sides of a join point, and thus both the resulting function and the first derivative are continuous over all segments.

We can get a more accurate idea of the increased smoothness of the Hermite form by rewriting the polynomial in the form

$$
\mathbf{p}(u) = \mathbf{b}(u)^T \mathbf{q},
$$

where the new blending functions are given by

$$
\mathbf{b}(u) = \mathbf{M}_H^T \mathbf{u} = \begin{bmatrix} 2u^3 - 3u^2 + 1 \\ -2u^3 + 3u^2 \\ u^3 - 2u^2 + u \\ u^3 - u^2 \end{bmatrix}.
$$

These four polynomials have none of their zeros inside the interval $(0, 1)$ and are much smoother than are the interpolating polynomial blending functions (see Exercise 11.16).

We can go on and define a bicubic Hermite surface patch through these blending functions,

$$\mathbf{p}(u, v) = \sum_{i=0}^{3} \sum_{j=0}^{3} b_i(u) b_j(v) \mathbf{q}_{ij},$$

where $\mathbf{Q} = [\mathbf{q}_{ij}]$ is the extension of $\mathbf{q}$ to surface data. At this point, however, this equation is just a formal expression. It is not clear what the relationship is between the elements of $\mathbf{Q}$ and the derivatives of $\mathbf{p}(u, v)$. Four of the elements of $\mathbf{Q}$ are chosen to interpolate the corners of the patch, whereas the others are chosen to match certain derivatives at the corners of the patch. In most interactive applications, however, the user enters point data rather than derivative data; consequently, unless we have analytic formulations for the data, usually we do not have these derivatives. However, the approach we took with the Hermite curves and surfaces will lead to the Bézier forms that we introduce in Section 11.6.

11.5.2 Geometric and Parametric Continuity

Before we discuss the Bézier and spline forms, we examine a few issues concerning continuity and derivatives. Consider the join point in Figure 11.15. Suppose that the polynomial on the left is $\mathbf{p}(u)$ and the one on the right is $\mathbf{q}(u)$. We enforce various continuity conditions by matching the polynomials and their derivatives at $u = 1$ for $\mathbf{p}(u)$, with the corresponding values for $\mathbf{q}(u)$ for $u = 0$. If we want the function to be continuous, we must have

$$\mathbf{p}(1) = \begin{bmatrix} p_x(1) \\ p_y(1) \\ p_z(1) \end{bmatrix} = \mathbf{q}(0) = \begin{bmatrix} q_x(0) \\ q_y(0) \\ q_z(0) \end{bmatrix}.$$

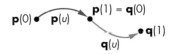

FIGURE 11.15 Continuity at the join point.

All three parametric components must be equal at the join point; we call this property C^0 **parametric continuity.**

When we consider derivatives, we can require, as we did with the Hermite curve, that

$$\mathbf{p}'(1) = \begin{bmatrix} p'_x(1) \\ p'_y(1) \\ p'_z(1) \end{bmatrix} = \mathbf{q}'(0) = \begin{bmatrix} q'_x(0) \\ q'_y(0) \\ q'_z(0) \end{bmatrix}.$$

If we match all three parametric equations and the first derivative, we have C^1 parametric continuity.

If we look at the geometry, however, we can take a different approach to continuity. In three dimensions, the derivative at a point on a curve defines the tangent line at that point. Suppose that instead of requiring matching of the derivatives for the two segments at the join point, we require only that their derivatives be proportional:

$$\mathbf{p}'(1) = \alpha \mathbf{q}'(0),$$

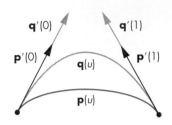

FIGURE 11.16 Change of magnitude in G^1 continuity.

for some positive number α. If the tangents of the two curves are proportional, then they point in the same direction, but they may have different magnitudes. We call this type of continuity G^1 **geometric continuity**.[6] If the two tangent vectors need only to be proportional, we have only two conditions to enforce, rather than three, leaving 1 extra degree of freedom that we can potentially use to satisfy some other criterion. We can extend this idea to higher derivatives and can talk about both C^n and G^n continuity.

Although two curves that have only G^1 continuity at the join points have a continuous tangent at the join points, the value of the constant of proportionality—or equivalently, the relative magnitudes of the tangents on the two sides of the join point—does matter. Curves with the same tangent direction but different magnitudes differ, as shown in Figure 11.16. The curves $\mathbf{p}(u)$ and $\mathbf{q}(u)$ share the same endpoints, and the tangents at the endpoints point in the same direction, but the curves are different. This result is exploited in many painting programs, where the user can interactively change the magnitude, leaving the tangent direction unchanged. However, in other applications, such as animation, where a sequence of curve segments describes the path of an object, G^1 continuity may be insufficient (see Exercise 11.11).

11.6   Bézier Curves and Surfaces

Comparing the Hermite form to the interpolating form is problematic; we are comparing forms with some similarities but with significant differences. Both are cubic polynomial curves, but the forms do not use the same data; thus, they cannot be compared on equal terms. We can use the same control-point data that we used to derive the interpolating curves to approximate the derivatives in the Hermite curves. The resulting Bézier curves are excellent approximations to the Hermite curves and are comparable to the interpolating curves because they have been obtained using the same data. In addition, because these curves do not need derivative information, they will be well suited for use in graphics and CAD.

11.6.1   Bézier Curves

Consider again the four control points: $\mathbf{p}_0$, $\mathbf{p}_1$, $\mathbf{p}_2$, and $\mathbf{p}_3$. Suppose that we still insist on interpolating known values at the endpoints with a cubic polynomial $\mathbf{p}(u)$:

$$\mathbf{p}_0 = \mathbf{p}(0),$$
$$\mathbf{p}_3 = \mathbf{p}(1).$$

---

6. G^0 continuity is the same as C^0 continuity.

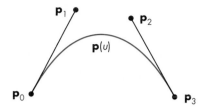

FIGURE 11.17 Approximating tangents.

Bézier proposed that rather than using the other two control points, $\mathbf{p}_2$ and $\mathbf{p}_3$, for interpolation, we use them to approximate the tangents at $u = 0$ and $u = 1$. In parameter space, we can use the linear approximations

$$\mathbf{p}'(0) \approx \frac{\mathbf{p}_1 - \mathbf{p}_0}{\frac{1}{3}} = 3(\mathbf{p}_1 - \mathbf{p}_0),$$

$$\mathbf{p}'(1) \approx \frac{\mathbf{p}_3 - \mathbf{p}_2}{\frac{1}{3}} = 3(\mathbf{p}_3 - \mathbf{p}_2),$$

as shown in Figure 11.17. Applying these approximations to the derivatives of our parametric polynomial, $\mathbf{p}(u) = \mathbf{u}^T\mathbf{c}$, at the two endpoints, we have the two conditions

$$3\mathbf{p}_1 - 3\mathbf{p}_0 = \mathbf{c}_1,$$
$$3\mathbf{p}_3 - 3\mathbf{p}_2 = \mathbf{c}_1 + 2\mathbf{c}_2 + 3\mathbf{c}_3,$$

to add to our interpolation conditions

$$\mathbf{p}_0 = \mathbf{c}_0,$$
$$\mathbf{p}_3 = \mathbf{c}_0 + \mathbf{c}_1 + \mathbf{c}_2 + \mathbf{c}_3.$$

At this point, we again have three sets of four equations in four unknowns that we can solve, as before, to find

$$\mathbf{c} = \mathbf{M}_B\mathbf{p},$$

where $\mathbf{M}_B$ is the **Bézier geometry matrix**

$$\mathbf{M}_B = \begin{bmatrix} 1 & 0 & 0 & 0 \\ -3 & 3 & 0 & 0 \\ 3 & -6 & 3 & 0 \\ -1 & 3 & -3 & 1 \end{bmatrix}.$$

The cubic Bézier polynomial is thus

$$\mathbf{p}(u) = \mathbf{u}^T\mathbf{M}_B\mathbf{p}.$$

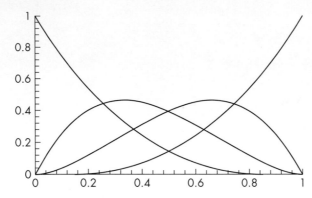

FIGURE 11.18   Blending polynomials for Bézier cubic.

We use this formula exactly as we did for the interpolating polynomial. If we have a set of control points, $\mathbf{p}_0, \ldots, \mathbf{p}_n$, we use $\mathbf{p}_0, \mathbf{p}_1, \mathbf{p}_2$, and $\mathbf{p}_3$ for the first curve; $\mathbf{p}_3, \mathbf{p}_4, \mathbf{p}_5$, and $\mathbf{p}_6$ for the second; and so on. It should be clear that we have C^0 continuity, but we have given up the C^1 continuity of the Hermite polynomial because we use different approximations on the left and right of a join point.

We can see important advantages to the Bézier curve by examining the blending functions in Figure 11.18. We write the curve as

$$\mathbf{p}(u) = \mathbf{b}(u)^T \mathbf{p},$$

where

$$\mathbf{b}(u) = \mathbf{M}_B^T \mathbf{u} = \begin{bmatrix} (1-u)^3 \\ 3u(1-u)^2 \\ 3u^2(1-u) \\ u^3 \end{bmatrix}.$$

These four polynomials are one case of the **Bernstein polynomials**,

$$b_{kd}(u) = \frac{d!}{k!(d-k)!} u^k (1-u)^{d-k},$$

which can be shown to have remarkable properties. First, all the zeros of the polynomials are either at $u = 0$ or at $u = 1$. Consequently, for each blending polynomial,

$$0 < b_{id}(u),$$

for $0 < u < 1$. Without any zeros in the interval, each blending polynomial must be smooth. We can also show that, in this interval (see Exercise 11.4),

$$b_{id}(u) \le 1,$$

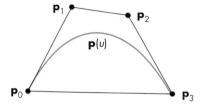

FIGURE 11.19   Convex hull and Bézier polynomial.

and

$$\sum_{i=0}^{d} b_{id}(u) = 1.$$

Under these conditions, the representation of our cubic Bézier polynomial in terms of its blending polynomials,

$$\mathbf{p}(u) = \sum_{i=0}^{3} b_i(u)\mathbf{p}_i,$$

is a convex sum. Consequently, $\mathbf{p}(u)$ must lie in the convex hull of the four control points, as shown in Figure 11.19. Thus, even though the Bézier polynomial does not interpolate all the control points, it cannot be far from them. These two properties, combined with the fact that we are using control-point data, make it easy to work interactively with Bézier curves. A user can enter the four control points to define an initial curve, and then can manipulate the points to control the shape.

11.6.2   Bézier Surface Patches

We can generate the **Bézier surface patches** through the blending functions. If $\mathbf{P}$ is a 4×4 array of control points,

$$\mathbf{P} = \left[\mathbf{p}_{ij} \right],$$

then the corresponding Bézier patch is

$$\mathbf{p}(u, v) = \sum_{i=0}^{3} \sum_{j=0}^{3} b_i(u) b_j(v) \mathbf{p}_{ij} = \mathbf{u}^T \mathbf{M}_B \mathbf{P} \mathbf{M}_B^T \mathbf{v}.$$

The patch is fully contained in the convex hull of the control points (Figure 11.20) and interpolates $\mathbf{p}_{00}$, $\mathbf{p}_{03}$, $\mathbf{p}_{30}$, and $\mathbf{p}_{33}$. We can interpret the other conditions as approximations to various derivatives at the corners of the patch.

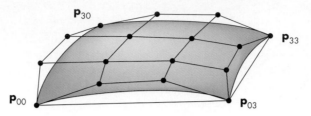

FIGURE 11.20 Bézier patch.

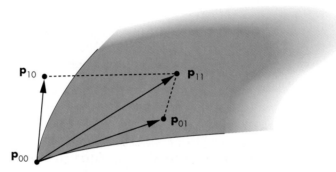

FIGURE 11.21 Twist at corner of Bézier patch.

Consider the corner for $u = v = 0$. We can evaluate $\mathbf{p}(u)$ and the first partial derivatives to find

$$\mathbf{p}(0, 0) = \mathbf{p}_{00},$$

$$\frac{\partial \mathbf{p}}{\partial u}(0, 0) = 3(\mathbf{p}_{10} - \mathbf{p}_{00}),$$

$$\frac{\partial \mathbf{p}}{\partial v}(0, 0) = 3(\mathbf{p}_{01} - \mathbf{p}_{00}),$$

$$\frac{\partial^2 \mathbf{p}}{\partial u \partial v}(0, 0) = 9(\mathbf{p}_{00} - \mathbf{p}_{01} + \mathbf{p}_{10} - \mathbf{p}_{11}).$$

The first three conditions are clearly extensions of our results for the Bézier curve. The fourth can be seen as a measure of the tendency of the patch to divert from being flat, or to **twist**, at the corner. If we consider the quadrilateral defined by these points (Figure 11.21), the points will lie in the same plane only if the twist is zero. Front Plate 3 uses Bézier patches to create a smooth surface from elevation data.

11.7 Cubic B-Splines

In practice, the cubic Bézier curves and surface patches are widely used. They have one fundamental limitation: At the join points (or patch edges, for surfaces), we have only C^0 continuity. If, for example, we were to use these curves to design our model-airplane cross sections, as shown in Section 11.2, and then were to attempt to build those cross sections, we might be unhappy with the way that the pieces met at the join points.

It might seem that we have reached the limit of what we can do with cubic parametric polynomials, and that if we need more flexibility, we have to either go to high-degree polynomials or shorten the interval and use more polynomial segments. Both of these tactics are possibilities—and there is another: We can use the same control-point data but not require the polynomial to interpolate any of these points. If we can come close to the control points and get more smoothness at the join points, we may be content with the result.

11.7.1 The Cubic B-Spline Curve

In this section, we illustrate a particular example of a B-spline curve and show how we can obtain C^2 continuity at the join points with a cubic. In Section 11.8, we give a short introduction to a more general approach to splines—an approach that is general enough to include the Bézier curves as a special case. Consider four control points in the middle of a sequence of control points: $\{\mathbf{p}_{i-2}, \mathbf{p}_{i-1}, \mathbf{p}_i, \mathbf{p}_{i+1}\}$. Our previous approach was to use these four points to define a cubic curve such that, as the parameter u varied from 0 to 1, the curve spanned the distance from $\mathbf{p}_{i-2}$ to $\mathbf{p}_{i+1}$, interpolating $\mathbf{p}_{i-2}$ and $\mathbf{p}_{i+1}$. Instead, suppose that as u goes from 0 to 1, we span only the distance between the middle two control points, as shown in Figure 11.22. Likewise, we use $\{\mathbf{p}_{i-3}, \mathbf{p}_{i-2}, \mathbf{p}_{i-1}, \mathbf{p}_i\}$ between $\mathbf{p}_{i-2}$ and $\mathbf{p}_{i-1}$, and $\{\mathbf{p}_{i-1}, \mathbf{p}_i, \mathbf{p}_{i+1}, \mathbf{p}_{i+2}\}$ between $\mathbf{p}_i$ and $\mathbf{p}_{i+1}$. Suppose that $\mathbf{p}(u)$ is the curve we use between $\mathbf{p}_{i-1}$ and $\mathbf{p}_i$, and $\mathbf{q}(u)$ is the curve to its left, used between $\mathbf{p}_{i-2}$ and $\mathbf{p}_{i-1}$. We can match conditions at $\mathbf{p}(0)$ with conditions at $\mathbf{q}(1)$. Using our standard formulation, we are looking for a matrix $\mathbf{M}$, such that the desired cubic polynomial is

$$\mathbf{p}(u) = \mathbf{u}^T \mathbf{M} \mathbf{p},$$

where $\mathbf{p}$ is the matrix of control points

$$\mathbf{p} = \begin{bmatrix} \mathbf{p}_{i-2} \\ \mathbf{p}_{i-1} \\ \mathbf{p}_i \\ \mathbf{p}_{i+1} \end{bmatrix}.$$

We can use the same matrix to write $\mathbf{q}(u)$ as

$$\mathbf{q}(u) = \mathbf{u}^T \mathbf{M} \mathbf{q},$$

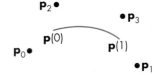

FIGURE 11.22 Four points that define a curve between the middle two points.

where

$$\mathbf{q} = \begin{bmatrix} \mathbf{p}_{i-3} \\ \mathbf{p}_{i-2} \\ \mathbf{p}_{i-1} \\ \mathbf{p}_i \end{bmatrix}.$$

In principle, we could write down a set of conditions on $\mathbf{p}(0)$ that would match conditions for $\mathbf{q}(1)$, and we could write equivalent conditions matching various derivatives of $\mathbf{p}(1)$ with conditions for another polynomial that starts there. For example, the condition

$$\mathbf{p}(0) = \mathbf{q}(1)$$

requires continuity at the join point, without requiring interpolation of any data. Enforcing this condition gives one equation for the coefficients of $\mathbf{M}$. There are clearly many sets of conditions that we can use; each set can define a different matrix.

We can take a shortcut to deriving the most popular matrix, by noting that we must use symmetric approximations at the join point. Hence, any evaluation of conditions on $\mathbf{q}(1)$ cannot use $\mathbf{p}_{i-3}$, because this control point does not appear in the equation for $\mathbf{p}(u)$. Likewise, we cannot use $\mathbf{p}_{i+1}$ in any condition on $\mathbf{p}(0)$. Two conditions that satisfy this symmetry condition are

$$\mathbf{p}(0) = \mathbf{q}(1) = \frac{1}{6}(\mathbf{p}_{i-2} + 4\mathbf{p}_{i-1} + \mathbf{p}_i),$$

$$\mathbf{p}'(0) = \mathbf{q}'(1) = \frac{1}{2}(\mathbf{p}_i - \mathbf{p}_{i-2}).$$

If we write $\mathbf{p}(u)$ in terms of the coefficient array $\mathbf{c}$,

$$\mathbf{p}(u) = \mathbf{u}^T \mathbf{c},$$

these conditions are

$$\mathbf{c}_0 = \frac{1}{6}(\mathbf{p}_{i-2} + 4\mathbf{p}_{i-1} + \mathbf{p}_i),$$

$$\mathbf{c}_1 = \frac{1}{2}(\mathbf{p}_i - \mathbf{p}_{i-2}).$$

We can apply the symmetric conditions at $\mathbf{p}(1)$:

$$\mathbf{p}(1) = \mathbf{c}_0 + \mathbf{c}_1 + \mathbf{c}_2 + \mathbf{c}_3 = \frac{1}{6}(\mathbf{p}_{i-1} + 4\mathbf{p}_i + \mathbf{p}_{i+1}),$$

$$\mathbf{p}'(1) = \mathbf{c}_1 + 2\mathbf{c}_2 + 3\mathbf{c}_3 = \frac{1}{2}(\mathbf{p}_{i+1} - \mathbf{p}_{i-1}).$$

We now have four equations for the coefficients of $\mathbf{c}$, which we can solve for a matrix $\mathbf{M}_S$, the **B-spline geometry matrix**,

$$\mathbf{M}_S = \frac{1}{6} \begin{bmatrix} 1 & 4 & 1 & 0 \\ -3 & 0 & 3 & 0 \\ 3 & -6 & 3 & 0 \\ -1 & 3 & -3 & 1 \end{bmatrix}.$$

This particular matrix yields a polynomial that has several important properties. We can see these properties by again examining the blending polynomials:

$$\mathbf{b}(u) = \mathbf{M}_S^T \mathbf{u} = \frac{1}{6} \begin{bmatrix} (1-u)^3 \\ 4 - 6u^2 + 3u^3 \\ 1 + 3u + 3u^2 - 3u^3 \\ u^3 \end{bmatrix}.$$

These polynomials are shown in Figure 11.23. We can show, as we did for the Bézier polynomials, that

$$\sum_{i=0}^{3} b_i(u) = 1,$$

and, in the interval $0 \le u \le 1$,

$$0 \le b_i(u) \le 1.$$

Thus, the curve must lie in the convex hull of the control points, as shown in Figure 11.24. Note that the curve is used for only part of the range of the convex hull. We defined the curve to have C^1 continuity; in fact, however, it

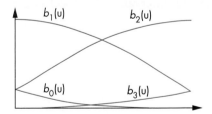

FIGURE 11.23 Spline-blending functions.

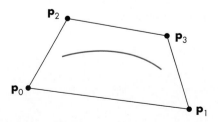

FIGURE 11.24 Convex hull for spline curve.

has C^2 continuity,[7] as we can verify by computing $\mathbf{p}''(u)$ at $u = 0$ and $u = 1$ and seeing that the values are the same for the curves on the right and left. It is for this reason that spline curves are so important. From a physical point of view, metal will bend such that the second derivative is continuous. From a visual perspective, a curve made of cubic segments with C^2 continuity will be seen as smooth, even at the join points.

Although we have used the same control-point data as those we used for the Bézier cubic to derive a smoother cubic curve, we must be aware that we are doing three times the work that we would do for Bézier or interpolating cubics. The reason is that we are using the curve between only control point $i - 1$ and control point i. A Bézier curve using the same data would be used from control point $i - 2$ to control point $i + 1$. Hence, each time we add a control point, a new spline curve must be computed, whereas for Bézier curves, we add the control points three at a time.

11.7.2 B-Splines and Basis

Instead of looking at the curve from the perspective of a single interval, we can gain additional insights by looking at the curve from the perspective of a single control point. Each control point contributes to the spline in four adjacent intervals. This property guarantees the locality of the spline; that is, if we change a single control point, we can affect the resulting curve in only four adjacent intervals. Consider the control point $\mathbf{p}_i$. In the interval between $u = 0$ and $u = 1$, it is multiplied by the blending polynomial $b_2(u)$. It also contributes to the interval on the left through $\mathbf{q}(u)$. In this interval, its contribution is $b_1(u + 1)$— we must shift the value of u by 1 to the left for this interval.

The total contribution of a single control point can be written as $B_i(u)\mathbf{p_i}$, where B_i is the function

$$
B_i(u) = \begin{cases}
0 & u < i - 2, \\
b_0(u + 2) & i - 2 \leq u < i - 1, \\
b_1(u + 1) & i - 1 \leq u < i, \\
b_2(u) & i \leq u < i + 1, \\
b_3(u - 1) & i + 1 \leq u < i + 2, \\
0 & u \geq i + 2.
\end{cases}
$$

This function is pictured in Figure 11.25. Given a set of control points $\mathbf{p}_0, \ldots,$ $\mathbf{p}_m$, we can write the entire spline with the single expression[8]

$$
\mathbf{p}(u) = \sum_{i=1}^{m-1} B_i(u)\mathbf{p}_i.
$$

---

7. If we are concerned with only G^2, rather than with C^2, continuity, we can use the extra degrees of freedom to give additional flexibility in the design of the curves; see Barsky [Bar83].
8. We determine the proper conditions for the beginning and end of the spline in Section 11.8.

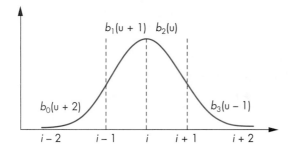

FIGURE 11.25 Spline basis function.

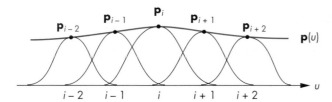

FIGURE 11.26 Approximating function over interval.

This expression shows that for the set of functions $B(u - i)$, each member is a shifted version of a single function, and the set forms a basis for all our cubic B-spline curves. Given a set of control points, we form a piecewise polynomial curve $\mathbf{p}(u)$ over the whole interval as a linear combination of basis functions. Figure 11.26 shows the function and the contributions from the individual basis functions. The general theory of splines that we develop in Section 11.8 expands this view by allowing higher-degree polynomials in the intervals and by allowing different polynomials in different intervals.

11.7.3 Spline Surfaces

B-spline surfaces can be defined in a similar way. If we start with the B-spline blending functions, the surface patch is given by

$$\mathbf{p}(u, v) = \sum_{i=0}^{3} \sum_{j=0}^{3} b_i(u) b_j(v) \mathbf{p}_{ij}.$$

This expression is of the same form as are those for our other surface patches, but as we can see from Figure 11.27, we use the patch over only the central area, and we must do nine times the work that we would do with the Bézier patch. However, because of inheritance of the convex-hull property and the additional continuity at the edges from the B-spline curves, the B-spline patch

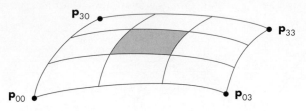

FIGURE 11.27   Spline surface patch.

is considerably smoother than a Bézier patch constructed from the same data would be.

11.8 General B-Splines

Suppose that we have a set of control points, $\mathbf{p}_0, \ldots, \mathbf{p}_m$. The general approximation problem is to find a function $\mathbf{p}(u) = [\ x(u) \quad y(u) \quad z(u)\ ]^T$, defined over an interval $u_{\min} \leq u \leq u_{\max}$, that is smooth and is close, in some sense, to the control points. Suppose we have a set of values $\{u_k\}$, called **knots**, such that

$$u_{\min} = u_0 \leq u_1 \leq \ldots \leq u_n = u_{\max}.$$

We call the sequence $u_0, u_1, \ldots, u_n$ the **knot array**.[9] In splines, the function $\mathbf{p}(u)$ is a polynomial of degree d between the knots,

$$\mathbf{p}(u) = \sum_{j=0}^{d} \mathbf{c}_{jk} u^j, \quad u_k < u < u_{k+1}.$$

Thus, to define a spline of degree d, we must define the $n(d+1)$ three-dimensional coefficients $\mathbf{c}_{jk}$. We get the required conditions by applying various continuity requirements at the knots and interpolation requirements at control points.

For example, if $d = 3$, then we have a cubic polynomial in each interval, and, for a given n, we must define $4n$ conditions. There are $n-1$ internal knots. If we want C^2 continuity at the knots, we have $3n-3$ conditions. If in addition we want to interpolate the $n+1$ control points, we have a total of $4n-2$ conditions. We can pick the other two conditions in various ways, such as by fixing the slope at the ends of the curve. However, this particular spline is global; we must solve a set of $4n$ equations in $4n$ unknowns, and each coefficient will depend on all the control points. Thus, although such a spline provides a smooth curve that

---

9. Most researchers call this sequence the *knot vector*, but that terminology violates our decision to use *vector* for only directed line segments.

interpolates the control points, it is not well suited to computer graphics and CAD.

11.8.1 Recursively Defined B-Splines

The approach taken in B-splines is to define the spline in terms of a set of basis, or blending, functions, each of which is nonzero over only the regions spanned by a few knots. Thus, we write the function $\mathbf{p}(u)$ as an expansion:

$$\mathbf{p}(u) = \sum_{i=0}^{m} B_{id}(u)\mathbf{p}_i,$$

where each function $B_{id}(u)$ is a polynomial of degree d, except at the knots, and is zero outside the interval $(u_{i_{\min}}, u_{i_{\max}})$. The name *B-splines* comes from the term *basis splines*, in recognition that the set of functions $\{B_{id}(u)\}$ forms a basis for the given knot sequence and degree. Although there are numerous ways to define basis splines, of particular importance is the set of splines defined by the **Cox-deBoor recursion**:[10]

$$B_{k0} = \begin{cases} 1, & u_k \leq u \leq u_{k+1}; \\ 0, & \text{otherwise} \end{cases}$$

$$B_{kd} = \frac{u - u_k}{u_{k+d} - u_k} B_{k,d-1}(u) + \frac{u_{k+d} - u}{u_{k+d+1} - u_{k+1}} B_{k+1,\,d-1}(u).$$

Each of the first set of functions, B_{k0}, is constant over one interval and is zero everywhere else; each of the second, B_{k1}, is linear over each of two intervals and is zero elsewhere; each of the third, B_{k2}, is quadratic over each of three intervals; and so on (Figure 11.28). In general, B_{kd} is nonzero over the $d+1$ intervals between u_k and u_{k+d+1}, and it is a polynomial of degree d in each of these intervals. At the knots, there is C^{d-1} continuity. The convex-hull property holds because

$$\sum_{i=0}^{m} B_{i,d}(u) = 1,$$

and

$$0 \leq B_{id}(u) \leq 1.$$

However, because each B_{id} is nonzero in only $d+1$ intervals, each control point can affect only $d+1$ intervals, and each point on the resulting curve is within the convex hull defined by these $d+1$ control points.

---

10. This formula is also known as the *deCasteljau recursion*.

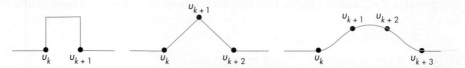

FIGURE 11.28   First three basis functions.

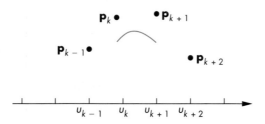

FIGURE 11.29   Uniform B-spline.

Note that careful examination of the Cox-deBoor formula shows that each step of the recursion is a linear interpolation of functions produced on the previous step. Linear interpolation of polynomials of degree k produces polynomials of degree $k + 1$.

A set of spline basis functions is defined by the desired degree and the knot array. Note that we need what appears to be $d - 1$ "extra" knot values to define our spline because the recursion requires u_0 through u_{n+d} to define splines from u_0 to u_{n+1}. These additional values are determined by conditions at the beginning and end of the whole spline.

Note that we have made no statement about the knot values other than that $u_k \leq u_{k+1}$. If we define any 0/0 term that arises in evaluating the recursion as equal to 1, then we can have repeated, or multiple, knots. If the knots are equally spaced, we have a **uniform spline**. However, we can achieve more flexibility by allowing not only nonuniform knot spacing but also repeated ($u_k = u_{k+1}$) knots. Let us examine a few of the possibilities.

11.8.2 Uniform Splines

Consider the uniform knot sequence $\{0, 1, 2, \ldots, n\}$. The cubic B-spline we discussed in Section 11.7 could be derived from the Cox-deBoor formula with equally spaced knots. We use the numbering that we used there (which is shifted from the Cox-deBoor indexing); between knots k and $k + 1$, we use the control points $\mathbf{p}_{k-1}$, $\mathbf{p}_k$, $\mathbf{p}_{k+1}$, and $\mathbf{p}_{k+2}$. Thus, we have a curve defined for only the interval $u = 1$ to $u = n - 1$. For the data shown in Figure 11.29, we define a curve that does not span the knots. In certain situations, such as that depicted in

Figure 11.30, we can use the periodic nature of the control-point data to define the spline over the entire knot sequence. These **uniform periodic B-splines** have the property that each spline basis function is a shifted version of a single function.

FIGURE 11.30 Periodic uniform B-spline.

11.8.3 Nonuniform B-Splines

Repeated knots have the effect of pulling the spline closer to the control point associated with the knot. If a knot at the end has multiplicity $d + 1$, the B-spline of degree d must interpolate the point. Hence, one solution to the problem of the spline not having sufficient data to span the desired interval is to repeat knots at the ends, forcing interpolation at the endpoints, and using uniform knots everywhere else. Such splines are called **open splines**.

The knot sequence $\{0, 0, 0, 0, 1, 2, \ldots, n - 1, n, n, n, n\}$ is often used for cubic B-splines. The sequence $\{0, 0, 0, 0, 1, 1, 1, 1\}$ is of particular interest, because, in this case, the cubic B-spline becomes the cubic Bézier curve. In the general case, we can repeat internal knots, and we can have any desired spacing of knots.

11.8.4 NURBS

In our development of B-splines, we have assumed that $\mathbf{p}(u)$ is the array $[\, x(u) \quad y(u) \quad z(u) \,]^T$. In two dimensions, however, we could have replaced it with simply $[\, x(u) \quad y(u) \,]^T$, and all our equations would be unchanged. Indeed, the equations remain unchanged if we go to four-dimensional B-splines. Consider a control point in three dimensions:

$$\mathbf{p}_i = [x_i \quad y_i \quad z_i].$$

The weighted homogeneous-coordinate representation of this point is

$$\mathbf{q}_i = w_i \begin{bmatrix} x_i \\ y_i \\ z_i \\ 1 \end{bmatrix}.$$

The idea is to use the weights w_i to increase or decrease the importance of a particular control point. We can use these weighted points to form a four-dimensional B-spline. The first three components of the resulting spline are simply the B-spline representation of the weighted points,

$$\mathbf{q}(u) = \begin{bmatrix} x(u) \\ y(u) \\ z(u) \end{bmatrix} = \sum_{i=0}^{n} B_{i,d}(u) w_i \mathbf{p}_i.$$

The w component is the scalar B-spline polynomial derived from the set of weights:

$$w(u) = \sum_{i=0}^{n} B_{i,d}(u) w_i.$$

In homogeneous coordinates, this representation has a w component that may not be equal to 1; thus, we must do a perspective division to derive the three-dimensional points:

$$\mathbf{p}(u) = \frac{1}{w(u)} \mathbf{q}(u) = \frac{\sum_{i=0}^{n} B_{i,d}(u) w_i \mathbf{p}_i}{\sum_{i=0}^{n} B_{i,d}(u) w_i}.$$

Each component of $\mathbf{p}(u)$ is now a rational function in u, and because we have not restricted the knots in any way, we have derived a **nonuniform rational B-spline (NURBS)** curve.

NURBS curves retain all the properties of our three-dimensional B-splines, such as the convex-hull and continuity properties. They have two other properties that make them of particular interest in computer graphics and CAD.

If we apply an affine transformation to a B-spline curve or surface, we get the same function as the B-spline derived from the transformed control points. Because perspective transformations are not affine, most splines will not be handled correctly in perspective viewing. However, the perspective division embedded in the construction of NURBS curves ensures that NURBS curves are handled correctly in perspective views.

Quadric surfaces are usually defined as algebraic implicit forms. If we are using nonrational splines, we can only approximate these surfaces. However, quadrics can be shown to be a special case of quadratic NURBS curve; thus, we can use a single modeling method, NURBS curves, for the most widely used curves and surfaces (see Exercises 11.14 and 11.15). Color Plate 5 shows the mesh generated by a NURBS modeling of the surfaces that make up the object in Color Plate 1. OpenGL ultimately renders this mesh with polygons. Color Plates 17 and 18 show a NURBS surface used to model moving water in an animated film from Dreamworks Animation Studio. In this example, a particle system (Chapter 10) was used to alter vertices in the mesh.

11.9   Rendering of Curves and Surfaces

Once we have defined a scene with curves and surfaces, we must find a way to render it. There are several approaches. In one, we compute points on the object that are the intersection of rays from the center of projection through pixels with the object. However, except for quadrics (Section 11.11), the intersection calculation requires the solution of nonlinear equations of too high a degree to be practical for real-time computation. A second approach involves evaluating the curve or surface at a sufficient number of points that we can approximate it with our standard flat objects. We focus on this approach for parametric polynomial curves and surfaces.

11.9.1 Polynomial Evaluation Methods

Suppose that we have a representation over our standard interval

$$\mathbf{p}(u) = \sum_{i=0}^{n} \mathbf{c}_i u^i, \quad 0 \le u \le 1.$$

We can evaluate $\mathbf{p}(u)$ at some set of values $\{u_k\}$, and we can use a polyline (or GL_LINE_STRIP) to approximate the curve. Rather than evaluate each term u^k independently, we can group the terms as

$$\mathbf{p}(u) = \mathbf{c}_0 + u(\mathbf{c}_1 + u(\mathbf{c}_2 + u(\ldots + \mathbf{c}_n u))).$$

This grouping shows that we need only n multiplications to evaluate each $p(u_k)$; this algorithm is known as **Horner's method**. For our typical cubic $\mathbf{p}(u)$, the grouping becomes

$$\mathbf{p}(u) = \mathbf{c}_0 + u(\mathbf{c}_1 + u(\mathbf{c}_2 + u\mathbf{c}_3)).$$

If the points $\{u_i\}$ are spaced uniformly, we can use the method of **forward differences** to evaluate $\mathbf{p}(u_k)$ using $O(n)$ additions and no multiplications. The forward differences are defined iteratively by the formulas

$$\Delta^{(0)}\mathbf{p}(u_k) = \mathbf{p}(u_k),$$

$$\Delta^{(1)}\mathbf{p}(u_k) = \mathbf{p}(u_{k+1}) - \mathbf{p}(u_k),$$

$$\Delta^{(m+1)}\mathbf{p}(u_k) = \Delta^{(m)}\mathbf{p}(u_{k+1}) - \Delta^{(m)}\mathbf{p}(u_k).$$

If $u_{k+1} - u_k = h$ is constant, then we can show that, if $\mathbf{p}(u)$ is a polynomial of degree n, then $\Delta^{(n)}\mathbf{p}(u_k)$ is constant for all k. This result suggests the strategy illustrated in Figure 11.31 for the scalar cubic polynomial

$$p(u) = 1 + 3u + 2u^2 + u^3.$$

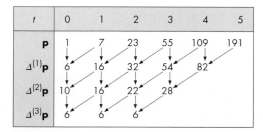

FIGURE 11.31 Construction of a forward-difference table.

t	0	1	2	3	4	5
p	1	7	23	55 → 109 → 191		
$\Delta^{(1)}$**p**	6	16	32 → 54 → 82			
$\Delta^{(2)}$**p**	10	16 → 22 → 28				
$\Delta^{(3)}$**p**	6 → 6 → 6					

FIGURE 11.32   Use of a forward-difference table.

We need the first $n + 1$ values of $p(u_k)$ to find $\Delta^{(n)}p(u_0)$. But, once we have $\Delta^{(n)}p(u_0)$, we can copy this value across the table and work upward, as shown in Figure 11.32, to compute successive values of $p(u_k)$, using the rearranged recurrence

$$\Delta^{(m-1)}(p_{k+1}) = \Delta^{(m)}p(u_k) + \Delta^{(m-1)}p(u_k).$$

This method is efficient, but is not without its faults: It applies only to a uniform grid, and it is prone to accumulation of numerical errors.

11.9.2   Recursive Subdivision of Bézier Polynomials

The most elegant rendering method performs recursive subdivision of the Bézier curve. The method is based on the use of the convex hull and never requires explicit evaluation of the polynomial. Suppose that we have a cubic Bézier polynomial (the method also applies to higher-degree Bézier curves). We know that the curve must lie within the convex hull of the control points. We can break the curve into two separate polynomials, $l(u)$ and $r(u)$, each valid over one-half of the original interval. Because the original polynomial is a cubic, each of these polynomials also is a cubic. Note that because each is to be used over one-half of the original interval, we must rescale the parameter u for l and r so that, as u varies over the range $(0, 1)$, $l(u)$ traces the left half of $\mathbf{p}(u)$, and $r(u)$ traces the right half of $\mathbf{p}$. Each of our new polynomials has four control points that both define the polynomial and form its convex hull. We denote these two sets of points by $\{l_0, l_1, l_2, l_3\}$ and $\{r_0, r_1, r_2, r_3\}$; the original control points for $\mathbf{p}(u)$ are $\{\mathbf{p}_0, \mathbf{p}_1, \mathbf{p}_2, \mathbf{p}_3\}$. These points and the two convex hulls are shown in Figure 11.33. Note that the convex hulls for l and r must lie inside the convex hull for p, a result known as the **variation-diminishing property** of the Bézier curve.

Consider the left polynomial. We can test the convex hull for flatness by measuring the deviation of l_1 and l_2 from the line segment connecting l_0 and l_3. If they are close, we can draw the line segment instead of the curve. If they are not close, we can divide l into two halves and test the two new convex hulls for flatness. Thus, we have a recursion that never requires us to evaluate

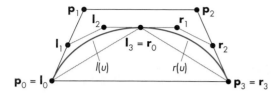

FIGURE 11.33 Convex hulls and control points.

points on a polynomial, but we have yet to discuss how to find $\{l_0, l_1, l_2, l_3\}$ and $\{r_0, r_1, r_2, r_3\}$. We shall find the hull for $l(u)$; the calculation for $r(u)$ is symmetric. We can start with

$$p(u) = u^T M_B \begin{bmatrix} p_0 \\ p_1 \\ p_2 \\ p_3 \end{bmatrix},$$

where

$$M_B = \begin{bmatrix} 1 & 0 & 0 & 0 \\ -3 & 3 & 0 & 0 \\ 3 & -6 & 3 & 0 \\ -1 & 3 & -3 & -1 \end{bmatrix}.$$

The polynomial $l(u)$ must interpolate $p(0)$ and $p\left(\frac{1}{2}\right)$; hence,

$$l(0) = l_0 = p_0,$$

$$l(1) = l_3 = p\left(\frac{1}{2}\right) = \frac{1}{8}(p_0 + 3p_1 + 3p_2 + p_3).$$

At $u = 0$, the slope of l must match the slope of p, but, because the parameter for p covers only the range $(0, \frac{1}{2})$, while u varies over $(0, 1)$, implicitly we have made the substitution $\bar{u} = 2u$. Consequently, derivatives for l and p are related by $d\bar{u} = 2du$, and

$$l'(0) = 3(l_1 - l_0) = p'(0) = \frac{3}{2}(p_1 - p_0).$$

Likewise, at the midpoint,

$$l'(1) = (l_3 - l_2) = p'\left(\frac{1}{2}\right) = \frac{3}{8}(-p_0 - p_1 + p_2 + p_3).$$

These four equations can be solved algebraically. Alternatively, this solution can be expressed geometrically, with the aid of Figure 11.34. Here, we construct

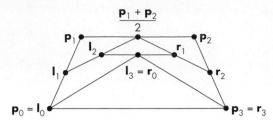

FIGURE 11.34   Construction of subdivision curves.

both the left and right sets of control points concurrently. First, we note that the interpolation condition requires that

$$\mathbf{l}_0 = \mathbf{p}_0,$$
$$\mathbf{r}_3 = \mathbf{p}_3.$$

We can verify by substitution in the four equations that the slopes on the left and right yield

$$\mathbf{l}_1 = \frac{1}{2}(\mathbf{p}_0 + \mathbf{p}_1),$$

$$\mathbf{r}_2 = \frac{1}{2}(\mathbf{p}_2 + \mathbf{p}_3).$$

The interior points are given by

$$\mathbf{l}_2 = \frac{1}{2}\left(\mathbf{l}_1 + \frac{1}{2}(\mathbf{p}_1 + \mathbf{p}_2)\right),$$

$$\mathbf{r}_1 = \frac{1}{2}\left(\mathbf{r}_2 + \frac{1}{2}(\mathbf{p}_1 + \mathbf{p}_2)\right).$$

Finally, the shared middle point is given by

$$\mathbf{l}_3 = \mathbf{r}_0 = \frac{1}{2}(\mathbf{l}_2 + \mathbf{r}_1).$$

The advantage of this formulation is that we can determine both sets of control points using only shifts (for the divisions by 2) and adds. However, one of the advantages of the subdivision approach is that it can be made adaptive, and only one of the sides may require subdivision at some point in the rendering. Also, note that, because the rendering of the curve need not take place until the rasterization stage of the pipeline and can be done in screen or window coordinates, the limited resolution of the display places a limit on how many times the convex hull needs to be subdivided (Exercise 11.18).

11.9.3 Rendering of Other Polynomial Curves by Subdivision

Just as any polynomial is a Bézier polynomial, it is also an interpolating polynomial, a B-spline polynomial, and any other type of polynomial for a properly selected set of control points. The efficiency of the Bézier subdivision algorithm is such that we usually are better off converting another curve form to Bézier form, and then using the subdivision algorithm. A conversion algorithm can be obtained directly from our curve formulations. Consider a cubic Bézier curve. We can write it in terms of the Bézier matrix $\mathbf{M}_B$ as

$$\mathbf{p}(u) = \mathbf{u}^T \mathbf{M}_B \mathbf{p},$$

where $\mathbf{p}$ is the **geometry matrix** of control points. The same polynomial can be written as

$$\mathbf{p}(u) = \mathbf{u}^T \mathbf{M} \mathbf{q},$$

where $\mathbf{M}$ is the matrix for some other type of polynomial and $\mathbf{q}$ is the matrix of control points for this type. We assume that both polynomials are defined over the same interval. The polynomials will be identical if we choose

$$\mathbf{q} = \mathbf{M}^{-1} \mathbf{M}_B \mathbf{p}.$$

For the conversion from interpolation to Bézier, the controlling matrix is

$$\mathbf{M}_B^{-1} \mathbf{M}_I = \begin{bmatrix} 1 & 0 & 0 & 0 \\ -\frac{5}{6} & 3 & -\frac{3}{2} & \frac{1}{3} \\ \frac{1}{3} & -\frac{3}{2} & 3 & -\frac{5}{6} \\ 0 & 0 & 0 & 1 \end{bmatrix}.$$

For the conversion between cubic B-splines and cubic Bézier curves, it is

$$\mathbf{M}_B^{-1} \mathbf{M}_S = \frac{1}{6} \begin{bmatrix} 1 & 4 & 1 & 0 \\ 0 & 4 & 2 & 0 \\ 0 & 2 & 4 & 0 \\ 0 & 1 & 4 & 1 \end{bmatrix}.$$

Figure 11.35 shows four control points and the cubic Bézier, interpolating, and spline polynomials. All three were generated with OpenGL's Bézier evaluators. The interpolating and spline forms were generated as Bézier curves, from the new control points derived from the matrices $\mathbf{M}_B^{-1} \mathbf{M}_I$ and $\mathbf{M}_B^{-1} \mathbf{M}_S$. Note that for the spline case, the resulting curve is generated between only the second and third of the original control points.

11.9.4 Subdivision of Bézier Surfaces

We can extend our subdivision algorithm to Bézier surfaces. Consider the cubic surface in Figure 11.36, with the 16 control points shown. Each four points in a row or column determine a Bézier curve that can be subdivided. However, our

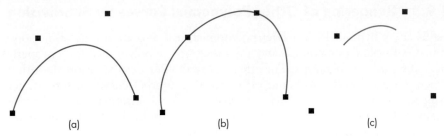

FIGURE 11.35   Cubic polynomials generated as Bézier curves by conversion of control points. (a) Bézier polynomial. (b) Interpolating polynomial. (c) B-spline polynomial.

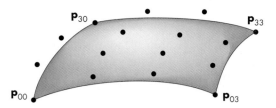

FIGURE 11.36   Cubic Bézier surface.

subdivision algorithm should split the patch into four patches, and we have no control points along the center of the patch. We can proceed in two steps.

First, we apply our curve-subdivision technique to the four curves determined by the 16 control points in the v direction. Thus, for each of $u = 0, \frac{1}{3}, \frac{2}{3}, 1$, we create two groups of four control points, with the middle point shared by each group. There are then seven different points along each original curve; these points are indicated in Figure 11.37 by circles. We see that there are three types of points: original control points that are kept after the subdivision (gray), original control points that are discarded after the subdivision (white), and new points created by the subdivision (black). We now subdivide in the u direction using these points. Consider the rows of constant v, where v is one of $0, \frac{1}{3}, \frac{2}{3}, 1$. There are seven groups of four points. Each group defines a Bézier curve for a constant v. We can subdivide in the u direction, each time creating two groups of four points, again with the middle point shared. These points are indicated in Figure 11.38. If we divide these points in four groups of 16, with points on the edges shared (Figure 11.39), each quadrant contains 16 points that are the control points for a subdivided Bézier surface.

Compared to the calculation for curves, the test for whether the new convex hull is flat enough to stop a subdivision process is more difficult. Many renderers use a fixed number of subdivisions, often letting the user pick the number. If a high-quality rendering is desired, we can let the subdivision continue until the projected size of the convex hull is less than the size of one pixel.

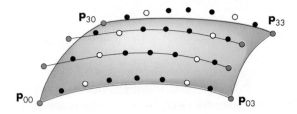

- New points created by subdivision
- Old points discarded after subdivision
- Old points retained after subdivision

FIGURE 11.37   First subdivision of surface.

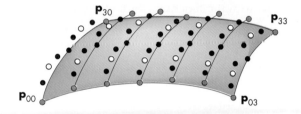

- New points created by subdivision
- Old points discarded after subdivision
- Old points retained after subdivision

FIGURE 11.38   Points after second subdivision.

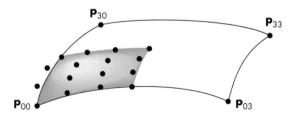

FIGURE 11.39   Subdivided quadrant.

11.10   The Utah Teapot

We conclude our discussion of parametric surfaces with an example of recursive subdivision of a set of cubic Bézier patches. The object that we show has become known as the **Utah teapot**. The data for the teapot were created at the University of Utah by Mike Newell for testing of various rendering algorithms. These data have been used in the graphics community for over 30 years. The teapot data consist of the control points for 32 bicubic Bézier patches. They are given in terms of 306 vertices (numbered from 1 to 306). The first 12 patches define the body of the teapot; the next four define the handle; the next four define the spout; the following eight define the lid; and the final four define the bottom. These data are widely available.

For purposes of illustration, let us assume that we want to subdivide each patch n times and, after these subdivisions, we will render the final vertices using either line segments or polygons passing through the four corners of each patch. Thus, our final drawing can be done with the function (for line segments)

```
typedef GLfloat point3[3];
void draw_patch(point3 p[4][4])
{
    glBegin(GL_LINE_LOOP);
        glVertex3fv(p[0][0]);
        glVertex3fv(p[3][0]);
        glVertex3fv(p[3][3]);
        glVertex3fv(p[0][3]);
    glEnd();
}
```

We build our patch subdivider from the curve subdivider for a cubic curve c, using our point3 type

```
void divide_curve(point3 c[4], point3 r[4], point3 l[4])
{
    int i;
    point3 t;
    for(i=0;i<3;i++)
    {
        l[0][i]=c[0][i];
        r[3][i]=c[3][i];
        l[1][i]=(c[1][i]+c[0][i])/2;
        r[2][i]=(c[2][i]+c[3][i])/2;
        t[i]=(l[1][i]+r[2][i])/2;
        l[2][i]=(t[i]+l[1][i])/2;
        r[1][i]=(t[i]+r[2][i])/2;
        l[3][i]=r[0][i]=(l[2][i]+r[1][i])/2;
    }
}
```

The patch subdivider is easier to write—but is slightly less efficient—if we assume that we have a matrix-transpose function transpose. This code is then

```
void divide_patch(point3 p[4][4], int n)
{
    point3 q[4][4], r[4][4], s[4][4], t[4][4];
    point3 a[4][4], b[4][4];
    int i,j, k;
    if(n==0) draw_patch(p);
    else
    {
        for(k=0; k<4; k++) divide_curve(p[k], a[k], b[k]);
        transpose(a);
        transpose(b);
        for(k=0; k<4; k++)
        {
            divide_curve(a[k], q[k], r[k]);
            divide_curve(b[k], s[k], t[k]);
        }
        divide_patch(q, n-1);
        divide_patch(r, n-1);
        divide_patch(s, n-1);
        divide_patch(t, n-1);
    }
}
```

A complete teapot-rendering program using shaded polygons is given in Appendix A. That program contains the teapot data.

The teapot is available as an object in the GLUT library with automatic generation of normals for shading. Here, we are interested in using it to demonstrate our recursive-subdivision algorithm. Figure 11.40 shows the teapot as a wire frame at three levels of subdivision, along with a simple rendering with constant shading. Note that the various patches have different curvatures and sizes; thus, carrying out all subdivisions to the same depth can create many unnecessarily small polygons.

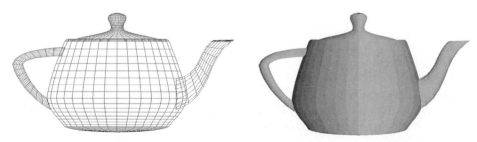

FIGURE 11.40   Rendered teapots.

The OpenGL Bézier curve functions that we introduce in Section 11.12 will allow us to render the patches through the API, using only a few function calls. These functions are usually implemented by means of recursive subdivision, but should be more efficient than an implementation in the user program would be.

11.11   Algebraic Surfaces

Although quadrics can be generated as a special case of NURBS curves, this class of algebraic objects is of such importance that it merits independent discussion. Quadrics are the most important case of the algebraic surfaces that we introduced in Section 11.1.

11.11.1   Quadrics

Quadric surfaces are described by implicit algebraic equations in which each term is a polynomial of the form $x^i y^j z^k$, with $i + j + k \leq 2$. Any quadric can be written in the form

$$q(x, y, z) = a_{11}x^2 + 2a_{12}xy + a_{22}y^2 + a_{33}z^2 + 2a_{23}yz + 2a_{13}xz$$
$$+ b_1 x + b_2 y + b_3 z + c = 0.$$

This class of surfaces includes ellipsoids, parabaloids, and hyperboloids. We can write the general equation in matrix form in terms of the three-dimensional column matrix $\mathbf{p} = [\, x \quad y \quad z \,]^T$ as the **quadratic form**

$$\mathbf{p}^T \mathbf{A} \mathbf{p} + \mathbf{b}^T \mathbf{p} + c = 0,$$

where

$$\mathbf{A} = \begin{bmatrix} a_{11} & a_{12} & a_{13} \\ a_{12} & a_{22} & a_{23} \\ a_{13} & a_{23} & a_{33} \end{bmatrix}, \qquad \mathbf{b} = \begin{bmatrix} b_1 \\ b_2 \\ b_3 \end{bmatrix}.$$

The 10 independent coefficients in $\mathbf{A}$, $\mathbf{b}$, and c determine a given quadric. However, for the purpose of classification, we can apply a sequence of rotations and translations that reduces a quadric to a standard form without changing the type of surface. In three dimensions, we can write such a transformation as

$$\mathbf{p}' = \mathbf{M}\mathbf{p} + \mathbf{d}.$$

This substitution creates another quadratic form with $\mathbf{A}$ replaced by the matrix $\mathbf{M}^T \mathbf{A} \mathbf{M}$. The matrix $\mathbf{M}$ can always be chosen to be a rotation matrix that such $\mathbf{D} = \mathbf{M}^T \mathbf{A} \mathbf{M}$ is a diagonal matrix. The diagonal elements of $\mathbf{D}$ can be used to determine the type of quadric. If, for example, the equation is that of an ellipsoid, the resulting quadratic form can be put in the form

$$a'_{11}x'^2 + a'_{22}y'^2 + a_{33}z'^2 - c' = 0,$$

where all the coefficients are positive. Note that because we can convert to a standard form by an affine transformation, quadrics are preserved by affine transformations and thus fit well with our other standard primitives.

11.11.2 Rendering of Surfaces by Ray Casting

Quadrics are easy to render because we can find the intersection of a quadric with a ray by solving a scalar quadratic equation. We represent the ray from $\mathbf{p}_0$ in the direction $\mathbf{d}$ parametrically as

$$\mathbf{p} = \mathbf{p}_0 + \alpha \mathbf{d}.$$

Substituting into the equation for the quadric, we obtain the scalar equation for α:

$$\alpha^2 \mathbf{d}^T \mathbf{A} \mathbf{d} + \alpha \mathbf{d}^T (\mathbf{b} + 2\mathbf{A}\mathbf{p}_0) + \mathbf{p}_0^T \mathbf{A} \mathbf{p}_0 + \mathbf{b}^T \mathbf{d} + c = 0.$$

As for any quadratic equation, we may find zero, one, or two real solutions. We can use this result to render a quadric into the frame buffer or as part of a ray-tracing calculation. In addition, we can apply our standard shading model at every point on a quadric because we can compute the normal by taking the derivatives

$$\mathbf{n} = \begin{bmatrix} \frac{\partial q}{\partial x} \\ \frac{\partial q}{\partial y} \\ \frac{\partial q}{\partial z} \end{bmatrix} = 2\mathbf{A}\mathbf{p} - \mathbf{b}.$$

This method of rendering can be extended to any algebraic surface. Suppose that we have an algebraic surface

$$q(\mathbf{p}) = q(x, y, z) = 0.$$

As part of the rendering pipeline, we cast a ray from the center of projection through each pixel. Each of these rays can be written in the parametric form

$$\mathbf{p}(\alpha) = \mathbf{p}_0 + \alpha \mathbf{d}.$$

Substituting this expression into q yields an implicit polynomial equation in α:

$$q(\mathbf{p}(\alpha)) = 0.$$

We can find the points of intersection by numerical methods, or for quadrics, by the quadratic formula. If we have terms up to $x^i y^j z^k$, we can have $i + j + k$ points of intersection, and the surface may require considerable time to render.

11.11.3 Subdivision Curves and Surfaces

Let us reexamine our subdivision formula from Section 11.9.2 from a slightly different perspective. We start with four points—$\mathbf{p}_0, \mathbf{p}_1, \mathbf{p}_2, \mathbf{p}_3$—and end up with

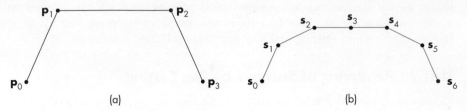

FIGURE 11.41   (a) Piecewise-linear curve determined by four points. (b) Piecewise-linear curve after one subdivision step.

seven points. We can call these new points $s_0, \ldots, s_6$. We can view each of these sets of points as defining a piecewise-linear curve, as in Figure 11.41.

We can use our subdivision formulas to relate the two sets of points:

$$s_0 = \mathbf{p}_0$$

$$s_1 = \tfrac{1}{2}(\mathbf{p}_0 + \mathbf{p}_1),$$

$$s_2 = \tfrac{1}{4}(\mathbf{p}_0 + 2\mathbf{p}_1 + \mathbf{p}_2),$$

$$s_3 = \tfrac{1}{8}(\mathbf{p}_0 + 3\mathbf{p}_1 + 3\mathbf{p}_2 + \mathbf{p}_3),$$

$$s_4 = \tfrac{1}{4}(\mathbf{p}_1 + 2\mathbf{p}_2 + \mathbf{p}_3),$$

$$s_5 = \tfrac{1}{2}(\mathbf{p}_2 + \mathbf{p}_3),$$

$$s_6 = \mathbf{p}_3.$$

The second curve is said to be a **refinement** of the first. As we saw in Section 11.9.2, we can continue the process iteratively and in the limit converge to the B-spline. However, in practice, we want to carry out only enough iterations so that the resulting piecewise-linear curve connecting the new points looks smooth. How many iterations we need to carry out depends on the size of the projected convex hull, which can be determined from the camera specifications. Thus, we have a method that allows us to render curves at different levels of detail.

These ideas and their benefits are not limited to B-splines. Over the past few years, a variety of methods for generating these **subdivision curves** have appeared. Some interpolate points—such as $\mathbf{p}_0$ and $\mathbf{p}_3$—while others do not interpolate any of the original points. But in all cases, the refined curves converge to a smooth curve.

11.11.4   Mesh Subdivision

The next issue we examine is how can we apply these ideas to surfaces. We saw one method in Section 11.9.2, but of even greater interest is how we might apply these ideas to meshes of polygons. A theory of **subdivision surfaces** has emerged that deals with both the theoretical and practical aspects of these ideas.

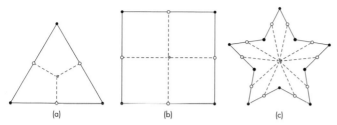

FIGURE 11.42   Polygon subdivision. (a) Triangle. (b) Rectangle. (c) Star-shaped polygon.

Rather than generating a general subdivision scheme, we shall focus on meshes of triangles and meshes of quadrilaterals. In practice, many modeling programs produce one of these types of meshes or a mesh consisting of only triangles and quadrilaterals. If we start with a more general mesh, we can also use tessellation to replace the original mesh with one consisting of only triangles or quadrilaterals.

We can form a quadrilateral mesh from an arbitrary mesh using the Catmull-Clark method. We divide each edge in half, creating a new vertex at the midpoint. We create an additional vertex at the **centroid** of each polygon, that is, the point that is the average of the vertices that form the polygon. We then form a quadrilateral mesh by connecting each original vertex to the new vertices on either side of it and connecting the two new vertices to the centroid. Figure 11.42 shows the subdivision for some simple polygons. Note that in each case the subdivision creates a quadrilateral mesh.

Once we have created the quadrilateral mesh, it is clear that successive subdivisions create a finer quadrilateral mesh. However, we have yet to do anything to create a smoother surface. In particular, we want to ensure as much continuity as possible at the vertices.

Consider the following procedure. First, we compute the average position of each polygon, its centroid. Then, we replace each vertex by the average of the centroids of all the polygons that contain the vertex. At this point, we have a smoother surface but one for which at vertices not of valence four, we can see sharp changes in smoothness. The Catmull-Clark scheme produces a smoother surface with one additional step. For each vertex not of valence 4, we replace it by

$$\mathbf{p} = \mathbf{p}_0 + \frac{4}{k}\mathbf{p}_1,$$

where $\mathbf{p}_0$ is the vertex position before the averaging step; $\mathbf{p}_1$ is its position after the averaging pass; and k is the valence of the vertex. The **valence** of a vertex is the number of polygons that share the vertex. This method tends to move edge vertices at corners more than other outer vertices. Figure 11.43 shows the sequence for a single rectangle. In Figure 11.43(a), the original vertices are black and the vertices at the midpoints of the edges are white. The centroid of the original polygon is the gray vertex at the center and the centroids of the subdivided polygons are shown as colored vertices. Figure 11.43(b) shows

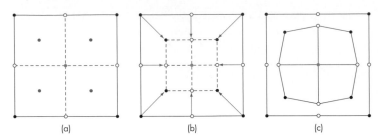

(a)   (b)   (c)

FIGURE 11.43   Catmull-Clark subdivision.

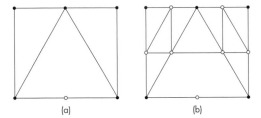

(a)   (b)

FIGURE 11.44   Loop subdivision. (a) Triangular mesh. (b) Triangles after one subdivision.

the movement of the vertices by averaging and Figure 11.43(c) shows the final Catmull-Clark subdivision after the correction factor has been applied.

This scheme does not work as well for meshes that start with all triangles because the interior vertices have high valences that do not change with refinement. For triangular meshes, there is a simple method called *Loop subdivision* that we can describe as a variant of the general scheme. We start by doing a standard subdivision of each triangle by connecting the bisectors of the sides to create four triangles. We proceed as before but use a weighted centroid of the vertices with a weight of $1/4$ for the vertex that is being moved and $3/8$ for the other two vertices that form the triangle. We can get a smoother surface by taking a weighted average of the vertex positions before and after the averaging step as we did for the Catmull-Clark scheme. Loop's method uses a weight of $\frac{5}{3} - \frac{8}{3}(\frac{3}{8} + \frac{1}{4}\cos(\frac{2\pi}{k}))^2$. Figure 11.44 shows a simple triangle mesh and the resulting mesh after the subdivision step.

The figures in Color Plate 29 were developed using subdivision surfaces. Figure 11.45 shows a sequence of meshes generated by a subdivision-surface algorithm and the rendered surface from the highest resolution mesh. Note that the original mesh contains polygons with different numbers of sides and vertices with different valences. Also, note that as the mesh is subdivided, each subdivision step yields a smoother surface.

We have not covered some tricky issues such as the data structures needed to ensure that when we insert vertices we get consistent results for shared edges. The references in Suggested Readings should help you get started.

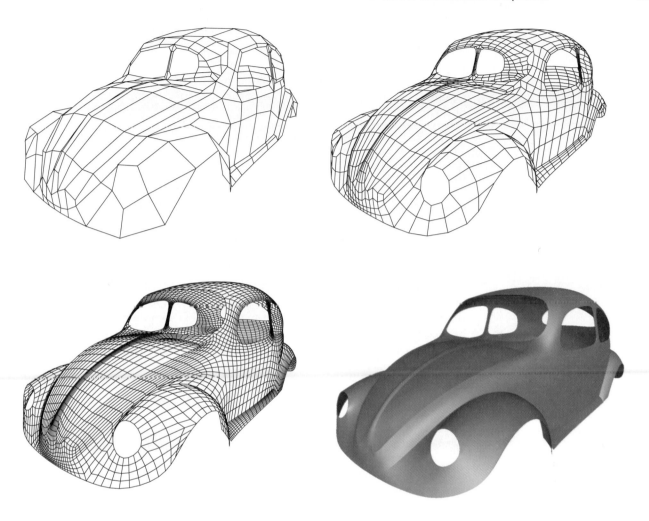

FIGURE 11.45 Successive subdivisions of polygonal mesh and rendered surface. (Images courtesy Caltech Multi-Res Modeling Group)

11.12 Curves and Surfaces in OpenGL

OpenGL supports Bézier curves and surfaces through mechanisms, called **evaluators**, that can be used to compute values for the Bernstein polynomials of any order. Evaluators do not require uniform spacing of control points, and because we can use Bézier curves and surfaces to generate other types of polynomial curves and surfaces by generating new control points, this mechanism is flexible. We can use evaluators to generate one-, two-, three-, and four-dimensional curves and surfaces. Curves use one-dimensional evaluators, which evaluate the Bernstein polynomials in one variable. We might use one-dimensional evaluators to define color maps or paths in time for animations. The GLU library uses this mechanism in four dimensions to provide NURBS curves. Two-dimensional evaluators evaluate the Bernstein polynomials in two variables and are used primarily to generate surfaces. In addition to defining curves and surfaces, the OpenGL evaluator functions can also provide colors, normals, and texture coordinates.

11.12.1 Bézier Curves

For curves, we define a one-dimensional evaluator through the function

```
glMap1f(type, u_min, u_max, stride, order, point_array)
```

as part of our initialization. The type parameter specifies the type of objects that we want to evaluate using Bézier polynomials. Options include three- and four-dimensional points, RGBA colors, normals, indexed colors, and one- through four-dimensional texture coordinates. The control-point data are in the array pointed to by point_array. The values u_min and u_max define the range of the parameter. The value of stride is the number of values of the parameter between curve segments. For example, in our cubic B-spline, we stride three points for each curve segment. The order parameter is 1 greater than the degree of the polynomial. Thus, for our cubic B-spline defined over (0, 1), we set up an evaluator for a three-dimensional curve by

```
point data[]={...}
glMap1f(GL_MAP2_VERTEX_3, 0.0, 1.0, 3, 4, data);
```

We can define multiple evaluators that are active at the same time and can use them to evaluate, for example, curves and normals at the same time. Each evaluator must be enabled through

```
glEnable(type);
```

Once an evaluator has been set up, whenever we need a value from the active evaluators, we use the function

```
glEvalCoord1f(u);
```

Thus, glEvalCoord1f can replace any combination of glVertex, glColor, and glNormal, depending on which evaluators have been enabled. Suppose that we have defined evaluators for the cubic Bézier curve over (0,10) and the array of control points. We can get 100 equally spaced points on the curve by the call

```
glBegin(GL_LINE_STRIP)
    for(i=0; i<100; i++) glEvalCoord1f( (float) i/100.0);
glEnd();
```

OpenGL provides an alternative if the values of u are equally spaced. In this case, we can use the functions

```
glMapGrid1f(100,0.0, 10.0);
glEvalMesh1(GL_LINE, 0, 100);
```

The first function sets up the uniform grid with 100 intervals; the second function generates the desired curve.

11.12.2 Bézier Surfaces

Bézier surfaces are generated in a manner similar to curves. We can use the functions glMap2 and glEvalCoord2, but now there are two parameters, u and v, to specify. For example, a bicubic Bézier surface over the region $(0, 1) \times (0, 1)$ can be set up with the function call

```
glMap2f(GL_MAP2_VERTEX_3, 0.0, 1.0, 3, 4, 0.0, 1.0, 12, 4, data);
```

We have to specify the order and stride for both parameters, allowing additional flexibility in defining the surface. Note that the stride for the second variable is 12 because the array data stores the information by rows. Hence, we step forward three floats to get the next element on the same row but must go through 12 floats to get to the element in the next column. The corresponding evaluator calls depend on whether we want to draw a mesh or to create a set of polygons for shading. For the mesh, we have to make sets of calls to the evaluator of the form

```
for(j=0; j<100; j++)
{
    glBegin(GL_LINE_STRIP);
        for(i=0; i<100; i++)
          glEvalCoord2f( (float) i/100.0, (float) j/100.0);
    glEnd();
    glBegin(GL_LINE_STRIP);
        for(i=0; i<100; i++)
          glEvalCoord2f( (float) j/100.0, (float) i/100.0);
    glEnd();
}
```

For quadrilaterals, the calls look like

```
for(j=0; j<99; j++)
{
    glBegin(GL_QUAD_STRIP);
    for(i=0; i<=100; i++)
    {
      glEvalCoord2f( (float) i/100.0, (float) j/100.0);
```

```
        glEvalCoord2f( (float) (i+1)/100.0, (float) j/100.0);
    }
    glEnd();
}
```

For uniform meshes, we can use `glMapGrid2` and `glEvalMesh2`. Thus, as part of the initialization, we specify

```
glMapGrid2f(100, 0.0, 1.0, 100, 0.0, 1.0);
```

As part of the display function, we call

```
glEvalMesh2(GL_FILL,0,100,0,100);
```

There is still a problem. Unless we enable lighting, if we display these polygons, we will see a flat filled area. We can enable lighting as in Chapter 6, but the shading calculations require the normals at the vertices. Although we could evaluate these normals ourselves by differentiating the appropriate polynomials, we can also ask OpenGL to generate normals automatically as the evaluators are used. We need only to enable the option

```
glEnable(GL_AUTO_NORMAL);
```

when we enable the lighting options.

11.12.3 Displaying the Teapot

We can display the teapot using OpenGL Bézier functions. Suppose that we first read in the vertex and patch information and place it in an array

```
GLfloat data[32][4][4];
```

If we want to display the teapot as a wire frame, we can simply initialize the grid:

```
void myinit()
{
  glEnable(GL_MAP2_VERTEX_3);
  glMapGrid2f(20, 0.0, 1.0, 20, 0.0, 1.0);
}
```

Then in the display callback, we draw the line segments:

```
for(k=0;k<32;k++)
{
```

```
glMap2f(GL_MAP2_VERTEX_3, 0, 1, 3, 4, 0, 1, 12, 4,
                 &data[k][0][0][0]);
for (j = 0; j <= 8; j++)
{
    glBegin(GL_LINE_STRIP);
    for (i = 0; i <= 30; i++)
        glEvalCoord2f((GLfloat)i/30.0, (GLfloat)j/8.0);
    glEnd();
    glBegin(GL_LINE_STRIP);
    for (i = 0; i <= 30; i++)
        glEvalCoord2f((GLfloat)j/8.0, (GLfloat)i/30.0);
    glEnd();
}
}
```

Note the necessity of setting up a map for each of the patches. To display a shaded teapot, we need a more complex initialization that enables lighting and sets the required material properties:

```
void myinit()
{
  glEnable(GL_MAP2_VERTEX_3);
  glEnable(GL_AUTO_NORMAL);
  glMapGrid2f(8, 0.0, 1.0, 8, 0.0, 1.0);
  glEnable(GL_DEPTH_TEST);

  glEnable(GL_LIGHTING);
  glEnable(GL_LIGHT0);

  glLightfv(GL_LIGHT0, GL_AMBIENT, ambient);
  glLightfv(GL_LIGHT0, GL_DIFFUSE, diffuse);
  glLightfv(GL_LIGHT0, GL_POSITION, position);

  glMaterialfv(GL_FRONT, GL_DIFFUSE, mat_diffuse);
  glMaterialfv(GL_FRONT, GL_AMBIENT, mat_ambient);
}
```

We can then render a teapot by two lines in display function:

```
for(k=0;k<32;k++)
{
    glMap2f(GL_MAP2_VERTEX_3, 0, 1, 3, 4, 0, 1, 12, 4,
                 &data[k][0][0][0]);
    glEvalMesh2(GL_FILL,0,8,0,8);
}
```

11.12.4 NURBS Functions

We can use evaluators to generate nonuniform spacing of points and to generate four-dimensional curves and surfaces. If we recall our earlier observation that we can change any of the polynomial forms to a Bézier form by generating a proper set of control points, then we see that we have all the information necessary to define NURBS curves and surfaces. Rather than have the application programmer go through all these steps, the OpenGL Utility library, GLU, provides a set of NURBS functions. These functions also allow the user to specify various additional parameters that enable finer control of the rendering. There are five NURBS functions for surfaces:

```
gluNewNurbsRenderer
gluNurbsProperty
gluBeginNurbsSurface
gluNurbsSurface
gluEndNurbsSurface
```

The first two functions set up a new NURBS object and define how we would like it rendered. The final three are used to generate the surface. For NURBS curves, the final three are replaced by the functions `gluBeginNurbsCurve`, `gluNurbsCurve`, and `gluEndNurbsCurve`.

The GLU library provides an additional useful facility called trimming curves. **Trimming curves** are closed curves that we can use to render a surface from which the areas defined by curves have been removed. Figure 11.46 illustrates a trimmed surface. The user can define a trimming curve either as a NURBS curve using `gluNurbsCurve` or as a piecewise linear curve, through the `gluPwlCurve` function. The trimming curves are defined after the call to `glNurbsSurface`, and their vertices are specified between calls to `glBeginTrim` and `glEndTrim`.

11.12.5 Quadrics

OpenGL supports several quadric objects—disks, cylinders, and spheres—through GLU. These objects can be treated like other graphical objects: They can be scaled, translated, rotated, shaded, and texture mapped. The quadric routines allow for automatic generation of normals and texture coordinates. OpenGL implements these objects by approximating them with polygons, although we can specify how many polygons are to be used in the approximation.

FIGURE 11.46   Trimmed surface.

Suppose that we want to use a cylinder for the base of the robot in Chapter 10 (see also Appendix A). The first step is to define a new quadric object by

```
GLUquadricObj *p;
p=gluNewQuadric();
```

We can then define how we would like the quadric to be rendered. For example, if we want a wire frame, using the present drawing color, we use the function call

```
gluQuadricDrawStyle(p, GLU_LINE);
```

We can now create the cylinder, centered at the origin, with its length along the y-axis, by using

```
gluCylinder(p, BASE_RADIUS, BASE_RADIUS, BASE_HEIGHT, 5, 5);
```

The first three parameters specify the top and bottom radii, and the height. The final two parameters specify by how many slices we divide each circle of constant y and into how many sections we slice the cylinder in the y direction.

Summary and Notes

Once again, we have only scratched the surface of a deep and important topic. Also once again, our focus has been on what we can do on a graphics system using a standard API such as OpenGL. From this perspective, there are huge advantages to using parametric Bézier curves and surfaces. The parametric form is robust and is easy to use interactively because the required data are points that can be entered and manipulated interactively. The subdivision algorithm for Bézier curves and surfaces gives us the ability to render the resulting objects to any desired degree of accuracy.

We have seen that, although Bézier surfaces are easy to render, splines can provide additional smoothness and control. The texts in Suggested Readings discuss many variants of splines that are used in the CAD community.

Quadric surfaces are used extensively with ray tracers, because solving for the points of intersection between a ray and a quadric requires the solution of only a scalar quadratic equation. Deciding whether the point of intersection between a ray and the plane determined by a flat polygon is inside the polygon can be more difficult than solving the intersection problem for quadric surfaces. Hence, many ray tracers allow only infinite planes, quadrics, and, perhaps, convex polygons.

Subdivision surfaces have become increasingly more important for two reasons. First, because commodity hardware can render polygons at such high rates, we can often achieve the desired smoothness using a large number of polygons that can be rendered faster than a smaller number of surface patches. However, future hardware may change this advantage if rendering of curved surfaces is built into the rasterizer. Second, because we can render a subdivision surface at any desired level of detail, we can often use subdivision very effectively by not rendering a highly subdivided surface when it projects to a small area on the screen.

Suggested Readings

The book by Farin [Far88] provides an excellent introduction to curves and surfaces. It also has an interesting preface in which Bézier discusses the almost simultaneous discovery by him and deCasteljau of the surfaces that bear Bézier's name. Unfortunately, deCasteljau's work was described in unpublished technical reports, so deCasteljau did not receive the credit he deserved for his work until recently. Books such as those by Rogers [Rog90], Foley [Fol90], Bartels [Bar87], and Watt [Wat01] discuss many other forms of splines. See Rogers [Rog00] for an introduction to NURBS.

The book by Faux [Fau80] discusses the coordinate-free approach to curves and surfaces and the Frenet frame.

Although the book edited by Glassner [Gla89] primarily explores ray tracing, the section by Haines has considerable material on working with quadrics and other algebraic surfaces.

There has been much recent activity on subdivision curves and surfaces. For some of the seminal work in the area, see [Che95], [Deb96], [Gor96], [Lev96], [Sei96], and [Tor96]. Our development follows [War04]. Catmull-Clark subdivision was proposed in [Cat78]. See also [War03] and [Sta03].

Exercises

11.1   Consider an algebraic surface $f(x, y, z) = 0$, where each term in f can have terms in x, y, and z of powers up to m. How many terms can there be in f?

11.2   Consider the explicit equations $y = f(x)$ and $z = g(x)$. What types of curves do they describe?

11.3   Suppose that you have a polynomial $p(u) = \sum_{k=0}^{n} c_k u^k$. Find a polynomial $q(v) = \sum_{k=0}^{n} d_k v^k$ such that, for each point of p in the interval (a, b), there is a point v in the range $0 \le v \le 1$, such that $p(u) = q(v)$.

11.4   Show that as long as the four control points for the cubic interpolating curve are defined at unique values of the parameter u, the interpolating geometry matrix always exists.

11.5   Show that in the interval $(0, 1)$, the Bernstein polynomials must be less than 1.

11.6 Verify the C^2 continuity of the cubic spline.

11.7 In Section 10.9, we showed that we can write a cubic polynomial as a cubic Bézier polynomial by choosing a proper set of control points or, equivalently, the proper convex hull. Using this fact, show how to render an interpolating curve using the Bézier renderer provided by OpenGL.

11.8 Find a homogeneous-coordinate representation for quadrics.

11.9 Suppose that we render Bézier patches by adaptive subdivision so that each patch can be subdivided a different number of times. Do we maintain continuity along the edges of the patches? Explain your answer.

11.10 Write an OpenGL program that will take as input a set of control points and that will produce the interpolating, B-spline, and Bézier curves for these data.

11.11 Suppose that you use a set of spline curves to describe a path in time that an object will take as part of an animation. How might you notice the difference between G^1 and C^1 continuity in this situation?

11.12 Extend the painting program from Chapter 3 to include Bézier curves. The user should be able to manipulate the control points interactively.

11.13 Derive a simple test for the flatness of a Bézier surface patch.

11.14 Derive the open rational quadratic B-spline with the knots $\{0, 0, 0, 0, 1, 1, 1, 1\}$ and the weights $w_0 = w_2 = 1$ and $w_1 = w$.

11.15 Using the result of Exercise 11.14, show that, if $w = \frac{r}{1-r}$, for $0 \le r \le 1$, you get all the conic sections. *Hint*: Consider $r < \frac{1}{2}$ and $r > \frac{1}{2}$.

11.16 Find the zeros of the Hermite blending functions. Why do these zeros imply that the Hermite curve is smooth in the interval $(0, 1)$?

11.17 What is the relationship between the control-point data for a Hermite patch and the derivatives at the corners of the patch?

11.18 For a 1024×1280 display screen, what is the maximum number of subdivisions that are needed to render a cubic polynomial surface?

11.19 Suppose you have three points, P_0, P_1, and P_2. First, connect successive points with parametric line segments where u ranges from 0 to 1 for each. Next, linearly interpolate between successive pairs of line segments by connecting points for the same value of u with a line segment and then using the same value of u to obtain a value along this new line segment. How can you describe the curve created by this process?

11.20 Extend Exercise 11.19 by considering four points. Linearly interpolate, first between the three curves constructed as in that exercise and, second, between the two curves thus created. Describe the final curve determined by the four points.

11.21 What happens in the cubic Bézier curve if the values of the control points P_0 and P_1 are the same?

11.22 Suppose that we divide a Bézier surface patch, first along the u direction, and that then in v we only subdivide one of the two patches we have created. Show how this process can create a gap in the resulting surface. Find a simple solution to this difficulty.

11.23 Write a program to carry out subdivision of triangular or quadrilateral meshes. When this is working correctly, add the averaging step to form a smoother surface.

ADVANCED RENDERING

In this final chapter, we consider a variety of alternative approaches to the pipeline rendering strategy supported by most hardware and software for interactive applications. We have multiple motivations for introducing these other approaches. We want to be able to incorporate effects, such as global lighting, that cannot be rendered in real-time environments. We also want to produce high-quality, high-resolution images that go beyond what is needed for standard computer displays.

First, we explore ray tracers. We then look at the rendering equation that provides a physical basis for global rendering. Although we cannot solve the rendering equation in general, we shall look at a special solution for a particular shading model that yields the radiosity approach to rendering.

We consider techniques for displaying large amounts of geometric data using parallel rendering on clusters of computers. These techniques will also allow us to create images with resolution greater than that of standard display devices.

We also introduce image-based rendering. Here we start with two-dimensional images and go backward to obtain three-dimensional information that can be used to create new images. These techniques combine elements of computer graphics, computer vision, and image processing.

12.1 Going Beyond Pipeline Rendering

Almost everything done so far has led us to believe that, given a scene description containing geometric objects, cameras, light sources, and attributes, we could render it in close to real time using available hardware and software. This view dictated that we would use a pipeline renderer of the type described by the OpenGL architecture and supported by graphics hardware. Although we have developed a reasonably large bag of tricks that enable us to handle most applications and get around many of the consequences of using the local shading model supported by such renderers, there are still limitations on what we can do. For example, there are many global lighting situations that we cannot approximate well with a pipeline renderer. We would also like to generate images with higher resolution than on a standard workstation and that contain fewer aliasing artifacts. In many situations, we are willing either to render at slower speeds or to use multiple computers to achieve these goals. In this chapter, we introduce a variety of techniques, all of which are of current interest both to researchers and practitioners.

First, we examine other rendering strategies that are based on the physics of image formation. Our original discussion of image formation was based on following rays of light. That approach is based on a very simple physical model and led to the ray tracing paradigm for rendering. We start by exploring this model in greater detail than in previous chapters and show how to get started writing your own ray tracer.

We can also take approaches to rendering, other than ray tracing, that are also based on physics. We shall examine an approach based on energy conservation and consider an integral equation, the **rendering equation**, that describes a closed environment with light sources and reflective surfaces. Although this equation is not solvable in general, we can develop a rendering approach called **radiosity** that satisfies the rendering equation when all surfaces are perfectly diffuse reflectors.

We shall also look at two approaches that are somewhere between physically correct and real-time renderers. One is the approach taken in RenderMan. The other is an approach to rendering that starts with images. Although these methods are different from each other, both have become important in the animation industry.

Finally, we turn to the problems of working with large data sets and high-resolution displays. These problems are related because large data sets contain detail that requires displays with a resolution beyond what we can get with standard CRTs and LCD panels. We shall consider solutions that use parallelism making use of commodity components, both processors and graphics cards.

12.2 Ray Tracing

In many ways, ray tracing is a logical extension to rendering with a local lighting model. It is based on our previous observation that of the light rays leaving a source, the only ones that contribute to our image are those that enter the lens of our synthetic camera and pass through the center of projection. Figure 12.1 shows several of the possible interactions with a single point source and perfectly specular surfaces. Rays can enter the lens of the camera directly from the source, from interactions with a surface visible to the camera, after multiple reflections from surfaces, or after transmission through one or more surfaces.

Most of the rays that leave a source do not enter the lens and do not contribute to our image. Hence, attempting to follow all rays from a light source is a time-wasting endeavor. However, if we reverse the direction of the rays and consider only those rays that start at the center of projection, we know that these **cast rays** must contribute to the image. Consequently, we start our ray tracer as shown

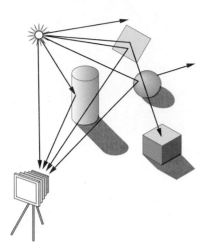

FIGURE 12.1   Rays leaving source.

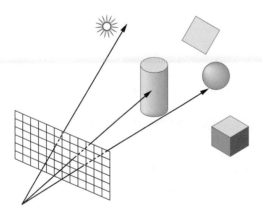

FIGURE 12.2   Ray-casting model.

in Figure 12.2. Here we have included the image plane, and we have ruled it into pixel-sized areas. Knowing that we must assign a color to every pixel, we must cast at least one ray through each pixel. Each cast ray either intersects a surface or a light source, or goes off to infinity without striking anything. Pixels corresponding to this latter case can be assigned a background color. Rays that strike surfaces—for now, we can assume that all surfaces are opaque—require us to calculate a shade for the point of intersection. If we were simply to compute the shade at the point of intersection, using the modified Phong model, we would produce the same image as would our local renderer. However, we can do much more.

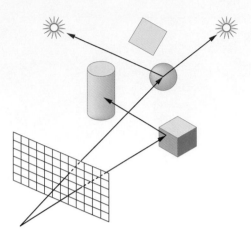

FIGURE 12.3   Shadow rays.

Note that the process that we have described thus far requires all the same steps as we use in our pipeline renderer: object modeling, projection, and visible-surface determination. However, as we saw in Chapter 7, the order in which the calculations are carried out is different. The pipeline renderer works on a vertex-by-vertex basis; the ray tracer works on a pixel-by-pixel basis.

In ray tracing, rather than immediately applying our reflection model, we first check whether the point of intersection between the cast ray and the surface is illuminated. We compute **shadow**, or **feeler, rays** (Figure 12.3) from the point on the surface to each source. If a shadow ray intersects a surface before it meets the source, the light is blocked from reaching the point under consideration, and this point is in shadow, at least from this source. No lighting calculation needs to be done for sources that are blocked from a point on the surface. If all surfaces are opaque and we do not consider light scattered from surface to surface, we have an image that has shadows added to what we have already done without ray tracing. The price we pay is the cost of doing a type of hidden-surface calculation for each point of intersection between a cast ray and a surface.

Suppose that some of our surfaces are highly reflective, like those shown in Figure 12.4. We can follow the shadow ray as it bounces from surface to surface, until it either goes off to infinity or intersects a source. Such calculations are usually done recursively and take into account any absorption of light at surfaces.

Ray tracing is particularly good at handling surfaces that are both reflecting and transmitting. Using our basic paradigm, we follow a cast ray to a surface (Figure 12.5) with the property that if a ray from a source strikes a point, then the light from the source is partially absorbed, and some of this light contributes to the diffuse reflection term. The rest of the incoming light is divided between a transmitted ray and a reflected ray. From the perspective of the cast ray, if a light source is visible at the intersection point, then we need to do three tasks. First, we must compute the contribution from the light source at the point, using our

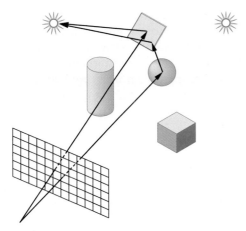

FIGURE 12.4   Ray tracing with a mirror.

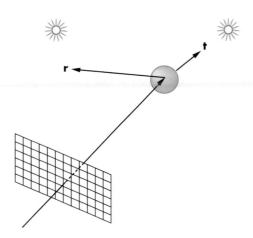

FIGURE 12.5   Ray tracing with reflection and transmission.

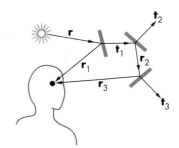

FIGURE 12.6   Simple ray-traced environments.

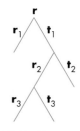

FIGURE 12.7   Ray tree corresponding to Figure 12.6.

standard reflection model. Second, we must cast a ray in the direction of a perfect reflection. Third, we must cast a ray in the direction of the transmitted ray. These two rays are treated just like the original cast ray; that is, they are intersected (if possible) with other surfaces, end at a source, or go off to infinity. At each surface that these rays intersect, additional rays may be generated by reflection and transmission of light. Figure 12.6 shows a single cast ray and the path it can follow through a simple environment. Figure 12.7 shows the **ray tree** generated. This tree shows which rays must be traced; it is constructed dynamically by the ray-tracing process.

Although our ray tracer uses the Phong model to include a diffuse term at the point of intersection between a ray and a surface, the light that is scattered diffusely at this point is ignored. If we were to attempt to follow such light, we would have so many rays to deal with that the ray tracer might never complete execution. Thus, ray tracers are best suited for highly reflective environments. Color Plate 23 was rendered with a public-domain ray tracer. Although the scene contains only a few objects, the reflective and transparent surfaces could not have been rendered correctly without the ray tracer. Also, note the complexity of the shadows in the scene, another effect created automatically by ray tracing.

12.3   Building a Simple Ray Tracer

The easiest way to describe a ray tracer is recursively, through a single function that traces a ray and calls itself for the reflected and transmitted rays. Most of the work in ray tracing goes into the calculation of intersections between rays and surfaces. One reason that it is difficult to implement a ray tracer that can handle a variety of objects is that as we add more complex objects, computing intersections becomes problematic. Consequently, most basic ray tracers support only flat and quadric surfaces.

We have seen the basic considerations that determine the ray-tracing process. Building a simple recursive ray tracer that can handle simple objects—quadrics and polyhedra—is quite easy. In this section, we shall examine the basic structure and the functions that are required. Details can be found in the references in Suggested Readings.

We need two basic functions. The recursive function `raytrace` follows a ray, specified by a point and a direction, and returns the shade of the first surface that it intersects. It will use the function `intersect` to find the location of the closest surface that the specified ray intersects.

12.3.1   Recursive Ray Tracing

Let us consider the procedure `raytrace` in pseudocode. We give it a starting point p and a direction d, and it returns a color c. In order to stop the ray tracer from recursing forever, we can specify a maximum number of steps max that it can take. We shall assume, for simplicity, that we have only a single light source whose properties, as well as the description of the objects and their surface properties, are all available globally. If there are additional light sources, we can add in their contributions in a manner similar to the way in which we deal with the single source.

```
color c = trace(point p, vector d, int step)
{

    color local, reflected, transmitted;
    point q;
    normal n;
```

```
    if(step > max) return(background_color);

    q = intersect(p, d, status);

    if(status == light_source) return(light_source_color);
    if(status == no_intersection) return(background_color);

    n = normal(q);
    r = reflect(q, n);
    t = transmit(q, n);

    local = phong(q, n, r);
    reflected = trace(q, r, step+1);
    transmitted = trace(q, t, step+1);

    return(local + reflected + transmitted);
}
```

Note that the calculation of reflected and transmitted colors must take into account how much energy is absorbed at the surface before reflection and transmission. If we have exceeded the maximum number of steps, we return a defined background color. Otherwise, we use intersect to find the intersection of the given ray with the closest object. This function must have the entire database of objects available to it, and it must be able to find the intersections of rays with all types of objects supported. Consequently, most of the time spent in the ray tracer and the complexity of the code is hidden in this function. We examine some of the intersection issues in Section 12.3.2.

If the ray does not intersect any object, we can return a status variable from intersect and return the background color from trace. Likewise, if the ray intersects the light source, we return the color of the source. If an intersection is returned, there are three components to the color at this point: a local color that can be computed using the modified Phong (or any other) model, a reflected color, and if the surface is translucent, a transmitted color. Before computing these colors, we must compute the normal at the point of intersection, as well as the direction of reflected and transmitted rays, as in Chapters 6 and 9. The complexity of computing the normal depends on the class of objects supported by the ray tracer, and this calculation can be part of the function raytrace.

The computation of the local color requires a check to see if the light source is visible from the point of closest intersection. Thus, we cast a feeler or shadow ray from this point toward the light source and check whether it intersects any objects. We can note that this process can also be recursive because the shadow ray might hit a reflective surface, such as a mirror, or a translucent surface, such as a piece of glass. In addition, if the shadow ray hits a surface that itself is illuminated, some of this light should contribute to the color at q. Generally, we ignore these possible contributions because they will slow the calculation significantly. Practical ray tracing requires that we make some compromises and is never quite physically correct.

Next, we have two recursive steps that compute the contributions from the reflected and transmitted rays starting at q using raytrace. It is these recursions that make this code a ray tracer rather than a simple ray-casting rendering in which we find the first intersection and apply a lighting model at that point. Finally, we add the three colors to obtain the color at p.

12.3.2 Calculating Intersections

Most of the time spent in a typical ray tracer is in the calculation of intersections in the function intersect. Hence, we must be very careful in limiting the objects to those for which we can find intersections easily. The general intersection problem can be expressed cleanly if we use an implicit representation of our objects. Thus, if an object is defined by the surface(s)

$$f(x, y, z) = f(\mathbf{p}) = 0,$$

and a ray from a point $\mathbf{p}_0$ in the direction $\mathbf{d}$ is represented by the parametric form

$$\mathbf{p}(t) = \mathbf{p}_0 + t\mathbf{d},$$

then the intersections are given for the values of t such that

$$f(\mathbf{p}_0 + t\mathbf{d}) = 0,$$

which is a scalar equation in t. If f is an algebraic surface, then f is a sum of polynomial terms of the form $x^i y^j z^k$. Finding the intersections reduces to finding all the roots of a polynomial. Unfortunately, there are only a few cases that do not require numerical methods.

One is quadrics. In Chapter 11, we saw that all quadrics could be written as the quadratic form

$$\mathbf{p} = \mathbf{p}^T \mathbf{A} \mathbf{p} + \mathbf{b}^T \mathbf{p} + c = 0.$$

Substituting in the equation for a ray leaves us with a scalar quadratic equation to solve for the values of t that yield zero, one, or two intersections. Because the solution of the quadratic equation requires only the taking of a single square root, ray tracers can handle quadrics without difficulty. In addition, we can eliminate those rays that miss a quadric object and those that are tangent to it before taking the square root, further simplifying the calculation.

Consider, for example, a sphere centered at $\mathbf{p}_c$ with radius r, which can be written as

$$(\mathbf{p} - \mathbf{p}_c) \cdot (\mathbf{p} - \mathbf{p}_c) - r^2 = 0.$$

Substituting in the equation of the ray

$$\mathbf{p}(t) = \mathbf{p}_0 + t\mathbf{d},$$

we get the quadratic equation

$$\mathbf{d} \cdot \mathbf{d} t^2 + 2(\mathbf{p}_0 - \mathbf{p}_c) \cdot \mathbf{d} t + (\mathbf{p}_0 - \mathbf{p}_c) \cdot (\mathbf{p}_0 - \mathbf{p}_c) - r^2 = 0.$$

Planes are also simple. We can take the equation for the ray and substitute it into the equation of a plane

$$\mathbf{p} \cdot \mathbf{n} + c = 0,$$

which yields a scalar equation that requires only a single division to solve. Thus, for the ray

$$\mathbf{p} = \mathbf{p}_0 + t\mathbf{d},$$

we find

$$t = -\frac{\mathbf{p}_0 \cdot \mathbf{n} + c}{\mathbf{n} \cdot \mathbf{d}}.$$

However, planes by themselves have limited applicability in modeling scenes. We are usually interested either in the intersection of multiple planes that form convex objects (polyhedra) or a piece of a plane that defines a flat polygon. For polygons, we must decide whether the point of intersection lies inside or outside the polygon. The difficulty of such a test depends on whether the polygon is convex and if not convex, whether it is simple. These issues are similar to the rendering issues that we discussed for polygons in Chapter 7. For convex polygons there are very simple tests that are similar to the tests for ray intersections with polyhedra that we consider next.

Although we can define polyhedra by their faces, we can also define them as the convex objects that are formed by the intersection of planes. Thus, a parallelepiped is defined by six planes and a tetrahedron by four. For ray tracing, the advantage of this definition is that we can use the simple ray-plane intersection equation to derive a ray-polyhedron intersection test.

We develop the test as follows. Let us assume that all the planes defining our polyhedron have normals that are outwardly facing. Consider the ray in Figure 12.8 that intersects the polyhedron. It can enter and leave the polygon only once. It must enter through a plane that is facing the ray and leave through a plane that faces in the direction of the ray. However, this ray must also intersect all the planes that form the polyhedron (except those parallel to the ray).

Consider the intersections of the ray with all the front-facing planes—that is, those whose normals point toward the starting point of the ray. The entry point must be the intersection farthest along the ray. Likewise, the exit point is the nearest intersection point of all the planes facing away from the start of the ray, and the entry point must be closer to the initial point than the exit point. If we consider a ray that misses the same polyhedron, as in Figure 12.9, we see that the farthest intersection with a front-facing plane is closer to the initial point than the closest intersection with a back-facing plane. Hence, our test is to find these possible entry and exit points by computing the ray-plane intersection points,

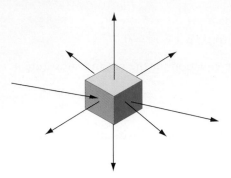

FIGURE 12.8 Ray intersecting a polyhedron with outward-facing normals shown.

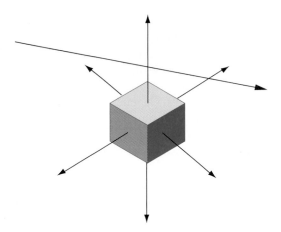

FIGURE 12.9 Ray missing a polyhedron with outward-facing normals shown.

in any order, and updating the possible entry and exit points as we find the intersections. The test can be halted if we ever find a possible exit point closer than the present entry point or a possible entry point farther than the present exit point.

Consider the two-dimensional example in Figure 12.10 that tests for a ray–convex polygon intersection in a plane. Here lines replace planes, but the logic is the same. Suppose that we do the intersections with the lines in the order 1, 2, 3, 4. Starting with line 1, we find that this line faces the initial point by looking at the sign of the dot product of the normal with the direction of the ray. The intersection with line 1 then yields a possible entry point. Line 2 faces away from the initial point and yields a possible exit point that is farther away than our present estimate of the entry point. Line 3 yields an even closer exit point but still one that is farther than the entry point. Line 4 yields a farther exit point that

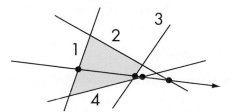

FIGURE 12.10   Ray intersecting a convex polygon.

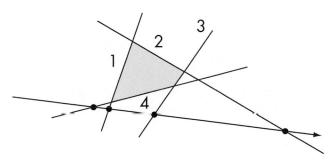

FIGURE 12.11   Ray missing a convex polygon.

can be discarded. At this point, we have tested all the lines and conclude that the ray passes through the polygon.

Figure 12.11 has the same lines and the same convex polygon but shows a ray that misses the polygon. The intersection with line 1 still yields a possible entry point. The intersections with lines 2 and 3 still yield possible exit points that are farther than the entry point. But the intersection with line 4 yields an exit point closer than the entry point, which indicates that the ray must miss the polygon.

12.3.3 Ray-Tracing Variations

Most ray tracers employ multiple methods for determining when to stop the recursive process. One method that is fairly simple to implement is to neglect all rays that go past some distance, assuming that such rays go off to infinity. We can implement this test by assuming that all objects lie inside a large sphere centered at the origin. Thus, if we treat this sphere as an object colored with a specified background color, whenever the intersection calculation determines that this sphere is the closest object, we terminate the recursion for the ray and return the background color.

Another simple termination strategy is to look at the fraction of energy remaining in a ray. When a ray passes through a translucent material or reflects from a shiny surface, we can estimate the fraction of the incoming energy that is in these outgoing rays and how much has been absorbed at the surface. If we add an energy parameter to the ray tracer

```
trace(point p, vector d, int steps, float energy),
```

then we need only to add a line of code to check if there is sufficient energy remaining to continue tracing a ray.

There are many improvements we can make to speed up a ray tracer or make it more accurate. For example, it is fairly simple to replace the recursion in the ray tracer with iteration. Frequently, much of the work in finding intersections can be avoided by the use of bounding boxes or bounding spheres, because the intersection with these objects can be done very quickly. Bounding volumes can often be used to group objects effectively.

Because ray tracing is a sampling method, it is subject to aliasing errors. As we saw in Chapter 8, aliasing errors occur when we do not have enough samples. However, in our basic ray tracer, the amount of work is proportional to the number of rays. Many ray tracers use a stochastic sampling method in which the decision as to where to cast the next ray is based upon the results of rays cast thus far. Thus, if rays do not intersect any objects in a particular region, few additional rays will be cast toward it, while the opposite holds for rays that are cast in a direction where they intersect many objects. This strategy is also used in RenderMan (Section 12.6). Although we could argue that stochastic sampling only works in a probabilistic sense—as there may well be small objects in areas that are not well sampled—it has the advantage that images produced by stochastic sampling tend not to show the moiré patterns characteristic of images produced using uniform sampling.

Ray tracing is an inherently parallel process, as every ray can be cast independently of every other ray. However, the difficulty is that every ray can potentially intersect any object. Hence, every tracing of a ray needs access to all objects. In addition, when we follow reflected and transmitted rays, we tend to lose any locality that might have helped us avoid a lot of data movement. Consequently, parallel ray tracers are best suited for shared-memory parallel architectures.

12.4　The Rendering Equation

Most of the laws of physics can be expressed as conservation laws, such as the conservation of momentum and the conservation of energy. Because light is a form of energy, an energy-based approach can provide an alternative to ray tracing. Consider the closed-environment picture in Figure 12.12. We see some surfaces that define the closed environment, some objects, and a light source inside. Physically all these surfaces are the same. Although each one may have different parameters, each obeys the same physical laws. Any surface can absorb some light and reflect some light. Any surface can be an emitter of light. From the ray-tracing perspective, we can say that the shades that we see are the result of an infinite number of rays bouncing around the environment, starting with

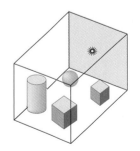

FIGURE 12.12 Closed environment with four objects and a light source.

sources and not ending until all the energy has been absorbed. However, when we look at the scene, we see the steady state; that is, we see surfaces each having its own shades. We do not see how the rays have bounced around; we see only the end result. The energy approach allows us to solve for this steady state directly, thus avoiding tracing many rays through many reflections.

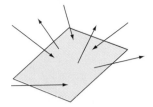

Let us consider just one surface, as in Figure 12.13. We see rays of light entering from many directions and other rays emerging, also possibly in all directions. The light leaving the surface can have two components. If the surface is a light source, then some fraction of the light leaving the surface is from emission. The rest of the light is the reflection of incoming light from other surfaces. Hence, the incoming light also consists of emissions and reflections from other surfaces.

FIGURE 12.13 A simple surface.

We can simplify the analysis by considering two arbitrary points $\mathbf{p}$ and $\mathbf{p}'$, as in Figure 12.14. If we look at the light arriving at and leaving $\mathbf{p}$, the energy must balance. Thus, the emission of energy, if there is a source at $\mathbf{p}$, and the reflected light energy must equal the incoming light energy from all possible points $\mathbf{p}'$. Let $i(\mathbf{p}, \mathbf{p}')$ be the intensity of light leaving the point $\mathbf{p}'$ and arriving at the point $\mathbf{p}$.[1] The rendering equation

$$i(\mathbf{p}, \mathbf{p}') = v(\mathbf{p}, \mathbf{p}')(\epsilon(\mathbf{p}, \mathbf{p}') + \int \rho(\mathbf{p}, \mathbf{p}', \mathbf{p}'')i(\mathbf{p}', \mathbf{p}'')d\mathbf{p}'')$$

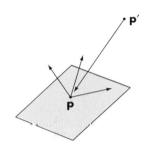

FIGURE 12.14 Light from $\mathbf{p}'$ arriving at $\mathbf{p}$.

expresses this balance. The intensity leaving $\mathbf{p}'$ consists of two parts. If $\mathbf{p}'$ is an emitter of light (a source), there is a term $\epsilon(\mathbf{p}, \mathbf{p}')$ in the direction of $\mathbf{p}$. The second term is the contribution of reflections from every possible point $(\mathbf{p}'')$ that are reflected at $\mathbf{p}'$ in the direction of $\mathbf{p}$. The reflection function $\rho(\mathbf{p}, \mathbf{p}', \mathbf{p}'')$ characterizes the material properties at $\mathbf{p}'$. The term $v(\mathbf{p}, \mathbf{p}')$ has two possible values. If there is an opaque surface between $\mathbf{p}$ and $\mathbf{p}'$, then the surface occludes $\mathbf{p}'$ from $\mathbf{p}$ and no light from $\mathbf{p}'$ reaches $\mathbf{p}$. In this case, $v(\mathbf{p}, \mathbf{p}') = 0$. Otherwise, we must account for the effect of the distance between $\mathbf{p}$ and $\mathbf{p}'$ and

$$v(\mathbf{p}, \mathbf{p}') = \frac{1}{r^2},$$

where r is the distance between the two points.

Although the form of the rendering equation is wonderfully simple, solving it is not an easy task. The main difficulty is the dimensionality. Because $\mathbf{p}$ and $\mathbf{p}'$ are points in three-dimensional space, $i(\mathbf{p}, \mathbf{p}')$ has six variables and ρ has nine. In addition, we have not included an additional variable for the wavelength of light, which would be necessary to work with color.

---

1. We are being careful to avoid introducing the units and terminology of radiometry. We see the intensity of light. Energy is the integral of intensity over time, but if the light sources are unchanging, we are in the steady state, and this distinction does not matter. Most references work with the energy or intensity per unit area (the **energy flux**) rather than energy or intensity.

There have been some efforts to solve a general form of the rendering equation by numerical methods. Most of these have been Monte Carlo methods that are somewhat akin to stochastic sampling. Recently, **photon mapping** has become a viable approach. Photon mapping follows individual photons, the carriers of light energy, from when they are produced at the light sources to when they are finally absorbed by surfaces in the scene. Photons typically go through multiple reflections and transmissions from creation to final absorption. The potential advantage of this approach is that it can handle complex lighting of the sort that characterizes real-world scenes.

When we discussed ray tracing, we argued that because such a small percentage of light emitted from sources reaches the viewer, tracing rays from a source is inefficient; however, photon mapping uses many clever strategies to make the process computationally feasible. In particular, photon mapping uses a conservation of energy approach combined with Monte Carlo methods. For example, consider what happens when light strikes a diffuse surface. As we have seen, the reflected light is diffused in all directions. In photon mapping, when a photon strikes a diffuse surface, a photon can be reflected or absorbed. Whether the photon is absorbed or not—and the specific angle of reflection, if it is reflected—is determined stochastically in a manner that yields the correct results on the average. Thus, what happens to two photons that strike a surface at the same place and with the same angle of incidence can be very different. The more photons that are generated from sources, the greater the accuracy but at the cost of tracing more photons.

There are special circumstances that simplify the rendering equation. For example, for perfectly specular surfaces, the reflection function is nonzero only when the angle of incidence equals the angle of reflection and the vectors lie in the same plane. Under these circumstances, ray tracing can be looked at as a method for solving the rendering equation.

The other special case that leads to a viable rendering method occurs when all surfaces are perfectly diffuse. In this case, the amount of light reflected is the same in all directions. Thus, the intensity function depends only on **p**. We examine this case in the next section.

12.5 Radiosity

One way to simplify the rendering equation is to consider an environment in which all the surfaces are perfectly diffuse reflectors. Because a perfectly diffuse reflector looks the same to all viewers, the corresponding reflection function is far simpler than the general cases considered by the rendering equation.

Note, however, that although a perfectly diffuse surface reflects light equally in all directions, even if the surface is flat, it can show variations in shading that are not shown when we render using the Phong lighting model. Suppose that we have a simple scene, such as that shown in Figure 12.15, in which all the surfaces are perfectly diffuse. If we render this scene with a distant light source,

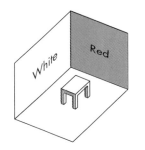

FIGURE 12.15 Simple scene with diffuse surfaces.

each polygon surface is rendered as a constant color. If this were a real scene, however, some of the diffuse reflections from the red wall would fall on the white wall, causing red light to be added to the white light reflected from those parts of the white wall that are near the red wall. Diffuse light reflected from the white wall would have a similar effect on the red wall. Our simple shading model has not considered these **diffuse–diffuse interactions**.

An ideal global renderer would capture these interactions. The radiosity method can approximate them very well using an energy approach that was originally used for solving problems in heat transfer.

The basic radiosity method breaks up the scene into small flat polygons, or **patches**, each of which can be assumed to be perfectly diffuse, and renders in a constant shade. What we must do first is to find these shades. Once we have found them, we have effectively assigned a color to each patch that is independent of the viewer. Effectively, we have assigned colors to a set of polygon patches in a three-dimensional environment. We can now place the viewer wherever we wish and render the scene in a conventional manner, using a pipeline renderer.

12.5.1 The Radiosity Equation

Let us assume our scene consists of n patches numbered from 1 to n. The radiosity of patch i, b_i is the light intensity (energy/unit time) per unit area leaving the patch. Typically, the radiosity would be measured in units such as $watts/meter^2$. Because we are measuring intensity at a fixed wavelength, we can think of a radiosity function $b_i(\lambda)$ that determines the color of patch i. Suppose that patch i has area a_i. Because we have assumed that each patch is a perfectly diffuse surface, the total intensity leaving patch i is $b_i a_i$. Following reasoning similar to that which we used to derive the rendering equation, the emitted intensity consists of an emissive component, also assumed to be constant across the patch, and a reflective component due to the intensities of all other patches whose light strikes patch i,

$$b_i a_i = e_i a_i + \rho_i \sum_{j=0}^{n} f_{ij} b_j a_j.$$

The term f_{ij} is called the **form factor** between patch i and patch j. It represents the fraction of the energy leaving patch j that reaches patch i. The form factor depends on how the two patches are oriented relative to each other, how far they are from each other, and whether any other patches occlude the light from patch j and prevent it from reaching patch i. We shall discuss the calculation of these factors in the next subsection. The reflectivity of patch i is ρ_i.

Because the form factors depend on the geometric relationship between pairs of patches, there is a simple relationship between the factors f_{ij} and f_{ji} known as the **reciprocity equation**:

$$f_{ij} a_i = f_{ji} a_j.$$

Substituting the reciprocity equation into the equation for the patch intensities, we find

$$b_i a_i = e_i a_i + \rho_i \sum_{j=0}^{n} f_{ij} b_j a_i.$$

We can now divide by a_i, obtaining an equation for the patch radiosity:

$$b_i = e_i + \rho_i \sum_{j=0}^{n} f_{ij} b_j.$$

This result is called the **radiosity equation**.

Assuming that we have computed the form factors, we have a set of n linear equations in the n unknown radiosities. Comparing this equation to the rendering equation, we can see that if the patches were made smaller and smaller, in the limit we would have an infinite number of patches. The sum would become an integral, and the resulting radiosity equation would be a special case of the rendering equation in which all surfaces are perfectly diffuse reflectors.

We can put these equations in matrix form by defining the column matrix of radiosities

$$\mathbf{b} = [b_i],$$

a column matrix of the patch emissions

$$\mathbf{e} = [e_i],$$

a diagonal matrix from the reflection coefficients

$$\mathbf{R} = [\, r_{ij} \,], \qquad a_{ij} = \begin{cases} \rho_i & \text{if } i = j; \\ 0 & \text{otherwise,} \end{cases}$$

and a matrix of the form factors

$$\mathbf{F} = [f_{ij}].$$

Now the set of equations for the radiosities becomes

$$\mathbf{b} = \mathbf{e} - \mathbf{RFb}.$$

We can write the formal solution as

$$\mathbf{b} = [\mathbf{I} - \mathbf{RF}]^{-1}\mathbf{e}.$$

12.5.2 Solving the Radiosity Equation

Although it can be shown that the radiosity equation must have a solution, the real difficulties are practical. A typical scene will have thousands of patches, so that solving the equations by a direct method, such as Gaussian elimination, usually is not possible. Most methods rely on the fact that the matrix $\mathbf{F}$ is sparse.

Most of its elements are zero because most patches are sufficiently far from each other so that almost none of the light that they emit or reflect reaches most other patches.

Solutions of sets of equations involving sparse matrices are based on iterative methods that require the multiplication of these sparse matrices, an efficient operation. Suppose that we use the equation for the patches to create the iterative equation

$$\mathbf{b}^{k+1} = \mathbf{e} - \mathbf{RFb}^k.$$

Each iteration of this equation requires the matrix multiplication $\mathbf{RFb}^k$, which, assuming $\mathbf{F}$ is sparse, requires $O(n)$ operations, rather than the $O(n^2)$ operations for the general case. In terms of the individual radiosities, we have

$$b_i^{k+1} = e_i - \sum_{j=1}^{n} \rho_i f_{ij} b_j^k.$$

This method, which is known as Jacobi's method, will converge for this problem regardless of the initial starting point $\mathbf{b}^0$.

In general, patches are not self-reflecting so that $f_{ij} = 0$. If we apply updates as soon as they are available, we obtain the Gauss-Seidel method:

$$b_i^{k+1} = e_i - \sum_{j=1}^{i-1} \rho_i f_{ij} b_j^{k+1} - \sum_{j=i+1}^{n} \rho_i f_{ij} b_j^k.$$

There is another possible iteration that provides additional physical insight. Consider the scalar formula

$$\frac{1}{1-x} = \sum_{i=0}^{\infty} x^i,$$

which holds if $|x| < 1$. The matrix form of this equation for $\mathbf{RF}$ is[2]

$$[\mathbf{I} - \mathbf{RF}]^{-1} = \sum_{i=0}^{\infty} (\mathbf{RF})^i.$$

Thus, we can write $\mathbf{b}$ as

$$\mathbf{b} = \sum_{i=0}^{\infty} (\mathbf{RF})^i \mathbf{e}$$

$$= \mathbf{e} + (\mathbf{RF})\mathbf{e} + (\mathbf{RF})^2 \mathbf{e} + (\mathbf{RF})^3 \mathbf{e} + \dots$$

---

2. The formula converges if the magnitudes of all the eigenvalues of $\mathbf{BF}$ are less than unity, a condition that must be true for the radiosity equation.

We can use this expression, terminating it at some point, to approximate **b**. Each term has an interesting physical interpretation. The first term, **e**, is the direct light emitted from each patch so that an approximate solution with just this term will show only the sources. The second term, (**RF**)**e**, adds in the light that is the result of exactly one reflection of the sources onto other patches. The next term adds on the contribution from double reflections and so on for the other terms.

12.5.3   Computing Form Factors

At this point, we have ways of solving for the patch radiosities that are reasonably efficient, but we have yet to discuss the calculation of the form factors. We start with a general derivation of an equation for the form factor between two patches, and then we shall look at how we might find approximate form factors using the tools that we have available.

Consider two perfectly diffuse flat patches, P_i and P_j, as in Figure 12.16, which we have drawn without any other patches that might cause occlusion. Each patch has a normal that gives its orientation. Although each patch emits light equally in all directions, the amount of light leaving two different points on P_j that reaches any point on P_i is different because of the different distances between two points on P_j and a point on P_i. Thus, to collect all the light from P_j that falls on P_i, we must integrate over all points on P_j. The same reasoning applies to two points on P_i that receive light from a point on P_j; they will receive a different amount of light, and thus to determine the light falling on P_i, we must also integrate over all points on P_i.

We can derive the required integral based on our understanding of diffuse shading from Chapter 6. Consider a small area on each patch, da_i and da_j. Each can be considered to be an ideal diffuse reflector (Figure 12.17). They are a distance r apart, where r is the distance between two points, $\mathbf{p}_i$ and $\mathbf{p}_j$, at the center of the two small areas. The light leaving da_j goes in the direction $\mathbf{d} = \mathbf{p}_i - \mathbf{p}_j$. However, the intensity of this light is reduced or foreshortened by $\cos \phi_j$, where ϕ_j is the angle between the normal for patch j and the vector $\mathbf{d}$. Likewise, the light arriving at da_i is foreshortened by $\cos \phi_i$, where ϕ_i is the angle between the normal for patch i and the vector $\mathbf{d}$. To obtain the desired form factor, f_{ij}, we must also account for the distance between the patches and the possibility of occlusion. We can do both by defining the term

$$o_{ij} = \begin{cases} 1 & \text{if } \mathbf{p}_j \text{ is visible from } \mathbf{p}_i, \\ 0 & \text{otherwise.} \end{cases}$$

Finally, by averaging over the total area of the patch, we obtain the form-factor equation

$$f_{ij} = \frac{1}{a_i} \int_{a_i} \int_{a_j} o_{ij} \frac{\cos \phi_i \cos \phi_j}{\pi r^2} da_i da_j.$$

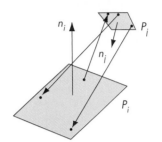

FIGURE 12.16   Two patches.

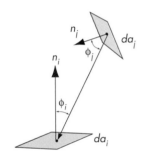

FIGURE 12.17   Foreshortening between two small patches.

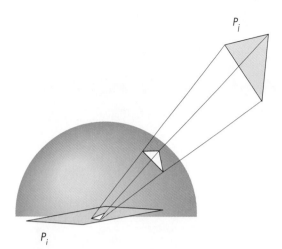

FIGURE 12.18   Projecting a patch on a hemisphere.

Although the form of this integral is simple, there are only a few special cases for which it can be solved analytically. For real scenes, we need numerical methods. Because there are n^2 form factors, most methods are a compromise between accuracy and time.

We shall sketch two approaches. The first method starts with the notion of two-step mappings that we used in our discussion of texture mapping in Chapter 8. Consider two patches again, this time with a hemisphere separating them as in Figure 12.18. Suppose that we want to compute the light from P_i that reaches P_j at a point $\mathbf{p}_i$. We center the hemisphere at this point and orient the patch so that the normal is pointing up. We can now project P_j onto the hemisphere and observe that we can use the projected patch for our computation of the form factor rather than the original patch. If we convert to polar coordinates, the form factor equation becomes simpler for the projected patch. However, for each small area of P_i, we have to move the hemisphere and add the contribution from each area.

A simpler approach for most graphics applications is to use a hemicube rather than a hemisphere, as shown in Figure 12.19. The hemicube is centered like the hemisphere, but its surface is divided into small squares called pixels. The light that strikes patch i is independent of the type of intermediate surface that we use. The advantage of the hemicube is that its surfaces are either parallel to or orthogonal to P_i. Consequently, it is straightforward to project P_j onto the hemicube and to compute the contribution of each pixel on the hemicube to the light that reaches point $\mathbf{p}_i$. Thus, if the surface of the hemicube is divided into m pixels, numbered 1 to m, then we can compute the contribution of those pixels that are projections of P_j and are visible from $\mathbf{p}_i$. We would then add them to

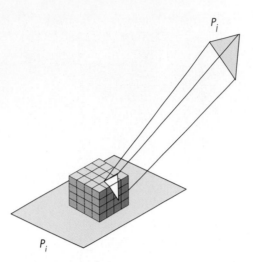

P_i

P_i

FIGURE 12.19   Projecting a patch on a hemicube and onto another patch.

form the **delta form factor** Δf_{ij}, which is the contribution of P_j to the small area da_i at the center of the hemicube. We then get the desired form factor by adding the contributions of all the delta form factors. The contributions from each pixel can be computed analytically once we know whether P_j projects on it, a calculation that is similar to the ray-tracing calculation required to determine whether an object is visible from a light source. The details are included in the references in Suggested Readings.

Another approach to computing form factors exploits our ability to use a graphics system to compute simple renderings very rapidly. Suppose that we want to compute f_{ij}. If we illuminate P_i with a known amount of light only from P_j, we will have an experimental measurement of the desired form factor. We can approximate this measurement by placing point light sources on P_j and then rendering the scene with whatever renderer we have available. Because of the possibility that another patch obscures P_i from P_j, we must use a renderer that can handle shadows.

12.5.4 Carrying Out Radiosity

In practice, radiosity rendering has three major steps. First, we divide the scene into a mesh of patches, as in Figure 12.20. This step requires some skill as more patches require the calculation of more form factors. However, it is the division of surfaces into patches that allows radiosity to yield images with subtle

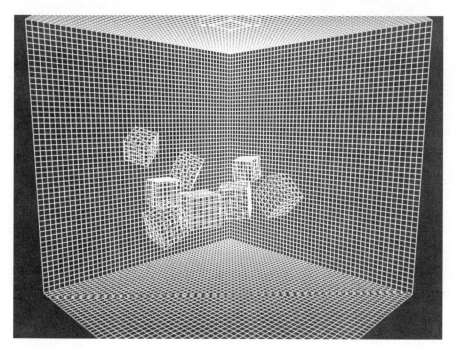

FIGURE 12.20   Division of surfaces into patches. (Courtesy of A. Van Pernis, K. Rasche, and R. Geist, Clemson University)

diffuse–diffuse interactions. Often the creation of the initial mesh can be done interactively, allowing the placement of more patches in regions such as corners between surfaces where we expect to see diffuse–diffuse interactions. Another approach is based on the observation that the radiosity of a large surface is equal to the area-weighted sum of the radiosities of any subdivision of it. Hence, we can start with a fairly rough mesh and refine it later (**progressive radiosity**). Once we have a mesh, we can compute the form factors, the most computationally intense part of the process.

Once we have the mesh and the form factors, we can solve the radiosity equation. We form the emission array **e** using the values for the light sources in the scene and assign colors to the surfaces, forming **R**. Now we can solve the radiosity equation to determine **b**.

The components of **b** act as the new colors of the patches. We can now place the viewer in the scene and render with a conventional renderer.

The image in Color Plate 24 was rendered using radiosity. It started with the initial mesh in Figure 12.20, which was then altered with a particle system to achieve a better set of patches. It shows the strength of radiosity for rendering interiors that are composed of diffuse reflectors.

12.6 RenderMan

There are other approaches to rendering that have arisen from the needs of the animation industry. Although interaction is required in the design of an animation, real-time rendering is not required when the final images are produced. Of greater importance is producing images free of rendering artifacts such as the jaggedness and moiré patterns that arise from aliasing. However, rendering the large number of frames required for a feature-length film cannot be done with ray tracers or radiosity renderers, even though animations are produced using large numbers of computers—**rendering farms**—whose sole task is to render scenes at the required resolution. In addition, neither ray tracers nor radiosity renderers alone produce images that have the desired artistic qualities.

The RenderMan interface is based on the use of the modeling–rendering paradigm that we introduced in Chapter 1. The design of a scene is done interactively, using simple renderers of the type that we discussed in Chapter 6. When the design is complete, the objects, lights, material properties, cameras, motion descriptions, and textures can be described in a file that can be sent to a high-quality renderer or to a rendering farm.

In principle, this off-line renderer could be any type of renderer. However, given the special needs of the animation industry, Pixar developed both the interface (RenderMan) and a renderer called Reyes that was designed to produce the types of images needed for commercial motion pictures. Like a ray tracer, Reyes was designed to work a pixel at time. Unlike a ray tracer, it was not designed to incorporate global lighting effects. By working a pixel at a time, Reyes collects all the light from all objects at a resolution that avoids aliasing problems. Reyes divides (**dices**) objects—both polygonal and curved—into **micropolygons**, which are small quadrilaterals that project to a size of about half of a pixel. Because each micropolygon projects to such a small area, it can be flat shaded, thereby simplifying its rendering. The smooth shading of surfaces is accomplished by coloring the micropolygons carefully during the dicing process.

Reyes incorporates many other interesting techniques. It uses random or stochastic sampling rather than point sampling to reduce visible aliasing effects. Generally, it works on small regions of the frame at one time to allow efficient use of textures. Note that even with its careful design, a single scene with many objects and complex lighting effects can take hours to render.

There are many renderers of this type available, some either public domain or shareware. Some renderers arc capable of incorporating different rendering styles within one product. Thus, we might use ray tracing on a subset of the objects that have shiny surfaces. Likewise, we might want to use radiosity on some other subset of the surfaces. In general, these renderers support a large variety of effects and allow the user to balance rendering time against sophistication and image quality.

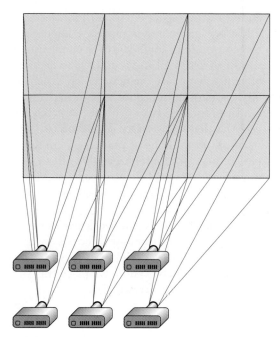

FIGURE 12.21 Power wall using six projectors.

12.7 Large-Scale Rendering

In many applications, particularly in the scientific visualization of large geometric data sets, we create images from data sets that might contain more than 500 million data points and generate more than 100 million polygons. This situation presents two immediate challenges. First, if we are to display this many polygons, how can we do so when typical monitor displays contain only about one million pixels. Second, if we have multiple frames to display, either from new data or because of transformations of the original data set, we need to be able to render this large amount of geometry faster than can be achieved even with high-end systems.

A popular solution to the display-resolution problem is to build a **power wall**, a large projection surface that is illuminated by an array of projectors (Figure 12.21), each with the resolution of a CRT (usually 1024 × 1280 or 1024 × 768). Generally the light output from the projectors is tapered at the edges, and the displays are overlapped slightly to created a seamless image. We can also create high-resolution displays from arrays of standard-size LCD panels, although at the cost of seeing small separations between panels, which can give the appearance of a window with multiple panes.

Our approach to both these problems is to use clusters of standard computers connected with a high-speed network. Each computer might have a commodity graphics card. Note that such configurations are one aspect of a major revolution in high-performance computing. Formerly, supercomputers were composed of expensive fast processors that usually incorporated a high degree of parallelism in their designs. These processors were custom designed and required special interfaces, peripheral systems, and environments that made them extremely expensive and thus affordable only by a few government laboratories and large corporations. Over the last few years, commodity processors have become extremely fast and inexpensive. The same technology has led to a variety of add-on graphics cards whose performance can be measured in millions of polygons per second and hundreds of millions of pixels per second. Computers assembled from such components can be connected by standard networks that run at gigabit-per-second rates. Thus, we can put together a cluster of these machines for a cost in the range of $1,000 to $3,000 per node.

However, there are multiple ways we can distribute the work that must be done to render a scene among the processors. We shall examine three possibilities. In this taxonomy, the key difference is where in the rendering process we assign, or sort, primitives to the correct areas of the display. Where we place this step leads to the designations **sort first**, **sort last**, and **sort middle**.

Suppose that we start with a large number of processors of two types: geometry processors and raster processors. This distinction corresponds to the two phases of the rendering pipeline that we discussed in Chapter 7. The geometry processors can handle front-end floating-point calculations, including transformations, clipping, and shading. The raster processors manipulate bits and handle operations such as scan conversion. Note that this distinction is somewhat historical, because the present general-purpose processors and graphics cards can each do either of these tasks. However, this distinction will help us organize the architectural possibilities.

12.7.1 Sort-Middle Rendering

Consider a group of geometry processors (each labeled with a G) and raster processors (each labeled with an R) connected as in Figure 12.22. Suppose that we have an application that generates a large number of geometric primitives. It can use multiple geometry processors in two obvious ways. It can run on a single processor and send different parts of the geometry generated by the application to different geometry processors. Alternatively, we can run the application on multiple processors, each of which generates only part of the geometry. At this point we need not worry about how the geometry gets to the geometry processors—as the best way is often application dependent—but on how to best employ the geometry processors that are available.

Assume that we can send any primitive to any of the geometry processors, each of which acts independently. When we use multiple processors in parallel, a major concern is **load balancing**, that is, having each of the processors do about the same amount of work so that none are sitting idle for a significant amount of time, thus wasting resources. One obvious approach would be to

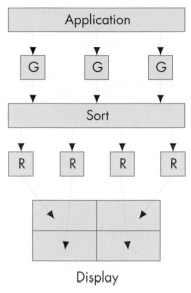

FIGURE 12.22   Sort-middle rendering.

divide the world-coordinate space equally among the processors. Unfortunately, this approach often leads to poor load balancing because in many applications the geometry is not uniformly distributed in the problem space. An alternative approach is to distribute the geometry uniformly among the processors as it is generated, independently of where the geometric objects are located. Thus, with n processors, we might send the first geometric entity to the first processor, the second to the second processor, the nth to the nth processor, the $(n + 1)$-st to the first processor, and so on. Now consider the raster processors. We can assign each of these to a different region of the frame buffer or, equivalently, assign each to a different region of the screen. Thus, each one renders a fixed part of the display.

Now the problem is how to assign the outputs of the geometry processors to the raster processors. Note that each geometry processor can process objects that could go anywhere on the display. Thus, we must sort their outputs and assign primitives that emerge from the geometry processors to the correct raster processors. Consequently, some sorting must be done before the raster stage. We refer to this architecture as *sort middle*.

This configuration was popular with high-end graphics workstations a few years ago when special hardware was available for each task and there were fast internal buses to convey information through the sorting step. Recent GPUs contain multiple geometry processors and multiple fragment processors and so can be looked at as sort-middle processors. We tend to regard a particular commodity card with a single GPU as a combination of one geometry processor and one raster processor, thus aggregating the parallelism inside the GPU. Now

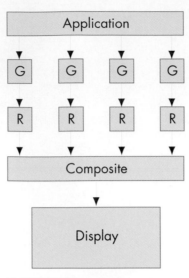

FIGURE 12.23   Sort-last rendering.

the problem is how to use a group of commodity cards or GPUs. If we can use a GPU or a CPU as either a geometry processor or a raster processor and connect them with a standard network, the sorting step in sort middle can be a bottleneck, and two other approaches have proved simpler.

12.7.2 Sort-Last Rendering

With sort-middle rendering, the number of geometry processors and the number of raster processors could be different. Now suppose that each geometry processor is connected to its own raster processor, as in Figure 12.23. This configuration would be what we would have with a collection of standard PCs, each with its own graphics card. Once again, let us not worry about how each processor gets the application data and instead focus on how this configuration can process the geometry generated by the application.

Just as with sort middle, we can load-balance the geometry processors by sending primitives to them in an order that ignores where on the display they might lie once they are rasterized. However, precisely because of this way of assigning geometry and lacking a sort in the middle, each raster processor must have a frame buffer that is the full size of the display. Because each geometry/raster pair contains a full pipeline, each pair produces a correct hidden-surface–removed image *for part of the geometry*. Figure 12.24 shows three images that are each correct, while the fourth shows how they must be combined to form a correct image containing all the geometry.

We can combine the partial images with a compositing step, as in Figure 12.25. For the compositing calculations, we need not only the images in the color

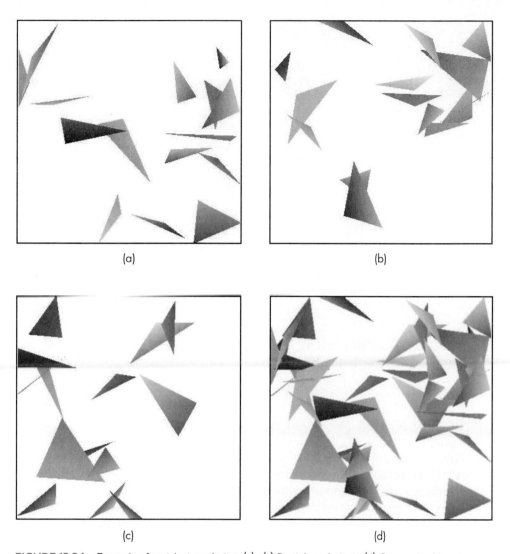

FIGURE 12.24 Example of sort-last rendering. (a)–(c) Partial renderings. (d) Composited image. (Courtesy of Ge Li, University of New Mexico)

buffers of the geometry processors but also the depth information because we must know for each pixel which of the raster processors contains the pixel corresponding to the closest point to the viewer.[3] Fortunately, if we are using our standard OpenGL pipeline, the necessary information is in the z buffer. For each

---

3. For simplicity, we are assuming that all the geometric objects are opaque.

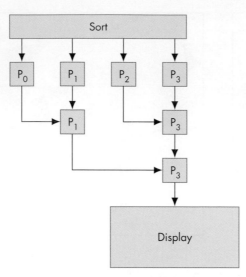

FIGURE 12.25 Binary-tree compositing.

pixel, we need only compare the depths in each of the z buffers and write the color in the frame buffer of the processor with the closest depth. The difficulty is determining how to do this comparison efficiently when the information is stored on many processors.

Conceptually, the simplest approach, sometimes called **binary-tree compositing**, is to have pairs of processors combine their information. Consider the example in Figure 12.26, where we have four geometry/raster pipelines, numbered 0 through 3. Processors 0 and 1 can combine their information to form a correct image for the geometry they have seen, while processors 2 and 3 do the same thing concurrently with their information. Let us assume that we form these new images on processors 1 and 3. Thus, processors 0 and 2 have to send *both* their color buffers *and* their z buffers to their neighbors (processors 1 and 3, respectively). We then repeat the process between processors 1 and 3, with the final image being formed in the frame buffer of processor 3. Note that the code is very simple. The geometry/raster pairs each do an ordinary rendering. The compositing step requires only the use of glReadPixels and some simple comparisons. However, in each successive step of the compositing process, only half the processors that were used in the previous step are still needed. In the end, the final image is prepared on a single processor.

There is another approach to the compositing step know as **binary-swap compositing** that avoids the idle processor problem. In this technique, each processor is responsible for one part of the final image. Hence, for compositing to be correct, each processor must see all the data. If we have n processors involved in the compositing, we can arrange them in a round-robin fashion as in Figure 12.26. The compositing takes n steps (rather than the log n steps

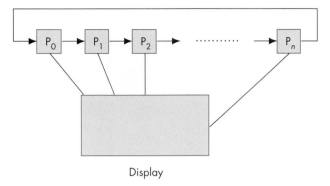

Display

FIGURE 12.26 Binary-swap compositing.

required by tree compositing). On the first step, processor 0 sends portion 0 of its frame buffer to processor 1 and receives portion n from processor n. The other processors do a similar send and receive of the portion of the color and depth buffers of their neighbors. At this point, each processor can update one area of the display that will be correct for the data from a pair of processors. For processor 0 this will be region n. On the second round, processor 0 will receive from processor n the data from region $n - 1$, which is correct for the data from processors n and $n - 1$. Processor 0 will also send the data from region n, as will the other processors for part of their frame buffers. All the processors will now have a region that is correct for the data from three processors. Inductively, it should be clear that after $n - 1$ steps, each processor has $1/n$ of the final image. Although we have taken more steps, far less data has been transferred than with tree compositing, and we have used all processors in each step.

12.7.3 Sort-First Rendering

One of the most appealing features of sort-last rendering is that we can pair geometric and raster processors and use standard computers with standard graphics cards. Suppose that we could decide first where each primitive lies on the final display. Then we could assign a separate portion of the display to each geometry/raster pair and avoid the necessity of a compositing network. The configuration might look like Figure 12.27. Here we have included a processor at the front end to make the assignment as to which primitives go to which processors.

This front-end sort is the key to making this scheme work. In one sense, it might seem impossible, since we are implying that we know the solution—where primitives appear in the display—before we have solved the problem for which we need the geometric pipeline. But things are not hopeless. Many problems are structured so that we may know this information in advance. We also can get the information back from the pipeline using glGetFloatv to find the mapping

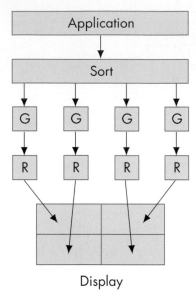

FIGURE 12.27   Sort-first rendering.

from world coordinates to screen coordinates. In addition, we need not always be correct. A primitive can be sent to multiple geometry processors if it straddles more than one region of the display. Even if we send a primitive to the wrong processor, that processor may be able to send it on to the correct processor. Because each geometry processor performs a clipping step, we are assured that the resulting image will be correct.

Sort-first rendering does not address the load-balancing issue, because if there are regions of the screen with very few primitives, the corresponding processors may not be very heavily loaded. However, sort-first rendering has one important advantage over sort-last rendering: It is ideally suited for generating high-resolution displays. Suppose that we want to display our output at a resolution much greater than we get with typical CRT or LCD displays that have a resolution in the range of 1 to 2 million pixels. Such displays are needed when we wish to examine high-resolution data that might contain more than 100 million geometric primitives.

One approach to this problem is to build a tiled display or power wall consisting of an array of standard displays (or tiles). The tiles can be CRTs, LCD panels, or the output of projectors. From the rendering perspective, we want to render an image whose resolution is the array of the entire display, which can exceed 4000 × 4000 pixels. Generally, these displays are driven by a cluster of PCs with commodity graphics cards. Hence, the candidate rendering strategies are sort first and sort last.

However, sort-last rendering cannot work in this setting because each geometry/rasterizer processor must have a frame buffer the size of the final image, and for the compositing step, extremely large amounts of data must be exchanged between processors. Sort-first renderers do not have this problem. Each geometry/processor pair need only be responsible for a small part of the final image, typically an image the size of a standard frame buffer.

12.8 Image-Based Rendering

Recently there has been a great deal of interest in starting with a set of two-dimensional images and either extracting three-dimensional information or forming new images from them. This problem has appeared in many forms over the years. Some of the most important examples in the past have included the following:

- Using aerial photographs to obtain terrain information.
- Using a sequence of two-dimensional X rays to obtain a three-dimensional image in computerized axial tomography (CT).
- Obtaining geometric models from cameras in robotics.
- Warping one image into another (morphing).

Newer applications have focused on creating new images from a sequence of stored images that have been carefully collected. For example, suppose that we take a sequence of photographs of an object—a person, a building, or a CAD model—and want to see the object from a different viewpoint. If we had a three-dimensional model, we would simply move the viewer or the object and construct the new image. But what can we do if we have only two-dimensional information? These problems all fit under the broad heading **image-based rendering**. Techniques involve elements of computer graphics, image processing, and computer vision.

12.8.1 A Simple Example

We can get some idea of the issues involved by considering the problem shown in Figure 12.28. On the left is a perspective camera located at a point $\mathbf{p}_1$, and on the right is a second located at $\mathbf{p}_2$. Consider a point $\mathbf{q}$ that is imaged by both cameras. Assuming that we know everything about these cameras—their locations, orientations, fields of view—can we determine $\mathbf{q}$ from the two images produced by the cameras? Figure 12.29 has a top view of a simplified version of the problem with the two cameras both located on the x-axis and with their image planes parallel at $z = d$. Using our standard equations for projections, we have the two relationships

$$\frac{x_1 - x_{p1}}{d} = \frac{x - x_1}{z},$$

$$\frac{x_2 - x_{p2}}{d} = \frac{x - x_2}{z}.$$

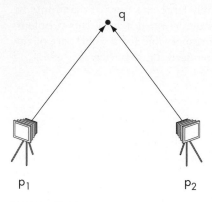

FIGURE 12.28   Two cameras imaging the same point.

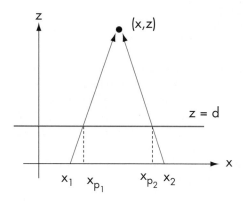

FIGURE 12.29   Top view of the two cameras.

These are two linear equations in the unknowns x and z that we can solve, yielding

$$z = \frac{d\,\Delta x}{\Delta x_p - \Delta x},$$

$$x = \frac{x_{p1}\Delta x - x_1\Delta x_p}{\Delta x_p - \Delta x},$$

where $\Delta x = x_2 - x_1$ and $\Delta x_p = x_{p2} - x_{p1}$.

Thus, we have determined **q** from the two images. This result does not depend on where the cameras are located; moving them only makes the equations a little more complex. Once we have **q** we can obtain an image from any viewpoint.

On closer examination, we can see some practical problems. First, there are numerical problems. Any small errors in the measurement of the camera position can cause large errors in the estimate of $\mathbf{q}$. Such numerical issues have plagued many of the traditional applications, such as terrain measurement. One way around such problems is to use more than two measurements and then to determine a best estimate of the desired position.

There are other potentially serious problems. For example, how do we obtain the points $\mathbf{p}_1$ and $\mathbf{p}_2$? Given the images from the two cameras, we need a method of identifying corresponding points. This problem is one of the fundamental problems in computer vision and one for which there are no perfect solutions. Note that if there is occlusion, the same point may not even be present in the two images, as shown in Figure 12.30.

Many early techniques were purely image-based, using statistical methods to find corresponding points. Other techniques were interactive, requiring the user to identify corresponding points. Recently, within the computer graphics community, there have been some novel approaches to the problem. We shall mention a few of the more noteworthy ones. The details of each are referenced in the Suggested Readings at the end of the chapter.

One way around the difficulties in pure image-based approaches has been to use geometric models rather than points for the registration. For example, in a real environment, we might know that there are many objects that are composed of right parallelepipeds. This extra information can be used to derive very accurate position information.

One use of image-based techniques has been to generate new images for a single viewer from a sequence of images. Variations of this general problem have been used in the movie industry, in providing new images in virtual reality applications, such as Apple's QuickTime VR, and for viewing objects remotely.

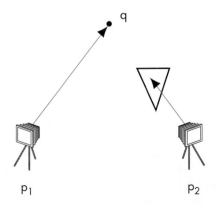

FIGURE 12.30   Imaging with occlusion.

Others have looked at the mathematical relationship between two-dimensional images and the light distribution in a three-dimensional environment. Each two-dimensional image is a sample of a four-dimensional light field. In a manner akin to how three-dimensional images are constructed from two-dimensional projections in computerized axial tomography, two-dimensional projections from multiple cameras can be used to reconstruct the three-dimensional world. Two of these techniques are known as the **lumigraph** and **light-field rendering**.

Summary and Notes

This chapter has illustrated that there are many approaches to rendering. The physical basis for rendering with global lighting is contained in the rendering equation. Unfortunately, it contains too many variables to be solvable for the general case, even by numerical methods. Radiosity and ray tracing can handle some global effects, although they make opposite assumptions on the types of surfaces that are in the scene. As GPUs become more and more powerful, they can handle much of the computation required by alternate rendering methods. Consequently, we may see less of a distinction than presently exists between pipeline approaches and all other rendering methods for real-time applications.

Although the speed and cost of computers make it possible to ray-trace scenes and do radiosity calculations that were not possible a few years ago, it appears that these techniques alone still have limited utility in the real world. If we look at what has been happening in the film, television, and game industries, it appears that we can create photorealistic imagery using a wealth of modeling methods and a variety of commercial and shareware renderers. However, there is a growing acceptance of the view that photorealism is not the ultimate goal. Hence, we see increasing interest in such areas as combining realistic rendering and computer modeling with traditional hand animation. The wide range of image-based methods fit in well with many of these applications.

Most of what we see on the consumer end of graphics is driven by computer games. It appears that no matter how fast and cheap processors are, the demands of consumers for more sophisticated computer games will continue to force developers to come up with faster processors with new capabilities. Most likely as high-definition television (HDTV) becomes more accepted, we will see a greater variety of high-resolution displays available at reasonable prices.

On the scientific side, the replacement of traditional supercomputers by clusters of commodity computers will continue to have a large effect on scientific visualization. The enormous data sets generated by applications run on these clusters will drive application development on the graphics side. Not only will these applications need imagery generated for high-resolution displays, but also the difficulties of storing these data sets will drive efforts to visualize these data as fast as they can be generated.

Suggested Readings

Ray tracing was introduced by Appel [App68] and popularized by Whitted [Whi80]. Many of the early papers on ray tracing are included in a volume by Joy and colleagues [Joy88]. The book by Glassner [Gla89] is particularly helpful if you plan to write your own ray tracer. Many of the tests for intersections are described in Haines's chapter in [Gla89] and in the *Graphics Gems* series [Gra90, Gra91, Gra92, Gra94, Gra95].

The Rendering Equation is due to Kajiya [Kaj86]. Radiosity is based on a method first used in heat transfer [Sie81]. It was first applied in computer graphics by Goral and colleagues [Gor84]. Since its introduction, researchers have done a great deal of work on increasing its efficiency [Coh85, Coh88, Coh93] and incorporating specular terms [Sil89]. The method of using point light sources to find form factors appeared in [Kel97]. Photon mapping has been popularized by Jensen [Jen01].

The RenderMan interface is described in [Ups89]. The Reyes rendering architecture was first presented in [Coo87]. Maya [Wat02] allows multiple types of renderers.

The sorting classification of parallel rendering was suggested by Molnar and colleagues [Mol94]. The advantages of sort-middle architectures were used in Silicon Graphics' high-end workstations such as the Infinite Reality Graphics workstations [Mon97]. The sort-last architecture was developed as part of the Pixel Flow architecture [Mol92]. Binary-swap compositing was suggested by [Ma94]. Software for sort-last renderings using clusters of commodity computers is discussed in [Hum01]. Power walls are described in [Her00, Che00].

Image-based rendering by warping frames was part of Microsoft's Talisman hardware [Tor96]. Apple's Quicktime VR [Che95] was based on creating new views from a single viewpoint from a 360-degree panorama. Debevec and colleagues [Deb96] showed that by using a model-based approach, new images from multiple viewpoints could be constructed from a small number of images. Other warping methods were proposed in [Sei96]. Work on the Lumigraph [Gor96] and light fields [Lev96] established the mathematical foundations for image-based techniques.

Exercises

12.1   Devise a test for whether a point is inside a convex polygon based on the idea that the polygon can be described by a set of intersecting lines in a single plane.

12.2   Extend your algorithm from Exercise 13.1 to polyhedra that are formed by the intersection of planes.

12.3 Derive an implicit equation for a torus whose center is at the origin. You can derive the equation by noting that a plane that cuts through the torus reveals two circles of the same radius.

12.4 Using the result from Exercise 13.3, show that you can ray-trace a torus using the quadratic equation to find the required intersections.

12.5 Consider a ray passing through a sphere. Find the point on this ray closest to the center of the sphere. *Hint:* Consider a line from the center of the sphere that is normal to the ray. How can you use this result for intersection testing?

12.6 We can get increased accuracy from a ray tracer by using more rays. Suppose that for each pixel, we cast a ray through the center of the pixel and through its four corners. How much more work does this approach require as compared to the one-ray-per-pixel ray tracer.

12.7 In the sort-middle approach to parallel rendering, what type of information must be conveyed between the geometry processors and raster processors?

12.8 What changes would you have to make to our parallel rendering strategies if we were to allow translucent objects?

12.9 One way to classify parallel computers is by whether their memory is shared among the processors or distributed so that each processor has its own memory that is not accessible to other processors. How does this distinction affect the various rendering strategies that we have discussed?

12.10 Extrapolate the simple example of imaging the same point from two viewers to the general case in which the two viewers can be located at arbitrary locations in three dimensions.

12.11 Build a simple ray tracer that can handle only planes and spheres. There are many interesting data sets available on the Internet with which to test your code.

12.12 Suppose that you have an algebraic function in which the highest term is $x^i y^j z^k$. What is the degree of the polynomial that we need to solve for the intersection of a ray with the surface defined by this function?

12.13 Consider again an algebraic function in which the highest term is $x^i y^j z^k$. If $i = j = k$, how many terms are in the polynomial that is created when we intersect the surface with a parametric ray?

12.14 For one or more OpenGL implementations, find how many triangles per second can be rendered. Determine what part of the rendering time is spent in hidden-surface removal, shading, texture mapping, and rasterization. If you are using a commodity graphics card, how does the performance that you measure compare with the specifications for the card?

12.15 Determine the pixel performance of your graphics card. Determine how many pixels per second can be read or written. Do the reading and writing of pixels occur at different rates? Is there a difference in writing texture maps?

12.16 Build a sort-last renderer using OpenGL for the rendering on each processor. You can do performance tests using applications that generate triangles or triangular meshes.

12.17 Explain why, as we add more processors, the performance of sort-first rendering will eventually get worse.

APPENDIX

SAMPLE PROGRAMS

This appendix contains the source code for many of the example programs that we developed in the text. These programs and others that are referred to in the text are also available at *www.cs.unm.edu/~angel* for updates. A makefile that should work on most Linux implementations is also available there, as are additional sample programs and some implementation notes. Other examples, including those in the *OpenGL Programming Guide* and GLUT, can be found starting from the OpenGL Web site (*www.opengl.org*).

OpenGL is standard on almost all workstations. For systems that use Microsoft Windows, the dynamic libraries for GL (OpenGL32.dll) and GLU (GLU32.dll) are in the system folder. The corresponding .lib files and include files are provided with language compilers such as Visual C++. The corresponding GLUT files (glut32.dll, glut32.lib, and glut.h) are available over the Web (see *www.opengl.org*). The drivers for particular graphics cards implement OpenGL using a combination of hardware and software. Thus, as long as the drivers are properly installed, using OpenGL is identical on all systems. Graphics cards differ in their performance and what extras they provide in the form of extensions.

Most Linux distributions provide the Mesa distribution of OpenGL (*www.mesa3D.org*) and include GLUT. Although Mesa is a pure software implementation of OpenGL (and includes the source for those interested in implementation issues), increasingly manufacturers of commodity graphics cards are providing Linux drivers that allow Linux users to take advantage of the cards' capabilities.

The programs that follow use the GLUT library for interfacing with the window system. The naming of the functions follows the *OpenGL Programming Guide* and the *GLUT Users Guide*. These programs share much of the same code. You should find functions, such as the reshape callback, the initialization function, and the main function, almost identical across the programs. Consequently, only the first instance of each function contains extensive comments.

In selecting all these programs, illustration of graphical principles, as opposed to efficiency, was the driving design criterion. You should find numerous ways to both extend these programs and make them run more efficiently. In some instances, the same visual results can be generated in a completely different manner, using OpenGL capabilities other than the ones we used in the sample program.

The programs that follow include

1. A program that generates 5,000 points on the Sierpinski gasket (Chapter 2).
2. A version of the gasket program using recursion (Chapter 2).
3. A three-dimensional recursive version of the gasket program (Chapter 2).
4. Marching-squares program (Chapter 2).
5. A program that illustrates the use of the mouse with GLUT (Chapter 3).
6. The simple paint program that we developed in Chapter 3.
7. A rotating-square program using both single and double buffering (Chapter 3).
8. A picking program using selection mode (Chapter 3).
9. The rotating-cube program from Chapter 4.
10. A rotating-cube program using vertex arrays (Chapter 4).
11. A rotating-cube program using a virtual trackball (Chapter 4).
12. The walk-through program from Chapter 5.
13. The program that generates approximations to a sphere by recursive subdivision generation from Chapter 6.
14. Mandelbrot set-generating program (Chapter 8).
15. Line drawing using Bresenham's algorithm (Chapter 8).
16. A rotating cube program with texture (Chapter 8).
17. A complete GLSL program (Chapter 9).
18. A program that defines and renders a scene graph using the simple scene-graph API from Chapter 10.
19. An interactive program that draws cubic Bézier curves from Chapter 11.

A.1   Sierpinski Gasket Program

```
/* two-dimensional Sierpinski gasket        */
/* generated using randomly selected vertices */
/* and bisection                             */

#include <GL/glut.h>

/* you may have to change the include to <glut.h> or
elsewhere depending on where it is stored on your system */

/* glut.h usually has includes for gl.h and glu.h */

void myinit()
{

/* attributes */
```

```
        glClearColor(1.0, 1.0, 1.0, 1.0); /* white background */
        glColor3f(1.0, 0.0, 0.0); /* draw in red */

/* set up viewing */
/* 50.0 x 50.0 camera coordinate window with origin lower left */

        glMatrixMode(GL_PROJECTION);
        glLoadIdentity();
        gluOrtho2D(0.0, 50.0, 0.0, 50.0);
        glMatrixMode(GL_MODELVIEW);
}

void display()
{
    /* A triangle */
    GLfloat vertices[3][2]={{0.0,0.0},{25.0,50.0},{50.0,0.0}};

    int i, j, k;
    int rand();        /* standard random number generator */
    GLfloat p[2] ={7.5, 5.0};  /* arbitrary initial point inside triangle */
    glClear(GL_COLOR_BUFFER_BIT);  /*clear the window */
    glBegin(GL_POINTS);

/* compute and plot 5000 new points */

    for( k=0; k<5000; k++)
    {
        j=rand()%3; /* pick a vertex at random */

     /* compute point halfway between selected vertex and old point */

        p[0] = (p[0]+vertices[j][0])/2.0;
        p[1] = (p[1]+vertices[j][1])/2.0;

    /* plot new point */

        glVertex2fv(p);

    }
    glEnd();
    glFlush(); /* clear buffers */
 }

int main(int argc, char** argv)
{

/* standard GLUT initialization */

    glutInit(&argc,argv);
```

```
        glutInitDisplayMode (GLUT_SINGLE | GLUT_RGB); /* default, not needed */
        glutInitWindowSize(500,500); /* 500 x 500 pixel window */
        glutInitWindowPosition(0,0); /* place window top left on display */
        glutCreateWindow("Sierpinski Gasket"); /* window title */
        glutDisplayFunc(display);
                    /* display callback invoked when window opened */
        myinit(); /* set attributes */
        glutMainLoop(); /* enter event loop */
}
```

A.2   Recursive Generation of Sierpinski Gasket

```
/* recursive subdivision of triangle to form Sierpinski gasket */
/* number of recursive steps given on command line */

#include <GL/glut.h>

/* initial triangle */

GLfloat v[3][2]={{-1.0, -0.58}, {1.0, -0.58}, {0.0, 1.15}};

int n;

void triangle( point2 a, point2 b, point2 c)

/* specify one triangle */
{
        glVertex2fv(a);
        glVertex2fv(b);
        glVertex2fv(c);
}

void divide_triangle(GLfloat *a, GLfloat *b, GLfloat *c, int m)
{

/* triangle subdivision using vertex numbers */

    GLfloat v0[2], v1[2], v2[2];
    int j;
    if(m>0)
    {
        for(j=0; j<2; j++) v0[j]=(a[j]+b[j])/2;
        for(j=0; j<2; j++) v1[j]=(a[j]+c[j])/2;
        for(j=0; j<2; j++) v2[j]=(b[j]+c[j])/2;
        divide_triangle(a, v0, v1, m-1);
```

```
        divide_triangle(c, v1, v2, m-1);
        divide_triangle(b, v2, v0, m-1);
    }
    else triangle(a,b,c); /* draw triangle at end of recursion */
}


void display()
{
    glClear(GL_COLOR_BUFFER_BIT);
    glBegin(GL_TRIANGLES);
    divide_triangle(v[0], v[1], v[2], n);
    glEnd();
    glFlush();
}

void myinit()
{
    glMatrixMode(GL_PROJECTION);
    glLoadIdentity();
    gluOrtho2D(-2.0, 2.0, -2.0, 2.0);
    glMatrixMode(GL_MODELVIEW);
    glClearColor (1.0, 1.0, 1.0, 1.0);
    glColor3f(0.0,0.0,0.0);
}

int main(int argc, char **argv)
{
    n=atoi(argv[1]); /* or set number of subdivision steps here */
    glutInit(&argc, argv);
    glutInitDisplayMode(GLUT_SINGLE | GLUT_RGB);
    glutInitWindowSize(500, 500);
    glutCreateWindow("Sierpinski Gasket");
    glutDisplayFunc(display);
    myinit();
    glutMainLoop();
}
```

A.3 Recursive Three-Dimensional Sierpinski Gasket

```
/* recursive subdivision of a tetrahedron to form 3D Sierpinski gasket */
/* number of recursive steps given on command line */

#include <stdlib.h>
#include <GL/glut.h>
```

```c
/* initial tetrahedron */

GLfloat v[4][3]={{0.0, 0.0, 1.0}, {0.0, 0.942809, -0.33333},
    {-0.816497, -0.471405, -0.333333}, {0.816497, -0.471405, -0.333333}};

GLfloat colors[4][3] = {{1.0, 0.0, 0.0}, {0.0, 1.0, 0.0},
                        {0.0, 0.0, 1.0}, {0.0, 0.0, 0.0}};

int n;

void triangle(GLfloat *va, GLfloat *vb, GLfloat *vc)
{
    glVertex3fv(va);
    glVertex3fv(vb);
    glVertex3fv(vc);
}

void tetra(GLfloat *a, GLfloat *b, GLfloat *c, GLfloat *d)
{
    glColor3fv(colors[0]);
    triangle(a, b, c);
    glColor3fv(colors[1]);
    triangle(a, c, d);
    glColor3fv(colors[2]);
    triangle(a, d, b);
    glColor3fv(colors[3]);
    triangle(b, d, c);
}

void divide_tetra(GLfloat *a, GLfloat *b, GLfloat *c, GLfloat *d, int m)
{

    GLfloat mid[6][3];
    int j;
    if(m>0)
    {
        /* compute six midpoints */

        for(j=0; j<3; j++) mid[0][j]=(a[j]+b[j])/2;
        for(j=0; j<3; j++) mid[1][j]=(a[j]+c[j])/2;
        for(j=0; j<3; j++) mid[2][j]=(a[j]+d[j])/2;
        for(j=0; j<3; j++) mid[3][j]=(b[j]+c[j])/2;
        for(j=0; j<3; j++) mid[4][j]=(c[j]+d[j])/2;
        for(j=0; j<3; j++) mid[5][j]=(b[j]+d[j])/2;

        /* create 4 tetrahedrons by subdivision */

        divide_tetra(a, mid[0], mid[1], mid[2], m-1);
        divide_tetra(mid[0], b, mid[3], mid[5], m-1);
```

```
        divide_tetra(mid[1], mid[3], c, mid[4], m-1);
        divide_tetra(mid[2], mid[4], d, mid[5], m-1);


    }
    else(tetra(a,b,c,d)); /* draw tetrahedron at end of recursion */
}


void display()
{
    glClear(GL_COLOR_BUFFER_BIT);
    glBegin(GL_TRIANGLES);
    divide_tetra(v[0], v[1], v[2], v[3], n);
    glEnd();
    glFlush();
}


void myReshape(int w, int h)
{
    glViewport(0, 0, w, h);
    glMatrixMode(GL_PROJECTION);
    glLoadIdentity();
    if (w <= h)
        glOrtho(-2.0, 2.0, -2.0 * (GLfloat) h / (GLfloat) w,
            2.0 * (GLfloat) h / (GLfloat) w, -10.0, 10.0);
    else
        glOrtho(-2.0 * (GLfloat) w / (GLfloat) h,
            2.0 * (GLfloat) w / (GLfloat) h, -2.0, 2.0, -10.0, 10.0);
    glMatrixMode(GL_MODELVIEW);
    glutPostRedisplay();
}


int main(int argc, char **argv)
{
    n=atoi(argv[1]); /* or enter number of subdivision steps here */
    glutInit(&argc, argv);
    glutInitDisplayMode(GLUT_SINGLE | GLUT_RGB | GLUT_DEPTH);
    glutInitWindowSize(500, 500);
    glutCreateWindow("3D Gasket");
    glutReshapeFunc(myReshape);
    glutDisplayFunc(display);
    glEnable(GL_DEPTH_TEST);
    glClearColor (1.0, 1.0, 1.0, 1.0);
    glutMainLoop();
}
```

A.4   Marching Squares

```c
/* generates contours using marching squares */

/* region size */

#define X_MAX 1.0
#define Y_MAX 1.0
#define X_MIN -1.0
#define Y_MIN -1.0

/* number of cells */

#define N_X 50
#define N_Y 50

/* contour value */

#define THRESHOLD 0.0

#include <GL/glut.h>

void display()
{
   double f(double,double);
   int cell(double, double, double, double);
   void lines(int, int, int, double, double, double, double);

   double data[N_X][N_Y];
   int i,j;
   int c;

   glClear(GL_COLOR_BUFFER_BIT);

/* form data array from function */

   for(i=0;i<N_X;i++) for (j=0;j<N_Y;j++)
     data[i][j]=f(X_MIN+i*(X_MAX-(X_MIN))/(N_X-1.0),
     Y_MIN+j*(Y_MAX-(Y_MIN))/(N_Y-1.0));

   /* process each cell */

   for(i=0;i<N_X;i++) for (j=0;j<N_Y;j++)
   {
     c=cell(data[i][j], data[i+1][j], data[i+1][j+1], data[i][j+1]);
     lines(c,i,j,data[i][j], data[i+1][j], data[i+1][j+1], data[i][j+1]);
   }
   glFlush();
}
```

```
/* define function f(x,y)       */

double f(double x, double y)
{

    double a=0.49, b=0.5;

    /* Ovals of Cassini  */

    return (x*x+y*y+a*a)*(x*x+y*y+a*a)-4*a*a*x*x-b*b*b*b;
}


/* define cell vertices */

int cell(double a, double b, double c , double d)
{
    int n=0;
    if(a>THRESHOLD) n+=1;
    if(b>THRESHOLD) n+=8;
    if(c>THRESHOLD) n+=4;
    if(d>THRESHOLD) n+=2;
    return n;
}



/* draw line segments for each case */

void lines(int num, int i, int j, double a, double b, double c, double d)
{
void draw_one(int, int, int, double, double, double, double);
void draw_adjacent(int, int, int, double, double, double, double);
void draw_opposite(int, int, int, double, double, double, double);
    switch(num)
    {
    case 1: case 2: case 4: case 7: case 8: case 11: case 13: case 14:
      draw_one(num, i,j,a,b,c,d);
      break;
    case 3: case 6: case 9: case 12:
      draw_adjacent(num,i,j,a,b,c,d);
      break;
    case 5: case 10:
      draw_opposite(num, i,j,a,b,c,d);
      break;
    case 0: case 15: break;
    }
}

void draw_one(int num, int i, int j, double a, double b, double c, double d)
```

```
{
  double x1, y1, x2, y2;
  double ox, oy;
  double dx, dy;
  dx=(X_MAX-(X_MIN))/(N_X-1.0);
  dy=(Y_MAX-(Y_MIN))/(N_Y-1.0);
  ox=X_MIN+i*(X_MAX-(X_MIN))/(N_X-1.0);
  oy=Y_MIN+j*(Y_MAX-(Y_MIN))/(N_Y-1.0);
    switch(num)
    {
    case 1: case 14:
      x1=ox;
      y1=oy+dy*(THRESHOLD-a)/(d-a);
      x2=ox+dx*(THRESHOLD-a)/(b-a);
      y2=oy;
      break;
    case 2: case 13:
      x1=ox;
      y1=oy+dy*(THRESHOLD-a)/(d-a);
      x2=ox+dx*(THRESHOLD-d)/(c-d);
      y2=oy+dy;
      break;
    case 4: case 11:
      x1=ox+dx*(THRESHOLD-d)/(c-d);
      y1=oy+dy;
      x2=ox+dx;
      y2=oy+dy*(THRESHOLD-b)/(c-b);
      break;
    case 7: case 8:
      x1=ox+dx*(THRESHOLD-a)/(b-a);
      y1=oy;
      x2=ox+dx;
      y2=oy+dy*(THRESHOLD-b)/(c-b);
      break;
    }
  glBegin(GL_LINES);
    glVertex2d(x1, y1);
    glVertex2d(x2, y2);
  glEnd();
}

void draw_adjacent(int num, int i, int j, double a, double b, double c,
double d)
{
  double x1, y1, x2, y2;
  double ox, oy;
  double dx, dy;
  dx=(X_MAX-(X_MIN))/(N_X-1.0);
  dy=(Y_MAX-(Y_MIN))/(N_Y-1.0);
```

```
  ox=X_MIN+i*(X_MAX-(X_MIN))/(N_X-1.0);
  oy=Y_MIN+j*(Y_MAX-(Y_MIN))/(N_Y-1.0);
  switch(num)
  {
    case 3: case 12:
      x1=ox+dx*(THRESHOLD-a)/(b-a);
      y1=oy;
      x2=ox+dx*(THRESHOLD-d)/(c-d);
      y2=oy+dy;
      break;
    case 6: case 9:
      x1=ox;
      y1=oy+dy*(THRESHOLD-a)/(d-a);
      x2=ox+dx;
      y2=oy+dy*(THRESHOLD-b)/(c-b);
      break;
  }
  glBegin(GL_LINES);
    glVertex2d(x1, y1);
    glVertex2d(x2, y2);
  glEnd();

}

void draw_opposite(int num, int i, int j, double a, double b, double c,
double d)
{
  double x1,y1,x2,y2,x3,y3,x4,y4;
  double ox, oy;
  double dx, dy;
  dx=(X_MAX-(X_MIN))/(N_X-1.0);
  dy=(Y_MAX-(Y_MIN))/(N_Y-1.0);
  ox=X_MIN+i*(X_MAX-(X_MIN))/(N_X-1.0);
  oy=Y_MIN+j*(Y_MAX-(Y_MIN))/(N_Y-1.0);
  switch(num)
  {
    case5:
      x1=ox;
      y1=oy+dy*(THRESHOLD-a)/(d-a);
      x2=ox+dx*(THRESHOLD-a)/(b-a);
      y2=oy;
      x3=ox+dx*(THRESHOLD-d)/(c-d);
      y3=oy+dy;
      x4=ox+dx;
      y4=oy+dy*(THRESHOLD-b)/(c-b);
      break;
    case 10:
      x1=ox;
      y1=oy+dy*(THRESHOLD-a)/(d-a);
```

```
          x2=ox+dx*(THRESHOLD-d)/(c-d);
          y2=oy+dy;
          x3=ox+dy*(THRESHOLD-a)/(b-a);
          y3=oy;
          x4=ox+dx;
          y4=oy+dy*(THRESHOLD-b)/(c-b);
          break;
    }
    glBegin(GL_LINES);
      glVertex2d(x1, y1);
      glVertex2d(x2, y2);
      glVertex2d(x3, y3);
      glVertex2d(x4, y4);
    glEnd();
}

void myReshape(int w, int h)
{
glViewport(0, 0, w, h);
glMatrixMode(GL_PROJECTION);
glLoadIdentity();
if (w <= h)
gluOrtho2D(X_MIN, X_MAX, Y_MIN * (GLfloat) h / (GLfloat) w,
Y_MAX * (GLfloat) h / (GLfloat) w);
else
gluOrtho2D(X_MIN * (GLfloat) w / (GLfloat) h,
X_MAX * (GLfloat) w / (GLfloat) h, Y_MIN, Y_MAX);
glMatrixMode(GL_MODELVIEW);
}

int main(int argc, char **argv)
{
    glutInit(&argc, argv);
    glutInitWindowSize(500, 500);
    glutCreateWindow("contour plot");
    glutReshapeFunc(myReshape);
    glutDisplayFunc(display);
    glClearColor(0.0,0.0,0.0,1.0);
    glColor3f(1.0,1.0,1.0);
    glutMainLoop();
}
```

A.5 Square Drawing Program

```
/* program illustrates the use of the GLUT library for
interfacing with a window system */
```

/* The program opens a window, clears it to black,
then draws a box at the location of the mouse each time the
left button is clicked. The right button exits the program.
The program also reacts correctly when the window is
moved or resized by clearing the new window to black.*/

```
#include <GL/glut.h>

/* globals */

GLsizei wh = 500, ww = 500; /* initial window size */
GLfloat size = 3.0;    /* half side length of square */


void drawSquare(int x, int y)
{

   y=wh-y;
   glColor3ub( (char) rand()%256, (char) rand()%256, (char) rand()%256);
   glBegin(GL_POLYGON);
      glVertex2f(x+size, y+size);
      glVertex2f(x-size, y+size);
      glVertex2f(x-size, y-size);
      glVertex2f(x+size, y-size);
   glEnd();
   glFlush();
}


/* reshaping routine called whenever window is resized
or moved */

void myReshape(GLsizei w, GLsizei h)
{

/* adjust clipping box */

   glMatrixMode(GL_PROJECTION);
   glLoadIdentity();
   glOrtho(0.0, (GLdouble)w, 0.0, (GLdouble)h, -1.0, 1.0);
   glMatrixMode(GL_MODELVIEW);
   glLoadIdentity();

/* adjust viewport and clear */

   glViewport(0,0,w,h);
   glClear(GL_COLOR_BUFFER_BIT);
   glFlush();
```

```
                    /* set global size for use by drawing routine */

                        ww = w;
                        wh = h;
                    }

                    void myinit()
                    {
                        glClearColor (0.0, 0.0, 0.0, 1.0);
                        glViewport(0,0,ww,wh);

                    /* Pick 2D clipping window to match size of screen window.
                    This choice avoids having to scale object coordinates
                    each time window is resized. */

                        glMatrixMode(GL_PROJECTION);
                        glLoadIdentity();
                        glOrtho(0.0, (GLdouble) ww , 0.0, (GLdouble) wh , -1.0, 1.0);

                    /* set clear color to black and clear window */

                        glClearColor (0.0, 0.0, 0.0, 1.0);
                        glClear(GL_COLOR_BUFFER_BIT);
                        glFlush();
                    }

                    void mouse(int btn, int state, int x, int y)
                    {
                        if(btn==GLUT_RIGHT_BUTTON && state==GLUT_DOWN)    exit(0);
                    }

                    /* display callback required by GLUT */

                    void display()
                    {}

                    int main(int argc, char** argv)
                    {

                        glutInit(&argc,argv);
                        glutInitDisplayMode (GLUT_SINGLE | GLUT_RGB);
                        glutCreateWindow("square");
                        myinit ();
                        glutReshapeFunc (myReshape);
                        glutMouseFunc (mouse);
                        glutMotionFunc(drawSquare);
                        glutDisplayFunc(display);
                        glutMainLoop();

                    }
```

A.6 Paint Program

```
/* simple painting program with text, lines, triangles,
rectangles, and points */


#define NULL 0
#define LINE 1
#define RECTANGLE 2
#define TRIANGLE  3
#define POINTS 4
#define TEXT 5

#include <GL/glut.h>

void mouse(int, int, int, int);
void key(unsigned char, int, int);
void display();
void drawSquare(int, int);
void myReshape(GLsizei, GLsizei);

void myinit();

void screen_box(int, int, int);
void right_menu(int);
void middle_menu(int);
void color_menu(int);
void pixel_menu(int);
void fill_menu(int);
int pick(int, int);

/* globals */

GLsizei wh = 500, ww = 500; /* initial window size */
GLfloat size = 3.0;    /* half side length of square */
int draw_mode = 0; /* drawing mode */
int rx, ry; /*raster position*/

GLfloat r = 1.0, g = 1.0, b = 1.0; /* drawing color */
int fill = 0; /* fill flag */

void drawSquare(int x, int y)
{

        y=wh-y;
        glColor3ub( (char) rand()%256, (char) rand()%256, (char) rand()%256);
        glBegin(GL_POLYGON);
                glVertex2f(x+size, y+size);
                glVertex2f(x-size, y+size);
```

```
                    glVertex2f(x-size, y-size);
                    glVertex2f(x+size, y-size);
            glEnd();
    }


/* reshaping routine called whenever window is resized
or moved */

void myReshape(GLsizei w, GLsizei h)
{

/* adjust clipping box */

        glMatrixMode(GL_PROJECTION);
        glLoadIdentity();
        glOrtho(0.0, (GLdouble)w, 0.0, (GLdouble)h, -1.0, 1.0);
        glMatrixMode(GL_MODELVIEW);
        glLoadIdentity();

/* adjust viewport and clear */

        glViewport(0,0,w,h);
        glClearColor (0.8, 0.8, 0.8, 1.0);
        glClear(GL_COLOR_BUFFER_BIT);
        display();
        glFlush();

/* set global size for use by drawing routine */

        ww = w;
        wh = h;
    }

void myinit()
{

 glViewport(0,0,ww,wh);


/* Pick 2D clipping window to match size of X window.
This choice avoids having to scale object coordinates
each time window is resized. */

        glMatrixMode(GL_PROJECTION);
        glLoadIdentity();
        glOrtho(0.0, (GLdouble) ww , 0.0, (GLdouble) wh , -1.0, 1.0);

/* set clear color to black and clear window */
```

```
         glClearColor (0.8, 0.8, 0.8, 1.0);
         glClear(GL_COLOR_BUFFER_BIT);
         glFlush();
}

void mouse(int btn, int state, int x, int y)
{
    static int count;
    int where;
    static int xp[2],yp[2];
    if(btn==GLUT_LEFT_BUTTON && state==GLUT_DOWN)
    {
       glPushAttrib(GL_ALL_ATTRIB_BITS);
       where = pick(x,y);
       glColor3f(r, g, b);
       if(where != 0)
       {
          count = 0;
          draw_mode = where;
       }
       else switch(draw_mode)
       {
         case(LINE):
           if(count--0)
           {
              count++;
              xp[0] = x;
              yp[0] = y;
           }
           else
           {
              glBegin(GL_LINES);
                 glVertex2i(x,wh-y);
                 glVertex2i(xp[0],wh-yp[0]);
              glEnd();
              draw_mode=0;
              count=0;
           }
           break;
         case(RECTANGLE):
           if(count == 0)
           {
              count++;
              xp[0] = x;
              yp[0] = y;
           }
           else
           {
              if(fill) glBegin(GL_POLYGON);
```

```
                          else glBegin(GL_LINE_LOOP);
                              glVertex2i(x,wh-y);
                              glVertex2i(x,wh-yp[0]);
                              glVertex2i(xp[0],wh-yp[0]);
                              glVertex2i(xp[0],wh-y);
                          glEnd();
                          draw_mode=0;
                          count=0;
                        }
                        break;
                  case (TRIANGLE):
                    switch(count)
                    {
                      case(0):
                        count++;
                        xp[0] = x;
                        yp[0] = y;
                        break;
                      case(1):
                        count++;
                        xp[1] = x;
                        yp[1] = y;
                        break;
                      case(2):
                        if(fill) glBegin(GL_POLYGON);
                        else glBegin(GL_LINE_LOOP);
                            glVertex2i(xp[0],wh-yp[0]);
                            glVertex2i(xp[1],wh-yp[1]);
                            glVertex2i(x,wh-y);
                        glEnd();
                        draw_mode=0;
                        count=0;
                    }
                    break;
                  case(POINTS):
                    {
                        drawSquare(x,y);
                        count++;
                    }
              break;
          case(TEXT):
            {
            rx=x;
            ry=wh-y;
            glRasterPos2i(rx,ry);
            count=0;
            }
                }
```

```
        glPopAttrib();
        glFlush();
      }
}

int pick(int x, int y)
{
    y = wh - y;
    if(y < wh-ww/10) return 0;
    else if(x < ww/10) return LINE;
    else if(x < ww/5) return RECTANGLE;
    else if(x < 3*ww/10) return TRIANGLE;
    else if(x < 2*ww/5) return POINTS;
 else if(x < ww/2) return TEXT;
    else return 0;
}

void screen_box(int x, int y, int s )
{
    glBegin(GL_QUADS);
      glVertex2i(x, y);
      glVertex2i(x+s, y);
      glVertex2i(x+s, y+s);
      glVertex2i(x, y+s);
    glEnd();
}

void right_menu(int id)
{
   if(id == 1) exit(0);
   else display();
}

void middle_menu(int id)
{

}

void color_menu(int id)
{
   if(id == 1) {r = 1.0; g = 0.0; b = 0.0;}
   else if(id == 2) {r = 0.0; g = 1.0; b = 0.0;}
   else if(id == 3) {r = 0.0; g = 0.0; b = 1.0;}
   else if(id == 4) {r = 0.0; g = 1.0; b = 1.0;}
   else if(id == 5) {r = 1.0; g = 0.0; b = 1.0;}
   else if(id == 6) {r = 1.0; g = 1.0; b = 0.0;}
   else if(id == 7) {r = 1.0; g = 1.0; b = 1.0;}
   else if(id == 8) {r = 0.0; g = 0.0; b = 0.0;}
}
```

```
void pixel_menu(int id)
{
   if (id == 1) size = 2 * size;
   else if (size > 1) size = size/2;
}

void fill_menu(int id)
{
   if (id == 1) fill = 1;
   else fill = 0;
}

void key(unsigned char k, int xx, int yy)
{
   if(draw_mode!=TEXT) return;
 glColor3f(0.0,0.0,0.0);
   glRasterPos2i(rx,ry);
   glutBitmapCharacter(GLUT_BITMAP_9_BY_15, k);
 /*glutStrokeCharacter(GLUT_STROKE_ROMAN,i); */
   rx+=glutBitmapWidth(GLUT_BITMAP_9_BY_15,k);

}

void display()
{
 int shift=0;
   glPushAttrib(GL_ALL_ATTRIB_BITS);
   glClearColor (0.8, 0.8, 0.8, 1.0);
   glClear(GL_COLOR_BUFFER_BIT);
   glColor3f(1.0, 1.0, 1.0);
   screen_box(0,wh-ww/10,ww/10);
   glColor3f(1.0, 0.0, 0.0);
   screen_box(ww/10,wh-ww/10,ww/10);
   glColor3f(0.0, 1.0, 0.0);
   screen_box(ww/5,wh-ww/10,ww/10);
   glColor3f(0.0, 0.0, 1.0);
   screen_box(3*ww/10,wh-ww/10,ww/10);
   glColor3f(1.0, 1.0, 0.0);
   screen_box(2*ww/5,wh-ww/10,ww/10);
   glColor3f(0.0, 0.0, 0.0);
   glBegin(GL_LINES);
       glVertex2i(wh/40,wh-ww/20);
       glVertex2i(wh/40+ww/20,wh-ww/20);
   glEnd();

   glBegin(GL_TRIANGLES);
       glVertex2i(ww/5+ww/40,wh-ww/10+ww/40);
       glVertex2i(ww/5+ww/20,wh-ww/40);
       glVertex2i(ww/5+3*ww/40,wh-ww/10+ww/40);
```

```
        glEnd();
        glPointSize(3.0);
        glBegin(GL_POINTS);
            glVertex2i(3*ww/10+ww/20, wh-ww/20);
        glEnd();
        glRasterPos2i(2*ww/5,wh-ww/20);
        glutBitmapCharacter(GLUT_BITMAP_9_BY_15, 'A');
        shift=glutBitmapWidth(GLUT_BITMAP_9_BY_15, 'A');
        glRasterPos2i(2*ww/5+shift,wh-ww/20);
        glutBitmapCharacter(GLUT_BITMAP_9_BY_15, 'B');
        shift+=glutBitmapWidth(GLUT_BITMAP_9_BY_15, 'B');
        glRasterPos2i(2*ww/5+shift,wh-ww/20);
        glutBitmapCharacter(GLUT_BITMAP_9_BY_15, 'C');
        glFlush();
        glPopAttrib();
}


int main(int argc, char** argv)
{
        int c_menu, p_menu, f_menu;

        glutInit(&argc,argv);
        glutInitDisplayMode (GLUT_SINGLE | GLUT_RGB);
        glutCreateWindow("square");
        glutDisplayFunc(display);
        c_menu = glutCreateMenu(color_menu);
        glutAddMenuEntry("Red",1);
        glutAddMenuEntry("Green",2);
        glutAddMenuEntry("Blue",3);
        glutAddMenuEntry("Cyan",4);
        glutAddMenuEntry("Magenta",5);
        glutAddMenuEntry("Yellow",6);
        glutAddMenuEntry("White",7);
        glutAddMenuEntry("Black",8);
        p_menu = glutCreateMenu(pixel_menu);
        glutAddMenuEntry("increase pixel size", 1);
        glutAddMenuEntry("decrease pixel size", 2);
        f_menu = glutCreateMenu(fill_menu);
        glutAddMenuEntry("fill on", 1);
        glutAddMenuEntry("fill off", 2);
        glutCreateMenu(right_menu);
        glutAddMenuEntry("quit",1);
        glutAddMenuEntry("clear",2);
        glutAttachMenu(GLUT_RIGHT_BUTTON);
        glutCreateMenu(middle_menu);
        glutAddSubMenu("Colors", c_menu);
        glutAddSubMenu("Pixel Size", p_menu);
        glutAddSubMenu("Fill", f_menu);
```

```
        glutAttachMenu(GLUT_MIDDLE_BUTTON);
        myinit ();
        glutReshapeFunc (myReshape);
        glutKeyboardFunc(key);
        glutMouseFunc (mouse);
        glutMainLoop();

}
```

A.7   Double-Buffering Example

```
/*
 *  double.c
 *  This program demonstrates double buffering for
 *  flicker-free animation.  The left and middle mouse
 *  buttons start and stop the spinning motion of the square.
 */
#include <GL/glut.h>
#include <stdlib.h>
#include <math.h>

#define DEGREES_TO_RADIANS 3.14159/180.0

static GLfloat spin = 0.0;
GLfloat x, y;
int singleb, doubleb;

void square()
{
    glBegin(GL_QUADS);
        glVertex2f(x,y);
        glVertex2f(-y,x);
        glVertex2f(-x,-y);
        glVertex2f(y,-x);
    glEnd();
}


void displayd()
{
    glClear (GL_COLOR_BUFFER_BIT);
    square();
    glutSwapBuffers ();
}

void displays()
{
    glClear (GL_COLOR_BUFFER_BIT);
```

```
    square();
    glFlush();
}

void spinDisplay ()
{
    spin = spin + 2.0;
    if (spin > 360.0) spin = spin - 360.0;
    x= 25.0*cos(DEGREES_TO_RADIANS * spin);
    y= 25.0*sin(DEGREES_TO_RADIANS * spin);
    glutSetWindow(singleb);
    glutPostRedisplay();
    glutSetWindow(doubleb);
    glutPostRedisplay();
}

void myinit ()
{
    glClearColor (0.0, 0.0, 0.0, 1.0);
    glColor3f (1.0, 1.0, 1.0);
    glShadeModel (GL_FLAT);
}

void mouse(int btn, int state, int x, int y)
{
     if(btn==GLUT_LEFT_BUTTON && state==GLUT_DOWN)
            glutIdleFunc(spinDisplay);
     if(btn==GLUT_MIDDLE_BUTTON && state==GLUT_DOWN) glutIdleFunc(NULL);
}

void myReshape(int w, int h)
{
    glViewport(0, 0, w, h);
    glMatrixMode(GL_PROJECTION);
    glLoadIdentity();
    if (w <= h)
    glOrtho (-50.0, 50.0, -50.0*(GLfloat)h/(GLfloat)w,
        50.0*(GLfloat)h/(GLfloat)w, -1.0, 1.0);
    else
    glOrtho (-50.0*(GLfloat)w/(GLfloat)h,
        50.0*(GLfloat)w/(GLfloat)h, -50.0, 50.0, -1.0, 1.0);
    glMatrixMode(GL_MODELVIEW);
    glLoadIdentity ();
}

/*  main loop
 *  open window with initial window size, title bar,
 *  RGBA display mode, and handle input events
 */
```

```
int main(int argc, char** argv)
{

    glutInit(&argc,argv);
    glutInitDisplayMode (GLUT_SINGLE | GLUT_RGB);
    singleb=glutCreateWindow("single buffered");
    myinit ();
    glutDisplayFunc(displays);
    glutReshapeFunc (myReshape);
    glutIdleFunc (spinDisplay);
    glutMouseFunc (mouse);
    glutInitDisplayMode (GLUT_DOUBLE | GLUT_RGB);
    doubleb=glutCreateWindow("double buffered");
    myinit ();
    glutDisplayFunc(displayd);
    glutReshapeFunc (myReshape);
    glutIdleFunc (spinDisplay);
    glutMouseFunc (mouse);

    glutMainLoop();

}
```

A.8   Selection-Mode Picking Program

```
#include <stdlib.h>
#include <stdio.h>
#include <GL/glut.h>


void init()
{
   glClearColor (0.0, 0.0, 0.0, 0.0);
}

void drawObjects(GLenum mode)
{
    if(mode == GL_SELECT) glLoadName(1);
    glColor3f(1.0, 0.0, 0.0);
    glRectf(-0.5, -0.5, 1.0, 1.0);
    if(mode == GL_SELECT) glLoadName(2);
    glColor3f(0.0, 0.0, 1.0);
    glRectf(-1.0, -1.0, 0.5, 0.5);
}

void display()
```

```
{
    glClear(GL_COLOR_BUFFER_BIT);
    drawObjects(GL_RENDER);
    glFlush();
}

/*  processHits prints out the contents of the
 *  selection array
 */
void processHits (GLint hits, GLuint buffer[])
{
    unsigned int i, j;
    GLuint ii, jj, names, *ptr;

    printf ("hits = %d\n", hits);
    ptr = (GLuint *) buffer;
    for (i = 0; i < hits; i++)
    { /*  for each hit  */
        names = *ptr;
        ptr+=3;
        for (j = 0; j < names; j++)
        { /*  for each name */
            if(*ptr==1) printf ("red rectangle\n");
            else printf ("blue rectangle\n");
            ptr++;
        }
        printf ("\n");
    }
}

#define SIZE 512

void mouse(int button, int state, int x, int y)
{
    GLuint selectBuf[SIZE];
    GLint hits;
    GLint viewport[4];

    if (button == GLUT_LEFT_BUTTON && state == GLUT_DOWN)
    {
    glGetIntegerv (GL_VIEWPORT, viewport);

    glSelectBuffer (SIZE, selectBuf);
    glRenderMode(GL_SELECT);

    glInitNames();
    glPushName(0);

    glMatrixMode (GL_PROJECTION);
```

```
            glPushMatrix ();
            glLoadIdentity ();
/* create 5x5 pixel picking region near cursor location */
            gluPickMatrix ((GLdouble) x, (GLdouble) (viewport[3] - y),
                        5.0, 5.0, viewport);
            gluOrtho2D (-2.0, 2.0, -2.0, 2.0);
            drawObjects(GL_SELECT);


            glMatrixMode (GL_PROJECTION);
            glPopMatrix ();
            glFlush ();

            hits = glRenderMode (GL_RENDER);
            processHits (hits, selectBuf);

            glutPostRedisplay();
            }
    }


    void reshape(int w, int h)
    {
        glViewport(0, 0, w, h);
        glMatrixMode(GL_PROJECTION);
        glLoadIdentity();
        gluOrtho2D (-2.0, 2.0, -2.0, 2.0);
        glMatrixMode(GL_MODELVIEW);
        glLoadIdentity();
    }

    void keyboard(unsigned char key, int x, int y)
    {
        switch (key)
        {
            case 27:
                exit(0);
                break;
        }
    }

/* main loop */
int main(int argc, char** argv)
{
    glutInit(&argc, argv);
    glutInitDisplayMode (GLUT_SINGLE | GLUT_RGB);
    glutInitWindowSize (500, 500);
    glutInitWindowPosition (100, 100);
    glutCreateWindow (argv[0]);
    init ();
```

```
    glutReshapeFunc (reshape);
    glutDisplayFunc(display);
    glutMouseFunc (mouse);
    glutKeyboardFunc (keyboard);
    glutMainLoop();
    return 0;
}
```

A.9   Rotating-Cube Program

```
/* rotating cube with color interpolation */

/* demonstration of use of homogeneous-coordinate
transformations and simple data structure for representing
cube from Chapter 4 */

/*colors are assigned to the vertices */
/*cube is centered at origin */

#include <stdlib.h>
#include <GL/glut.h>


 GLfloat vertices[][3] = {{-1.0,-1.0,-1.0},{1.0,-1.0,-1.0},
 {1.0,1.0,-1.0}, {-1.0,1.0,-1.0}, {-1.0,-1.0,1.0},
 {1.0,-1.0,1.0}, {1.0,1.0,1.0}, {-1.0,1.0,1.0}};

 GLfloat colors[][3] = {{0.0,0.0,0.0},{1.0,0.0,0.0},
 {1.0,1.0,0.0}, {0.0,1.0,0.0}, {0.0,0.0,1.0},
 {1.0,0.0,1.0}, {1.0,1.0,1.0}, {0.0,1.0,1.0}};

void polygon(int a, int b, int c, int d)
{

/* draw a polygon via list of vertices */

 glBegin(GL_POLYGON);
 glColor3fv(colors[a]);
 glVertex3fv(vertices[a]);
 glColor3fv(colors[b]);
 glVertex3fv(vertices[b]);
 glColor3fv(colors[c]);
 glVertex3fv(vertices[c]);
 glColor3fv(colors[d]);
 glVertex3fv(vertices[d]);
 glEnd();
}
```

```
void colorcube()
{

/* map vertices to faces */

polygon(0,3,2,1);
polygon(2,3,7,6);
polygon(0,4,7,3);
polygon(1,2,6,5);
polygon(4,5,6,7);
polygon(0,1,5,4);
}

static GLfloat theta[] = {0.0,0.0,0.0};
static GLint axis = 2;

void display()
{

/* display callback, clear frame buffer and z buffer,
   rotate cube and draw, swap buffers */

 glClear(GL_COLOR_BUFFER_BIT | GL_DEPTH_BUFFER_BIT);
 glLoadIdentity();
 glRotatef(theta[0], 1.0, 0.0, 0.0);
 glRotatef(theta[1], 0.0, 1.0, 0.0);
 glRotatef(theta[2], 0.0, 0.0, 1.0);

 colorcube();

 glFlush();
 glutSwapBuffers();
}

void spinCube()
{

/* idle callback, spin cube 2 degrees about selected axis */

 theta[axis] += 2.0;
 if( theta[axis] > 360.0 ) theta[axis] -= 360.0;
 /* display(); */
 glutPostRedisplay();
}

void mouse(int btn, int state, int x, int y)
{

/* mouse callback, selects an axis about which to rotate */
```

```
if(btn==GLUT_LEFT_BUTTON && state == GLUT_DOWN) axis = 0;
if(btn==GLUT_MIDDLE_BUTTON && state == GLUT_DOWN) axis = 1;
if(btn==GLUT_RIGHT_BUTTON && state == GLUT_DOWN) axis = 2;
}

void myReshape(int w, int h)
{
    glViewport(0, 0, w, h);
    glMatrixMode(GL_PROJECTION);
    glLoadIdentity();
    if (w <= h)
        glOrtho(-2.0, 2.0, -2.0 * (GLfloat) h / (GLfloat) w,
            2.0 * (GLfloat) h / (GLfloat) w, -10.0, 10.0);
    else
        glOrtho(-2.0 * (GLfloat) w / (GLfloat) h,
            2.0 * (GLfloat) w / (GLfloat) h, -2.0, 2.0, -10.0, 10.0);
    glMatrixMode(GL_MODELVIEW);
}

int main(int argc, char **argv)
{
    glutInit(&argc, argv);

/* need both double buffering and z buffer */

    glutInitDisplayMode(GLUT_DOUBLE | GLUT_RGB | GLUT_DEPTH);
    glutInitWindowSize(500, 500);
    glutCreateWindow("colorcube");
    glutReshapeFunc(myReshape);
    glutDisplayFunc(display);
    glutIdleFunc(spinCube);
    glutMouseFunc(mouse);
    glEnable(GL_DEPTH_TEST); /* Enable hidden-surface removal */
    glutMainLoop();
}
```

A.10 Rotating Cube Using Vertex Arrays

```
/* rotating cube with color interpolation */

/* demonstration of use of homogeneous-coordinate
transformations and simple data structure for representing
cube from Chapter 4 */
/* colors are assigned to the vertices */
/* cube is centered at origin */

#include <stdlib.h>
#include <GL/glut.h>
```

```
GLfloat vertices[] = {-1.0,-1.0,-1.0,1.0,-1.0,-1.0,
1.0,1.0,-1.0, -1.0,1.0,-1.0, -1.0,-1.0,1.0,
1.0,-1.0,1.0, 1.0,1.0,1.0, -1.0,1.0,1.0};

GLfloat colors[] = {0.0,0.0,0.0,1.0,0.0,0.0,
1.0,1.0,0.0, 0.0,1.0,0.0, 0.0,0.0,1.0,
1.0,0.0,1.0, 1.0,1.0,1.0, 0.0,1.0,1.0};

GLubyte cubeIndices[]={0,3,2,1,2,3,7,6,0,4,7,3,1,2,6,5,4,5,6,7,0,1,5,4};


static GLfloat theta[] = {0.0,0.0,0.0};
static GLint axis = 2;

void display()
{
/* display callback, clear frame buffer and z buffer,
   rotate cube and draw, swap buffers */

 glClear(GL_COLOR_BUFFER_BIT | GL_DEPTH_BUFFER_BIT);
 glLoadIdentity();
 glRotatef(theta[0], 1.0, 0.0, 0.0);
 glRotatef(theta[1], 0.0, 1.0, 0.0);
 glRotatef(theta[2], 0.0, 0.0, 1.0);

 glDrawElements(GL_QUADS, 24, GL_UNSIGNED_BYTE, cubeIndices);

 glBegin(GL_LINES);
   glVertex3f(0.0,0.0,0.0);
   glVertex3f(1.0,1.0,1.0);
 glEnd();
 glFlush();
 glutSwapBuffers();
}

void spinCube()
{

/* idle callback, spin cube 2 degrees about selected axis */

 theta[axis] += 2.0;
 if( theta[axis] > 360.0 ) theta[axis] -= 360.0;
 glutPostRedisplay();
}

void mouse(int btn, int state, int x, int y)
{

/* mouse callback, selects an axis about which to rotate */
```

```
  if(btn==GLUT_LEFT_BUTTON && state == GLUT_DOWN) axis = 0;
  if(btn==GLUT_MIDDLE_BUTTON && state == GLUT_DOWN) axis = 1;
  if(btn==GLUT_RIGHT_BUTTON && state == GLUT_DOWN) axis = 2;
}

void myReshape(int w, int h)
{
    glViewport(0, 0, w, h);
    glMatrixMode(GL_PROJECTION);
    glLoadIdentity();
    if (w <= h)
        glOrtho(-2.0, 2.0, -2.0 * (GLfloat) h / (GLfloat) w,
            2.0 * (GLfloat) h / (GLfloat) w, -10.0, 10.0);
    else
        glOrtho(-2.0 * (GLfloat) w / (GLfloat) h,
            2.0 * (GLfloat) w / (GLfloat) h, -2.0, 2.0, -10.0, 10.0);
    glMatrixMode(GL_MODELVIEW);
}

int main(int argc, char **argv)
{

/* need both double buffering and z buffer */

    glutInit(&argc, argv);
    glutInitDisplayMode(GLUT_DOUBLE | GLUT_RGB | GLUT_DEPTH);
    glutInitWindowSize(500, 500);
    glutCreateWindow("colorcube");
    glutReshapeFunc(myReshape);
    glutDisplayFunc(display);
    glutIdleFunc(spinCube);
    glutMouseFunc(mouse);
    glEnable(GL_DEPTH_TEST); /* Enable hidden--surface--removal */
    glEnableClientState(GL_COLOR_ARRAY);
    glEnableClientState(GL_NORMAL_ARRAY);
    glEnableClientState(GL_VERTEX_ARRAY);
    glVertexPointer(3, GL_FLOAT, 0, vertices);
    glColorPointer(3,GL_FLOAT, 0, colors);
    glColor3f(1.0,1.0,1.0);
    glutMainLoop();
}
```

A.11   Rotating Cube with a Virtual Trackball

```
/* rotating cube demo with trackball*/

#include <math.h>
#include <GL/glut.h>
```

```
#define bool int
#define false 0
#define true 1


int  winWidth, winHeight;

float  angle = 0.0, axis[3], trans[3];
bool  trackingMouse = false;
bool  redrawContinue = false;
bool    trackballMove = false;

/* draw the cube */

GLfloat vertices[][3] = {
    {-1.0,-1.0,-1.0}, {1.0,-1.0,-1.0}, {1.0,1.0,-1.0}, {-1.0,1.0,-1.0},
    {-1.0,-1.0,1.0}, {1.0,-1.0,1.0}, {1.0,1.0,1.0}, {-1.0,1.0,1.0}
};

GLfloat colors[][3] = {
    {0.0,0.0,0.0},{1.0,0.0,0.0}, {1.0,1.0,0.0}, {0.0,1.0,0.0},
    {0.0,0.0,1.0}, {1.0,0.0,1.0}, {1.0,1.0,1.0}, {0.0,1.0,1.0}
};

void polygon(int a, int b, int c , int d, int face)
{

   /* draw a polygon via list of vertices */

   glBegin(GL_POLYGON);
     glColor3fv(colors[a]);
     glVertex3fv(vertices[a]);
     glVertex3fv(vertices[b]);
     glVertex3fv(vertices[c]);
     glVertex3fv(vertices[d]);
   glEnd();
}

void colorcube()
{

    /* map vertices to faces */

    polygon(1,0,3,2,0);
    polygon(3,7,6,2,1);
    polygon(7,3,0,4,2);
    polygon(2,6,5,1,3);
    polygon(4,5,6,7,4);
    polygon(5,4,0,1,5);
}
```

```
/* These functions implement a simple trackball-like motion control */

float lastPos[3] = {0.0F, 0.0F, 0.0F};
int curx, cury;
int startX, startY;

void trackball_ptov(int x, int y, int width, int height, float v[3])
{
    float d, a;

    /* project x,y onto a hemisphere centered within width, height */
    v[0] = (2.0F*x - width) / width;
    v[1] = (height - 2.0F*y) / height;
    d = (float) sqrt(v[0]*v[0] + v[1]*v[1]);
    v[2] = (float) cos((M_PI/2.0F) * ((d < 1.0F) ? d : 1.0F));
    a = 1.0F / (float) sqrt(v[0]*v[0] + v[1]*v[1] + v[2]*v[2]);
    v[0] *= a;
    v[1] *= a;
    v[2] *= a;
}


void mouseMotion(int x, int y)
{
    float curPos[3], dx, dy, dz;

    trackball_ptov(x, y, winWidth, winHeight, curPos);
if(trackingMouse)
{
    dx = curPos[0] - lastPos[0];
    dy = curPos[1] - lastPos[1];
    dz = curPos[2] - lastPos[2];

    if (dx || dy || dz) {
    angle = 90.0F * sqrt(dx*dx + dy*dy + dz*dz);

    axis[0] = lastPos[1]*curPos[2] - lastPos[2]*curPos[1];
    axis[1] = lastPos[2]*curPos[0] - lastPos[0]*curPos[2];
    axis[2] = lastPos[0]*curPos[1] - lastPos[1]*curPos[0];

    lastPos[0] = curPos[0];
    lastPos[1] = curPos[1];
    lastPos[2] = curPos[2];
        }
}

    glutPostRedisplay();
}

void startMotion(int x, int y)
```

```c
{
    trackingMouse = true;
    redrawContinue = false;
    startX = x; startY = y;
    curx = x; cury = y;
    trackball_ptov(x, y, winWidth, winHeight, lastPos);
    trackballMove=true;
}
void stopMotion(int x, int y)
{

    trackingMouse = false;

    if (startX != x || startY != y) {
    redrawContinue = true;
        } else {
    angle = 0.0F;
    redrawContinue = false;
    trackballMove = false;
        }
}


void display()
{
    glClear(GL_COLOR_BUFFER_BIT|GL_DEPTH_BUFFER_BIT);

    /* view transform */

    if (trackballMove) {
     glRotatef(angle, axis[0], axis[1], axis[2]);

    }
 colorcube();
    glutSwapBuffers();
}


void mouseButton(int button, int state, int x, int y)
{
 if(button==GLUT_RIGHT_BUTTON) exit(0);
 if(button==GLUT_LEFT_BUTTON) switch(state)
 {
    case GLUT_DOWN:
    y=winHeight-y;
    startMotion( x,y);
    break;
    case GLUT_UP:
    stopMotion( x,y);
```

```
        break;
        }
}

void myReshape(int w, int h)
{
    glViewport(0, 0, w, h);
    winWidth = w;
    winHeight = h;
}

void spinCube()
{
    if (redrawContinue) glutPostRedisplay();
}

int main(int argc, char **argv)
{
    glutInit(&argc, argv);
    glutInitDisplayMode(GLUT_DOUBLE | GLUT_RGB | GLUT_DEPTH);
    glutInitWindowSize(500, 500);
    glutCreateWindow("colorcube");
    glutReshapeFunc(myReshape);
    glutDisplayFunc(display);
    glutIdleFunc(spinCube);
    glutMouseFunc(mouseButton);
    glutMotionFunc(mouseMotion);
    glEnable(GL_DEPTH_TEST);
    glMatrixMode(GL_PROJECTION);
    glLoadIdentity();
    glOrtho(-2.0, 2.0, -2.0, 2.0, -2.0, 2.0);
    glMatrixMode(GL_MODELVIEW);
    glutMainLoop();
}
```

A.12 Moving Viewer

```
/* rotating cube with viewer movement from Chapter 5 */
/* cube definition and display similar to rotating-cube
program */

/* we use the Lookat function in the display callback to point
the viewer, whose position can be altered by the x, X, y, Y, z,
and Z keys */
/* the perspective view is set in the reshape callback */

#include <stdlib.h>
#include <GL/glut.h>
```

```
GLfloat vertices[][3] = {{-1.0,-1.0,-1.0},{1.0,-1.0,-1.0},
{1.0,1.0,-1.0}, {-1.0,1.0,-1.0}, {-1.0,-1.0,1.0},
{1.0,-1.0,1.0}, {1.0,1.0,1.0}, {-1.0,1.0,1.0}};

GLfloat colors[][3] = {{0.0,0.0,0.0},{1.0,0.0,0.0},
{1.0,1.0,0.0}, {0.0,1.0,0.0}, {0.0,0.0,1.0},
{1.0,0.0,1.0}, {1.0,1.0,1.0}, {0.0,1.0,1.0}};

void polygon(int a, int b, int c , int d)
{
 glBegin(GL_POLYGON);
  glColor3fv(colors[a]);
  glVertex3fv(vertices[a]);
  glVertex3fv(vertices[b]);
  glVertex3fv(vertices[c]);
  glVertex3fv(vertices[d]);
 glEnd();
}

void colorcube()
{
 polygon(0,3,2,1);
 polygon(2,3,7,6);
 polygon(0,4,7,3);
 polygon(1,2,6,5);
 polygon(4,5,6,7);
 polygon(0,1,5,4);
}

static GLfloat theta[] = {0.0,0.0,0.0};
static GLint axis = 2;
static GLdouble viewer[]= {0.0, 0.0, 5.0}; /* initial viewer
                                                   location */

void display()
{

 glClear(GL_COLOR_BUFFER_BIT | GL_DEPTH_BUFFER_BIT);

/* update viewer position in model-view matrix */

 glLoadIdentity();
 gluLookAt(viewer[0],viewer[1],viewer[2], 0.0, 0.0, 0.0,
                                        0.0, 1.0, 0.0);

/* rotate cube */

 glRotatef(theta[0], 1.0, 0.0, 0.0);
 glRotatef(theta[1], 0.0, 1.0, 0.0);
```

```
    glRotatef(theta[2], 0.0, 0.0, 1.0);
    colorcube();

    glFlush();
    glutSwapBuffers();
}

void mouse(int btn, int state, int x, int y)
{
 if(btn==GLUT_LEFT_BUTTON && state == GLUT_DOWN) axis = 0;
 if(btn==GLUT_MIDDLE_BUTTON && state == GLUT_DOWN) axis = 1;
 if(btn==GLUT_RIGHT_BUTTON && state == GLUT_DOWN) axis = 2;
 theta[axis] += 2.0;
 if( theta[axis] > 360.0 ) theta[axis] -= 360.0;
 display();
}

void keys(unsigned char key, int x, int y)
{

/* use x, X, y, Y, z, and Z keys to move viewer */

    if(key == 'x') viewer[0]-= 1.0;
    if(key == 'X') viewer[0]+= 1.0;
    if(key == 'y') viewer[1]-= 1.0;
    if(key == 'Y') viewer[1]+= 1.0;
    if(key == 'z') viewer[2]-= 1.0;
    if(key == 'Z') viewer[2]+= 1.0;
    display();
}

void myReshape(int w, int h)
{
 glViewport(0, 0, w, h);

/* use a perspective view */

 glMatrixMode(GL_PROJECTION);
 glLoadIdentity();
 if(w<=h) glFrustum(-2.0, 2.0, -2.0 * (GLfloat) h/ (GLfloat) w,
      2.0* (GLfloat) h / (GLfloat) w, 2.0, 20.0);
 else glFrustum(-2.0, 2.0, -2.0 * (GLfloat) w/ (GLfloat) h,
      2.0* (GLfloat) w / (GLfloat) h, 2.0, 20.0);

/* or we can use gluPerspective */
/* gluPerspective(45.0, w/h, 1.0, 10.0); */

 glMatrixMode(GL_MODELVIEW);
}
```

```
int main(int argc, char **argv)
{
 glutInit(&argc, argv);
 glutInitDisplayMode(GLUT_DOUBLE | GLUT_RGB | GLUT_DEPTH);
 glutInitWindowSize(500, 500);
 glutCreateWindow("colorcube");
 glutReshapeFunc(myReshape);
 glutDisplayFunc(display);
 glutMouseFunc(mouse);
 glutKeyboardFunc(keys);
 glEnable(GL_DEPTH_TEST);
 glutMainLoop();
}
```

A.13   Sphere Program

```
/* Recursive subdivision of tetrahedron (Chapter 6). Three display
modes: wire frame, constant, and interpolative shading. */

/* program also illustrates defining materials and light sources
in init() */

/* mode 0 = wire frame, mode 1 = constant shading,
mode 3 = interpolative shading */

#include <stdlib.h>
#include <GL/glut.h>


typedef float point[4];

/* initial tetrahedron */

point3 v[]={{0.0, 0.0, 1.0}, {0.0, 0.942809, -0.33333},
      {-0.816497, -0.471405, -0.333333}, {0.816497, -0.471405, -0.333333}};

static GLfloat theta[] = {0.0,0.0,0.0};

int n;
int mode;


void triangle( point3 a, point3 b, point3 c)

/* display one triangle using a line loop for wire frame, a single
normal for constant shading, or three normals for interpolative shading */
{
    if (mode==0) glBegin(GL_LINE_LOOP);
```

```
    else glBegin(GL_POLYGON);
        if(mode==1) glNormal3fv(a);
        if(mode==2) glNormal3fv(a);
        glVertex3fv(a);
        if(mode==2) glNormal3fv(b);
        glVertex3fv(b);
        if(mode==2) glNormal3fv(c);
        glVertex3fv(c);
    glEnd();
}

void normal(point3 p)
{

/* normalize a vector */

    double sqrt();
    float d =0.0;
    int i;
    for(i=0; i<3; i++) d+=p[i]*p[i];
    d=sqrt(d);
    if(d>0.0) for(i=0; i<3; i++) p[i]/=d;
}

void divide_triangle(point3 a, point3 b, point3 c, int m)
{

/* Triangle subdivision using vertex numbers.
Right-hand rule applied to create outward-pointing faces. */

    point3 v1, v2, v3;
    int j;
    if(m>0)
    {
        for(j=0; j<3; j++) v1[j]=a[j]+b[j];
        normal(v1);
        for(j=0; j<3; j++) v2[j]=a[j]+c[j];
        normal(v2);
        for(j=0; j<3; j++) v3[j]=b[j]+c[j];
         normal(v3);
        divide_triangle(a, v1, v2, m-1);
        divide_triangle(c, v2, v3, m-1);
        divide_triangle(b, v3, v1, m-1);
        divide_triangle(v1, v3, v2, m-1);
    }
    else triangle(a,b,c); /* draw triangle at end of recursion */
}

void tetrahedron( int m)
```

```
{

/* apply triangle subdivision to faces of tetrahedron */

    divide_triangle(v[0], v[1], v[2], m);
    divide_triangle(v[3], v[2], v[1], m);
    divide_triangle(v[0], v[3], v[1], m);
    divide_triangle(v[0], v[2], v[3], m);
}

void display()
{

/* displays all three modes, side by side */

    glClear(GL_COLOR_BUFFER_BIT | GL_DEPTH_BUFFER_BIT);
    glLoadIdentity();
    mode=0;
    tetrahedron(n);
    mode=1;
    glTranslatef(-2.0, 0.0,0.0);
    tetrahedron(n);
    mode=2;
    glTranslatef( 4.0, 0.0,0.0);
    tetrahedron(n);


    glFlush();
}

void myReshape(int w, int h)
{
    glViewport(0, 0, w, h);
    glMatrixMode(GL_PROJECTION);
    glLoadIdentity();
    if (w <= h)
        glOrtho(-4.0, 4.0, -4.0 * (GLfloat) h / (GLfloat) w,
            4.0 * (GLfloat) h / (GLfloat) w, -10.0, 10.0);
    else
        glOrtho(-4.0 * (GLfloat) w / (GLfloat) h,
            4.0 * (GLfloat) w / (GLfloat) h, -4.0, 4.0, -10.0, 10.0);
    glMatrixMode(GL_MODELVIEW);
    display();
}


void myinit()
{
    GLfloat mat_specular[]={1.0, 1.0, 1.0, 1.0};
```

```
    GLfloat mat_diffuse[]={1.0, 1.0, 1.0, 1.0};
    GLfloat mat_ambient[]={1.0, 1.0, 1.0, 1.0};
    GLfloat mat_shininess={100.0};
    GLfloat light_ambient[]={0.0, 0.0, 0.0, 1.0};
    GLfloat light_diffuse[]={1.0, 1.0, 1.0, 1.0};
    GLfloat light_specular[]={1.0, 1.0, 1.0, 1.0};

/* set up ambient, diffuse, and specular components for light 0 */

    glLightfv(GL_LIGHT0, GL_AMBIENT, light_ambient);
    glLightfv(GL_LIGHT0, GL_DIFFUSE, light_diffuse);
    glLightfv(GL_LIGHT0, GL_SPECULAR, light_specular);

/* define material properties for front face of all polygons */

    glMaterialfv(GL_FRONT, GL_SPECULAR, mat_specular);
    glMaterialfv(GL_FRONT, GL_AMBIENT, mat_ambient);
    glMaterialfv(GL_FRONT, GL_DIFFUSE, mat_diffuse);
    glMaterialf(GL_FRONT, GL_SHININESS, mat_shininess);

    glShadeModel(GL_SMOOTH); /* enable smooth shading */
    glEnable(GL_LIGHTING); /* enable lighting */
    glEnable(GL_LIGHT0);   /* enable light 0 */
    glEnable(GL_DEPTH_TEST); /* enable z buffer */
    glClearColor (1.0, 1.0, 1.0, 1.0);
    glColor3f (0.0, 0.0, 0.0);
}

int main(int argc, char **argv)
{
    n=atoi(argv[1]);
    glutInit(&argc, argv);
    glutInitDisplayMode(GLUT_SINGLE | GLUT_RGB | GLUT_DEPTH);
    glutInitWindowSize(500, 500);
    glutCreateWindow("sphere");
    myinit();
    glutReshapeFunc(myReshape);
    glutDisplayFunc(display);
    glutMainLoop();
}
```

A.14 Mandelbrot Set Program

```
#include <stdio.h>
#include <stdlib.h>
#include <GL/glut.h>

/* default data*/
```

```
/* can enter other values via command line arguments */

#define CENTERX -0.5
#define CENTERY 0.5
#define HEIGHT 0.5
#define WIDTH 0.5
#define MAX_ITER 100

/* N x M array to be generated */

#define N 500
#define M 500

float height = HEIGHT; /* size of window in complex plane */
float width = WIDTH;
float cx = CENTERX; /* center of window in complex plane */
float cy = CENTERY;
int max = MAX_ITER; /* number of interations per point */

int n=N;
int m=M;

/* use unsigned bytes for image */

GLubyte image[N][M];

/* complex data type and complex add, mult, and magnitude functions
   probably not worth overhead */

typedef float complex[2];

void add(complex a, complex b, complex p)
{
    p[0]=a[0]+b[0];
    p[1]=a[1]+b[1];
}

void mult(complex a, complex b, complex p)
{
    p[0]=a[0]*b[0]-a[1]*b[1];
    p[1]=a[0]*b[1]+a[1]*b[0];
}

float mag2(complex a)
{
    return(a[0]*a[0]+a[1]*a[1]);
}
```

```
void form(float a, float b, complex p)
{
    p[0]=a;
    p[1]=b;
}

void display()
{
    glClear(GL_COLOR_BUFFER_BIT);
    glDrawPixels(n,m,GL_COLOR_INDEX, GL_UNSIGNED_BYTE, image);
}


void myReshape(int w, int h)
{
    glViewport(0, 0, w, h);
    glMatrixMode(GL_PROJECTION);
    glLoadIdentity();
    if (w <= h)
    gluOrtho2D(0.0, 0.0, (GLfloat) n, (GLfloat) m* (GLfloat) h /
                        (GLfloat) w);
    else
    gluOrtho2D(0.0, 0.0, (GLfloat) n * (GLfloat) w / (GLfloat) h,
                        (GLfloat) m);
    glMatrixMode(GL_MODELVIEW);
    display();
}

void myinit()
{
    float redmap[256], greenmap[256],bluemap[256];
    int i;

    glClearColor (1.0, 1.0, 1.0, 1.0);
    gluOrtho2D(0.0, 0.0, (GLfloat) n, (GLfloat) m);

/* define pseudocolor maps, ramps for red and blue,
   random for green */


    for(i=0;i<256;i++)
    {
        redmap[i]=i/255.;
        greenmap[i]=rand()%255;
        bluemap[i]=1.0-i/255.;
    }

    glPixelMapfv(GL_PIXEL_MAP_I_TO_R, 256, redmap);
```

```
            glPixelMapfv(GL_PIXEL_MAP_I_TO_G, 256, greenmap);
            glPixelMapfv(GL_PIXEL_MAP_I_TO_B, 256, bluemap);
}


main(int argc, char *argv[])
{
    int i, j, k;
    float x, y, v;
    complex c0, c, d;

    scanf("%f", &cx); /* center x */
    scanf("%f", &cy); /* center y */
    scanf("%f", &width); /* rectangle width */
    height=width; /* rectangle height */
    scanf("%d",&max); /* maximum iterations */

    for (i=0; i<n; i++) for(j=0; j<m; j++)
    {

/* starting point */

    x= i *(width/(n-1)) + cx -width/2;
    y= j *(height/(m-1)) + cy -height/2;

    form(0,0,c);
    form(x,y,c0);

/* complex iteration */

    for(k=0; k<max; k++)
        {
        mult(c,c,d);
        add(d,c0,c);
        v=mag2(c);
        if(v>4.0) break; /* assume not in set if mag > 4 */
        }

/* assign gray level to point based on its magnitude */
        if(v>1.0) v=1.0; /* clamp if > 1 */
        image[i][j]=255*v;
    }


    glutInit(&argc, argv);
    glutInitDisplayMode(GLUT_SINGLE | GLUT_RGB );
    glutInitWindowSize(N, M);
    glutCreateWindow("mandlebrot");
    myinit();
```

```
     glutReshapeFunc(myReshape);
     glutDisplayFunc(display);

     glutMainLoop();


}
```

A.15 Bresenham's Algorithm

```
#define BLACK 0
#include <GL/glut.h>
#include <stdio.h>


void draw_pixel(int ix, int iy, int value)
{
  glBegin(GL_POINTS);
    glVertex2i( ix, iy);
  glEnd();
}

bres(int x1,int y1,int x2,int y2)
{
  int dx, dy, i, e;
  int incx, incy, inc1, inc2;
  int x,y;

  dx = x2 - x1;
  dy = y2 - y1;

  if(dx < 0) dx = -dx;
  if(dy < 0) dy = -dy;
  incx = 1;
  if(x2 < x1) incx = -1;
  incy = 1;
  if(y2 < y1) incy = -1;
  x=x1;
  y=y1;

  if(dx > dy)
    {
      draw_pixel(x,y, BLACK);
      e = 2*dy - dx;
      inc1 = 2*( dy -dx);
      inc2 = 2*dy;
```

```
            for(i = 0; i < dx; i++)
            {
               if(e >= 0)
               {
                  y += incy;
                  e += inc1;
               }
               else e += inc2;
               x += incx;
               draw_pixel(x,y, BLACK);
            }
         }
         else
         {
            draw_pixel(x,y, BLACK);
            e = 2*dx - dy;
            inc1 = 2*( dx - dy);
            inc2 = 2*dx;
            for(i = 0; i < dy; i++)
            {
               if(e >= 0)
               {
                  x += incx;
                  e += inc1;
               }
               else e += inc2;
               y += incy;
               draw_pixel(x,y, BLACK);
            }
         }
      }

void display()
{
    glClear(GL_COLOR_BUFFER_BIT);
    bres(200, 200, 100, 50);
    glFlush();
}

void myinit()
{
    glClearColor(1.0, 1.0, 1.0, 1.0);
    glColor3f(1.0, 0.0, 0.0);
    glPointSize(1.0);
    glMatrixMode(GL_PROJECTION);
    glLoadIdentity();
    gluOrtho2D(0.0, 499.0, 0.0, 499.0);
}
```

```
void main(int argc, char** argv)
{

/* standard GLUT initialization */

    glutInit(&argc,argv);
    glutInitDisplayMode (GLUT_SINGLE | GLUT_RGB); /* default, not needed */
    glutInitWindowSize(500,500); /* 500x500 pixel window */
    glutInitWindowPosition(0,0); /* place window top left on display */
    glutCreateWindow("Bresenham's Algorithm"); /* window title */
    glutDisplayFunc(display); /* display callback invoked when window opened
*/

    myinit(); /* set attributes */

    glutMainLoop(); /* enter event loop */
}
```

A.16   Rotating Cube with Texture

```
#include <stdlib.h>
#include <GL/glut.h>
GLfloat planes[]= {-1.0, 0.0, 1.0, 0.0};
GLfloat planet[]= {0.0, -1.0,  0.0, 1.0};
GLfloat vertices[][3] = {{-1.0,-1.0,-1.0},{1.0,-1.0,-1.0},
    {1.0,1.0,-1.0}, {-1.0,1.0,-1.0}, {-1.0,-1.0,1.0},
    {1.0,-1.0,1.0}, {1.0,1.0,1.0}, {-1.0,1.0,1.0}};
GLfloat colors[][4] = {{0.0,0.0,0.0,0.5},{1.0,0.0,0.0,0.5},
    {1.0,1.0,0.0,0.5}, {0.0,1.0,0.0,0.5}, {0.0,0.0,1.0,0.5},
    {1.0,0.0,1.0,0.5}, {1.0,1.0,1.0,0.5}, {0.0,1.0,1.0,0.5}};

void polygon(int a, int b, int c, int d)
{
    glBegin(GL_POLYGON);
    glColor4fv(colors[a]);
    glTexCoord2f(0.0,0.0);
    glVertex3fv(vertices[a]);
    glColor4fv(colors[b]);
    glTexCoord2f(0.0,1.0);
    glVertex3fv(vertices[b]);
    glColor4fv(colors[c]);
    glTexCoord2f(1.0,1.0);
    glVertex3fv(vertices[c]);
    glColor4fv(colors[d]);
    glTexCoord2f(1.0,0.0);
    glVertex3fv(vertices[d]);
    glEnd();
}
```

```
void colorcube()
{

/* map vertices to faces */

    polygon(0,3,2,1);
    polygon(2,3,7,6);
    polygon(0,4,7,3);
    polygon(1,2,6,5);
    polygon(4,5,6,7);
    polygon(0,1,5,4);
}

static GLfloat theta[] = {0.0,0.0,0.0};
static GLint axis = 2;

void display()
{
    glClear(GL_COLOR_BUFFER_BIT | GL_DEPTH_BUFFER_BIT);
    glLoadIdentity();
    glRotatef(theta[0], 1.0, 0.0, 0.0);
    glRotatef(theta[1], 0.0, 1.0, 0.0);
    glRotatef(theta[2], 0.0, 0.0, 1.0);
    colorcube();
    glutSwapBuffers();
}

void spinCube()
{
    theta[axis] += 2.0;
    if( theta[axis] > 360.0 ) theta[axis] -= 360.0;
    glutPostRedisplay();
}

void mouse(int btn, int state, int x, int y)
{
    if(btn==GLUT_LEFT_BUTTON && state == GLUT_DOWN) axis = 0;
    if(btn==GLUT_MIDDLE_BUTTON && state == GLUT_DOWN) axis = 1;
    if(btn==GLUT_RIGHT_BUTTON && state == GLUT_DOWN) axis = 2;
}

void myReshape(int w, int h)
{
    glViewport(0, 0, w, h);
    glMatrixMode(GL_PROJECTION);
    glLoadIdentity();
    if (w <= h)
        glOrtho(-2.0, 2.0, -2.0 * (GLfloat) h / (GLfloat) w,
```

```
                2.0 * (GLfloat) h / (GLfloat) w, -10.0, 10.0);
        else
            glOrtho(-2.0 * (GLfloat) w / (GLfloat) h,
                2.0 * (GLfloat) w / (GLfloat) h, -2.0, 2.0, -10.0, 10.0);
        glMatrixMode(GL_MODELVIEW);
}

void key(unsigned char k, int x, int y)
{
    if(k == '1') glutIdleFunc(spinCube);
    if(k == '2') glutIdleFunc(NULL);
    if(k == 'q') exit(0);
}

int main(int argc, char **argv)
{
    GLubyte image[64][64][3];
    int i, j, r, c;
    for(i=0;i<64;i++)
    {
      for(j=0;j<64;j++)
      {
        c = ((((i&0x8)==0)^((j&0x8))==0))*255;
        image[i][j][0]= (GLubyte) c;
        image[i][j][1]= (GLubyte) c;
        image[i][j][2]= (GLubyte) c;
      }
    }
    glutInit(&argc, argv);
    glutInitDisplayMode(GLUT_DOUBLE | GLUT_RGB | GLUT_DEPTH);
    glutInitWindowSize(500, 500);
    glutCreateWindow("colorcube");
    glutReshapeFunc(myReshape);
    glutDisplayFunc(display);
    glutIdleFunc(spinCube);
    glutMouseFunc(mouse);
    glEnable(GL_DEPTH_TEST);
    glEnable(GL_TEXTURE_2D);
    glTexImage2D(GL_TEXTURE_2D,0,3,64,64,0,GL_RGB,GL_UNSIGNED_BYTE, image);
    glTexParameterf(GL_TEXTURE_2D,GL_TEXTURE_WRAP_S,GL_REPEAT);
    glTexParameterf(GL_TEXTURE_2D,GL_TEXTURE_WRAP_T,GL_REPEAT);
    glTexParameterf(GL_TEXTURE_2D,GL_TEXTURE_MAG_FILTER,GL_NEAREST);
    glTexParameterf(GL_TEXTURE_2D,GL_TEXTURE_MIN_FILTER,GL_NEAREST);
    glutKeyboardFunc(key);
    glClearColor(1.0,1.0,1.0,1.0);
    glutMainLoop();
}
```

A.17 GLSL Example

```c
/* display teapot with vertex and fragment shaders */
/* sets up elapsed time parameter for use by shaders */

#include <stdio.h>
#include <stdlib.h>
#include <GL/glut.h>


const float nearVal    = 1.0f;
const float farVal     = 300.0f;
const float lightPos[3] = {3.0f, 3.0f, 3.0f};

int width  = 512;
int height = 512;

GLint        program = 0;
GLint        timeParam;

/* shader reader */
/* creates null terminated string from file */

char* readShaderSource(const char* shaderFile)
{
    struct stat statBuf;
    FILE* fp = fopen(shaderFile, "r");
    char* buf;

    stat(shaderFile, &statBuf);
    buf = (char*) malloc(statBuf.st_size + 1 * sizeof(char));
    fread(buf, 1, statBuf.st_size, fp);
    buf[statBuf.st_size] = ' ';
    fclose(fp);

    return buf;
}

/* error printing function */

static void checkError(GLint status, const char *msg)
{
    if (!status)
    {
    printf("%s\n", msg);
    exit(EXIT_FAILURE);
    }
}
```

```
/* standard OpenGL initialization */

static void init()
{
    const float teapotColor[]     = {0.3f, 0.5f, 0.4f, 1.0f};
    const float teapotSpecular[]  = {0.8f, 0.8f, 0.8f, 1.0f};
    const float teapotShininess[] = {80.0f};

    glMaterialfv(GL_FRONT, GL_AMBIENT_AND_DIFFUSE, teapotColor);
    glMaterialfv(GL_FRONT, GL_SPECULAR, teapotSpecular);
    glMaterialfv(GL_FRONT, GL_SHININESS, teapotShininess);

    glClearColor(1.0f, 1.0f, 1.0f, 1.0f);

    glMatrixMode(GL_MODELVIEW);
    glLoadIdentity();
    glTranslate(0.0f, 0.0f, 10.0f);

    glLightfv(GL_LIGHT0, GL_POSITION, lightPos);
    glEnable(GL_LIGHTING);
    glEnable(GL_LIGHT0);
    glEnable(GL_DEPTH_TEST);
}

/* GLSL initialization */

static void initShader(const GLchar* vShaderFile, const GLchar* fShaderFile)
{
    GLint vShader = 0;
    GLint fShader = 0;
    GLint status = 0;

    /* read shader files */

    GLchar* vSource = readShaderSource(vShaderFile);
    GLchar* fSource = readShaderSource(fShaderFile);

    /* create program and shader objects */

    vShader = glCreateShaderObject(GL_VERTEX_SHADER);
    fShader = glCreateShaderObject(GL_FRAGMENT_SHADER);
    program = glCreateProgramObject();

    /* attach shaders to the program object */

    glAttachObject(program, vShader);
    glAttachObject(program, fShader);

    /* read shaders */
```

```
        glShaderSource(vShader, 1, &vShaderFile, NULL);
        checkError(status, "Failed to read vertex shader");
        glShaderSource(fShader, 1, &fShaderFile, NULL);
        checkError(status, "Failed to read vertex shader");

        /* compile shaders */

        glCompileShader(vShader);
        glCompileShader(fShader);

        /* error check */

        glGetObjectParameteriv(vShader, GL_OBJECT_COMPILE_STATUS, &status);
        checkError(status, "Failed to compile the vertex shader.");

        glGetObjectParameteriv(fShader, GL_OBJECT_COMPILE_STATUS, &status);
        checkError(status, "Failed to compile the fragment shader.");

        /* link */

        glLinkProgram(program);

        glGetObjectParameteriv(program, GL_OBJECT_LINK_STATUS, &status);
        checkError(status, "Failed to link the shader program object.");

        /* use program object */

        glUseProgramObject(program);

        /* set up uniform parameter */

        timeParam = glGetUniformLocation(program, "time");
    }

static void draw()
{

    /* send elapsed time to shaders */

    glUniform1f(timeParam, glutGet(GLUT_ELAPSED_TIME));

    glClear(GL_COLOR_BUFFER_BIT | GL_DEPTH_BUFFER_BIT);

    glTranslatef(0.0f, 0.0f, -10.0f);
    glutSolidTeapot(2.0);
    glutSwapBuffers();
}

static void reshape(int w, int h)
```

```
{
    width  = w;
    height = h;


    glMatrixMode(GL_PROJECTION);
    glLoadIdentity();
    gluPerspective(45.0, (double)width / (double)height, nearVal, farVal);
    glMatrixMode(GL_MODELVIEW);
    glLoadIdentity();
    glViewport(0, 0, width, height);

    glutPostRedisplay();
}

static void keyboard(unsigned char key, int x, int y)
{
    switch (key) {
    case 27:
    case 'Q':
    case 'q':
        exit(EXIT_SUCCESS);
        break;
    default:
        break;
    }
}


int main(int argc, char** argv)
{
    glutInit(&argc, argv);
    glutInitDisplayMode(GLUT_RGBA | GLUT_DOUBLE | GLUT_DEPTH);
    glutInitWindowSize(width, height);
    glutCreateWindow("Simple GLSL example");
    glutDisplayFunc(draw);
    glutReshapeFunc(reshape);
    glutKeyboardFunc(keyboard);

    init();
    initShader("vPhong.glsl","fPassThrough.glsl");

    glutMainLoop();
}

/* the following code is for the vertex and fragment shaders */
/* shader code is assumed to be in separate files */
```

```
// Vphong.glsl
// modified Phong vertex shader

uniform float time;

void main()
{
    gl_Position = gl_ModelViewProjectionMatrix * gl_Vertex;

    vec4 eyePosition = gl_ModelViewMatrix * gl_Vertex;
    vec4 eyeLightPos = gl_LightSource[0].position;

    vec3 eyeNormalVec = normalize(gl_NormalMatrix * gl_Normal);
    vec3 eyeLightVec = normalize(eyeLightPos.xyz - eyePosition.xyz);
    vec3 eyeViewVec = -normalize(eyePosition.xyz);
    vec3 eyeHalfVec = normalize(eyeLightVec + eyeViewVec);

    float Kd = max(dot(eyeLightVec, eyeNormalVec), 0.0);
    float Ks = pow(dot(eyeNormalVec, eyeHalfVec),
    gl_FrontMaterial.shininess);
    float Ka = 1.0;

    gl_FrontColor = Kd * gl_FrontLightProduct[0].diffuse +
              Ks * gl_FrontLightProduct[0].specular +
          gl_FrontLightModelProduct.sceneColor;
}


// fPassThrough.glsl
// Pass through fragment shader.

void main()
{
    gl_FragColor = gl_Color;
}
```

A.18   Scene-Graph Example

```
//scene.cc

#include "Scene.h"

#define BaseRadius 0.2
#define Radius 0.08
#define BaseLen 1
#define UpLen 0.6
#define LowLen 0.6
```

```
#define EyeRadius 0.04
#define ChairLegLen 0.55

int main(int argc, char **argv)
{

  float v[][3]={{-0.3,-0.2,0.0},{0.3, -0.2, 0.0},
        {0.3, 0.2, 0.0},{-0.3, 0.2, 0.0} };

  //light nodes
  Light *Light1=new Light;
  Light *Light2=new Light;
  TurnOff *Off1=new TurnOff(Light1);
  TurnOff *Off2=new TurnOff(Light2);

  //setting light values :
  Light1->SetValue(POSITION, -2, -3, 1.5, 1);
  Light1->SetValue(SPOT_DIRECTION, 2, 3, -1.5);
  Light1->SetValue(CUTOFFANGLE, 40.0);
  Light1->TurnOn();

  Light2->SetValue(POSITION, 5, 5, 5, 0);
  Light2->SetValue(SPECULAR, 1.0, 1.0, 1.0, 1.0);
  Light2->SetValue(DIFFUSE, 1.0, 1.0, 1.0, 1.0);
  Light2->TurnOn();


  //nodes for camera:
  Camera *Camera1=new Camera(PERSPECTIVE);

  Camera1->SetValue(POSITION, 2.2, 0.9, 3);
  Camera1->SetValue(AIMAT, 0, 0, 0);
  Camera1->SetValue(UPDIRECTION, 0, 1, 0);
  Camera1->SetValue(ASPECT, 1);
  Camera1->SetValue(NEAR, 1);
  Camera1->SetValue(FAR, 20);
  Camera1->SetValue(YANGLE, 50);

  //nodes for robot:
  Material *RobotMat=new Material;
  Material *EyeMat=new Material;

  Cylinder *Base=new Cylinder;
  Sphere *Head=new Sphere;
  Sphere *EyeL=new Sphere;
  Sphere *EyeR=new Sphere;
  Cylinder *UpperArmL=new Cylinder;
  Cylinder *UpperArmR=new Cylinder;
  Cylinder *LowerArmL=new Cylinder;
```

```
Cylinder *LowerArmR=new Cylinder;
Cylinder *UpperLegL=new Cylinder;
Cylinder *UpperLegR=new Cylinder;
Cylinder *LowerLegL=new Cylinder;
Cylinder *LowerLegR=new Cylinder;
Polygon *Paper=new Polygon;

Transformation *EyeLTrans=new Transformation;
Transformation *EyeRTrans=new Transformation;
Transformation *HeadTrans=new Transformation;
Transformation *UpArmLTrans=new Transformation;
Transformation *UpArmRTrans=new Transformation;
Transformation *LowArmTrans=new Transformation;
Transformation *UpLegLTrans=new Transformation;
Transformation *UpLegRTrans=new Transformation;
Transformation *LowLegTrans=new Transformation;
Transformation *BaseTrans=new Transformation;

//robot value:
RobotMat->SetValue(DIFFUSE, 0.0, 0.0, 1.0, 1.0);
RobotMat->SetValue(AMBIENT, 0.0, 0.0, 1.0, 1.0);
RobotMat->SetValue(SPECULAR, 1.0, 1.0, 1.0, 1.0);
RobotMat->SetValue(SHININESS, 100.0);

EyeMat->SetValue(DIFFUSE, 1.0, 1.0, 1.0, 1.0);
EyeMat->SetValue(AMBIENT, 1.0, 1.0, 1.0, 1.0);
EyeMat->SetValue(SPECULAR, 1.0, 1.0, 1.0, 1.0);
EyeMat->SetValue(SHININESS, 100.0);
Base->SetValue(HEIGHT, BaseLen);
Base->SetValue(RADIUS, BaseRadius);
Head->SetValue(RADIUS, BaseRadius);
EyeL->SetValue(RADIUS, EyeRadius);
EyeR->SetValue(RADIUS, EyeRadius);
UpperArmL->SetValue(HEIGHT, UpLen);
UpperArmL->SetValue(RADIUS, Radius);
LowerArmL->SetValue(HEIGHT, LowLen);
LowerArmL->SetValue(RADIUS, Radius);
UpperArmR->SetValue(HEIGHT, UpLen);
UpperArmR->SetValue(RADIUS, Radius);
LowerArmR->SetValue(HEIGHT, LowLen);
LowerArmR->SetValue(RADIUS, Radius);
UpperLegL->SetValue(HEIGHT, UpLen);
UpperLegL->SetValue(RADIUS, Radius);
LowerLegL->SetValue(HEIGHT, LowLen);
LowerLegL->SetValue(RADIUS, Radius);
UpperLegR->SetValue(HEIGHT, UpLen);
UpperLegR->SetValue(RADIUS, Radius);
LowerLegR->SetValue(HEIGHT, LowLen);
LowerLegR->SetValue(RADIUS, Radius);
```

```
Paper->SetVerticesv(v, 4);
Paper->SetMaterial(EyeMat);

EyeLTrans->SetValue(TRANSLATION, BaseRadius-EyeRadius/2, 0, 0, 0);
EyeLTrans->SetValue(ROTATION, 30, 0, 0, 1, 1);
EyeRTrans->SetValue(TRANSLATION, BaseRadius-EyeRadius/2, 0, 0, 0);
EyeRTrans->SetValue(ROTATION, -30, 0, 0, 1, 1);
HeadTrans->SetValue(TRANSLATION, 0, 0, BaseLen+BaseRadius+BaseRadius/3, 0);
UpArmLTrans->SetValue(TRANSLATION, 0, 0, -UpLen, 0);
UpArmLTrans->SetValue(ROTATION, -45, 0, 1, 0, 1);
UpArmLTrans->SetValue(TRANSLATION, 0, BaseRadius+Radius, BaseLen, 2);
UpArmRTrans->SetValue(TRANSLATION, 0, 0, -UpLen, 0);
UpArmRTrans->SetValue(ROTATION, -45, 0, 1, 0, 1);
UpArmRTrans->SetValue(TRANSLATION, 0, -(BaseRadius+Radius), BaseLen, 2);
LowArmTrans->SetValue(TRANSLATION, 0, 0, -UpLen, 0);
LowArmTrans->SetValue(ROTATION, -45, 0, 1, 0, 1);
UpLegLTrans->SetValue(TRANSLATION, 0, 0, -UpLen, 0);
UpLegLTrans->SetValue(ROTATION, -90, 0, 1, 0, 1);
UpLegLTrans->SetValue(TRANSLATION, 0, BaseRadius+Radius, 0, 2);
UpLegRTrans->SetValue(TRANSLATION, 0, 0, -UpLen, 0);
UpLegRTrans->SetValue(ROTATION, -100, 0, 1, 0, 1);
UpLegRTrans->SetValue(TRANSLATION, 0, -(BaseRadius+Radius), 0, 2);
LowLegTrans->SetValue(TRANSLATION, 0, 0, -UpLen, 0);
LowLegTrans->SetValue(ROTATION, 95, 0, 1, 0, 1);
BaseTrans->SetValue(ROTATION, -90, 1, 0, 0, 0);
BaseTrans->SetValue(ROTATION, -10, 0, 0, 1, 1);

Head->SetTransform(HeadTrans);
EyeL->SetTransform(EyeLTrans);
EyeR->SetTransform(EyeRTrans);
EyeR->SetMaterial(EyeMat);
EyeL->SetMaterial(EyeMat);
UpperArmL->SetTransform(UpArmLTrans);
LowerArmL->SetTransform(LowArmTrans);
UpperArmR->SetTransform(UpArmRTrans);
LowerArmR->SetTransform(LowArmTrans);
UpperLegL->SetTransform(UpLegLTrans);
LowerLegL->SetTransform(LowLegTrans);
UpperLegR->SetTransform(UpLegRTrans);
LowerLegR->SetTransform(LowLegTrans);
Base->SetTransform(BaseTrans);

Paper->SetTransform(ROTATION, 20, 0, 1, 0, 0);
Paper->SetTransform(TRANSLATION, 0.05, -0.15, -0.2, 1);

//set relationship in robot:
RobotMat->AddChild(Light1);
Light1->AddChild(Base);
```

```
Base->AddChild(Off1);
Off1->AddChild(Light2);
Light2->AddChild(Head);
Head->AddChild(Off2);
Head->AddChild(EyeL);
Head->AddChild(EyeR);

Base->AddChild(UpperArmL);
UpperArmL->AddChild(LowerArmL);
Base->AddChild(UpperArmR);
UpperArmR->AddChild(LowerArmR);
Base->AddChild(UpperLegL);
UpperLegL->AddChild(LowerLegL);
Base->AddChild(UpperLegR);
UpperLegR->AddChild(LowerLegR);
LowerArmR->AddChild(Paper);

//nodes for chair:
Cube *Seat=new Cube(0.7, 0.06, 0.7);
Line *Leg1=new Line;
Line *Leg2=new Line;
Line *Leg3=new Line;
Line *Leg4=new Line;
DrawStyle *LegStyle=new DrawStyle;
Color *ChairColor=new Color;

//chair value:
float v1[][3]={{-0.3, 0, 0.3},{-0.35, -1*ChairLegLen, 0.3}};
float v2[][3]={{0.3, 0, 0.3},{0.35, -1*ChairLegLen, 0.3}};
float v3[][3]={{0.3, 0, -0.3},{0.35, -1*ChairLegLen, -0.3}};
float v4[][3]={{-0.3, 0, -0.3},{-0.35, -1*ChairLegLen, -0.3}};

ChairColor->SetValue(RED);
Seat->SetTransform(TRANSLATION, 0, -0.15, 0, 0);
LegStyle->SetValue(LINEWIDTH, 7);
Leg1->SetStyle(LegStyle);
Leg1->SetVerticesv(v1);
Leg2->SetStyle(LegStyle);
Leg2->SetVerticesv(v2);
Leg3->SetStyle(LegStyle);
Leg3->SetVerticesv(v3);
Leg4->SetStyle(LegStyle);
Leg4->SetVerticesv(v4);
Seat->AddChild(Leg1);
Seat->AddChild(Leg2);
Seat->AddChild(Leg3);
Seat->AddChild(Leg4);
ChairColor->AddChild(Seat);
```

```
//transformation nodes for both robot and chair:
Transformation *Trans1=new Transformation;

Trans1->SetValue(TRANSLATION, -0.5, 0, 0, 2);

Trans1->AddChild(ChairColor);
Trans1->AddChild(RobotMat);

//root node:
Node *Root=new Node;

Root->AddChild(Trans1);
Root->AddChild(Camera1);

//viewer:
GLViewer *MyViewer=new GLViewer;

MyViewer->Init(argc, argv);
MyViewer->SetValue(BACKCOLOR, GRAY);
MyViewer->SetValue(BUFFER, DOUBLE);
MyViewer->CreateWin("Working Hard", 500, 500);

GLViewer *MyViewer2=new GLViewer;

MyViewer2->Init(argc, argv);
MyViewer2->SetValue(BACKCOLOR, MAGENTA);
MyViewer2->CreateWin("Working Hard2", 200, 200);
MyViewer2->SetValue(BUFFER, DOUBLE);

MyViewer->Show(Root);
MyViewer2->Show(Root);
return 0;
}
```

A.19 Program for Drawing Bézier Curves

```
/*
  curves.c

  Bézier curve drawing program


     q - Quit the program
     c - Clear the screen
     e - Erase the curves
     b - Draw Bezier curves

*/
```

```
#include <GL/glut.h>

void keyboard(unsigned char key, int x, int y);

#define MAX_CPTS  25    /* fixed maximum number of control points */

GLfloat cpts[MAX_CPTS][3];
int ncpts = 0;
static int width = 500, height = 500;    /* window width and height */


void drawCurves()
{
    int i;
    for(i=0; i<ncpts-3; i +=3)
    {
        /* draw the curve using OpenGL evaluators */

        glMap1f(GL_MAP1_VERTEX_3, 0.0, 1.0, 3, 4, cpts[i]);
        glMapGrid1f(30, 0.0, 1.0);
        glEvalMesh1(GL_LINE, 0, 30);
    }
    glFlush();
}


void display()
{
    int i;
    glClear(GL_COLOR_BUFFER_BIT);


    glBegin(GL_POINTS);
    for (i = 0; i < ncpts; i++)
        glVertex3fv(cpts[i]);
    glEnd();

    glFlush();
}


void mouse(int button, int state, int x, int y)
{
    float wx, wy;

    if (button == GLUT_LEFT_BUTTON && state == GLUT_DOWN)
    {
```

```
          /* translate back to our coordinate system */
          wx = (2.0 * x) / (float)(width - 1) - 1.0;
          wy = (2.0 * (height - 1 - y)) / (float)(height - 1) - 1.0;


          /* see if we have room for any more control points */
          if (ncpts == MAX_CPTS) return;

          /* save the point */
          cpts[ncpts][0] = wx;
          cpts[ncpts][1] = wy;
          cpts[ncpts][2] = 0.0;
          ncpts++;

          /* draw the point */
          glColor3f(0.0, 0.0, 0.0);
          glPointSize(5.0);
          glBegin(GL_POINTS);
              glVertex3f(wx, wy, 0.0);
          glEnd();
          glFlush();
      }
}

void keyboard(unsigned char key, int x, int y)
{
    switch (key)
    {
        case 'q': case 'Q':
            exit(0);
            break;
        case 'c': case 'C':
            ncpts = 0;
            glutPostRedisplay();
            break;
        case 'e': case 'E':
            glutPostRedisplay();
            break;
        case 'b': case 'B':
            drawCurves();
            break;
    }
}

void reshape(int w, int h)
{
    width = w;
    height = h;
```

```
        glMatrixMode(GL_PROJECTION);
        glLoadIdentity();
        glOrtho(-1.0, 1.0, -1.0, 1.0, -1.0, 1.0);
        glMatrixMode(GL_MODELVIEW);
        glViewport(0, 0, w, h);
    }

    int main(int argc, char **argv)
    {
        glutInit(&argc, argv);
        glutInitDisplayMode(GLUT_RGB);
        glutInitWindowSize(width, height);
        glutCreateWindow("curves");
        glutDisplayFunc(display);
        glutMouseFunc(mouse);
        glutKeyboardFunc(keyboard);
        glutReshapeFunc(reshape);
        glClearColor(1.0, 1.0, 1.0, 1.0);
        glColor3f(0.0, 0.0, 0.0);
        glPointSize(5.0);
        glEnable(GL_MAP1_VERTEX_3);
        glutMainLoop();
    }
```

SPACES

Computer graphics is concerned with the representation and manipulation of sets of geometric elements, such as points and line segments. The necessary mathematics is found in the study of various types of abstract spaces. In this appendix, we review the rules governing three such spaces: the (linear) vector space, the affine space, and the Euclidean space. The **(linear) vector space** contains only two types of objects: scalars, such as real numbers, and vectors. The **affine space** adds a third element: the point. **Euclidean spaces** add the concept of distance.

The vectors of interest in computer graphics are directed line segments and the n-tuples of numbers that are used to represent them. In Appendix C, we discuss matrix algebra as a tool for manipulating n-tuples. In this appendix, we are concerned with the underlying concepts and rules. It is probably helpful to think of these entities (scalars, vectors, points) as abstract data types, and the axioms as defining the valid operations on them.

B.1 Scalars

Ordinary real numbers and the operations on them are one example of a **scalar field**. Let S denote a set of elements called **scalars**, α, β, ... Scalars have two fundamental operations defined between pairs. These operations are often called addition and multiplication and are symbolized by the operators $+$ and $\cdot$,[1] respectively. Hence, for $\forall \alpha, \beta \in S, \alpha + \beta \in S$, and $\alpha \cdot \beta \in S$. These operations are associative, commutative, and distributive, $\forall \alpha, \beta, \gamma \in S$:

$$\alpha + \beta = \beta + \alpha,$$

$$\alpha \cdot \beta = \beta \cdot \alpha,$$

$$\alpha + (\beta + \gamma) = (\alpha + \beta) + \gamma,$$

---

1. Often, if there is no ambiguity, we can write $\alpha\beta$ instead of $\alpha \cdot \beta$.

$$\alpha \cdot (\beta \cdot \gamma) = (\alpha \cdot \beta) \cdot \gamma,$$

$$\alpha \cdot (\beta + \gamma) = (\alpha \cdot \beta) + (\alpha \cdot \gamma).$$

There are two special scalars—the additive identity (0) and the multiplicative identity (1)—such that $\forall \alpha \in S$:

$$\alpha + 0 = 0 + \alpha = \alpha,$$

$$\alpha \cdot 1 = 1 \cdot \alpha = \alpha.$$

Each element α has an additive inverse, denoted $-\alpha$, and a multiplicative inverse, denoted $\alpha^{-1} \in S$, such that

$$\alpha + (-\alpha) = 0,$$

$$\alpha \cdot \alpha^{-1} = 1.$$

The real numbers using ordinary addition and multiplication form a scalar field, as do the complex numbers (under complex addition and multiplication) and rational functions (ratios of two polynomials).

B.2   Vector Spaces

A vector space, in addition to scalars, contains a second type of entity: **vectors**. Vectors have two operations defined: vector–vector addition and scalar–vector multiplication. Let u, v, w denote vectors in a vector space V. Vector addition is defined to be closed $(u + v \in V, \forall u, v \in V)$, commutative $(u + v = v + u)$, and associative $(u + (v + w) = (u + v) + w)$. There is a special vector $\mathbf{0}$ (the **zero vector**) defined such that $\forall u \in V$:

$$u + \mathbf{0} = u.$$

Every vector u has an additive inverse denoted by $-u$ such that

$$u + (-u) = \mathbf{0}.$$

Scalar–vector multiplication is defined such that for any scalar α and any vector u, αu is a vector in V. The scalar–vector operation is distributive. Hence,

$$\alpha(u + v) = \alpha u + \alpha v,$$

$$(\alpha + \beta)u = \alpha u + \beta u.$$

The two examples of vector spaces that we use are geometric vectors (directed line segments) and the n-tuples of real numbers. Consider a set of directed line segments that we can picture as shown in Figure B.1. If our scalars are real numbers, then scalar–vector multiplication changes the length of a vector but not that vector's direction (Figure B.2).

Vector–vector addition can be defined by the **head-to-tail axiom**, which we can visualize easily for the example of directed line segments. We form the vector

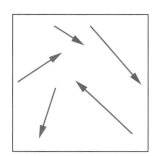

FIGURE B.1   Directed line segments.

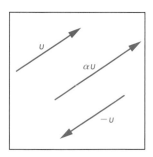

FIGURE B.2   Scalar–vector multiplication.

$u + v$ by connecting the head of u to the tail of v, as shown in Figure B.3. You should be able to verify that all the rules of a vector field are satisfied.

The second example of a vector space is n-tuples of scalars—usually, real or complex numbers. Hence, a vector can be written as

$$v = (v_1, v_2, \ldots, v_n).$$

Scalar–vector multiplication and vector–vector addition are given by

$$u + v = (u_1, u_2, \ldots, u_n) + (v_1, v_2, \ldots, v_n)$$
$$= (u_1 + v_1, u_2 + v_2, \ldots, u_n + v_n),$$
$$\alpha v = (\alpha v_1, \alpha v_2, \ldots, \alpha v_n).$$

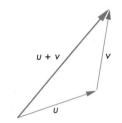

FIGURE B.3 Head-to-tail axiom for vectors.

This space is denoted $\mathbf{R}^n$ and is the vector space in which we can manipulate vectors using matrix algebra (Appendix C).

In a vector space, the concepts of linear independence and basis are crucial. A **linear combination** of n vectors $u_1, u_2, \ldots, u_n$ is a vector of the form

$$u = \alpha_1 u_1 + \alpha_2 u_2 + \ldots + \alpha_n u_n.$$

If the only set of scalars such that

$$\alpha_1 u_1 + \alpha_2 u_2 \ldots + \alpha_n u_n = 0$$

is

$$\alpha_1 = \alpha_2 = \ldots = \alpha_n = 0,$$

then the vectors are said to be **linearly independent**. The greatest number of linearly independent vectors that we can find in a space gives the **dimension** of the space. If a vector space has dimension n, any set of n linearly independent vectors form a **basis**. If $v_1, v_2, \ldots, v_n$ is a basis for V, any vector v can be expressed uniquely in terms of the basis vectors as

$$v = \beta_1 v_1 + \beta_2 v_2 + \ldots + \beta_n v_n.$$

The scalars $\{\beta_i\}$ give the **representation** of v with respect to the basis v_1, $v_2, \ldots, v_n$. If $v'_1, v'_2, \ldots, v'_n$ is some other basis (the number of vectors in a basis is constant), there is a representation of v with respect to this basis; that is,

$$v = \beta'_1 v'_1 + \beta'_2 v'_2 + \ldots + \beta'_n v'_n.$$

There exists an $n \times n$ matrix $\mathbf{M}$ such that

$$\begin{bmatrix} \beta'_1 \\ \beta'_2 \\ \vdots \\ \beta'_N \end{bmatrix} = \mathbf{M} \begin{bmatrix} \beta_1 \\ \beta_2 \\ \vdots \\ \beta_N \end{bmatrix}.$$

We derive **M** in Appendix C. This matrix gives a way of changing representations through a simple linear transformation involving only scalar operations for carrying out matrix multiplication. More generally, once we have a basis for a vector space, we can work only with representations. If the scalars are real numbers, then we can work with n-tuples of reals and use matrix algebra, instead of doing operations in the original abstract vector space

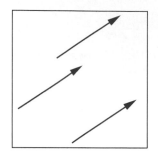

FIGURE B.4   Identical vectors.

B.3   Affine Spaces

A vector space lacks any geometric concepts, such as location and distance. If we use the example of directed line segments as the natural vector space for our geometric problems, we get into difficulties because these vectors, just like the physicist's vectors, have magnitude and direction but have no position. The vectors in Figure B.4 are identical.

If we think of this problem in terms of coordinate systems, we can express a vector in terms of a set of basis vectors that define a **coordinate system**. Figure B.5(a) shows three basis vectors emerging from a particular reference point, the **origin**. The location of the vectors in Figure B.5(b) is equally valid, however, because vectors have no position. In addition, we have no way to express this special point, because our vector space has only vectors and scalars as its members.

We can resolve this difficulty by introducing an affine space that adds a third type of entity—points—to a vector space. The points $(P, Q, R, \ldots)$ form a set. There is a single new operation, **point–point subtraction**, that yields a vector. Hence, if P and Q are any two points, the subtraction

$$v = P - Q$$

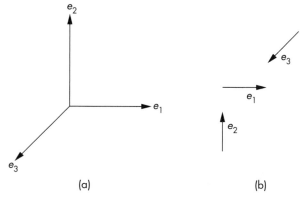

(a)   (b)

FIGURE B.5   Coordinate system. (a) Basis vectors located at the origin. (b) Arbitrary placement of basis vectors.

always yields a vector in V. Conversely, for every v and every P, we can find a Q such that the preceding relation holds. We can thus write

$$Q = v + P,$$

defining a vector–point addition. A consequence of the head-to-tail axiom is that for any three points P, Q, R,

$$(P - Q) + (Q - R) = (P - R).$$

If we visualize the vector $P - Q$ as the line segment from the point Q to the point P, using an arrow to denote direction, the head-to-tail axiom can be drawn as shown in Figure B.6.

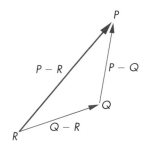

FIGURE B.6 Head-to-tail axiom for points.

Various properties follow from affine geometry. Perhaps the most important is that if we use a frame, rather than a coordinate system, we can specify both points and vectors in an affine space. A **frame** consists of a point P_0 and a set of vectors $v_1, v_2, \ldots, v_n$ that defines a basis for the vector space. Given a frame, an arbitrary vector can be written uniquely as

$$v = \alpha_1 v_1 + \alpha_2 v_2 + \ldots + \alpha_n v_n,$$

and an arbitrary point can be written uniquely as

$$P = P_0 + \beta_1 v_1 + \beta_2 v_2 + \ldots + \beta_n v_n.$$

The two sets of scalars, $\{\alpha_1, \ldots, \alpha_n\}$ and $\{\beta_1, \ldots, \beta_n\}$, give the representations of the vector and point, respectively, with each representation consisting of n scalars. We can regard the point P_0 as the origin of the frame; all points are defined from this reference point.

If the origin never changes, we can worry about only those changes of frames corresponding to changes in coordinate systems. In computer graphics, however, we usually have to deal with making changes in frames and with representing objects in different frames. For example, we usually define our objects within a physical frame. The viewer, or camera, can be expressed in terms of this frame, but as part of the image-creation process, it is to our advantage to express object positions with respect to the camera frame—a frame whose origin usually is located at the center of projection.

B.4 Euclidean Spaces

Although affine spaces contain the necessary elements for building geometric models, there is no concept of how far apart two points are or of what the length of a vector is. Euclidean spaces have such a concept. Strictly speaking, a Euclidean space needs to contain only vectors and scalars.

Suppose that E is a Euclidean space. It is a vector space containing scalars $(\alpha, \beta, \gamma, \ldots)$ and vectors $(u, v, w, \ldots)$. We assume that the scalars are the ordinary real numbers. We add a new operation—the **inner (dot) product**—that combines two vectors to form a real. The inner product must satisfy the properties that for any three vectors u, v, w and scalars α, β,

$$u \cdot v = v \cdot u,$$

$$(\alpha u + \beta v) \cdot w = \alpha u \cdot w + \beta v \cdot w,$$

$$v \cdot v > 0 \text{ if } v \neq 0,$$

$$0 \cdot 0 = 0.$$

If

$$u \cdot v = 0,$$

then u and v are **orthogonal**. The magnitude (length) of a vector is usually measured as

$$|v| = \sqrt{v \cdot v}.$$

Once we add affine concepts, such as points, to the Euclidean space, we naturally get a measure of distance between points because for any two points P and Q, $P - Q$ is a vector, and hence

$$|P - Q| = \sqrt{(P - Q) \cdot (P - Q)}.$$

We can use the inner product to define a measure of the angle between two vectors:

$$u \cdot v = |u||v| \cos \theta.$$

It is easy to show that $\cos \theta$ as defined by this formula is 0 when the vectors are orthogonal, lies between −1 and +1, and has magnitude 1 if the vectors are parallel ($u = \alpha v$).

B.5   Projections

We can derive several of the important geometric concepts from the use of orthogonality. The concept of **projection** arises from the problem of finding the shortest distance from a point to a line or plane. It is equivalent to the following problem. Given two vectors, we can take one of them and divide it into two parts, one parallel and one orthogonal to the other vector, as shown in Figure B.7 for directed line segments. Suppose that v is the first vector and w is the second. Then, w can be written as

$$w = \alpha v + u.$$

The parallel part is αv, but for u to be orthogonal to v, we must have

$$u \cdot v = 0.$$

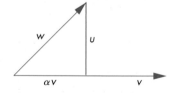

FIGURE B.7 Projection of one vector onto another.

Because u and v are defined to be orthogonal,

$$w \cdot v = \alpha v \cdot v + u \cdot v = \alpha v \cdot v,$$

allowing us to find

$$\alpha = \frac{w \cdot v}{v \cdot v}.$$

The vector αv is the projection of w onto v, and

$$u = w - \frac{w \cdot v}{v \cdot v} v.$$

We can extend this result to construct a set of orthogonal vectors from an arbitrary set of linearly independent vectors.

B.6 Gram-Schmidt Orthogonalization

Given a set of basis vectors, $a_1, a_2, \ldots, a_n$, in a space of dimension n, it is relatively straightforward to create another basis $b_1, b_2, \ldots, b_n$ that is **orthonormal**, that is, a basis in which each vector has unit length and is orthogonal to each other vector in the basis, or mathematically:

$$b_i \cdot b_j = \begin{cases} 1 & \text{if } i = j, \\ 0 & \text{otherwise.} \end{cases}$$

Hence, there is no real loss of generality in using orthogonal (Cartesian) coordinate systems.

We proceed iteratively. We look for a vector of the form

$$b_2 = a_2 + \alpha b_1,$$

which we can make orthogonal to b_1 by choosing α properly. Taking the dot product, we must have

$$b_2 \cdot b_1 = 0 = a_2 \cdot b_1 + \alpha b_1 \cdot b_1.$$

Solving, we have

$$\alpha = -\frac{a_2 \cdot b_1}{b_1 \cdot b_1}$$

and

$$b_2 = a_2 - \frac{a_2 \cdot b_1}{b_1 \cdot b_1} b_1.$$

We have constructed the orthogonal vector by removing the part parallel to b_1—that is, the projection of a_2 onto b_1.

The general iterative step is to find a

$$b_k = a_k + \sum_{i=1}^{k-1} \alpha_i b_i$$

that is orthogonal to $b_1, \ldots, b_{k-1}$. There are $k-1$ orthogonality conditions that allow us to find

$$\alpha_i = -\frac{a_k \cdot b_i}{b_i \cdot b_i}.$$

We can normalize each vector, either at the end of the process by replacing b_i by $b_i/|b_i|$ or, more efficiently, by normalizing each b_i as soon as possible.

Suggested Readings

There are many excellent books on linear algebra and vector spaces. For practitioners of computer graphics, the preferred approach is to start with vector-space ideas and to see linear algebra as a tool for working with general vector spaces. Unfortunately, most of the linear algebra textbooks are concerned with only the Euclidean spaces of n-tuples, $\mathbf{R}^n$. See Bowyer and Woodwark [Bow83] and Banchoff and Werner [Ban83].

Affine spaces can be approached in a number of ways. See Foley [Fol90] for a more geometric development.

Exercises

B.1   Prove that the complex numbers form a scalar field. What are the additive and multiplicative identity elements?

B.2   Prove that the rational functions form a scalar field.

B.3   Prove that the rational functions with real coefficients form a vector space.

B.4   Prove that the number of elements in a basis is unique.

B.5   Consider a set of n real functions $\{f_i(x)\}$, $i = 1, \ldots, n$. Show how to form a vector space of functions with these elements. Define *basis* and *dimension* for this space.

B.6   Show that the set of polynomials of degree up to n form an n-dimensional vector space.

B.7   The most important Euclidean space is the space of n-tuples, $a_1, \ldots, a_n$: $\mathbf{R}^n$. Define the operations of vector addition and scalar–vector multiplication in this space. What is the dot product in $\mathbf{R}^n$?

B.8   Suppose that you are given three vectors in $\mathbf{R}^3$. How can you determine whether they form a basis?

B.9   Consider the three vectors in $\mathbf{R}^3$: $(1, 0, 0)$, $(1, 1, 0)$, and $(1, 1, 1)$. Show that they are linearly independent. Derive an orthonormal basis from these vectors, starting with $(1, 0, 0)$.

MATRICES

In computer graphics, the major use of matrices is in the representation of changes in coordinate systems and frames. In the studies of vector analysis and linear algebra, the use of the term *vector* is somewhat different. Unfortunately, computer graphics relies on both these fields, and the interpretation of *vector* has caused confusion. To remedy this situation, we use the terms *row matrix* and *column matrix*, rather than the linear algebra terms of *row vector* and *column vector*. We reserve the *vector* to denote directed line segments and occasionally, as in Appendix B, to denote the abstract-data–type vector that is an element of a vector space.

This appendix reviews the major results that you will need to manipulate matrices in computer graphics. We almost always use matrices that are 4×4. Hence, the parts of linear algebra that deal with manipulations of general matrices, such as the inversion of an arbitrary square matrix, are of limited interest. Most implementations instead implement inversion of 4×4 matrices directly in the hardware or software.

C.1 Definitions

A **matrix** is an $n \times m$ array of scalars, arranged conceptually as n rows and m columns. Often, n and m are referred to as the row and column **dimensions** of the matrix, and if $m = n$, we say that the matrix is a **square matrix** of dimension n. We use real numbers for scalars almost exclusively, although most results hold for complex numbers as well. The elements of a matrix $\mathbf{A}$ are the members of the set of scalars, $\{a_{ij}\}$, $i = 1, \ldots, n, j = 1, \ldots, m$. We write $\mathbf{A}$ in terms of its elements as

$$\mathbf{A} = [\, a_{ij} \,].$$

The **transpose** of an $n \times m$ matrix $\mathbf{A}$ is the $m \times n$ matrix that we obtain by interchanging the rows and columns of $\mathbf{A}$. We denote this matrix as $\mathbf{A}^T$, and it is given as

$$\mathbf{A}^T = [\, a_{ji} \,].$$

The special cases of matrices with one column ($n \times 1$ matrix) and one row ($1 \times m$ matrix) are called **column matrices** and **row matrices**, respectively. We denote column matrices with lowercase letters:

$$\mathbf{b} = [\, b_i \,].$$

The transpose of a row matrix is a column matrix; we write it as $\mathbf{b}^T$.

C.2   Matrix Operations

There are three basic matrix operations: scalar–matrix multiplication, matrix–matrix addition, and matrix–matrix multiplication. You can assume that the scalars are real numbers, although all these operations are defined in the same way when the elements of the matrices and the scalar multipliers are of the same type.

Scalar–matrix multiplication is defined for any size matrix $\mathbf{A}$; it is simply the element-by-element multiplication of the elements of the matrix by a scalar α. The operation is written as

$$\alpha\mathbf{A} = [\, \alpha a_{ij} \,].$$

We define **matrix–matrix addition**, the sum of two matrices, by adding the corresponding elements of the two matrices. The sum makes sense only if the two matrices have the same dimensions. The sum of two matrices of the same dimensions is given by the matrix

$$\mathbf{C} = \mathbf{A} + \mathbf{B} = [\, a_{ij} + b_{ij} \,].$$

For **matrix–matrix multiplication**, the product of an $n \times l$ matrix $\mathbf{A}$ by an $l \times m$ matrix $\mathbf{B}$ is the $n \times m$ matrix

$$\mathbf{C} = \mathbf{AB} = [\, c_{ij} \,],$$

where

$$c_{ij} = \sum_{k=1}^{l} a_{ik} b_{kj}.$$

The matrix–matrix product is thus defined only if the number of columns of $\mathbf{A}$ is the same as the number of rows of $\mathbf{B}$. We say that $\mathbf{A}$ premultiplies $\mathbf{B}$, or $\mathbf{B}$ postmultiplies $\mathbf{A}$.

Scalar–matrix multiplication obeys a number of simple rules that hold for any matrix $\mathbf{A}$ and for scalars α and β, such as

$$\alpha(\beta\mathbf{A}) = (\alpha\beta)\mathbf{A},$$

$$\alpha\beta\mathbf{A} = \beta\alpha\mathbf{A},$$

all of which follow from the fact that our matrix operations reduce to scalar multiplications on the scalar elements of a matrix. For matrix–matrix addition, we have the **commutative** property. For any $n \times m$ matrices $\mathbf{A}$ and $\mathbf{B}$:

$$\mathbf{A} + \mathbf{B} = \mathbf{B} + \mathbf{A}.$$

We also have the **associative** property, which states that for any three $n \times m$ matrices $\mathbf{A}$, $\mathbf{B}$, and $\mathbf{C}$:

$$\mathbf{A} + (\mathbf{B} + \mathbf{C}) = (\mathbf{A} + \mathbf{B}) + \mathbf{C}.$$

Matrix–matrix multiplication, although associative,

$$\mathbf{A}(\mathbf{BC}) = (\mathbf{AB})\mathbf{C},$$

is almost never commutative. So not only is it almost always the case that $\mathbf{AB} \neq \mathbf{BA}$ but also one product may not even be defined when the other is. In graphics applications, where matrices represent transformations such as translation and rotation, these results express that the order in which you carry out a sequence of transformations is important. A rotation followed by a translation is not the same as a translation followed by a rotation. However, if we do a rotation followed by a translation followed by a scaling, we get the same result if we first combine the scaling and translation, preserving the order, and then apply the rotation to the combined transformation.

The identity matrix $\mathbf{I}$ is a square matrix with 1s on the diagonal and 0s elsewhere:

$$\mathbf{I} = [\, a_{ij} \,], \qquad a_{ij} = \begin{cases} 1 & \text{if } i = j, \\ 0 & \text{otherwise.} \end{cases}$$

Assuming that the dimensions make sense,

$$\mathbf{AI} = \mathbf{A},$$

$$\mathbf{IB} = \mathbf{B}.$$

C.3 Row and Column Matrices

The $1 \times n$ and $n \times 1$ row and column matrices are of particular interest to us. We can represent either a vector or a point in three-dimensional space,[1] with respect to some frame, as the column matrix

$$\mathbf{p} = \begin{bmatrix} x \\ y \\ z \end{bmatrix}.$$

---

1. The homogeneous-coordinate representation introduced in Chapter 4 distinguishes between the representation of a point and the representation of a vector.

We use lowercase letters for column matrices. The transpose of $\mathbf{p}$ is the row matrix

$$\mathbf{p}^T = [\, x \quad y \quad z \,].$$

Because the product of an $n \times l$ and a $l \times m$ matrix is an $n \times m$ matrix, the product of a square matrix of dimension n and a column matrix of dimension n is a new column matrix of dimension n. Our standard mode of representing transformations of points is to use a column matrix of two, three, or four dimensions to represent a point (or vector) and a square matrix to represent a transformation of the point (or vector). Thus, the expression

$$\mathbf{p}' = \mathbf{A}\mathbf{p}$$

yields the representation of a transformed point (or vector), and expressions such as

$$\mathbf{p}' = \mathbf{A}\mathbf{B}\mathbf{C}\mathbf{p}$$

describe sequences, or **concatenations**, of transformations. Note that because the matrix–matrix product is associative, we do not need parentheses in this expression.

Many graphics books prefer to use row matrices to represent points. If we do so, using the fact that the transpose of a product can be written as

$$(\mathbf{A}\mathbf{B})^T = \mathbf{B}^T \mathbf{A}^T,$$

then the concatenation of the three transformations can be written in row form as

$$\mathbf{p}'^T = \mathbf{p}^T \mathbf{C}^T \mathbf{B}^T \mathbf{A}^T.$$

The professed advantage of this form is that in English we read the transformations in the order in which they are performed: first $\mathbf{C}$, then $\mathbf{B}$, then $\mathbf{A}$. Almost all the scientific, mathematics, and engineering literature, however, uses column matrices rather than row matrices. Consequently, we prefer the column form. Although the choice is conceptually simple, in practice you have to be careful regarding which one your API is using because not only is the order of transformations reversed but also the transformation matrices themselves must be transposed.

C.4 Rank

In computer graphics, the primary use of matrices is as representations of points and of transformations. If a square matrix represents the transformation of a point or vector, we are often interested in whether or not the transformation is reversible or **invertible**. Thus, if

$$\mathbf{q} = \mathbf{A}\mathbf{p},$$

we want to know whether we can find a square matrix $\mathbf{B}$ such that

$\mathbf{p} = \mathbf{Bq}$.

Substituting for $\mathbf{q}$,

$\mathbf{p} = \mathbf{Bq} = \mathbf{BAp} = \mathbf{Ip} = \mathbf{p}$

and

$\mathbf{BA} = \mathbf{I}$.

If such a $\mathbf{B}$ exists, it is the **inverse** of $\mathbf{A}$, and $\mathbf{A}$ is said to be **nonsingular**. A noninvertible matrix is **singular**. The inverse of $\mathbf{A}$ is written as $\mathbf{A}^{-1}$.

The fundamental result about inverses is as follows: *The inverse of a square matrix exists if and only if the determinant of the matrix is nonzero.* Although the determinant of $\mathbf{A}$ is a scalar, denoted by $|\mathbf{A}|$, its computation, for anything but low-dimensional matrices, requires almost as much work as does computation of the inverse. These calculations are $O(n^3)$ for an n-dimensional matrix. For the two-, three-, and four-dimensional matrices of interest in computer graphics, we can compute determinants by Cramer's rule and inverses using determinants, or we can use geometric reasoning. For example, the inverse of a translation is a translation back, and thus the inverse of a translation matrix must be a translation matrix. We pursued this course in Chapter 4.

For general nonsquare matrices, the concept of rank is important. We can regard a square matrix as a row matrix whose elements are column matrices or, equivalently, as a column matrix whose elements are row matrices. In terms of the vector-space concepts of Appendix B, the rows of an $n \times m$ matrix are elements of the Euclidean space $\mathbf{R}^m$, whereas the columns are elements of $\mathbf{R}^n$. We can determine how many rows (or columns) are **linearly independent**. The row (column) **rank** is the maximum number of linearly independent rows (columns), and thus *for an $n \times n$ matrix, the row rank and the column rank are the same and the matrix is nonsingular if and only if the rank is n.* Thus, a matrix is invertible if and only if its rows (and columns) are linearly independent.

C.5 Change of Representation

We can use matrices to represent changes in bases for any set of vectors satisfying the rules of Appendix B. Suppose that we have a vector space of dimension n. Let $\{u_1, u_2, \ldots, u_n\}$ and $\{v_1, v_2, \ldots, v_n\}$ be two bases for the vector space. Hence, a given vector v can be expressed as either

$v = \alpha_1 u_1 + \alpha_2 u_2 + \ldots + \alpha_n u_n$

or

$v = \beta_1 v_1 + \beta_2 v_2 + \ldots + \beta_n v_n$.

Thus, $(\alpha_1, \alpha_2, \ldots, \alpha_n)$ and $(\beta_1, \beta_2, \ldots, \beta_n)$ are two different representations of v, and each can be expressed, equivalently, as a vector in the Euclidean space $\mathbf{R}^n$ or as a column matrix of dimension n. When we are working with representations, rather than with the vectors, we have to be careful to make sure that our notation reflects the difference. We write the representations of v as either

$$\mathbf{v} = [\, \alpha_1 \quad \alpha_2 \quad \ldots \quad \alpha_n \,]^T$$

or

$$\mathbf{v}' = [\, \beta_1 \quad \beta_2 \quad \ldots \quad \beta_n \,]^T,$$

depending on which basis we use.

We can now address the problem of how we convert from the representation $\mathbf{v}$ to the representation $\mathbf{v}'$. The basis vectors $\{v_1, v_2, \ldots, v_n\}$ can be expressed as vectors in the basis $\{u_1, u_2, \ldots, u_n\}$. Thus, there exists a set of scalars γ_{ij} such that

$$u_i = \gamma_{i1} v_1 + \gamma_{i2} v_2 + \ldots + \gamma_{in} v_n, \quad i = 1, \ldots, n.$$

We can write the expression in matrix form for all u_i as

$$\begin{bmatrix} u_1 \\ u_2 \\ \vdots \\ u_n \end{bmatrix} = \mathbf{A} \begin{bmatrix} v_1 \\ v_2 \\ \vdots \\ v_n \end{bmatrix},$$

where $\mathbf{A}$ is the $n \times n$ matrix:

$$\mathbf{A} = [\, \gamma_{ij} \,].$$

We can use column matrices to express both $\mathbf{v}$ and $\mathbf{v}'$ in terms of the vectors' representations as

$$\mathbf{v} = \mathbf{a}^T \begin{bmatrix} u_1 \\ u_2 \\ \vdots \\ u_n \end{bmatrix},$$

where

$$\mathbf{a} = [\, \alpha_i \,].$$

We can define $\mathbf{b}$ as

$$\mathbf{b} = [\, \beta_i \,],$$

and we can write $\mathbf{v}'$ as

$$\mathbf{v}' = \mathbf{b}^T \begin{bmatrix} v_1 \\ v_2 \\ \vdots \\ v_n \end{bmatrix}.$$

The matrix $\mathbf{A}$ relates the two bases, so we find by direct substitution that

$$\mathbf{b}^T = \mathbf{a}^T \mathbf{A}.$$

The matrix $\mathbf{A}$ is the **matrix representation** of the change between the two bases. It allows us to convert directly between the two representations. Equivalently, we can work with matrices of scalars rather than with abstract vectors. For geometric problems, although our vectors may be directed line segments, we can represent them by sets of scalars, and we can represent changes of bases or transformations by direct manipulation of these scalars.

C.6 The Cross Product

Given two nonparallel vectors, u and v, in a three-dimensional space, the cross product gives a third vector, w, that is orthogonal to both. Regardless of the representation, we must have

$$w \cdot u = w \cdot v = 0.$$

We can assign one component of w arbitrarily because it is the direction of w, rather than the length, that is of importance, leaving us with three conditions for the three components of w. Within a particular coordinate system, if u has components $\alpha_1, \alpha_2, \alpha_3$, and v has components $\beta_1, \beta_2, \beta_3$, then in this system, the **cross product** is defined as

$$\mathbf{w} = \mathbf{u} \times \mathbf{v} = \begin{bmatrix} \alpha_2\beta_3 - \alpha_3\beta_2 \\ \alpha_3\beta_1 - \alpha_1\beta_3 \\ \alpha_1\beta_2 - \alpha_2\beta_1 \end{bmatrix}.$$

Note that vector w is defined by u and v; we use their representation only when we wish to compute w in a particular coordinate system. The cross product gives a consistent orientation for $u \times v$. For example, consider the x-, y-, and z-axes as three vectors that determine the three coordinate directions of a right-handed coordinate system.[2] If we use the usual x- and y-axes, the cross product $x \times y$ points in the direction of the positive z-axis.

---

2. A right-handed coordinate system has positive directions determined by the thumb, index finger, and middle finger of the right hand used for the x-, y-, and z-axes, respectively. Equivalently, on a piece of paper, if positive x points left to right and positive y points bottom to top, then positive z points out of the page.

C.7   Eigenvalues and Eigenvectors

Square matrices are operators that transform column matrices into other column matrices of the same dimension. Because column matrices can represent points and vectors, we are interested in questions such as, When does a transformation leave a point or vector unchanged? For example, every rotation matrix leaves a particular point—the fixed point—unchanged. Let us consider a slightly more general problem. When does the matrix equation

$$\mathbf{Mu} = \lambda \mathbf{u}$$

have a nontrivial solution for some scalar λ, that is, a solution with $\mathbf{u}$ not being a matrix of zeros? If such a solution exists, then $\mathbf{M}$ transforms certain vectors $\mathbf{u}$—its **eigenvectors**—into scalar multiples of themselves. The values of λ for which this relationship holds are called the **eigenvalues** of the matrix. Eigenvalues and eigenvectors are also called **characteristic values** and **characteristic vectors**, respectively. These values characterize many properties of the matrix that are invariant under such operations as changes in representation.

We can find the eigenvalues by solving the equivalent matrix equation

$$\mathbf{Mu} - \lambda \mathbf{u} = \mathbf{Mu} - \lambda \mathbf{Iu} = (\mathbf{M} - \lambda \mathbf{I})\mathbf{u} = \mathbf{0}.$$

This equation can have a nontrivial solution if and only if the determinant[3]

$$|\mathbf{M} - \lambda \mathbf{I}| = 0.$$

If $\mathbf{M}$ is $n \times n$, then the determinant yields a polynomial of degree n in λ. Thus, there are n roots, some of which may be repeated or complex. For each distinct eigenvalue, we can then find a corresponding eigenvector. Note that every multiple of an eigenvector is itself an eigenvector so that we can choose an eigenvector with unit magnitude. Eigenvectors corresponding to distinct eigenvalues are linearly independent. Thus, if all the eigenvalues are distinct, then any set of eigenvectors corresponding to the distinct eigenvalues forms a basis for an n-dimensional vector space.

If there are repeated eigenvalues, the situation can be more complex. However, we need not worry about these cases for the matrices we shall use in graphics. Thus, if $\mathbf{R}$ is a 3×3 rotation matrix and $\mathbf{p} = [\, x \quad y \quad z \,]^T$ is the fixed point, then

$$\mathbf{Rp} = \mathbf{p}.$$

Thus, every rotation matrix must have an eigenvalue of 1. This result is the same whether we work in three dimensions or use the four-dimensional homogenous-coordinate representation in Chapter 4.

---

3. The general statement, known as the Fredholm alternative, states that the n linear equations in n unknowns $\mathbf{Ax} = \mathbf{b}$ have a unique solution if and only if $|\mathbf{A}| \neq 0$. If $|\mathbf{A}| = 0$, there are multiple nontrivial solutions.

Suppose that $\mathbf{T}$ is a nonsingular matrix. Consider the matrix

$$\mathbf{Q} = \mathbf{T}^{-1}\mathbf{MT}.$$

Its eigenvalues and eigenvectors are solutions of the equation

$$\mathbf{Qv} = \mathbf{T}^{-1}\mathbf{MTv} = \lambda\mathbf{v}.$$

But if we multiply by $\mathbf{T}$, this equations becomes

$$\mathbf{MTv} = \lambda\mathbf{Tv}.$$

Thus, the eigenvalues of $\mathbf{Q}$ are the same as those of $\mathbf{M}$, and the eigenvectors are the transformations of the eigenvectors of $\mathbf{M}$. The matrices $\mathbf{M}$ and $\mathbf{Q}$ are said to be **similar**. Many of the transformations that arise in computer graphics involve similar matrices. One interpretation of this result is that changes of coordinate systems leave fundamental properties, such as the eigenvalues, unchanged. If we can find a similarity transformation that converts $\mathbf{M}$ to a diagonal matrix $\mathbf{Q}$, then the diagonal elements of $\mathbf{Q}$ are the eigenvalues of both matrices.

Eigenvalues and eigenvectors have a geometric interpretation. Consider an ellipsoid, centered at the origin, with its axes aligned with the coordinate axes. It can be written as

$$\lambda_1 x^2 + \lambda_2 y^2 + \lambda_3 z^2 = 1$$

for positive values of λ_1, λ_2, and λ_3, or in matrix form

$$[\,x \quad y \quad z\,] \begin{bmatrix} \lambda_1 & 0 & 0 \\ 0 & \lambda_2 & 0 \\ 0 & 0 & \lambda_3 \end{bmatrix} \begin{bmatrix} x \\ y \\ z \end{bmatrix} = 1.$$

Thus, λ_1, λ_2, and λ_3 are both the eigenvalues of the diagonal matrix and the inverses of the lengths of the major and minor axes of the ellipsoid. If we apply a change of coordinate system through a rotation matrix, we create a new ellipsoid that is no longer aligned with the coordinate axes. However, we have not changed the length of axes of the ellipse, a property that is invariant under coordinate system changes.

Suggested Readings

Some of the standard references on linear algebra and matrices include Strang [Str93] and Banchoff and Werner [Ban83]. See also Rogers and Adams [Rog90] and the *Graphics Gems* series [Gra90, Gra91, Gra92, Gra94, Gra95].

The issue of row versus column matrices is an old one. Early graphics books [New73] used row matrices. The trend now is to use column matrices [Fol90], although a few books still use row representations [Wat00]. Within the API, it may not be clear which is being used, because the elements of a square matrix can be represented as a simple array of n^2 elements. Certain APIs, such as OpenGL, allow only postmultiplication of an internal matrix by a user-defined matrix; others, such as PHIGS, support both pre- and postmultiplication.

Exercises

C.1   In $\mathbf{R}^3$, consider the two bases $\{(1, 0, 0), (1, 1, 0), (1, 1, 1)\}$ and $\{(1, 0, 0), (0, 1, 0), (0, 0, 1)\}$. Find the two matrices that convert representations between the two bases. Show that they are inverses of each other.

C.2   Consider the vector space of polynomials of degree up to 2. Show that the sets of polynomials $\{1, x, x^2\}$ and $\{1, 1 + x, 1 + x + x^2\}$ are bases. Give the representation of the polynomial $1 + 2x + 3x^2$ in each basis. Find the matrix that converts between representations in the two bases.

C.3   Suppose that $\mathbf{i}$, $\mathbf{j}$, and $\mathbf{k}$ represent the unit vectors in the x, y, and z directions, respectively, in $\mathbf{R}^3$. Show that the cross product $u \times v$ is given by the matrix

$$u \times v = \begin{vmatrix} \mathbf{i} & \mathbf{j} & \mathbf{k} \\ u_1 & u_2 & u_3 \\ v_1 & v_2 & v_3 \end{vmatrix}.$$

C.4   Show that, in $\mathbf{R}^3$,

$$|u \times v| = |u||v|| \sin \theta|,$$

where θ is the angle between u and v.

C.5   Find the eigenvalues and eigenvectors of the two-dimensional rotation matrix

$$\mathbf{R} = \begin{bmatrix} \cos \theta & -\sin \theta \\ \sin \theta & \cos \theta \end{bmatrix}.$$

C.6   Find the eigenvalues and eigenvectors of the three-dimensional rotation matrix

$$\mathbf{R} = \begin{bmatrix} \cos \theta & -\sin \theta & 0 \\ \sin \theta & \cos \theta & 0 \\ 0 & 0 & 1 \end{bmatrix}.$$

SYNOPSIS OF OPENGL FUNCTIONS

D.1 Specifying Simple Geometry

```
void glVertex[234][sifd](TYPE xcoordinate, TYPE ycoordinate,...)
void glVertex[234][sifd]v(TYPE *coordinates)
```

specifies the position of a vertex in two, three, or four dimensions. The coordinates can be specified as shorts s, ints i, floats f, or doubles d. If the v is present, the argument is a pointer to an array containing the coordinates.

```
void glBegin(glEnum mode)
```

initiates a new primitive of type mode and starts the collection of vertices. mode includes GL_POINTS, GL_LINES, and GL_POLYGON.

```
void glEnd()
```

terminates a list of vertices.

```
void glutStrokeCharacter(void* font, int char)
```

renders the character with ASCII code char at the current raster position using the stroke font given by font. Fonts include GLUT_STROKE_MONO_ROMAN and GLUT_STROKE_ROMAN.

```
void glRect[sifd](TYPE x1, TYPE y1, TYPE x2, TYPE y2)
void glRect[sifd]v(TYPE *v1, TYPE *v2)
```

specifies a two-dimensional axis-aligned rectangle by the x, y coordinates of the diagonally opposite vertices (or pointers to the vertices) using the standard data types.

```
void glutWireTeapot(GLdouble size)
void glutSolidTeapot(GLdouble size)
```

generates a Utah teapot including normals and texture coordinates of size.

D.2 Attributes

```
void glPolygonMode(glEnum faces, glEnum mode)
```

sets the desired mode for polygon rendering for the faces (GL_FRONT, GL_BACK, GL_FRONT_AND_BACK). mode can be GL_POINTS, GL_LINES, or GL_FILL.

```
void glColor3[b i f d ub us ui](TYPE r, TYPE g, TYPE b)
void glColor4[b i f d ub us ui](TYPE r, TYPE g, TYPE b, TYPE a)
void glColor[34][b i f d ub us ui]v(TYPE *color)
```

sets the present RGB (or RGBA) colors. Valid types are byte (b), int (i), float (f), double (d), unsigned byte (ub), unsigned short (us), and unsigned int (ui). The maximum and minimum values of the floating-point types are 1.0 and 0.0, respectively, whereas the maximum and minimum values of the discrete types are those of the type, for example, 255 and 0 for unsigned bytes.

```
void glClearColor(GLclampf r, GLclampf g, GLclampf b, GLclampf a)
```

sets the present RGBA clear color used when clearing the color buffer. Variables of type GLclampf are floating-point numbers between 0.0 and 1.0.

```
void glIndexi[s i f d ub](TYPE index)
```

sets the present color index.

```
void glutSetColor(int index, float r, float g, float b)
```

sets the RGB values for color index.

```
void glPointSize(GLfloat size)
```

sets the point size attribute in pixels.

```
void glPushAttrib(GLbitfield mask)
void glPopAttrib()
```

pushes to and pops from the attribute stack. Attribute groups, such as `GL_LINE_BIT` and `GL_POLYGON_BIT`, are combined using logical OR to form `mask`. All attributes can be pushed using `GL_ALL_ATTRIBUTE_BITS`.

`void glPolygonOffset(GLfloat factor, GLfloat units)`

offsets polygon depths by a linear combination of `factor` and `units`. The multiplicative constants in the computation depend on the slope of the polygon and the precision of the depth values.

D.3　Working with the Window System

`void glFlush()`

forces any buffered OpenGL commands to execute.

`void glutInit(int *argc, char **argv)`

initializes GLUT. The arguments from `main` are passed in and can be used by the application.

`int glutCreateWindow(char *title)`

creates a window on the display. The string `title` can be used to label the window. The return value provides a reference to the window that can be used when there are multiple windows.

`void glutInitDisplayMode(unsigned int mode)`

requests a display with the properties in `mode`. The value of `mode` is determined by the logical OR of options, including the color model (`GL_RGB`, `GLUT_INDEX`) and buffering (`GL_SINGLE`, `GL_DOUBLE`).

`void glutInitWindowSize(int width, int height)`

specifies the initial height and width of the window in pixels.

`void glutInitWindowPosition(int x, int y)`

specifies the initial position of the top-left corner of the window in pixels.

```
void glViewport(int x, int y, GLsizei width, GLsizei height)
```

specifies a `width` × `height` viewport in pixels whose lower-left corner is at (x, y) measured from the origin of the window.

```
void glutMainLoop()
```

cause the program to enter an event-processing loop. It should be the last statement in `main`.

```
void glutDisplayFunc(void (*func)(void))
```

registers the display function `func` that is executed when the window needs to be redrawn.

```
void glutPostRedisplay()
```

requests that the display callback be executed after the current callback returns.

```
void glutSwapBuffers()
```

swaps the front and back buffers.

```
void glutSetWindow(int id)
```

sets the current window to the window with identifier `id`.

D.4   Interaction

```
void glutMouseFunc(void *f(int button, int state, int x, int y)
```

registers the mouse callback function `f`. The callback function returns the button (GLUT_LEFT_BUTTON, GLUT_MIDDLE_BUTTON, GLUT_RIGHT_BUTTON), the state of the button after the event (GLUT_UP, GLUT_DOWN), and the position of the mouse relative to the top-left corner of the window.

```
void glutReshapeFunc(void (*f)(int width, int height))
```

registers the rehape callback function `f`. The callback function returns the height and width of the new window. The reshape callback invokes a display callback.

```
void glutKeyboardFunc(void (*f)(char key, int width, int height))
```

registers the keyboard callback function f. The callback function returns the ASCII code of the key pressed and the position of the mouse.

```
void glutIdleFunc(void (*f)(void))
```

registers the display callback function f that is executed whenever there are no other events to be handled.

```
int glutCreateMenu(void (*f)(int value))
```

returns an identifier for a top-level menu and registers the callback function f that returns an integer value corresponding to the menu entry selected.

```
void glutSetMenu(int id)
```

sets the current menu to the menu with identifier id.

```
void glutAddMenuEntry(char *name, int value)
```

adds an entry with the string name displayed to the current menu. value is returned to the menu callback when the entry is selected.

```
void glutAttachMenu(int button)
```

attaches the current menu to the specified mouse button.

```
void glutAddSubMenu(char *name, int menu)
```

adds a submenu entry name to the current menu. The value of menu is the identifier returned when the submenu was created.

```
void glutTimerFunc(int delay, void (*f)(int v), int value)
```

registers the timer callback function f and delays the event loop by delay milliseconds. After the timer counts down, f is executed with the parameter v. value is available to f.

```
void glutMotionFunc(void (*f)(int x, int y))
```

registers the motion callback function f. The position of the mouse is returned by the callback when the mouse is moved with at least one of the mouse buttons depressed.

```
void glutPassiveMotionFunc(void (*f)(int x, int y))
```

registers the motion callback function f. The position of the mouse is returned by the callback when the mouse is moved.

D.5   Enabling Features

```
void glEnable(GLenum feature)
```

enables an OpenGL feature. Features that can be enabled include GL_DEPTH_TEST, GL_LIGHTING, GL_LIGHTi, GL_TEXTURE_1D, GL_TEXTURE_2D, GL_TEXTURE_3D, GL_LINE_SMOOTH, GL_POLYGON_SMOOTH, GL_POINT_SMOOTH, GL_BLEND, GL_LINE_STIPPLE, GL_POLYGON_STIPPLE GL_FOG, and GL_NORMALIZE.

```
void glDisable(GLenum feature)
```

disables an OpenGL feature.

D.6   Transformations

```
void glMatrixMode(GLenum mode)
```

specifies which matrix will be affected by subsequent transformations. mode can be GL_MODELVIEW, GL_PROJECTION, or GL_TEXTURE.

```
void glLoadIdentity()
```

sets the current transformation matrix to an identity matrix.

```
void glPushMatrix()
void glPopMatrix()
```

pushes to and pops from the matrix stack corresponding to the current matrix mode.

```
void glRotate[fd](TYPE angle, TYPE dx, TYPE dy, TYPE dz)
```

alters the current matrix by a rotation of angle degrees about the axis (dx, dy, dz). TYPE is either GLfloat or GLdouble.

```
void glTranslate[fd](TYPE x, TYPE y, TYPE z)
```

alters the current matrix by a displacement of (x, y, z). TYPE is either GLfloat or GLdouble.

```
void glScale[fd](TYPE sx, TYPE sy, TYPE sz)
```

alters the current matrix by a scaling of (sx, sy, sz). TYPE is either GLfloat or GLdouble.

```
void glLoadMatrix[fd](TYPE *m)
```

loads the 16-element array of TYPE GLfloat or GLdouble as the current matrix. The elements of m are assumed to be in column major order.

```
void glMultMatrix[fd](TYPE *m)
```

postmultiplies the current matrix by the 4-*times* array obtained from the 16-element array of TYPE GLfloat or GLdouble. The elements of m are assumed to be in column major order.

D.7 Viewing

```
void glOrtho(GLdouble left, GLdouble right, GLdouble bottom,
    GLdouble top, GLdouble near, GLdouble far)
```

defines an orthographic viewing volume with all parameters measured from the center of the projection plane.

```
void gluOrtho2D(GLdouble left, GLdouble right, GLdouble bottom,
    GLdouble top)
```

defines a two-dimensional viewing rectangle in the plane $z = 0$.

```
void gluLookAt(GLdouble eyex, GLdouble eyey, GLdouble eyez,
    GLdouble atx, GLdouble aty, GLdouble atz
    GLdouble upx, GLdouble upy, GLdouble upz)
```

postmultiplies the current matrix by a matrix determined by a viewer at the eye point looking at the at point with the specified up direction.

---

void glFrustum(GLdouble left, GLdouble right, GLdouble bottom,
    GLdouble top, GLdouble near, GLdouble far)

defines a perspective viewing volume with all parameters measured from the center of projection (the origin) in camera coordinates.

---

void gluPerspective(GLdouble fov, GLdouble aspect,
                    GLdouble near, GLdouble far)

defines a perspective viewing volume using the *y* direction field of view fov measured in degrees, the aspect ratio of the front clipping plane, and the near and far distances.

D.8   Defining Discrete Primitives

void glRasterPos[234][sifd](TYPE xcoord, TYPE ycoord,...)
void glRasterPos[234][sifd]v(TYPE *coordinates)

specifies a raster position. The parameters are the same as for glVertex.

---

void glutBitmapCharacter(void* font, int char)

renders the character with ASCII code char at the current raster position using the raster font given by font. Fonts include GLUT_BITMAP_TIMES_ROMAN_10 and GLUT_BITMAP_TIMES_ROMAN_8_BY_13. The raster position is incremented by the width of the character.

---

void glBitmap(GLsizei width, GLsizei height, GLfloat x0, GLfloat y0,
            GLfloat xi, GLfloat yi, GLubyte *bits)

renders a width × height bitmap bits. The bitmap is offset by x0, y0 from the current raster position, which is incremented by xi, yi after the bitmap is rendered.

---

glReadPixels(GLint x, GLint y, GLsizei width, GLsizei height,
            GLenum format, GLenum type, GLvoid *image)

reads a width × height rectangle of pixels from the present read buffer starting at x, y into the array image. The pixels are in the specified format in the read buffer and written as the specified data type.

```
glDrawPixels(GLsizei width, GLsizei height, GLenum format, GLenum type,
          GLvoid *image)
```

renders a width × height rectangle of pixels from the array image. The pixels are written in the specified format and read as the specified data type.

```
glCopyPixels(GLint x, GLint y, GLsizei width, GLsizei height,
          GLenum buffer)
```

copies a width × height block of pixels from buffer starting at the current raster position to a block starting at x, y in the same buffer.

```
glPixelStore[id](GLenum param, TYPE value)
```

sets the pixel store parameter param to value. Parementers include GL_UNPACK_SWAP_BYTES, GL_PACK_SWAP_BYTES, GL_PACK_ALIGNMENT, and GL_UNPACK_ALIGNMENT.

```
glPixelMap[ui us f]v(GLenum map, GLint size, TYPE *array)
```

sets up a pixel map with the size elements in array for the specified type of pixels. The values for map include GL_PIXEL_MAP_R_TO_R (or G_TO_G or B_TO_B) and GL_PIXEL_MAP_I_TO_R (or I_TO_G or I_TO_B).

D.9 Display Lists

```
void glNewList(GLunint name, GLenum mode)
```

starts a new display list with identifier name. The value of mode determines if the list is placed on the server with (GL_COMPILE_AND_EXECUTE) or without (GL_COMPILE_AND_EXECUTE) executing the list.

```
void glEndList()
```

ends the specification of a display list.

```
void glCallList(GLunint name)
```

executes display list name.

void glListBase(GLunint offset)

sets the offset for glCallLists.

---

void glCallLists(GLsizei num, GLenum type, GLvoid* lists)

executes num display lists using the integer identifiers stored in the array lists of type. The offset set by glListBase (default 0) is added to each identifier.

GLuint glGenLists(GLsizei n)

returns the first of n consecutive integers that are available for display list identifiers.

D.10 Picking

GLint glRenderMode(GLenum mode)

sets the render mode to mode (GL_RENDER, GL_SELECTION, GL_FEEDBACK). The return value after entering normal mode gives the number of hits from selection mode or the number of primitives from feedback mode.

---

void glSelectBuffer(GLsizei n, GLunint *buff)

specifies the array buff of n integers to place selection data.

---

void glInitNames()

initializes the name stack.

---

void glPushName(GLuint name)

pushes name on the name stack.

---

void glPopName()

pops the top name from the name stack.

```
void glLoadName(GLuint name)
```

replaces the top of the name stack with name.

```
void gluPickMatrix(GLdouble x, GLdouble y, GLdouble w,
    GLdouble h, GLint *vp)
```

creates a projection matrix for picking that restricts rendering to a w × h area centered at (x, y) in window coordinates within the viewport vp.

D.11 Lighting

```
void glNormal[bsidf](TYPE dx, TYPE dy, TYPE dz)
void glNormal[bsidf]v(TYPE *v)
```

sets the present normal vector either directly as (dx, dy, dz) or by a pointer to the array v.

```
void glLight[if](GLenum light, GLenum param, TYPE value)
void glLight[if]v(GLenum light, GLenum param, TYPE *v)
```

sets scalar and vector parameter param for light source light.

```
void glLightModel[if](GLenum param, TYPE value)
void glLightModel[if]v(GLenum param, TYPE *value)
```

sets light model properties for param (GL_LIGHT_MODEL_AMBIENT, GL_LIGHT_MODEL_LOCAL_VIEWER, GL_LIGHT_MODEL_TWO_SIDE).

```
void glMaterial[if](GLenum face, GLenum param, TYPE value)
void glMaterial[if]v(GLenum face, GLenum param, TYPE *value)
```

sets parameter param for face (GL_FRONT, GL_BACK, GL_FRONT_AND_BACK).

D.12 Texture Mapping

```
glTexImage2D[ui us f]v(GLenum target, GLint level, GLint iformat,
    GLsizei width, GLsizei height, GLint border, GLenum format
    GLenum type, GLvoid *texels)
```

sets up a two-dimensional texture of height × width texels of type and format. The array texels is of format iformat. A border of 0 or 1 texels can be specified.

```
glTexCoord[1234][sifd](TYPE scoord, TYPE tcoord,....)
glTexCoord[1234][sifd]v(TYPE *vcoord)
```

specifies texture coordinates either directly though scoord, tcoord, . . . or through the array vcoord.

```
glTexParameter[if](GLenum target, GLenum param, TYPE value)
glTexParameter[if]v(GLenum target, GLenum param, TYPE *value)
```

sets the texture parameter param to value for texture of type target (GL_TEXTURE_ 1D, GL_TEXTURE_2D, or GL_TEXTURE_3D)

```
gluBuild2DMipmaps(GLenum target, GLint iformat, GLint width,
    GLint height, GLenum format, GLenum type, void *texels)
```

builds and loads a set of mipmaps. Parameters are the same as for glTexImage2D.

```
glTexEnv[if](GLenum target, GLenum param, TYPE value)
glTexEnv[if]v(GLenum target, GLenum param, TYPE *value)
```

sets texture parameter param to value; target must be GL_TEXTURE_ENV.

```
glTexGen[ifd](GLenum texcoord, GLenum name, TYPE param)
glTexGen[ifd]v(GLenum texcoord, GLenum name, TYPE *param)
```

sets up automatic texture coordinate generation for coordinate texcoord (GL_ S, GL_T, GL_R, or GL_Q). If name is GL_TEXTURE_GEN_MODE, then param specifies the method for generating the coordinate values (GL_SPHERE_MAP, GL_REFLECTION_ MAP, GL_NORMAL_MAP). If name is GL_OBJECT_LINEAR or GL_EYE_LINEAR, then param is an array containing the values that determine a plane.

```
glGenTextures(GLsizei n, GLuint name)
```

returns in name the first integer of n unused integers for texture-object identifiers.

```
glBindTexture(GLenum target, GLuint name)
```

binds name to texture of type target (GL_TEXTURE_1D, GL_TEXTURE_2D, GL_ TEXTURE_3D, GL_TEXTURE_CUBE_MAP,)

```
glDeleteTextures(GLsizei n, GLuint 8namearray)
```

deletes n texture objects from the array namearray that holds texture-object names.

D.13   State and Buffer Manipulation

void glDrawBuffer(GLenum buffer)

selects the color buffer buffer for rendering.

---

void glLogicOp(GLenum op)

selects one of the 16 logical writing modes if the feature GL_COLOR_LOGIC_OP is enabled. Modes include replacement (GL_COPY), the default, and exclusive OR (GL_XOR).

---

glHint(GLenum option, GLenum hint)

requests that hint be applied to option.

---

glDepthMask(GLboolean flag)

sets flag to make the depth buffer read-only (GL_FALSE) or writable (GL_TRUE).

---

glAccum(GLenum operation, GLfloat value)

defines the operation (GL_ACCUM, GL_LOAD, GL_RETURN, GL_ADD, GL_MULT) performed by the accumulation buffer using the constant value.

D.14   Vertex Arrays

void glEnableClientState(GLenum array)

enables one of the arrays. Choices include GL_VERTEX_ARRAY, GL_COLOR_ARRAY, GL_TEXTURE_COORDINATE_ARRAY, and GL_NORMAL_ARRAY.

---

void glDisableClientState(GLenum array)

disables one of the arrays.

```
void glVertexPointer(GLint dim, GLenum type. GLsizei stride, GLvoid *array)
void glColorPointer(GLint dim, GLenum type. GLsizei stride, GLvoid *array)
void glNormalPointer(GLint dim, GLenum type. GLsizei stride, GLvoid *array)
void glTexCoordPointer(GLint dim, GLenum type. GLsizei stride, GLvoid *array)
```

specifies data for arrays. The data are in array of type with dimension dim. stride is the number of bytes between consecutive data values (0 indicates that the data are packed in the array).

---

void glDrawElements(GLenum mode, GLsizei n, GLenum type, void *indices)

draws elements of the standard OpenGL types (mode), such as GL_POLYGON or GL_LINES, using n indices from the array indices of type GL_UNSIGNED_BYTE, GL_UNSIGNED_SHORT, or GL_UNSIGNED_INT.

D.15   Blending Functions

void glBlendFunc(GLenum source, GLenum destination)

sets the source and destination blending factors. Options include GL_ONE, GL_ZERO, GL_SRC_COLOR, GL_SRC_ALPHA, GL_ONE_MINUS_SRC_COLOR, GL_ONE_MINUS_SRC_ALPHA, GL_DST_COLOR, GL_ONE_MINUS_DST_COLOR, GL_DST_ALPHA, and GL_ONE_MINUS_DST_ALPHA.

---

void glFog[if](GLenum param, TYPE value)
void glFog[if]v(GLenum param, TYPE value)

sets fog parameter param to value. Parameters include GL_FOG_MODE (GL_LINEAR, GL_EXP, GL_EXP2), GL_FOG_COLOR, and GL_FOG_DENSITY.

D.16   Query Functions

void glGetBooleanv(GLenum name, GLboolean *param)
void glGetIntegerv(GLenum name, GLinteger *param)
void glGetFloatv(GLenum name, GLfloat *param)
void glGetDoublev(GLenum name, GLdouble *param)
void glGetPointerv(GLenum name, GLvoid **param)

writes the present value of the parameter name into param.

D.17   Curve and Surface Functions

void glMap1[fd](GLenum entity, TYPE u0, TYPE u1, GLint stride, GLint order,
                TYPE *data)
void glMap2[fd](GLenum entity, TYPE u0, TYPE u1, GLint ustride,
                GLint uorder, TYPE v0, TYPE v1, GLint vstride,
                GLint vorder, TYPE *data)

sets up an evaluator for entity (GL_MAP{12}_VERTEX_{234}, GL_MAP{12}_NORMAL, GL_MAP{12}_COLOR_{34}) over the range (u0, u1) and (v0, v1) using a Bernstein polynomial of degree order-1. There are stride variables of TYPE between successive data points in the array data.

```
void glEvalCoord1[fd](TYPE u)
void glEvalCoord1[fd]v(TYPE u)
void glEvalCoord2[fd](TYPE u, TYPE v)
void glEvalCoord2[fd]v(TYPE u, TYPE v)
```

forces the evaluation of maps for the given values of u and v.

```
void glMapGrid1[fd](GLint n, TYPE u0, TYPE u1)
void glMapGrid2[fd](GLint n, TYPE u0, TYPE u1, GLint m, TYPE v0, TYPE v1)
```

sets up an equally spaced grid of n partitions between u0 and u1 (and of m partitions between v0 and v1).

```
void glEvalMesh1(GLenum mode, GLint first, GLint last)
void glEvalMesh2(GLenum mode, GLint ufirst, GLint ulast,
                GLint vfirst, GLint vlast)
```

renders in mode (GL_LINE, GL_POINT, GL_FILL) all enabled evaluators from first to last.

D.18 GLU Quadrics

```
GLUquadricObj* gluNewQuadric()
```

returns a pointer to a new quadric object.

```
void gluQuadricDrawStyle(GLUquadricObj *obj, GLenum style)
```

sets the drawing style (GLU_POINT, GLU_LINE, GLU_FILL, GLU_SILHOUETTE) for quadric object obj.

```
void gluQuadricNormals(GLUquadricObj *obj, GLenum mode)
void gluQuadricTexture(GLUquadricObj *obj, GLboolean mode)
```

sets the automatic normal (GLU_NONE, GLU_FLAT, GLU_SMOOTH) or texture coordinate generation (GLU_TRUE,GLU_FALSE) mode for quadric object obj.

```
void gluSphere(GLUquadricObj *obj, GLdouble radius, GLint slices,
               GLint stacks)
```

defines quadric object obj as a sphere of radius using slices lines of longitude and stacks lines of latitude.

```
void gluCylinder(GLUquadricObj *obj, GLdouble base, GLdouble top,
                 GLdouble height, GLint slices, GLint stacks)
```

defines quadric object obj as a centered cylinder with height along the z-axis, base radius and top radius using stacks lines in the z-direction, and slices lines around the cylinder.

D.19   GLSL Functions

```
GLuint glCreateProgram()
```

creates an empty program object and returns an identifier for it.

```
GLuint glCreateShader(GLenum type)
```

creates an empty shader object of type GL_VERTEX_SHADER or GL_FRAGMENT_SHADER and returns an identifier for it.

```
void glShaderSource(GLuint shader, GLsizei nstrings, const GLchar **strings,
                    const GLint *lengths)
```

identifies the source code for shader as coming from an array of nstrings strings of lengths characters. If the shader is a single null-terminated string then nstrings is 1 and lengths is NULL.

```
void glCompileShader(GLuint shader)
```

compiles shader object shader.

```
void glAttachObject(GLunit program, GLuint shader)
```

attaches shader object shader to program object program.

```
void glLinkProgram(GLuint program)
```

links together the application and shaders in program object program.

```
GLint glGetAttributeLocation(GLuint program, const char *name)
```

returns the index of the attribute name from the linked program object name.

```
void glVertexAttribute[1234][sfd](GLunint index, TYPE value1,
                                  TYPE value2,...)
void glVertexAttribute[123][sfd]v(GLunint index, TYPE *value)
```

specifies the value of the vertex attribute with the specified index.

```
GLint glGetUniformLocation(GLuint program, const GLchar *name)
```

returns the index of uniform variable name from the linked program object program.

```
void glUniform[1234][if](GLint index, TYPE value)
void glUniform[1234][if]v(GLint index, GLsizei num, TYPE value)
void glUniformMatrix[234]f(GLint index, GLsizei num, GLboolean transpose,
                          const GLfloat *value)
```

sets the value of a uniform variable, array, or matrix with the specified index. For the array and matrix, num is the number of elements to be changed.

REFERENCES

Ado85   Adobe Systems, Inc., *PostScript Language Reference Manual*, Addison-Wesley, Reading, MA, 1985.

Ake88   Akeley, K., and T. Jermoluk, "High Performance Polygon Rendering," *Computer Graphics*, 22(4), 239–246, 1988.

Ake93   Akeley, K., "Reality Engine Graphics," *Computer Graphics*, 109–116, 1993.

Ang90   Angel, E., *Computer Graphics*, Addison-Wesley, Reading, MA, 1990.

Ang04   Angel, E., *OpenGL, A Primer,* Addison-Wesley, Reading, MA, 2004.

ANSI85   American National Standards Institute (ANSI), *American National Standard for Information Processing Systems—Computer Graphics—Graphical Kernel System (GKS) Functional Description*, ANSI, X3.124-1985, ANSI, New York, 1985.

ANSI88   American National Standards Institute (ANSI), *American National Standard for Information Processing Systems—Programmer's Hierarchical Interactive Graphics System (PHIGS)*, ANSI, X3.144-1988, ANSI, New York, 1988.

App68   Appel, A., "Some Techniques for Shading Machine Renderings of Solids," *Spring Joint Computer Conference*, 37–45, 1968.

Arn96   Arnold, K., and J. Gosling, *The Java Programming Language,* Addison-Wesley, Reading, MA, 1996.

Ban83   Banchoff, T., and J. Werner, *Linear Algebra Through Geometry*, Springer-Verlag, New York, 1983.

Bar93   Barnsley, M., *Fractals Everywhere,* Second Edition, Academic Press, San Diego, CA, 1993.

Bar83   Barsky, B. A., and C. Beatty, "Local Control of Bias and Tension in Beta-Splines," *ACM Transactions on Graphics,* 2(2), 109–134, 1983.

Bar87   Bartels, R. H., C. Beatty, and B. A. Barsky, *An Introduction to Splines for Use in Computer Graphics and Geometric Modeling*, Morgan Kaufmann, Los Altos, CA, 1987.

Bli76   Blinn, J. F., and M. E. Newell, "Texture and Reflection in Computer Generated Images," *CACM,* 19(10), 542–547, 1976.

Bli77   Blinn, J. F., "Models of Light Reflection for Computer-Synthesized Pictures," *Computer Graphics,* 11(2), 192–198, 1977.

Bow83   Bowyer, A., and J. Woodwark, *A Programmer's Geometry*, Butterworth, London, 1983.

Bre63   Bresenham, J. E., "Algorithm for Computer Control of a Digital Plotter," *IBM Systems Journal*, January, 25–30, 1965.

Bre87   Bresenham, J. E., "Ambiguities in Incremental Line Rastering," *IEEE Computer Graphics and Applications*, May, 31–43, 1987.

Car78   Carlbom, I., and J. Paciorek, "Planar Geometric Projection and Viewing Transformations," *Computing Surveys*, 10(4), 465–502, 1978.

Cas96   Castleman, K. C., *Digital Image Processing*, Prentice Hall, Englewood Cliffs, NJ, 1996.

Cat75   Catmull, E., "A Hidden-Surface Algorithm with Antialiasing," *Computer Graphics*, 12(3), 6–11, 1975.

Cat78   Catmull, E., and J. Clark, "Recursively Generated B-Spline Surfaces on Arbitrary Topological Meshes," *Proceedings of Computer-Aided Design 10*, 350–355, 1978.

Cha98   Chan, P., and R. Lee, *The Java Class Libraries: Java.Applet, Java.Awt, Java.Beans* (Vol. 2), Addison-Wesley, Reading, MA, 1998.

Che95   Chen, S. E., "Quicktime VR: An Image-Based Approach to Virtual Environment Navigation," *Computer Graphics*, 29–38, 1995.

Che00   Chen, K. L. et al., "Building and Using a Scalable Display Wall System," *IEEE Computer Graphics and Applications*, 20(4), 29–37, 2000.

Cla82   Clark, J. E., "The Geometry Engine: A VLSI Geometry System for Graphics," *Computer Graphics*, 16, 127–133, 1982.

Coh85   Cohen, M. F., and D. P. Greenberg, "The Hemi-Cube: A Radiosity Solution for Complex Environments," *Computer Graphics*, 19(3), 31–40, 1985.

Coh88   Cohen, M. F., S. E. Chen, J. R. Wallace, and D. P. Greenberg, "A Progressive Refinement Approach to Fast Radiosity Image Generation," *Computer Graphics*, 22(4), 75–84, 1988.

Coh93   Cohen, M. F., and J. R. Wallace, *Radiosity and Realistic Image Synthesis*, Academic Press Professional, Boston, MA, 1993.

Coo82   Cook, R. L., and K. E. Torrance, "A Reflectance Model for Computer Graphics," *ACM Transactions on Graphics*, 1(1), 7–24, 1982.

Coo87   Cook, R. L., L. Carpenter, and E. Catmull, "The Reyes Image Rendering Architecture," *Computer Graphics*, 21(4), 95–102, July 1987.

Cro81   Crow, F. C., "A Comparison of Antialiasing Techniques," *IEEE Computer Graphics and Applications*, 1(1), 40–48, 1981.

Cro97   Crossno, P. J., and E. Angel, "Isosurface Extraction Using Particle Systems," *IEEE Visualization*, 1997.

Deb96   Debevec, P. E., C. J. Taylor, and J. Malik, "Modeling and Rendering Architecture from Photographs: A Hybrid Geometry- and Image-Based Approach," *Computer Graphics*, 11–20, 1996.

DeR88   DeRose, T. D., "A Coordinate Free Approach to Geometric Programming," SIGGRAPH Course Notes, *SIGGRAPH*, 1988.

DeR89   DeRose, T. D., "A Coordinate Free Approach to Geometric Programming," *Theory and Practice of Geometric Modeling*, W. Strasser and H. P. Seidel (Eds.), Springer-Verlag, Berlin, 1989.

Dre88   Drebin, R. A., L. Carpenter, and P. Hanrahan, "Volume Rendering," *Computer Graphics*, 22(4), 65–74, 1988.

Ebe01   Eberly, D. H., *3D Game Engine Design*, Morgan Kaufmann, San Francisco, CA, 2001.

Ebe02   Ebert, D., F. K. Musgrave, D. Peachey, K. Perlin, and S. Worley, *Texturing and Modeling, A Procedural Approach*, Third Edition, Morgan Kaufman, San Francisco, CA, 2002.

End84   Enderle, G., K. Kansy, and G. Pfaff, *Computer Graphics Programming: GKS—The Graphics Standard*, Springer-Verlag, Berlin, 1984.

Eng68   Engelbart, D. C., and W. K. English, "A Research Center for Augmenting Human Intellect," *Fall Joint Computer Conference*, Thompson Books, Washington, DC, 1968.

Far88   Farin, G., *Curves and Surfaces for Computer Aided Geometric Design*, Academic Press, New York, 1988.

Fau80   Faux, I. D., and M. J. Pratt, *Computational Geometry for Design and Manufacturing*, Halsted, Chichester, England, 1980.

Fern03 Fernando, R., and M. J. Kilgard, *The Cg Tutorial: The Definitive Guide to Programmable Real-Time Graphics*, Addison-Wesley, Reading, MA, 2003.

Fern04 Fernando, R., *GPU Gems: Programming Techniques, Tips, and Tricks for Real-Time Graphics*, Addison-Wesley, Reading, MA, 2004.

Fol90   Foley, J. D., A. van Dam, S. K. Feiner, and J. F. Hughes, *Computer Graphics*, Second Edition, Addison-Wesley, Reading, MA, 1990 (C Version 1996).

Fol94   Foley, J. D., A. van Dam, S. K. Feiner, J. F. Hughes, and R. Phillips, *Introduction to Computer Graphics*, Addison-Wesley, Reading, MA, 1994.

Fos96   Fosner, R., *OpenGL Programming for Windows 95 and Windows NT*, Addison-Wesley, Reading, MA, 1996.

Fou82   Fournier, A., D. Fussell, and L. Carpenter, "Computer Rendering of Stochastic Models," *CACM*, 25(6), 371–384, 1982.

Fuc77   Fuchs, H., J. Duran, and B. Johnson, "A System for Automatic Acquisition of Three-Dimensional Data," *Proceedings of the 1977 NCC*, AFIPS Press, 49–53, Montvale, NJ, 1977.

Fuc80   Fuchs, H., Z. M. Kedem, and B. F. Naylor, "On Visible Surface Generation by A Priori Tree Structures," *SIGGRAPH 80*, 124–133, 1980.

Gal95   Gallagar, R. S., *Computer Visualization: Graphics Techniques for Scientific and Engineering Analysis*, CRC Press, Boca Raton, FL, 1995.

Gla89   Glassner, A. S. (Ed.), *An Introduction to Ray Tracing*, Academic Press, New York, 1989.

Gla95   Glassner, A. S., *Principles of Digital Image Synthesis*, Morgan Kaufmann, San Francisco, 1995.

Gol83   Goldberg, A., and D. Robson, *Smalltalk–80: The Language and Its Implementation*, Addison-Wesley, Reading, MA, 1983.

Gon87 Gonzalez, R., and P. Wintz, *Digital Image Processing*, Second Edition, Addison-Wesley, Reading, MA, 1987.

Gor84 Goral, C. M., K. E. Torrance, D. P. Greenberg, and B. Battaile, "Modeling the Interaction of Light Between Diffuse Surfaces," *Computer Graphics (SIGGRAPH 84)*, 18(3), 213–222, 1984.

Gor96 Gortler, S. J., R. Grzeszczuk, R. Szeliski, and M. F. Cohen, "The Lumigraph," *Computer Graphics*, 43–54, 1996.

Gou71 Gouraud, H., "Computer Display of Curved Surfaces," *IEEE Trans. Computers*, C-20, 623–628, 1971.

Gra90 *Graphics Gems I*, Glassner, A. S. (Ed.), Academic Press, San Diego, CA, 1990.

Gra91 *Graphics Gems II*, Arvo, J. (Ed.), Academic Press, San Diego, CA, 1991.

Gra92 *Graphics Gems III*, Kirk, D. (Ed.), Academic Press, San Diego, CA, 1992.

Gra94 *Graphics Gems IV*, Heckbert, P. (Ed.), Academic Press, San Diego, CA, 1994.

Gra95 *Graphics Gems V*, Paeth, A. (Ed.), Academic Press, San Diego, CA, 1995.

Gra03 Gray, K., *The Microsoft DirectX 9 Programmable Graphics Pipeline*, Microsoft Press, 2003.

Hal89 Hall, R., *Illumination and Color in Computer Generated Imagery*, Springer-Verlag, New York, 1989.

Har96 Hartman, J., and J. Wernecke, *The VRML 2.0 Handbook*, Addison-Wesley, Reading, MA, 1996.

Hea04 Hearn, D., and M. P. Baker, *Computer Graphics*, Third Edition, Prentice Hall, Englewood Cliffs, NJ, 2004.

Hec84 Heckbert, P. S., and P. Hanrahan, "Beam Tracing Polygonal Objects," *Computer Graphics*, 18(3), 119–127, 1984.

Hec86 Heckbert, P. S., "Survey of Texture Mapping," *IEEE Computer Graphics and Applications*, 6(11), 56–67, 1986.

Her79 Herman, G. T., and H. K. Liu, "Three-Dimensional Display of Human Organs from Computed Tomograms," *Computer Graphics and Image Processing*, 9, 1–21, 1979.

Her00 Hereld, M., I. R. Judson, and R. L. Stevens, "Tutorial: Introduction to Building Projection-Based Tiled Display Systems," *IEEE Computer Graphics and Applications*, 20(4), 22–26, 2000.

Hil01 Hill, F. S., Jr., *Computer Graphics*, Second Edition, Prentice Hall, Upper Saddle River, NJ, 2001.

Hop83 Hopgood, F. R. A., D. A. Duce, J. A. Gallop, and D. C. Sutcliffe, *Introduction to the Graphical Kernel System: GKS*, Academic Press, London, 1983.

Hop91 Hopgood, F. R. A., and D. A. Duce, *A Primer for PHIGS*, John Wiley & Sons, Chichester, England, 1991.

Hum01 Humphreys, G., M. Elridge, I. Buck, G. Stoll, M. Everett, and P. Hanrahan, "WireGL: A Scalable Graphics System for Clusters," *SIGGRAPH 2001*, 129–140.

ISO88 International Standards Organization, *International Standard Information Processing Systems—Computer Graphics—Graphical Kernel System for Three*

Dimensions (GKS-3D), ISO Document Number 8805:1988(E), American National Standards Institute, New York, 1988.

Jar76   Jarvis, J. F., C. N. Judice, and W. H. Ninke, "A Survey of Techniques for the Image Display of Continuous Tone Pictures on Bilevel Displays," *Computer Graphics and Image Processing,* 5(1), 13–40, 1976.

Jen01   Jensen, H. W., "Realistic Image Synthesis Using Photon Mapping," AK Peters, Natick, MA, 2001.

Joy88   Joy, K. I., C. W. Grant, N. L. Max, and L. Hatfield, *Computer Graphics: Image Synthesis*, Computer Society Press, Washington, DC, 1988.

Kaj86   Kajiya, J. T., "The Rendering Equation," *Computer Graphics,* 20(4), 143–150, 1986.

Kel97   Keller, H., "Instant Randiosity," *Computer Graphics*, 49–56, 1997.

Kil94a   Kilgard, M. J., "OpenGL and X, Part 3: Integrated OpenGL with Motif," *The X Journal,* SIGS Publications, July/August 1994.

Kil94b   Kilgard, M. J., "An OpenGL Toolkit," *The X Journal,* SIGS Publications, November/December 1994.

Kil96   Kilgard, M. J., *OpenGL Programming for the X Windows System*, Addison-Wesley, Reading, MA, 1996.

Knu87   Knuth, D. E., "Digital Halftones by Dot Diffusion," *ACM Transactions on Graphics,* 6(40), 245–273, 1987.

Kov97   Kovatch, P. J., *The Awesome Power of Direct3D/DirectX*, Manning Publications Company, Greenwich, CT, 1997.

Kui99   Kuipers, J. B., *Quaternions and Rotation Sequences*, Princeton University Press, Princeton, NJ, 1999.

Las87   Lasseter, J., "Principles of Traditional Animation Applied to 3D Computer Animation," *Computer Graphics*, 21(4), 33–44, 1987.

Lev88   Levoy, M., "Display of Surface from Volume Data," *IEEE Computer Graphics and Applications,* 8(3), 29–37, 1988.

Lev96   Levoy, M., and P. Hanrahan, "Light Field Rendering," *Computer Graphics*, 31–42, 1996.

Lia84   Liang, Y., and B. Barsky, "A New Concept and Method for Line Clipping," *ACM Transactions on Graphics*, 3(1), 1–22, 1984.

Lin68   Lindenmayer, A., "Mathematical Models for Cellular Interactions in Biology" *Journal of Theoretical Biology,* 18, 280–315, 1968.

Lin01   Linholm, E., M. J. Kilgard, and H. Morelton, "A User-Programmable Vertex Engine," *SIGGRAPH 2001,* 149–158.

Lor87   Lorensen, W. E., and H. E. Cline, "Marching Cubes: A High Resolution 3D Surface Construction Algorithm," *Computer Graphics,* 21(4), 163–169, 1987.

Ma94   Ma, K. L., J. Painter, C. Hansen, and M. Krogh, "Parallel Volume Rendering Using Binary-Swap Compositing," *IEEE Computer Graphics and Applications,* 14(4), 59–68, 1994.

Mag85   Magnenat-Thalmann, N., and D. Thalmann, *Computer Animation: Theory and Practice*, Springer-Verlag, Tokyo, 1985.

Man82   Mandelbrot, B., *The Fractal Geometry of Nature*, Freeman Press, New York, 1982.

Mat95   The MathWorks, *Student Edition of MatLab Version 4 Users Guide,* Prentice Hall, Englewood Cliffs, NJ, 1995.

Max51   Maxwell, E. A., *General Homogeneous Coordinates in Space of Three Dimensions*, Cambridge University Press, Cambridge, England, 1951.

Mia99   Miamo, J., *Compressed Image File Formats*, ACM Press, New York, 1999.

Mol92   Molnar, S., J. Eyles, and J. Poulton, "PixelFlow: High-Speed Rendering Using Image Composition," *Computer Graphics*, 26(2), 231–240, 1992.

Mol94   Molnar, S., M. Cox, D. Ellsworth, and H. Fuchs, "A Sorting Classification of Parallel Rendering," *IEEE Computer Graphics and Applications*, 26(2), 231–240, 1994.

Mol02   Möller, T., and E. Haines, *Real-Time Rendering*, Second, Edition, AK Peters, Natick, MA, 1999.

Mon97   Montrym, J., D. Baum, D. Dignam, and C. Migdal, "InfiniteReality: A Real-Time Graphics System," *Computer Graphics*, 293–392, 1997.

Mur94   Murray, J. D., and W. Van Ryper, *Encyclopedia of Graphics File Formats*, O'Reilly and Associates, Sebastopol, CA, 1994.

New73   Newman, W. M., and R. F. Sproull, *Principles of Interactive Computer Graphics*, McGraw-Hill, New York, 1973.

Nie94   Nielson, J., *Usability Engineering*, Academic Press, New York, 1994.

Nie97   Nielson, G. M., H. Hagen, and H. Muller, *Scientific Visualization: Overviews, Methodologies, and Techniques*, IEEE Computer Society, Piscataway, NJ, 1997.

Ope04a   OpenGL Architecture Review Board, *OpenGL Programming Guide*, Fourth Edition, Addison-Wesley, Reading, MA, 2001.

Ope04b   OpenGL Architecture Review Board, *OpenGL Reference Manual*, Fourth Edition, Addison-Wesley, Reading, MA, 2001.

OSF89   Open Software Foundation, *OSF/Motif Style Guide,* Prentice Hall, Englewood Cliffs, NJ, 1989.

Ost94   Osterhaut, J., *Tcl and the Tk Toolkit,* Addison-Wesley, Reading, MA, 1994.

Pap81   Papert, S., *LOGO: A Language for Learning*, Creative Computer Press, Middletown, NJ, 1981.

Pav95   Pavlidis, T., *Interactive Computer Graphics in X,* PWS Publishing, Boston, MA, 1995.

Per89   Perlin, K., and E. Hoffert, "Hypertexture," *Computer Graphics,* 23(3), 253–262, 1989.

PHI89   PHIGS+ Committee, "PHIGS+ Functional Description, Revision 3.0," *Computer Graphics,* 22(3), 125–218, July 1998.

Pho75   Phong, B. T., "Illumination for Computer Generated Scenes," *Communications of the ACM*, 18(6), 311–317, 1975.

Pei88   Peitgen, H. O., and S. Saupe (Ed.), *The Science of Fractal Images,* Springer-Verlag, New York, 1988.

Pik84   Pike, R., L. Guibas, and D. Ingalls, "Bitmap Graphics," *Computer Graphics*, 18(3), 135–160, 1984.

Por84   Porter, T., and T. Duff, "Compositing Digital Images," *Computer Graphics,* 18(3), 253–259, 1984.

Pra78   Pratt, W. K., *Digital Image Processing*, Wiley, New York, 1978.

Pru90   Prusinkiewicz, P., and A. Lindenmayer, *The Algorithmic Beauty of Plants,* Springer-Verlag, Berlin, 1990.

Ree83   Reeves, W. T., "Particle Systems—A Technique for Modeling a Class of Fuzzy Obejcts," *Computer Graphics*, 17(3), 359–376, 1983.

Rey87   Reynolds, C. W., "Flocks, Herds, and Schools: A Distributed Behavioral Model," *Computer Graphics*, 21(4), 25–34, 1987.

Rie81   Riesenfeld, R. F., "Homogeneous Coordinates and Projective Planes in Computer Graphics," *IEEE Computer Graphics and Applications*, 1(1), 50–56, 1981.

Rog85   Rogers, D. F., *Procedural Elements for Computer Graphics,* Second Edition, McGraw-Hill, New York, 1998.

Rog90   Rogers, D. F., and J. A. Adams, *Mathematical Elements for Computer Graphics,* McGraw-Hill, New York, 1990.

Rog00   Rogers, D. F., *An Introduction to NURBS: With Historical Perspective,* Morgan Kaufmann, San Francisco, CA, 2000.

Ros04   Rost, R. J., *OpenGL Shading Language*, Addison-Wesley, Reading, MA, 2003.

Sch88   Schiefler, R. W., J. Gettys, and R. Newman, *X Window System,* Digital Press, Woburn, MA, 1988.

Sch97   Schneiderman, B., *Designing the User Interface: Strategies for Effective Human–Computer Interaction,* Third Edition, Addison-Wesley, Reading, MA, 1997.

Sch98   Schroeder, W., K. Martin, and B. Lorensen, *The Visualization Toolkit*, Prentice Hall, Upper Saddle River, NJ, 1998.

Shi02   Shirley, P., *Fundamentals of Computer Graphics,* AK Peters, Natick, MA, 2002.

Sho98   Shoemaker, K., "Animating Rotation with Quaternion Curves," *Computer Graphics*, 19(3), 245–254, 1985.

Sei96   Seitz, S. M., and C. R. Dyer, "View Morphing," *Computer Graphics*, 21–30, 1996.

Seg92   Segal, M., and K. Akeley, *The OpenGL Graphics System: A Specification,* Version 1.0, Silicon Graphics, Mountain View, CA, 1992.

Sie81   Siegel, R., and J. Howell, *Thermal Radiation Heat Transfer,* Hemisphere, Washington, DC, 1981.

Sil89   Sillion, F. X., and C. Puech, "A General Two-Pass Method Integrating Specular and Diffuse Reflection," *Computer Graphics,* 22(3), 335–344, 1989.

Smi84   Smith, A. R., "Plants, Fractals and Formal Languages," *Computer Graphics,* 18(3), 1–10, 1984.

Sta03   Stam, J., and C. Loop, "Quad/Triangle Subdivision," *Computer Graphics Forum 22,* 1–7, 2003.

Str93   Strang, G., *Introduction to Linear Alegbra,* Wellesley-Cambridge Press, Wellesley, MA, 1993.

Sut63   Sutherland, I. E., *Sketchpad, A Man–Machine Graphical Communication System, SJCC,* 329, Spartan Books, Baltimore, MD, 1963.

Sut74a   Sutherland, I. E., and G. W. Hodgeman, "Reentrant Polygon Clipping," *Communications of the ACM*, 17, 32–42, 1974.

Sut74b   Sutherland, I. E., R. F. Sproull, and R. A. Schumacker, "A Characterization of Ten Hidden-Surface Algorithms," *Computer Surveys*, 6(1), 1–55, 1974.

Swo00   Swoizral, H., K. Rushforth, and M. Deering, *The Java 3D API Specification*, Second Edition, Addison-Wesley, Reading, MA, 2000.

Tor67   Torrance, K. E., and E. M. Sparrow, "Theory for Off–Specular Reflection from Roughened Surfaces," *Journal of the Optical Society of America*, 57(9), 1105–1114, 1967.

Tor96   Torborg, J., and J. T. Kajiya, "Talisman: Commodity Realtime 3D Graphics for the PC," *Computer Graphics*, 353–363, 1996.

Tuf83   Tufte, E. R., *The Visual Display of Quantitative Information*, Graphics Press, Cheshire, CT, 1983.

Tuf90   Tufte, E. R., *Envisioning Information*, Graphics Press, Cheshire, CT, 1990.

Tuf97   Tufte, E. R., *Visual Explanations*, Graphics Press, Cheshire, CT, 1997.

Ups89   Upstill, S., *The RenderMan Companion: A Programmer's Guide to Realistic Computer Graphics*, Addison-Wesley, Reading, MA, 1989.

Van94   Van Gelder, A., and J. Wilhelms, "Topological Considerations in Isosurface Generation," *ACM Transactions on Graphics*, 13(4), 337–375, 1994.

War03   Warren, J., and H. Weimer, *Subdivision Methods for Geometric Design*, Morgan Kaufmann, San Francisco, CA, 2003.

War04   Warren, J., and S. Schaefer, "A Factored Approach to Subdivision Surfaces," *IEEE Computer Graphics and Applications*, 24(3), 74–81, 2004.

Wat92   Watt, A., and M. Watt, *Advanced Animation and Rendering Techniques*, Addison-Wesley, Wokingham, England, 1992.

Wat98   Watt, A., and F. Policarpo, *The Computer Image*, Addison-Wesley, Wokingham, England, 1998.

Wat00   Watt, A., *3D Computer Graphics*, Third Edition, Addison-Wesley, Wokingham, England, 2000.

Wat02   Watkins, A., *The Maya 4 Handbook*, Charles River Media, Hingham, MA, 2002.

Wer94   Wernecke, J., *The Inventor Mentor*, Addison-Wesley, Reading, MA, 1994.

Wes90   Westover, L., "Footprint Evaluation for Volume Rendering," *Computer Graphics*, 24(4), 367–376, 1990.

Whi80   Whitted, T., "An Improved Illumination Model for Shaded Display," *Communications of ACM*, 23(6), 343–348, 1980.

Wit94a   Witkin, A. P., and P. S. Heckbert, "Using Particles to Sample and Control Implicit Surfaces," *Computer Graphics*, 28(3), 269–277, 1994.

Wit94b   Witkein, A. (Ed.), *An Introduction to Physically Based Modeling*, Course Notes, *SIGGRAPH 94*, 1994.

Wol91   Wolfram, S., *Mathematica*, Addison-Wesley, Reading, MA, 1991.

Wri97   Wright, R. S., Jr., and M. Sweet, *OpenGL Superbible*, Waite Group Press, Corte Madera, CA, 1997.

Wys82   Wyszecki, G., and W. S. Stiles, *Color Science*, Wiley, New York, 1982.

FUNCTION INDEX

This index includes only the first appearance of those functions that are used in the text. The complete list of OpenGL functions is contained in the *OpenGL Reference Manual* and the GLUT documentation. The function are grouped according to their inclusion in the GL, GLU, or GLUT libraries. Functions with multiple forms, such as glVertex, are listed once. Appendix D contains a synopsis of these functions.

GL Functions

glAccum, 432
glAttachObject, 463
glBegin, 42
glBitMap, 391
glBlendFunc, 427
glBindtexture, 417
glCallList, 110
glCallLists, 111
glClear, 77
glClearColor, 63
glColor, 63
glColorMaterial, 315
glColorPointer, 191
glCompileShader463
glCopyPixels, 393
glCreateProgram, 463
glCreateShader, 463
glDeleteTextures, 418
glDepthFunc, 358
glDepthMask, 428
glDrawBuffer, 143
glDrawElements, 191
glDrawPixels, 393
glEnable, 84
glEnableClientState, 190
glEnd, 42
glEndList, 110
glEvalCoord, 616
glEvalMesh, 617
glFlush, 44
glFog, 431
glFrustum, 257
glGenLists, 111
glGenTextures, 418
glGetIntegerv, 128
glGetFloatv, 511
glGetUnifromLocation, 464
glHint, 414
glIndex, 65

glInitNames, 126
glLight, 312
glLightModel, 313
glLinkProgram, 464
glListBase, 114
glLoadIdentity, 70
glLoadMatrix, 214
glLoadName, 126
glLogicOp, 147
glMap, 616
glMapGrid, 617
glMaterial, 314
glMatrixMode, 70
glMultMatirx, 217
glNewList, 110
glNormal, 302
glOrtho, 69
glPixelMap, 393
glPixelStore, 394
glPointSize, 66
glPolygonOffset, 267
glPopAttrib, 111
glPopMatrix, 111
glPopName, 126
glPushAttrib, 111
glPushMatrix, 111
glPushName, 126
glRasterPos, 389
glReadBuffer, 143
glReadPixels, 393
glRect, 149
glRotate, 214
glScale, 214
glSelectBuffer, 126
glShadeModel, 305
glShaderSource, 463
glTexCoord, 410
glTexEnv, 413
glTexGen, 416
glTexImage, 409
glTexParameter, 411

glTranslate, 113
glUniform, 464
glUseProgram, 464
glVertex, 41
glVertexAttrib, 464
glVertexPointer, 191
glViewport, 73

GLU functions

gluBeginNurbsSurface, 620
gluBuild2DMipmaps, 413
gluCylinder, 621
gluEndNurbsSurface, 620
gluEndTrim, 620
gluLookAt, 251
gluNewNurbsRenderer, 620
gluNewQuadric, 621
gluNewTess, 350
gluNurbsProperty, 620
gluNurbsSurface, 620
gluOrtho2D, 69
gluPerspective, 258
gluPickMatrix, 127
gluQuadricDrawStyle, 621
gluTessBeginContour, 350
gluTessEndPolygon, 350
gluTessEndContour, 350
gluTessBeginPolygon, 350
gluTessVertex, 350

GLUT functions

glutAddMenuEntry, 123
glutAddSubMenu, 124
glutAttachMenu, 123
glutBitmapCharacter, 115
glutCreateMenu, 123
glutCreateWindow, 72
glutDisplayFunc, 75
glutIdleFunc, 122
glutInit, 72
glutInitDisplayMode, 72
glutInitWindowPosition, 72
glutInitWindowSize, 72
glutKeyboardFunc, 121
glutMainLoop, 74
glutMotionFunc, 120
glutMouseFunc, 116
glutPostRedisplay, 122
glutReshapeFunc, 117
glutSetColor, 65
glutSetWindow, 122
glutSolidCube, 498
glutStrokeCharacter, 115
glutSwapBuffers, 142
glutTimerFunc, 144

SUBJECT INDEX

A

abstract data type (ADT), 161
    geometric, 162
accumulation buffer, *see* buffer, accumulation
acuity, 18
additive color model, 60–61
affine
    addition (sum), 163–164
    space, 160, 725, 728–729
    transformation, *see* transformation, affine
algebraic surface, *see* surface, algebraic
aliasing, 27, 330, 363, 405, 437–443
    spatial-domain, 365
    time-domain, 365
alpha , 63
    blending, 425
    channel, 425
ambient
    light, 290–291
    refection, 295
angle
    critical, *see* critical angle
    Euler, 222
    incidence, 302–303
    of view, *see* field of view
    reflection, 302–303
animation, 140, 512–513
    key-frame, 467, 513
antialiasing, 363–365, 428–430, 433
aperture, *see* lens, aperture
API, *see* application programmer's interface
application programmer's interface (API)21, 39
    functions, 47–48
applet, 548–549
architecture
    graphics, 29–34
    pipeline, 30–34
    von Neumann, 29
area averaging, 364
articulated model, 512

aspect ratio, 26, 73–74
associative, 737
ATI38, 492
at point, 250
attractor, 396
attributes, 58–66, 514–515
    binding, 59
    functions, 47
    vertex *see* vertex, attribute
axis-aligned bounding box, *see* bounding box
axonometric projection, *see* projection
azimuth, 252

B

back-end processing, 34
back-face removal, 356–357
backing store, 387
back-to-front rendering, 361, 430–431
band-limited, 439
basis, 168
    splines, 594–595
Bernstein polynomials, 588437–443
Bezier
    blending functions, 587–588
    curve, *see* curve, Bezier
    geometry matrix, 587
    surface, *see* surface, Bezier
bilinear interpolation, *see* interpolation
binary spatial–partition, 541–543
binormal vector, 488
bit block, 57, 146, 384
    transfer (bitblt), 57, 384
bitmap, 388
    font, 391–393
bitplane, 380
black box, 47, 324
blending, *see* compositing
    factors, 426
    patch, 582
    polynomials (functions), 579–580

Blinn-Phong reflection model, 299
bounding box (rectangle), 338–339
   volume338–339
Bresenham's algorithm, 346–348
brightness, 18, 370
browser, 547
B-spline
   blending functions, 593
   curve, *see* curve, B-spline
   geometry matrix, 593
   surface, *see* surface, B-spline
buffer, 379–381
   accumulation, 389, 432–437
   auxiliary, 381
   back, 142, 381, 389
   color, 6, 389
   color index, 381
   depth, *see* z-buffer
   destination, 384
   frame, 389
   front, 142, 381
   left, 389
   right, 389
   source, 384
   stencil, 381, 389
   writing (drawing), 384–388
   z, *see* z-buffer
bump
   mapping, 27, 400, 433–434, 487–492
   function, 487
byte code, 548

C

CAD, *see* computer–aided design
callback (function), 106
   display, 75, 121–122
   keyboard, 121
   idle, 121–122
   motion (move), 120
   mouse, 116
   reshape, 117–118
   timer, 144–145
camera,, 11–12
   bellows, 19
   frame *see* frame, camera
   pinhole, 15–18
   specification
   synthetic, model , 19–21, 66–69
canonical view volume, *see* view volume
cast ray, *see* ray, cast
cathode-ray tube (CRT), 1, 7–10, 361
   calligraphic, 8
   interlaced, 8
   random scan, 8
   shadow mask, 8
   vector, 8
Catmull-Clark subdivision, 614
cell, 87

center of projection (COP), 20, 234
central processing unit (CPU), 7
CERN,547
Cg, 94, 454
characteristic
   value, 742
   vector, 742
centroid, 613
child node, *see* node, child
choice device, 104
chromatic dispersion, 485
chromaticity, 368–369
   coordinates, 368–369
clamping, 426
client, 107
   -server graphics, 107,
   -server network, 107
clipping, 32, 330
   Cohen–Sutherland, 331–333, 340–341
   curve, 339
   Liang–Barsky, 333–335, 340–341
   line-segment, 330–335
   pipeline
   polygon, 335–337
   Sutherland–Hodgeman, 335–337, 340–341
   text, 339–340
   three-dimensional, 340–343
   window (rectangle), 21, 32, 70
cluster, 543
coefficient of restitution, 494, 562
Cohen–Sutherland clipping, *see* clipping,
       Cohen–Sutherland
collision, 560–563
   detection, 560
   elastic, 561
   inelastic, 561
color, 60–66, 366–371
   additive, 60–61
   balancing, 395
   buffer, *see* buffer, color
   complementary (CMY, CMYK)61, 367, 370
   cone, 369
   gamut, 62
   HLS, 369
   indexed, 62, 64–65
   Lab, 367
   lookup table, 64–65, 394–395
   matrix, 369–370
   palette, 64
   primary, 18
   raster, 391
   RGB (RGBA, RGBα), 6, 62–64, 366–369
   solid (cube), 61
   subtractive, 61
   XYZ, 367–369
   YUV, 367
commutative, 737
complex arithmetic, 396
components, 168

compositing, 425–432
  binary-swap, 652
  binary-tree, 652
compression, 383
  range, 486
  ratio, 383
computer-aided design (CAD), 3
computer graphics, 1
  applications, 2–5
  interactive, 99
concatenation, 32
  of transformations, *see* transformation
concave polygon, 335
cones, 18
  sensitivity, 18
constant shading, *see* shading, flat
constraint, 560–563
  hard, 560
  soft, 560, 563
constructive solid geometry (CSG), 168,
      539–541
contour curve, 86
control
  functions, 47–48, 71–76
  (data) point, 576, 603
convex, 164
  hull, 164, 589, 603
convolution, 434
  matrix (kernel), 434
coordinate system, 45–46, 168–184, 728
  camera, 180–181
  change of, 173–174
  clip, 180–181
  device (physical), 46
  eye, 180–181
  model, 180–181, 498
  normalized-device (NDC), 180–181, 330
  object, 180–181, 417–418, 498
  raster, 391
  right-handed, 165
  screen, 46, 180–181, 329
  texture, 402, 415
  viewing, 248
  window, 46, 180–181, 328
  world (application, problem), 45 , 180–181
COP, *see* center of projection
cornea, 18
Cox-deBoor recursion, 597
CPU, *see* central processing unit
Cramer's rule, 739
critical angle, 483
cross product, 164–165, 741
CSG, *see* constructed solid geometry
CTM, *see* current transformation matrix
cube map, 480–486
culling, 262, 330, 356–357
current transfromation matrix (CTM),
  213
cursor, 102, 150–151

curve
  Bezier, 586–589
    subdivision, 604
  B-spline, 591–594, 596–600
    open, 599
    uniform (periodic), 598–599
  Hermite, 583–585
  interpolating, 577–580
  NURBS, 599–600,
  parametric polynomial, 573–574
    cubic, 576–580
  piecewise linear, 87
  rendering (scan conversion), 600–605
  segment, 574
  space-filling, 96
  subdivision, 604, 611–612
  trimming, 620
curvature, 570

D

DAG, *see* directed acyclic graph
dark field, 371
data tablet, 103
DDA (digital differential analyzer), 344
  algorithm, 344–346
decal, 414
deCasteljau recursion, 597
decision variable, 346
degree of freedom, 103, 193, 195, 504, 512
dependent variable, 569
depth
  buffer, *see* z-buffer
  cueing, 431
  of field, 17, 436–437
  of frame buffer, *see* frame buffer
  sort, 361–363
descender, 392
destintion
  bit, 386
  blending factor, 427
  buffer, *see* buffer, destination
  pixel146
determinant, *see* matrix, determinant
device-independent graphics, 45
diffuse (perfectly diffuse), 295
  -diffuse interaction, 639
  reflection, 295–296
  surface, 288–289
digital light projection (DLP), 9
dimension, 165, 727
  $2\frac{1}{2}$ data set, 263, 266
dimetric projection, *see* projection, axonometric
diminution, 239
directed acyclic graph (DAG), 501
direction
  angles, 211
  cosines, 211
  of projection (DOP), 67, 234

DirectX (Direct3D), 46, 94, 523
display, 7, 365–373
    list (file), 29–30, 108–114
    memory, 108
    processor, 29–30, 108,
displacement function, 487
distance
    far, 26, 257–259
    near, 26, 257–259
distributive, 725
dither, 371–372
DLP, see *digital light projection*
dot (inner) product, 164
double buffering, 142–144
driver, 21
dual–ported memory
dynamics (inverse dynamics), 512–513

E

edge, 500
    silhouette, see silhouette edge
eigenvalue, 222, 742
eigenvector, 222, 742
elevation, 252
embossing, 433–434
Encapsulated PostScript (EPS), 382
energy
    function, 563
    flux, 637
environment mapping, 27, 400, 419–425
Ethernet, 546
Euclidean space, 160, 725, 729–730
Euler's method, 558–559
    improved, 560
evaluators, 104, 615
event mode, see input mode
event
    display, 121–122
    idle, 121–122
    keyboard, 121
    mouse, 116
    move (motion), 116, 120
        passive, 116
    processing
    queue, 106
    reshape, 117–188
    window, 119
exclusive or (XOR) see writing mode, XOR
explicit form, 86, 569
extent, 125, 338
eye point, 250

F

facet, 185
feedback, 126
feeler ray, see ray, shadow
field of view, 16, 26,

fill
    area, 52
    flood, 351–352
    odd-even, 351
    scan-line, 351
    and sort, 351–352
filter (linear), 412
film plane, 25
fixed point, 196
flat shading, see shading, flat
flood fill, see fill, flood
focal length, 18, 25
fog, 431–432
    factor, 431
font, 56, 111–115,
    bitmap, see bitmap font
    monotype, 114, 392
    proportional, 114, 392
    raster, 391–392
forces
    attractive, 556–557
    contact, 563
    drag (damping), 555
    gravity, 554
    repulsive, 556–557
    spring, 554–556
foreshortening, 211
    nonuniform, 254
form factor, 639, 642–644
    delta, 644
forward difference, 601
Fourier analysis, 439
fractal
    geometry, 95
    mountain, 95
fragment, 33
    processing, 33, 329–330
    shader (program), 34, 457–458, 474–477
frame, 168–184, 729
    camera (eye), 171, 181, 234
    change of, 177–179
    Frenet, 573
    model, 171, 181, 498
    object, 171, 181, 498
    texture, 490
    world, 171, 181
frame buffer, 6
    depth, 6
    precision, 6
    resolution, 6
Frendel equation, 484
Frenet frame, see frame, Frenet
friend, 517
front buffer, see buffer, front
front-end processing, 34, 328
front-to-back rendering, 361, 430–431
frustum, 257
full color, 6

G

gamma correction, 370–371
gamut, *see* color, gamut
Gaussian elimination, 640
Gauss-Seidel method, 641
geometric
    continuity, 585–586
    optics13
geometry, 31, 187
    coordinate-free, 159–166
    fractal, *see* fractal geometry
    matrix, 578
    node, 525
    processing, 326–328
geometry engine, 34, 228, 372
GIF, 380, 382, 547
GKS (Graphical Kernel System), 93
    -3D, 247
GL, 93
GLSL *see* OpenGL Shading Language
global
    lighting, *see* lighting, global
    rendering, *see* rendering, global
GLU (GL Utility) library, 49
GLUT (GL Utility toolkit), 49, 71–76
    fonts, 114–115,
Gouraud shading, *see* shading, Gouraud
GP-GPU, 493
GPU *see* graphics processing unit
gradient vector, 301
Gram-Schmidt orthogonalization, 731–732
graph, 500
    directed, 500
    scene, 29, 521–539
graphics processing unit (GPU), 34, 152, 445,
        492
graphics server, 107

H

half angle, 299
halftoning, 371–372
halfway vector, 299
head-to-tail axiom (rule), 158–159, 726
height field, 263
Hermite
    blending functions, 584
    curve, *see* curve, Hermite
    geometry matrix, 584
    surface, *see* surface, Hermite
hidden-surface removal, 27, 84–85, 260–262,
        327, 352–363
    image–space algorithm, 260–261, 353–354
    object–space algorithm, 260–261, 353
hierarchical model, 499–505, 519
high-definition television (HDTV), 658
histogram, 394
hit list, 126

HLS, *see* color, HLS
homogeneous coordinates, 174–177, 192
    transformations, 200–207
homomorphic, 171, 467–468
Hooke's law, 555
Horner's method, 601
HSR, *see* hidden-surface removal
HTML (hypertext markup language), 546–547
hue, 369
human-computer interaction (HCI), 145
human visual system, 15, 18–19, 60
hypermedia, 546–547

I

icon, 122
illumination function,
    , 289
image, 10
    compositing
    digital, 381–384
    formation, 11–20
    luminance (monochrome), 394
    processing, 395, 434–435
image-oriented implementation324
imaging extensions, 435–436
imaging subset, 435
immediate mode, 59, 109
implicit
    function visualization, 85
    form, 571–572
    surface, 301
in–betweening, 513
independent variable, 569
index of refraction, 482
inner product, *see* dot product
input
    devices, 100–106
        logical, 101, 104
        physical, 101–103
    functions, 47–48
    modes, 105–106
        event, 106
        request, 105
        sample, 105
instance, 137, 208, 498
    table, 138
    transformation, *see* transformation, instance
interaction, 99
interlaced, *see* cathode ray tube
International Standards Organization (ISO),
        545
Internet, 545–549
Internet Explorer, 4
interpolative shading, *see* shading, interpolative
interpolation, 576
    bilinear, 189–190
    blending functions, 579–580
    curve, *see* curve, interpolating

interpolation *(cont.)*
    geometry matrix, 578
    surface, *see* surface, interpolating
inward (outward) facing, 186
iris, 18
isometric projection, *see* projection,
        axonometric
isosurface, 563

J

Jacobi's method, 641
JAVA, 93–94, 548–549
    -3D, 46, 523, 549
jitter, 377, 433
join point, 575
joint angle, 501–502
joy stick, 103
JPEG, 380, 383, 547

K

keyboard device, 101
key-frame animation, *see* animation, key-frame
kinematics (inverse kinematics), 512–513
knot, 596
    array, 596
Koch
    curve, 96
    snowflake, 96

L

Lamertian surface, 295–296
Lambert's law, 295–296
latency, 31
lateral inhibition, 305
LCD, see *liguid-crystal display*, 8
leaf, 501
LED, see *light-emitting diode*
left–child right–sibling structure, 508–512
Lempel-Ziv algorithm, 383
lens, 18
Liang–Barsky clipping, *see* clipping, Liang–
        Barsky
light12
    -field rendering, 658
    -material interaction, 286–289
    node, 528
    pen103
    refracted
    source, 287, 289–293
        distant, 292–293
        OpenGL, *see* OpenGL, light sources
light-emitting diode (LED, 8
lighting
    local, 317
    global, 317–318

lightness, 369
lightpen, 103
line, 51, 162
    implicit form, 571
    loop, 52
    parametric form, 163
    segment, 51, 163
    directed, 158
    strip, 52
linear
    function, 193
    combination, 727
    filter, *see* filter
    independence, 165, 727, 739
liquid crystal display (LCD), 8
load balancing, 649
load matrix, 217
local lighting, *see* lighting, local
locator device, 104
logic operation, 146–147,
logicaldevice
    , 104
LOGO, 22
look-at function, 250–251
lookup table, *see* color lookup table
Loop subdivision, 614
lumigraph, 658
luminance
    function, 290
    image, *see* image, luminance

M

Mach bands, 306
Macintosh, 4, 49, 100, 152
magnitude (vector), 158–159, 162
Mandelbrot set, 395–398
mapping
    methods, 399–401
    normal, 489
    normalization, 485–486
    spherical, 421–423
marching
    cubes, 98
    squares, 86–92
masking, 390
master coordinates, *see* cooordinates, model
material, 293–298
    node, 529
matrix, 735
    addition, 736
    column, 737
    concatenation, 738
    determinant, 739
    dimension, 735
    identity, 737
    inverse, 739
    mode, 70

model-view, 70, 182
multiplication, 736
normal, 470
orthogonal, 203
projection, 70, 267–279
rank, 738
representation, 168, 176, 741
    change of, 173–180, 739–740
row, 737
shear, 204
singular (nonsingular), 739
square, 735
translation, 201
texture, 415
transpose, 735
Maxwell triangle, 98
measure, 105
membership function, 571
member
    private, 517
    protected, 517
    public, 517
menu, 122–124
    hierarchical, 123
    pop-up, 123,
Mercator projection, *see* projection, Mercator
message, 514–515
mesh (polygonal), 97, 262–264
    simplification
    subdivision, 612–615
method, 514–515
Microsoft
    Windows, 4, 49, 72, 94, 100, 152
    High Level Shading Language (HLSL), 454
mipmap, 412–414
mode
    copy146
    exclusive or (XOR), 147, 150, 385, 387–388
    feedback, 126
    input, 105
    matrix, *see* matrix, mode
    replacement, 146
    selection, 125
    writing, 147, 385–387
model coordinates, *see* coordinates, model
model frame, *see* frame, model
model-view matrix
modeling326–327, 497
    -rendering paradigm, 28–29
moir/'e pattern, 372, 413, 439, 636
Monte Carlo methods, 638
monochrome, 18
monotype, *see* font, monotype
morphing, 467–468
Mosaic, 547
motion blur, 436
mouse, 101–102
multirendering, 432

multitexturing, 418

N

name stack, *see* stack, name
NCSA, 547
Netscape, 4, 547
Newell, Mike, 608
Newton
    method, 550
    laws, 469, 550, 552–557
node, 500
    child, 501
    class, 523
    dynamic, 511
    parent, 501
    root, 500
    separator, 521
    terminal, 501
nonuniform foreshortening, 254
normal
    vector, 166, 300–301, 488
    map *see* mapping, normal
normalization map *see* map, normalization
normalization transformation, *see*
    transformation
NTSC (National Television Systems
    Committee), 367
n-tuple, 170–171
numerical instability, 559
NURBS (nonuniform rational B-spline) *See*
    curve, NURBS
NVIDIA, 38, 492
Nyquist
    frequency, 438
    sampling theorem, 438, 442

O

object, 11–12
    geometric, 158–159, 520
    graphical, 513
    tessellator, 350
object-oriented
    implementation, 324–325
    programming
Occum's razor, 87
octree, 544–545
odd-even
    fill, 349
    test, 369
opacity, 63, 425
opaque surface, 287
Open Inventor, 565
OpenGL, 1, 24–25, 93
    API, 41, 46–49,
    Architectural Review Board ARB), 453
    attributes, 58–66

OpenGL *(cont.)*
  bit operations, 388–392
  blending, 427–432
  buffers, 380–381, 389–390
    current drawing, 390
    current read, 390
  camera positioning, 242–247
  color, 65–66, 389
  compositing, 427–432
  curves, 615–617
  extensions, 435, 452–454
  frames, 180–184
  light sources, 312–314
  materials, 314–316
  NURBS, 620
  pipeline
  pixel operations, 393–394
  primitives, 50–54
  projections, 256–259, 268–274, 278–279
  quadrics, 620–621
  Shading Language (GLSL), 94, 449,
      454–463
    data types, 459–462
    execution, 458–459
    functions, 462–463
    linking, 463–464
    operators, 462–463
    samplers, 477–482
  surfaces, 615–621
  texture mapping, 408–418
  transformation matrices, 212–216
  types, 42
  viewing, 66–70
Open Scene Graph, 523
orthogonal, 164, 730
  matrix
  projection, *see* projection, orthographic
orthographic projection, *see* projection,
      orthographic
orthonormal, 731
outcode, 331, 341
oval of Cassini, 86, 92,
overlay planes, 151

P

pack, 390
palette, *see* color palette
painter's algorithm, 361–363
parallel view, *see* viewing, parallel
parametric
  continuity, 585–586
  form, 166, 301, 572
  plane, 165–166
  polynomial curve, *see* curve, parametric
  surface, *see* surface
parent node, *see* node, parent
particle
  Newtonian, 552–557

system, 468–469, 551–557
  solving, 557–560
patch, 639
  surface, *see* surface, patch
pen plotter, 22
  model, 22–24
penalty function, 563
penumbra, 292
performance, 34–35
perspective
  division, 255
  matrix, 254
  normalization, 274–278
perspective transformation, *see* transformations,
      perspective
perspective view, *see* viewing, perspective
PHIGS (Programmer's Hierarchical Interactive
      Graphics System)93,
  viewing, 247–250
Phong
  modified reflection model, 298–299,
      449–451470–473
  reflection model, 293–299, 449
  shading, *see* shading, Phong
photon mapping, 15, 638
physically–based modeling, 551–557
pick device, 104
picking, 124–131, 399
pinhole camera, *see* camera, pinhole
pipeline,, 30, 48
  architecture, *see* architecture, pipeline
  arithmetic, 30
  geometric, 31
  pixel, 389–390
  programmable, 33–34
  renderer
  transformation
pitch, 154, 251
Pixar, 28, 35, 423
pixel6
  map, 390
  test, 390
planar geometric projection, *see* projection
plane, 165
point, 41
  at *see* at point
  eye *see* eye point
  -point subtraction, 159, 728
  -vector addition, 159–161
  source, 13, 291–292
pointing device, 10, 101, 116–119
polygon, 52–54
  convex, 52–53
  offset, 266–267
  simple, 52
polygonal shading, *see* shading, polygonal
polyhedra, 633–634
polyline, 52
polynomial curve, 573

pop, 111
  matrix, 217
PostScript (PS),
  22, 382
  Encapsulated (EPS), 382
power wall, 647
preimage, 404
primary colors, *see* colors, primary
primitives, 50–54
  assembly, 32, 327
  curved, 58
  functions, 47
  geometric, 50
  line loop, 52
  line segment, 51
  line strip, 52
  point, 51
  quadrilateral, 54
    strip, 54
  polygon, 52–54
  raster (image), 50
  text, 56–58, 112–115
  three-dimensional, 166–167
  triangle, 54
    fan, 54
    strip, 54
principal face, 235
procedural method, 549–563
program object, 463
projection, 16, 165, 730–731
  axonometric, 237–238
    dimetric, 237
    isometric, 237
    trimetric, 237
  Mercator, 407
  normalization, 268, 343
  oblique, 238–239, 271–274
  OpenGL, 1
  orthogonal (orthographic), 236–239,
    255–256
    multiview, 236–237
  parallel, 236–239
  perspective239–240, 252–255
  planar geometric, 234
  plane (surface), 20, 258
projector, 20
protocol, 545–546
  Internet (IP), 546
  Transmission Control (TCP), 546
pseudocolor, 394
push111
  matrix, 217

Q

quadratic form, 610
quadric surface, *see* surface, quadric
quadtree, 543–544
quantization, 444

quaterion, 224–227
query functions, 47–48
QuickTime VR, 657

R

radiosity, 14, 318–319, 638–645
  equation, 639–642
  progressive, 645
rank, *see* matrix, rank
raster, 6
  operation (raster op)
  position, 115, 389
raster text, *see* text
rasterization, 33, 326, 328–229, 343–353
ray, 14, 163
  cast, 627
  casting, 611
  -polygon intersection, 633
  shadow (feeler), 628
  tracing, 14, 318, 626–636
    recursive, 630–632
  tree, 629
read-only memory (ROM)
reciprocity equation, 639
reconstruction, 437, 442–443
recursive subdivision, 77–84, 309–312,
    602–604
refinement, 612
reflection, *see* transformations
  mapping, 400, 420–423, 480–482
    sphere, 421–423
refraction, 482–485
refresh, 8
register, 75, 116
relative positioning, 102
  device, 102
rendering, 323–326
  equation, 286, 626, 636–638
  farm, 646
  global, 625
  image-based, 655–658
  large-scale, 647–655
  multipass (multirendering, 424, 432,
    436–437
  parallel, 648
  sort-first, 648
  sort-last, 648, 650–652
  sort-middle, 648–650, 653–655
RenderMan, 28, 35, 450–451, 646–647
replication, 57, 440
request mode, *see* input mode
resolution, 18
restitution, *see* coefficient of restitution
retained mode, 109
retina, 18
Reyes, 646
RGB (RGBA, RGBα) color, *see* color, RGB
right-hand rule, 186

right-handed coordinate system, *see* coordinate
    system
rigid-body transformation, *see* transformations
rods, 18
roll, 152, 251
rotation, *see* transformation, rotation
rubberbanding, 145–146, 385
Runge–Kutta method, 560

S

sample mode, *see* input mode
sampler, 477-482
sampling, 437–443
    aperture, 441
    stochastic
    texture, 412
    theory, 437–443
saturation, 63, 369
scalar, 158, 725–726
    field, 160, 726
    -vector multiplication, 160, 726
    visualization, *see* visualization, scalar
scaling, *see* transformations
    matrix, 202
scan conversion, 328, 343–353
    line segment, 343–348
    polygon, 348–351
    curves
scanline, 325
    algorithm, 355
    fill, 355
scatter, 286
scene graph, *see* graph, scene
scientific visualization, *see* visualization,
    scientific
scissoring, 340
screen coordinates, *see* coordinates, screen
seed point, 351
selection, 125–126
separable surface, *see* surface, separable
server, 107
set
    difference, 540
    intersection, 540
    union, 540
shader, 450
    object, 463
shading, 27, 285
    flat (constant), 304–305
    Gouraud, 306
    interpolative, 306
    language, 450
    nonphotorealistic473
    per fragment, 308
    Phong, 308–309, 470–473
        per-vertex versus per-fragment, 474–476
    polygonal, 304–309
    smoothv306-307

shadow, 279–281
    generation
    ray, *see* ray, shadow
    polygonv280–281
shape grammar
shear, *see* transformation, shear
    matrix, 204
shininess, 297
shrinkwrap, 164
Sierpinski gasket, 39–40, 43, 76–85
silhouette edge, 317, 473
Silicon Graphics (SGI), 34, 228, 372
simple polygon, *see* polygon, simple
singular, *see* matrix, singular
singularity, 352
Sketchpad, 99
slidebar, 104, 122, 145
smoothness, 575
Snell's law, 482
sort
    first, *see* rendering, sort-first
    and hidden-surface removal, 354–355
    last, *see* rendering, sort-last
    middle, *see* rendering, sort-middle
source
    bit, 386
    blending factor, 427
    buffer, *see* buffer, source
    pixel, 146
spaceball, 103
span, 355
spectrum, 13, 438
specular (perfectly specular)
    reflection, 297
    surface, 288–289, 297
splatting
spline
    curve, *see* curve, spline
    open, *see* curve, spline
    surface, *see* surface, spline
    uniform (periodic), *see* curve, spline
spotlight, 292
stability, 575–576
stack, 111
    name, 126
state machine, 48–49
stencil buffer, *see* buffer, stencil
stiff equation, 559
stipple patterns, 361
string device, 104
stroke device, 104
stroke text, *see* text, stroke
structure (PHIGS), *see* PHIGS, struture
subtractive color model, 61
Sun Microsystems, 94
supersampling, 433
surface
    algebraic, 572, 610–611
    Bezier, 589–590

subdivision, 605–606
B-spline, 591–599
  NURBS, 27, 599–600
Hermite, 585
interpolating, 581–583
parametric polynomial, 574
patch, 574, 583
  bicubic, 581
quadric, 610–611, 632
rendering, 605–607
separable, 583
subdivision, 612–614
tensor-product, 583
Sutherland, Ivan, 99
Sutherland–Hodgeman clipping, *see* clipping,
    Sutherland–Hodgeman
swizzling, 462
symbol, 498-499
  -instance table, 499
synthetic camera, *see* camera, synthetic

T

tangent
  plane, 301
  space, 489
  vector, 488
Taylor's theorem, 558
tessellation, 58, 167, 350
texel
text, 56–58
  raster, 57–58,
  stroke, 56–57
texture, 27
  aliasing, 405
  coordinates, *see* coordinates, texture
  generation, 418–419
  magnification, 412
  mapping, 400–408, 477–482
    linear, 405
    two-part, 406–408
  matrix, 415
  minification, 412
  modulation, 413
  object, 417–418
  sampling, 412–414
three-color theory, 60
3DLabs, 38, 492
throughput, 31
TIFF, 380, 382–383
timer, 144
toolkit, 145
topology, 187
touch
  pad, 103
  -sensitive screen, 103
trackball, 101–102
  virtual, 219–221

transformation, 192
  affine, 192–194
  color, 369–370
  concatenation of, 204–212
  functions, 47–48
  implementation
  instance, 208–209
  node, 537
  normalization, 247–250
  OpenGL, 212–215
    order, 215
  perspective, 254
    normalization, 274–278
  reflection, 199
  rigid-body, 197
  rotation, 196–197, 202–203
    fixed point, 196, 205–207
    incremental, 223-224
    general, 207, 209–212
    smooth, 222-223
  translation, 195, 200–201
  scaling, 197–199, 201–202
  shear, 204–205
translation, *see* transformation, translation
    matrix
transmitted light, 482
translucent, 329, 425
  surface, 288–289
transparency, 63, 425
traversal, *see* tree traversal
tree, 500
  BSP, 541–543437–443
  CSG, 539–541
  expression, 451
  shade, 451–452
  traversal, 503–504
    backward in-order, 532
    in-order, 543
    pre-order, 505
    post-order, 541
    stack-based, 505–507
triad, 8
trigger, 105
trimetric projection, *see* projection, axonometric
trimming curve, *see* curve, trimming
tristimulus value, 60, 366
true color, 6
turtle graphics, 96
twist, 252, 590
typeface, 391

U

umbra, 292
unpack, 390
URL (uniform resource locator), 547
user interface, 218–219
Utah teapot, 415, 608–610

V

vanishing point, 37
variation–diminishing property, 602
vector, 158–159
  inverse, 159
  magnitude, 158–159
  space (linear), 159, 725–728
  sum, 159
  -vector addition, 159–160
  visualization, *see* visualization, vector
  zero, 159
vertex, 11, 24, 41
  array, 190–192
  attribute, 464
  list, 187
  normal, 306
  processing, 31–32
  shader (program), 34, 454–457
very-large-scale integrated (VLSI) circuits, 3
viewer, 11–12
  class, 532
viewing, 233–262
  API, 247–252
  axonometric, 237–238
    dimetric, 237
    isometric, 237
    trimetric, 237
  classical, 26, 233–240
  computer, 240–241
  coordinates, *see* coordinates, viewing
  functions, 47–48
  oblique, 238–239, 342
  orthogonal (orthographic), 67–69, 236–237
    multiview, 236–237
  parallel, 234
  perspective, 234, 239–240
    one-point, 37, 239–240
    three-point, 239–240
    two-point, 37, 239–240
  rectangle, 70
  two-dimensional, 69–71
  volume, 69, 327
    canonical
view-orientation matrix, 248
view-plane normal (VPN), 247
viewport, 73–74, 328

view-reference point (VRP), 247
view-up vector (VUP), 247
virtual reality (VR)
visible-surface algorithm, 84, 327
visibility testing, 541
VLSI, *see* very-large scale integrated circuit
volumetric data set, *see* data set, volumetric
voxel, 544
VRML (Virtual Reality Modeling Language),
    523, 548

W

wgl
white noise, 419
widget, 104, 145
winding number, 349–350
World Wide Web, 547
window, 71
  management, 122
  screen, 71
  system, 72
  coordinates, *see* coordinates, window
wire frame, 27
world (problem) coordinates, *see* coordinate
    system, world
writing mode, 386
  XOR, 147, 150

X

X Window system, 4, 49, 72, 95, 100, 108,
    152, 546
Xerox Palo Alto Research Center (PARC), 152

Y

yaw, 251
y–x algorithm, 355

Z

z-buffer, 381, 389
  algorithm, 84–85, 260–262, 357–359
  and scan conversion, 359–361
zip file, 384

Back Plate 1 Rendering of hierarchical robot figure.

(Courtesy of University of New Mexico.)

Back Plate 2 Sphere computer by recursive subdivision of tetrahedron. Triangle colors assigned randomly.

(Courtesy of University of New Mexico.)

Back Plate 3 Shadows from a cube onto ground. Computed by two passes over the data with viewpoint shifted between viewer and light source.

(Courtesy of University of New Mexico.)

Back Plate 4 Visualization of thermohaline flows in the Carribean Sea using streamtubes colored by water temperature.

(Courtesy of David Munich, High Performance Computing Center, University of New Mexico.)

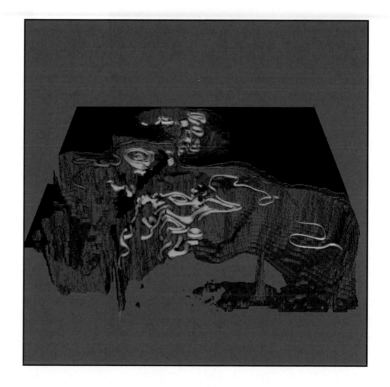

CL

006.
66
ANG